# KEYSTONE OF JUSTICE

# THE PENNSYLVANIA SUPERIOR COURT

Commonwealth of Pennsylvania
Pennsylvania Historical and Museum Commission
for the Pennsylvania Superior Court
Harrisburg 2000

**Commonwealth of Pennsylvania**

Tom Ridge, Governor

**Superior Court of Pennsylvania**

Stephen J. McEwen Jr., President Judge

**Pennsylvania Historical and Museum Commission**

Janet S. Klein, Chairman

Brent D. Glass, Executive Director

www.phmc.state.pa.us

# TABLE OF CONTENTS

# FOREWORD

The word *judge* inspires in most members of the citizenry the vision of a robed individual high upon the courtroom bench who, while presiding over the trial of a cause, holds in constant view the jury, the witnesses, and the spectators, all the while employing an especially watchful eye over the lawyers in the case. *Justice* for the parties and to their cause, of course, is the sole and single goal of the trial judge.

The term *appellate judge,* on the other hand, fails to trigger any particular image or view, for the members of the appellate judiciary generally labor in the anonymity appropriate to en banc deliberation and to decisions made following argument in courtrooms to which the public is invited but seldom finds its way.

Such obscurity belies the critical role of the intermediate appellate judiciary as architects of the jurisprudential landscape, since the consideration of appeals poses a dual challenge—it must present in bright and vivid color a clear and certain decision in each appeal tendered to it, while portraying in lighter hues and suggestive tones principles upon which the Supreme Court may deliberate and even rely, as that highest court tempers the jurisprudence of the Commonwealth and unceasingly undertakes to mold a body of law in which the strongest feel restraint and the humblest find trust.

It has been said that the Superior Court of the twentieth century in its decisions and, more particularly, when called upon to adjust a prevailing principle or to craft an innovative notion, has rendered exceptional service in the pursuit of justice—a most exacting and inexact of tasks—and has, as well, been an eloquent voice of the jurisprudence of reason. Whether the Court has in fact so achieved remains for legal historians to remark, but sure and certain it is that the Judges of the Court have aspired to do so.

The jurisprudence of reason would also wisely be a goal of the Judges of the Superior Court during the twenty-first century, for they are certain to encounter challenges and to confront demands posed by a technology of such speed that each day is a New Age, by an artificial intelligence uninhibited by intuition or conscience, and by such biogenetic engineering as appears to defy even Heaven.

Our concern for the future must not, however, exceed our confidence that mankind through reliance upon the law will prevail, a notion so aptly expressed by scientist/philosopher Freeman J. Dyson in a work as mighty as it is obscure, *Disturbing the Universe.*[1]

> Man cannot play God and still stay sane. And the progress of biology is inescapably placing in man's hands the power to play God. But from these two facts it does not follow that there is no hope for us. We still can choose to be masters of our fate. To deny to any man the power to

---

1. Freeman J. Dyson, *Disturbing the Universe* (New York: Harper & Row, 1979), 172.

play God, it is not necessary to forbid him to experiment and explore. It is necessary only to make strict laws placing the applications of his knowledge under public control.

History records that such demands upon and challenges to the efficacy of the law have been as constant and relentless as the law has been impervious and triumphant. That the law is so fundamental as to be the foundation for, and thereby essential to the survival of, civilization was ever so brilliantly expressed by Robert Bolt in his master-piece, *A Man for All Seasons*,[2] as he bespoke the efficacy of *law and its ministers* through the response of Chancellor Thomas More to the taunting challenge of son-in-law Roper:

> MORE: [Would you] cut a great road through the law to get after the Devil?
>
> ROPER: I'd cut down every law in England to do that!
>
> MORE: And when the last law was down, and the Devil turned round on you—where would you hide, Roper, the laws all being flat? This country's planted thick with laws from coast to coast. . .and if you cut them down. . .d'you really think you could stand upright in the winds that would blow then? Yes, I'd give the Devil benefit of law, for my own safety's sake.

And so it is that, as we enter the new century, we declare our debt to our esteemed colleague Judge Patrick R. Tamilia for his monumental effort in producing this history, and bid our successors:

> The wish: That the following account of the efforts of this Court during the century since it was founded will well serve you as a guide; and
>
> The prayer: That your success will be equal to our wishes.

***Stephen J. McEwen Jr.***
*President Judge*
*Superior Court of Pennsylvania*
*December 31, 1999*

---

2. Robert Bolt, *A Man for All Seasons: A Play in Two Acts* (New York: Random House, 1960), 1.6.

# ACKNOWLEDGEMENTS

A ny book which attains publication is a work product that brings together the efforts and contributions of many people. I believe the contributions of those persons involved in this volume were of such significance that, without them, the book would not have been produced within the timeframe achieved, nor would it have contained the detailed historic scope which we sought.

First, I wish to thank Chief Justice John P. Flaherty for his support and approval of the funds, budgeted by Superior Court, needed to involve the Pennsylvania Historical and Museum Commission Publications Department. This eliminated the necessity of obtaining outside funding which always presents a problem for members of the judiciary. It also gives greater authenticity to the book, *Keystone of Justice: The Pennsylvania Superior Court,* since it is a product of the unified judiciary of Pennsylvania, published within Commonwealth resources.

Next, it is incumbent to reaffirm that which is written in the Introduction, that the vision and imagination of Superior Court President Judge Stephen J. McEwen Jr., and his complete support for the project, in a large measure contributed to the ability of the authors to recreate the court's history within a limited timeframe and entirely as a Superior Court product. The alternative would have been to obtain researchers and writers from universities, law schools, or other sources.

John Hare, Esquire, co-author of the book, was indispensable in both researching and writing the historical content. John was meticulous in keeping with the format and outline I prepared for approval by the court, which detailed the relationship of the court and its judges to the political climate and the social, economic, and cultural conditions of the twentieth century. John's involvement eliminated the initial plan to obtain research interns to obtain the historical infrastructure thereby saving time and effort in bringing the book to completion in a consistent framework. His involvement in a graduate program in history at Princeton University, while also officially working per diem for the court in his court research, was the ideal arrangement. Since John previously worked as my law clerk, our thinking patterns and work relationship were such as to create the best possible cooperative result.

The other indispensable person in this process was Lauren Posati, Esquire, my administrative law clerk. Her involvement entailed being the intermediary between me and all other parties involved in the project. She reviewed every one of the multiple drafts, editing and correcting continuously, working with the publisher and editor on an almost daily basis, and assigning parts of the drafts to each of our clerks to cross check and review the hundreds of citations, references, and excerpts for accuracy and applicability. Lauren's training in journalism and her nineteen years' experience with the judiciary as my administrative law clerk prepared her superbly for any and all of the demands I placed on her, or which she initiated herself, in relation to the unification and completion of the book. My office has always maintained a current status as to our caseload on both a monthly and yearly basis, which entails authoring an average of

250 written memoranda or opinions yearly. Lauren is the coordinator of that effort and, during the years involved in the work on the book, there has been no abatement in our work for the court.

The other person on my staff who was intricately involved in every step of the work is my lead secretary, Lori Rexa. Lori, through her skills with the word processor, computer, printer, electronic mail, and the fundamental work of producing hard copies, discs, and literally thousands of rewrites and corrections, permitted us to maintain pace with every facet related to the book. Assisting her in this process was our part-time secretary, Sandra Michalski. Also, my three law clerks, Patrick O'Leary, Maureen Farrar and Michele Routh, constantly were called into service, proofreading and checking case citations to verify their accuracy and content. In that respect, the cooperation of Kathryn Bann, the Superior Court Recorder, in assisting us in locating volumes of the Superior Court Reports containing induction ceremonies, memorial services and the chronology of court membership, was also valuable.

I wish to express appreciation to Judges John Hester, James Cavanaugh and Justice Frank Montemuro Jr., who were the designated review committee for the book's first draft. Their readings and subsequent comments were extremely helpful in pointing out technical and content defects, but more importantly, in applauding the effort and giving assurance that the book would contribute to the history of the Pennsylvania judiciary and document the valuable asset epitomized by Superior Court. Judge John Brosky, who has been identified as the semi-official court photographer, is deserving of praise for the contribution of many photographs of court personnel and activities, far more than we could possibly use, which adds presence and interest to the book.

Dr. Charles Thrall, Superior Court's legal systems coordinator, played an important role in reviewing our documentation of the computer system development of the past twenty years. Without that implementation and continued growth, the ability of Superior Court to maintain its progress, in relation to the dramatic changes in the law and expanding appellate litigation, would have been stifled. As a participant in this development, Dr. Thrall was an indispensable source for tracking that development. We also express our appreciation to Nancy McGowan, administrative assistant to former President Judge James Rowley, who accumulated numerous clippings, documents, and biographies from a number of sources such as newspapers, county bar associations, and historical societies, which were utilized in creating the publication, compiled at the direction of Judge Rowley, *100 Years of Justice,* a brief history of the first century of the Pennsylvania Superior Court.

The support of Joseph Mittleman, former Superior Court executive administrator, is also appreciated for his cooperation and that of the court staff and resources he made available on demand.

Finally, the production of this book required the expert skills of many persons on the staff of the Pennsylvania Historical and Museum Commission. Dr. Brent D. Glass, in an early meeting with various members of the staff, was encouraging of our project, and detailed the types of services and support his staff members and departments could supply. The early support and assistance of Harry Parker, chief of the Division of Archives and Manuscripts, initiated our search of the Pennsylvania archives relating to court records, and was instrumental in the acquisition of much original data. To Heidi Mays and Michael Sherbon, associate archivists, we express appreciation for their efforts in identifying, organizing and obtaining archive photographs that illustrate the text of the book. Thereafter, when the book progressed far enough that publication became a reality, the assistance of Diane Reed, chief of publications, became the primary source of our melding much disparate material into cohesive and intelligible book form. Her encouragement and leadership made the task exciting and gratifying. The close editing provided by Fred J. Lauver, editor, in the copy/editing process was valuable and indispensable in achieving the degree of reliability, credibility, and compliance with historical publication standards, which we could not achieve on our own. The layout and design work by Susan Gahres, the final step before printing, brought the book to its final form and imparted the format which increased its readability and interest as a historical reference which tells the story of the Superior Court.

To my wife, Betty J. Tamilia, I owe her thanks and appreciation for tolerating the many hours in the evenings, weekends, and on vacation I spent buried in reading, writing, and reviewing materials for the book, or working on matters relating to my caseload on the court, to compensate for time taken during office hours working on the book or traveling to sources where data was stored.

Despite the best efforts of all involved, I am certain there will be errors of commission and omission and to the degree this has occurred, I accept full responsibility. To the extent the results are fulfilling and commendable, it can be attributed to the exceptional support of those listed above and others who remain unnamed.

*Patrick R. Tamilia*
*Judge*
*Superior Court of Pennsylvania*

# INTRODUCTION

In 1895, the creation of the Superior Court of Pennsylvania came about as a result of crisis in appellate proceedings, which were solely the domain of the Supreme Court of Pennsylvania. As early as the Constitutional Convention of 1873, relief for the Supreme Court was considered, but the debate failed to develop a consensus as to how that relief could be achieved. Again in 1895, following legislative organization of a judiciary general committee, creation of an intermediate court of appellate jurisdiction to relieve the Supreme Court of an overwhelming backlog was considered. With the advent of the Industrial Revolution and an era historians call the "Gilded Age", the progress of Pennsylvania, if not the nation, was being impeded by lack of a definitive judicial system, represented at its top by an effective process of appellate review. The legislature did what the constitutional convention could not do; that is, create a legislative court of appeals which relieved the Supreme Court of its backlog. In doing so, it expedited appeals and provided a vehicle for the rapidly developing industrial state to construe legislation, resolve disputes, and give guidance to evolving concepts and principles of law in economics, crime, family, torts, and government affairs.

Pennsylvania is considered by historians to be the arsenal of democracy and the engine of industrial might of America from the Civil War through World War II and beyond. No democratic industrial society can develop without a sophisticated legal and judicial system to provide for prompt, fair resolution of disputes, and create an avenue for the people to air their grievances, and the means for government to carry out and establish social policy pronounced through laws promulgated by the legislature.

The foundations in Pennsylvania had been laid with one of the best and earliest constitutions and the first Supreme Court in the nation. The industrialization of the Gilded Age and the wealth it created, accompanied by the negative consequences of laissez-faire policies, a disproportionate distribution of the wealth generated, and the widespread corruption, graft, and special legislation, impacted heavily upon the judicial system and ultimately on the Supreme Court. The pressures generated by the burgeoning appeals demanded the relief, which was afforded by creation of the Superior Court. Progressive legislation and a sound legal and judicial system were necessary to prevent this revolution from self-destructing.

As the Constitutional Convention of 1873 seriously debated issues of relief for the Supreme Court, all of which failed, the seeds for the creation of the Superior Court were planted and the record made of the means suggested by which this could be achieved. Despite increasing the Supreme Court from five justices to seven, and some limitations on jurisdiction, the relief provided by the convention of 1873 was short lived and, by the 1890s, the overload of the Supreme Court again became a significant issue in Pennsylvania politics and law. Spurred by efforts of bar leaders and others, the legislature organized a judiciary general committee in 1895 to consider the plight of the Supreme Court and to generate proposals for its relief. Quickly, proposals were considered, and in rapid succession, most fell by the wayside. In January 1895, the significant bills for creation of a Superior Court were introduced, drawing heavily on concepts developed in the 1873 convention. Over several months the legislation took the form and substance which provided for the type of court, the number of judges, the jurisdiction to be exercised, and the court's relationship to the Supreme Court, the trial courts, and how and where it would decide cases. Chapter I delineates the story of this decades-long process from the Constitutional Convention of 1873, and the legislative enactment of June 24, 1895 which established the Superior Court. The court functioned within that structure without change until the Constitutional Convention of 1968 and the amendments of 1978.

Following its creation in 1895, the Superior Court quickly embarked upon its charge on every front and soon brought the Supreme Court the relief that was expected. It survived its last test of viability when the vote of the Pennsylvania Bar Association to abolish the court was defeated by one vote in 1909. Over the next one hundred years, it participated in review of every facet of business, industry, social change, and development which occurred in Pennsylvania. From early rulings on the relation of workers to employers, women and child labor, crime and punishment, negligence and tort actions, contracts and family law, the path for development and resolution of the ever-expanding legal and judicial base of our society passed through the Superior Court. The story of this progress, which will unfold in the following pages, is a chronicle of the twentieth century and a kaleidoscope of some of the most remarkable changes in society in the history of mankind. The work of the court tracks progress from horse and buggy to moon flights, in employment from totally adversarial labor relations to shared and legally protected rights, and from a criminal justice system, which was at best primitive, to one where the true meaning of constitutional protections was implemented. Children and women went from being treated as chattel to become protected and equal, race relations which were harsh and demeaning acquired the protection of law, and the rights of consumers became safeguarded in the market place, with a cap being placed on corruption, bribery, and exploitation of the people. The progressive legislation from 1900 through the "Little New Deal" of the Great Depression, the impact of the war years, followed by the postwar boom and the accompanying changes in values in every conceivable respect, challenged and tested the Superior Court in its role as the filter and crystallizer of every change occurring in society.

In reviewing the initial selection of the men who were called to serve on this court, we have learned that their ability and character were of the highest quality. While politics played its role in the creation of the court and the determination of its membership, the court, once it became functional, took on the character of its collective membership, which was representative of and subservient to the needs of the people. Early members of the court derived values, character and direction from participation in or exposure to the great American conflict, the Civil War. Four veterans of that war served on the first court created in 1895. One suffered the loss of an arm and another the loss of a leg in battles of that war. The philosophy underlying the progressive era at the turn of the century which led to the curtailment of corruption, monopoly and trusts, and looked to the betterment of the condition of women, children, and the family became the court's driving force. The character and philosophy of those men is illustrative of the fact some were drawn from the state legislature, the Congress, district attorney positions, while three judges of the court served as governors of Pennsylvania, and one was a United States senator. Many previously served as trial judges and several went on to be elected to the Pennsylvania Supreme Court. Through succeeding decades, Superior Court judges served in World War I, the Second World War, Korea, and Vietnam, and in peacetime of the years between the wars. More recently, women have come to serve on the court, which in the coming years will add significant balance and fresh viewpoints to a formerly all-male institution.

The court continued to make its impact felt in the years following World War I dealing with sedition, prohibition, economic depression, labor unrest, the destabilization of World War II, the post-war booms and the civil rights movement. It guided many of the changes in criminal law, civil actions, and the revolution in family law. In that respect, the court is still a work in progress.

In 1995, this court embarked on its centennial celebration, which included many special sessions throughout the Commonwealth. In preparation for these observations, President Judge James E. Rowley undertook the creation of an abbreviated history of the Superior Court, which included a description of centennial activities and photographs of the full court as it existed in 1995. To some extent that effort inspired the desire and interest in providing a more definitive history of the court, in documenting it before many of the records were lost, and in capturing the experiences of the judges who played a major role during the second half of the last century.

In 1996, Judge Stephen J. McEwen Jr., assumed the position of president judge, and shortly thereafter, discussion arose amongst the judges about preserving the activities and records of the court in a more significant fashion. The court initially was concerned that the attempt to compile a history of the court's first one hundred years would be difficult and enormously time consuming due to the lack of access to data and information on the court. Although the court had access to reported cases and the legislative history and materials available in the Pennsylvania Bureau of Archives and History, more personal details about the individual judges and the role of the court in developing state, national, and world affairs would be difficult to obtain.

About this time, the Speaker of the Pennsylvania House of Representatives, Matthew J. Ryan, was moving forward on the preparation of a biographical history of the Pennsylvania speakers between 1682 and 1998. From this effort, Judge McEwen was motivated to pursue a similar project for the Superior Court.

In 1996, the Superior Court Archives Committee, composed of this author and Judge John P. Hester, was created. Judge McEwen then consulted the Speaker and Jean Schmedlen, director of the Speaker's project, to request their assistance and to advise the court about making contact with legislative and state officials who could assist in the serious search for the history and documents of the Superior Court. This resulted in meetings with Jean Schmedlen and Harry Parker, chief archivist of the Pennsylvania Historical and Museum Commission. Thereafter, this author involved his staff members, particularly John Hare, Esquire, and Lauren Posati, Esquire, in the mechanical process of deep research. The research began with the Pennsylvania Archives and later expanded to legislative reports, newspaper accounts and the solicitation of state and local bar association records, reports, and accounts from the various counties whence Superior Court judges came. Additionally, to preserve a living history, this author undertook to prepare an oral history of present and past Superior Court Judges still living. While these histories will not be the basis for any current report on the court, they may be significant to future archivists or historians. Since the ultimate result of this effort would be of limited value unless it was formalized in writing, the work took on a life of its own and naturally evolved into the product, which follows. Needless to say, without the vision, energy and commitment of President Judge McEwen, this undertaking would not have succeeded.

In a serendipitous circumstance, John Hare, Esquire, this author's law clerk, expressed great interest in the project. John was interested in graduate work in history and was pursuing acceptance to leading universities for a program leading to an M.A. and Ph.D. in legal history. Following meetings with the chief of the Pennsylvania Bureau of Archives and History, Harry Parker, the Archives Committee and John began accumulating original data on the court from the Archives in Harrisburg. Among the materials gathered were the court's original orders, first opinions, original rules, conference minutes, and the early documents and materials of a developing court. Upon return to Pennsylvania from the University of California at Berkley, where he completed the master's program, John was placed under contract with the court to do basic research from materials contained in the *New York Times*, the *Philadelphia Public Ledger*, historical treatises on Pennsylvania and the Pennsylvania Bureau of Archives and History. John's involvement was of such importance that I have constituted him as co-author of this book.

I outlined the format of the book to detail the background of every judge who served, and to relate the creation and evolution of the court to the various eras and epochs through which the state and nation passed during the court's first century.

The book on the court's history was to track the significant and relevant sociological, political, national, and business developments of the times. In this fashion, we would not be focusing on the individual biographies of judges of the court, but rather would flesh out those biographies with important decisions the court rendered during a time and century covering some of the most dynamic and important changes in Pennsylvania, the United States, and the world. The material, as it relates to the politics, the law, and the socio-economic development of Pennsylvania, proved to be deeply interesting and exciting. It fully confirmed our belief that the Superior Court of Pennsylvania was created at a propitious time. Its existence over one hundred years paralleled and contributed to the enormous role the industrialization of this country, much of which was centered in Pennsylvania, played in making the United States the foremost country in the world and the bastion of democracy and free enterprise. As anticipated, the decisions of this court tracked the history of Pennsylvania and the United States for over one hundred years with significant impact. This court was not a passive viewer of history, but rather an active participant in shaping history.

In the epilogue leading to the twenty-first century, I believe it necessary to briefly document what has occurred in the Superior Court since 1995 and what changes we can foresee. Clear trends indicate that computerization of the court and public accessibility to our process will increase. Within the past twenty years, the court went from typewriter to word processor to computer and e-mail. We have a court computer database which provides immediate access to our filed opinions, and a Web site, on which the opinions are posted, the court schedule displayed, and information about the court, its judges, procedures, and history are available. The court also uses an electronic docketing/case management system, which provides for immediate recall of all docket entries necessary to schedule and track cases. The acceleration of appeals and the increase in their volume has led to the exploration of new and different means of expediting cases, both argued and submitted. These means are being evaluated and adopted without losing the focus and critical review which have been the hallmark of the court from its inception. Additionally, beginning last year, court en banc proceedings were televised for the first time on Pennsylvania's government access cable television network.

Training of judges is becoming increasingly important. The character and composition of the court has inevitably changed with the evolution of generations from the Civil War era which now includes post-World War II baby boom members. The children of the "baby boomers", the "Y" generation, will match and perhaps exceed the population explosion during the post-World War II years. This alone will mark a radical change in the court's practices and procedures during the first half of the twenty-first century. The first African American was not appointed and later elected to the court until seventy-one years after its inception. It was eighty-six years before a woman was appointed and later elected to the court. Now the court has five women serving on the court with more to be anticipated in the coming years. The future composition of the court, as in the past, will reflect the makeup and political/social values of the citizens of Pennsylvania. Its decisions will continue to interpret and refine the legislation, which is at the core of the appellate review process.

Pennsylvania incorporates many, if not most, of the attributes and problems of our nation with its varied and substantial mix of rural and urban communities, industries, educational and scientific institutions, and agrarian and service activities. Fortunately for Pennsylvania, the Superior Court was created as a statewide court rather than a district court, which had been proposed from time to time. The statewide structure has provided a uniform approach to decision making and allows different concepts and philosophies to be melded into a universal whole that better integrates the decisions of the court and makes for stronger and more credible precedents.

In 1968, with the enactment of a new state constitution, the first since 1874, the Superior Court was established as a constitutional court. This step confirmed the court's excellence and necessity as an intermediate appellate court and proved the soundness of the decision to create the court by its founders in 1895. In many ways this permits the Superior Court to be the final word in most cases and strengthens the role of the Pennsylvania Supreme Court in ultimately deciding policy and constitutional issues. To the extent possible, we have tracked decisions of this court that have had a measurable impact on our society and the law. In incontrovertible fashion, it is evident the Superior Court has been a great clarifier and originator of concepts in the law, acting as a filter for new and changing philosophies and legal principles by which the Pennsylvania Supreme Court and other jurisdictions throughout the country can crystallize new principles at the cutting edge of change.

The expectations of the creators of the Superior Court have been fulfilled beyond what might have been hoped and the court's historical basis provides a strong foundation for continuation into the twenty-first century and beyond.


*Patrick R. Tamilia*
*Judge*
*Superior Court of Pennsylvania*

Pennsylvania, "The Laboratory of Industrial Society". Producing Bessemer steel at the Pennsylvania Steel Company in Steelton, Dauphin County c. 1895 *(Hagley Museum and Library)*.

# CHAPTER ONE

# ORIGINS OF THE SUPERIOR COURT: 1873-1895

Fifty thousand square miles of fertile farms and bustling coal fields spanning two great industrial cities, Pennsylvania in the last half of the nineteenth century was among the most prosperous economic regions on earth. At the outset of the Civil War, the state's mechanical industries were twice as productive as those of the entire South, and Philadelphia was the nation's preeminent industrial center. All of the anthracite and most of the bituminous coal consumed by the Union war machine was mined in Pennsylvania and, led by the booming mills of Pittsburgh, the state produced 80 percent of the North's iron. After the war as well, Pennsylvania remained the keystone of the American industrial arch. In 1880, it produced 84 percent of the nation's coke, and it remained the chief supplier of coal, iron, and steel until the turn of the century. For much of this period, it was also the nation's principal source of lumber and oil. By the 1870s, the Pennsylvania Railroad was the world's largest freight carrier and perhaps the most powerful corporation in America. Throughout the Gilded Age, Pennsylvania was indeed the "Laboratory of Industrial Society."[1]

Although this industrial might created tremendous wealth and power for many Pennsylvanians, it also had negative consequences. Two of these consequences, in particular, led to the creation of the Superior Court. First, industrialization generated unprecedented corruption. In the years following the Civil War, new corporate wealth commercialized Pennsylvania politics, and the state acquired a national reputation for graft and bribery. The legislature was especially notorious. Since the state had no general incorporation law, grants of corporate power required special legislation. Legislators sold their votes to corporations and then extracted bribes by threatening to enact laws hostile to corporate interests. The amount of special legislation was staggering; of 9,230 acts passed by the legislature between 1866 and 1873, 8,700 were special or local acts. Most were passed with little study or debate, and their merit was assessed solely by commercial value.

In his 1871 inaugural address, Governor John White Geary declared, "Special legislation is the great and impure fountain of corruption, private speculation and public wrong. It has become a reproach to republican government, and is one of the most alarming evils of the times."[2] Many Pennsylvanians agreed with Geary, and, on October 10, 1871, they overwhelmingly passed a referendum calling for a constitutional

---

1. This reference to Pennsylvania, as well as the statistics which preceded it, are found in Philip S. Klein and Ari Hoogenboom, *A History of Pennsylvania*, 2d ed. (University Park: Pennsylvania State University, 1980), 277-315.

2. *Pennsylvania Archives*, Fourth Series, VIII, 1127-31.

convention to combat political corruption.[3] Although the Superior Court was not established until 1895, its roots can be traced to this convention.

The second factor caused by industrialization—a dramatic increase in the Supreme Court's caseload—ensured that proposals to create an intermediate appellate court would play a leading role at the convention. Throughout the latter half of the nineteenth century, the increasing complexity of commercial relationships, and the resulting litigation increase, placed tremendous pressure upon the state judiciary. This pressure was manifested most visibly in the caseload of the Supreme Court, which grew dramatically in the four years preceding the convention. In 1869, for instance, 568 cases came before the high court, but by 1872, the number had grown to 778, an increase of nearly 40 percent.[4] More significant, however, was the burgeoning number of unresolved cases remaining on the Supreme Court's docket at the end of each year. This number increased nearly 80 percent, from 128 in 1869 to 231 in 1872.[5] On the eve of a convention called to combat legislative corruption, relief of the Supreme Court's caseload became an important issue in state politics.

## THE CONSTITUTIONAL CONVENTION OF 1873

At noon on Tuesday, November 12, 1872, convention delegates assembled on the floor of the House of Representatives in Harrisburg. After completing organizational tasks, the convention adjourned and reconvened in Philadelphia on January 7, 1873. Elected to "revise and amend the constitution,"[6] the delegates brought to their work a variety of viewpoints and agendas, and the debates in the ten months that followed were both wide-ranging and heated.[7] Yet, it was generally agreed that the state judiciary was no longer equipped to deal with the myriad of challenges presented by Pennsylvania's headlong industrialization. According to delegate David Craig of New Castle:

> The peculiar law in relation to the railway system, the railways themselves, the law relative to all corporations, the vast increase in the subjects of commercial law arising out of operations of these corporations, have precipitated new and entangling questions upon the courts which our fathers of the judiciary knew not of. . . . It is all new, and yet our courts stand still where they were forty years ago. It has seemed to me, sir, that everything in this world progresses except the judiciary system.[8]

3. Wayland F. Dunaway, *A History of Pennsylvania* (New York, 1948), 443 ("For some time there had been a growing feeling that the legislature was corrupt, that the evils of special legislation and the temptation connected therewith to commercialize politics should be removed, and that the constitution should be modernized to meet the new conditions that had arisen."). See also, Robert Woodside, *Pennsylvania Constitutional Law* (Sayre, Pa.: Murrelle Printing Co., 1985), 576-77; and Klein and Hoogenboom, *A History of Pennsylvania*, 356-57. The referendum was passed by a vote of 328,000 to 70,000. Rosalind L. Branning, *Pennsylvania Constitutional Development* (Pittsburgh: University of Pittsburgh Press, 1960), 56.

4. *Debates of the Convention to Amend the Constitution of Pennsylvania, 1872-1873* (hereinafter *Debates*) (Harrisburg, Pa.: Benjamin Singerly, State Printer, 1873), vol. III, 641 (statement of Delegate-at-Large William H. Armstrong on April 28, 1873).

5. See note 4.

6. Pa. Act of April 11, 1872, PL 53, sec. 1. The only limitations placed on the convention were that it could not modify the Declaration of Rights contained in the Constitution of 1838, and it could not create a separate court of equity. Journal of the Convention of 1872-1873, part I, 20-21.

7. The contentious nature of the proceedings was assured by the structure established by the legislature for electing delegates. Of the 133 delegates sent to the convention, 99 were elected from senatorial districts (three from each of the thirty-three districts), twenty-eight were elected at large from across the state, and

William A. Armstrong, Republican congressman and chairman of the Judiciary Committee, Constitutional Convention, 1873.

George W. Woodward, Democratic delegate
from Philadelphia, former Chief Justice,
Pennsylvania Supreme Court.

The delegates viewed relief of the Supreme Court's caseload burden as the first priority of judicial reform. Indeed, it may well have been "the one purpose . . . in which . . . the entire Convention concur[red]."[9] In order to consider amendments to the judiciary article (Article V) of the constitution, the convention established a judiciary committee. Its chairman was William H. Armstrong, Republican congressman and delegate-at-large from Williamsport. While all members of the committee recognized the need to assist the Supreme Court in easing its caseload, they were hardly unanimous on how best to achieve that goal. From the outset, the central issue of contention was whether and in what form an intermediate appellate court should be added to the courts enumerated in the Pennsylvania Constitution.[10] In the following months, the committee considered and debated a number of proposals. One proposal was submitted by George W. Woodward, Democratic delegate from Philadelphia, who had played a leading role in formulating the judicial article at the Constitutional Convention of 1838. Woodward served for ten years as president judge of the Fourth Judicial District, and served on the Pennsylvania Supreme Court for fifteen years, including four years as chief justice. His proposal, which was endorsed by a significant minority of the judiciary committee, recommended dividing the state into a number of appellate circuits, not to exceed twelve. A judge would then be appointed to each circuit and sit, with at least two judges from the common pleas courts, in judgment of appeals from the counties in the circuit. The common pleas judges serving on the circuit court would be selected on a rotating basis

---

six were elected at large from Philadelphia. Democrats and Republicans were to share equally the at-large delegate positions, and in each of the senatorial districts, the minority party was assured at least one of the three delegate seats. Branning, *Pennsylvania Constitutional Development,* 56-7. As a result, the convention was nearly equally divided between Democrats and Republicans, with the latter possessing only a slight majority. Editorial, *Pittsburgh Gazette,* October 18, 1872. The fierce debates at the convention might also be attributed to the fact that 103 of the 133 delegates were lawyers. Branning, supra note 3, 61.

8. *Debates,* vol. III, 708.

9. *Debates,* vol. III, 640.

10. The Constitution of 1838 stated that "the judicial power of this Commonwealth shall be vested in a Supreme Court, in Courts of Common Pleas, Courts of Oyer and Terminer and General Jail Delivery, Courts of Quarter Sessions of the Peace, Orphan's Courts and Magistrates Courts." Pennsylvania Constitution (1838), art. V, sec. 1.

and, although no judge could pass on a case he decided at trial, he might sit with the circuit court as an "assessor." The proposed court required a quorum of three judges, and likely would be composed of five or more. It would be empowered to order a new trial or affirm the judgment of the common pleas court as it saw fit, with appeals proceeding to the Supreme Court. According to Woodward, this manner of review would discourage appeals and ultimately lighten the burden upon the Supreme Court, which would thus be enabled to consider only cases presenting significant legal issues.[11]

Opponents of Woodward's plan argued that twelve different tribunals would result in a lack of conformity in the law, and that inclusion of common pleas judges would deprive the court of desired impartiality in reviewing common pleas decisions.[12] A majority of the judiciary committee ultimately rejected Woodward's proposal, and its rationale for doing so can be inferred from the following statement of Chairman Armstrong:

> The court is itself in constant rotation. Judges A and B may sit in the circuit court at this term, and Judges C and D may sit at the next; it lacks stability; there is no certainty in its decision, even within itself. But the evil becomes greatly exaggerated, when you consider that there are many such districts; and the gentleman himself proposes twelve. Then you have substantially twelve separate distinct intermediate courts, all making their own decisions in their own way, diverse and different from one another, and none of them of authority anywhere beyond its own district, and not of much authority there, for the judges within each district will consider that one is as able to decide as another, and it might frequently happen that a case which was decided by two judges, a majority of a quorum in the same circuit, might be reversed by three or four judges the very next term, and in the same circuit, and thus no certainty could be had within itself, and its decisions could command no respect beyond it, further than a well considered opinion, new from a judge of the court of common pleas of recognized ability, is entitled to respectful consideration, not as authority, but as the opinion of a lawyer entitled to respect.[13]

The judiciary committee also considered a number of other proposals, none of which attracted significant support. One such proposal called for an intermediate appellate court consisting of common pleas judges from across the state to assemble en banc in individual districts. Rather than establishing a new court, another proposal recommended the addition of three to five justices to the five-member Supreme Court. The expanded court would then be divided into two sections, one to sit in the east and one to sit in the west. Where a section decided a case unanimously, its judgment would stand as the judgment of the whole court, but where a section was not unanimous, the two sections would reunite and sit in judgment of the case. Finally, the committee considered and rejected a plan offered by Delegate John Broomall of Delaware County, which provided that no judges or courts should be added to the judiciary, but sought instead to require that existing Supreme Court justices sit longer and write shorter opinions.[14]

Having rejected these proposals, the judiciary committee submitted its own

---

11. *Debates*, vol. III, 653-63.
12. *Debates*, vol. III, 664-729.
13. *Debates*, vol. III, 644.
14. *Debates*, vol. III, 677-81.

report in March of 1873 calling for the creation of an intermediate court possessing both appellate and original jurisdiction.[15] In exercising the former, the proposed court would consist of eight judges who would be elected rather than appointed, and one justice of the Supreme Court who would be appointed by the remainder of that court and sit as chief justice of the intermediate court. A quorum of five was necessary for the court to convene, and the Supreme Court justice would sit as chief justice only when the intermediate court sat en banc. All cases involving less than $2,000 were subject to the proposed court's appellate jurisdiction. The committee believed that the $2,000 jurisdictional limit, which encompassed the majority of appellate cases in the mid-nineteenth century, would significantly reduce the Supreme Court's caseload without unduly usurping its jurisdictional prerogative. Cases exceeding $2,000 would proceed directly to the Supreme Court, since the committee felt that such cases would end up before the high court in any event. The committee report also provided that cases involving less than $2,000, but more than $500, would proceed through the intermediate court, but the right of appeal to the Supreme Court would be absolute. Cases involving less than $500 could not be appealed so long as the judgment of the intermediate court was unanimous. An exception to this rule was provided where the intermediate court certified the case for appeal to the Supreme Court. Finally, where the court was not unanimous in a case involving less than $500, an appeal could be taken, since such cases presumably involved issues sufficiently difficult to warrant review by the court of last resort.[16]

The proposed court's original jurisdiction, which was clearly intended as subordinate to its appellate jurisdiction, would be exercised in a given case by a single judge, who would enter the county in which the case arose and preside in the manner of a common pleas judge. To ensure that a judge exercising original jurisdiction would not later review his own judgment under the court's appellate jurisdiction, the judiciary committee provided that all appeals from the exercise of original jurisdiction would proceed directly to the Supreme Court. As to the remainder of the court's exercise of original jurisdiction, however, the committee was exceedingly vague. For instance, it provided only that the court should sit at least once per year, and that the legislature could increase the frequency of sessions as it saw fit. Further, unlike its specific pronouncements regarding the types of cases subject to appellate jurisdiction, the committee declined to specify what cases might fall within the court's original jurisdiction.[17] According to Chairman Armstrong, "What cases or class of cases should be embraced in such jurisdiction is a question of mere detail, which may be in some measure determined by the Constitution, or left wholly to the Legislature."[18] Nonetheless, it appears from Armstrong's subsequent comments that the committee intended original jurisdiction to attach in cases where it would be difficult or improper for a common pleas court to sit in judgment:

> There are cases which it is not for the public interest that local judges should try. Let them be classified and designated by law, and the jurisdiction vested in the circuit court—such are contested election cases, and cases which the common pleas judges are now by law disqualified from trying; such are the majority of those cases in which change of

---

15. Three members of the committee, Delegates Daniel Kaine, Samuel A. Purviance, and James L. Reynolds, filed dissenting reports. *Debates,* vol. III, 189-91. Two others, Delegates Woodward and Broomall, gave notice of their intention to file such reports at a later date.

16. *Debates,* vol. III, 639-53.

17. See note 16.

18. *Debates,* vol. III, 650.

A bark peeler's load during the logging era of the Gilded Age.

venue is asked, and if unfortunately in any district there be a question as to the ability or fitness of a particular judge, the suitors ought to have a right to say, "there is a court where I can avoid what I apprehend from the decisions of such a local judge."[19]

Under convention debate rules, committee proposals were to be read three times, with the first reading to take place before the committee of the whole.[20] Pursuant to these rules, the judiciary committee's report was presented to the committee of the whole by Chairman Armstrong on March 27, 1873. He began by noting the committee's unanimous agreement "that the Supreme Court, as a matter of absolute necessity, and imperatively urgent, must have some relief."[21] "It is not a matter of any great importance by what name it may be called," Armstrong continued, "whether it be a superior court, or a circuit court, or an appellate court. . . . By whatever name it may be designated, the purpose of it is to devise a practical and thorough relief to the Supreme Court."[22] In support of his appeal to the delegates, Armstrong also cited the dramatic increase in the Supreme Court's caseload in the preceding four years,[23] and noted that the five-member court had disposed of more than five hundred cases in each of the past three years.[24] "The Supreme Court of Pennsylvania," he declared, "is working more

19. See note 18.
20. *Journal of the Convention, 1872-73*, part I, 57.
21. *Debates,* vol. III, 640.
22. See note 21.
23. *Debates,* vol. III, 641.
24. *Debates,* vol. III, 642.

industriously and doing more work than the court of appeals of the State of New York or any of our sister states."[25] He continued:

> The judges of that court are overworked in body and in mind, and it is a marvel of persistent energy and endurance that they perform their work to the extent and as well as they do.
>
> I appeal to the intelligent judgment of every member of this Convention, can this state of things continue with fairness and justice to the judicial administration of the State? Is there not a continuing ration of increase?
>
> Do not the *remanets* [unresolved cases] increase, year by year, by a rapidly increasing percentage?[26]

Pressing his argument, Armstrong returned to the experience of New York:

> If we do not relieve the Supreme Court we shall go on step by step until the *remanets* of the State will accumulate to that degree that we shall be compelled, as they were in the State of New York, to organize, by a change of the Constitution, a commission of appeal, who shall consider and decide the *remanets* of the State, and who there are now going on year by year to decide them, and which, when decided, are certified to the court of appeals and become the judgment of that court, although none of its judges have participated in making the decisions, a misfortune imposed upon them by inexorable necessity; and a like necessity already casts its dark shadow upon the judicial administration of our State. It is to the State of New York an admitted and much deplored evil. It is a misfortune which must overtake us if we be not wise to be warned by their experience. It has introduced into their adjudicated law a series of decisions which the court of last resort had no lot nor part in making, and which must be open to the revision of the court of appeals when similar questions arise—and to end in long lists of cases "over-ruled or doubted"—for no set of judges acting distinctly and separately one from another can bring their minds to run in the same channel—and if opinions of the commissioners differ from their own, they will be in the direct line of cases over-ruled.[27]

Armstrong also sought to defend the specific provisions of the committee report from a variety of criticisms. Countering claims that adding a Supreme Court justice to the intermediate court would deprive the high court of one of its members and thus weaken its manpower, Armstrong directed the delegates' attention to the committee's recommendation that the Supreme Court should be increased by two justices. Additionally, he argued, "the judge thus taken from the supreme court to sit as chief justice of the circuit court will add dignity to that court, give popular confidence to its administration and its decisions, and keep the two appellate courts of the state in close accord, in harmony, and unity of decision."[28] Moreover, countering the argument of Del-

---

25. See note 24.
26. See note 24.
27. *Debates,* vol. III, 652-53.
28. *Debates,* vol. III, 652.

egate Samuel A. Purviance of Allegheny County that the $500 minimum limit for appeals from the intermediate court unduly deprived litigants of access to the Supreme Court, Armstrong reiterated that such appeals were permitted where the intermediate court's judgment is not unanimous and stated that such a provision ensured "that no man's case, much or little, rich or poor, should be debarred from the consideration of the Supreme Court, if there was anything in his case which deserved the consideration of that court."[29] Again responding to claims that the proposed court operated to limit access to the Supreme Court, Armstrong stated that "we are careful to deny to no suitor the right to be heard in the court of last resort, if there be in his case anything which, after hearing in the intermediate court, shall present any question upon which competent judicial minds can reasonably doubt. And even this limitation upon the right to appeal to the highest court of the State is fixed at a point which is liberal and cannot be oppressive, and which, in the judgment of many men of good judgment, is more liberal than expedient."[30] Finally, in order to assure delegates that the authoritative case law of the state would remain only "that which has passed in review and been established by the Supreme Court," Armstrong emphasized the committee's recommendation that opinions of the intermediate court "shall not be published . . . as authoritative decisions."[31]

Armstrong also argued that the benefits of the proposed court would extend beyond the realm of civil cases. Noting that under current law criminal defendants, unlike civil litigants, were required to seek special *allocatur* before the Supreme Court in order to obtain any review, Armstrong argued that "[t]he rights of personal liberty, and life, and reputation, are thus placed in subordinate relation to the courts as compared with purely civil rights."[32] The committee's report, he believed, would remedy this anomaly:

> With the establishment of the proposed intermediate court, jurisdiction to review criminal appeals, under reasonable and proper restrictions, but far more liberal than exist at present, might be safely and ought to be vested in that court. It is demanded no less by enlightened public policy than by the higher sense of justice which pervades the public mind. It ought no longer to be that there shall be unobstructed public highway to the court of appeals for the value of a herring, but a devious and difficult path to an appellate court where life, and liberty, and reputation, which is dearer than both, are brought to the arbitrament of the law.[33]

While Armstrong repeatedly emphasized the virtues of the proposed court's appellate jurisdiction, he offered only a halfhearted defense of the committee's recommendation that the court also exercise original jurisdiction. In this regard, Armstrong apparently recognized that many delegates were extremely hostile to the idea of a state-wide court with original jurisdiction. Three factors caused this hostility. First was the apparently widespread belief that the assertion of original jurisdiction would infringe upon the prerogatives of the common pleas courts. Armstrong himself admitted that the common pleas judges with whom he spoke were unanimous in feeling that the

---

29. *Debates,* vol. III, 646.
30. *Debates,* vol. III, 640.
31. *Debates,* vol. III, 645.
32. *Debates,* vol. III, 647.
33. See note 32.

Drake Oil Well, Titusville, Pennsylvania. Discovery of oil by Edwin Drake in 1859 was one of the sources of Pennsylvania's industrial might.

committee's proposal "will diminish the influence of the common pleas; you reduce us to inferior courts; you take away our dignity; you destroy us in the estimation of the people." Although Armstrong dismissed these claims as "merely personal considerations,"[34] his halting support of the committee's proposal regarding original jurisdiction seems to be at least partially in response to such claims.

An unhappy chapter of Pennsylvania's legal history also generated hostility toward the committee's recommendation regarding original jurisdiction. In 1827, the *nisi prius* court sitting in Philadelphia was reconstituted as a "circuit court" and extended to the other counties of the state. The judges bitterly resented the hardships of circuit duty, and they repeatedly postponed cases in order to avoid their responsibilities. Since circuit duty arose only once yearly, a single postponement effectively delayed a case for a year. As postponements multiplied, administration of the court deteriorated. Ultimately, the court broke down under the resistance of its own judges and it was abolished after nine years. Memories of this debacle apparently endured and the delegates at the convention in 1873 proved resistant to resurrecting a statewide court with original jurisdiction. The third factor that caused hostility was the view among many delegates that a statewide court with original jurisdiction would encourage plaintiffs from one county to issue writs in that county and compel the appearance of defendants from another county. Armstrong declared this fear "a total misconception" and attempted to allay it by reiterating that a circuit judge sitting with original jurisdiction acts precisely as would a common pleas judge in the same county.[35] Nonetheless, he seems to have concluded under the weight of criticism that the provisions regarding original jurisdiction were expendable in order to save those regarding appellate jurisdiction. Throughout his discussion of the committee's proposal, he emphasized that the

34. *Debates,* vol. III, 651.
35. *Debates,* vol. III, 648.

two jurisdictional provisions were severable, and at times, he invited the convention to disregard the provisions establishing original jurisdiction. For instance, he stated that "[i]f the circuit court of original jurisdiction does not commend itself to [your] approval, strike it out, for it is so distinctly separate that, by a single amendment . . . it is wholly eliminated from the report."[36] Moreover, he encouraged the committee of the whole to await further readings of the proposal, as well as the remainder of the judiciary committee's plan regarding the judiciary, before it judged the proposed intermediate court. "[T]hen," he continued:

> if the original jurisdiction does not commend itself to the judgment of the Convention, let it be stricken out; but I do say that in my judgment the appellate jurisdiction is the most advantageous and important suggestion which this committee has been able to make. In my judgment, it is worth all the other sections together. The others are minor and unimportant compared with this.[37]

Despite Armstrong's impassioned defense of the judiciary committee's proposal, and his plea for restraint in judging its original jurisdiction provisions, a key objection had remained unanswered. Specifically, opponents of the proposal had argued throughout the convention that the committee's plan would allow a multiplicity of appeals that would cause delay in the administration of justice. According to one opponent, George W. Biddle, Democrat of Philadelphia:

> I do not believe that any suitor desires or ought to have the right to keep his case in successive courts, after it has been fairly heard and the law correctly pronounced. I think the delay of justice a monstrous evil. . . . I can not understand that it is the right of a freeman to be used as a sort of shuttlecock between the battledores of successive appellate courts, to be knocked about from one to the other. I do not believe it is a right he should possess. . . . I am, therefore, opposed to an intermediate court in the sense of a steppingstone to the reaching of a final adjudication.[38]

Biddle's concern that "successive appellate courts" would result in "the delay of justice" was echoed by others who hoped to maintain the strict dichotomy between a set of courts vested exclusively with original jurisdiction and a single high court vested with final, appellate jurisdiction. The most prominent advocate of this view was delegate and ex-U.S. Senator Charles R. Buckalew of Columbia County, who emerged as the father of the Constitution of 1874. In rejecting the idea of an intermediate appellate court, Buckalew stated:

> I for one shall be compelled to vote against establishing a new system in Pennsylvania. I believe that our system of courts of first and final jurisdiction, which we have always had in Pennsylvania is capable of indefinite application and expansion; that it will do for a country of ten millions of people as well as for one of half a million; that it can be taken by the people of this State and carried forward indefinitely in the fu-

---

36. *Debates,* vol. III, 641.

37. *Debates,* vol. III, 652. Prior to the end of debate, Delegate John Mann of Coudersport rose and declared his belief that the legislature was the proper body to create a new court, and that it had the power to do so if the people found it desirable. *Debates,* vol. III, 703-05.

38. *Debates,* vol. III, 688.

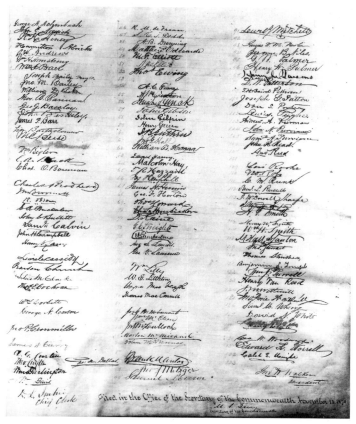

The signatures of the delegates to the Constitutional Convention of 1874 signified the completion of the work of the convention.

ture, even to that supposable period of time when our population shall be equal to the whole population of the United States at its present time.[39]

Buckalew's view that the two-tiered court system should be maintained was also shared by prominent attorney Mortimer F. Elliot, Democratic delegate from Wellsboro:

> The two cardinal principles of our present system which I desire to see maintained and perpetuated are, first, that there shall be one court of original jurisdiction for the trial of all civil actions; and, secondly, that there shall be one appellate court to which the causes tried in the court of original jurisdiction shall be directly taken, and when that court has pronounced its judgment in any case, that case shall be at an end forever.[40]

The belief of Biddle, Buckalew, Elliot, and other delegates that creation of an

39. Buckalew's comments are recalled in the context of a subsequent debate. *Legislative Record*, Pennsylvania General Assembly, June 6, 1895, vol. 2, 3915.

40. Pennsylvania, *Report of the Special Committee on the Constitution*, 1910, 270.

intermediate appellate court would cause multiple appeals and result in delayed justice ultimately proved determinative, and the proposed court was defeated by a vote of sixty-two to twenty-two.[41] Thus ended the first concerted effort to establish an intermediate appellate court in Pennsylvania.

Having rejected the creation of a new court, the convention opted instead to expand the Supreme Court and limit the types of cases presented to it. First, the convention provided that the five-member court should be expanded by two justices,[42] to be chosen at the general election of 1874.[43] The tenure of justices was also increased from fifteen to twenty-one years, after which they could not be re-elected.[44] Further, the delegates removed the Supreme Court's *nisi prius* jurisdiction, which had been granted when the separate *nisi prius* court was abolished.[45] The convention also sharply limited the court's remaining original jurisdiction, approving its exercise only in cases of injunction where a corporation is a defendant, of habeas corpus, of mandamus to courts of inferior jurisdiction, and of quo warranto to all state officers. The result was that the court's appellate jurisdiction, to be exercised only by appeal, on writ of error, or writ of certiorari, became nearly exclusive.[46] Finally, to ensure that the justices' time was spent adjudicating cases before the Supreme Court, the convention directed that "no duties not judicial are to be imposed upon any of the judges of said court."[47]

Despite the convention's efforts, these measures proved insufficient, and in the following two decades, the tide of appellate litigation continued to engulf the Supreme Court. In 1873, the year the constitutional convention had declined to create an intermediate appellate court, 678 cases were brought before the Supreme Court on writs of errors. Of this number, 226 were either dismissed for failure to prosecute (non prossed) or discontinued. Thus, the five-member court was required to adjudicate 452 cases, or approximately ninety per justice. By 1894, the number of writs totaled 1,106, of which 189 were either non prossed or discontinued.[48] With 915 cases remaining, each of the seven justices was required to adjudicate approximately 130. Thus, the decision of the Constitutional Convention of 1873 to ease the Supreme Court's backlog by adding two justices had proven erroneous, as the workload per justice increased by nearly 50 percent in the following two decades.

## RENEWED EFFORTS TO RELIEVE THE SUPREME COURT

By the 1890s, relief of the Supreme Court's onerous caseload once again loomed as a significant issue in Pennsylvania politics, and lawyers and others familiar with the judiciary became increasingly aware of the need for reform. "We are confident," declared the *Legal Intelligencer*, "that to anyone who has given the subject intelligent consideration, the necessity for the relief of the Supreme Court [is a fact which] the profession and the client needed no argument to support."[49] Representatives also decried the condition of the Supreme Court on the floor of the legislature. According to Representative Emmett E. Cotton of Allegheny County:

---

41. *Report of the Special Committee on the Constitution*, 1910, 728.

42. Pennsylvania Constitution (1873), art. V, sec. 2.

43. *A Statement and Exposition of the Changes Contained in the New Constitution of Pennsylvania* (Philadelphia, 1873), 5.

44. See note 42.

45. *Statement and Exposition,* 6.

46. Pennsylvania Constitution (1838), art. V, sec. 3.

47. See note 45.

48. Table prepared by a Mr. Taylor, crier of the Superior Court, and attached to a speech presented to the state bar by Judge John B. McPherson on June 30, 1897. *Fifteenth Annual Report of the Pennsylvania Bar Association* (1897), 139.

49. *Legal Intelligencer* (Philadelphia), vol. 53, no. 30: 308.

I do not believe there is a lawyer in the State of Pennsylvania who has given this subject any consideration that is not perfectly satisfied of the necessity of some sort of relief for the Supreme Court of this State. . . . It cannot be contradicted that the [court] today must in every year consider and decide upon not less than nine hundred cases. Taking three hundred working days in the year, it would give that court three cases each day to consider, digest and write opinions upon. I am informed that one of the judges of that court, when they adjourned for their vacation of sixty days, took seventy-one cases with him for the purpose of writing his opinions during that vacation. Now, the lawyers all know that no lawyer or man that was ever born on the earth can carefully consider and try one case for each working day of the year, and do it properly—or half do it. That is unquestioned, so far as the question of necessity is concerned.[50]

Representative Edward P. Gould of Erie County agreed:

[B]y reason of the great amount of business thrown upon the Supreme Court, the standing of the Supreme Court today is lower, whereas, in the past it stood at the head of any judiciary in the Union, whereas it today is scarcely recognized as an authority, because the judges today do not have time to prepare the reports they want to. Nine-tenths of the opinions of the Supreme Court are decided on some side issue and the main legal questions are avoided.[51]

The issue of judicial reform had also been a primary concern of the Pennsylvania Bar Association, quite literally, from the beginning. Indeed, in his presidential address to the association at its first annual meeting, John W. Simonton stated the following:

One other subject, and only one, shall I take the time now to refer to; and that is a matter which has been in the minds, I know, of many of the members of the Bar, and which has been frequently referred to, and spoken of to many of us by members of the Supreme Court; and that is the question with reference to what has been styled "relief of the Supreme Court." I think we all know and feel, and I don't think any persons feel it more than the members of the Supreme Court themselves, that the magnitude of the business which comes before that Court is

---

50. *Legislative Record*, May 31, 1895, vol. 2, 3339.

51. *Leg. Record*, May 31, 1895, vol. 2, 3339. A number of other representatives shared the view expressed by Cotton and Gould. For instance, Representative Benjamin K. Focht stated:

I have been told by lawyers of the State of Pennsylvania who frequently have cases in the Supreme Court . . . that they can get no more than thirty minutes to argue any case. Now, if that court is so overcrowded that you can get but thirty minutes time in which your lawyer can argue the case which you have spent your money to have taken to the Supreme Court, and which means so much to you, I think we should turn to the constitution and see whether we can't get some relief. *Leg. Record*, May 31, 1895, vol. 2, 3340.

Similarly, Representative Samuel B. Cochrane noted that he had been "told by the lawyers of [another] county that cases are not and cannot be fully considered in our present Supreme Court on account of the great press of business in that court, and that much injustice is done to litigants on that account." *Leg. Record*, May 31, 1895, vol. 2, 3341.

such that they have not been able for some years, and are not now able, to transact it in the manner they desire to do, and as they think it ought to be done, and as the Bar of the State generally think it ought to be done.[52]

Spurred by the efforts of bar leaders and others, the legislature organized the Judiciary General Committee in 1895 to take testimony regarding the plight of the Supreme Court and to consider proposals for its relief. In short order, a variety of proposals emerged. One such proposal, suggested to the committee by former Pennsylvania Supreme Court Justice Christopher Heydrick, recommended prohibiting any appeal to the Supreme Court where the amount in controversy was less than five hundred dollars.[53] In such a case, the adjudication of the common pleas court would be final. Proponents of "Heydrick's bill" argued that it would reduce the caseload of the Supreme Court by two-fifths.[54] Almost immediately, however, the bill came under attack. According to Representative Gould, Heydrick's proposal was "one of the most dangerous bills that was ever presented to the Legislature. . . . It made the judge an autocrat. If he [improperly] favored any client or suitor at that court that he saw fit, in cases under the limit, there was no redress."[55] The bill was also seen as discriminatory against the poor, who, it was argued, would be precluded from access to the Supreme Court simply because their case did not exceed the $500 limit.[56] Moreover, an executive committee of the bar, convened at the inaugural meeting to consider reform proposals, conducted a caseload study and concluded that Heydrick's proposal "would be inadequate in affording the necessary relief from the pressure of business now upon the Supreme Court."[57] On this basis, Heydrick's bill was rejected by the judiciary general committee. A similar bill, submitted by Representative Walter T. Merrick on behalf of the Tioga County Bar Association and seeking to lower the appeal threshold to $300, also failed. Further, a Senate bill proposed increasing the Supreme Court by two justices and splitting it into two divisions. However, this bill was rejected as a violation of Article V of the state constitution, which, as amended by the Convention of 1873, fixed the number of justices to sit on the Supreme Court at seven.[58]

In addition to bills seeking to increase the Supreme Court or modify its jurisdiction, a number of bills also proposed creation of new intermediate courts. Bills authored by Representatives James L. Young and Allen Simpson, for instance, contemplated the creation of two appellate courts, which would consider all appeals, with strict limitations on subsequent appeals to the Supreme Court. These bills were abandoned after legislators expressed concern over the expense necessary to create two new courts.[59]

## THE SUPERIOR COURT EMERGES

On January 21, 1895, a far more significant bill was introduced by Representative George Kunkel. The ensuing debate over Kunkel's bill proved lengthy and at times bitter, and it resulted in significant alterations to the measure as originally drafted.

---

52. *First Annual Report of the Pennsylvania Bar Association* (Philadelphia, 1895), 30.
53. *Leg. Record*, May 31, 1895, vol. 2, 3339.
54. *Leg. Record*, May 31, 1895, vol. 2, 3338.
55. See note 53.
56. For instance, Representative Gould stated, "If this was a poor man's court, I don't know what a poor man's court is." *Leg. Record*, May 31, 1895, vol. 2, 3339.
57. *First Annual Report*, Pa. Bar Assoc., 60.
58. *Legal Intelligencer*, discussion of S.B. 257, vol. 52, 103.
59. *First Annual Report,* Pa. Bar Assoc., 60.

Farming with steam power. A great and continuing source of industrial might in Pennsylvania.

Nonetheless, Kunkel's bill ultimately evolved into the act that created the Superior Court. In order to trace this evolution, it is necessary to review the bill's legislative history.

As originally drafted by Judge John B. McPherson and introduced by Kunkel, the bill was entitled "An Act to establish circuit courts of appeal; relating to their constitution, officers, jurisdiction, powers and practice to the reports of their decisions, to the compensation of the judges and other officers and to costs on appeal from their judgments."[60] Most importantly, as the title implies, the bill contemplated circuit courts, rather than a single intermediate court presiding at different locations throughout the state. Under Section 1, the state was to be divided into six circuits. In delineating the jurisdiction of these circuits, however, the section offered two alternatives. Under the first, the circuits would be established exclusively according to geography:

> The first circuit comprises the counties of Philadelphia, Bucks and Delaware.

> The second circuit comprises the counties of Chester, Montgomery, Berks, Lebanon, Schuylkill, Carbon, Monroe, Northampton and Lehigh.

> The third circuit comprises the counties of Lancaster, York, Adams, Franklin, Fulton, Cumberland, Dauphin, Perry, Juniata, Centre, Huntingdon, Blair, Cambria, Somerset, Bedford and Clearfield.

> The fourth circuit comprises the counties of Lycoming, Union, Snyder, Mifflin, Montour, Columbia, Luzerne, Sullivan, Wyoming, Lackawanna, Wayne, Pike, Bradford, Susquehanna and Northumberland.

---

60. *Leg. Record*, January 21, 1895, vol. 1, 545.

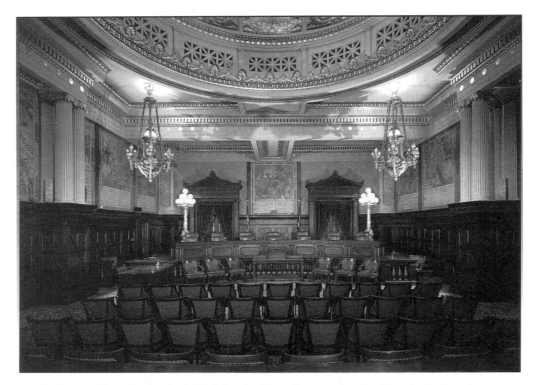

The Supreme Court Chamber, Capitol Building, Harrisburg, Pennsylvania, site of Superior Court sessions since 1906.

The fifth circuit comprises the counties of Erie, Warren, Forest, Crawford, Mercer, Venango, Lawrence, Butler, Beaver, Clarion, Jefferson, Clinton, Cameron, Elk, McKean, Potter and Tioga.

The sixth circuit comprises the counties of Allegheny, Westmoreland, Washington, Greene, Fayette, Armstrong and Indiana.[61]

The second alternative set forth under Section 1 also utilized counties as the basic organizing structure for the circuits, but it sought to divide the appellate caseload emanating from the state's most populous counties. Specifically, it placed a greater number of counties in the first and sixth circuits, which continued to encompass Philadelphia and Allegheny counties, but it split the caseloads from those counties between the first and second and fifth and sixth circuits, respectively. Section 2 provided that each circuit court would be staffed by common pleas judges from the counties in that circuit, and that no more than seven such judges could sit at one time. Section 4 further provided that all seven judges shall preside over appeals "[w]henever it is reasonably possible," although five judges would constitute a quorum for purposes of conducting

---

61. The proposed act was reprinted in its entirety in *The Legal Intelligencer* on January 18, 1895, 26-27, three days before it was introduced into the legislature by Representative Kunkel. The *Intelligencer* said of the bill:

It is possible that the draft of the bill as printed today may be improved on, as it is an exceedingly difficult matter to formulate such a far reaching measure. It is essential, while providing the necessary relief for the Supreme Court, to secure to any intermediary court a degree of power and dignity essential to an ideal appellate tribunal. This has been done in the draft presented. *Legal Intelligencer,* January 18, 1895, 28.

The Supreme Court Chamber, City Hall, Philadelphia, Pennsylvania—location of Superior Court sessions beginning in 1895.

court business. Under Section 5, the circuit courts were directed to conduct at least two sessions per year in each county. Section 9 prohibited the exercise of any original jurisdiction, but declared that the new courts "shall have exclusive and final appellate jurisdiction" over appeals from the following types of cases:  proceedings commenced before a justice of the peace, magistrate, or alderman; proceedings commenced in the court of quarter sessions; proceedings commenced in the court of oyer and terminer and general jail delivery (except in cases of felonious homicide, which were appealable directly to the Supreme Court); negligence actions for personal injury, regardless of whether the injury resulted in death; actions either at law or in equity in which the sole question related to pleading or practice; all other actions in which the amount in controversy is less than $500; and in any case which would otherwise be appealable directly to the Supreme Court (except those involving felonious homicide), where the parties file a stipulation that the appeal will be resolved by the circuit court. Even where the case fell into one of these categories, however, it nonetheless could be appealed to the Supreme Court where it involved a challenge to the circuit court's jurisdiction, a question relating to the state or federal constitution, or where the circuit court or a Supreme Court justice agreed that further review was necessary.[62]

As these provisions indicate, Kunkel's bill as originally drafted proposed creation of a series of intermediate courts to sit in final adjudication of a wide class of appeals that would otherwise end up before the Supreme Court. By utilizing common pleas judges to staff the new circuit courts, the bill was intended to avoid the expense of hiring additional judges, and by requiring the courts to sit at least biannually in each

62. *Legal Intelligencer,* January 18, 1895, 26.

county, the bill perceived an administration of justice that would be accessible and responsive to the needs of litigants throughout the state. These two features—the use of common pleas judges and the adjudication of appeals in every county—were critical aspects of Kunkel's original bill. Nonetheless, over the next two months, the House judiciary general committee revised the bill significantly, and it emerged in March without either feature. Although no record remains of the proceedings before the judiciary general committee, its rationale for abandoning the two salient features of Kunkel's original bill can be inferred from the grounds upon which bills incorporating similar features were decisively rejected by the judiciary committee at the Constitutional Convention of 1873. As noted, at least two proposals calling for the establishment of circuit courts staffed by common pleas judges had been presented to the convention. The most prominent of these, introduced by Judge Woodward, called for the creation of twelve circuit courts, each of which would be staffed by one appointed judge and two common pleas judges from the same circuit. The principal objection to the circuit court provision was that it would result in a lack of conformity in the law.[63] Chairman Armstrong of the judiciary committee, for example, decried the "evil" of "separate distinct intermediate courts, all making their own decisions in their own way, diverse and different from one another, and none of them of authority anywhere beyond its own district."[64] The proposal to include common pleas judges on the circuit courts met a similar fate at the convention. In addition to the claim that the rotating nature of appointments to the court resulted in instability, delegates argued that in order to maintain the desired objectivity, common pleas judges should not sit in review of common pleas decisions, especially where those decisions were rendered by colleagues on the same common pleas bench.[65] The result of these criticisms was that, despite Woodward's influence as former chief justice and principal drafter of the judiciary article of the 1838 constitution, his proposal was rejected, as was the other measure calling for a similar court, before reaching the floor of the convention.

It is likely that these criticisms contributed to the decision of the judiciary general committee to divest Kunkel's bill of its provisions for a circuit court staffed with common pleas judges, for when the bill emerged from the judiciary general committee in March it had changed substantially. As had occurred at the convention in 1873, the committee opted for a single intermediate court to be staffed exclusively by appellate judges, and it revised Kunkel's bill accordingly. The new bill, enumerated H.B. 130, received the unanimous support of the committee and the endorsement of the state bar.[66] Nonetheless, the bill underwent further change as it passed through the legislative process.

On March 20, 1895, Kunkel presented his bill for a second reading to the House.[67] Section 1, as revised by the judiciary general committee, provided in relevant part:

> Section 1. Be it enacted by the Senate and House of Representatives of the Commonwealth of Pennsylvania in General Assembly met, and it is hereby enacted by the authority of the same, that a court of intermediate appeal is hereby established to be called the appellate court and to be composed of five judges learned in the law who shall be elected by

---

63. *Debates*, vol. III, 664-729.

64. *Debates*, vol. III, 644.

65. See note 63.

66. Although the records of the committee no longer exist, its unanimous support of H.B. 130, as well as the endorsement of the state bar, is noted. *Leg. Record*, May 31, 1895, vol. 2, 3337.

67. The legislative rule requiring bills to be considered in the committee of the whole was dispensed with and the bill was presented directly to the legislature. *Leg. Record*, March 20, 1895, vol. 1, 1129.

Charles R. Buckalew, former U.S. senator and father of the 1874 Constitution—the most prominent antagonist to creation of an intermediate court.

the qualified electors of the State. . . . Its jurisdiction shall extend throughout the Commonwealth and the first judges thereof shall be appointed by the Governor before the first day of July, one thousand eight hundred and ninety five, by and with the advise and consent of the Senate if in session, and shall hold their office until the first Monday of January, one thousand eight hundred and ninety six. The term of office of the elected judges shall be ten years, to begin on the first Monday of January following their election.

Section 2 of the revised bill provided that priority of commission for the first judges would be determined by lot, and that the president judge thereafter would be the member whose commission has priority, either in time or as the result of the lot. The section also provided that the court should sit with all five judges, but that four would constitute a quorum. Section 2 was agreed to without amendment. Section 3 provided in relevant part:

The said appellate court may fix the time and places when and where it will meet except that it must meet at least once a year in the cities of Philadelphia, Pittsburg[h] and Harrisburg.[68]

The failure of Section 3 to provide with more specificity where the court should meet prompted several legislators to seek amendments mandating that the court sit in their districts. The first was Representative Charles P. O'Malley, who sought to add

---

68. *Leg. Record*, March 20, 1895, vol. 1, 1129.

Representative George Kunkel introduced H.B. 130, which after modification, became the legislation establishing the Superior Court in 1895.

Scranton to the list of enumerated cities. According to O'Malley, "Scranton is the metropolis of northeastern Pennsylvania and its facilities for holding a court of this kind are equal with those, if not superior, to any other city in that section of the State, and a great part of the legislation from that section would come to that court. I think it should be one of the cities in which this court should be held." Kunkel opposed the amendment on the basis that requiring the court to sit in more than three cities would impose an onerous burden. "[T]he citizens of this Commonwealth," he argued, "will get very poor service out of a court that is required to travel from place to place throughout the entire year." Moreover, he noted, the court could still sit at Scranton if it so desired, because Section 3 "leaves the matter of sitting at other places entirely within the discretionary power of the court." Representative Jerome B. Niles also appeared at first to oppose the amendment, arguing that "if you fix other places besides the three mentioned there would of necessity have to be new prothonotaries, new offices and additional expenses." But, he continued, "[i]f we are to have a court at Scranton I would like to have one at Williamsport, because the people who live in my section would have to travel clear to Lake Erie and clear from Lake Erie, would have to travel to these places of meeting now fixed in this bill."[69] Seizing the opportunity to secure an ally, Representative O'Malley withdrew his amendment and immediately replaced it with one adding both Scranton and Williamsport to the cities contemplated by Section 3. "[N]ow I am for the amendment," declared Representative Emerson Collins, who continued:

> It does seem to me that if we are to establish a new circuit court, or a new appellate court, in order to relieve the Supreme Court, we might as

---

69. *Leg. Record*, March 20, 1895, vol. 1, 1130.

well establish a court that would relieve the people from the necessity of traveling as far as they are now compelled to travel in order to have the superior court review the decisions of the lower court. . . . Certainly, Scranton, representing the great northeastern section and Williamsport the great northwestern section of the State should be places where this court should sit, and I trust the amendment will prevail.[70]

Referring to O'Malley's amendment, Representative John H. Fow of Philadelphia then rose and sarcastically offered his own amendment:

> Mr. Speaker, I am in favor of the amendment and I would even go farther than that if it was necessary. If it was in order I would move an amendment to the amendment providing that the court be furnished with a horse and buggy and stop at every town throughout the Commonwealth and dispense law.[71]

Without comment, the Speaker submitted O'Malley's amendment to the House, and it passed by a vote of sixty-seven to fifty-nine.[72] Thereafter, Kunkel read into the record Sections 4, 5, and 6, which provided, respectively, that the Supreme Court prothonotary shall operate in the same capacity for the new appellate court, that the new court shall have the power to issue "every lawful writ and process necessary," and that the decisions of the court shall be published by the state reporter in volumes entitled *Pennsylvania Appellate Reports.*[73]

Next, Kunkel turned to Section 7, which set forth the jurisdictional power of the new court. In significant respects, this section resembled the jurisdictional provision of Kunkel's original bill. Like its predecessor, Section 7 provided the court with no original jurisdiction, except insofar as necessary to issue writs of habeas corpus. It further provided that the court was to have "exclusive and final appellate jurisdiction" over the following types of cases:

a)  proceedings commenced in the court of quarter sessions of the peace;

b)  proceedings commenced in the court of oyer and terminer and general jail delivery (except in cases of felonious homicide);

c)  all other actions in which the amount in controversy does not exceed $1,000;

d)  proceedings commenced in orphan's court;

e)  any appeal which the parties have stipulated may be adjudicated by the appellate court.

Despite the fact that cases of these types were vested in the "exclusive and final jurisdiction" of the new court, Section 7 further provided that appeal could be taken to

---

70. See note 69.
71. See note 69.
72. See note 69.
73. *Leg. Record*, March 20, 1895, vol. 1, 1133.

Allegheny County Court House, Pittsburgh, Pennsylvania. Site of Supreme Court Chamber and Superior Court sessions from 1895 to 1918.

the Supreme Court when such cases involved a question relating to the jurisdiction of the court or provisions of the federal or state constitutions, or when the court or a Supreme Court justice expressly allowed such an appeal.[74]

Clause (c) of Section 7 quickly became the subject of controversy. The controversy centered on two factors. First, the delegates disagreed sharply on whether a lesser monetary threshold would adequately relieve the Supreme Court. Debate on this question began when Representative Niles offered an amendment reducing the amount in controversy requirement to $500. "I am conscientious in offering this amendment," he declared, "believing that when the absolute right of appeal is limited to five hundred dollars that the Supreme Court will be relieved to such an extent that it will be entirely satisfactory." Representative Fow agreed, arguing "that if a special allocatur was allowed in cases under five hundred dollars by the Supreme Court there would be no need to pass a bill of this character. I believe that the Supreme Court would be aided to a sufficient extent by making the limit five hundred dollars." Kunkel opposed Niles' amendment, noting that Section 7(c) "was carefully considered by the Committee on Judiciary General, and advice upon it was received from some of the brightest lawyers in the State."[75] Nonetheless, Fow persisted:

> Mr. Speaker, if this amendment does not prevail this act might as well
> be entitled, "An act to relieve the Supreme Court of all work," because
> the vast majority of cases that are taken up with the Supreme Court

74. *Leg. Record*, March 20, 1895, vol. 1, 1134.
75. See note 74.

This leaded stained glass window, depicting the Pennsylvania seal, was originally installed in the Supreme Court Chamber in the Allegheny County Court House in 1888 (*see previous page*) and is the only remaining vestige of that courtroom.

involve a principle, and of the vast amount of cases taken there a great majority of them involve less than five hundred dollars. Of one thousand one hundred and thirty eight cases taken to the Supreme Court, seventy percentum of them involved an amount less than five hundred dollars.[76]

Representative D. Smith Talbot agreed "that the great majority of cases that are taken up from the lower courts to the Supreme Court are under five hundred dollars."[77]

More contentious than the effect of clause (c) on the Supreme Court's caseload, however, was the issue of whether establishing a $1,000 threshold for appeals deprived poorer litigants of access to the Supreme Court. This issue arose at the outset of the debate. For instance, in offering his amendment, Niles hoped that it would "test the sense of the House as to whether five hundred dollars is not better for the people than one thousand." Representative Talbot argued that "[i]f this amendment is voted down then we will be establishing a court for the rich people of the state, who have great sums of money involved in litigation."[78] In response to such claims, Representative John L. Mattox argued:

The limit of one thousand dollars is not too hard. It has been said that if this limit was established that this would be considered a bill against the poor man. My experience and observation have been that it is very rare that a poor man wants to appeal his case to the Supreme Court. It is usually the rich corporations that want to appeal to that court. Almost invariably in our courts the poor man, as he is called, wins his

76. See note 74.
77. See note 74.
78. See note 74.

suit, and the corporation, in order to annoy him, in order to compel him to settle, takes the case to the Supreme Court. He has not the money to pay for paper books and attorneys and is compelled to settle. So it is my candid opinion that the limit should remain where it is, and instead of being a detriment to the poor man would be to his interest.[79]

Kunkel also opposed Niles' amendment on the following basis:

The question arose before the committee [of judiciary general] as to how the jurisdiction was to be denied by a monied value. It was at first suggested that the jurisdiction be limited to cases involving $500 dollars or less. It was replied by some of the members of the committee that this would be regarded as a court created in the interest of the money power of the State. A litigant who had sued for no more than five hundred dollars would be confined to the jurisdiction of this new court, while he who had the suit involving an amount greater than five hundred dollars would be entitled to go to the highest court of the State. . . .

[However,] [i]f you limit this jurisdiction to five hundred dollars then you will allow the corporation and wealthy litigant to go to the Supreme Court of the State and take the adverse party either to Pittsburg[h], Philadelphia, or Harrisburg, to have his case reviewed. Whilst if you pass the bill in the condition it now is, making the limit one thousand dollars, then the corporation who has that amount of money involved in controversy must go to one of these places named, to wit: Philadelphia, Pittsburg(h), Scranton, Williamsport or Harrisburg, places convenient for the adverse party.[80]

Following Kunkel's argument, a vote was taken and Niles' amendment was defeated. Yet, the debate over Section 7 was far from over. As soon as Niles' amendment had been defeated, Representative Ward R. Bliss of Delaware County offered an amendment to delete from Section 7 the provision allowing appeal to the Supreme Court where a case raised a question under the Pennsylvania Constitution. "Every lawyer knows," he argued in support of the amendment, "that since our new Constitution was adopted almost every case involving a thousand dollars . . . can be made to have a constitutional question, and the lawyers who cannot show that [a] case involves a construction of some of the provisions of our Constitution, [are] very poor lawyer[s] indeed. To put that provision in this act," he continued, "is simply to render this whole court useless and cumbersome, and there would not be a case of any consequence tried that would not be appealable to the Supreme Court. Such a bill will not relieve the Supreme Court one particle," Bliss concluded, "and the multitude of cases that arise in the cities and towns of the State . . . will simply be so much longer and so much more expensive before they can be finally decided."[81] Rising to oppose the amendment offered by Bliss, Kunkel argued that:

[i]t was the thought of the friends of this bill that the highest court in the State was the proper court to pass upon constitutional questions, and I don't believe there is a member of the bar upon the floor of this House, or any layman, who will take issue with me on that subject.[82]

---

79. See note 74.
80. See note 74.
81. *Leg. Record*, March 20, 1895, vol. 1, 1135.82.
82. See note 81.

Tioga County Representative Walter T. Merrick, a leading opponent of H.B. 130. Merrick presented the last attempt to defeat the bill.

Representative Richard Salinger agreed with Kunkel that "it is right and proper that questions involving the construction of the Constitution should be left to the Supreme Court, where it is now."[83] Similarly, Representative Fow concluded that "if there is a constitutional question involved it should go to the Supreme Court." Representative Niles also opposed the amendment because, by effectively allowing concurrent jurisdiction over constitutional questions, it might lead to the anomalous situation in which "the appellate court would decide the Constitution one way and the Supreme Court might determine it another."[84] In the end, the majority of legislators sided with these latter views, and the amendment proposed by Bliss was defeated.[85]

None of the remaining eight sections of H.B. 130 were amended on second reading. Section 8 set forth the practice of the new court in some detail. Section 9 established procedures regarding the costs of appeal. Section 10 provided that a case could be certified for appeal to the Supreme Court by any three judges of the new court. Section 11 set the salaries of the judges at $7,500. Section 12 determined the effective date of the proposed act and provided for membership to the bar of the new court. Section 13 provided that the new court had jurisdiction over all appeals commenced on or after July 1, 1895. Section 14 provided that the proposed act would not apply to any actions which were not "hereinbefore made reviewable by the said appellate court." Section 15 repealed all inconsistent acts.[86]

---

83. See note 81.
84. *Leg. Record,* March 20, 1895, vol. 1, 1137.
85. *Leg. Record,* March 20, 1895, vol. 1, 1138.
86. *Leg. Record,* March 20, 1895, vol. 1, 1138-39.

The final amendment to H.B. 130 at its reading on March 20 was directed at its title. Interestingly, although the committee on judiciary general had revised the bill to provide for a single appellate court, its title had remained "An Act to establish circuit courts of appeals."[87] When this title was reread on March 20, Kunkel proposed to amend the title to provide for a single "intermediate court of appeal." This amendment was accepted, as was the remainder of H.B. 130 on second reading.[88]

Kunkel returned the bill to the House floor for its third and final reading on May 31, 1895.[89] Almost immediately, Representative Merrick moved that the House go into a committee of the whole to consider his amendment reducing the salaries of the proposed court's judges from $7,500 to $5,000.[90] Merrick, who by this time had emerged as a leading opponent of H.B. 130, had supported the Heydrick bill and sponsored an alternative plan on behalf of the Tioga County Bar Association. Thus, it is not surprising that in supporting his amendment to reduce salaries, Merrick also assailed the entirety of H.B. 130. His comments touched off an acrimonious debate over the merits of the bill, which began when Merrick stated the following:

> Mr. Speaker, before the House agrees to go into committee of the whole for the purpose of considering this amendment I would like to say that in the early part of this session the House was reminded by executive message that we should be careful and not go into any extravagance. It is now proposed to create an entirely new court which was not recognized by the constitutional convention, and which the Legislature until today has refused to create. The proposition is not only to create this court but to create it with extravagant salaries. It proposes to bestow upon these five judges a salary of seven thousand five hundred dollars per year, which is only five hundred dollars less than the jud[g]es of the Supreme Court receive. . . .
>
> When you gentlemen of this House go back to your constituents who labor upon the farm from one year's end to another, and who, after having spent a lifetime in tilling the soil, succeed in accumulating the sum, possibly, of five thousand dollars, will then find your justification for voting to insert this amendment in this bill. . . .
>
> After all, gentlemen, there is no necessity for the creation of a court of this kind. The people of the State are not demanding it, and the only persons who are demanding it are the politicians and the judges who are to reap this magnificent salary. They have come here from all over the State of Pennsylvania. There is hardly a county in the great Commonwealth that has not a favorite son who has the ambition planted in his breast to serve the State at that salary.[91]

Representative Courtlandt K. Bolles of Philadelphia was the first to respond to Merrick:

> I want to ask the gentleman if he does not think this is not a question of extravagance or economy, but it is a question whether this State can

---

87. *Leg. Record*, January 21, 1895, vol. 1, 545.
88. *Leg. Record*, March 20, 1895, vol. 1, 1139.
89. *Leg. Record*, May 31, 1895, vol. 2, 3335.
90. *Leg. Record*, May 31, 1895, vol. 2, 3336.
91. See note 90.

afford to create this court. He starts out with the assumption that this court is not necessary, he is opposed to it. Therefore, he undertakes to reduce the salary of the judges, provided the court shall be created. This court is a Supreme Court for a certain class of actions, which it [is] proposed shall be heard before it. Now is it a dignified proceeding for the State of Pennsylvania, if it creates a court of that dignity, to say the judges of that court shall receive a less salary than due the judges of the court in the county of Philadelphia? . . . The necessity for this court was urged before the committee which reported this bill. A former judge of the Supreme Court gave to that committee a concise statement of the business that had to be transacted, and no member who listened to his argument should doubt for a moment, [in] the interest for justice in the State of Pennsylvania, and in the interest of persons whose causes were to be determined by a higher tribunal, that the Supreme Court should receive some adequate relief. It was generally conceded that the number of cases which that court had to consider was impossible, in a specific time, to give to each case the consideration that it deserves; that the time was too limited for the proper consideration of all cases coming before that court. We are considering today whether this court shall be established or whether it shall not. If it is not necessary, do not establish it. If it is a necessity do not be guilty of this paltry sort of economy which would only result in placing those judges in an undignified position.[92]

Representative Fow, who had supported lowering the proposed court's jurisdictional limit to $500 upon the bill's second reading, rejected Merrick's claim of "extravagance," and argued that the court "will be cheaper for the poor man because [it] will sit in different portions of the State, and it will be cheaper to have a hearing in this court than it would be to go to Philadelphia, Pittsburg[h] or Harrisburg as it is now necessary . . . before this present Supreme Court." Referring to Merrick, Fow also stated that he was "surprised that a member of the bar should so belittle his profession as to undertake to cheapen the price of a judge. If the judges of the Supreme Court are worthy of the money," Fow concluded, "then the judges who are to sit in this poor man's Supreme Court are also worthy to receive the amount of money which [was] assigned to them in this bill."[93] Representative Kunkel, again rising to defend his bill, agreed with Fow's comparison between the proposed court and the Supreme Court:

I submit that the only line of demarcation between the Supreme Court and the court sought to be created by this bill is indicated by the amount of money involved in the litigation. That is the only difference between these two courts, and I submit that this is really and substantially a second Supreme Court in this State, and if it is to be established at all it ought to be surrounded by the same dignity and its members paid for their services the same price, or, at least, the salary that is provided by this bill.[94]

Kunkel also questioned Merrick's motives in presenting his amendment:

[T]here can be no other object in view by the gentleman in offering this amendment than to retard passage of this bill. Every member of this

92. See note 90.
93. See note 90.
94. *Leg. Record*, May 31, 1895, vol. 2, 3337.

House knows that if we go into a committee of the whole and reduce these salaries that this bill will have to lie over to be printed and its passage will be delayed. So, I believe that the purpose and object of this amendment is not so much a matter of economy as it is to permit the gentleman to go before his people and point out to them the record that he has made for himself in offering this amendment, and also for the purpose of defeating this bill or delaying its passage through this house.[95]

Rising to a question of privilege, Merrick responded:

[M]y motives have been impugned by the gentleman from Dauphin. I wish to say that he has no right to impugn my motives. . . . I offered this amendment because I believed that the interest of the people of the State of Pennsylvania demanded that some such amendment should be offered to this bill. . . .

It is not a poor man's court by any manner of means. What poor man in the State of Pennsylvania would ask you, gentlemen, to provide another court through which he must drag his case which he is obliged to take through to the end. What poor man in this State would ask this Legislature to provide a court of delay—and that is what this court might be called.[96]

A number of representatives again rose in opposition to Merrick. Representative Edward Gould was first, declaring that "if there ever was a necessity for the creation of any office, it is this one." Gould further indicated that his county's bar association was in unanimous support of the bill.[97] In urging the defeat of Merrick's amendment, Representative George Cotton also stated that "[i]f it is the desire of this House to create a court of appellate jurisdiction, in which shall be decided the rights, the liberties and property of the citizens of this State, you must make it a respectable court. You must not make it ridiculous by the salary you pay the judges," he continued, "I do not think it is the desire of this House to create an absurd, ridiculous, puppet court." Moreover, rejecting Merrick's claim that the court would impose an undue burden on Pennsylvania taxpayers, Representative Peter James declared, "I am ready to pay my portion of the tax that this court would put upon the state, and pay it cheerfully, as I am always willing to pay for what I know to be necessary." Representative Walter H. Parcels agreed, stating that "when money is paid for a thing that is needed, it is not an extravagance and cannot be so interpreted. If there was anything ever needed in Pennsylvania," Parcels argued, "it is a court of this character[,] a poor man's court . . . where a case can be settled and speedily settled."[98]

Following these comments, a vote was taken on Merrick's amendment seeking to reduce the proposed salaries to $5,000, and it was defeated by a vote of 107 to forty-one.[99] Merrick then proposed an amendment reducing the salaries to $6,000, and this amendment was defeated, without discussion, by a vote of 108 to 30.[100] Upon the defeat of this final amendment, H.B. 130 was submitted to the House for final passage,

---

95. See note 94.
96. *Leg. Record*, May 31, 1895, vol. 2, 3337-38.
97. See note 96.
98. *Leg. Record*, May 31, 1895, vol. 2, 3339.
99. *Leg. Record*, May 31, 1895, vol. 2, 3341.
100. *Leg. Record*, May 31, 1895, vol. 2, 3342.

and it passed by a vote of 140 to 20.[101] The bill was then sent to the Senate for concurrence.

The Senate version of the intermediate court bill, S.B. 916, was introduced for reading on June 5, 1895, by Senator John C. Grady of Philadelphia. In the course of this reading, the bill was amended in four significant respects. The two most important amendments were directed at Section 1, which, in addition to the portion set forth above, provided:

> The first elected judges of the court shall be chosen at the general election in November, one thousand eight hundred and ninety five, and the five candidates who then receive the highest vote shall be declared elected. But no elector may vote either then or at any subsequent election for more than four candidates upon one ballot for the said office. If at any subsequent election four judges are to be elected, no elector may vote for more than three candidates upon one ballot, and if three judges are to be elected no elector may vote for more than two upon one ballot, and if two judges are to be elected no elector may vote for more than one upon one ballot. . . .[102]

This provision, which was extremely important given the heavy Republican majority in Pennsylvania, was intended to ensure that the minority party would fill at least one seat on the court at all times. Upon the reading of Section 1, Senator Samuel J. M. McCarrell of Dauphin County offered an amendment to increase the number of judges to seven and the number for which an elector may vote to six. Although McCarrell's amendment was passed without discussion,[103] Democratic Senator Henry D. Green of Berks County subsequently offered an amendment to reduce to five the number of candidates a single elector could choose.[104] In support of this amendment, Green argued:

> Mr. President, I want to say for the party that I represent that if this court is to be composed of seven judges it is no more than fair that the minority should be entitled to two representatives on that bench. That certainly is not asking much. I think I am speaking the sentiments of the Democrats here and the Democrats in the House. If it is not changed there will not be a Democratic vote passed for this bill, although many of them favor it. All we want is fair play.[105]

Senator Grady then moved to amend Green's amendment by restoring to six the number of candidates an elector may choose. The matter was put to a vote, and Grady's motion, which effectively restored the provisions of McCarrell's original amendment, was passed twenty-three to five.[106] As a result of these amendments, S.B. 916 called for a court of seven judges, six of whom could be from the same political party.

The next important amendment was directed at Section 3. Unlike its counterpart in the House bill, which directed the court to sit in Philadelphia, Pittsburgh, Har-

---

101. *Leg. Record,* May 31, 1895, vol. 2, 3342-43.

102. See note 101.

103. *Leg. Record,* June 5, 1895, vol. 2, 3700. Upon the passage of McCarrell's amendment, the remainder of the act's references to "five" judges was amended to provide for "seven."

104. *Leg. Record,* June 5, 1895, vol. 2, 3704.

105. See note 104.

106. See note 104.

Governor Daniel H. Hastings, who signed the Superior Court legislation into law
on June 24, 1895; thereafter appointed the first seven members of the court.

risburg, Scranton, and Williamsport, Section 3 of S.B. 916 provided that the court "shall hold its meetings in the City of Harrisburg exclusively."[107] Senator William U. Brewer offered an amendment to make the Senate bill conform with the House bill, and it was passed without discussion.[108] The final significant amendment also addressed a difference between the House and Senate bills. Unlike H.B. 130, which referred to the new court as "the appellate court," S.B. 916 identified it in the alternative as "the (appellate) superior court."[109] Following the reading of Section 4, Senator Grady offered an amendment to strike the word "appellate" from the bill's references to the new court.[110] From that point forward, the proposed court was known as the Superior Court. No other significant changes were made to the bill by the Senate on the reading of June 5.[111]

At noon the following day, June 6, 1895, S.B. 916 was read for the final time. Following the reading, Senator Green resumed his argument from a day earlier that the elector provisions of Section 3 should be amended to provide the minority party with two of the seven new judgeships.

---

107. *Leg. Record*, June 5, 1895, vol. 2, 3701, citing S.B. 916, sec. 3.

108. *Leg. Record*, June 5, 1895, vol. 2, 3701.

109. *Leg. Record*, June 5, 1895, vol. 2, 3700, citing S.B. 916, sec. 1.

110. See note 108.

111. The only other amendments to the bill included the following: Section 2, providing that "the full bench of *five* judges shall sit" whenever reasonably possible (emphasis added), was amended to reflect the increase in the court's membership to seven. *Leg. Record*, June 5, 1895, vol. 2, 3700; Section 3, referring to "*the* county" in which the court shall sit (emphasis added), was amended to "each county" to reflect the addition of Philadelphia, Pittsburgh, Scranton, and Williamsport to the designated meeting places of the court. *Leg. Record*, June 5, 1895, vol. 2, 3701; Section 8, providing that where a money judgment is collected upon execution, the court "may make an order of restitution and may enforce the same by execution," was

Mr. President, speaking for the minority side of this Senate, as well as for the minority side, as far as I know, of the House, I think this bill is not a fair bill, and we will not support it unless a fair representation is given to the minority party on this bench. . . . The majority party is not entitled to more than five out of seven judges. . . . Therefore, I ask unanimous consent to strike out the word "six" [in Section 3] and in lieu thereof insert the word "five." This will give the minority party in Pennsylvania a small representation on the bench, which they are certainly entitled to. If it is to be a party bench the other party should now say nay; they have five out of the seven. If we would be asking for something unreasonable it would be perfectly right to ignore our requests. I therefore ask unanimous consent to amend the bill.[112]

Despite Green's plea, objections were heard and his request for unanimous consent was defeated by the heavily Republican Senate. The bill was then submitted for final passage, and it succeeded by a vote of thirty-six to seven.[113]

Hours later, the bill was returned to the House for concurrence. Following a reading of the Senate amendments, and as the final vote approached, leading opponents of the bill launched a last effort to bring about its defeat. The first to speak was Representative Merrick, who declared that "there is no necessity for the establishment of such a court as this [and even] if it must be established five judges are sufficient. When we go before the people in our next State campaign," he argued, "we will have this thing to answer for. The people of Pennsylvania do not want new offices created by the wholesale in this manner and with extravagant salaries."[114] Merrick continued:

I don't believe there is a lawyer upon the flo[o]r of this House that feels deep down in his heart but [t]hat this is a departure from an old and established system . . . . [W]hy should the State of Pennsylvania depart from her old standard, why should it depart from the simplest system in the Union and adopt a cumbersome one? It simply means another court to drag cases through. As a lawyer, I say it will benefit the profession, I admit it freely, but beyond the lawyers who practice before this court, I say it will benefit no one in Pennsylvania. There is no crying demand for it . . . . [I]t is simply a demand for place.[115]

Thus, he concluded, the Superior Court "should be defeated upon economic ground[s], it should be defeated because it is not a proper way to provide relief for the Supreme Court of Pennsylvania. It is too expensive a way, both to the litigant and to the State." Next to speak was Representative Andrew L. Fritz of Columbia County, who opposed H.B. 130 on numerous grounds.

I have been inquiring as to whether or not [the bill] is necessary and I have found very few, not even among the judges themselves, who think

---

amended by removal of the words following "restitution"; Section 10, providing that "any *three* of the judges" may certify a case for review before the Supreme Court (emphasis added), was amended to "four" to reflect the increase in the court's membership to seven; Section 12, empowering the court to establish "the times of all meetings," was amended to conform to H.B. 130, which provided that "the times and places of all subsequent meetings [were] to be fixed by this act and the court itself." *Leg. Record,* June 5, 1895, vol. 2, 3703.

112. *Leg. Record,* June 5, 1895, vol. 2, 3843.

113. See note 112.

114. *Leg. Record,* June 6, 1895, vol. 2, 3914.

115. See note 114.

it is necessary and who favor its passage. . . . Some of the greatest and
best legal lights of the State at the present time are opposed to the
provisions of this bill. . . .[116]

It has been said that this intermediate court is necessary for the relief
of the judges of the Supreme Court, [but] [t]his was the talk twenty
years ago when the Constitution of this State was adopted—when the
able men of that convention decided against an intermediate court.[117]

Again referring to the Constitutional Convention of 1873, Fritz argued that
"[s]ome of the greatest legal minds which this State has produced" believed that the
most desirable judicial system is one which possesses lower courts of original jurisdiction and a single court of appellate jurisdiction.[118] According to Fritz, such a system:

has been handed down to us by our forefathers, as the best judicial
system which has yet been devised by man. It has stood the test of a
century. Shall we now begin to tear it to pieces and try some new method
which will be unpopular with the people, dilatory and very expensive?[119]

Fritz also claimed that the proposed court would disadvantage the poor litigant:

[Y]ou will see that it is a bad law for the poor man who is determined
that the Supreme Court should decide his case. He must first have the
case decided by the intermediate court and after the long delay and
expense he is then compelled to carry it up to the Supreme Court. Is it
right that we should pass a law which will discriminate against the
interest of the poor classes of people of this Commonwealth? . . .

The five hundred dollar case of the poor man may involve principles
which if properly decided will do more good than the five thousand dollar case of the millionaire . . . and if we pass a law to deprive him of this
right [to pursue an appeal to the Supreme Court] we are taking away
from him that personal privilege and liberty which the founders of this
great government intended that all should enjoy. The high and the low,
the rich and the poor, should all be treated alike.[120]

Fritz further stated his belief that, regardless of the monetary threshold for
further appeals, there would be no finality to the intermediate court's decisions because properly framed appeals could always succeed in finding their way to the Supreme Court. "This result can be brought around," he argued, "by any lawyer who handles
his case carefully."[121] In concluding his remarks, Fritz returned to the issue of the Supreme Court's caseload, and offered his own remedy:

[W]e hear the cry of "overburdened courts" and "worn out judges." Let
all of our courts adopt more strict rules, which will stop the intentional

---

116. See note 114.
117. *Leg. Record*, June 6, 1895, vol. 2, 3915.
118. *Leg. Record*, June 6, 1895, vol. 2, 3914.
119. See note 117.
120. See note 117.
121. See note 117.

delay, and the lists will become small. The courts then will not be over-burdened with business because a large number of cases which now are taken into court for the purpose of delay would be settled by the parties. Our courts would then not be overburdened and no one would think of establishing a new court.[122]

Following these remarks, Representative Bolles invoked the vote of May 31, which passed H.B. 130 and sent it to the Senate, and stated that "[t]his House has already, by a decisive vote, decided upon the necessity for this court."[123] Therefore, dismissing the attack upon the merits of the bill by Merrick and Fritz, he reminded his colleagues that the topic under debate was simply whether the House would finally concur in the Senate amendments. Thereafter, he turned to the most prominent of those amendments, and stated the following:

> The Senate has seen fit to amend this bill by providing seven instead of five judges, and I think the change is a wise one and the House should concur in the change, because, if this court is worth establishing at all, it is worth making it right.[124]

The debate was concluded by Representative P. M. Lytle of Huntingdon County, who, although he had voted in the affirmative on May 31, indicated that he could not support the Senate amendment increasing the court from five to seven members. "I will perhaps have to explain to my constituents how I came to vote for the proposition at all," he stated, "but I don't want to be placed in the position of having to explain to them why I voted for five judges in the first place and then afterwards for seven."[125] Following Lytle's remarks, a final vote was taken and the House concurred in the Senate amendments by a vote of 120 to 53.[126]

Having been passed by both chambers of the legislature, the bill was signed into law by Governor Daniel H. Hastings on June 24, 1895, to be effective the first day of July. As finally enacted, the Superior Court Act provided that the court would exercise jurisdiction throughout the Commonwealth, and that it would consist of seven judges learned in the law, who were to be elected for ten year terms beginning on the first Monday of January following the election. The court was permitted to establish the times and locations of its sessions, except that it must meet at least once a year in Philadelphia, Pittsburgh, Harrisburg, Scranton, and Williamsport. All seven members of the court were to sit in judgment of cases whenever reasonably possible, but four would constitute a quorum to conduct business when necessary. The act granted the Superior Court no original jurisdiction, but it provided for appellate jurisdiction over all civil actions involving $1,000 or less. All appeals involving felonious homicide or the right to public office, or in which the attorney general was involved, were appealable directly to the Supreme Court. Appeals were allowed from the Superior Court where its jurisdiction was challenged, and issues of federal or state constitutional law were appealable to the Supreme Court as a matter of right. Appeals to the Supreme Court were also permitted where authorized by four members of the Superior Court or a single justice of the Supreme Court. If the parties to a case stipulated that the Superior Court's

---

122. *Leg. Record*, June 6, 1895, vol. 2, 3916.
123. See note 122.
124. See note 122.
125. See note 122.
126. *Leg. Record*, June 6, 1895, vol. 2, 3916-17. Although the vote was recorded as 119-54, Representative Earl Pomeroy subsequently raised a question of privilege to change his vote on the basis that he had acted "under a misapprehension." *Leg. Record*, June 6, 1895, vol. 2, 3920.

judgment was final, no further appeal was allowed, and the parties could also agree to grant the Superior Court jurisdiction of a case that would otherwise belong to the Supreme Court.[127]

## ASSESSING THE EFFORT

The Superior Court Act was the product of a long and contentious debate over the need for, and parameters of, an intermediate appellate court in the Pennsylvania judiciary. In the decades prior to 1895, opponents had successfully raised a number of objections to such a court. The most common objections were that an intermediate court would prove unnecessary and expensive. Another prominent objection, and one which played a key role in defeating the judiciary committee's proposal at the convention in 1873, was that addition of an intermediate court would cause a multiplicity of appeals and ultimately delay justice. Related to this claim was the argument that an intermediate court would remove finality from appellate judicial decisions, since an aggrieved party might pursue a subsequent appeal to the Supreme Court. Opponents also argued that a new court would disadvantage the poor. This objection took one of two forms. First, it was claimed that the addition of successive stages in the appellate process would increase the costs of hiring attorneys and printing documentary materials, and thus the poor would be less likely to pursue even meritorious actions. Secondly, it was claimed that jurisdictional limits based upon the amount in controversy unduly limited the access of the poor to the Supreme Court. Another objection was that decisions of different appellate courts would inevitably conflict, and that this danger was especially pronounced where a similar issue arises in two cases which fall on different sides of the monetary threshold and thus proceed to different appellate courts. Finally, opponents of an intermediate court appealed to history, arguing that such a court violated Pennsylvania's time-honored dichotomy between an array of trial courts vested with original jurisdiction and a single high Supreme Court vested with final, appellate jurisdiction. All of these objections arose repeatedly at the convention in 1873, in the intervening two decades, and in the legislative debates of 1895. Confronted by such diverse and persistent opposition, the effort to achieve an intermediate appellate court nonetheless reached fruition with the creation of the Superior Court.

Yet, the achievement grows larger still when it is recalled that even the proponents of an intermediate court disagreed sharply on its form. The most prominent alternative to a single court staffed with appellate judges was a multiplicity of circuit courts staffed with common pleas judges. Courts of this latter type had received the support of a significant minority of the judiciary committee in 1873, and, it must be remembered, precisely such courts were contemplated by the original version of H.B. 130. Thus, circuit courts had been prime competitors in the effort to advance a successful appellate court proposal. Other proposals also competed, including a bill introduced at the convention seeking to establish two intermediate courts with jurisdiction over all appeals, and from which subsequent appeals were strictly limited. Numerous other proposals directed at increasing the Supreme Court or modifying its jurisdiction had also attained prominence, and the convention ultimately rejected an intermediate court in favor of one such proposal. All of these options were again available to the legislature in 1895. Yet, just as it had overcome the significant criticism lodged against intermediate courts in general, the Superior Court model surfaced against these specific alternatives.

---

127. The act is nicely summarized in the James E. Rowley Pamphlet, *100 Years of Justice: The Superior Court of Pennsylvania's First Century* (Superior Court of Pennsylvania: March 1995), 3.

This chapter has sought to demonstrate the reasons for that success. Not surprisingly, the Superior Court that emerged in 1895 was profoundly shaped by the historical process in which it evolved. The agent driving that historical process is clear: as the records of the Constitutional Convention of 1873 and the legislature in 1895 indicate beyond question, relief of the Supreme Court's caseload was the primary impetus behind efforts at institutional reform of Pennsylvania's judiciary throughout the last half of the nineteenth century. While this fact explains the necessity for reform, however, it does not explain how the course of that reform led to the Superior Court.

The answer manifests itself when the Convention of 1873 is revisited. First, it is important to recall that the convention, wary of the multiplicity of appeals and conflicting decisions perceived to be associated with intermediate courts, opted to expand the Supreme Court and modify its jurisdiction. By the early 1890s, the caseload of each justice had increased by nearly 50 percent, and the failure of the convention's efforts was apparent. With proposals directed at altering the Supreme Court demonstrably in error, the same majority that had always recognized the need to relieve the Supreme Court began to consider proposals for another layer of courts to filter appeals. A second factor related to the convention also enabled legislators in 1895 to consider such proposals. Under the Pennsylvania Constitution of 1838, Article V vested the judicial power of the Commonwealth "in a supreme court, in courts of common pleas, courts of oyer and terminer and general jail delivery, courts of quarter sessions of the peace, orphans' courts and magistrates' courts."[128] In 1873, the convention added to this list "other courts as the general assembly may from time to time establish."[129] The fortuitous result of this change was that the very convention which declined to create an intermediate court expanded the power of the legislature in a manner that allowed it to create precisely such a court two decades later.

Thus, the convention's unsuccessful modification of the Supreme Court compelled reformers to consider an intermediate court, and the convention's modification of the constitution's text empowered the legislature, for the first time, to create such a court. For these reasons, reformers focused upon intermediate courts, and they began to consider the two models most familiar to the common law, circuit courts and unified courts. At this point, several factors intervened to dispose reformers in favor of the latter. The first appears to have been the law's natural prejudice against inconsistency. As noted, the principal criticism lodged against circuit court proposals was that the various circuits would render conflicting decisions. Although this criticism was also leveled at intermediate courts generally, the possibility of conflicting opinions was obviously perceived as greater in the case of six or more co-equal courts than in the case of a single appellate court reviewable by the Supreme Court.

The second factor that militated in favor of a single intermediate court was the attachment to circuit court proposals of provisions for staffing by common pleas judges. This implicated another natural prejudice of the law, namely, the desire to avoid the appearance of partiality. Justice could hardly be blind, it was argued, if common pleas judges were reviewing the work of their colleagues on the common pleas bench.

The final factor that led to the endorsement of a single intermediate court was Pennsylvania's particularly unsatisfactory experience with circuit courts. The *nisi prius* court, which had been established in 1827 and met with complete failure in the nine years of its existence, was referred to on several occasions by delegates and legislators opposed to circuit courts.

Having thus limited the options to a single intermediate court, it is not surpris-

---

128. Pa. Constitution (1838), art. V, sec. 1
129. Pa. Constitution (1873), art. V, sec. 1.

ing that the Superior Court emerged as it did in 1895. Of course, as with any process involving large components of historical and political contingency, the process that culminated in the creation of the Superior Court is not explainable with scientific exactitude. It is undeniable that numerous other significant yet incalculable factors operated to shape the particulars of the new court. For instance, the requirement that the court sit in Williamsport appears to have resulted solely from an effort to silence the objection of a legislator from that city to an amendment directing the court to sit in Scranton. Had a legislator from Erie been quicker to his feet, it is possible that his hometown would have hosted the court on its visits to the northwest section of the state. Such contingencies are unknowable, especially from a sterile vantage point one hundred years in the future. What remains clear is that the Superior Court emerged in 1895 from a historical process that deemed it necessary. Our careful analysis of this process illustrates the legislature at its best, whereby free and open debate weighed every option, ultimately determining what appeared to be the most effective and viable model in service of the public interest. With a new century approaching, it remained to be seen whether the court would fulfill the aspirations of those who labored so assiduously to make it a reality.

The first Superior Court, as appointed in 1895. L-R (seated): Edward N. Willard, President Judge Charles E. Rice, John J. Wickham, Henry J. McCarthy. L-R (standing): James A. Beaver, George B. Orlady, Howard J. Reeder.

# Chapter Two

# The First Court: 1895-1910

## The Political Climate and Its Impact on the Composition of the Court

In an article dated November 4, 1895, the *New York Times* surveyed upcoming elections in states around the nation. Turning to the Pennsylvania general election scheduled for the next day, the *Times* noted the Superior Court race and found little of "live interest," given "the enormous Republican majorities in the State in the last seven years."[1] The *Times* estimate of Republican strength was accurate, yet that strength had endured for far longer than seven years. Indeed, by 1895, Republicans had dominated Pennsylvania politics for more than three decades, and that dominance would continue into the midst of the Great Depression, nearly forty years in the future. Not surprisingly, these seven decades of Republican rule profoundly influenced the selection of Superior Court judges.

Republican control of state politics was premised on several factors. The most important of these was the Civil War. Initially, Pennsylvania's participation in a Republican-led conflict against a solidly Democratic South generated significant hostility against the state's Democrats. Indeed, as the war consumed tens of thousands of the state's young men, Democrats who opposed the cause were increasingly seen as traitors. While the tactic of labeling Democrats as disloyal "Copperheads" was utilized throughout the North, it was especially effective in Pennsylvania because a large portion of the state's Democrats had opposed the war and resisted the draft. Moreover, the Union army and postwar veterans' organizations were heavily Republican, and men who served in those groups often abandoned any prewar Democratic allegiances they possessed. Finally, in the period of Reconstruction following the war, atrocities committed by unrepentant Southern Democrats against black Republicans infuriated Pennsylvanians and further diminished the standing of the Democratic Party.

The extraordinary power of industrial concerns in Pennsylvania also contributed to the rise of the Republican Party. The single most important political issue to the state's iron, steel, and textile manufacturers was the enactment of protective tariffs, which the manufacturers believed would eliminate foreign competition. Republicans were more prominently associated with the issue of tariffs than Democrats, and, in return, they received substantial industrial backing. In addition to bankrolling Repub-

---

1. *New York Times*, 5 Nov. 1895, p. 1, col. 3.

lican campaigns, the state's large businesses influenced their employees, many of whom were recent immigrants dependent upon their jobs, to vote Republican.

Yet, many northern states experienced the Civil War and industrial power without being dominated for generations by the Republican Party. The distinguishing factor in Pennsylvania was the existence of one of the nation's great political machines. Through the power of this machine, "Governors and Presidents were made, and the political life of not only the State but the Nation were influenced."[2] Simon Cameron was the machine's most powerful early leader. Always excelling in "spoilsmanship, opportunism, and political chicanery," Cameron began his ascendancy in the 1820s by utilizing his friendship with Governor John A. Shulze to secure lucrative state printing and construction contracts.[3] Thereafter, he diversified into railroading, banking, and iron manufacturing. Despite his extensive business interests, however, Cameron's passion was politics, and he indulged that passion in a number of capacities, including United States senator (1845-49, 1857-61 and 1867-77), secretary of war (1861-62) and minister to Russia (1862) in the Lincoln administration. Throughout his career, Cameron's one consistent political position was support for protective tariffs and this position earned him the enduring support of Pennsylvania's industrialists. Cameron's contacts with Lincoln also proved valuable. During the war, he served as the president's chief consultant on federal patronage in Pennsylvania, a position that gave him tremendous influence in the state's booming wartime economy. Cameron utilized this position to reward his allies and punish his enemies.

After Lincoln's assassination, President Johnson retained Cameron as his patronage consultant in Pennsylvania. Following the war, Cameron solidified his control of the Republican Party through patronage, the support of big business, and by engineering the election of his supporters to important state posts, including governor. By manipulating the nomination process at all levels of government, he also gained control of the legislature, and thus the election of United States Senators and the apportionment of congressional districts.[4]

The machine constructed by Cameron, and presided over by subsequent political bosses, the most prominent of whom was Matthew Quay,[5] endured for more than seventy years. Its dominance was so complete that the Democratic Party was largely destroyed as a viable entity in state politics. Between 1860 and 1932, Pennsylvania did not vote for a single Democratic presidential candidate, only one Democrat served as governor between 1861 and 1934, and the state had no Democratic senators from 1875 to 1934. In the end, it took the Great Depression to again make Pennsylvania a two-party state.

---

2. George P. Donehoo, *Pennsylvania; A History* (New York City: 1926), 1491-92.

3. Philip Klein and Ari Hoogenboom, *A History of Pennsylvania* (University Park: Pennsylvania State University, 1973), 291.

4. In 1873, a legislature and governor, Cameron-controlled, combined to pass a new congressional reapportionment act, a model of gerrymandering, which limited Democrats to a maximum of nine of Pennsylvania's twenty-seven congressional seats. Of 1,452 acts passed by the same legislature, 1,389 were either special or local, and many benefited Pennsylvania corporations. One such bill, for instance, passed unanimously in both houses, permitted the Pennsylvania Railroad to increase its capital stock without limit. Klein and Hoogenboom, *A History of Pennsylvania*, 356.

5. Quay, from Beaver, Pa., served as an Indian fighter, colonel in the Civil War, Pennsylvania state legislator, secretary of state, treasurer, and, finally, United States senator. For an article recognizing Quay "as one of the greatest political generals of the age," see *New York Times*, 17 Nov. 1895, p. 22, col. 6 to p. 23, col. 8. See also, Wayland F. Dunaway, *A History of Pennsylvania* (New York: 1948), 456-78.

# NEW JUDGES

## FOR THE SUPERIOR COURT

### Governor Hastings Names the Prize Winners To-Day.

Governor Hastings this afternoon announced the following appointments for Judges of the Superior Court: Gen. James A. Beaver, Bellefonte; Charles E. Rice, Wilkes-Barre; Howard J. Reeder, Easton; George B. Orlady, Huntingdon; John J. Wickham, Beaver; E. N. Willard, Scranton; Henry J. McCarthy, Philadelphia. The new judges will meet in Harrisburg to-morrow afternoon for organization.

The Governor stated to-day when inquiry was made as to his tender of a position upon the Superior Bench to the Hon. J. Hay Brown, of Lancaster, that it was true the position had been tendered Mr. Brown and accepted by him. He subsequently declined solely for personal and family reasons that were entirely creditable to him, and the regret of the Governor is that the reasons for his declination could not be overcome. The Governor further stated that he deeply regretted Mr. Brown's declination, because his well known ability and experience would have made him a most useful member of the court.

---

## LEGAL INTELLIGENCE.

#### INJUNCTION AGAINST ACCEPTANCE OF A SCHOOLHOUSE DISSOLVED.

#### NEW SUPERIOR COURT IN SESSION

#### BEGINNING OF NOVEMBER TERM OF THE CRIMINAL COURTS.

#### PEPPER ESTATE REPORT CONFIRMED

Judgment, without execution, was entered on judgment notes yesterday in the Common Pleas as follows:

A. Wilt & Sons against Louis P. Hickman, $2000, note dated Oct. 31, 1894, payable in one year.

Thomas Taylor against M. Newkirk, $1700, note dated 26th ult., payable in six days.

In the Orphans' Court yesterday the settlement of estates for the November term was begun. There are 169 estates on the lists.

##### IN THE SUPERIOR COURT.

The new Superior Court began its sessions in the Supreme Court room, on the fourth floor of the City Hall. The judges were all attired in black silk gowns, similar to those worn by the Justices of the Supreme Court. Tastefully arranged on the bench in front of each judge was a handsome basket of flowers, which had been presented by the Five O'clock Club, of which Judge McCarthy is a member. There was a large gathering of members of the Bar, but there were no ceremonies attending the opening.

CHARLES E. RICE,
President Judge of the Superior Court.

After the Court had been convened promptly at 11 o'clock, President Judge Rice made the announcement that members of the Bar who had been admitted to practice in the Supreme Court prior to July 1, 1895, would be permitted to practice before the Superior Court without further order. After this announcement the business of the Court was at once proceeded with, by the calling of the regular list of cases.

The first three cases on the list—The City of Philadelphia, to use McCann, against the North Pennsylvania Railroad Company, appellant, appealed from C. P. No. 4 (two cases), and the city of Philadelphia, to use Pugh, use Kelly, against the Philadelphia and Reading Railroad Company, appellant, appeal from C. P. No. 4—were continued until December 23.

Argument was heard in the cases of Morgan against Wolstencraft, appellant, appeal from C. P. No. 4, and Kraemer against Guarantee T. and S. D. Co. (Kitchenman, appellant), appeal from C. P. No. 4, and non pros. was entered in the case of Barnes et al., executors, vs. Ruby et al. (Ruby et al., appellants), appeal from C. P. No. 4.

The case of Forider et al. vs. Kirchner (Gallagher, appellant), appeal from C. P. No. 3, was continued, and in re vacation of portion of Melon street—Philadelphia and Reading Railroad Terminal's appeal, appeal from the Quarter Sessions—was being argued when the Court adjourned, and argument will be resumed when court resumes to-morrow. There will be no session to-day.

##### COMMON PLEAS.

---

(left) The *Harrisburg Telegraph*, 27 June 1895, announces Governor Daniel H. Hastings' appointment of the first seven judges to the Superior Court.

(right) The *Philadelphia Legal Intelligencer*, 5 Nov. 1895, details early cases presented to the court as oral argument in Philadelphia. President Judge Charles E. Rice presided.

## The First Appointees to the Court

Given this political dominance, it is not surprising that six of the first seven appointees to the Superior Court were Republicans. Indeed, only Section 1 of the Superior Court Act, which reserved one seat to the minority party by providing that each elector could vote for only six of the seven candidates, prevented the court from being entirely Republican.[6] On June 28, 1895, the appointments were made by Governor Daniel H. Hastings, a product of the powerful Republican machine.[7] Hastings first appointed Charles E. Rice as president judge. Rice was born on September 15, 1846, in Fairfield, New York, and graduated from Hamilton College in 1867 and Albany Law School in 1869. Thereafter, he moved to Pennsylvania and was admitted to the bar at Wilkes-Barre in 1870. He was elected district attorney in 1876, and three years later he was elected judge of the Eleventh Judicial District. He became president judge of the Eleventh District in 1880, and was reelected in 1889. Following his appointment as president judge of the Superior Court, Rice was elected to a full ten-year term on November 5, 1895, and was reelected in 1905. In February 1915, Rice announced that he would retire when his second term ended in January 1916. In a letter to the Luzerne County Bar Association, which had endorsed him for reelection, Rice explained his decision to retire:

> I would like to remain in judicial service as long as I can do the work. I have no wish to leave it in order to enjoy the ease that would follow.
>
> No feeling of that kind enters into the determination of the question of my candidacy for reelection. But although I am in fair condition now, my bodily health, as has been demonstrated, is unreliable.
>
> Taking this into consideration with my age, the probability of my being as capable of long sustained mental effort as a Judge ought to be, for any considerable part of the new term, is, to speak within bounds, not strong.
>
> I will not dwell on these personal matters. It is enough to say they have led me to a definite conclusion as to what my duty to the court and to the people of the Commonwealth, who have so generously honored me, requires.
>
> Accordingly, much as I shall regret severance from association and work which have been agreeable to me I have determined not to be a candidate for re-election.[8]

Despite Rice's emphasis on his health and age, there was considerable speculation at the time that his decision to retire was caused by a 1913 change in the state's

---

6. This provision of the Superior Court Act was challenged by the Commonwealth on the basis that it unconstitutionally abridged the fundamental right to vote. The Supreme Court rejected this argument and declared the Superior Court Act constitutional in *Pennsylvania v. Reeder*, 171 Pa. 505 (1895). This decision, filed on October 17, 1895, was reported in the *Pittsburgh Legal Journal*, October 23, 1895, p. 107-11.

7. Endorsed by Quay, Hastings was elected in 1894 by a plurality of 240,000 votes, the largest to date in a gubernatorial election. He served as governor until January 1899. Howard M. Jenkins, ed., *Pennsylvania: Colonial and Federal; A History, 1608-1907* (Philadelphia, 1907) 194, 200-01.

8. The letter is quoted in the *Philadelphia Public Ledger*, 18 Feb. 1915, p. 3, col. 7.

election law, which replaced party nominations with primary elections.[9] Citing unnamed "political observers," for instance, the *Philadelphia Public Ledger* suggested that Rice did not want to "engage in an unseemly scramble [and] spend large sums of money for the office," as required by a primary election.[10] Whatever its cause, Rice's decision to retire proved final, and he left office at the expiration of his second term, in January 1916. Rice's tenure as president judge, twenty years and seven months, remains the longest in the Superior Court's history.[11]

Governor Hastings' next appointment was James Addams Beaver, the former governor who was instrumental in Hastings' early political career.[12] Beaver was born in Millerstown, Perry County, on October 21, 1837. As a youth, he studied at Pine Grove Academy, Centre County, and, in 1856, at the age of eighteen, he graduated from Jefferson College. Following graduation, he moved to Bellefonte, where he began the study of law. He was admitted to the bar of Centre County in January 1859. When the Civil War erupted, Beaver was commissioned a first lieutenant in the Second Pennsylvania Volunteers. He proved to be an excellent soldier, and was promoted to lieutenant colonel of the Forty-fifth Pennsylvania Volunteers. He resigned that post on September 4, 1862, to become Colonel of the 148th Pennsylvania Volunteers. He was wounded in combat at Chancellorsville, Spotsylvania, and Cold Harbor. On August 25, 1864, Beaver lost his right leg at Ream's Station, Virginia. His bravery resulted in a promotion to brigadier general, and he was mustered out on December 22, 1864. Following an unsuccessful campaign in 1882, he was elected governor in 1886. Beaver's tenure as governor was marked by a willingness to consider new approaches to various problems. For instance, he appointed a number of commissions to study law reform. One such commission revised and codified laws relating to the poor, another revised laws relating to public highways, and a third considered the regulation of coal usage to reduce waste.[13] He also enthusiastically commissioned a study that recommended the construction of a canal between Lake Erie and the Ohio River. In endorsing the study's conclusions, Beaver declared:

> If the waters of Lake Erie and the Ohio were connected by a canal such as is proposed and shown to be entirely feasible, and if the present canal from Albany to Buffalo were enlarged so as to admit vessels of the same size, these links would secure a chain of inter-waterway communication between New York and New Orleans, which would be invaluable for commercial purposes and in times of war would furnish an entirely safe means of communication between these important termini and all interior points. It would in addition give us control for defensive purposes of our lake front, which we do not now have and which it is doubtful whether we can secure in any other way under present treaty stipulations.[14]

9. The new statute, the Non-Partisan Ballot Law, sought to diminish the influence of political organizations in the selection of judges. Pa. Act of July 24, 1913, PL 1001. It is discussed more fully in Chapter 3.

10. *Philadelphia Public Ledger*, 19 Feb. 1915, p. 6, col. 3.

11. At his memorial service on July 17, 1919, Judge Orlady placed on the record Judge Rice's service of production on the court, as follows:

> During his administration, 10,823 appeals were disposed of. He filed 617 per curiam and 1,169 individual opinions; affirming 1,272, reversing 364, and quashing 150 appeals. He dissented in 82 judgments and filed 42 dissenting opinions.

12. As governor in 1889, Beaver elevated Hastings to state prominence by appointing him to administer relief efforts following the Johnstown Flood. Hastings' efficient administration of more than three million dollars in aid made him a rising force in the Republican Party, and he was elected governor in 1894. Jenkins, *Pennsylvania: Colonial and Federal*, 201.

13. Jenkins, *Pennsylvania: Colonial and Federal*, 191.

14. Jenkins, *Pennsylvania: Colonial and Federal*, 192-93.

The first business conference of the court is detailed in the minutes of the July 24, 1895, session in Harrisburg *(Pa. Archives)*.

Following his appointment to the Superior Court, Beaver was elected to a full ten-year term on November 5, 1895, and reelected in 1905. He served until his death on January 31, 1914.

Hastings' next Republican appointment was George B. Orlady, who was born in Petersburg, Huntingdon County, on February 22, 1850. Orlady graduated from Washington and Jefferson College in 1869, and he received a medical degree from Jefferson College in 1871. Following a brief tenure as a medical doctor, he moved to Hollidaysburg and undertook the study of law. He was admitted to the bar of Blair County in January 1875, and to the bar of Huntingdon County in March 1876. In 1878, and twice thereafter, he was elected district attorney of Huntingdon County. Following his appointment to the Superior Court, he was elected to a full term in November 1895, and was reelected in 1905 and 1915. Throughout his tenure on the court, Orlady was opposed by the state's liquor interests. This opposition peaked in the election of 1915, when opponents of Prohibition mounted a vigorous, although unsuccessful, campaign against him.[15] Upon the retirement of Judge Rice in January 1916, Orlady became president judge of the Superior Court. He served in that capacity until his death in 1925.

John J. Wickham was Hastings' fourth appointment to the Superior Court. Born in County Meath, Ireland, on May 14, 1844, Wickham emigrated to America at five years of age and settled in Beaver. A telegraphy enthusiast as a teenager, he enlisted in the Military Telegraph Corps during the Civil War. In July 1862, while serving with the Twenty-third Brigade as a cipher expert, he was captured during the Battle of Murfreesboro, Tennessee, by the forces of Confederate General Nathan Bedford Forrest. He remained a prisoner for several months, ending his captivity at the notorious Libby Prison. Following his exchange, he continued in the telegraph corps until 1867. Returning home, he was admitted to the bar in Beaver, and practiced there until 1884, when he was elected president judge of the Thirty-sixth Judicial District. He was reelected in 1894. Following his appointment to the Superior Court, he was elected to a full term on November 5, 1895. In June 1898, Wickham's house was struck by lightning, and it caught fire. While attempting to subdue the flames, he suffered a stomach hemorrhage. A week later, he fell unconscious and remained in that condition until his death on June 18, 1898.[16]

Hastings also appointed Edward Newell Willard to the Superior Court. Willard was born on April 2, 1835, graduated from Yale Law School in 1857, and was admitted to the bar of Luzerne County the same year. He was a Captain in the Civil War, ending his service as judge advocate of the Second Division, Fifth Army Corps. He was appointed Register in Bankruptcy in 1867. Following his appointment, Willard served on the Superior Court until his resignation in 1897. Thereafter, he continued to practice in Luzerne County until his death on March 3, 1910.

Howard J. Reeder, Hastings' final Republican appointment, was born on December 11, 1843. In 1860, at the age of sixteen, he entered Princeton College as a sophomore. He graduated from Princeton College. During the Civil War, he served as a lieutenant in the First Regiment, United States Infantry, and as a captain in the 153rd Pennsylvania Volunteers. In July 1863, he participated in the battles of Chancellorsville and Gettysburg. Upon being mustered out in 1864 and following service in the offices of Reeder and Green, he entered Harvard Law School to complete his legal studies. He was elected judge of the Third Judicial District in 1884 and served in that capacity until his appointment to the Superior Court. He served on the court until his death on December 28, 1898 at the age of fifty-three.

---

15. *Philadelphia Public Ledger*, 20 Sept. 1915, p. 8, col. 7.
16. Wickham's obituary was published in the *Philadelphia Inquirer* on June 18, 1898, p. 1, col. 3.

Hastings' sole Democratic appointee was Henry J. McCarthy, who was born in Philadelphia on October 11, 1845. Upon his graduation from high school in 1862, McCarthy undertook the study of law in the office of Judge William A. Porter. Admitted to practice in 1866, he associated with Philadelphia Solicitor William Nelson West, and was instrumental in bringing about the downfall of the Gas Trust. Although appointed to the Superior Court in 1895, McCarthy did not receive the nomination of his party for the general election. In 1898, he was appointed judge of the First Judicial District, and subsequently elected to a full term. In his fifteen years on the trial bench, McCarthy was reversed but once by the Supreme Court.[17] Beginning in the spring of 1903, an excess of work caused McCarthy to suffer "from complete nervous exhaustion." When bed rest did not relieve the condition, he was directed by his physician to recuperate in Atlantic City, New Jersey. He complied with the directions, but returned to Philadelphia in early July. Although his family and friends did not notice the seriousness of his condition, Judge McCarthy grew ever weaker, and he died of a heart attack three weeks later, on July 21, 1903. Mourning the passing, Mayor Weaver of Philadelphia declared that "[t]he city has lost in him an upright and a most fearless judge."[18]

Taken together, these biographical sketches indicate that the judges of the first court were men of varied backgrounds. Of the seven appointees, four had served as trial judges, four were Civil War veterans, three were law school graduates, and one had served as district attorney. The court also included a former governor and a physician. Finally, the judges ranged in age from forty-four to sixty.

## THE WORK OF THE COURT BEGINS

On June 28, 1895, three days before the Superior Court Act became effective, the appointed judges gathered in Harrisburg to establish operating procedures for the new court. Similar meetings occurred throughout the summer and fall. Court rules were modeled on those of the Supreme Court, and the two courts arranged to share prothonotaries in Philadelphia, Harrisburg, and Pittsburgh.[19] The Superior Court designated its own prothonotaries in Williamsport and Scranton.[20] Finally, the judges established the new court's schedule and divided the state's counties among the five regions established by the Superior Court Act.[21]

The court conducted its first argument session on November 4, 1895, at 11:00

---

17. McCarthy was among Philadelphia's most noted after-dinner speakers, and a lifelong student of classical history. He was president of the Five O'Clock Club, a Mason, a member of the Penn and Columbia Clubs, and a director of the Commonwealth Title and Trust Company.

18. McCarthy's obituary appeared in the *Philadelphia Inquirer* on July 22, 1903, p. 1, col. 2.

19. The prothonotaries in Philadelphia, Harrisburg, and Pittsburgh were Charles S. Greene, William Pearson, and George Pearson, respectively. *Smull's Legislative Hand Book and Manual* (Harrisburg, Pa.: 1895), 38a.

20. The prothonotaries appointed by the court in Williamsport and Scranton were Benjamin S. Bentley and Samuel H. Stevens. See note 19.

21. The judges determined that while sitting at Philadelphia, they would hear appeals from the counties of Berks, Bucks, Chester, Delaware, Lancaster, Lehigh, Montgomery, Northampton, Philadelphia, and Schuylkill. By 1910, the Philadelphia district also included the counties of Bedford, Blair, Bradford, Carbon, Centre, Clearfield, Franklin, Fulton, Huntingdon, Lebanon, McKean, Monroe, Northumberland, Potter and Wyoming. The Scranton district consisted of Bradford, Carbon, Columbia, Lackawanna, Luzerne, Montour, Pike, Susquehanna, Wayne, and Wyoming. By 1910, Bradford, Carbon, and Wyoming Counties had been transferred to the Philadelphia district. The Williamsport district consisted of Cameron, Centre, Clearfield, Clinton, Elk, Lycoming, McKean, Northumberland, Potter, Snyder, Sullivan, Tioga, and Union Counties. By 1910, Centre, Clearfield, McKean, Northumberland and Potter Counties had been transferred to Philadelphia, and Snyder County was transferred to Harrisburg. The Harrisburg district included the counties of

## SUPERIOR COURT SESSION

### Opens at 11 O'clock Today in the Federal Building.

### HOW THE JUDGES WILL ACT

**Court Etiquette Provides That Everybody Shall Rise When the Crier Announces the Judges' Entrance—Particulars of the Duties of the Body.**

The first session of the superior court of Pennsylvania will begin in this city today in the Federal building. Twice has the court sat in Philadelphia while the seven members were holding an appointive office, but the session which begins here today is the first since the judges were elected to their high office by the people.

At 11 o'clock the court will open and will continue in session all this week and probably during three days of next week.

Etiquette of the supreme court of the United States, lately adopted by the supreme court of Pennsylvania will be followed in the superior court. When the judges enter the chamber the crier will strike his desk with a gavel and formally announce, "The honorable, the president judge and the associate judges of the superior court of Pennsylvania." Lawyers and spectators will be standing while this announcement is made and will not be seated until the judges occupy their chairs. The method of practice will be the same as that before the supreme court.

## SUPERIOR COURT OPENED.

### First Session of That Body Held in Pittsburg—Gave Up a Lover for Nothing.

The first session of the superior court for the Fifth district was opened in the supreme court rooms yesterday morning. The justices present were: President Judge Charles E. Rice, and Associate Justices John J. Wickham, Howard J. Reeder, Peter P. Smith and Geo. B. Orlady. Justices James A. Beaver and E. N. Willard will put in an appearance to-day. The session yesterday was a short one. The entire list for Allegheny county was called over and only five cases were heard. There seemed to be very few lawyers prepared to argue their cases, and the court adjourned for the day at 2 o'clock.

The first case argued was the appeal of T. Milnor McDonough from common pleas No. 1. James Fitzsimmons appeared for him, and he had the honor of making the first argument before the superior court in this district.

## SUPERIOR COURT

### FIRST SITTING IN THIS CITY

### Governor and Mrs. Hastings Will Give a Dinner to the Judges.

The Superior Court began its first sitting for this district in the Supreme Court room at 10 o'clock this morning. All the judges were present. On the right of Presiding Judge Rice sat Judges Willard, Beaver and Orlady, and on his left Judges Reeder and Smith. Promptly at 10 o'clock W. K. Taylor, of Philadelphia, the crier of the new court, announced the judges, who filed in and took their places, the lawyers and others assembled in the court room rising. They wear the judicial gowns and are a fine looking body of men.

There was no ceremony, and the Court at once began business. The list was called over and argument was commenced in the case of the E. Keeler Company against Schott, an appeal from the common pleas of Juniata county. There is no limitation as to the time counsel shall occupy as in the Supreme Court, and this case consumed more than an hour.

The cases of George Gearhart versus Middlesex township, Cumberland county; and John Reed versus Richland Water Company, appeal, Lebanon county, were non-prossed. The case of the West Branch Lumberman's Exchange against D. A. Lutz et al., was continued until the 18th. Other cases continued were those of Zion's Church against A. H. Light, Lebanon county, and Overseers of Susquehanna township against the Overseers of Monroe township, Junata county.

There was a large attendance of the members of the Dauphin County Bar this morning. All wanted to see how the new Court conducted business. Samuel Collins, of Philadelphia, is the tipstaff of this court, the appointment being permanent. No decisions were handed down to-day. This evening Governor and Mrs. Hastings will entertain the Court, Judges Simonton and McPherson and a few others at dinner at the Executive Mansion. There will be covers for sixteen.

News clippings from the *Scranton Tribune*, 13 Jan. 1896 (top left), the *Harrisburg Telegraph*, 10 Mar. 1896 (right), and the *Pittsburg Post*, 7 Apr. 1896 (bottom left), announce the first sessions of the Superior Court in each of those cities.

A.M., in the Supreme Court's courtroom at City Hall in Philadelphia. A lawyer present in court that day recalled the scene as the judges entered the courtroom:

> When the seven members of the Bench of the Superior Court filed into the Supreme Court-room on the fourth floor of the City Hall at 11 o'clock this morning, the scene was an impressive one. . . . They stood by their chairs as the Crier in the most solemn manner opened the Court for the first time, and then in the usual formula called down the blessings of God on "this honorable Court."
>
> On the desks before each of the new Judges were huge baskets of flowers sent by the Five O'clock Club as a token of the respect in which Judge Henry J. McCarthy, . . . one of its members, was held. . . . [T]hroughout the session of the Court the perfume from the roses, violets, and other sweet smelling flowers filled the air.
>
> President Judge Rice was naturally seated in the center, while on his right were Judges Edward N. Willard, Howard J. Reeder, and Henry J. McCarthy, and on his left were Judges James A. Beaver, John J. Wickham, and George B. Orlady. They all wore the regulation black gowns and looked to be just what was expected of them, a fine and imposing body of men. They went to work at once, and the business of the day was transacted with a despatch that was note worthy.[22]

Following its inaugural meeting, the court met five more times in Philadelphia in November and December.[23] On the first three Mondays in January 1896, it met at the federal courtroom in the post office at Scranton. Thereafter, it met at the courtroom in the federal building at Williamsport on the first three Mondays in February. It also met at the Supreme Court courtroom in Harrisburg on the first three Mondays in March, and at the Supreme Court courtroom in Pittsburgh on the first three Mondays in both April and May. On May 18, 1896, while in the Pittsburgh region, the court also began its practice of holding "special" sessions by convening in Erie.[24] With slight variations, the court maintained this schedule until 1917, when it stopped sitting at Williamsport.[25]

---

Adams, Bedford, Blair, Cumberland, Dauphin, Franklin, Fulton, Huntingdon, Juniata, Lebanon, Mifflin, Perry and York. By 1910, Bedford, Blair, Huntingdon and Lebanon Counties had been transferred to Philadelphia, and Harrisburg had obtained Snyder County. The Pittsburgh district included the counties of Allegheny, Armstrong, Beaver, Butler, Cambria, Clarion, Crawford, Erie, Fayette, Forest, Greene, Indiana, Jefferson, Lawrence, Mercer, Somerset, Venango, Warren, Washington and Westmoreland. This district had not changed by 1910.

22. *Philadelphia Public Ledger*, 4 Nov. 1895, p. 1, col. 3. The court adjourned for the day at 3:00 p.m.

23. On November 18, 1895, while sitting at Philadelphia, the court decided the first case to be published in the new *Superior Court Reports*. In *Benevolent Order of Active Workers v. Smith*, 1 Pennsylvania Superior Court 1 (1895), appellee, the secretary of a fraternal society, returned dues to members of the society rather than pay them over to the society, which was subject to an assignment by appellant. The trial court held that appellee had properly returned the dues, and the Superior Court reversed on the basis that appellee, as an agent of the society, was required to pay the dues into its treasury. 1 Pa. Super. 3-4.

24. On December 27, 1895, while the court was in between its Philadelphia and Scranton sessions, Judge Rice took the oath of office as the first president judge. He was sworn in at Wilkes-Barre by Judge Woodward, president judge of Luzerne County. *Philadelphia Inquirer*, 28 Dec. 1895, p. 1, col. 4.

25. In 1904, the court began sitting at Williamsport in March, instead of February, and in 1908, the Williamsport sessions were shifted back to February and Scranton sessions were held in March. After 1916, the Williamsport district was abolished and its counties were transferred to Harrisburg.

The February 1899 motion for admission of McKean County attorney Fred D. Gallup to practice before the Superior Court, having completed a two-year clerkship with J. W. Bouton, is one of the earliest on record.

## THE FIRST ELECTION AND EARLY TURNOVER OF JUDGES

Even as the new court began sitting, its personnel started to change. Although the first change—the replacement of Judge McCarthy—was formalized by the general election of November 5, 1895, it was determined several months earlier. In the late summer of 1895, the Republicans and Democrats held nominating conventions for the November general election. Each party nominated six candidates for the Superior Court. The six candidates offered by the Republicans were those appointed by Governor Hastings. The Democrats, however, refused to nominate McCarthy, Hastings' sole Democratic appointee. Instead, they offered a slate of new candidates, including Judge William Yerkes of Bucks County, Judge Patrick Magee of Allegheny County, and Judge Peter P. Smith of Lackawanna County.

By refusing to nominate McCarthy, the Democratic Party ensured that the fall general election would result in the court's first personnel change. On November 5, 1895, as expected, the Republicans won an overwhelming victory, carrying the state by a plurality of more than 180,000 votes.[26] The six Republican nominees were elected to full ten-year terms,[27] but the identity of the sole Democrat elected to the court was at first unclear. The day after the election, November 6, 1895, with returns still trickling in, the *New York Times* opined:

---

26. On the morning after the elections, with returns still trickling in, the *New York Times* published a headline entitled, "Republicans in Pennsylvania: They Carry the State by the Usual Majority." 6 Nov. 1895, p. 4, col. 6.

27. The order of election for the Republicans, from most votes to least, was Beaver, Willard, Wickham, Rice, Reeder, and Orlady. *Philadelphia Inquirer*, 9 Nov. 1895, p. 4, col. 2.

Judge Peter P. Smith          Judge William W. Porter          Judge Dimner Beeber

Judge Yerkes of Bucks will probably be the minority representative on the Superior Court Bench. The returns indicate that he will run far ahead of his colleagues all through the eastern section of the State, and unless Judge Magee, of Allegheny, polls a heavy vote in Western Pennsylvania, Yerkes election is assured. Magee is a cousin of Chris L. Magee, the Republican banker of Allegheny County, who made a special effort to secure the election of his relative.[28]

The same day, the *Philadelphia Inquirer* noted that the "choice for Democratic Judge apparently lies between Magee, of Allegheny; Smith, of Lackawanna; and Yerkes, of Bucks, with chances favoring the former."[29] Despite the predictions of these leading newspapers, Peter Smith emerged victorious. On November 7, 1895, the *Inquirer* declared that "Judge Peter P. Smith (Dem.), of Lackawanna is elected . . . by about 2000 plurality over his next competitor, Judge Yerkes. Judge Magee's failure to get a substantial vote in Philadelphia destroyed his chances of winning the coveted position."[30] The next day, the *Times* stated that Smith had a plurality of 2,500 to 3,000 votes over Yerkes.[31] Smith's election was assured, but the controversy continued. In an article entitled "Judges Puzzled Over Returns," published on November 9, the *Inquirer* noted that election officials were investigating "discrepancies" in the votes of both Smith and Yerkes.[32] Finally, in an article published a week later, the Republican *Inquirer* alleged fraud:

> The vote by which Judge Smith is declared to have been elected to the Superior Court has created astonishment, suspicion and indignation throughout the State.

28. See note 26.
29. *Philadelphia Inquirer*, 6 Nov. 1895, p. 8, col. 1.
30. *Philadelphia Inquirer*, 7 Nov. 1895, p. 1, col. 1.
31. *New York Times*, 8 Nov. 1895, p. 1, col. 6.
32. *Philadelphia Inquirer*, 9 Nov. 1895, p. 4, col. 2.

Judge John I. Mitchell

Judge Thomas A. Morrison *(photo courtesy of John M. Woodburn, Esq., and Dione Bell Hayes, great-great-grandson and great-granddaughter, respectively, of Judge Morrison).*

In Lackawanna county Myers, the Democratic candidate for State Treasurer, received only 4,269 votes. Smith, one of the Democratic candidates for Superior Judge, received 7,712 votes. The vote for the other Democratic candidates for Judge ran from 2,629 to 2,794. In Luzerne county Smith got 12,360 votes, running several thousand ahead of the other Democratic candidates. In the two counties the Smith voters are charged with cutting the other Democratic candidates to the extent of 3,300 votes.

In Schuylkill county it is said that the Democratic voters did not know anything about Smith until a few days before the election, when suddenly the boys, as with one voice, began to whoop it up for him.

In Philadelphia Myers received 42,020 votes to Smith 43,420, leading all the Democratic candidates for Judge except Yerkes, who received 46,500 votes, only 3,080 more votes than Smith, when, without some hocus-pocus arrangement, he would naturally have received many thousands more votes than Smith. In Allegheny county Smith ran away ahead of the other Democratic candidates for Judge, except Magee. As personally he was entirely unknown to the voters of many of the counties, it is apparent that he received 6,214 more votes than Yerkes, according to the returns, only because some influence set up the slate and slashed the Democratic ticket in Smith's behalf.[33]

---

33. *Philadelphia Inquirer*, 16 Nov. 1895, p. 6, col. 1,2.

Nothing came of these fraud allegations, however, and Smith took his seat on the Superior Court bench. He was born in 1851, admitted to the bar in 1874, and served as district attorney of Wayne County from 1875 to 1878. In 1892, he was appointed judge of the Forty-fifth Judicial District, in which capacity he served until 1894. After replacing McCarthy in 1895,[34] Smith served for ten years. In 1905, he was retired from the court pursuant to the provisions of the Act of May 11, 1901, which provided for the removal of judges who were unable to perform their judicial duties due to mental or physical disability. Judge Smith died in 1909.

Smith's replacement of McCarthy was only the first of many personnel changes on the early court. Although Judges Rice, Beaver, and Orlady served long tenures, the occupants of the remaining four seats changed no less than seven times in the ten years after Smith replaced McCarthy. It is necessary to identify the new judges before turning to a review of the significant cases they, and the original members of the court, decided. The first change following Smith's election occurred on September 14, 1897, when William W. Porter was appointed to replace Judge Willard. Porter was born on May 5, 1856, the son of Justice William A. Porter of the Supreme Court and the grandson of David Rittenhouse Porter, twice governor of Pennsylvania. He graduated from the University of Pennsylvania in 1875, and thereafter studied law under his father. He was admitted to the bar in 1877, and devoted his early career to the practice of corporate and estate law. Following his appointment to the Superior Court, Porter served until January 27, 1903, when he resigned and returned to private practice.

Porter's seat was filled on March 11, 1903, by the appointment of another Republican, John J. Henderson. Henderson was born in Allegheny County on September 23, 1843, and educated at Meadville Academy and Allegheny College. Thereafter, he served in the Civil War, and was honorably discharged in June 1865.[35] Two years later, he was admitted to the bar of Crawford County, and he was elected district attorney in 1872. In 1887, he was elected president judge of the Thirtieth Judicial District and served in that capacity until January 1898. Following his appointment to the Superior Court, Henderson was elected to a full term in November 1903, as the nominee of the Republican, Prohibition, and Progressive Parties. He was reelected in 1913 and 1923, and served until his death on December 12, 1928.

The deaths of two of the court's original members resulted in further personnel changes. When Judge Wickham died on June 18, 1898, he was replaced by Republican William D. Porter, who was born in New Cumberland, West Virginia, on January 3, 1849. Porter was educated at the University of Pennsylvania, receiving a law degree in 1868. He was admitted to the Allegheny County bar on January 5, 1870. In 1883, he was elected district attorney of Allegheny County and reelected in 1886. In 1891, he was appointed judge of the court of common pleas, Fifth Judicial District, and elected to succeed himself in the fall. Following his appointment to the Superior Court, he was elected in November 1898, and reelected in 1908 and 1918. In this latter campaign, he also received the nomination of the Democratic Party. Following the death of Judge Orlady, Porter became president judge and served in that capacity until his death in February 1930.

---

34. On November 9, 1895, the Five O'Clock Club had a dinner for Judge McCarthy to "Speed [his] Parting" from the bench. The next day the *Inquirer* reported that "it is doubtful if fun was ever in greater force in the history of the club." The article gives some indication as to why McCarthy was not favored by the Democratic Convention several months earlier. In addition to the fact that he was appointed by a Republican governor, McCarthy seemed to have extensive contacts in the state's Republican hierarchy. More than a few members of this hierarchy spoke on his behalf at the Five O'Clock Club. Among them were Judges Rice, Wickham, Beaver, Philadelphia Mayor Warwick, and many others. *Philadelphia Inquirer*, 10 Nov. 1895, p. 4, col. 2.

35. As reported in the *Meadville Tribune* at a testimonial for Judge Henderson in 1927, Professor Christopher B. Coleman, detailing Judge Henderson's life, remarked about the judge's presence at the Ford Theater in Washington, D.C., when President Lincoln was shot.

The seat occupied by Judge Reeder changed three times within four years after his death on September 28, 1898. At Scranton, Pennsylvania, on January 9, 1899, President Judge Rice, in speaking for the court at the Memorial Session upon the death of Judge Howard J. Reeder, stated:

> Judge Reeder was one of the seven men appointed as the first judges of this court upon its organization three and one-half years ago and it is a forcible remainder [sic] of the vicissitude, and uncertainties of life that since his death, but three of the original members of the court remain on this bench.

The first of these changes occurred on January 2, 1899, when Dimner Beeber replaced Reeder. Beeber was born on March 8, 1854, in Muncy, Lycoming County. In 1874, he graduated from the Pennsylvania College at Gettysburg, and he was admitted to the Lycoming and Philadelphia bars two years later. In 1894, he became a member of the firm of Jones, Carson, and Beeber. On the day of Beeber's appointment to the Superior Court, January 9, 1899, he participated in the court's session at Scranton. After the session, he wrote to a family member: "I have just finished my first day's listening on the bench and must confess I have not yet seized the knack of grasping instantly the point of the case as it is presented to the court. I hope to do better in the hereafter."[36] Beeber served until January 1900, when he was denied the nomination of the Republican Party to succeed himself.

Beeber was succeeded by John I. Mitchell. Judge Mitchell was born July 28, 1838 in Tioga County, Pennsylvania. He attended Buchnell University in Lewisburg, Pennsylvania and taught for a short time thereafter. Upon the outbreak of the Civil War, he raised a company for service in the war and became a captain in Company A, 136th Pennsylvania Volunteers. Following the war, he read law and was admitted to practice in 1864. In 1868, he was elected district attorney of Tioga County, but before the expiration of his term, he was elected to the state legislature where he served for five years. Thereafter, he returned to the practice of law and soon was elected to both the Forty-fifth and Forty-sixth Congress. As his last congressional term neared expiration, he was nominated and elected to the position of United States Senator, in which capacity he served for six years, from March 4, 1881 to retirement in 1887. He was elevated to the bench of the Fourth Judicial District in 1888, where he served until January 1900 when he resigned to take a seat on the Superior Court, to which he was elected in November 1899. He was on the bench in Scranton for one session, after which, upon returning to his home on January 24, 1900, he was stricken by paralysis. He resigned on November 28, 1902 and died August 20, 1907.

Thomas A. Morrison was appointed to succeed Mitchell one month later. Morrison was born in Pleasantville, Venango County, on May 4, 1840. He was educated at the State Normal School in Edinboro, and in July 1862, he enlisted in the 121st Volunteers. Five months later, at the Battle of Fredericksburg, he lost his left arm and received other serious wounds, as a result of which he was discharged. Returning home, he served as treasurer of Venango County from 1868 to 1869. Thereafter, he was admitted to the bar and practiced in Pleasantville until 1879, at which time he moved to Smethport. In September 1887, he was appointed judge of the Fourth Judicial District. He was elected to a full term in 1897, and became president judge on September 10, 1901. On December 30, 1902, he assumed office in the Superior Court, succeeding Judge Mitchell, and was elected to a full term in 1903. He retired from the bench in January 1914 and died in Smethport on August 26, 1916.

---

36. Beeber to "Joe," 9 January 1899, Historical Society of Pennsylvania, Philadelphia.

Finally, John B. Head was elected to replace Judge Smith in November 1905. Born in Latrobe on April 4, 1855, Head was educated in the public schools and at Mt. Saint Mary's College, Emmitsburg, Maryland. Following his graduation in 1873, he returned home and was admitted to the bar in 1880. He practiced law until his election to the Superior Court in November 1905. Winning the fourth seat in a field with only three Republicans, he was the final Democrat elected to the bench until 1934.[37] He was reelected in 1915 with the endorsement of the Republican Party, and served until poor health forced his sudden retirement in April 1922.[38]

## THE COURT AT WORK: ECONOMIC REGULATION

Not surprisingly, the most important cases decided by the early court involved the uneasy place of the new industrial economy in the state regulatory structure. In resolving these cases, the court was required to mediate between profoundly different theories of government. At issue was the fundamental question of whether and to what extent the economy could be regulated. On the one hand, captains of industry and other advocates of laissez faire argued that the economy, operating upon its own principles of supply and demand, should not be restrained by legislation. On the other, reformers of all types, alarmed at the rapid growth of powerful corporations, asserted that the onerous consequences of headlong industrialization necessitated extensive legislative intervention. The opposing sides repeatedly brought their claims before the Superior Court, and the court's response depended most often on the specific goals of the economic regulation at issue. In distinguishing between permissible and impermissible goals, the court in its first years played a critical role in defining the proper relationship between the judiciary, the legislature, and the economy.

The court took its most restrictive stance with regard to statutes seeking to regulate the employment relationship. Such statutes, which today are quite commonplace, were the result of a highly-politicized effort by Gilded Age labor reformers to remedy the power imbalance inherent in industrial employment. The primary goal of these reformers, both in Pennsylvania and nationally, was to achieve legislation regulating the wage contract and labor conditions. In particular, they advocated a shorter work day, legislation limiting sweat shops by prohibiting manufacturing in tenements, wage laws abolishing payment in scrip and requiring regular pay schedules, laws banning employers from discriminating against union organizing efforts, and laws regulating the manner in which miners' wages were determined, including restrictions upon how, when, and by whom coal was weighed.[39] By advancing their cause in legislatures, rather than before executive officials or the courts, labor reformers believed they could exercise the power of the ballot to remedy the oppressive industrial system.[40]

Beginning in the 1840s and 1850s, the Pennsylvania legislature responded to the efforts of reformers with a series of protective labor laws. In 1849, for instance, it declared that ten hours constituted "a legal day's labor" for all workers in cotton, woolen, silk, paper, bagging, and flax factories,[41] and six years later it mandated that no em-

---

37. Head received barely half the votes (305,218) of Republicans Rice (626,226), Beaver (610,394), and Orlady (591,592). *Smull's Legislative Hand Book* (1906), 367.

38. In 1915, Head was elected without a party designation pursuant to the Non-Partisan Ballot Law, which is discussed infra.

39. William E. Forbath, "The Shaping of the American Labor Movement," *Harvard Law Review* 102 (1989), 1111, 1132.

40. According to Forbath, "[t]hese reform campaigns were testing grounds for the proposition that workers could use the ballot to 'engraft republican principles' on property and industry." See note 39, citing McNeill, "The Problem of Today," in *The Labor Movement: The Problem of Today* (G. McNeill, 1891), 460.

41. Pa. Act of April 21, 1849, PL 671, sec. 2.

No. *1 November* Term, *1895*
~~Supreme~~ Superior COURT OF PENNSYLVANIA,

EASTERN DISTRICT.

*Anna C. Deipel Exrx*

*vs*

*Richard M. Johnson*

*Appellant*

## APPEAL AND AFFIDAVIT.

FILED
IN THE SUPERIOR COURT.
JUL 15 1895

*W. E. Doster*
*J. D. Hoffman*

---

IN THE COURT OF COMMON PLEAS OF SCHUYLKILL COUNTY.

Cordea Seff            )
                       )
        vs             )    No. 106 November Term, 1891.
                       )
E. Lowenstein          )

SCHUYLKILL COUNTY, SS.;

    I, James R. Deegan, Prothonotary of said Court; do hereby certify that the Plaintiff in this cause has on the 15th day of July 1895 appealed from the judgment of this Court to the Superior Court of Pennsylvania, and has duly entered into a recognizance as required by law in the sum of Two Thousand Dollars ($2000.00) with Max Rubinsky and I. Laubenstein as her sureties, and that said Bond or Recognizance remains on file in my office.

    In Testimony Whereof I have hereunto set my hand and affixed the seal of the said Court, this Seventh day of August A. D., 1895.

*James R. Deegan*
Prothonotary.

---

In the ~~Supreme~~ Superior Court of Pennsylvania,
~~FOR THE EASTERN DISTRICT.~~

*Cordea Seff*
Plaintiff

*vs,*

*E. Lowenstein*

Defendant.

Court of *Common Pleas*
of the County of *Schuylkill*
*November* Term, 18*91*

No. *106*

Enter Appeal on behalf of *the Plaintiff*
from *Judgment* of the Court of *Common Pleas*
of the County of *Schuylkill in above cause*

*To Charles S. Greene, Protho'y Sup. Ct. E. D.*

*The Prothonotary*
*yours truly*

County of *Schuylkill* ss.

*Cordea Seff* being duly *sworn* saith that the above Appeal is not intended for delay, but because she firmly believes that she has suffered injustice by the judgment from which she desires to appeal.

*sworn* and subscribed,
this *15th* day *July* A. D. 18*95*

*James R. Deegan*
Pro'thy.

These documents depict the first appeal filed with the Superior Court. Note the scratch-out of "Supreme Court" and insertion of "Superior Court," as printed Superior Court forms were not yet available (*Pa. Archives*).

ployee under the age of twenty-one could be employed in such factories for more than sixty hours per week.[42] By statutes enacted in 1881 and 1891, the legislature further decreed that miners' wages be paid in "lawful money of the United States," rather than in goods purchased at a company store.[43] In 1893, the legislature created the office of factory inspector, and required that any business employing women or children must post notices, for the inspector's examination, indicating the number of work hours per day required of employees.[44] In 1897, the permissible work hours of adult females were limited to twelve per day and sixty per week.[45] Also in 1897, the legislature passed a law prohibiting corporations from discharging employees because of membership in lawful labor organizations.[46] The same year, it prohibited mine owners from screening bituminous coal, and thus reducing its weight, before the tonnage was credited to a miner's account.[47] Subsequent legislation also mandated an eight-hour day for employees of the state or municipal corporations.[48]

These measures, and a number of others aimed at mitigating the evils of industrial employment, were enacted by the legislature pursuant to the police power of the Pennsylvania Constitution.[49] In 1900, the Superior Court described this power as follows:

> The police power of the state is difficult of definition, but it has been held by the courts to be the right to prescribe regulations for the good order, peace, health, protection, comfort, convenience and morals of the community which does not violate the provisions of the organic law. . . . Its essential quality as a government agency is that it imposes upon persons and property burdens designed to promote the safety and welfare of the public at large.[50]

Article XVI, Section 3, of the 1874 state constitution declares that "the exercise of the police power of the State shall never be abridged." Despite its breadth, however, the police power has always been subject to judicial review, and legislative exercise of the power might be invalidated where it infringes upon constitutional rights.[51] This limitation upon the police power had significant implications for the efforts of reformers to achieve protective labor legislation. Indeed, despite their early successes, reformers soon found that courts were far more hostile to their cause than legislatures.

Judges throughout the 1880s and 1890s proved quite willing to invalidate laws that sought to regulate the employment relationship. Nationwide, more than sixty such laws were struck down by the turn of the century, and, by 1920, the number exceeded three hundred.[52] The courts' hostility to protective labor legislation resulted primarily from two factors. First, many judges during the late nineteenth century believed that such legislation sought group advantage, not equality. Specifically, these judges, the vast majority of whom were middle and upper-class Republicans, saw labor laws as invidious class legislation seeking to benefit employees at the expense of employers,

---

42. Pa. Act of May 7, 1855, PL 472
43. Pa. Act of June 29, 1881, PL 147; Pa. Act of May 20, 1891, PL 96.
44. Pa. Act of June 3, 1893, PL 276.
45. Pa. Act of April 29, 1897, PL 30.
46. Pa. Act of June 4, 1897, PL 116.
47. Pa. Act of July 15, 1897, PL 286.
48. Pa. Act of July 26, 1897, PL 418.
49. See *Commonwealth v. Beatty,* 15 Pa. Super. 5, 15 (1900).
50. See note 49.
51. See e.g., *Mugler v. Kansas,* 123 U.S. 623 (1887).
52. Forbath, "The Shaping of the American Labor Movement", 102 *Harvard Law Review,* 1133.

Boys separating shale from coal in the "breakers" of a hard coal mining region. Note the supervisor carrying a rod for discipline or coercion *(Pa. Archives)*.

and thus violating constitutional prohibitions against special legislation.[53] Moreover, they argued, such laws threatened the constitutional values of limited government and respect for property.[54] The second and most important theory utilized by the courts to declare labor legislation unconstitutional, and thus invalidate legislative exercises of the police power, was "liberty of contract," which derived from the freedom and property guarantees of state and federal constitutions. Courts repeatedly held that liberty of contract meant that employers and employees possessed a constitutional right to decide on terms and conditions of employment without legislative interference.[55]

The interrelation of these concepts—the police power, special class legislation, and liberty of contract—was central to the cases brought before the Superior Court as it began the critical work of enunciating the role of government in Pennsylvania's economy. The result was a line of cases that probably constitute the first court's most important work. The first of these cases was *Showalter v. Ehlan*,[56] in which the court considered

53. Article III, Section 7 of the Pennsylvania Constitution declares that "The General Assembly shall not pass any local or special law . . . regulating labor, trade, mining or manufacturing."

54. Forbath, "The Shaping of the American Labor Movement," 1133, n. 79.

55. The most famous judicial enunciation of this doctrine was *Lochner v. New York*, 198 U.S. 45 (1905), in which the United States Supreme Court invalidated a New York statute prohibiting employment in the state's bakeries for more than sixty hours per week. According to the court, the "freedom of master and employee to contract with each other in relation to their employment, and in defining the same, cannot be prohibited or interfered with, without violating the Federal Constitution." *Lochner v. New York*, 63-64. So significant is this case that the period it represents, enduring into the 1930s, has been known ever since as the Lochner Era.

56. 5 Pa. Super. 242 (1897) (Wickham, J.).

an 1891 law requiring payment of miners' wages in cash.[57] The law was intended to outlaw the practice, utilized by mining companies across the state, of paying miners in goods from a company store. In a brief opinion, the unanimous Superior Court struck down the law as an unconstitutional violation of liberty of contract:

> The act is an infringement alike of the right of the employer and the employee; more than this, it is an insulting attempt to put the laborer under the legislative tutelage, which is not only degrading to his manhood, but subversive of his rights as a citizen of the United States.[58]

A more prominent case decided a year later, *Commonwealth v. Brown*,[59] involved both liberty of contract and the special legislation prohibitions of the state constitution. In *Brown*, the court considered the constitutionality of P.L. 286,[60] which regulated the manner in which coal was weighed and credited to miners' accounts. Prior to the enactment of P.L. 286, it was common practice in the mining industry to pass coal sent to the surface over a screen which separated slag and dust from lump coal measuring one and one-half inches or greater.[61] Since miners were credited only with the weight of coal remaining atop the screen, some mine operators were encouraged to utilize special screens which broke coal lumps apart as they were unloaded, thus reducing the amount credited to the miner.[62] P.L. 286 outlawed this practice, declaring as follows:

> That it shall be unlawful for any mine owner, lessee or operator of any bituminous coal mine in this commonwealth, employing miners at bushel or ton rates, or other quantity, to pass the output of coal mined by said miners over any screen or other device which shall take any part of the weight, value or quantity thereof, before the same shall have been weighed and duly credited to the employee sending the same to the surface, and accounted for at the legal rate of weight fixed by the laws of the commonwealth.[63]

Thus, rather than outlawing only the use of improper screens, the act prohibited all screening before coal was credited to a miner. The indictment at issue in *Brown* charged that on September 24, 1897, the defendant, owner of a bituminous mine in Boston, Allegheny County, screened one hundred bushels of coal before crediting it to a miner's account. The defendant claimed, inter alia, that P.L. 286 deprived him of contract and property rights guaranteed by the state and federal constitutions. Following trial, the jury returned a special verdict finding that, if P.L. 286 was constitutional, the defendant had violated it, but if the act was unconstitutional, he was not guilty.[64] Following the special verdict, the trial court deemed the act an unconstitutional violation of liberty of contract, and the Commonwealth appealed.

The court began its analysis by noting that "[t]he most important question in the case is, whether the legislature had power to enact such a law."[65] To resolve this

---

57. Pa. Act of May 20, 1891, PL 96
58. 5 Pa. Super. 248, citing *Godcharles v. Wigeman*, 113 Pa. 431 (1886) (invalidating a similar 1881 statute).
59. 8 Pa. Super. 339 (1898) (Rice, J.).
60. Pa. Act of July 15, 1897, "An Act requiring the weighing of bituminous coal before screening, and providing a penalty for the violation thereof."
61. 8 Pa. Super. 348-49.
62. 8 Pa. Super. 349.
63. The act further provided for fines of $100 to $500 and imprisonment not to exceed ninety days.
64. 8 Pa. Super. 341-42.
65. 8 Pa. Super. 350.

Women winding transformer coils at Westinghouse Electric and Manufacturing Co., East Pittsburgh, in the early years of the twentieth century *(Pa. Archives)*.

issue, the court turned to the scope of the police power. "[I]n the exercise of the police power of the state," it began, "[the legislature] may enact laws in the interest of public morals, and to protect the lives, health and safety of persons following specified callings, and thus indirectly interfere with freedom of contract."[66] "These and other limitations which might be referred to," the court continued, "show that the right of the citizen to contract is not beyond legislative control."[67]

Yet, the court also found that this "legislative control" of contracts was limited by a number of constitutional provisions. These provisions included the following:

> Section 1, article 1, declar[ing]: "All men are born equally free and independent and have certain inherent and indefeasible rights, among which are those of enjoying and defending life and liberty, of acquiring, possessing and protecting property and reputation, and of pursuing their own happiness." Section 9 of the same article declares that no person can "be deprived of his life, liberty or property unless by the judgment of his peers or the law of the land." Section 7, article 3, declares as follows: "The General Assembly shall not pass any local or special law . . . regulating labor, trade, mining or manufacturing."[68]

According to the court, liberty of contract was implied in these provisions, and it operated to limit the police power. The court continued:

---

66. 8 Pa. Super. 352.

67. See note 66. As examples, Rice noted the legislature's ability to regulate the manner in which contracts are evidenced, declare that certain persons are incapable of entering contracts, outlaw contracts which are deemed contrary to public morals, and regulate contracts involving public business. 8 Pa. Super. 351.

68. 8 Pa. Super. 350-51.

Not only is the right of property protected against arbitrary encroachments by the legislature, but also the right of contract necessarily involved in it. The general rule is, that private parties, able to contract and willing to contract, may freely make such contracts concerning their property or labor, not contrary to good morals or public policy, as they may deem for their best interests; the instances where the legislature may interfere to abridge or deny this valuable right are exceptional, and such interference must have some reason for their justification other than the mere judgment of the legislature that the contract is not for the best interests of one or the other of the parties to it.[69]

On the basis of this "general rule" of liberty of contract, the court declared P.L. 286 unconstitutional. "If one mine owner or operator sees fit to offer to pay his employees upon the basis of the weight of the lump of coal remaining in the screen," the court asserted, "no substantial reason can be given for denying the parties the right to bind themselves by an agreement upon those terms. "[T]he parties being free to contract," the court continued, "are at liberty to alter or abandon the basis of compensation or to increase the rate, or, if they cannot agree upon terms, to refuse to contract altogether."[70]

While the court's invalidation of P.L. 286 was premised mainly upon a contract analysis, it was also based on Article III, Section 7, of the state constitution, which provides that "the General Assembly shall not pass any local or special law . . . regulating labor, trade, mining or manufacturing." Initially, the court noted that under P.L. 286 "one class of citizens is singled out and denied the rights which others enjoy."[71] Liberty of contract made available to all classes the means of resisting oppressive employment, the court concluded, "and we are not convinced that there is such inequality between these special classes of employees and employers as requires or justifies special legislative restriction of the liberty guaranteed to one as well as the other by the constitution."[72]

The court further enunciated this concern with special legislation two years later in *Commonwealth v. Clark*,[73] in which the court again invalidated a statute regulating the employment relationship. At issue in *Clark* was P.L. 116,[74] which prohibited corporations from discharging or threatening to discharge employees because of lawful union membership. Upon defendant's motion, the trial court quashed the indictment on the basis that P.L. 116 was enacted in violation of Article III, Section 7, of the state constitution. Before addressing this finding, the court noted that the issue of whether the act violated liberty of contract, although contested at trial, was not properly before the court since it had not been addressed by the defendant on appeal or ruled upon by the trial court.[75] Nonetheless, the court left little doubt as to how the issue would be resolved in a proper case:

[I]t will be well worthy the most serious and dispassionate consideration, whether a law forbidding the employer to prescribe the terms upon which he will take or retain another in his employment, or the employee to dictate the terms upon which he will enter or remain in the

---

69. See note 66.
70. 8 Pa. Super. 357.
71. 8 Pa. Super. 353.
72. See note 70.
73. 14 Pa. Super. 435 (1900) (Rice, J.).
74. Pa. Act of June 4, 1897.
75. 14 Pa. Super. 439.

Merchant Charles K. Godshall, about 1916, in the Reading Market, Philadelphia, during the era when statutes regulating food handling and sale were construed by the court.

employment of another, is not such an unwarranted interference with freedom of contract as to be an infringement of the liberty guaranteed to one as well as the other by the constitution.[76]

Turning to the question at issue, the court determined that P.L. 116 was clearly a law "regulating labor, trade, mining or manufacturing" within the meaning of Article III, Section 7. Thus, the only remaining question was whether it was a special law. The court began its analysis of this issue by finding that the law was "unquestionably" class legislation, since it applied only to corporations and their employees. It noted, "class legislation is not necessarily special legislation within the meaning of the prohibitory provisions of our state constitution."[77] Indeed, following a review of relevant case law, the court found that classification is within legislative authority under the police power where it is based on "genuine and substantial distinctions" between classes, and where it applies to all members of a class.[78] Applying this standard to P.L. 116, the court concluded:

---

76. Apparently referring to the defendant's failure to argue the issue on appeal, Rice also noted that "[i]llegitimate and unconstitutional practices get their first footing in that way, namely, by silent approaches." See note 75, citing *Boyd v. U.S.* 116 U.S. 616, 635 (1886).

77. 14 Pa. Super. 440.

78. 14 Pa. Super. 441, citing *Ayars Appeal* 122 Pa. 266 (1889), *In re Sugar Notch Borough* 192 Pa. 349 (1899), *Seabolt v. Commissioners of Northumberland County,* 187 Pa. 318, (1898), *Commonwealth ex rel. Fell v. Gilligan* 195 Pa. 504 (1900), and *Clark's Estate* 195 Pa. 520 (1900).

East Ohio Street and the City of Allegheny office building at the time Pittsburgh's petition came before the Superior Court, consolidating Allegheny and Pittsburgh into one municipality.

[I]t extends protection to employees of corporations in their right to form or join labor organizations, whilst denying the same protection to the employees of individuals, firms and limited partnerships; it deprives corporations of the right to discharge employees for a certain cause, even though this right be expressly reserved in the contract of employment; whilst leaving individuals, firms and limited partnerships free to discharge their employees for the same cause or at will, provided no contract or law against conspiracy be violated. As has been well said arbitrary selection can never be justified by calling it classification.[79]

Invalidating P.L. 116 as "a special law within the true intent and meaning of the constitution," the court also rejected the claim that passage of the act had been a legitimate exercise of the police power:

If it be said that legislation for the protection of employees as a class against coercion or unfair and unconscionable dealings on the part of employers as a class is a valid exercise of the police power of the state, the plain answer is that, even if the soundness of this general principle is conceded, it does not apply here, because the act under consideration does not apply alike to all the members of the two classes, namely employers and employees.[80]

As *Showalter, Brown,* and *Clark* indicate, the early court viewed employment regulations narrowly.[81] A prominent exception to this narrow view occurred in 1900 in the case of *Commonwealth v. Beatty.* In *Beatty,* the court reviewed an employer's conviction under the Act of April 29, 1897, P.L. 30, which prohibited the employment of adult women for more than twelve hours per day. The court began by noting that the law was

In the Court of Common Pleas No. *3* of Allegheny Co.

*W. F. Pollock*

vs.

*Joseph Carr & Geo. A. Carr, trading as Joseph Carr & Bro.*

:
:
:
:
:
:

Appeal to the Court of Common
Pleas No. *3* for the County of
Allegheny, Pa.

No. *145* of *Aug.* Term 189*5*

To George Pearson,

    Prothonotary of the Superior Court:

    July *10,* 1895.

        I hereby certify that the proper appeal,
affidavit and recognizance in the sum of *one Thousand* dollars
has been duly filed in the above stated case in my office,
as required by an Act entitled "An Act to establish an intermediate court of appeal; regulating its constitution, officers
jurisdiction, powers, practice, and its relation to the Supreme
Court and other courts; providing for the reports of its decisions, the compensation of the Judges and other officers
and the practice and costs on appeals from its judgments."
Approved the twenty-fourth day of June, A. D. 1895.

                    *J J McQuillty*

                    Prothonotary of Allegheny
                             Co.

This document denotes the first appeal taken from a court in Allegheny County, July 10, 1895
(*Pa. Archives*).

enacted after "extended legislative examination into the management of our varied industrial institutions."[82] The court also discussed the breadth of the police power, and found that "[t]he length of time a laborer shall be subjected to the exhaustive exertion of physical labor is as clearly within legislative control as is the governmental inspection of boilers, machinery, etc., to avoid accidents . . . [and] to preserve the health of laborers."[83]

More importantly, however, P.L. 30 was intended to protect women. The court continued:

> It is undisputed that some employments may be admissible for males and yet improper for females, and regulations recognizing and forbidding women to engage in such would be open to no reasonable objection. . . . Sex imposes limitations to excessive or long-continued physical labor as certainly as does minority, and the arrested development of children is no more dangerous to the state, than debilitating so large a class of our citizens as adult females by undue and unreasonable physical labor.[84]

> Adult females are a class distinct as minors, separated by natural conditions from all other laborers, and are so constituted as to be unable to endure physical exertion and exposure to the extent and degree that it is not harmful to adult males; and employments which under favorable conditions are not injurious, are rightly limited as to time by this statute, so as not to become harmful by prolonged engagements.[85]

Having distinguished female from male laborers, the court thus concluded that P.L. 30 was not an unconstitutional special law because "it applies to all adult females alike throughout the state."[86] Further, citing *Brown* for the proposition that "indirect" interferences with liberty of contract were permissible, the court concluded that the law was a valid exercise of the police power.[87]

As with the Superior Court's decisions in *Showalter*, *Brown* and *Clark*, the resolution of *Beatty* was completely consistent with Lochner Era jurisprudence. Indeed, like the Superior Court in 1900, courts nationwide sanctioned legislative use of the police power to protect supposed vulnerable groups within the working class, although such protection was not permissible when extended to adult male workers. As William Forbath has noted:

> The police power, courts often declared, could be invoked to protect "dependent" or "vulnerable" groups within the labor force, but it could not constitutionally reach the inequalities of fortune and power that arose from the "fact that some men are possessed of industrial property and others are not." The courts' relative hospitality toward hour laws for women and children encouraged and ratified within labor circles a gender-based division of the working class.[88]

---

82. 15 Pa. Super. 14.
83. 15 Pa. Super. 16.
84. 15 Pa. Super. 18.
85. 15 Pa. Super. 19.
86. 15 Pa. Super. 20.
87. See note 84.
88. Forbath, "The Shaping of the American Labor Movement," 1144.

Although modern courts are far more receptive to such regulations, these cases remain important in Pennsylvania constitutional law.[89] Taken together, they indicate that the legislature's ability to promulgate economic regulations under the police power is subject to substantive constitutional limitations. They are also among the most important cases ever decided on the scope of personal liberty under the state constitution. Indeed, they stand for the proposition that liberty means more than simply the freedom to move about; it also includes the right to earn a living in any lawful manner, to pursue any lawful trade or calling, and to work upon terms and conditions of one's choosing.

There are notable cases that have been extremely influential. *Commonwealth v. Brown*, for instance, is the sole case cited by the *Pennsylvania Law Encyclopedia* for the following propositions:

> The right of personal liberty means more than mere freedom of locomotion. It includes and comprehends, among other things, freedom of speech, the right of self defense against lawful violence, the right to live and work where one wishes, the right of a person to earn his livelihood in any lawful calling, the right to pursue any lawful trade or avocation, and the right to freely buy and sell as others may.[90]

> As a general rule, private parties, able to contract and willing to contract, may freely make such contracts concerning their property or labor, not contrary to good morals or public policy, as they may deem for their best interests; the instances where the legislature may interfere to abridge or deny this valuable right are exceptional, and such interference must have some reason for their justification other than the mere judgment of the legislature that the contract is not for the best interests of one or the other of the parties to it.[91]

In reviewing economic regulations not involving the employment relationship, the court took an expansive view of legislative authority under the police power. In *Commonwealth v. Mintz*,[92] for instance, the court considered P.L. 37, which required that junk shops and dealers in second-hand goods conducting business in the state's cities keep adequate records of their transactions.[93] The court began its analysis by emphasizing "that the attitude of the courts is not one of hostility to acts whose constitutionality is attacked. On the contrary, all the presumptions are in their favor, and the courts are not to be astute in finding or sustaining objections."[94] Finding the act a valid exercise of the police power, the court concluded:

> The regulation of this class of dealers is within the police power of the state, and the legislative judgment in prescribing rules and imposing penalties in conducting such a business is to be made effectual by the courts unless it is clearly in violation of the constitution.

> The business of keeping a junk shop or second-hand store is a proper subject for legislative control. Such a business appeals to the necessity

---

89. As discussed infra, these cases, like *Lochner* and its progeny, were repudiated in the 1930s.
90. *Pennsylvania Law Encyclopedia*, "Constitutional Law," sec. 123, p. 437.
91. *Pennsylvania Law Encyclopedia*, "Constitutional Law," sec. 202, p. 67.
92. 19 Pa. Super. 283 (1902).
93. Pa. Act of April 11, 1899.
94. Pa. Act of April 11, 1899, 284.

and cupidity of the needy and criminal classes in furnishing a market for unsalable articles and it is within the common knowledge of men that the business is most actively conducted in the cities.[95]

Similarly, in a case decided the same year, which upheld a statute prohibiting the sale of adulterated food, the court stated, "Police power is not a mere phrase. It is a potent reality and embraces within its comprehensive grasp everything relating to the safety, welfare, health and comfort of the people of the commonwealth."[96] In a series of five cases between 1900 and 1905, the court also upheld statutes prohibiting the sale of oleomargarine colored to resemble butter. In the last of these cases, *Commonwealth v. Mellet*,[97] the court discussed at length the relationship between the judiciary and the legislature. The court noted the following:

> The rule of law upon this subject appears to be that, except where the constitution has imposed limits upon the legislative power, it must be considered as practically absolute, whether it operate[s] according to natural justice or not in any particular case. The courts are not the guardians of the rights of the people of the state, except as those rights are secured by some constitutional provision which comes within the judicial cognizance. The protection against unwise and oppressive legislation, within constitutional bounds, is by an appeal to the justice and patriotism of the representatives of the people. If this fails, the people in their sovereign capacity can correct the evil; but courts cannot assume their rights. The judiciary can only arrest the execution of a statute when it conflicts with the constitution. It cannot run a race of opinions upon points of right, reason, and expediency with the law-making power.[98]

Quoting from the holding of Justice John M. Harlan in an earlier Pennsylvania case involving a similar statute, the court concluded, "If all that can be said of this legislation is that it is unwise, or unnecessarily oppressive to those manufacturing or selling wholesome oleomargarine, as an article of food, their appeal must be to the legislature, or to the ballot box, not to the judiciary."[99]

As these cases indicate, the court generally took an expansive view of legislative authority to regulate the economy under the police power. The court only interceded when economic regulations infringed upon the perceived liberty of employers and employees to fashion the terms of the employment relationship. In these cases, the court held, the police power must yield to constitutional provisions regarding liberty of contract and special legislation. In cases not involving employment, the court generally declined to substitute its judgment for that of the legislature.

---

95. Pa. Act of April 11, 285. Similarly, in *Commonwealth v. Muir*, 1 Pa. Super. 578 (1896), the court held that an act regulating public lodging houses was a valid exercise of the police power.

96. *Commonwealth v. Seiler*, 20 Pa. Super. 260, 262 (1902) (Beaver, J.).

97. 27 Pa. Super. 41 (1905) (Rice, P.J.). The other four cases are *Commonwealth v. Leslie*, 20 Pa. Super. 529 (1902), *Commonwealth v. Schollenberger* 17 Pa. Super. 218 (1901), *Commonwealth v. Diefenbacher*, 14 Pa. Super. 264 (1900), and *Commonwealth v. Vandyke*, 13 Pa. Super. 484 (1900).

98. 27 Pa. Super. 53-54, citing *Cooley on Constitutional Limitations*, 7th ed., ch. 7, sec. 4, 232.

99. 27 Pa. Super. 54, citing *Powell v. Pennsylvania*, 127 U.S. 678 (1888).

A column for the new (present) state Capitol Building in Harrisburg. *Commonwealth v. Sanderson* was the first case in a series before the Superior Court arising from fraud involving construction of the Capitol (see footnote 119) *(Pa. Archives).*

## STATE AUTHORITY OVER POLITICAL SUBDIVISIONS

The court also decided a number of important cases that did not involve economic regulation. *Pittsburg's Petition,*[100] for instance, involved a number of issues relating to the constitutional powers of state government, and it was ultimately resolved by the United States Supreme Court. At issue was a lower court decree consolidating the cities of Pittsburgh and Allegheny. On November 11, 1905, Governor Samuel Pennypacker issued a proclamation convening the General Assembly in an extraordinary session to meet January 15, 1906. The proclamation was issued pursuant to Article IV, Section 12, of the state constitution, which provides that the governor "may on extraordinary occasions, convene the general assembly." The constitution further provides, at Article III, Section 25, that "when the general assembly shall be convened in special session there shall be no legislation upon subjects other than those designated in the proclamation of the governor calling such session." Pursuant to this latter provision, the proclamation of November 11 designated seven subjects for consideration by the legislature. The first of these was an act "to enable contiguous cities in the same counties to be united in one municipality in order that the people may avoid the unnecessary burdens of maintaining separate city governments." On January 15, 1906, the governor issued a second proclamation which designated four "additional subjects" for legislative consideration. The final one of these was an act "to enable cities that are now, or may hereafter be contiguous or in close proximity, including any intervening land, to be united in one municipality." The latter proclamation also provided that the fourth sub-

---

100. 32 Pa. Super. 210 (1906) (Orlady, J.). At the time of this case, the spelling of "Pittsburgh" did not include the letter "h."

ject was "a modification of the first subject in the original call, and is added in order that the legislation may be enacted under either of them as may be deemed wise."[101]

In January, the legislature convened as directed and passed an act nearly identical to the one suggested by the second proclamation. Thereafter, pursuant to the act, the city of Pittsburgh filed a petition in the Court of Quarter Sessions of Allegheny County praying for the consolidation of Pittsburgh and Allegheny. Residents of Allegheny filed exceptions, which were dismissed. In conformity with the act, the court then ordered an election, and, by a combined vote of 54 percent to 46 percent, the residents of Pittsburgh and Allegheny approved consolidation. The court of quarter sessions then ordered "that the city of Allegheny, the lesser city, be annexed and consolidated with the city of Pittsburg, the greater or larger city." The residents of Allegheny appealed this decree on the basis that, inter alia, the statute authorizing consolidation arose only under the second proclamation, and thus violated the mandate of Article III, Section 25, that subjects to be considered at a special session must be raised in "the proclamation of the governor calling such session." The statute was also challenged on the basis that it violated due process guarantees by permitting the electors of a larger city to annex by their votes a lesser city, over the protest of a majority of the lesser city's electors.

In rejecting these claims, the court found that its authority did not extend to the executive and legislative actions at issue. The court disposed of the appellants' first claim on the following basis:

> The form in which the general assembly is to be convened, the requisites of the proclamation, and the measure of the notice to be given to the members of that body are not prescribed by the constitution, hence no challenge lies to either the necessity for such a meeting, or the correctness of the precedent notice. Had the governor chosen to issue as many proclamations to consider legislation as there were subjects embraced in the two he did issue, it would be at most a matter of form and not of substance. . . . While it is mandatory upon the executive to designate the subjects to be considered by the general assembly, it is outside our duty to go beyond the words of the law to inquire whether all of the other precedent formalities have in fact been complied with.[102]

The court began its analysis of the appellants' due process claim by noting that judicial review of legislation is warranted only where the constitution is offended, and that all challenges to legislative authority not based on the constitution must be asserted through the political process. He also found that the legislature had been convened pursuant to the constitution, and that its authority to regulate cities was unquestioned. Thus, the court would not recognize the appellants' challenge to the statute at issue.[103] Importantly, the decision in *Pittsburg's Petition* also turned on the respective power of residents and the state to effect the organization of municipalities. "These local governments," the court concluded, "are mere auxiliaries to, and in the aggregate they constitute the commonwealth at large which through its legislature may, at will, create, change, reorganize, consolidate or abolish them, and that wholly irrespective of the wishes or consent of those composing the local body politic."[104]

---

101. 32 Pa. Super. 215-17.

102. 32 Pa. Super. 217.

103. 32 Pa. Super. 226-27, stating, "Restraints on the legislative power of control must be found in the constitution of the state, or they must rest alone in the legislative discretion. If the legislature acts injuriously . . . the people must be looked to, to right through the ballot box all these wrongs."

104. 32 Pa. Super. 227.

Following the rejection of their appeal, appellants continued to pursue their case, first to the Pennsylvania Supreme Court. In affirming, the Supreme Court quoted at length from the Superior Court's opinion.[105] Thereafter, appellants commenced an action in federal court claiming that the process by which Pittsburgh and Allegheny were consolidated violated the due process guarantees of the United States Constitution. The case was ultimately heard by the United States Supreme Court, which rejected appellants' due process claim. Like the Superior Court, the United States Supreme Court emphasized the extent of state authority over its political subdivisions:

> The State . . . may take without compensation such property, hold it itself, or vest it in other agencies, expand or contract the territorial area . . . repeal the charter and destroy the corporation. All this may be done, conditionally or unconditionally, with or without the consent of the citizens, or even against their protest. In all these respects the State is supreme, and its legislative body, conforming its actions to the state constitution, may do as it will unrestrained by any provision of the Constitution of the United States.[106]

*Pittsburg's Petition* remains an important case in Pennsylvania constitutional law. Most importantly, it has been cited repeatedly for the proposition that cities and municipalities are not sovereigns, and that their duties may be expanded or limited, or the agencies themselves completely abolished, at the discretion of the state.[107] It also has been cited as the seminal case in delineating the authority of governors to convene special legislative sessions.[108]

## CRIMINAL LAW

The court also decided a number of important cases in the realm of criminal law. Five of these cases, which might be identified collectively as the "Capitol Fraud" cases, involved an elaborate scheme to defraud the state in connection with the furnishing of its new capitol.[109] The cases remain among the most notorious in Pennsylvania history due primarily to the prominence of the defendants, including State Treasurer William L. Mathues, Auditor General William P. Snyder, James M. Shumaker, superintendent of public grounds and buildings, and Joseph M. Huston, a prominent Philadelphia architect who was hired to furnish the interior of the capitol.[110] The fifth defendant, John H. Sanderson, was a contractor hired to provide the furnishings.

Each defendant had a vital role in the complicated conspiracy. Mathues and

---

105. *Pittsburg's Petition*, 217 Pa. 227, 66 A. 348 (1907). The Supreme Court rejected the appellants' due process claim on the basis that it was "completely answered in . . . the opinion of the learned judge speaking for the Superior Court."

106. *Hunter v. City of Pittsburgh*, 207 U.S. 161, 178-79 (1907).

107. See e.g., *City of Chester v. Commonwealth Department of Transportation*, 495 Pa. 382, 434 A.2d 695 (1981), *Genkinger v. New Castle*, 368 Pa. 547, 84 A.2d 303 (1951), *Murray v. Philadelphia*, 364 Pa. 157, 71 A.2d 280 (1950), *Henderson v. Delaware River Joint Toll Bridge Commission*, 362 Pa. 475, 66 A.2d 843 (1949), *Kline v. Harrisburg*, 362 Pa. 438, 68 A.2d 182 (1949).

108. See Robert Woodside, *Pennsylvania Constitutional Law* (Sayre, Pa.: Murrelle Printing Co., 1985), 277-78.

109. The state capitol building was completely destroyed by fire on February 2, 1897. In 1901, the legislature appropriated $4 million for a new capitol, to be completed by 1907. Klein and Hoogenboom, *A History of Pennsylvania*, 422-24.

110. The case received extensive exposure in the *New York Times*. See e.g., articles of March 8, 1910, p. 2, col. 4, March 4, 1911, p. 4, col. 2, and May 24, 1911, p. 1, col. 6.

Nos. 3 & 4 Nov. Term, 1895.
Philadelphia.

Phila. to the use of

McCann,

vs:

North Penn. R. R. Co.,

Appellant.

RICE, P. J.

Opinion affirming judg-
ments of Common Pleas No. 4
of Phila. Co.

*Filed February 20. 1896.*

---

1

IN THE SUPERIOR COURT OF PENNSYLVANIA.

-----o-----

City of Philadelphia, to
the use of
John McCann,
vs:
The North Penn. R. R. Co.
Appellant.

No.s 3 and 4 Nov. Term, 1895.
Philadelphia.

APPEAL from judgments of court
of common pleas No. 4 of Philadelphia county for want of
sufficient affidavits of defence to writs of <u>sci. fa.</u> upon municipal liens for sewer-
ing.

These two cases differ somewhat from Philadelphia to
the use of Kelly, v: P. & R. R. Co., but not so as to require different judgments. The claims were filed against
two lots of ground on opposite sides of Cadwallader street,
near the terminus of the defendant railroad, in the City of
Philadelphia. One lot is described on the map as a freight
yard, and in the affidavit of defence as "a carload delivery yard for bulk potatoes, apples and other merchandise of
like character."

The learned judge below, in an able opinion, has clearly defined, and pointed out the distinctions between the
different species of taxation, and has shown that property,
such as these, belonging to a railroad company is liable to
ordinary annual taxation for city purposes under the local
act of April 21, 1858 (P. L. 385) and possibly would be liable to such taxation under general laws. Perhaps its liability to general taxation would not be conclusive upon the
question of its liability to special assessments for local
improvements.

But as the
questions raised are discussed at length in an opinion filed
herewith, in Phila. v: P. & R. R. R. Co., it is unnecessary
to go over the same ground again. We are of opinion that
the court was right in entering judgment in each case for
the plaintiff.

The judgments are affirmed.

The legal backing and an excerpt from the first opinion filed by the court *(Pa. Archives).*

Snyder, two of the three members of a board vested with extensive authority over bids for state contracts, manipulated the bidding process so that they could award the furnishings contract to Sanderson.[111] Specifically, they mandated on the bid solicitation, or schedule, which was publicized on May 10, 1904, that the state would pay only a certain amount for numerous items.[112] The amounts listed were well below market value. Moreover, the schedule indicated that payment would be made "per foot" for sofas, tables, and legislative rostrums, which constituted a significant portion of the furnishing project. Apparently believing that this method of payment contemplated the customary measure of linear feet, no contractors but Sanderson bid on this portion of the contract.

On June 7, 1904, Sanderson was awarded the entire contract, despite the fact that each of the forty-one items on the schedule was to be contracted separately.[113] Thereafter, pursuant to the conspiracy, Sanderson submitted invoices based on the square footage, not linear footage, of the furniture delivered, and many charges exceeded the square-foot amount.[114] Sanderson's charges were then authorized by the other defendants in their various capacities. In total, Sanderson delivered sixty-five sofas, eighty oblong tables, twenty-four oval tables, fifty round tables, seven square tables, and a number of other items of furniture.[115] He was paid $5,376,308.52 on a contract that Huston had advised would cost between $500,000 and $800,000.[116] The scheme was discovered in 1906, after new Treasurer William H. Berry became suspicious and ordered independent estimates of the contracting work.[117] All five defendants were subsequently convicted of conspiracy, the overt act in each case being the presentation, certification, settlement, and payment of fraudulent invoices.[118] They received fines and sentences ranging from six months to two years. Following their convictions, all defendants appealed, and the resulting Superior Court opinions encompassed nearly two hundred reporter pages.

The first and most significant of the "Capitol Fraud" cases was *Commonwealth v. Sanderson*,[119] which involved no less than fifty-six allegations of error. The most important of these concerned Sanderson's claim at trial that he was entitled to bill the state per square foot for the furniture he provided. His claim was based on the argument that, since the state drafted the contract, the ambiguous phrase "per foot" should be construed in his favor. Yet, in support of this claim he offered "no evidence whatever"

---

111. The Board of Commissioners of Public Grounds and Buildings, which included the governor, treasurer, and auditor general, was created by the Pa. Act of May 26, 1895, PL 22. The act was passed pursuant to Article III, Section 12 of the state constitution, which mandated public bidding for all contracts to provide items utilized by state government, and to maintain state buildings. Under the act, bidding for contracts was to be competitive, and the schedule was to indicate the maximum the state would pay for each item. PL 22.

112. *Commonwealth v. Sanderson*, 40 Pa. Super. 416, 455 (1909) (Porter, J.).

113. See note 112.

114. For instance, Sanderson's bill recited that the rostrum in the senate caucus room measured 1,910 square feet, but at trial it was established that the rostrum was only 907 square feet; similarly he billed for the rostrum in the house caucus room based upon 3,022 square feet; but trial evidence established that it was only 1,176 square feet. 40 Pa. Super. 466. Moreover, the fair market value of both rostrums was established as $4,000, but the state paid $90,748 for them. 40 Pa. Super. 471.

115. 40 Pa. Super. 456.

116. 40 Pa. Super. 471. The state subsequently brought a civil suit seeking $5,000,000 against the defendants, the estate of Sanderson, who died in 1910, his company, and its sureties. The suit was settled for $1,300,000. *New York Times*, 4 Mar. 1911, p. 4, col. 2.

117. Berry initially became suspicious after hearing that fifteen men had laid $90,000 dollars worth of parquet flooring in just two weeks. Thereafter, he obtained independent estimates for the work done in his office. The estimates revealed that the work on his ceiling, originally estimated at $550, actually cost the state $5,500, and that oak wainscoting worth $1,800 had cost $15,500. Klein and Hoogenboom, *A History of Pennsylvania*, 423-24. Governor Pennypacker testified at the trials of the defendants. 40 Pa. Super. 465.

118. Mathues, Snyder, Shumaker, and Sanderson were tried together. Huston's case was severed and he was tried separately. 40 Pa. Super. 450.

119. 40 Pa. Super. 416.

that payment by the square foot was customary in the furniture industry under contracts providing for payment "per foot." Moreover, there was only one similar contract on record, and that contract was "made by appellant to the state, under the schedule of 1898-1899, when he construed the term 'per foot' as meaning linea[r] foot of the sofa."[120] In response to Sanderson's argument, the Commonwealth sought to clarify the ambiguous phrase "per foot" by introducing evidence of the fair market value of the furniture provided. This evidence, the Commonwealth maintained, would demonstrate that the definition offered by Sanderson "would result in an exorbitant and unconscionable contract." The evidence was admitted, but only insofar as it impacted upon the sincerity of Sanderson's defense, i.e., that he could not be guilty of fraud because he reasonably believed that "per foot" meant "per square foot."[121]

Having found no state authority on point, the court turned to an analogous decision of the United States Supreme Court to address Sanderson's claim that evidence of fair market value was improperly admitted at trial. In *Hume v. United States*, plaintiff was awarded a contract to provide the federal government with shucks. Although the government traditionally bought shucks by the "hundredweight," the schedule on which plaintiff entered a bid included the word "pounds."[122] Thereafter, plaintiff attempted to enforce the contract at sixty cents *per pound* of shucks. At trial in federal district court, the government was permitted to counter plaintiff's claim by introducing evidence that the fair market value of shucks was not more than $35 per ton. Thus, plaintiff's claim sought thirty-five times the market value of the goods he provided. Rejecting this claim, the Supreme Court held:

> In order to guard the public against losses and injuries arising from the fraud or mistake or rashness or indiscretion of their agents, the rule requires of all persons dealing with public officers, the duty of inquiring as to their power and authority to bind the government; and persons so dealing must necessarily be held to a recognition of the fact that governments agents are bound to fairness and good faith as between themselves and their principal. . . .[123]

Moreover, the Supreme Court continued, if the plaintiff "intended to induce the agents of the government to contract to pay for these shucks thirty-five times their highest market value, and the agents of the government knowingly entered such a contract, it will not be denied that such conduct would be fraudulent and the agreement vitiated accordingly." In affirming the decision of the trial court, the Supreme Court concluded that plaintiff "designed to commit the agents of the government to a contract, 'such as no man in his senses and not under delusion would make on the one hand, and as no honest and fair man would accept on the other,' and [this] is fatal to his recovery according to the letter of the contract."[124]

Applying *Hume* to the facts at issue, the Superior Court concluded:

> Sanderson is presumed to have known the market value of the furniture which he was to furnish under the contract. Knowing this did he believe that the state officers, in using the term "per foot" in the con-

---

120. 40 Pa. Super. 466.
121. 40 Pa. Super. 467.
122. 40 Pa. Super. 468, citing *Hume v. United States*, 132 U.S. 406 (1889).
123. 40 Pa. Super. 469, quoting Hume, 132 U.S. 414-15.
124. See note 123.

tract, intended to pay him, at the rate fixed, for each square foot of surface in the sofas furnished under the contract, if such a construction would lead to an extortionate and unconscionable bargain? If he did not believe that the agents of the state so understood the contract, then his contention at trial as to the meaning of the term "per foot" in the schedule was not made in good faith. The evidence was, therefore, admissible, as against Sanderson.[125]

As this passage indicates, the court invoked the ruling of *Hume* to conclude that Sanderson had a duty to assess the subjective intentions of the state officials with whom he was dealing. Because of this duty, even assuming he did not know of the agents' fraudulent intentions, if he believed they intended to pay him per linear foot, a subsequent claim that he expected payment per square foot was necessarily in bad faith.[126] *Sanderson* is particularly notable for this imposition of a heightened duty in contracts involving state agents.[127] The remainder of appeals in the "Capitol Fraud" cases, all of which were rejected by the court, were highly publicized, but of little legal significance.[128]

The court also rendered a series of decisions in the prominent criminal case of *Commonwealth v. House*, in which city attorney William H. House and assistant city attorney W.C. Moreland conspired to embezzle more than $26,000 from the City of Pittsburgh. The men were indicted in 1896, and Moreland plead guilty and received a sentence of three years in state prison. Although House was brought to trial on six counts, five were abandoned by the Commonwealth. The remaining count alleged that House was an accessory to the embezzlement perpetrated by Moreland. Following his first trial, House was convicted, but the Superior Court reversed the conviction on the basis that a juror who voted to convict House was the part owner of a newspaper that had repeatedly expressed the opinion that House was guilty of embezzlement.[129] Following retrial on the same count, House was again convicted, but the Superior Court reversed this conviction as well, finding that House was improperly denied the right to

---

125. 40 Pa. Super. 470.

126. The court also concluded that if Sanderson believed that the agents intentionally used an ambiguous term in order to pay him an exorbitant amount, "then he knew that the agents of the state were guilty of a palpable dereliction of their duty to their principal and that the contract would be fraudulent in its very inception." See note 125. Thereafter, the court reviewed the evidence of fair market value, and found that it "conclusively established that the construction of the term, 'per foot,' contended for by Sanderson, when applied to the subject-matter would unquestionably render the contract unconscionable." 40 Pa. Super. 471. On this basis, the court affirmed the trial court's decision to allow evidence of fair market value to rebut Sanderson's construction of the phrase "per foot." 40 Pa. Super. 484.

127. For instance, the Supreme Court cited *Sanderson* in affirming the dismissal of a distiller's claim for reimbursement of transportation expenses based on an alleged oral contract with representatives of the state liquor control board. See *Commonwealth v. Seagram Distillers Corp.*, 379 Pa. 411, 109 A.2d 184 (1954) ("It was incumbent upon the representatives of Seagram to ascertain the extent of the authority of the Director of Operations to bind the Board by any oral agreement."). The Pa. Supreme Court has also applied this principle in a number of other cases subsequent to *Sanderson*. See e.g., *Charleroi Lumber Co. v. Bentleyville Borough School Dist.*, 334 Pa. 424, 433 (1939) ("Persons contracting with a governmental agency must, at their peril, know the extent of the power of its officers making the contract.").

128. The same day it decided *Sanderson*, the court also handed down its opinion in *Commonwealth v. Snyder*, 40 Pa. Super. 485 (1909), in which it addressed and rejected thirty claims of trial error, all of which challenged evidentiary rulings and jury instructions. *Commonwealth v. Mathues*, 40 Pa. Super. 546 (1909), and (1911). *Commonwealth v. Shumaker*, 40 Pa. Super. 547 (1909), were also affirmed, in brief opinions, on the basis that they raised the same issues that were disposed of in *Sanderson*. On March 3, 1911, the last conviction was affirmed in *Commonwealth v. Huston*, 46 Pa. Super. 172 (1911). Several of these opinions were affirmed per curiam by the Pennsylvania Supreme Court. See *Commonwealth v. Shumaker*, 227 Pa. 347, 76 A. 1118 (1910); *Commonwealth v. Snyder*, 227 Pa. 346, 76 A. 1119 (1910); *Commonwealth v. Huston*, 232 Pa. 209, 81 A. 1135.

129. 3 Pa. Super. 304 (1897) (Smith, J.).

be present in the courtroom when the jury was charged.[130] While House's third trial was pending, on January 28, 1898, Moreland received a pardon from Governor Hastings. When House was again brought to trial, he raised the pardon of Moreland, and argued that it precluded his conviction as an accessory since the criminal liability of an accessory depends upon the guilt of the principal. House also argued that the pardon not only completely effaced the guilt of the principal, but that it also "extirpates and blots out the offense itself."[131] Since no offense remained, House argued, the charge against him should be dismissed. The trial court sustained the Commonwealth's demurrer to the motion for dismissal, and House was again convicted. On appeal, he reasserted the claim that Moreland's pardon precluded his conviction as an accessory.[132]

As happened in so many of its early cases, the Superior Court found little precedent to guide its decision. The unanimous court began by citing *Diehl v. Rodgers* in which the Supreme Court held that a pardon relieved "all penal consequences of crime whether by common law or by statute."[133] The court also surveyed a number of cases from the United States Supreme Court and other states that considered the scope of protection afforded to an individual who receives a pardon.[134] Yet, neither *Diehl* nor the other cases addressed whether the protections of a pardon extended beyond the person receiving it. As a result, the court looked to general principles, and concluded that clemency decisions were based upon the particular facts and circumstances of individual cases. Applying this principle to Moreland's pardon, the court found that "executive clemency was extended to him for reasons which were presumably personal to him and upon the record as it then stood."[135] Since Moreland's pardon was "personal to him," the court concluded, it would not exonerate House of accessory liability:

> The argument of appellant would lead to the conclusion that a pardon granted to one person should extend to and be enjoyed by others, in regard to whom there might not be any mitigating facts, and who would receive a benefit through a grace they had never sought, and of which they might not have any knowledge.

> The special nature of the crime, the previous character, age, or health of the offender, the restitution of property, the discovery of evidence not available at the time of trial, or other impelling reasons might justly move the executive, through the exercise of his discretionary power, to favor a particular petitioner, while others who participated in the same crime might not be able to furnish the slightest argument to justify a similar leniency.[136]

Another important criminal case decided by the early court involved state regulation of the practice of religion and the authority of courts to review regulations pro-

---

130. 6 Pa. Super. 92 (1897) (Rice, J.).

131. 10 Pa. Super. 259 (1899) (Orlady, J.).

132. 10 Pa. Super. 263.

133. 10 Pa. Super. 264, citing *Diehl v. Rodgers*, 169 Pa. 316 (1895), which involved the competency of a witness who had been convicted of perjury and later pardoned. When the witness attempted to testify at a subsequent trial, an objection was made that, under the criminal code, a perjury conviction forever disqualified the testimony of an individual so convicted. The pardon was raised in response to the objection, and the witness was permitted to testify. Finding the testimony competent, the Pa. Supreme Court held that the power of granting clemency, vested in the governor by the constitution, could not be limited by legislation.

134. 10 Pa. Super. 264-65.

135. 10 Pa. Super. 266.

136. See note 135.

*E. H. Griffith v. George Knarr* was the earliest decision by the Superior Court. In it the court upheld the decision of the Court of Common Pleas of Clearfield County involving a dispute over the sale of a stagecoach and horses. The docket entry was date March 25, 1896.

mulgated by political subdivisions. In *Wilkes-Barre v. Garabed*,[137] a member of the Salvation Army was convicted and fined for violating a city ordinance which prohibited the playing of musical instruments in public places without a permit from the mayor's office. The member, Joseph Garabed, was arrested while beating a drum in order to draw a crowd to a sidewalk sermon offered by the Army.[138] Garabed challenged his conviction on the basis that the ordinance under which he was convicted violated the religious liberty guarantee of the state constitution.[139] He also challenged the ordinance on due process and equal protection grounds.[140]

Addressing Garabed's religious liberty claim, the court began by distinguishing between religious beliefs and religious practices. Although the former is inviolate, it stated the latter are subject to regulation. To support this conclusion, the court offered a hypothetical: "Suppose one believed that human sacrifices were a necessary part of religious worship, would it be seriously contended that the civil government under which he lived could not interfere to prevent a sacrifice?"[141] The court then looked to a Michigan case, and summarily rejected Garabed's claim:

> Religious liberty does not include the right to introduce and carry out every scheme or purpose which persons see fit to claim as part of their religious system. While there is no legal authority to constrain belief, no one can lawfully stretch his own liberty of action so as to interfere with that of his neighbors, or violate peace and good order. The whole criminal law would be practically superseded if, under pretext of liberty of conscience, the commission of crime is made a religious dogma.[142]

The majority of the court also rejected Garabed's due process and equal protection claims. Initially, it found that the challenged ordinance was a legitimate exercise of the police power delegated to the municipality by the state. Relying on precedent from other states, the court held that this power included the "authority to make regulations as to the time, mode, and circumstances under which parties shall assert, enjoy, or exercise their rights."[143] To deny this power," the court concluded, "would be to turn the streets over to the will and pleasure of the mob. . . . The ordinance is a discretionary preventative to avoid what would reasonably be expected to happen if the use of [musical] instruments was not restrained."[144] Rejecting Garabed's equal protection claim, the court also found that the "ordinance applies to all of the public streets or places in the city; it is not directed against the defendant or the organization he represents, or any other person or body of men."[145] Finally, the court turned to the argument that the ordinance violated due process protections because it placed the decision to grant per-

---

137. 11 Pa. Super. 355 (1899) (Orlady, J.).

138. The record indicates that the Salvation Army believed that it was divinely commanded "to go into the streets and there preach the gospel." It further appears that beating a drum was the preferred method of drawing a crowd to the sermons. 11 Pa. Super. 369. The group's petition for a permit had been denied by the city.

139. Article I, Section 4, provides, "All men have a natural and indefeasible right to worship Almighty God according to the dictates of their own consciences; . . . no human authority can, in any case whatever, control or interfere with the rights of the conscience; and no preference shall ever be given by law to any religious establishments or modes of worship."

140. 11 Pa. Super. 366.

141. 11 Pa. Super. 355, citing *Reynolds v. United States*, 98 U.S. 145 (1878).

142. 11 Pa. Super. 366, citing *In re Frazee*, 63 Mich. 396 (1886).

143. 11 Pa. Super. 369, citing *Commonwealth v. Davis*, 140 Mass. 485 (1886), and *State v. Freeman*, 38 N.H. 426 (1859).

144. 11 Pa. Super. 373.

145. 11 Pa. Super. 370.

mits exclusively within the mayor's discretion. To the contrary, the court held, the ordinance was not "unreasonable, impartial or oppressive because the power is to be exercised by the mayor, as he may deem expedient, which is equivalent to saying in his discretion, and which implies that it must be done with a sound discretion and according to law."[146]

In dissent, Judge Beeber, joined by Judge W.W. Porter, argued that the challenged ordinance violated the equal protection mandate of the fourteenth amendment. The dissent's specific target was the scope of discretionary power vested in the mayor. The argument in this regard was premised on the noted case of *Yick Wo v. Hopkins*,[147] in which the United States Supreme Court invalidated a series of San Francisco ordinances requiring that no one could establish a laundry in the city "without having obtained the consent of the board of supervisors, except the same be located in a building constructed either of brick or stone." Although he acknowledged that the precise holding of *Yick Wo* turned on the fact that the ordinances were enforced almost exclusively against Chinese proprietors, and that no biased enforcement was demonstrated by Garabed in the instant case, Beeber nonetheless saw a broader holding by the United States Supreme Court. Indeed, he wrote, "the greater part of the opinion . . . was devoted to showing the invalidity of the ordinances on the ground that they lodged an unrestrained and arbitrary power with a single individual."[148] Applying this holding to the Wilkes-Barre ordinance, Beeber saw a clear violation of equal protection:

> [The ordinance] divides all persons who desire to make music upon the streets into two classes by an arbitrary line, upon one side of which are those who are permitted to play upon instruments or beat upon drums by the mere will and pleasure of the mayor, and upon the other side are those who are not permitted, or have been permitted and then refused, by the mere will and pleasure of the mayor. Both classes are alike in this, that they enjoy or are denied a permissible line of conduct at the mere will of the mayor, and this without any regard whatever as to the character of the individuals or circumstances under which they desire to do this allowable act.[149]

Beeber searched in vain for binding Pennsylvania authority to support his conclusion. Having found none, he could offer only "the preponderance of the authorities of this country and the general policy of our own state."[150]

---

146. 11 Pa. Super. 372. The court also described the respective power of the legislature and judiciary regarding municipal ordinances:

The general assembly is a co-ordinate branch of the state government, and within the prescribed limits, so are the lawmaking municipal corporation[s]. It is no more competent for the judiciary to interfere with the legislative acts of one than the other. When acting within their powers, or exercising a discretionary power, the courts are not warranted in interfering unless the power is abused to the oppression of the citizens, or for an equally good reason. 11 Pa. Super. 368-69.

Garabed has been repeatedly cited for the proposition that the state has extensive authority to delegate decisional power to political subdivisions, and that courts will not interfere where the subdivision's exercise of that power is reasonable. See *Gima v. Hudson Coal Co.*, 310 Pa. 480, 165 A. 850 (1933); and *Upper Moreland Township v. Ivymor Contractors, Inc.*, 20 Pa. Cmwlth. 66, 341 A.2d 214 (1975).

147. 118 U.S. 356 (1886).
148. 11 Pa. Super. 375 (Beeber, dissenting).
149. 11 Pa. Super. 377-78.
150. See note 149.

## JUVENILE LAW

In response to the national child welfare movement to better the treatment of children who became involved in criminal activity or who were neglected by their parents, and the creation of the first juvenile court in Cook County, Chicago, Illinois, the Pennsylvania legislature promulgated P.L. 279, on May 21, 1901. By 1903, the first of many cases testing and interpreting this juvenile act reached the Superior Court. In *Mansfield's Case*,[151] the Superior Court found the act to be unconstitutional. The act was entitled "An act to regulate the treatment and control of dependent, neglected and delinquent children under the age of sixteen years; providing for the establishment of juvenile courts, and regulating the practice before such courts; providing for the appointment of probation officers . . ." and ancillary matters necessary to the functioning of a juvenile court. The court found the act was flawed in several respects: because of the attempt to change the jurisdiction of the courts of oyer and terminer and quarter sessions and create a new court in violation of the constitution; because children were brought to the court on petition, without indictment or without verified affidavit; and because of the vagueness of the designation of a child as dependent, neglected or delinquent. The court also opined:

> There is also a grave question whether this act does not come into conflict with the fourteenth amendment to the constitution of the United States, which took away from any state the power to "deny to any person within its jurisdiction the equal protection of the laws."[152]

The court went on to say:

> The motives of those whose influence procured this legislation are worthy of the highest commendation, those who labor to shield the young from evil influences benefit humanity; but benevolent enterprises must be carried out in a constitutional manner. The act of 1901 is an exotic, transplanted from a foreign soil, and sufficient care was not exercised to accommodate it to the conditions prescribed by our organic law.[153]

The judgment of the Philadelphia Juvenile Court was reversed and the child was ordered discharged from custody.

The juvenile court movement at that time had considerable impetus and very soon new legislation was promulgated to overcome the objections to the constitutionality of the act of 1901. Thereafter, a new and legally correct juvenile act was created on April 23, 1903, P.L. 274.

In *Commonwealth v. Fisher*,[154] the Superior Court reviewed a case arising from delinquency charges pursuant to the act of 1903. The act was entitled an act "[d]efining the powers of the several courts of quarter sessions of the peace, within this commonwealth, with reference to the care, treatment and control of dependent, neglected, incorrigible and delinquent children, under the age of sixteen, and providing for the means in which such power may be exercised." The court stated:

---

151. 22 Pa. Super. 224 (1903) (W. D. Porter, J.).
152. 22 Pa. Super. 234.
153. 22 Pa. Super. 235.
154. 27 Pa. Super. 175 (1905) (Beaver, J.).

A mere comparison of these two several acts [acts of 1901 and 1903] by their titles shows a very marked and clear distinction between them. The title of the former act was held by us to be defective in several particulars which have been carefully avoided in the act now under consideration. The former act provides expressly for the establishment of juvenile courts. The present act simply defines the power of the courts of quarter sessions already in existence.[155]

The court went on to say:

[N]o new court is created and the ancient court of quarter sessions, which is older than all the constitutions of Pennsylvania, is given thereby not greater but different powers from those previously exercised.

The court of quarter sessions has for many years exercised jurisdiction over the settlement of paupers, over the relation of a man to his wife and children in desertion cases, in surety of the peace cases, in the granting of liquor licenses and in very many of the ways in which the public welfare is involved, where there is neither indictment nor trial by jury.[156]

In affirming the Superior Court decision, the Pennsylvania Supreme Court in *Commonwealth v. Fisher* said that as to the due process issue, the state, pursuant to the parens patriae power, may adopt any process as a means of placing its hands on the child to lead it into one of its courts. "When the child gets there and the court, with the power to save it, determines on its salvation, and not its punishment, it is immaterial how it got there. The act simply provides how children who ought to be saved may reach the court to be saved."[157]

The Supreme Court also found the right to jury trial is not violated by the act and the procedure adopted by the legislature, where the child is not charged with a crime nor placed on trial, is to prevent trial. The court also found the purpose of the act was reformation and not punishment and the state as parens patriae had the right to save a child from prosecution and punishment.

With these pronouncements the foundation and procedures creating the juvenile justice system were established and provided the legal process by which juvenile cases were handled in the courts of Pennsylvania until the philosophy underwent modification in 1965, pursuant to the United States Supreme Court decision in *In re Gault*, infra (Chapter V).

Thus, this court paved the way to the introduction in Pennsylvania of one of the most far reaching social revolutions ever undertaken, the philosophy and product of which will reverberate in a dynamic and unrestrained manner into the twenty-first century. All subsequent legislation, including the acts of 1933, 1972, and most recently 1995, continues the underlying thrust of the act of 1903 and the philosophy elaborated upon by this court in *Fisher*, supra.

---

155. 27 Pa. Super. 178.
156. 27 Pa. Super. 181.
157. 213 Pa. 48, 53, 62 A. 198, 200 (1905).

| County. | APPEALS ENTERED IN | | | |
| | Supreme Court. | | | Superior Court. |
| | 1873 | 1894. | 1896. | 1896. |
|---|---|---|---|---|
| Adams | 2 | 0 | 0 | 2 |
| Allegheny | 99 | 225 | 109 | 87 |
| Armstrong | 9 | 13 | 8 | 7 |
| Berks | 7 | 33 | 17 | 14 |
| Bucks | 5 | 3 | 1 | 1 |
| Blair | 16 | 7 | 5 | 2 |
| Beaver | 4 | 3 | 5 | 5 |
| Butler | 0 | 13 | 4 | 14 |
| Bedford | 4 | 3 | 2 | 3 |
| Bradford | 7 | 11 | 1 | 3 |
| Centre | 3 | 13 | 3 | 5 |
| Carbon | 0 | 0 | 3 | 1 |
| Clinton | 3 | 4 | 2 | 3 |
| Clarion | 1 | 5 | 0 | 1 |
| Chester | 11 | 19 | 10 | 14 |
| Cameron | 1 | 1 | 0 | 0 |
| Cambria | 5 | 8 | 3 | 3 |
| Crawford | 12 | 8 | 5 | 3 |
| Columbia | 7 | 4 | 4 | 1 |
| Clearfield | 1 | 6 | 9 | 8 |
| Cumberland | 9 | 18 | 10 | 7 |
| Dauphin | 10 | 36 | 19 | 7 |
| Delaware | 9 | 17 | 13 | 13 |
| Elk | 2 | 4 | 3 | 0 |
| Erie | 16 | 9 | 3 | 2 |
| Forest | 1 | 4 | 0 | 0 |
| Fulton | 2 | 1 | 1 | 1 |
| Fayette | 3 | 20 | 9 | 1 |
| Franklin | 2 | 3 | 1 | 3 |
| Greene | 5 | 6 | 5 | 2 |
| Huntingdon | 6 | 12 | 5 | 7 |
| Indiana | 4 | 2 | 2 | 2 |
| Juniata | 2 | 2 | 1 | 3 |
| Jefferson | 1 | 2 | 4 | 3 |
| Lehigh | 12 | 5 | 5 | 2 |
| Lebanon | 7 | 6 | 6 | 10 |
| Luzerne | 20 | 24 | 13 | 11 |
| Lycoming | 8 | 7 | 12 | 14 |
| Lawrence | 3 | 4 | 6 | 1 |
| Lancaster | 19 | 28 | 21 | 20 |
| Lackawanna | ★ | 24 | 23 | 22 |
| Mercer | 3 | 4 | 3 | 6 |
| Monroe | 3 | 6 | 3 | 1 |
| Montour | 4 | 0 | 1 | 1 |
| Mifflin | 4 | 0 | 1 | 0 |
| Montgomery | 7 | 26 | 14 | 3 |
| McKean | 3 | 7 | 3 | 2 |
| Northampton | 8 | 15 | 3 | 6 |
| Northumerland | 14 | 8 | 5 | 5 |
| Philadelphia | 200 | 299 | 184 | 94 |
| Pike | 4 | 0 | 2 | 0 |
| Perry | 2 | 0 | 3 | 3 |
| Potter | 0 | 1 | 4 | 0 |
| Snyder | 3 | 4 | 1 | 1 |
| Sullivan | 0 | 2 | 1 | 1 |
| Somerset | 4 | 5 | 6 | 1 |
| Schuylkill | 24 | 22 | 11 | 16 |
| Susquehanna | 3 | 6 | 0 | 2 |
| Tioga | 4 | 1 | 0 | 3 |
| Union | 7 | 6 | 1 | 2 |
| Venango | 8 | 23 | 4 | 2 |
| Wayne | 1 | 2 | 2 | 1 |
| Warren | 10 | 14 | 4 | 1 |
| Wyoming | 9 | 1 | 4 | 3 |
| Washington | 6 | 16 | 10 | 10 |
| Westmoreland | 6 | 16 | 20 | 10 |
| York | 3 | 7 | 10 | 1 |
| | 678 | 1104 | 653 | 483 |

*Luzerne.

An accounting of the number of appeals from each county to the Superior and Supreme Courts following the Superior Court's first year.

## *FAMILY LAW*

In the first decade of its existence, the Superior Court took up the review of appeals from cases involving divorce, support, custody, and estates. Much of what this court reviewed and decided was a continuation of established principles and statutory interpretations previously promulgated by the Supreme Court. A few examples serve to illustrate those progressions and do not represent any departure or innovation of prior law. In *Davidov v. Bail*,[158] the court held that the duty to provide necessaries arises from the common law duty to furnish such in accordance with the needs of the family and social station in life. This is derivative of ecclesiastical law, ingrained in English law and incorporated into the common law and statutory law of Pennsylvania.[159]

In *Henkel's Estate*,[160] this court held that parents cannot bargain away rights of children to support. In *Evans's Estate*,[161] the court held that the right to claim a family exemption is permitted only if partners are living in a family relationship.

A major acceleration of appellate review in family law matters followed a historical change in the divorce code promulgated by the legislature in 1980 and the custody act in 1985. While a complete and separate treatise is required to fully document the impact of these changes and their review and implementation by this court, we will survey the more significant rulings of Superior Court in Chapter VII.

## *DIVORCE LAW*

Prior to 1785 in Pennsylvania, divorces were granted by petition of the governor or by special acts of the State Assembly. The first divorce code in Pennsylvania was enacted in 1785 (Smith's Law 343), which provided for divorce from bonds of matrimony or bed and board upon the grounds of impotency, bigamy, adultery, desertion or marriage upon false rumor of death. Upon adoption of the constitution of 1838, in Article I, Section 14, the legislature was deprived of any power to legislate annulment of marriage in any case where the courts were empowered to grant a decree of divorce.

Legislative divorces continued where the facts would not warrant a decree under the act of 1785, but were eliminated entirely under the constitution of 1815. The sole jurisdiction was conferred upon the courts of common pleas, with appeal to the Supreme Court. Numerous amendments occurred between 1785 and 1815 which were incorporated in the act of 1815. Upon creation of the Superior Court, appellate jurisdiction was conferred on this court. A later codification occurred on May 2, 1929, P.L. 1237. This codification, while changing procedure and substantive law, retained the basic principles as set forth in the law of 1785.[162] Again, through amendments between 1929 and 1980, no substantial change occurred in the law. As a result of the dramatic changes in culture, economics, values, and various civil rights movements, beginning in 1970 in California and sweeping the country for the two decades following, a revolutionary change in the laws of divorce occurred. Pennsylvania enacted the 1980 Divorce Code, which for the first time eliminated fault as a necessary ground for divorce, and adopted totally new concepts regarding the acquisition and distribution of marital property. These will be discussed in Chapter VII.

---

158. 23 Pa. Super. 579 (1903).
159. 48 P.S. sec. 116, "Proceedings in case of debts constructed for necessaries."
160. 13 Pa. Super. 337 (1900).
161. 21 Pa. Super. 430 (1902)
162. *The Pennsylvania Divorce Law* (9th reprint, 1996), commentary by Hubert I. Teitelbaum preceding 23 P.S., 343.

In the century between the creation of the Superior Court in 1895 and the present, the Superior Court played a central role in interpreting, refining and applying the law of marriage, divorce, support and custody. In *Fay v. Fay*[163] the court found no change in the proof required under the Act of 1895, which for the first time gave the right to the husband for divorce on the ground of indignities. The husband was required to show not only that his condition was rendered intolerable and his life burdensome, but that this consequence was caused by cruel and barbarous treatment—both statutory elements were required to concur.[164] However, cruelty by a husband directed to his wife must endanger her life, whereas cruelty by the wife need only render his condition intolerable. This disparity between husband and wife continued until *Sklan v. Sklan*[165] which interpreted the Act of June 28, 1923, as conferring equally upon husband and wife the right to divorce *a vinculo matrimonii* for cruelty and indignities. In *Krug v. Krug*[166] the court said:

> The act clearly distinguishes between cruel and barbarous treatment upon the one hand, and indignities to the person upon the other, as causes for divorce, and requires that the first shall endanger life. A single act of cruelty may be so severe and with such attending circumstances of atrocity as to justify a divorce. No single act of indignity to the person is sufficient cause for a divorce; there must be such a course of conduct or continued treatment as renders the wife's condition intolerable and life burdensome. The indignities need not be such as to endanger life or health; it is sufficient if the course of treatment be of such a character as to render the condition of any woman [or man] of ordinary sensibility and delicacy of feeling intolerable and her [or his] life burdensome.[167]

## Success and Criticism

These cases represent but a handful of the appeals decided by the Superior Court in its first years of operation. Indeed, between 1895 and 1908, the court adjudicated 4,991 appeals. Applications for allocatur totaled 765, and of these, 584 were refused and 181 were allowed. Of the 181 decisions reviewed by the Supreme Court, 121 were affirmed and 60 were reversed. Thus, the Superior Court was found to have erred in 60 of the first 4,991 cases it decided.

This court's caseload increased most significantly beginning in 1899, when its jurisdictional amount was increased to $1,500.[168] The following table sets forth the total number of appeals filed in the Superior and Supreme Courts between 1899 and 1907:

|  | *1899* | *1900* | *1901* | *1902* | *1903* | *1904* | *1905* | *1906* | *1907* | *Total* |
|---|---|---|---|---|---|---|---|---|---|---|
| Supreme Court | 664 | 555 | 579 | 574 | 546 | 564 | 602 | 597 | 634 | 5315 |
| Superior Court | 609 | 581 | 569 | 536 | 531 | 630 | 570 | 565 | 586 | 5177 |
| Total Appeals Filed | 1273 | 1136 | 1148 | 1100 | 1177 | 1194 | 1172 | 1162 | 1220 | 10,492 |

---

163. 27 Pa. Super. 328 (1905)
164. Abraham L. Freedman, Maurice Freedman, *Law of Marriage and Divorce in Pennsylvania*, vol. 2 (Philadelphia: G.T. Bisel Co., 1957), 642.
165. 110 Pa. Super. 226 (1933) (Cunningham, J.).
166. 22 Pa. Super. 572 (1903) (W.D. Porter, J.).
167. See note 166.
168. Pa. Act of May 5, 1899, PL 248.

In considering these statistics, it is important to recall that in the years immediately preceding 1895, the Supreme Court averaged more than 1,200 cases per year.[169]
As the above table indicates, that number was cut in half by 1899. Thus, in addition to
the fact that it disposed of a large number of cases with a relatively low reversal rate,
the Superior Court also succeeded in reducing the Supreme Court's caseload. Nonetheless, it did not escape significant criticism. This criticism arose most prominently from
a committee appointed by the state bar association to study reform of the appellate
courts.[170] In June, 1909, this committee, designated the Special Committee on the Constitution of the Courts in Pennsylvania, submitted a report to the annual meeting of
the bar association in which it recommended the following:

1) That the Superior Court be abolished.

2) That the judges of the Supreme Court be increased to fourteen by the
transfer of the Superior Court judges thereto.

3) That the judges sit in two divisions of seven judges each, at the seat
of government.

4) That where there is a dissenting opinion the cause shall be put down
for argument before the full bench or court *en banc.*[171]

The reasons offered in support of the committee's report echoed those advanced
by critics of an intermediate court at the constitutional convention in 1873, and reiter-
ated when the Superior Court was created in 1895. First, committee members argued
that the court's judgments were not "decisive of the law" because they "may be over-
thrown years after innocent parties have acted upon them. The deluge of cases on final
appeal is great enough," they continued, "and there is sufficient diversity among them
without burdening the shelves of the profession with an interminable series of reports
of the decisions of a court, which, though binding upon the inferior tribunals, are inde-
cisive of the law." Secondly, the members claimed that by allowing a series of appeals
from court to court "the law may be established by an insignificant number of judges
against nearly the whole current of judicial opinion."[172] In support of this claim, they
cited a New York case in which a trial court decision was affirmed by a four judge panel
of the Appellate Division, only to be reversed by a four to three vote of the Court of
Appeals.[173] In the view of the committee, this case represented the unfortunate situation in which "the law was established by four judges against the opinion of seven
others."[174] The committee also noted a Pennsylvania case in which the Superior Court's
unanimous affirmance of a trial court decision was overturned by the Supreme Court
on a vote of five to two.[175] Again, this case was cited because a minority of the judges

---

169. Pamphlet, James E. Rowley, *100 Years of Justice: The Superior Court of Pennsylvania's First Century; 1895-1995* (Superior Court of Pennsylvania: March 1995), 2.

170. The subcommittee consisted of Chairman Harold M. McClure, F.C. McGirr, C.M. Clement, H.C.
Niles, and H.S.P. Nichols. *Pennsylvania Bar Association Reports* (15th Ann. ed., 1909), 487.

171. "Report of the Special Committee on the Constitution of Courts in Pennsylvania," June 2, 1909,
186. Since the number of justices on the Supreme Court was limited by the constitution to seven, the committee also recommended a constitutional amendment.

172. "Report of the Special Committee," June 2, 1909, 189-90.

173. "Report of the Special Committee," June 2, 1909, 189, citing *Roberson v. Rochester Folding Box Co.*,
171 N.Y. 538 (1902).

174. See note 172.

175. "Report of the Special Committee," June 2, 1909, 190, citing *Louchheim v. Somerset Building &
Loan Association*, 211 Pa. 499 (1905).

who considered it determined its outcome. Finally, the committee argued that because the court's decisions were subject to review by the Supreme Court, they resulted in a delay in the administration of justice.[176]

Despite the thrust of these criticisms, however, the committee did not consider the court a failure. Instead, it simply believed that the court's time had passed:

> As a temporary contrivance for the relief of the Supreme Court the Superior Court has fulfilled the expectations of its founders and justified its establishment. This has been due to the painstaking, conscientious performance of their duties by the learned gentlemen who have graced and ornamented its Bench. But there is no reason for its continuance as a permanent institution if its obvious and inherent defects can be cured, its judges placed in a position worthy of them and their decisions be given the weight and authority they deserve.[177]

Following submission of the report, the bar association referred the matter to its Committee on Judicial Procedure for a vote on whether to submit the recommendations to the full membership of the association. The committee considered the recommendations for nearly a year before voting five to four to reject them.[178] In a report submitted to the bar association on May 12, 1910, the majority addressed the criticisms raised by the Special Committee on the Constitution of the Courts. As to the claim that the Superior Court's decisions were not "decisive of the law," the majority noted that Supreme Court decisions were subject to the same criticism. Indeed, the Supreme Court's "own decisions have been, and if the courts were consolidated, doubtless would be, overruled, modified, distinguished and explained, so that it may be perhaps fairly said that they, too, are not decisive of the law."[179] Similarly, the majority deemed irrelevant the claim that multiple appeals allowed a fewer number of judges to overturn the decision of a greater number:

> This is a result which occurs under many circumstances and is almost inseparable from any system. The present complaint is not that the law is not correctly decided, but that the decisions are not final in the sense of becoming authoritative precedents. If the finality and decisiveness of the decision is the element which is to be desired, it can make no difference by what number of judges it is rendered, so long as it establishes the law of the State. The decision of the Supreme Court remains the decision of the Supreme Court, and it would seem to make no difference how many inferior tribunals or judges had decided to the contrary.[180]

---

176. "Report of the Special Committee," June 2, 1909, 190-91. The subcommittee also argued that because the court traveled it was "inconvenient, annoying, tiresome and expensive," and these factors made it unappealing "to able men of independent income who might otherwise be willing to accept positions on its Bench." "Report of the Special Committee," June 2, 1909, 191.

177. "Report of the Special Committee," June 2, 1909, 192.

178. Four members of the committee did not vote. Of the remaining quorum of nine, those voting against the recommendations were Chairman H.B. Gill, C.J. Hepburn, Russell Duane, Maurice W. Sloan, and William B. Linn. Voting in favor were Reynolds D. Brown, Gustavus Remak Jr., Horace M. Rumsey, and Thomas James Meagher. See Reports of the Committee on Judicial Procedure on the Proposed Consolidation of the Supreme and the Superior Courts of the Commonwealth of Pennsylvania, May 12, 1910, Superior Court File, Jenkins Law Library, Philadelphia, 6, 8.

179. Reports of the Committee on Judicial Procedure, May 12, 1910, 4.

180. Reports of the Committee on Judicial Procedure, May 12, 1910, 5.

Finally, the majority addressed the claim that multiple appeals resulted in a delay in the administration of justice. Noting that only 181 cases were appealed from the Superior Court between 1895 and 1908, they found that "[t]his does not seem to be a sufficient number to entitle the result to be styled a serious delay in the administration of justice." Moreover, they stated, "It is not clear that merely by consolidating the courts the hearing of appeals will be expedited."[181] In voting to retain the present system, the committee majority concluded:

> the superior court accomplished the object for which it was constituted, and that the reasons assigned for the consolidation of the courts do not in the light of the actual facts warrant the conclusion that it would be wise to abandon the present system for the purpose of establishing an unwieldy tribunal of fourteen judges with an amount of work which it might be difficult for them to properly perform, and which could not long cope with any increase in the business to be done.[182]

The majority's report ended the effort within the state bar to abolish the Superior Court, and no similar effort has arisen since. Yet, the effort remains significant because it tells us a great deal about perceptions of the court in the early years of this century. Most importantly, although the opposing sides in the state bar effort disagreed on the continuing usefulness of the court, both sides agreed that it achieved its principal goal, relief of the Supreme Court's caseload burden. Moreover, the court's contributions to the state's case law were never questioned, and even its critics conceded that the court's "painstaking, conscientious performance . . . fulfilled the expectations of its founders and justified its establishment." In its first fifteen years, the court accomplished a great deal.

Although notable, however, this success belongs to a phase of the court's history that was profoundly different from those that followed. As we have seen, the court's early history was shaped by factors that made Pennsylvania virtually unique in the nation. The state's industrialization, rivaled only by that of New York, created unprecedented corruption. This corruption necessitated a constitutional convention that laid the groundwork for the creation of an intermediate court by amending the judiciary article of the state constitution and by demonstrating the inadequacy of an expanded Supreme Court. Industrialization also dramatically increased the Supreme Court's caseload, and this caseload expansion provided the direct impetus for creation of the Superior Court. In addition to industrialization, the Pennsylvania Republican machine was perhaps the most powerful in the nation, and its influence shaped the court by dictating the party affiliation of the vast majority of its members. Although these factors—corruption, industrialization, and Republican political dominance—were present in many states, they were exceptionally powerful in Pennsylvania, and each contributed to the emergence of the court in 1895, and to its structure and operation in the years prior to 1910. In the decades that followed, however, the particular influence of these factors diminished, and the work of the court was increasingly shaped by events that occurred far outside the borders of Pennsylvania.

181. See note 180.
182. See note 180.

The Superior Court in 1915.
L-R (seated): George B. Orlady, Charles E. Rice (President Judge), William D. Porter. L-R (standing): Frank M. Trexler, John B. Head, John J. Henderson, John W. Kephart.

# CHAPTER THREE

# PROGRESSIVISM, PROHIBITION, AND WAR: 1911-1930

## *PROGRESSIVISM*

The Superior Court entered a distinct phase in its history in the two decades after 1910. Its enabling statute was repeatedly amended by the legislature, and its membership changed ten times. Yet, the greatest change was in the types of cases brought before the court. As we have seen, the court's major cases prior to 1910 involved primarily state issues—the relationship between the legislature and the economy, the respective powers of the branches of state government, the duties of contractors dealing with state officials, the effect of gubernatorial pardons, and state authority over its political subdivisions. While these issues arose in many states, they were resolved by the Superior Court with little reference to, or interference from, events that were occurring outside of Pennsylvania. This changed dramatically in the years after 1910. Indeed, for decades thereafter, national and even international events shaped the work of the court to a remarkable degree.

The first such event was Progressivism, which swept across the nation as the nineteenth century gave way to the twentieth. Although a contentious and diverse group, Progressives shared a belief that positive governmental intervention was necessary to remedy the evils of rapid industrialization and urbanization. Building on the efforts of early reformers, they advocated a broad array of measures aimed at protecting laborers. But Progressives also looked beyond labor laws and envisioned a comprehensive program of societal reform that combated corruption and benefited virtually all members of the poor and working classes. In Pennsylvania, Progressivism was especially strong. Indeed, the only time between 1860 and 1932 that the state voted for a non-Republican presidential candidate was in 1912, when it favored Progressive Theodore Roosevelt by a plurality of nearly 50,000 votes. This political strength translated into legislative success. In 1905, 1909, and 1915, Progressives enacted child labor laws,[1] and in 1913, they secured passage of a women's labor law.[2] They placed regulatory

---

1. The Child Labor Act of 1905 raised the minimum age for factory and mine workers to fourteen and prohibited night work for children except in continuous industries (glass factories and foundries); the Child Labor Law of 1909 restricted child labor to ten hours per day and fifty-eight hours per week; the Child Labor Law of 1915 made fourteen the minimum age in all establishments, prohibited night work for children, restricted hours to nine per day and fifty-one hours per week, provided a lengthy list of dangerous occupations, and mandated the completion of the sixth-grade for any fourteen or fifteen year old working child. The latter of these laws, the Pa. Act of May 13, 1915, PL 286, is considered more fully infra.

2. The Female Employment Act of 1913 provided that girls, defined as females under the age of twenty-one, could not work more than fifty-four hours per week. Pa. Act of July 25, 1913, PL 286. This act is considered more fully infra.

duties within the state government by creating the Department of Labor and Industry,[3] and the Public Service Commission,[4] and in 1911, they passed the Sproul Act, which established a highway system maintained exclusively by the state.[5] Importantly, in 1915, they also secured passage of a comprehensive workmen's compensation law and established a bureau to administer claims.[6] A number of relief measures were also passed, including the Mother's Assistance Act,[7] the Old Age Commission Act,[8] the World War Veteran's Compensation Act,[9] and the General Poor Relief Act.[10] In 1921, the legislature created the Department of Public Welfare, and two years later it enacted the Administrative Code, which grouped 139 state agencies into 15 departments, established the budget system, and standardized state purchases, salaries, and positions. Some of the most important decisions rendered by the Superior Court between 1911 and 1930 involved the constitutionality and construction of these Progressive statutes.

In addition to Progressive-Era social legislation, the outbreak of World War I in August 1914, and the entry of the United States less than three years later, profoundly influenced the types of cases brought before the Superior Court. Although wars are generally perceived as national events, they present state courts with a variety of challenging issues. Citizens sue foreign nationals during wartime on contracts executed in the state, they resist the draft and incite insurrection, they divorce while out of state, and they die in combat overseas. These and many other activities invoke questions of both state and federal law. In resolving such questions, the Superior Court rendered an important and far-reaching series of decisions.

Even the court's work in the realm of criminal law, usually the most domestic of concerns, involved important issues that transcended state borders. Many of these issues arose from prosecutions under the Brooks Law, Pennsylvania's most important Prohibition enforcement law. As convictions under the Brooks Law increased dramatically in the early years of Prohibition, the Superior Court was called upon to define the relationship of state law to the Eighteenth Amendment and the federal Volstead Act. This relationship necessarily involved difficult issues relating to concurrent jurisdiction and interstate commerce. Also, in the realm of criminal law, the court was repeatedly required to review the sedition convictions of Socialists and Communists in the wake of the Bolshevik Revolution in 1917. These cases posed difficult questions relating to the scope of personal freedoms guaranteed by the state constitution.

These factors—Progressivism, world war, Prohibition, and foreign-inspired domestic unrest—shaped the work of the Superior Court in the two decades after 1910. Indeed, perhaps at no time in the court's history has it decided more cases involving issues of national and international significance. This is most apparent from the fact that the United States Supreme Court reviewed a larger proportion of Superior Court decisions between 1911 and 1930 than at any other time before or since. Before turning to these cases, it is necessary to introduce the new judges who joined the court.

---

3. Pa. Act of May 27, 1913, PL 10.
4. Pa. Act of July 26, 1913, PL 1374.
5. Pa. Act of May 25, 1911, PL 100.
6. Pa. Act of June 2, 1915, PL 736.
7. Pa. Act of May 23, 1913, PL 118.
8. Pa. Act of May 21, 1923, PL 189.
9. Pa. Act of May 19, 1923, PL 236.
10. Pa. Act of May 17, 1925, PL 762.

## NEW ADDITIONS/REPLACEMENTS TO THE COURT

The first change in the court's membership followed the death of Judge Beaver on January 31, 1914. He was succeeded by John W. Kephart, who was born on November 12, 1872, in Wilmore, Cambria County. Kephart was educated at the Soldier's School in McAlisterville, at Allegheny College, and at Dickinson Law School. He later served as president of the Dickinson Alumni Association and associate advisor of the Dickinson Law School. He was admitted to the bar of Cambria County in 1895 and engaged in general practice, but concentrated on corporate law. From 1907 until 1914, Kephart served as solicitor of Cambria County. On November 4, 1913, he was elected to the Superior Court on the Republican ticket and served for five years. In 1918, he became the first Superior Court judge elected justice of the state Supreme Court.

The second change on the court occurred in February 1914, when Frank M. Trexler, a Republican from Allentown, was appointed to replace Judge Morrison. Trexler was born on January 9, 1861. He received bachelor's and master of arts degrees from Muhlenberg College. He began the practice of law in Allentown in 1882, and served as city solicitor for eleven years. In 1890, he was elected president of the Allentown Y.M.C.A. and served in that capacity for nearly forty years. From 1902 to 1913, he served as President Judge of the Lehigh County Court of Common Pleas. While serving on the trial court, in 1910, he received a doctor of laws degree from Muhlenberg. Following his appointment to the Superior Court, Trexler was elected to full ten-year terms in 1914 and 1924. He served as an associate judge until February 10, 1930, when, upon the death of Judge William D. Porter, he became President Judge of the Superior Court. He served until 1934.

Upon Judge Rice's retirement in January 1916, he was replaced by J. Henry Williams, who had been elected the previous November. Williams was born in Philadelphia in 1866. He was educated in the public and private schools of the city and thereafter read law. Following his admission to the bar, he practiced generally in the court of common pleas and orphans' court. He also served as master and referee in many cases, and as trustee and executor of many estates. Later in his career, he assisted in the preparation of *The American and English Encyclopedia of Law*. Williams was extremely active in Philadelphia social circles. He was the historian of the Grand Lodge of Masons at its 125th anniversary celebration, and a member of the Union League, Art Club, the Law Association and Law Academy of Philadelphia, the Young Republicans, Pen and Pencil Club, and the West Philadelphia Club.[11] It appears that Williams' residency in Philadelphia was an important factor in the decision of the Republican Party to endorse him for the Superior Court. In late July 1915, the *Philadelphia Public Ledger* reported that the "agreement as to Mr. Williams is a recognition of the point that Philadelphia, which originates such a large percentage of the business coming before the Superior Court, should have representation in that higher court." The article also reported the claim of a member of a committee of lawyers supporting Williams that "[w]e have received assurances that a majority of the Philadelphia bar will support Mr. Williams. Mr. Williams, therefore, is Philadelphia's candidate, and with that support we will work for support in other counties."[12] The committee received the necessary support, and Williams was elected in the fall of 1915. He served until his death on October 24, 1919.

The next change occurred on January 9, 1919, when William Huestis Keller was appointed to fill the vacancy occasioned by Judge Kephart's election to the Su-

---

11. *Philadelphia Inquirer*, 25 Oct. 1919, p. 2, col. 8.
12. *Philadelphia Public Ledger*, 28 July 1915, p. 3, col. 5.

Judge J. Henry Williams

preme Court. Keller was born in Montgomery County, Maryland, on August 11, 1869. After attending the public schools in Bellefonte, Pennsylvania, and Bellefonte Academy, he graduated from Franklin and Marshall College in 1891. Thereafter, he attended law school at George Washington University, and received an LL.B. in 1893. He was admitted to the bar of Lancaster County on August 22, 1893, and practiced with his father's firm, Coyle and Keller. He was a delegate to the Republican National Conventions of 1908 and 1912. He also had five children, the oldest of whom was killed in France during World War I. On May 10, 1915, Keller was appointed first deputy attorney general by Governor Brumbaugh, and he served in that capacity until his appointment to the Superior Court in 1919. He was elected to a full term in 1919, and reelected in 1929. On January 7, 1935, he followed Judge Trexler as President Judge, and served until his death on January 16, 1945. During his tenure on the court, Judge Keller was well known for the clarity of his legal opinions. In his important 1985 text on Pennsylvania Constitutional Law, former Superior Court Judge Robert E. Woodside said of Judge Keller:

> In an era when books, speeches and sermons were longer than today, President Judge William Keller, one of Pennsylvania's most respected appellate court judges of his or any other time, demonstrated in his opinions how even the most difficult and involved principles of law could be established and expressed clearly, accurately and succinctly on a few pages.[13]

---

13. Robert Woodside, *Pennsylvania Constitutional Law* (Sayre, Pa.: Murrelle Printing Co., 1985), 35, footnote designated by * (also noting that "Judge Keller did practically all his own research and wrote all his opinions in longhand.").

On November 5, 1919, William B. Linn was appointed upon the death of Judge Williams. Linn was born in Ephrata, Lancaster County, on December 20, 1871. He attended, and later taught in, the public schools. In 1897, he received a law degree from the University of Pennsylvania. He practiced in Philadelphia, serving as senior counsel of the Baltimore and Ohio Railroad and as a partner in the firm of Gill and Linn. He also served as president of the Art Club and was active in a number of community affairs in Philadelphia. Upon Linn's appointment to the Superior Court in 1919, the *Philadelphia Public Ledger* opined:

> Mr. Linn in a special manner represents the Philadelphia bar in its most dignified and honorable aspect. Far from being a narrow legal pendant unknown outside of his profession and his practice, he has taken a prominent part in those things that make the city a more amenable place to live in and at the same time has attained that distinction in his own profession that makes his recognition one that honors the bar as well as himself.[14]

Following his appointment, Linn was elected, as a Republican, to a full term in 1920. While on the court, he was a prominent advocate of abolishing the unanimity requirement for jury verdicts and allowing for verdicts found by only three-fourths or five-sixths of the jurors. Responding to those who sought to abolish the jury system completely, he published a lengthy article in 1929 in which he reviewed literature on the subject and found "no substantial objection to trial by jury that cannot be reasonably expected to be removed by a modification of the rule requiring unanimity."[15] Despite Linn's efforts, the unanimity requirement remained. On February 23, 1932, he was appointed to the state Supreme Court to fill the vacancy caused by the death of Justice Emory A. Walling. He was the second Superior Court judge to become a justice of the Supreme Court. In the fall of 1932, he was elected to a full term of twenty-one years.

The next change occurred in April 1922, when Judge Head resigned because of poor health. Head was the only Democrat to serve on the court between 1905 and 1934, and he was replaced on April 12, 1922, by the appointment of Republican Robert S. Gawthrop. Gawthrop was born in Embreeville, Chester County, on October 20, 1878. He graduated from West Chester High School in 1897, and received a bachelor's degree from the University of Pennsylvania in 1901. He studied law in the office of Thomas S. Butler of West Chester, and was admitted to the bar of Chester County in 1904. He served as district attorney of that county from 1909 to 1911, and also served as chairman of the Republican County Committee. On May 11, 1915, he was appointed by Governor Brumbaugh as judge of the Chester County Court of Common Pleas. He served in that capacity until January 1916. From January 1919, until his appointment to the Superior Court, he served as first deputy attorney general. When summoned to the governor's office in April 1922, Gawthrop had no idea that he was about to be appointed to the Superior Court.[16] He quickly accepted the appointment and was subsequently elected to a full term. Although he ran for reelection in the fall of 1931, he finished fourth in a race with three open seats. Gawthrop was the first Superior Court judge to lose a bid for reelection after serving a full term.

---

14. *Philadelphia Public Ledger*, 7 Nov. 1919, p. 12, col. 3. The *Ledger* also published a brief biographical account of Linn on November 6, 1919, p. 5, col. 4.

15. *Philadelphia Public Ledger*, 28 Dec. 1929, p. 6, col. 5.

16. *Philadelphia Public Ledger*, 13 Apr. 1922, p. 3, col. 7.

On November 3, 1925, Jesse E. B. Cunningham was elected to the Superior Court to replace Judge Orlady, who retired at the end of his third term. Cunningham was elected as the candidate of the Republican, Prohibition, and Socialist Parties. He was born in Johnstown on December 19, 1868, the grandson of John Cunningham, one of the founders of Blairsville, Pennsylvania. He was awarded a bachelor's degree from Washington and Jefferson College, and later received honorary master of arts and doctor of laws degrees from that school. Cunningham was admitted to the Westmoreland County bar in 1893. He was elected district attorney of Westmoreland County in 1900, and reelected in 1903. Four years later, he was appointed second deputy attorney general in 1907. In that capacity, he participated in the prosecution of the Capitol Fraud Cases, and was subsequently appointed first deputy attorney general. He served until his resignation in 1915. It appears that Cunningham resigned due to disappointment that he was not named attorney general by Governor Brumbaugh. Instead, Francis Shrunk Brown was appointed, and Cunningham's was only one in a series of high-level resignations. Thereafter, Cunningham remained in Harrisburg, where he engaged in private practice with Charles H. Bergner, who was solicitor for the Pennsylvania Railroad. The new partnership also represented a number of other large corporate interests.[17] Following his election to the Superior Court in 1925, Cunningham served his full term and ran for reelection in 1935. In his reelection campaign, Cunningham was opposed by a Democratic candidate whose party had been strengthened by the Depression. Despite concerted opposition, however, Cunningham won reelection, and he served on the court until his death in 1942.

On January 28, 1929, Thomas J. Baldridge was appointed to replace Judge Henderson. Baldridge was born in Hollidaysburg on April 5, 1872, the son of Howard Malcolm Baldridge, a prominent attorney. He attended Andover Academy in Massachusetts, Bucknell University, and the law school of the University of Pennsylvania. On March 11, 1895, he was admitted to the bar of Blair County, and remained in private practice until January 15, 1910, when he was appointed president judge of the Blair County Court of Common Pleas. He was elected to a full term in 1911. Thereafter, he was appointed by Governor Brumbaugh to a commission organized to revise orphans' court practice and the laws relating to decedents' estates. The commission's work resulted in a new decedents' estate law in 1917. In December 1925, while still a member of the commission, Baldridge also served on the orphans' court while another judge was convalescing. He was the only judge from Blair County to sit on the orphans' court of that judicial district in its fifty-year existence.[18] On January 18, 1927, he resigned his position on the orphans' court commission to become Governor Fisher's attorney general. Baldridge resigned that position in 1929, when he was appointed to the Superior Court. He was elected to a full term in the fall of 1929, and reelected in 1939. He served until 1947.[19]

On February 18, 1930, J. Frank Graff was appointed upon the death of Judge Porter. Graff was born in Worthington, Armstrong County, on December 28, 1888. He

17. *Philadelphia Public Ledger*, 16 Feb. 1915, p. 6, col. 4.

18. *Philadelphia Public Ledger*, 27 Dec. 1925, p. 7, col. 2.

19. An interesting anecdote concerning Judge Baldridge appeared in the *Altoona Mirror* on October 8, 1995 announcing it would begin carrying a weekly article by Letitia Baldridge on social conduct. There it reported:

> Letitia Baldrige [*sic*], who has served as an adviser to five first ladies, brings her weekly column on how to survive in today's world to the Altoona Mirror. . . . Baldrige began her work in the White House during the Kennedy administration. She has since written numerous books on manners.

PENNSYLVANIA

SAMUEL B. RAMBO
SUPERINTENDENT

OFFICE OF
SUPERINTENDENT OF PUBLIC GROUNDS & BUILDINGS
HARRISBURG

January 15, 1912.

Hon. William Pearson,

Prothonotary, Supreme and Superior Courts,
Commonwealth of Pennsylvania,

Harrisburg, Pa.

Dear Sir:-

According to the requirements of the Act of Assembly approved March 26, 1895, (P.L. 1895, pp 22, etc.) relative to contracts for supplies, stationery, fuel, furniture, furnishings, distribution of documents, repairs, alterations, or all other matters or things needed by the State Government and the Executive Mansion, you are respectfully notified as the head of your Department to furnish me a list (NOT LATER THAN FEBRUARY 15, 1912.) of the above matters or things that may be required by your Department during the fiscal year beginning on the first Tuesday of June, A.D. 1912.

The above list is required to be in detail, giving as far as practicable a description of everything needed by your Department during the coming year. It should include all items whether or not they are on our present Schedule. The description of items on our present Schedule should include the Item Numbers, but the new items should be accompanied by the estimated cost and fully described.

A material reduction is to be made in the size of the Schedule this year. Only such articles as are actually used by the Departments will be included - all unnecessary articles will be omitted. Therefore, it is imperative that the list contain only your actual requirements. This can be accomplished by careful reference to the statements furnished you by the Superintendent of Public Grounds and Buildings each month, showing the amount and character of supplies furnished your Department in the past.

Promptness in attending to this matter is necessary.

Very truly yours,

*Samuel B. Rambo.*

Superintendent.

The January 1912 directive to the Superior Court from the superintendent of Public Grounds and Buildings regarding contracts for all purchases to be made by the court.

graduated from Mercersburg Academy in 1907, and Princeton University in 1911. He then studied law for two years at Harvard Law School and completed the third year at the University of Pittsburgh. In 1914, he enlisted as a private in the Pennsylvania National Guard. He later served as a lieutenant while stationed on the Mexican border, and as judge advocate of the 56th Infantry Brigade at Camp Hancock, Georgia. During World War I, he served overseas with the 28th Division, and was promoted to captain, and later major. After the war, Graff returned home to Armstrong County, and ultimately became a partner in the firm of Ralston and Graff. On November 6, 1923, he was elected to the Court of Common Pleas of Armstrong County as the candidate of the Republican, Prohibition, and Socialist Parties. On February 18, 1930, he was appointed to the Superior Court, but resigned three months later.

Baldrige says some of her early etiquette lessons came from Hollidaysburg in the 1940s and 1950s during family visits to her great uncle and aunt, the late Judge Thomas Baldrige and Anne Baldrige.

"They had a 19th century house and very lovely things and no children," Baldrige says. "So when my family would visit them (from her home state of Nebraska) we had to be well behaved."

The train engine explosion that killed engineer H. K. Thomas on May 11, 1905, is an example of rampant industrial accidents during the Gilded Age.

On June 24, 1930, John G. Whitmore was appointed to replace Judge Graff. Whitmore was born in 1868 in Ridgway, Elk County. He was a lifelong friend of John S. Fisher, who as governor in 1930 honored Whitmore, then age 62, with the Superior Court appointment to finish the remaining six months of Graff's term. The move surprised many in the state Republican Party who assumed that Fisher would appoint the Republican primary winner, John Drew. Whitmore left the court at the end of his appointive term in January 1931. [20]

## THE COURT AT WORK: PROGRESSIVE LEGISLATION

The Superior Court contributed more to the development of workmen's compensation law than perhaps any other social legislation passed during the Progressive Era.[21] Prior to the twentieth century in the United States, employees injured at work had only one option for legal redress, a common law negligence action against their employers. Like other personal injury plaintiffs, the employees had the burden of proof, and this burden often proved insurmountable. Worse yet, employers had available an effective "trinity of defenses," the fellow servant doctrine, assumption of risk, and contributory negligence.[22] This combination of the employees' heavy burden and the employers' potent defenses created an extremely unjust situation in which thousands of

---

20. *Philadelphia Inquirer*, 25 June 1930, p. 1, col. 5.

21. The designation "workmen's compensation" did not become "workers' compensation" until statutory revisions of the 1960s.

22. Edward J. O'Connell, "Intentional Employer Misconduct and Pennsylvania's Exclusive Remedy Rule After *Poyser v. Newman Co.*: A Proposal for Legislative Reform," 49 U. Pitt. L. Rev. 1127, 1131 (1988), citing William L. Prosser, *Handbook of the Law of Torts*, 3d ed., (St. Paul: West Publishing Co., 1964), sec. 81.

injured employees could neither work nor receive compensation.

As industrial accidents increased throughout the Gilded Age, the inequities of the common law system became glaring, and, by 1910, states began responding with comprehensive workmen's compensation statutes.[23] Under these statutes, employees forfeited their common law right to bring personal injury actions in exchange for expedited compensation, and employers were declared immune from common law liability for workplace accidents in exchange for agreeing to provide compensation regardless of fault. The drafters of these statutes believed that they would afford some measure of financial relief to injured workers while at the same time providing employers with an economic incentive to improve workplace safety.

Although it lagged behind other industrial states, Pennsylvania joined the workmen's compensation movement in 1915, when an amendment was added to the state constitution empowering the general assembly to enact laws requiring employers to pay reasonable compensation to employees for injuries arising in the course of employment.[24] Pursuant to the amendment, the legislature enacted P.L. 736, which sought to "correct the very generalized evils" of the common law system by affording "an employe and his dependents prompt, expeditious and immediate relief in case of injury or death."[25] The new statute also established a board to adjudicate claims and provided that "[a]ny appeal from a decision of the board to the Court of Common Pleas and from there to the Supreme or Superior Court, shall take precedence over all other civil cases."[26] Despite its worthy goal, however, P.L. 736 created a number of problems. Most importantly, by establishing an entirely new structure for the compensation of injured employees, the statute necessarily impacted other laws that also related to the compensation of injuries. In addressing whether and to what extent the overlapping laws conflicted, the Superior Court rendered a number of important decisions.

The most notable of these decisions was *Liberato v. Royer & Herr*,[27] which was finally resolved by Justice Oliver Wendell Holmes and the United States Supreme Court. The sequence of events underlying *Liberato* began on February 9, 1916, when Guiseppi Liberato was killed in Dauphin County while in the course of his employment.[28] He died without spouse or issue. Thereafter, his parents, Italians who never resided in the United States, filed a workmen's compensation claim in Pennsylvania. The board ultimately awarded the parents $820, and the court of common pleas affirmed.[29]

The employer appealed to the Superior Court on the basis that the award of compensation violated Section 310 of the Worker's Compensation Act, which provided that "[a]lien widowers, parents, brothers, and sisters not residents of the United States, shall not be entitled to any compensation." Apparently recognizing the difficulty pre-

---

23. In 1910, New York became the first state to enact a workmen's compensation statute, and more than twenty states quickly followed suit. By 1913, more than half of the nation's population lived in jurisdictions with workmen's compensation statutes. *Poyser v. Newman Co.*, 1131-32.

24. Pa. Constitution (1874), art. III, sec. 21 (1915).

25. Pa. Act of June 2, 1915, PL 736. The need for such a law was recognized in Pennsylvania prior to 1915. For instance, in an earlier address to the legislature, Governor John K. Tener called for "the creation of an industrial accidents commission to consist of seven members to inquire into the subject of fair compensation for those injured and the families of those killed in the mines, factories, stores and upon railroads, ships wharves and in all industrial establishments." George P. Donehoo, *Pennsylvania; A History* (New York City: 1926), 1559.

26. Pa. Act of June 2, 1915, PL 736, sec. 425.

27. 81 Pa. Super. 403 (1923) (Porter, J.).

28. The court's opinion does not indicate the nature of the accident that claimed Liberato's life.

29. The board at first refused the claim on the basis that the plaintiffs were nonresident aliens, but the court of common pleas remanded and the board was constrained to find in favor of the plaintiffs. Decisions of the board were appealable to the court of common pleas pursuant to Section 409 of PL 736, which provided that "on a question of law . . . appeal may be taken to the courts."

sented by Section 310, the Liberatos argued that the provision conflicted with a treaty existing between Italy and the United States. Article 3 of the treaty provided:

> The citizens of each of the high contracting parties shall receive in the states and territories of the other, the most constant protection and security for their persons and property, and for their rights including that form of protection granted by any state or national law which establishes a civil responsibility for injuries or for death caused by negligence or fault and gives to the relatives or heirs of the injured party a right of action which shall not be restricted on account of the nationality of said relatives or heirs, and shall enjoy in this respect the same rights and privileges as are, or shall be, granted to nationals, provided that they submit themselves to the conditions imposed on the latter.[30]

Rejecting the Liberatos' argument, a unanimous Superior Court began by emphasizing that the treaty applied only to "death caused by negligence or fault." Yet, the plaintiffs, the court found, were not attempting to recover for such a death; instead, they commenced an action under the Workmen's Compensation Act, and that statute constituted a contract between their son and his employer that they would abide by its terms.[31] According to the court:

> When Guiseppi Liberato accepted the provisions of article 3 of the [statute], he covenanted that if he should suffer an injury in the course of his employment and death therefrom resulted, his parents (these claimants) should not be entitled to compensation, if at the time of such injury they were aliens and not residents of the United States. These claimants are attempting to assert a right under the statute, but in violation of the contract by the statute authorized.[32]

The court also rejected the argument, which the trial court found persuasive, that Guiseppi's contract was not binding on the rights of his parents. "If this contention is to prevail," the court held, "then it logically follows that, for the same reason, neither widow, children or parents (whether resident citizens or nonresident aliens) are bound by the contract authorized by the statute. . . . This would plainly be the equivalent of declaring to be invalid the beneficent provisions of the statute. . . ."[33] For this reason, the court reversed the award of compensation to Guiseppi Liberato's parents.[34] On appeal, the Supreme Court affirmed on the basis of the Superior Court opinion.[35]

Thereafter, the Liberatos pursued their case in the federal courts, and in 1926, the United States Supreme Court granted certiorari.[36] Like the Superior Court's analysis, the Supreme Court's opinion turned on the fact that the workmen's compensation statute created a contract between employers and employees. The Supreme Court declared:

---

30. 81 Pa. Super. 406-07. (The treaty was executed on November 18, 1871, and amended on February 13, 1913.)

31. 81 Pa. Super. 410. (When the parties accept the provisions of Article 3 of the statute, their relations become contractual, and their rights are to be determined under the provisions of that article.)

32. 81 Pa. Super. 408.

33. 81 Pa. Super. 408-09.

34. 81 Pa. Super. 411.

35. *Liberato v. Royer & Herr*, 281 Pa. 227 (1924).

36. *Liberato v. Royer & Herr*, 270 U.S. 535 (1926) (Holmes, J.).

Typical view of coal miners encompassing three generations
*(PHMC, Anthracite Heritage Museum).*

[T]he Compensation Act offers a plan different from the common law and the workman is free not to come in under it. If he does, of course all benefits dependent on the new arrangement are matters of agreement and statutory consequences of agreement and cannot be carried further than the contract and statute go. One of those benefits is compensation irrespective of the cause of death, but it is confined to residents. . . .

We are of opinion that the Treaty was construed rightly by the Courts below.[37]

In the seven decades since *Liberato* was decided, it has been cited repeatedly for the proposition that parties in an employment relationship may voluntarily contract away certain of their rights to sue in tort,[38] and that where the Workmen's Compensation Act applies, the remedies provided therein are exclusive.[39]

The Superior Court was also called upon to define the relationship between state workmen's compensation law and the Federal Employers' Liability Act. Under well-established precedent of the United States Supreme Court, the federal act applied where there was "an element of interstate commerce" in an injured worker's employ-

---

37. *Liberato v. Royer & Herr*, 270 U.S. 538.

38. See e.g., *Repyneck v. Tarantino*, 403 Pa. 300, 303 (1961); *Agostin v. Pittsburgh Steel Foundry Corp.*, 354 Pa. 543, 554 (1946) (Patterson concurring).

39. See e.g., *McIntyre v. Lavino Co.*, 344 Pa. 163, 168 (1942); *Staggers v. Dunn-Mar Oil & Gas Co.*, 312 Pa. 269, 275 (1933); *Persing v. Citizens Traction Co.*, 294 Pa. 230, 234 (1928); *Miller v. Reading Co.*, 292 Pa. 44, 47 (1928); *Ford v. A.E. Dick*, 288 Pa. 140, 151 (1927).

ment.[40] In a series of cases, the Superior Court resolved conflicts concerning the applicability of this rule. The most important of these cases were *Martini v. Director General of Railroads*[41] and *Lamlein v. Director General of Railroads*.[42] In *Martini*, the plaintiff lost sight in one eye when he was hit by a flying piece of steel while trying to repair a ladder track in Philadelphia. Rejecting the employer's claim that plaintiff was engaged in interstate commerce at the time of the accident, the Workmen's Compensation Board rendered an award to plaintiff under the state statute. The court of common pleas affirmed the board's decision. On appeal, the Superior Court reversed. The court began by noting that since a question of federal law was involved, the court was not bound by the board's findings of fact.[43] Reexamining the evidence, the court found that, although it was not clear which ladder track the plaintiff was injured on, all three tracks in defendant's rail yard "were at all times used and available both for interstate and intrastate traffic." Thus, the court concluded, each of the ladder tracks was necessarily "an instrumentality of interstate commerce," and the board erred in rendering an award under state law.[44] The same day, the court also decided *Lamlein*, in which the plaintiff's son was killed while employed as a brakeman on a local freight train running between Bethlehem and Philadelphia. At the time of the accident, which occurred at Perkasie on July 3, 1919, both cars attached to the train were used only in intrastate commerce, and one of the cars struck and killed the decedent while it was being placed in the yard. The Workmen's Compensation Board rendered an award to the plaintiff under the state statute on the basis that defendant failed to carry his burden of establishing that the decedent was engaged in interstate commerce at the time of his death. On appeal, the Superior Court again reversed. Surveying numerous decisions of the United States Supreme Court, the court adopted the "constituents of interstate commerce" test. Under this test, "if there be an assertion of the claim or remedy growing out of an occurrence in which there are constituents of interstate commerce the burden of explanation and avoidance is on him who asserts the claim or remedy, not on the railway company to which it is directed."[45] The court then noted that, regardless of the fact that it ran only between two Pennsylvania cities, the train was "carrying freight consigned to or from more than half a dozen different states and Canada." As a result, it held, the "constituents" test was satisfied and the board improperly imposed upon defendant the burden of proving interstate commerce.[46] On this basis, the court reversed the decision of the Workmen's Compensation Board. Taken together, *Martini* and *Lamlein* indicate that the "instrumentality" and "constituents" tests of federal law precluded state workmen's compensation awards where the slightest component of interstate commerce is involved in workplace accidents.[47] These rulings have remained authoritative in the realm of workmen's compensation for the past eight decades.

Finally, in 1919, the court rendered a workmen's compensation decision that was ultimately codified by the legislature. The difficult issue in *Chovic v. Pittsburgh Crucible Steel Co.*,[48] and the companion case of *Turkovic v. Pittsburgh Crucible Steel Co.*,[49] was how to define "loss of use" under Article III of the Workmen's Compensation

---

40. See *Philadelphia & Reading Railway Co. v. Polk*, 256 U.S. 332, 334 (1921) ("It is to be remembered that it is the declaration of the cases that if there is an element of interstate commerce in a traffic or employment it determines that remedy of the employee.").
41. 77 Pa. Super. 529 (1921) (Linn, J.).
42. 77 Pa. Super. 534.
43. 77 Pa. Super. 531.
44. See note 42.
45. 77 Pa. Super. 537, citing *Philadelphia & Reading Railway Co. v. Polk*, 256 U.S. 332 (1921).
46. 77 Pa. Super. 538.
47. See also, *Zimmerman v. Western Union Tel. Co.*, 77 Pa. Super. 127 (1921).
48. 71 Pa. Super. 350 (1919).
49. 71 Pa. Super. 354.

Act, which provided in relevant part that "[p]ermanent loss of the use of a hand, arm, foot, leg or eye, shall be considered as the equivalent of the loss of such hand, arm, foot, leg or eye."[50] While the plaintiff in *Chovic* was employed in defendant's mill, his right hand was crushed by a steel plate. As a result of the accident, he suffered numerous broken bones and retained very little grasping power in his hand. An award was rendered in favor of the plaintiff. On appeal to the Superior Court, the employer argued that because the plaintiff retained some function in his right hand he had not sustained "loss of the use of a hand" within the meaning of Section 306. Finding no guidance in the workmen's compensation statute or case law, the court devised its own test for determining whether the plaintiff's injury satisfied the mandate of Section 306. "Whether a man has lost the use of a hand," the court held, "depends upon whether the hand has become useless in any employment for which that particular man is mentally and physically qualified."[51] Since this question was a matter of fact, not law, the court refused to disturb the ruling of the workmen's compensation referee.

For nearly twenty years after the court's ruling, the so-called "industrial use" test of *Chovic* was utilized repeatedly by courts to determine "loss of use" under state workmen's compensation law. In 1937, the legislature codified this test in P.L. 1552, which provided that loss of use means "industrial loss of use." Two years later, the legislature removed this test from the statute and replaced it with a similar test, "loss of use for all practical intents and purposes."[52] Even after it was replaced, however, courts continued to rely on the test set forth in *Chovic*.[53]

As with the workmen's compensation statute, the early development of public utility law was decisively influenced by Superior Court decisions. In order to limit the fraud and overreaching that plagued the utility industry in Pennsylvania, the legislature in 1913 enacted the Public Service Company Law.[54] Most importantly, the law established the Public Service Commission and vested it with "general administrative power and authority . . . to supervise and regulate all public service companies doing business within this Commonwealth."[55] As originally enacted, the law also provided that appeals from rulings of the commission were to be taken to the Court of Common Pleas of Dauphin County. Two years later, by the Act of June 3, 1915, P.L. 779, the legislature substituted the Superior Court as the tribunal of appellate jurisdiction. This substitution was challenged in *West Virginia Pulp & Paper Co. v. Public Service Commission*,[56] the first of several important public utility cases decided by the early court. In *West Virginia Pulp*, plaintiff appealed after the commission authorized an increase in the rates charged by several railroads for the transportation of wood pulp. The railroad companies, as intervenors, sought to quash the appeal on the basis that P.L. 779 was unconstitutional. They argued, inter alia, that since the Public Service Commission was not a court, P.L. 779 granted original rather than appellate jurisdiction to the Superior Court. Thus, it was contended, the law violated the "spirit of our Constitution," by which the judiciary was sharply divided between courts of original jurisdiction and courts of appellate jurisdiction.[57] The intervenors also argued that P.L. 779 vio-

---

50. 71 Pa. Super. 351, citing paragraph (c), sec. 306, art. III (Porter, J.).

51. 71 Pa. Super. 353.

52. Pa. Act of June 21, 1939, PL 520.

53. *Krasznay v. Milton Ross Metals Co.*, 204 Pa. Super. 94 (1964); see also, *Curran v. Walter E. Knipe and Sons*, 185 Pa. Super. 540, 546 (1958) (Woodside, J.) ("Apparently following the *Chovic* case, the courts applied the 'industrial use' interpretation to some cases occurring both before and after the period when the legislature directed it to be applied.").

54. Pa. Act of July 26, 1913, PL 1374.

55. Pa. Act of July 26, 1913, PL 1374, art. V, sec. 1.

56. 61 Pa. Super. 552 (1915) (Henderson, J.).

57. It is not entirely clear how the intervenors reconciled their argument with the fact that the Superior Court received original jurisdiction in the act that established it.

THE SUPERIOR COURT OF PENNSYLVANIA.

Philadelphia, August 20, 1917.

William Pearson, Esq.,

    Prothonotary Superior Court,

        Harrisburg, Pa.

Dear Mr. Pearson:

    As you know the Legislature passed an Act authorizing the transfer from the Dauphin County Court to the Superior Court of all undisposed of appeals from the decrees of the Public Service Commission.  I understand the Superior Court is anxious to have as many of the Public Service cases disposed of at their October Session in Philadelphia as will be agreeable to counsel concerned.

    Will you kindly send me a list of all the appeals entered on your docket from the Public Service Commission and I will then take up the matter with Judge Orlady as to whether orders of transfers will be made advancing these cases to the Philadelphia Session.

    With kind regards to Homer and yourself

WM TAYLOR

Letter to the Superior Court Prothonotary from the calendar control official regarding the scheduling and transfer of appeals cases from the Public Service Commission to the Superior Court.

lated the special legislation prohibition of Article III, Section 7, of the constitution by attempting to confer jurisdiction over a special type of cases, namely, appeals from the Public Service Commission.

The Superior Court rejected the intervenors' claims. Initially, the court concluded that the act did not confer original jurisdiction:

> All of the cases so authorized to be heard by the Superior Court are first heard and determined by the Public Service Commission and the inquiry in the Superior Court is limited to the case as found in the record of the proceedings before the commission. The trial in the Superior Court is in fact, therefore, an appellate review.[58]

The court also concluded that even if the jurisdiction granted was original, nothing in the constitution prohibited such a grant. Referring to the language of the intervenors' argument, the court held, "There is no warrant for an appeal to the spirit of [the Constitution] independently of language therein out of which such spirit necessarily arises."[59] Finally, the court rejected the intervenors' claim that P.L. 779 violated the special legislation prohibition of the state constitution. The court began its analysis of

---

58. 61 Pa. Super. 563-64.
59. 61 Pa. Super. 564.

Low wages and long hours were typical for women in many manufacturing and production industries, such as this food preparation plant at H. J. Heinz and Company, Pittsburgh. The Superior Court upheld new laws written to help protect women and children in the workplace *(Carnegie Library of Pittsburgh)*.

this issue by noting that public service companies constitute a separate class of businesses because they affect "all the interests of the people to a greater or a less degree, controlling large capital; having their existence by the permission of the Commonwealth and exercising special privileges by legislative grant and constituting necessary monopolies to a greater or less degree."[60] These "substantial distinctions" meant that public service companies were a separate class for legislative purposes, the court held, and P.L. 779 was therefore general legislation.[61] The court's ruling in *West Virginia Pulp* established beyond question its jurisdiction over appeals from the Public Service Commission.

A year later, the court upheld the constitutionality of the Public Service Company Law. In *Relief Electric Co.'s Petition*,[62] the plaintiff petitioned the commission for a certificate of public convenience authorizing it to begin providing electricity to the borough of Washington. Such a certificate was required for all contracts entered between public service companies and municipalities. In support of its petition, plaintiff established that it had secured an ordinance allowing it to occupy the streets of Washington. Thereafter, the West Penn Lighting Company intervened on the basis that it

---

60. 61 Pa. Super. 565-66.

61. 61 Pa. Super. 566, citing *Wheeler v. Philadelphia*, 77 Pa. 338 (1875), and *Seabolt v. Commissioners of Northumberland County*, 187 Pa. 318 (1898), for the proposition that legislation for a class distinguished from a general subject will not be deemed special legislation.

62. The full citation is *Relief Electric Light, Heat and Power Company's Petition*, 63 Pa. Super. 1 (1916) (Kephart, J.). The same issue was presented in a companion case decided the same day, *East End Electric Light, Heat and Power Company's Petition*, 63 Pa. Super. 16 (1916).

had served Washington for a number of years at reasonable rates. Following a hearing, the commission denied plaintiff's request for a certificate of public convenience. On appeal from the commission's decision, plaintiff challenged the Public Service Company Law on a number of constitutional bases. Most importantly, it argued that the legislature lacked the constitutional authority to regulate utility companies, and that the commission's decision violated the contract clauses of the state and federal constitutions because it deprived plaintiff of the opportunity to perform the contract with Washington and to pursue the business for which it was chartered.

A six-member majority of the court rejected both claims.[63] Initially, the majority found that since utility companies had a "peculiar relation" to the public interest, they could be regulated under the state's police power. This conclusion was based in large part on Pennsylvania's experience with utility companies:

> Unrestricted competition in such utilities has been, by experience, definitely shown to be ultimately unwholesome for the community. The invariable rule in such cases, in companies of this character, is that in addition to the cutting and destruction of rates and other practices entirely outside of the range of sound business, one company is absorbed and the surviving company recoups its loss through excessive charges, at the expense of an unprotected public.[64]

The court also found that the state had a particular interest in restraining competition among utility companies because of the "highly dangerous" nature of their business. "It is hardly necessary to say," the court noted, "that if this business could be dealt in generally by a large number of different concerns in competition, the streets and alleys in the municipality would be veritable death-traps for pedestrians."[65] Since it was reasonably intended to protect the health of the citizenry, the Public Service Company Law was upheld as a valid exercise of the state's constitutional police power. The court also rejected plaintiff's contract claim on the basis that corporate charters "are made and accepted in subordination to the police power of the State, which cannot be bargained away by the legislature."[66]

*Relief Electric* has been cited repeatedly to validate state regulation of public utilities. Most importantly, it stands for the proposition that such regulation falls within the proper exercise of the state's police power. This holding was applied by the Superior Court forty years later in *Pittsburgh v. Pennsylvania PUC*, a case which involved the constitutionality of the Public Utility Commission, the modern successor of the Public Service Commission.[67] *Relief Electric* has also been cited for the principle that contracts made by utility companies are subordinate to the state's exercise of the police power.[68]

---

63. 63 Pa. Super. 16. Judge Henderson dissented without opinion.

64. 63 Pa. Super. 11.

65. 63 Pa. Super. 11-12.

66. 63 Pa. Super. 7. Kephart also rejected plaintiff's contract claim regarding its corporate charter on the basis that the charter had not been recorded in the county in which Washington was located. 63 Pa. Super. 15-16.

67. See *Pittsburgh v. Pennsylvania PUC*, 182 Pa. Super. 551, 578 (1956) ("[T]he commission's delegated authority to regulate public utility rates . . . is derived from the police power of the state and is a valid exercise thereof.").

68. See *Burke v. Bryant*, 283 Pa. 114, 119 (1925) ("It is a well recognized principle of law that all contracts are made in subordination to a prospective exercise of the police power within legitimate limits by the state."); *New Street Bridge Co. v. Public Service Commission*, 271 Pa. 19, 34 (1921) ("We need not review the authorities sustaining the power of the commission as a government agency to control contracts of this nature, or to exercise regulatory control over service companies.").

IN THE SUPERIOR COURT OF PENNSYLVANIA

July 19, 1916.

It is ordered that the fees to be charged by the Prothonotaries of the Superior Court, as compensation for services rendered, not specified by acts of assembly, shall not be in excess of those mentioned in the following schedule:

IN THE SUPERIOR COURT OF PENNSYLVANIA

SCHEDULE OF FEES.

| | |
|---|---|
| Issuing Writ of Certiorari,................................. | $12.00 |
| "    "    " Habeas Corpus,............................. | 12.00 |
| "    "    " Mandamus,............................... | 12.00 |
| Petitions,................................................ | 1.00 |
| Discontinuance (if record has been sent up),............... | 5.00 |
| (if record has not been sent up),.......... | 4.00 |
| Non pres,................................ | 3.00 |
| Certificates of Transfer and of Orders due to Prothonotary, where transfer is made,............................. | 2.00 |
| Short Certificate (certifying attorney has been admitted to practice before Superior Court),................... | 1.00 |
| Certificate to Practice in another State,................. | 1.00 |
| Registration of attorneys to take final examination,........ | 1.00 |
| Admission of Attorneys,................................... | 5.00 |
| (Two Dollars of which shall be paid to the Crier). | |
| Certified copies of opinions per page (size 8x13). Average 350 words per page, first copy, per page...... | .40 |
| Additional copies, per page........................... | .15 |
| Transcript of Record when Writ of Error is taken to United States Supreme Court, per page, first ten pages,...... | .50 |
| each succeeding page,........... | .25 |
| Certifying case from Superior to Supreme Court in case where the appeal is erroneously taken to the Superior Court | 6.00 |
| No charge for affixing seal to any paper connected with proceedings in Court. | |

BY THE COURT.

CERTIFIED FROM THE RECORD.

IN TESTIMONY WHEREOF, I have hereunto set my hand and the seal of said Court, at Philadelphia, this 19th day of July, A. D. 1916.

*William A. Stone*
Prothonotary.

The July 1916 fee schedule established for services rendered by the Superior Court Prothonotary.

An even more important decision in the realm of public utility law was *Ben Avon Borough v. Ohio Valley Water Co.*,[69] which ultimately established a federal constitutional standard for judicial review of administrative decisions. In *Ben Avon*, the Public Service Commission instituted an investigation upon a complaint filed by the plaintiff/borough charging the defendant/water company with demanding unreasonable rates. Pursuant to the statute that created it, the commission determined the value of the company's property and fixed rates based on that value. The company appealed, arguing that the valuation upon which the commission established rates was much too low. This insufficient valuation, it was argued, deprived the company of a reasonable return on its investment and thus amounted to a confiscation of property without due process of law.[70]

A unanimous Superior Court reversed the order of the Public Service Commission. The lengthy opinion began by noting the "grave importance" of the commission's

---

69. 68 Pa. Super. 561 (1917) (Kephart, J.).
70. 68 Pa. Super. 575-76.

statutory duty to establish equitable utility rates. "A rate that is too low may deprive the members of the corporation of property that cannot be returned," the court found, "and if too high, the public is unjustly deprived of property."[71] The court then engaged in an extensive reevaluation of both the facts and the law applied by the commission in establishing its valuation. The court concluded that the valuation of the company's property was insufficient and remanded to the commission with directions to establish rates that would allow a 7 percent return on the company's investment.[72]

The borough then appealed, and the Pennsylvania Supreme Court reversed the determination of the Superior Court, finding that since there was sufficient evidence to sustain the commission's conclusion, no abuse of discretion occurred, and the Superior Court had improperly substituted its judgment for that of the commission.[73] The water company then appealed to the United States Supreme Court, arguing that the decision of the Pennsylvania Supreme Court operated to deprive it of an opportunity for judicial review of its allegation of confiscation. Since the decision of the Supreme Court precluded the Superior Court from conducting a review of the whole record, the company argued it denied them of due process of law. The United States Supreme Court agreed with this contention and reversed the Pennsylvania Supreme Court. "In all such cases," the court held, "if the owner claims confiscation of his property will result, the State must provide a fair opportunity for submitting that issue to a judicial tribunal for determination upon its own independent judgment as to both law and facts; otherwise the order is void because it is in conflict with the due process clause, Fourteenth Amendment."[74] The case was then remanded to the Pennsylvania Supreme Court, which, in turn, remanded it to the Superior Court with instructions that "said court determine, upon its own independent judgment as to the law and the facts involved, whether the order of the Public Service Commission of which the [water company] complains is confiscatory, and to make such disposition . . . as is required by the opinion of the Supreme Court of the United States."[75] In its opinion on remand, the Superior Court stated that it "complied with the order and have again reviewed the record and now adopt the conclusions stated in our former opinion as our present judgment of the law and the facts involved."[76] The borough again appealed, and the Pennsylvania Supreme Court affirmed the decision of the Superior Court.[77]

In the years after the United States Supreme Court validated the standard of review enunciated by the Superior Court, *Ben Avon* became the constitutional guidepost for courts examining administrative decisions. The "*Ben Avon* Doctrine," as it came to be known, was cited on dozens of occasions by the United States Supreme Court, other federal courts, and numerous state courts for the proposition that due process required independent judicial review of confiscation claims, and that such review encompassed reassessment of both the facts and law determined by an administrative agency.[78] Although it appears that this doctrine was ultimately supplanted by a standard permitting affirmance where administrative factual determinations are supported

---

71. 68 Pa. Super. 576.
72. 68 Pa. Super. 593.
73. *Ben Avon Borough v. Ohio Valley Water Co.,* 260 Pa. 289, 309 (1918).
74. *Ohio Valley Water Co. v. Ben Avon Borough*, 253 U.S. 287, 289 (1920).
75. The text of the order can be found at 75 Pa. Super. 290, 293 (1921).
76. 75 Pa. Super. 294.
77. *Ben Avon Borough v. Ohio Valley Water Co,* 271 Pa. 346 (1921).
78. See e.g., *State Corporation Commission of Kansas v. Wichita Gas*, 290 U.S. 561 (1934) (federal constitutional due process requires "independent judgement of the courts as to both law and facts."); *United Railways v. West*, 280 U.S. 234 (1930) (due process requires "independent judgment as to both law and facts."); *Pennsylvania Railroad v. Driscoll*, 336 Pa. 310 (1939); *Allegheny Steel v. New York Central Railroad*, 324 Pa. 353 (1936); *Pusey's Estate*, 321 Pa. 248 (1936); *Shirk v. Lancaster*, 313 Pa. 158 (1933).

The Superior Court in 1922. L-R: William B. Linn, Frank M. Trexler, William D. Porter, George B. Orlady (President Judge), John J. Henderson, William H. Keller, Robert S. Gawthrop.

by substantive evidence,[79] *Ben Avon* has never been overruled, and it has been cited by the Pennsylvania Supreme Court as recently as 1992.[80]

In addition to its decisions in workmen's compensation and public utility cases, the Superior Court also upheld the validity of statutes aimed at protecting women and child laborers. As we saw in the previous chapter, the doctrine of liberty of contract compelled the court to invalidate a series of general employment regulations in the last decade of the nineteenth century. Yet, even in that era, the court proved more receptive to statutes regulating the employment of women and children. For instance, in *Commonwealth v. Beatty*,[81] the court upheld an employer's conviction under an act prohibiting the employment of adult women for more than twelve hours per day.[82] Although it often spoke in general terms,[83] the court's opinion clearly turned on the fact that the statute protected women. For instance, the court wrote:

> It is undisputed that some employments may be admissible for males and yet improper for females, and regulations recognizing and forbidding women to engage in such would be open to no reasonable objection. . . . Sex imposes limitations to excessive or long-continued physical labor as certainly as does minority, and the arrested development of children is no more dangerous to the state, than debilitating so large a class of our citizens as adult females by undue and unreasonable physical labor.[84]

Although the court's decision in *Beatty* appears to be at odds with its invalidation of other employment regulations, it was in fact completely consistent with the jurisprudence of the era. Indeed, like the Superior Court in 1900, courts nationwide sanctioned legislative use of the police power to protect supposed vulnerable groups within the working class, although such protection was not permissible when extended

---

79. See e.g., *Surrick v. Zoning Hearing Board*, 11 Pa. Cmwlth. 607 (1974) ("[T]he United States Supreme Court has tended to ignore the *Ben Avon* doctrine in latter cases and had usually applied the substantive evidence rule to findings of fact made by administrative agencies.").

80. See *Foster v. Mutual Fire*, 531 Pa. 598 (1992).

81. 15 Pa. Super. 5 (1900) (Orlady, J.).

82. Pa. Act of April 29, 1897, PL 30.

83. For instance, in discussing the breadth of the police power, Judge Orlady noted that "[t]he length of time a laborer shall be subjected to the exhaustive exertion of physical labor is as clearly within legislative control as is the governmental inspection of boilers, machinery, etc., to avoid accidents . . . [and] to preserve the health of laborers." 15 Pa. Super. 16.

84. 15 Pa. Super. 18.

to adult male workers.[85] In light of this national trend, it is not surprising that the court upheld sweeping new employment regulations that were enacted on behalf of women and children in the Progressive Era. In 1915, for instance, the court upheld the Female Employment Act, which prohibited the employment of women under the age of twenty-one after 9:00 p.m., or for more than fifty-four hours in one week.[86] The same year, with Pennsylvania leading the nation in the number of working children, the legislature passed a new Child Labor Act, which made fourteen the minimum age for employment in all establishments, prohibited the employment of children under the age of sixteen before 6:00 a.m. or after 8:00 p.m., required the completion of the sixth grade for fourteen and fifteen-year-old working children, and prohibited employment in a lengthy list of dangerous occupations.[87] The constitutionality of the act was considered by the court in 1917 in the case of *Commonwealth v. Wormser.*[88] Rejecting a liberty of contract claim by an employer convicted of violating the act, the court stated that "[w]hat is a reasonable time within which children should be excluded from places of labor is a legislative question. It can hardly be contended that the State is without authority to protect persons of immature years from exposure to the danger and exhausting toil of factories."[89] In concluding, the court also noted:

> The fact that legislation of this character is of comparatively recent origin is not an argument against its validity. Law is an expanding science and the social order is in a constant process of evolution. That may become an important subject of legislation in the present condition of society which was ignored or regarded a matter of little consequence in years gone by.[90]

The court's statement in *Wormser* was equally applicable to all Progressive-Era social legislation. Whether compensating injured employees, regulating public utility companies, or protecting women and children from onerous working conditions, this legislation did indeed reflect "a constant process of evolution." By validating and construing the new laws, the Superior Court profoundly shaped that evolution.

---

85. As William Forbath has noted:

> The police power, courts often declared, could be invoked to protect "dependent" or "vulnerable" groups within the labor force, but it could not constitutionally reach the inequalities of fortune and power that arose from the "fact that some men are possessed of industrial property and others are not." The courts' relative hospitality toward hour laws for women and children encouraged and ratified within labor circles a gender-based division of the working class. William E. Forbath, "The Shaping of the American Labor Movement," 102 *Harv. L. Rev.* 1144.

86. *Commonwealth v. Mecca Cooperative Co.*, 60 Pa. Super. 314 (1915), upholding the Pa. Act of July 25, 1913, PL 1024.

87. Pa. Act of May 13, 1915, PL 286.

88. 67 Pa. Super. 444 (1917) (Henderson, J.).

89. 67 Pa. Super. 448.

90. See note 89. The Superior Court's decision was affirmed in *Commonwealth v. Wormser*, 260 Pa. 44 (1918).

## PROHIBITION

Long before the Eighteenth Amendment was ratified, prohibition of the sale of alcoholic beverages was a significant issue in Pennsylvania politics. As early as 1854, it failed in a statewide referendum by only 5,000 votes, out of a total 322,000 cast. In 1887, the legislature submitted to the electorate a constitutional amendment calling for Prohibition, but the amendment failed. When the issue arose on a national level in 1918, Pennsylvania ratified the Eighteenth Amendment by a plurality of more than 100,000 votes. Yet, even after Congress passed the Volstead Act to enforce the amendment, Pennsylvania enacted no enforcement measures of its own for nearly four years. In the meantime, as Prohibition cases flooded the courts, violators were prosecuted under the Brooks High License Law, a statute enacted in 1887, the same year the state prohibition amendment failed of passage.[91] The Brooks Law consisted of two discreet provisions: it established a licensing procedure for those interested in selling alcohol; and it prohibited all unlicensed sales.[92] Although the Brooks Law was always seen as a proper exercise of the state's police power, its continuing validity was called into question with the enactment of the Eighteenth Amendment and the Volstead Act. In particular, opponents of the Brooks Law argued that it was preempted by the federal laws. This question was presented to the appellate courts of Pennsylvania for the first time in 1921, when a series of five cases reached the Superior Court.

The first and most important of these cases was *Commonwealth v. Vigliotti*,[93] in which the defendant was convicted of selling "Jamaica Ginger," a beverage containing 88 percent alcohol. On appeal, Vigliotti argued that the Eighteenth Amendment and the Volstead Act superseded and thus invalidated the Brooks Law. The court began by noting that, pursuant to its first section, the Eighteenth Amendment made Prohibition "obligatory throughout the United States and therefore render[ed] inoperative every legislative act permitting what the section prohibits."[94] The court also recited the declaration of Section 2 that "Congress and the several states shall have concurrent power to enforce this article by appropriate legislation."[95] Since Pennsylvania had concurrent authority to enforce Prohibition, the question thus became whether the Brooks Law was "appropriate legislation." To answer this question, the court examined the intent of the law. "It had two purposes," it found, "to permit the granting of licenses to sell to some persons, and to forbid all other persons from dealing in the merchandise described."[96] Since the Eighteenth Amendment outlawed the use of alcohol, the court found that it invalidated the licensing provisions of the Brooks Law. Yet, this was not the end of the case. The court next found that the two purposes of the state law were severable, and that the latter purpose "tends to accomplish that which the federal legislation undertakes to do and is in no way inconsistent with or contradictory of the federal law." Since this part of the Brooks Law was "compatible" with the amendment, the court held it was "appropriate legislation" under Section 2. On this basis, the Superior Court affirmed Vigliotti's conviction,[97] and it applied this ruling to the other four cases raising the same issue.[98]

---

91. For an article discussing the judiciary's difficulty in coping with the volume of prohibition cases, see "Dry Cases Congest Courts in Penna.," *Philadelphia Public Ledger*, 30 Jan. 1929, p. 3, col. 1.

92. Pa. Act of May 13, 1887, PL 108.

93. 75 Pa. Super. 366 (1921) (Henderson, J.).

94. 75 Pa. Super. 369.

95. 75 Pa. Super. 370.

96. 75 Pa. Super. 375.

97. 75 Pa. Super. 377-78, 381. The court also disposed of Vigliotti's allegations of trial error.

98. See *Commonwwealth v. Vigliotti* (Vigliotti 2), 75 Pa. Super. 381 (1921); *Commonwealth v. Williams,*

Thereafter, Vigliotti continued to pursue his appeal. On May 26, 1921, the Pennsylvania Supreme Court affirmed the holding of the Superior Court, finding that "the [Brooks Law] is adapted to serve as an instrument with which to perform, at least in part, this State's right and obligation to enforce, 'by appropriate legislation,' the 18th Amendment."[99] A year later, the United States Supreme Court granted certiorari. In affirming the state courts, Justice Louis Brandeis found that the Brooks Law was "primarily a prohibitory law; and its prohibitory features are not so dependent upon those respecting license as to be swept away by the Eighteenth Amendment and the Volstead Act."[100] Moreover, he concluded:

> [It] does not purport to authorize or sanction anything which the Eighteenth Amendment or the Volstead Act prohibits. And there is nothing in it which conflicts with any provision of either. It is merely an additional instrument which the State supplies in the effort to make prohibition effective. That the State may by appropriate legislation exercise its police power to that end was expressly provided in [Section] 2 of the Amendment. . . . That the Brooks Law as construed is appropriate legislation is likewise clear.[101]

For the remaining years of Prohibition, *Vigliotti* was perhaps the most influential case in the nation construing concurrent federal and state authority to enforce the Eighteenth Amendment. It was cited more than a dozen times by the United States Supreme Court for the proposition that the amendment did not invalidate state laws that were not inconsistent with it.[102] In no less than seven of those cases, lower court rulings were affirmed or dismissed per curiam on the authority of *Vigliotti*.[103] Under Pennsylvania law, the case was equally significant.[104] Most importantly, in 1936, it was utilized by the Pennsylvania Supreme Court to reject a constitutional challenge to the newly established Liquor Control Board and State Store system.[105]

---

75 Pa. Super. 382 (1921); *Commonwealth v. Krizon,* 75 Pa. Super. 383 (1921); and *Commonwealth v. Mondalek,* 75 Pa. Super. 384 (1921).

99. *Commonwealth v. Vigliotti*, 271 Pa. 10, 15 (1921).

100. *Vigliotti v. Pennsylvania*, 258 U.S. 403, 408 (1922).

101. See note 100.

102. See *McCormick v. Brown*, 286 U.S. 131 (1932); *Donnelley v. United States*, 276 U.S. 505 (1928); *United States v. One Ford Coupe Auto*, 272 U.S. 321 (1926); *Van Oster v. Kansas*, 272 U.S. 465 (1926); *Hebert v. Louisiana*, 272 U.S. 312 (1926); *Barnes v. New York*, 266 U.S. 581 (1924); *Moore v. Idaho*, 264 U.S. 569 (1924); *Molinari v. Maryland*, 263 U.S. 685 (1924); *Walser v. City of Sioux Falls*, 263 U.S. 678 (1923); *Campbell v. North Carolina*, 262 U.S. 728 (1923); *Chandler v. Texas*, 260 U.S. 708 (1923); *United States v. Lanza*, 260 U.S. 377 (1922); *Edwards v. Georgia*, 258 U.S. 613 (1923).

103. See *Barnes, Moore, Molinari, Walser, Campbell, Chandler, Edwards*, supra.

104. See *Premier Cereal & Beverage Co. v. Pennsylvania Alcohol Permit Board*, 292 Pa. 127 (1928); *Commonwealth v. Dabbierio*, 290 Pa. 174 (1927); *Commonwealth v. Dietz*, 285 Pa. 511 (1926); *Hazle Drug Co. v. Wilner*, 284 Pa. 361 (1925); *Commonwealth v. Alderman*, 275 Pa. 483 (1923).

105. In *Commonwealth v. Stofchek*, 322 Pa. 513 (1936), the appellant argued that, by assuming responsibility for the sale of intoxicating liquors, the state had exceeded its constitutional authority to legislate under the police power. Citing *Vigliotti*, the Supreme Court rejected this claim on the basis that "one of [the police power's] well known objects is the protection of public health, and laws prohibiting the import, export, sale or transfer of articles deleterious to the public, such as intoxicating liquors are valid under it."

## SEDITION

Following the Bolshevik Revolution in October 1917, the United States experienced a dramatic increase in the number of groups calling for its violent overthrow. Because these groups, consisting primarily of Communists and Socialists, often focused on organized labor, they were especially active in industrially powerful Pennsylvania. As this activity increased, the state responded by passing a broad sedition act. As amended, the act defined "sedition" as "any writing, publication, printing, cartoon, utterance, or conduct, either individually or in connection or combination with any other person or persons, the intent of which is: (a) To make or cause to be made any outbreak or demonstration of violence against this State or against the United States; (b) To encourage any person or persons to take any measures or engage in any conduct with a view of overthrowing or destroying or attempting to overthrow or destroy, by any force or show or threat of force, the Government of this State or of the United States."[106] Primarily because it outlawed certain "utterance[s]" in addition to conduct, the Sedition Act proved extremely controversial. In a series of cases decided between 1922 and 1931, the Superior Court upheld the act against a number of constitutional challenges.

The first of these cases was *Commonwealth v. Blankenstein*,[107] in which the defendant, an alien and member of the Communist Party, was arrested in Pittsburgh while in possession of numerous documents calling for the violent overthrow of the state and federal governments. In order to establish the defendant's motive, the Commonwealth called as a trial witness one Lennon, who explained the agenda of the Communist Party, and the methods by which it sought to advance that agenda. The defendant presented no evidence and he was convicted of sedition. On appeal, he claimed the Sedition Act violated numerous provisions of the Pennsylvania Constitution, including: Article I, Section 1, guaranteeing freedom and independence, the right to life and property, the right to acquire and possess property and reputation, and the right to pursue happiness; Article I, Section 2, guaranteeing the right of the people to alter, reform or abolish their government in any manner they think proper; Article I, Section 20, guaranteeing the right to assemble for the common good and to petition for redress of common grievances or other proper purposes; and Article III, Section 20, forbidding the passage of bills containing more than one subject. The defendant also challenged the competency of Lennon to present testimony regarding the Communist Party.[108]

On appeal, the Superior Court rejected all of the defendant's claims. The court began by finding that the general freedom and property guarantees of Article I, Section 1, apply "only to those who live under the Constitution and are obedient to the laws of the Commonwealth," and do not extend to violations of the criminal law. "Nor was the second section of the article," the court continued, "intended to be permission to residents of other states or foreign countries to come into this Commonwealth for the purpose of altering, reforming or abolishing the government. The power to make such changes is in the citizens of Pennsylvania." The court found the defendant's claim to the contrary incredible. "That the Commonwealth has authority," it stated, "to enact legislation intended to preserve the stability of the government and to prevent the incitement of tumult tending to disturb the public peace and conduct tending to treason

---

106. Pa. Act of June 26, 1919, PL 639, as amended by the Pa. Act of May 10, 1921, PL 435. Congress also passed a sedition act in 1918 as part of the Second Espionage Act, 40 Stat. 553, but it was repealed by Congress in 1921, 41 Stat. 1359, 1360. Congress did not enact another sedition law until 1940. Thus, between 1921 and 1940, sedition was prosecuted as a state offense.

107. 81 Pa. Super. 340 (1923).

108. 81 Pa. Super. 341-42.

cannot be seriously questioned."[109] The court also noted, "[f]reedom of speech does not include the right of solicitation to commit a felony."[110] Next, the court found that the act had a single subject, sedition, and therefore that it complied with Article III, Section 20's prohibition of bills with multiple subjects.[111] Having rejected defendant's challenges to the constitutionality of the Sedition Act, the court also addressed the claim that Lennon's testimony was incompetent and relied on two noted cases to reject this claim.

The first case, *In re Debs*,[112] involved Eugene V. Debs, a socialist and anti-war activist convicted of inciting insubordination and mutiny during World War I. At Debs' trial, the convictions of other activists and a prominent anti-war proclamation were introduced into evidence, and the government argued that since Debs had expressed approval of the activists and the proclamation, the evidence helped the jury to understand the import of his activities and intentions. The second case relied on by the court was *Hester v. Commonwealth*,[113] in which evidence was introduced against a member of the "Molly McGuires," a militant organization of coal miners, to explain the purposes and motives of the organization. The trial court permitted the evidence on the basis that it helped to explain the defendant's motive for committing the felony at issue in the trial. Based on *Debs* and *Hester*, the court found, "A qualified witness is permitted to state a relevant fact not generally known but known by him because of his training and experience and this is so although the witness may not be regarded as an expert whose opinion would be admissible on a hypothetical inquiry."[114] Thus, the court held Lennon's testimony was properly admitted to explain the Communist Party, and defendant properly was convicted.[115]

Five years later, the court utilized its holding in *Blankenstein* to reject a claim that the Sedition Act violated the free speech guarantee of the state constitution. *Commonwealth v. Widovich*[116] involved the sedition convictions of four members of the Workers' Party of America, a branch of the Third International of Moscow, a communist group.[117] Three of the defendants were naturalized citizens of the United States, and the fourth had commenced the naturalization process. In anticipation of the ninth anniversary of the Soviet Union, the defendants, who were living in Beaver County, engaged in a variety of activities aimed at fomenting a Communist revolution against both the state and federal governments. One of the activities for which they were indicted and subsequently convicted was teaching by "word of mouth" from several books, including *The Theory and Practice of Leninism*, *The A.B.C. of Communism*, and *Manifesto of the Communist International*.

On appeal from their convictions, the defendants argued, inter alia, that the Sedition Act violated Article I, Section 7, of the state constitution, which guarantees that "every citizen may freely speak, write and print on any subject, being responsible for the abuse of that liberty." The Superior Court quickly rejected this claim. "A complete answer to [their] contention," the court held, "is found in a single sentence from the opinion in *Commonwealth v. Blankenstein*, supra,—'Freedom of speech does not include the right of solicitation to commit a felony.'"[118] The court also noted that the

---

109. 81 Pa. Super. 342.
110. 81 Pa. Super. 343. The opinion does not indicate whether defendant raised a free speech claim under Article I, Section 7 of the state constitution.
111. 81 Pa. Super. 343.
112. 249 U.S. 211 (1919).
113. 85 Pa. 139 (1878) (Henderson, J.).
114. 81 Pa. Super. 345.
115. 81 Pa. Super. 346.
116. 93 Pa. Super. 323 (1928) (Cunningham, J.). Widovich, the defendant whose name appears in the caption of the case, was not apprehended, and the trial proceeded against his four co-defendants.
117. 93 Pa. Super. 328.
118. 93 Pa. Super. 331-32, citing, *Blankenstein*, 81 Pa. Super. 343.

trial court properly charged the jury that defendants were not to be convicted because "they merely uttered certain sentiments." Instead, conviction was permissible only if "they had uttered certain things and have been guilty of doing certain things, the intent of which is the forcible overthrow of the government."[119] Finding the evidence in this regard sufficient against three of the four defendants, the Superior Court affirmed their convictions. The fourth defendant was discharged.[120] Thereafter, an appeal was taken to the Pennsylvania Supreme Court, which affirmed the decision of the Superior Court. The United States Supreme Court denied certiorari.[121]

A free speech challenge to the Sedition Act was also rejected by the Superior Court in *Commonwealth v. Lazar*.[122] In that case, the defendant, a naturalized citizen, addressed a crowd in Philadelphia on behalf of the Communist candidate for President of the United States. The defendant stated the following:

> This government murdered Sacco and Vanzett[i]. . . . This government is a strikebreaking government. . . . Let us teach our young workers in time of war to shoot down the people who ordered us to shoot on other people. . . . The only government in the world is the Russian Soviet. . . . We could not get into power by participating in the election campaign, in order for the Communists to get into power, it is necessary to have a revolution, only by a revolution can they gain the power in this country. . . . When the minority will refuse to submit to the will of the majority, and will use force and violence against the majority, then naturally the majority of the people will have to use force in order to combat the force of the minority.[123]

The defendant was convicted of sedition, and he appealed. In affirming the conviction, the court left little doubt that defendant's statements were beyond the protection of constitutional free speech guarantees. "The language used," the court held, "was a clear abuse of the inestimable privilege of free speech and was inimical to the public welfare. . . . [defendant's] ranting utterances clearly had for their purpose the undermining of the stability, and the usurping of the powers, by force, of the constituted authority."[124]

In addition to his free speech claim, the defendant also argued that he was not intending to incite *present* revolutionary action. In support of his claim, he directed the court's attention to *Schenck v. U.S.*, in which Justice Holmes said, "The question in every case is whether the words used are used in such circumstances and are of such a nature as to create a clear and present danger that they will bring about the substantive evils that Congress has a right to prevent."[125] Rejecting defendant's claim, the court noted a subsequent case in which the United States Supreme Court held that Holmes' statement was not applicable where, as in the instant case, "the legislative body itself has previously determined the danger of substantive evils arising from utterances of a specific character."[126] Continuing to quote from this latter case, the court held:

---

119. 93 Pa. Super. 332.
12093 Pa. Super. 338-39.
121. *Muselin v. Pennsylvania*, 280 U.S. 518 (1929).
122. 103 Pa. Super. 417 (1931) (Baldridge, J.).
123. 103 Pa. Super. 420.
124. 103 Pa. Super. 422-23.
125. 249 U.S. 47, 52 (1919).
126. 103 Pa. Super. 423, citing *Gitlow v. N.Y.*, 268 U.S. 652 (1925).

That utterances inciting to the overthrow of organized government by unlawful means present a sufficient danger of substantive evil to bring their punishment within the range of legislative discretion is clear. Such utterances, by their very nature, involve danger to the public peace and to the security of the state. They threaten breaches of the peace and ultimate revolution. And the immediate danger is none the less real and substantial because the effect of a given utterance cannot be accurately foreseen. . . . It cannot reasonably be required to defer the adoption of measures for its own peace and safety until the revolutionary utterances lead to actual disturbances of the public peace or imminent and immediate danger of its own destruction; but [the state] may, in the exercise of its judgment, suppress the threatened danger in its incipiency.[127]

Finally, the court found that the language of the Sedition Act "fixe[d] a definite and precise standard for the conduct of individuals."[128] On this basis, the defendant's claim that the act violated the Fourteenth Amendment of the United States Constitution was rejected. Thereafter, the Pennsylvania Supreme Court refused allocatur and the United States Supreme Court denied certiorari.[129]

Taken together, *Blankenstein*, *Widovich*, and *Lazar* validated the Pennsylvania Sedition Act against a variety of constitutional challenges. In fact, they remained perhaps the most important cases defining sedition under state law until 1940, when the Sedition Act was suspended by operation of law upon Congressional enactment of the Smith Act, a federal sedition law.[130]

## WAR CASES

The Superior Court also decided a series of diverse and important cases arising from World War I. The impact of war on state law is difficult to overstate. Under the so-called "War Power," the federal government is granted sweeping authority to regulate domestic affairs, and to mobilize the economy in the war effort. Numerous businesses are aggrieved by the new assertions of federal power, and they respond with a multitude of constitutional claims that begin in state courts. In addition to these cases pitting private enterprise against the government, numerous disputes between private parties are generated by war. During wartime, for instance, federal law suspends normal relations between citizens of belligerent nations. When peace is restored, private rights and remedies are revived, and citizens attempt to assert claims that arose before or during the war. Many of these claims, having arisen under state law, present complicated legal issues to state courts.

Particularly because of the state's massive industrial contributions to the war effort, Pennsylvania corporations were dramatically influenced by economic regulations promulgated under the War Power. The most significant of these regulations was the Fuel and Food Control Act, more widely known as the Lever Act.[131] This act created

---

127. 103 Pa. Super. 423, quoting *Gitlow*, 268 U.S. 669.

128. 103 Pa. Super. 424, quoting *Commonwealth v. Widovich*, 295 Pa. 311, 323 (1929), in which then-Justice Kephart affirmed the Superior Court's resolution in the same case.

129. *Lazar v. Pennsylvania*, 286 U.S. 532 (1932).

130. It was not until 1954, in *Commonwealth v. Nelson*, 377 Pa. 58, 63 (1954), that the Pennsylvania Sedition Act was deemed superseded by the Smith Act in 1940.

131. Pa. Act of August 10, 1917, c. 53, 40 St.L. 276, 284.

The Superior Court in 1929. L-R (seated): Frank M. Trexler, William D. Porter (President Judge), William H. Keller. L-R (standing): Jesse E. B. Cunningham, William B. Linn, Robert S. Gawthrop, Thomas J. Baldridge.

the United States Fuel Administration, which was vested with extensive authority to ensure the production and distribution of coal at reasonable prices. The act also authorized the president "to fix the price of coal and coke . . . during the war or for such part of said time as in his judgment may be necessary."[132] The constitutionality of the Lever Act was validated by the United States Supreme Court in a highly important case that began in the bituminous fields of Pennsylvania and passes through the Superior Court.

In *Highland v. Russell Car & Snow Plow Co.*,[133] the plaintiff, a Clearfield County coal company, agreed to supply the defendant with a quantity of coal at $3.60 per ton. The coal was shipped by the plaintiff between October 23, 1917, and February 14, 1918. However, by a proclamation dated August 21, 1917, President Woodrow Wilson had exercised his authority under the Lever Act and declared that coal in the Pennsylvania region encompassing Clearfield County must be sold at two dollars per ton. On October 27, 1917, the president increased the allowable sale price to $2.45. The defendant paid the plaintiff the price set forth by the president, and the plaintiff commenced an action to recover the original contract price of $3.60 per ton. The plaintiff received a jury verdict, but the trial court granted judgment non obstante verdicto on the ground that the price established under the Lever Act was controlling. The plaintiff appealed, arguing that the Lever Act invalidated his agreement with the defendant and thus violated the contract clause of the United States Constitution. The plaintiff also claimed the Lever Act deprived him of property (the unrecovered contract price) without due process of law.

A unanimous Superior Court rejected these claims. The court began by noting that the Lever Act and the subsequent executive orders issued under it were valid exercises of congressional authority under the War Power. Rejecting the plaintiff's con-

132. Pa. Act of August 10, 1917, sec. 25.
133. 87 Pa. Super. 235 (1926) (Gawthrop, J.).

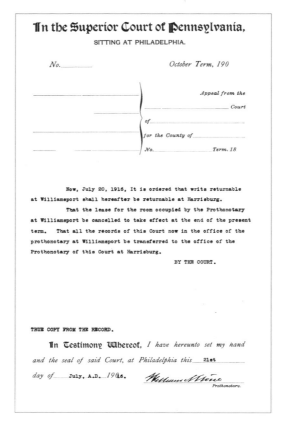

**In the Superior Court of Pennsylvania,**

SITTING AT PHILADELPHIA.

No._____

*October Term, 190*

*Appeal from the*

_____ *Court*

*of*_____

*for the County of*_____

*No.*_____ *Term. 18*

Now, July 20, 1916, It is ordered that writs returnable
at Williamsport shall hereafter be returnable at Harrisburg.

That the lease for the room occupied by the Prothonotary
at Williamsport be cancelled to take effect at the end of the present
term. That all the records of this Court now in the office of the
prothonotary at Williamsport be transferred to the office of the
Prothonotary of this Court at Harrisburg.

BY THE COURT.

TRUE COPY FROM THE RECORD.

**In Testimony Whereof,** *I have hereunto set my hand
and the seal of said Court, at Philadelphia this* 21st
day of July, A.D. 1916. *William N Stone*
                                                    *Prothonotary.*

This order of July 20, 1916 eliminated the Williamsport sessions of Superior Court,
closed the Williamsport office, and transferred the records to Harrisburg.

tract claim, the court held "[e]ven in times of peace private contract rights must yield to the public welfare where the latter is appropriately declared and defined and the two conflict."[134] "There would seem to be even greater justification," the court continued, "for interference with contract and property rights of individuals under the war power."[135] Moreover, the court noted that the Lever Act did not force plaintiff to sell its coal; it merely provided that if it chose to do so, the sale must be at a certain price. Plaintiff's due process claim also failed, the court held, because "[f]ixing a price at which a commodity may be sold is not a taking. Nor does it require a party to give up his property without adequate compensation." Finally, the court held that the contract relied upon by plaintiff was never valid because it was entered subsequent to, and therefore in violation of, the president's executive order of August 21, 1917, which established a coal price of two dollars per ton.[136] For all of these reasons, the court affirmed the judgment in favor of the defendant. On appeal, the Pennsylvania Supreme Court affirmed.[137] The Supreme Court rejected each of the defendant's claims. Like the Superior Court, the Supreme Court found that the Lever Act was a proper exercise of congressional author-

---

134. 87 Pa. Super. 238, citing *Union Dry Goods v. Georgia Public Service Commission*, 248 U.S. 372 (1919); *Armour Packing Co. v. U.S.*, 209 U.S. 56 (1908); *Hudson County Water Co. v. McCarter*, 209 U.S. 349 (1908).

135. 87 Pa. Super. 238.

136. 87 Pa. Super. 240.

137. *Highland v. Russell Car & Snow Plow Co.*, 288 Pa. 230 (1927) (Kephart, J.).

The Superior Court in 1930. L-R (seated): William H. Keller, Frank M. Trexler (President Judge), William B. Linn. L-R (standing): Thomas J. Baldridge, Robert S. Gawthrop, Jesse E. B. Cunningham, J. Frank Graff.

ity under the War Power. "A fair construction of the Constitution," the court held, "should leave no doubt as to the supreme power of Congress when war exists and that Congress may delegate powers such as these [in the Lever Act] to the president."[138] Moreover, the court continued, "the sections of the Lever Act, under consideration, may be upheld under the war powers, having a direct relation thereto, to which contracts made during the war are subject."[139]

Thereafter, the plaintiff pursued his case in federal court, again challenging the Lever Act as a violation of liberty of contract. He also continued to argue that Congress had no power to establish or authorize the president to prescribe prices for coal without providing just compensation for those who, in the absence of regulation, might have sold their coal for a higher price. In 1929, the case reached the United States Supreme Court. Rejecting the plaintiff's contract claim, the Supreme Court held that it "is also well-established by the decisions of this court that such liberty is not absolute or universal and that Congress may regulate the making and performance of such contracts whenever reasonably necessary to effect any of the great purposes for which the national government was created."[140] Moreover, the court held, "[u]nder the Constitution and subject to the safeguards there set for the protection of life, liberty and property, the Congress and the President exert the war power of the nation, and they have wide discretion as to the means to be employed successfully to carry on." On this basis, the Supreme Court upheld the constitutionality of the Lever Act and affirmed the decisions of the Pennsylvania state courts.[141]

138. 288 Pa. 235.
139. 288 Pa. 237.
140. *Highland v. Russell Car and Snow Plow Company,* 279 U.S. 253, 261 (1929).
141. 279 U.S. 261-62.

Judge John G. Whitmore

*Highland* has the rare distinction of standing for two important propositions of constitutional law. First, it has been cited repeatedly as indicating that freedom of contract, far from an absolute, is subject to a great variety of legislative restraints. Most importantly, when it conflicts with the power and duty of the state to safeguard its property and citizens, freedom of contract may be regulated and limited to the extent which reasonably may be necessary to carry that power and duty into effect.[142] In this regard, *Highland* was relied upon by the United States Supreme Court in the landmark case of *West Coast Hotel Co. v. Parrish*,[143] which signaled the demise of liberty of contract as a substantive restraint on economic regulations. Finally, *Highland* has been cited as indicative of the scope of congressional and the presidential authority under the War Power.[144]

In addition to claims challenging governmental authority during wartime, disputes between private parties following a war also present significant challenges to state courts. Perhaps the most difficult of these challenges involve the application of statutes of limitations to claims arising before or during a war. Although it is well settled that such statutes are suspended during "a state of war," determining the date on which the suspension ends with regard to different nations often proves difficult. Due to the unprecedented international scope of World War I, this question arose re-

---

142. See e.g., *Berman v. Parker*, 348 U.S. 26 (1954); *Virginian Railway Co. v. System Federation No. 40*, 300 U.S. 515 (1937); *Continental Illinois National Bank & Trust v. Chicago, Rock Island & Pacific Railroad*, 294 U.S. 648, 680 (1935); *Hartford Accident & Indemnity Co. v. N.O. Nelson Mfg. Co.*, 291 U.S. 352 (1934); *Stephenson v. Binford*, 287 U.S. 251 (1932).

143. 300 U.S. 379, 392 (1937) ("The courts have recognized a wide latitude for the legislature to determine the necessity for protecting the peace, health, safety, morals and general welfare of the people. Where there is no reasonable ground for supposing that the legislature's determination is not supported by the facts, or that its judgment is one of speculation rather than from experience, its findings are not reviewable.").

144. See e.g., *E.I. DuPont De Nemours & Co. v. Hughes*, 50 F. 2d 821 (3rd Cir. 1931); *U.S. v. City of Philadelphia*, 56 F. Supp. 862 (1944).

peatedly before the Superior Court during the 1920s. In *Zeliznik v. Lytle Coal Co.*,[145] for instance, the court considered a workmen's compensation claim brought by the widow and child of a coal miner killed in Pennsylvania during the course of his employment. The employee, a native of Austria-Hungary, was killed in Schuylkill County on August 20, 1917, while in the employ of the Lytle Coal Company. His widow and child were residents of Austria-Hungary who never entered the United States. The coal company argued in defense that since the family's claim was not filed until 1921, it was untimely under the one-year statute of limitations contained in the state workmen's compensation statute. Although it acknowledged that the limitation period was suspended during the war because the United States and Austria-Hungary were belligerents, the company argued that the region occupied by the decedent's family fell within the borders of Czechoslovakia, which became independent of Austria-Hungary and was recognized as such by the United States in September 1918. Thus, it was argued, the family had one year from that time to file their claim, and that the subsequent filing in 1921 was untimely. The Workmen's Compensation Board rejected this claim and rendered an award to the family.

The question presented on appeal to the Superior Court was whether the recognition of Czechoslovakia, which was not at war with the United States, revived the statute of limitations against citizens of that country. The court began its analysis of this question by noting that the action of the United States in recognizing the independence of Czechoslovakia "cannot be doubted and the courts are bound by such action." Yet, this conclusion did not resolve the case. The court went on to examine whether Czechoslovakia was actually independent of the Austro-Hungarian Empire. Such independence, it held, could be achieved only by "secession successfully maintained or by treaty."[146] Czechoslovakia had achieved neither by 1918. Although acknowledging that "[a] rebellion was in progress against the parent government and armies were in the field asserting by force the independence," the court nonetheless concluded, "the extent of the territory over which the new republic was subsequently to exercise sovereignty had not then been effectively determined."[147] Since the territorial question was not resolved until treaties were ratified in 1921, the court held a state of war "technically existed" until that time between the United States and the empire encompassing Czechoslovakia. Thus, the workmen's compensation statute of limitations was not revived until 1921, and the claim of decedent's family, which was filed the same year, was timely.[148]

The court considered a similar issue four years later in *Arnold v. Ellison*,[149] which involved an assumpsit action by a German textile company against a Philadelphia importer for payment on a series of orders made by the latter between March 7 and June 20, 1914. Payment on the first order was due June 22, 1914. The defendant never received the payment, and it finally brought suit on October 2, 1924. In defense, the defendant raised the six-year statute of limitations on contract actions. Although the defendant conceded that the statute of limitations was suspended as of April 6, 1917, when the war between the United States and Germany began, it argued that the statute was revived on July 14, 1919, when the War Trade Board issued an order granting a general license to citizens of this country to resume trade and communications with citizens of Germany. This order, the defendant argued, allowed the plaintiff to commence his action at any time on or after the date it was issued. Alternatively, the

---

145. 82 Pa. Super. 489 (1924) (Henderson, J.).
146. 82 Pa. Super. 491.
147. 82 Pa. Super. 491-92.
148. 82 Pa. Super. 492.
149. 96 Pa. Super. 118 (1929) (Cunningham, J.).

defendant argued that the statute was revived no later than July 2, 1921, when a Joint Resolution of Congress declared the war at an end. In either case, the defendant argued, plaintiff's claim was entirely or substantially barred. The Court of Common Pleas of Philadelphia County rejected the defendant's claims and entered an award in favor of the plaintiff. The defendant appealed.

The Superior Court began its analysis by stating the question at issue:

> Whether or not this [plaintiff's claim] was too late depends primarily upon the determination of the question when the state of war existing between this country and Germany was legally terminated, and, secondarily, upon the inquiry whether private remedies available to citizens of the two countries became actionable prior to that date.[150]

Citing federal precedent, the court noted that a state of war is terminated only when the belligerent nations exchange ratifications of a peace treaty, which occurred between the United States and Germany on November 11, 1921. The court then considered whether this "general rule" was altered by the defendant's claims relating to the order of the War Trade Board or the Joint Resolution of Congress. Rejecting the first claim, the court looked to the statute authorizing the Trade Board's order, the Trading With the Enemy Act, Section 7(b), of which provided that "nothing in this act shall be deemed to authorize the prosecution of any suit or action at law or in equity in any court within the United States by an enemy or ally of enemy prior to the end of the war."[151] The act further defined "end of the war" as meaning "the date of proclamation of exchange of ratifications of the treaty of peace."[152] Thus, the defendant's first claim was denied because the statute which authorized the order he cited endorsed, rather than rejected, the rule that the war did not end until treaty ratifications were exchanged. The defendant's claim that a Joint Declaration of Congress ended the war also failed on this basis. "A state of war cannot be terminated by a mere declaration by one of the belligerents," the Superior Court held. "The actual termination of a war is a mutual matter evidenced by a treaty, duly ratified by both parties, and it cannot properly be said that a war has ended until the ratifications have been exchanged."[153] Since Germany and the United States exchanged ratifications on November 14, 1921, the court concluded that the war did not end until that date. Thus, the plaintiff's claim was filed approximately two years and eleven months after the end of the war, and since less than two years and ten months had lapsed between when payment on the first contract was due and the start of the war, the claim was filed more than three months before the six-year statute of limitations expired. On this basis, the trial court's award in favor of the plaintiff was affirmed.

Zeleznik and Arnold became important precedents for determining when a war ends for purposes of state statutes of limitations. In the wake of World War II, for instance, Zeleznik was cited by a federal court for the proposition that "[w]ar can only end by treaty of peace between the belligerent countries, and while war continues the courts of each belligerent are closed to nationals of the other country. Statute of limitations will not be permitted to run against an alien."[154]

---

150. 96 Pa. Super. 121.
151. 40 Statutes at Large 411, Chap. 106.
152. 96 Pa. Super. 123.
153. 96 Pa. Super. 124.
154. *Frabutt v. N.Y., Chicago and St. Louis Railroad Co.*, 84 F. Supp. 460, 465 (U.S.D.C., W.D. Pa. 1949).

As the foregoing cases demonstrate, a diverse array of national and international factors shaped the work of the court in the two decades after 1910. In turn, the court's rulings helped to shape both state and federal law. Many of these rulings, especially those construing the workmen's compensation and public utility statutes, contributed to the development of new areas of law that remain important today. Even the court's decisions relating to Prohibition, war, and sedition outlived the events that gave rise to them, and established precedents that became useful to other courts and other events.

## CRIMINAL LAW

A final case warrants consideration. This case involved the practice of numerous judges in Philadelphia conducting criminal trials without juries. While this practice is today quite commonplace, it was strictly prohibited under the common law. Despite the prohibition, however, Judge Edwin O. Lewis of the Philadelphia Court of Common Pleas began to conduct nonjury criminal trials in March 1926, and his experiment was soon replicated by a number of other Philadelphia judges. Judge Lewis believed that the "prime advantage of [nonjury trials] would be improvement in the administration of criminal justice. We would have prompt trials of those charged with crime, very few appeals and speedy punishment while the crimes were still fresh in the public mind."[155] The practice was employed for more than a year before it was challenged on appeal. Finally, in 1927, the case of *Commonwealth v. Hall* reached the Superior Court.[156] The case involved the assault indictment of James Hall, who waived his right to a jury trial and was convicted by Judge Lewis.

On appeal, Hall argued that he was constitutionally entitled to a trial by jury, regardless of the fact that he had waived that right. The Superior Court agreed. Following a lengthy review of relevant authorities and an examination of the constitutional mandate of jury trials for all criminal cases, the court concluded "that the learned Judge of the court below was without jurisdiction to try and determine the issues of fact involved, without the intervention of a jury." The court concluded that the judiciary must not initiate a change in the legal system as important as that attempted by Lewis. "Until the Legislature does by statute confer jurisdiction upon the court to try issues of fact in criminal cases without the aid of a jury," the court noted, "the courts are without jurisdiction to so proceed." Nor did it matter that Hall had waived his right to a jury trial, since the trial court lacked jurisdiction to honor the waiver. Finally, the court deemed irrelevant Lewis' claim that trials without juries expedited the administration of justice and saved both time and money. "Such arguments," the court held, "ought not to have weight with the courts and thus induce them to usurp legislative functions."[157] For these reasons, the Superior Court reversed Hall's conviction, although it meant that numerous other convictions also had to be overturned. The Commonwealth appealed, and the state Supreme Court affirmed, stating, "We agree with the Superior Court that, if this revolution in judicial procedure is at all permissible, the legislature must ordain it; in the present situation, for the courts to first make the change would amount to judicial legislation, a practice which we in Pennsylvania strive to avoid."[158] Thus ended what the press dubbed "Judge Lewis' experiment" of "trials minus jury,"[159]

---

155. Lewis' statement, made in March 1926, is quoted in the *Philadelphia Public Ledger*, 7 Oct. 1927, p. 1, col. 4.

156. 91 Pa. Super. 485 (1927) (Porter, J.).

157. 91 Pa. Super. 494

158. *Commonwealth v. Hall*, 291 Pa. 341, 354 (1928).

159. See e.g., *Philadelphia Public Ledger*, 7 Oct. 1927, p. 1, col. 4.

and *Hall* was repeatedly cited in the following years for the proposition that the right to a jury trial in criminal cases may not be waived.[160] Finally, in 1935, the legislature enacted P.L. 319, which provided for waiver of jury trials in criminal cases,[161] and six years later the Superior Court sustained the constitutionality of the statute.[162]

## THE CHANGE CONTINUES

Like the quality of the court's work, the quantity remained high in the years after 1910. Indeed, while the court averaged approximately 575 cases per year in its first fifteen years, this number had grown to 615 by 1917. Yet, the case load of the Supreme Court, which was already cut in half in the years following 1895, continued to decline. While the high court decided 634 cases in 1907, this number was 575 by 1917.[163] Thus, despite the Commonwealth's continued growth, the workload of the Supreme Court experienced an absolute decline. By the early 1920s, this decline allowed the court to routinely clear its docket. Indeed, by 1925, the high court's docket had been cleared for four years in a row, and members of the bar were boasting that "probably no other appellate court in the country has such a splendid record."[164] This was a marked improvement over the condition prevailing before the Superior Court was established, when the Supreme Court often had more than 100 cases remaining on its docket at the end of each year.

Personnel turnover, different types of cases, and an expanding caseload were not the only changes the court experienced between 1911 and 1930. Most importantly, its jurisdiction also expanded significantly. In 1923, for instance, the court's jurisdictional limit was increased to $2,500.[165] It also received exclusive jurisdiction over appeals from the Public Service Commission in 1915[166] and the Workmen's Compensation Board.[167] As a result of these changes, the Superior Court's jurisdiction by 1930 included all civil cases in which the amount in controversy did not exceed $2,500, all criminal cases except felonious homicides, all cases from the Public Service Commission, and all workmen's compensation cases. Cases involving questions of constitutionality could be appealed from the Superior Court to the Supreme Court as of right, but all other appeals were subject to the discretion of the Supreme Court.

In the years after 1910, the legislature also amended the Superior Court Act in a number of respects. Judges salaries and staff allowances were repeatedly raised,[168]

---

160. See e.g., *Commonwealth v. Dillworth*, 431 Pa. 479 (1968), and *Commonwealth v. Robinson*, 317 Pa. 321 (1935).

161. Pa. Act of June 11, 1935, PL 319. In 1968, this statute was recodified as Rule 1101 of the Code of Criminal Procedure.

162. See *Commonwealth v. Kramer,* 146 Pa. Super. 91 (1941).

163. *Philadelphia Public Ledger*, 13 May 1918, p. 9, col. 4.

164. *Philadelphia Public Ledger*, 28 June 1925, p. 2, col. 1, citing the remarks of former Judge Theodore Jenkins.

165. Pa. Act of March 2, 1923, PL 2, amending the Pa. Act of May 5, 1899, PL 248.

166. Pa. Act of June 3, 1915, PL 779.

167. Pa. Act of April 5, 1929, PL 173, amending the Pa. Act of June 2, 1915, PL 736. Prior to 1929, the Superior Court shared jurisdiction with the Supreme Court.

168. On April 9, 1915, the legislature increased to $2,500 the amount judges could be reimbursed for "stenographers, typewriters, or clerks." The act also shifted responsibility for supplying the court with dockets, books, and stationary from the secretary of the Commonwealth to the superintendent of Public Printing and Binding, and for supplying "other necessary supplies" from the secretary to the Board of Public Grounds and Buildings." Pa. Act of April 9, 1915, PL 45, amending Section 9, Pa. Act of May 5, 1899, as amended by the Act of April 17, 1905. Fours years later, the legislature authorized Superior Court judges to hire briefers and investigators, and increased the staff reimbursement amount to $3,500. Pa. Act of June 18, 1919, PL 246, amending the Pa. Act of May 5, 1899, PL 248, as amended by the Act of April 9, 1915, PL 77. Interestingly, in

and the original act was clarified to provide that seniority of reelected judges would be determined by date of first election rather than by casting lots.[169] The court was also permitted to designate two of its members to write opinions, rather than sit and hear cases, during sessions.[170] Further, the legislature replaced the mandatory language of the original act and provided that the court "*may* meet once a year in the cities of Philadelphia, Pittsburgh, Harrisburg, Scranton, and Williamsport." Finally, the legislature directed the court to appoint its own prothonotaries in Philadelphia, Harrisburg, and Pittsburgh.[171]

Between 1911 and 1916, the court maintained its prior schedule, sitting at Williamsport in February, Scranton and Harrisburg in March, Pittsburgh in April and May, and Philadelphia in October, November, and December. In 1917, the court stopped sitting at Williamsport. Two years later, bills were introduced in the legislature to make Harrisburg the permanent seat of the Supreme and the Superior Courts. While the bills were under consideration, the *Philadelphia Public Ledger* conducted a statewide survey of lawyers. According to the *Ledger*, the majority favored Harrisburg as the permanent home of the appellate courts.[172] Nonetheless, the bills were defeated in the legislature, and the Superior Court continued to meet at Scranton, Harrisburg, Pittsburgh, and Philadelphia. Finally, in 1929, a bill was introduced proposing construction in Philadelphia of a building for the sole use of the appellate courts while sitting in that city.[173] This bill was also defeated, and the Superior Court continued to meet at City Hall while in Philadelphia.

Two other significant proposals were directed at the court. The first emerged from the Commission on Constitutional Amendment and Revision, which was appointed in 1919 by innovative Governor William C. Sproul to study constitutional reform and report its recommendations.[174] The so-called Sproul Commission was comprised of many of the state's leading politicians and legal scholars and, after a year of deliberations, it proposed 132 changes that touched nearly every article of the constitution.[175] As to the judiciary article, the commission proposed an amendment that would have made the Superior Court a constitutional court.[176] According to Hampton L. Carson, the former

1920 and 1921, the Office of Prothonotary in Philadelphia was vacant, leading a city newspaper to question whether the job was anything more than a "convenient retiring place for superannuated politicians and others, providing them with a comfortable salary and nothing to do." *Philadelphia Public Ledger,* 23 Jan. 1923, p. 10, col. 1.

169. This new provision, the Pa. Act of May 6, 1915, PL 155, clarified Section 2 of the original Superior Court Act, which provided only that "the successful candidates shall cast lots for priority of commission."

170. Pa. Act of May 6, 1915, PL 156, amending Pa. Act of June 24, 1895.

171. Pa. Act of May 6, 1915, PL 156. The court previously shared prothonotaries with the Supreme Court.

172. *Philadelphia Public Ledger,* 18 May 1918, p. 9, col. 1.

173. *Philadelphia Public Ledger,* 12 Feb. 1929, p. 8, col. 1.

174. The Commission was authorized by the Pa. Act of June 4, 1919, PL 388. Although a product of the Republican machine, Sproul was thoroughly progressive. In addition to his emphasis on constitutional reform, Sproul consolidated and improved the state's education system, developed a state highway system, created the Department of Public Welfare, and reorganized the banking and insurance departments, the National Guard, and the executive staff. See Philip Klein and Ari Hoogenboom, *A History of Pennsylvania* (University Park: Pennsylvania State University, 1973), 442.

175. Commission on Constitutional Amendment and Revision, *Report of the Commission to the General Assembly,* December 15, 1920, 5-7. The chairman of the commission was Attorney General William Schaffer. The commission's members included United States Senator George Wharton Pepper, former Attorney General Hampton Carson, and future Governor Gifford Pinchot, among others. For a description of the commission's work, see Rosalind L. Branning, *Pennsylvania Constitutional Development* (Pittsburgh: University of Pittsburgh Press, 1960), 130-32.

176. *Report of the Commission,* 46. This amendment, designated Section 5, also provided that Superior Court judges would be elected for a term of twenty-one years, and that no judge may be reelected. For an article reporting the proposed judicial changes, see "Change in Courts' Status Proposed: Constitutional Revi-

attorney general and chairman of the subcommittee that proposed judicial changes, such an amendment was warranted because "the superior court had been so long in existence and discharging so satisfactorily its appellate duties . . . that that court had justified its right to be regarded as a constitutional court."[177] Subsequent discussions among commission members also reveals that the Superior Court was viewed in a favorable light. For instance, in declaring that he would vote against a proposal to increase the Supreme Court from seven to nine justices, Judge Edward J. Fox of Northampton County stated, "I confirm what has been stated on the floor here that so far as my observation goes since the supreme court has been relieved by the creation of the superior court that the work is not of such a character that the supreme court requires any relief by adding additional justices."[178] Commission member James Reed agreed:

> Are those two judges needed on the [Supreme Court] bench? Well, some of us doubt it. I know one justice of the supreme court who when the summer vacation came said that he was absolutely out of work. He did not have a thing to do; he walked a little, he tried to play golf, read until his eyes gave out, and then nearly four months after he had written his last opinion he was no better than, to use his own expression, a tramp. He did not have a thing to do that interested him. There is no overwork. I do not think there is any demand for relief. The superior court has relieved the supreme court of a great deal of work, and, of course, you do not make the court any more respected by the people by adding to its number. So that coming back to the original position it seems to me that upon the theory of changing this Constitution as little as possible, and only where there is a manifest evil to overcome, or a necessity to be met, that we should not make this change.[179]

Sentiments like those expressed by Fox and Reed prevailed, and the commission defeated the proposal to increase the Supreme Court.[180] Ultimately, the commission submitted its proposed amendments to the general assembly, along with a call for a constitutional convention to incorporate the amendments. Many Pennsylvanians, however, opposed the calling of a convention. Conservatives feared that the social unrest, which often followed war, would cause the convention to be dominated by radicals, and liberals believed that Governor Sproul would appoint the entirety of the relatively conservative members of the commission as convention delegates.[181] Opposed on two sides, the call for a convention was defeated on a statewide referendum by nearly 100,000 votes.[182] Although the Superior Court would not be incorporated into the constitution for nearly half a century thereafter, the work of the commission in 1920 reveals a great deal about the court's growing status. In 1910, it will be recalled, a single vote prevented the state bar association from calling for the court's abolition. Less than a decade later, the leading political and legal figures of Pennsylvania agreed that the court had "justified its right" to become part of the constitution.

---

sion Commission Asked to Make Superior Court Constitutional Body," *Philadelphia Public Ledger*, 15 Nov. 1920, p. 8, col. 1.

177. Commission on Constitutional Amendment and Revision, *Proceedings of the Commission*, vol. I, January 20, 1920, 307.

178. *Proceedings of the Commission*, vol. I, 313.

179. *Proceedings of the Commission*, vol. I, 316.

180. *Proceedings of the Commission*, vol. I, 318.

181. *Pennsylvania Constitutional Development*, 132.

182. *Pennsylvania Constitutional Development*, 132, citing *Smull's Legislative Handbook*, 1921-22, 763.

A final attempt to change the court resulted from the desperation of Democrats to secure representation on the court. In 1913, the legislature enacted the Nonpartisan Ballot Law, which provided that candidates for judicial office would appear on primary ballots without party designations, and that electors could vote only for as many candidates as there were seats to fill.[183] This law ensured that, regardless of party affiliation, only the candidate for each seat who received the highest vote at the primary would appear on the ballot at the general election.[184] By placing nominating power in the electorate, the law was intended to diminish the influence of political organizations in selecting judges. Nonetheless, the law did not prove helpful to the Democrats. As noted, the original Superior Court Act sought to ensure at least one minority representative on the bench by providing that electors could vote for only six of the seven judges. In keeping with this original provision, a 1907 law provided that where two vacancies occurred on the court, electors could vote for only one candidate, and a 1913 law further provided that where four vacancies occurred, electors could vote for only three candidates. On June 1, 1915, consistent with the intention of the Nonpartisan Ballot Law to diminish the influence of politics in judicial elections, the legislature repealed the laws providing for minority representation on the Superior Court bench.[185] Although the Nonpartisan Ballot Law was ultimately repealed as ineffective, the laws providing for minority representation on the Superior Court were not reinstated.[186]

Without these protective laws, the Democrats found it impossible to secure a seat on the court. Indeed, no Democrat was elected after 1905, when Judge Head won the fourth open seat in a field with only three Republicans,[187] and this trend continued until 1934. By 1929, the Democrats were desperate. In that year, two seats opened on the Superior Court, and Henry C. Niles and George F. Douglas won the Democratic primary election in September. If the 1907 law had remained in effect, electors would have been to able to vote for only one of their party's candidates, and either Niles or Douglas would have stood a greatly improved chance of election. Yet, the law had been repealed in 1915, and Pennsylvania's heavy Republican majority made the election of either Niles or Douglas extremely unlikely. Officials of the Democratic State Committee considered challenging the constitutionality of the legislature's decision to repeal the minority representation laws.[188] With no time remaining for a legal challenge, however, Niles and Douglas took an extreme measure shortly before the general election. Based upon an apparent agreement between the men, Douglas withdrew from the race, thereby allowing the Democratic Committee to concentrate its efforts and resources on securing Niles' election. Both men also made a public appeal to the voters to abide by "the old custom" of electing one candidate from each party.[189] Voters disregarded this

---

183. Pa. Act of June 24, 1913, PL 1001. Section 5 of the act provided that electors could vote for "no greater number of persons for nomination to any office than the number for which he could vote at the succeeding [general] election for the same office."

184. Since the Nonpartisan Ballot Law essentially ensured that primary victors would win the general election, it was widely criticized. See e.g., *Philadelphia Public Ledger*, 10 Oct. 1915, p. 12, col. 2 ("Under [the law as interpreted], the three Judges of the Superior Court have been elected already, the placing of their names on the ballot for the election on November 2 being a mere formality, for they will have no opposition."). By removing judges from the controversy of partisan politics, the law also appeared to reduce voter interest in judicial elections. See e.g., *Philadelphia Public Ledger*, 31 Oct. 1918, p. 8, col. 1 ("[I]t has been the universal experience in Pennsylvania that ever since the passage of the nonpartisan judicial ballot law a lamentable large proportion of the voters overlook or neglect the duty of voting for judges."); and *Philadelphia Public Ledger*, 26 July 1914, p. 1, col. 4. ("Interest Lagging in Judicial Contest").

185. Pa. Act of May 13, 1915, PL 100.

186. The Nonpartisan Ballot Law was repealed by the Pa. Acts of 1921, PL 423 and PL 426.

187. Head received barely half the votes of Judges Rice, Beaver, and Orlady. In 1915, Head was reelected without a party designation pursuant to the Nonpartisan Ballot Law.

188. See *Philadelphia Public Ledger*, 10 Oct. 1929, p. 10, col. 7.

189. See note 188 and *Philadelphia Public Ledger*, 12 Oct. 1929, p. 2, col. 4 (noting that "Philadelphia

appeal, however, and Republicans Baldridge and Keller each received nearly ten times the votes cast for Niles.[190] Yet, even as Democrats were engaging in desperate measures to secure a single seat on the court, an event had already begun that would transform the fortunes of their party. This event—the Great Depression—began a process that would elevate the Democrats to a prominence that Niles and Douglas could not have imagined.

---

Democrats are not inclined to agree with the logic of [this appeal].").
190. The votes were as follows: Keller, 287,920; Baldridge, 274,904; Niles, 33,460. *Philadelphia Public Ledger*, 6 Nov. 1929, p. 1, col. 5.

The Superior Court in 1933.
L. to R. (seated): William H. Keller, Frank M. Trexler (President Judge), Jesse E. B. Cunningham. L. To R. (standing): William M. Parker, Thomas J. Baldridge, Joseph Stadtfeld, Arthur H. James.

# Chapter Four

# The Great Depression, the "Little New Deal," and a Return to War: 1931-1950

## The Great Depression

Like the two decades prior to 1930, the two decades that followed were dominated by issues of national importance. Yet, the legislation that accompanied Progressivism and Prohibition, and the new legal questions that arose from World War I, were only a dress rehearsal for what followed. Beginning in the early 1930s, Congress enacted sweeping new laws aimed at remedying the social and economic inequalities exposed by the Great Depression. This legislation, which was replicated during Pennsylvania's "little New Deal," had no precedent in the common law and courts found little guidance in attempting to construe and apply it. Moreover, as the broad new statutes accumulated, the legislature was required to delegate an ever-increasing amount of responsibility to administrative bodies, and courts were repeatedly called upon to distinguish between legitimate delegations of rule-making authority and unconstitutional delegations of legislative authority. Finally, like the legislation of the New Deal, the scope of World War II was unprecedented, and for years after the fighting ended, courts were dealing with its effects. Not surprisingly, these factors—the Depression, the New Deal, and World War II—influenced the work of the Superior Court to a remarkable degree between 1931 and 1950.

As its name suggests, the Great Depression was the most devastating economic crisis in American history. Although its precise causes have long been the subject of debate, there is little question that the Depression was triggered by deep structural flaws in the nation's economy. Too few companies controlled too much of the market, demand could not keep pace with the exploding supply of consumer goods, banks did not have sufficient reserves to cover bad loans, and America was too dependent on foreign trade. The consequences of these flaws became dramatically apparent beginning with the stock market crash of "Black Tuesday," October 29, 1929. Less than three years later, the market retained barely 10 percent of its 1929 value.[1] Worse yet, banks failed by the hundreds, farmers lost their land by the thousands, and unemployment soared to more than 25 percent of the nation's workforce. When the conservative efforts of Herbert Hoover failed to relieve the crisis, the nation turned to Franklin Roosevelt in

---

1. On August 31, 1929, the *New York Times* list of industrials was 449; on July 8, 1932, it was fifty-eight. Philip S. Klein and Ari Hoogenboom, *A History of Pennsylvania*, 2d ed. (University Park: Pennsylvania State University, 1980), 449.

A common sight in the Great Depression—an unemployment line *(Carnegie Library of Pittsburgh)*.

the fall of 1932. When his own moderate measures proved insufficient, the pragmatic Roosevelt, beginning in the spring of 1935, initiated the most radical phase of the New Deal. States followed suit, and the resulting flood of legislation transformed existing law and involved the government in the lives of the citizenry to an unprecedented degree.

Although it is difficult to overstate the impact of the Great Depression on nearly every segment of American life, the most important changes occurred in the areas of social legislation, labor relations, and politics. Change in the first of these areas was motivated primarily by the need to relieve the tremendous problem of unemployment. The main federal unemployment measure, the Social Security Act, was proposed by President Roosevelt and passed by Congress in 1935. In addition to establishing a system of old age relief and a pension fund for workers, the act created a comprehensive program of employer-funded unemployment insurance.[2] In a pattern repeated throughout the New Deal, Pennsylvania followed Congress' lead and enacted its own unemployment compensation law in 1936. Like its federal counterpart, Pennsylvania's new statute had no precedent in the common law, and its construction was a central task of the Superior Court.

The second significant impact of the Great Depression was in labor relations, and change in this realm was especially resonant in heavily unionized Pennsylvania. Until the Depression, corporations were the preeminent powers in American life. Neither consumers nor labor unions were any match for the political and economic might

2. The act also provided for aid to dependent children. Act of August 14, 1935, 49 Stat. 635, 42 U.S.C. 901, et seq. In addition to securing passage of the Social Security Act, Roosevelt also sought to combat unemployment by establishing work relief agencies, including the Civilian Conservation Corps, the Works Progress Administration, and the Civil Works Administration.

```
                 IN THE SUPERIOR COURT OF PENNSYLVANIA
                            HARRISBURG DISTRICT


                                 OATH


          I do solemnly swear that I will support, obey and
     defend the Constitution of the United States, and the Con-
     stitution of this Commonwealth, and that I will discharge
     the duties of my office with fidelity;  that I have not paid
     or contributed, or promised to pay or contribute, either
     directly or indirectly, any money or other valuable thing,
     to procure my appointment, except for necessary and proper
     expenses expressly authorized by law;  that I have not know-
     ingly violated any election law of this Commonwealth, or
     procured it to be done by others in my behalf;  that I will
     not knowingly receive, directly or indirectly, any money or
     other valuable thing for the performance or non-performance
     of any act or duty pertaining to my office, other than the
     compensation allowed by law.


     Sworn to and subscribed before   )
     me on this 25th day of Oct.       )
                                       )
     in the year 1937                  )
                                       )  Herbert A. Schaffner (Signed)
                                          Herbert A. Schaffner


        Wm. M. Hargest
             President Judge
             12th Judicial District
```

The oath of office administered to Herbert A. Schaffner, the newly appointed prothonotary of the Superior Court's Harrisburg District *(Pennsylvania State Archives)*.

wielded by big business. This began to change in the early 1930s, however, as labor, energized by economic despair, exerted mounting political pressure on the Roosevelt administration. Beginning in 1935, Roosevelt responded with a series of measures aimed at curtailing corporate power. He proposed so-called "soak the rich" taxation, which in the highest brackets reached 75 percent of income. More importantly for labor, however, was the National Industrial Recovery Act (NIRA),[3] which guaranteed the rights of workers to organize and bargain collectively. Although this act was invalidated by the Supreme Court in 1935, it was replaced by a more sweeping statute, the National Labor Relations Act, commonly known as the Wagner Act.[4] This act restored the guarantees of the NIRA and established the National Labor Relations Board, which was

---

3. Pa. Act of June 16, 1933, 48 Pa. Stat. 195.
4. Pa. Act of July 5, 1935, 49 Pa. Stat. 449.

vested with broad authority to force employers to recognize and bargain with legitimate unions. In 1932 Congress passed the Norris-LaGuardia Act[5] to sharply limit the practice, utilized by courts nationwide, of granting broad labor injunctions that prohibited unions from engaging in many forms of collective activity. Pennsylvania replicated the Wagner and Norris-LaGuardia Acts by passing the Labor Relations Act[6] and the Labor Anti-Injunction Act.[7] Taken together, these statutes transformed labor relations by granting unions broad new rights to organize, strike, picket, and bargain collectively. The result was that, by 1940, unions were able to compete with previously invincible corporate power. In construing these broad and unprecedented new statutes, the Superior Court rendered a series of important decisions.

Significantly, the new labor statutes did more than alter the power balance of labor relations. They also signaled an attack that would roll back the jurisprudence of the Gilded Age. As we saw in Chapter 1, the Superior Court in the 1890s and 1900s, like courts nationwide, invalidated protective labor laws under the doctrine of "liberty of contract." As noted, this doctrine held that employers and employees possessed the right, guaranteed by the due process clauses of the state and federal constitutions, to fashion the terms of the employment relationship without legislative interference. As the inequality in bargaining power between large corporations and industrial workers became more apparent, the doctrine of "liberty of contract" eroded, and it finally disappeared as labor unions gained power in the 1930s. By the time Pennsylvania's new labor statutes were enacted, it was widely recognized that the industrial employment relationship was hardly characterized by "liberty of contract." In its public policy declaration, for instance, the Labor Anti-Injunction Act recognized that "the individual unorganized worker is commonly helpless to exercise actual liberty of contract and to protect his freedom of labor, and thereby to obtain acceptable terms and conditions of employment."[8]

Similarly, the Labor Relations Act declared that "[u]nder prevailing economic conditions, individual employes do not possess full freedom of association or actual liberty of contract."[9] The same view was endorsed by the judiciary in the 1930s, and the Superior Court would never again invalidate an employment regulation on the basis that it violated "liberty of contract."

Although the new social and labor legislation profoundly altered the common law and spawned a new activist government that has endured to the present, perhaps the greatest change wrought by the Great Depression was political. Reeling from economic despair, large blocs of traditional Republicans saw hope in the innovative new programs advocated by Roosevelt and his Democratic supporters. Nationwide, laborers, immigrants, and blacks who had voted Republican since the Civil War felt that their party had abandoned them in favor of corporate interests and the status quo. In turn, by the millions, they abandoned the Republican Party. In 1932, Robert Vann, a prominent black lawyer and editor of the widely read *Pittsburgh Courier*, captured the sentiment perfectly when he told a black audience to "go home and turn Lincoln's picture on the wall. The debt has been paid in full."[10] By 1934, Philadelphia blacks joined their Pittsburgh counterparts in bolting the Republican Party, Democratic allegiance among Italian-Americans doubled to more than 50 percent, and in 1936, every ward in Philadelphia with a foreign-born majority voted Democratic. Although Republicanism

---

5. Pa. Act of March 23, 1932, 47 Pa. Stat. 70.
6. Pa. Act of June 1, 1937, PL 1168.
7. Pa. Act of June 2, 1937, PL 1198.
8. See note 7, sec. 206d.
9. See note 6, sec. 101b.
10. Klein and Hoogenboom, *A History of Pennsylvania*, 455-56.

Judge James B. Drew, elected to Superior Court in 1930, served until June 1931, when he was appointed to the Supreme Court.

in Pennsylvania remained a powerful force—the state was one of only five to vote against Roosevelt in 1932—it nonetheless relinquished its stranglehold on state politics. In 1934 voters elected a Democratic United States senator for the first time since the 1870s, and a Democratic governor for the first time in the twentieth century. The new governor, George H. Earle, spoke for all of the state's Democrats when he declared in 1934 that "I literally rode into office on the coat-tails of President Roosevelt, and I have no hesitation in saying so."[11] Not surprisingly, the Democratic insurgency altered the political make-up of the Superior Court, which entered the 1930s composed entirely of Republicans. Although this insurgency was slow and fitful, it laid the groundwork for more significant Democratic inroads in the decades that followed. Before turning to important cases decided by the court between 1930 and 1950, it is necessary to consider these political changes.

## THE MEMBERS OF THE COURT

The new decade began just as the 1920s had ended, with a series of Republican appointments. In January 1931, James B. Drew filled the seat vacated by Judge Whitmore when the term of his appointment expired. Drew was born in Pittsburgh on April 27, 1877. He was educated in the public schools, and graduated from Columbia University with A.M. and LL.B. degrees. Later in his career, he was also awarded honorary LL.D. degrees from Duquesne University, the University of Pittsburgh, St. Francis College, and Dickinson College. In 1900 Drew was admitted to the New York bar, and two years later he was admitted to the bar of Allegheny County. From 1906 to 1912, he was assistant city solicitor of Pittsburgh. In November 1911, he was elected judge of the Allegheny County Court and served in that capacity until 1920. During World War I, he also served as a captain in the United States Army. In the fall of 1919, he was elected judge of the Court of Common Pleas of Allegheny County. He was reelected in 1929, and served in that capacity until his election to the Superior Court on November 4, 1930. He served only until June 1931, when he was appointed to the Supreme Court by Gov-

---

11. Klein and Hoogenboom, *A History of Pennsylvania*, 457.

ernor Gifford Pinchot. Although he was quickly confirmed, however, Drew refused to resign his seat on the Superior Court for more than two months, during which neither court was in session. There was considerable speculation that Drew refused to resign until after August 4, the deadline for entry in the September primary elections, in order to enable Governor Pinchot to make a long-term appointment to replace him.[12]

Whether or not it was designed for political advantage, Drew's refusal to resign until after the primary registration allowed Pinchot to make a long-term appointment. The Governor responded by appointing Republican Joseph Stadtfeld on November 7, 1931. Stadtfeld was born in New York City on August 12, 1861. His family thereafter relocated to Pittsburgh, and he was educated in the public schools, including Pittsburgh Central High School. He was admitted to the bar of Allegheny County in 1886, and engaged in private practice. In 1914 Stadtfeld was appointed city solicitor of Pittsburgh, but declined the appointment to remain in private practice, where he remained until his appointment to the Superior Court. He served as vice-president of the Pennsylvania Bar Association in 1928, and as president of the Allegheny County Bar Association from 1927 to 1929. He was also a director of Kaufmann's Department Stores and a member of the Concordia Club. On June 24, 1930, Governor Fisher appointed Stadtfeld judge of the Court of Common Pleas of Allegheny County. However, in the September primary election, he was defeated for a full term. The following year, he was appointed to the Superior Court by Governor Pinchot. He was elected to a full ten-year term in the fall of 1932. In that election, in which three seats were open, Judge Stadtfeld, along with Judges Parker and James, was victorious at the expense of Judge Gawthrop, who became the first Superior Court judge to lose a bid for reelection after serving a full term. Stadtfeld was reelected in 1942 when his Democratic opponent was Michael Musmanno, who went on to become one of Pennsylvania's most noted jurists. Stadtfeld served until his death on December 12, 1943.

On February 23, 1932, William M. Parker was appointed by Governor Pinchot to replace Judge Linn, who was appointed to the Supreme Court the same day. Parker, a Republican from Venango County, was born on December 19, 1870. He graduated from Oil City High School and Princeton University. He also received an LL.D. from Grove City College. Following college, he returned home and taught mathematics in the Grove City schools for two years. In January 1895, he was admitted to the Venango County bar. In 1925 he was elected judge of the court of common pleas. In 1932 Governor Pinchot, who had been seeking an opportunity to promote Parker, elevated him to the Superior Court. After his appointment, Parker was elected to a full term in the fall of 1932, and served until his resignation on December 11, 1940.

On November 8, 1932, Republican Arthur H. James was elected to fill the vacancy caused by the resignation of Judge Gawthrop. James was born in Plymouth, Luzerne County, on July 14, 1883. As a youth, he was employed as a breaker boy and mule driver for local mining companies. He graduated from Plymouth High School in 1901 and entered Dickinson Law School the same year, graduating with the class of 1904. He was admitted to the bars of Cumberland and Luzerne Counties and thereafter engaged in general practice. He was elected district attorney of Luzerne County in 1919, and reelected in 1923. He resigned in 1926, after his election as lieutenant governor. He served in that capacity from January 18, 1927 until January 20, 1931, when he left office upon the expiration of his term. In the fall of 1932, he was elected to the Superior Court, and served until 1938. In the spring of that year, he defeated Gifford

---

12. See article entitled "Judicial Ethics," *Philadelphia Public Ledger*, 3 Aug. 1931, p. 2, col. 3 (noting the "widespread belief that Judge Drew has made himself a party to a political bargain concerning this position and in doing so has raised a distinct question of judicial ethics and propriety.").

Pinchot in the Republican gubernatorial primary and was elected governor in the fall general election. In addition to substantial industrial backing, James had benefited from Democratic factionalism and the hostility of small businessmen and white-collar workers to New Deal legislation. James shared this hostility, despite the fact that he began his working career in the coal mines. During the 1938 gubernatorial campaign, he threatened to "make a bonfire of all the laws passed by the 1937 legislature." He also promised to reduce "confiscatory" taxes to "bring business back to Pennsylvania." As these statements suggest, James was an ardent supporter of big business during his tenure as governor. Most importantly, he established the Department of Commerce to attract new business to the state. Not surprisingly, he also proved to be an opponent of organized labor. To save money, he cut the number of state factory inspectors from one hundred to fifty-nine, quarry inspectors from thirteen to seven, and elevator inspectors from twenty-one to nineteen. He also cut the budget of the Public Utility Commission by one-third, abolished 2,000 state jobs, and delayed the construction of state facilities. He further emasculated the Labor Relations Act by giving the state secretary of labor a veto over decisions of the labor relations board. In March 1941, he sent state troopers to break a strike at Bethlehem Steel. Eight months later, during a coal strike, he promised support to any federal effort to "break the deadlock in defense production caused by short-sighted labor leaders." He also refused a request from the Fayette County sheriff to intervene when fourteen pickets were wounded by gunfire at a mine owned by the Frick Company. In 1944, after the expiration of his term, James was reappointed to the Superior Court by new Governor Edward Martin, who was elected with James' support. However, James was defeated in his bid for a full term on the court at the 1944 general election.

In 1934, in addition to electing a governor and United States senator, Democrats elected Chester H. Rhodes to the Superior Court. Rhodes, who defeated Frank Trexler's bid for reelection by less than 100,000 votes, was the first Democrat elected to the court since 1905, and the first ever elected without the assistance of a minority-representation statute. He was born in Gouldsboro, Wayne County, on October 19, 1887. He was educated in the public schools, and graduated from Lehigh University with a B.A. in 1910 and an M.A. in 1912. On October 4, 1913, he was admitted to the Monroe County bar. He engaged in general practice in Stroudsburg, and served as county solicitor of Monroe County from 1918 to 1920. He was elected district attorney in 1919, and served until he was elected to the House of Representatives in 1922. He was reelected to the general assembly in 1924, 1926, 1928, 1930, and 1932. Following his election to the Superior Court in 1934, Rhodes was reelected in 1944 and 1954. In the 1944 campaign, he defeated two Republicans, former Judge and Governor Arthur James and incumbent Judge Frank Graff. On March 1, 1947, Rhodes became president judge of the court and served in that capacity until his retirement in 1964. During his career, Rhodes also served as a member of the advisory board of the Pennsylvania Military College. He received honorary doctor of law degrees from the Military College in 1938, Muhlenberg College in 1949, Gettysburg College in 1956, and Dickinson School of Law in 1959. In 1955 he received the Meritorious Service Medal of the Commonwealth of Pennsylvania.

Unfortunately for the Democrats, there remained little opportunity to follow Rhodes' success in 1934 with another electoral victory. Since six of the seven judges on the court were either elected or reelected in the five years prior to 1934, only one seat opened within the next five years. In this intervening period, Pennsylvania voted for a Democratic presidential candidate for the first time since the Civil War, yet there was only one Superior Court race upon which to focus this Democratic strength. In the fall of 1935, the Democrats mounted a concerted campaign on behalf of their candidate,

The Superior Court in 1939. L. to. R. (seated): Jesse E. B. Cunningham, William H. Keller (President Judge), Thomas J. Baldridge. L. to R. (standing): Chester H. Rhodes, Joseph Stadtfeld, William M. Parker, William E. Hirt.

Deputy Attorney General Robert Myers, against the reelection bid of Judge Cunningham. Feeling the pressure of this Democratic opposition, Judge Cunningham stated the following a week before the election:

> It will be a sad day for this Commonwealth if our courts ever become a football of partisan politics. That the Democratic State machine is now striving to take a long step in that direction is too clear for argument. . . . The underlying issue in my case is whether I am to be unseated to make a place upon the bench of the Superior Court not for want of outstanding and eminent Democratic lawyers of the State, of whom there are hundreds, but for the treasurer of the present State Democratic Committee as an exponent of experimental extravagance and fallacious theories of state government.[13]

Although Cunningham prevailed in the election, the fact that he feared the efforts of the "Democratic State machine" suggests a great deal about the rising power of the Democratic Party in the midst of the Depression. By the time the next seats opened, however, that power had receded, and the next four judges to be elected were Republicans.

---

13. *Philadelphia Public Ledger*, 31 Oct. 1935, p. 12, col. 3.

On March 8, 1939, new Governor James named his own replacement on the court, Republican William E. Hirt. Hirt was born in Erie on May 13, 1881. He was educated at Erie High School and Princeton University. He also received an honorary D.C.L. from Thiel College. From March 1, 1920, until his appointment to the Superior Court, he served as judge of the Court of Common Pleas of Erie County. During his career, Hirt was active in many organizations. He served as vice-president of the Erie Community Chest, director of the Child-Parent Department of the Erie Welfare Bureau, director of the Erie Boys' Club, president of the Erie School Board, and he was a member of the Masons and the Knights of Pythias. In 1939, when Hirt was elevated to the Superior Court, it was rumored that his primary competitor for the appointment was Judge Sara M. Soffel of Allegheny County, Pennsylvania's first female judge and the first female law graduate of the University of Pittsburgh.[14] Instead of Soffel, however, Hirt received the appointment. He was elected to a full term in the fall of 1939, and reelected in 1949.

On April 15, 1941, Charles H. Kenworthey was appointed by Governor James to replace Judge Parker. Kenworthey was born in Milford, Pike County, on March 7, 1901. He graduated from Milford High School and the University of Pennsylvania in 1922 with a B.A. and in 1925 with an LL.B. He was admitted to the bar in 1929, and ultimately became a partner in the Philadelphia firm of Evans Bayard & Frick. From 1937 to 1941 he served as chief counsel for the Pennsylvania Medical Society. He was also a member of the state Supreme Court's Procedural Rules Committee, the Pennsylvania Bar Association Committee on the Work of the American Law Institute, the Philadelphia Volunteer Defender Society, the Juristic Society, and the University of Pennsylvania Law Alumni Association. Following his appointment to the Superior Court, Kenworthey was elected to a full term on November 4, 1941. In winning the election, Kenworthey defeated Democrat and future State Supreme Court Justice Michael Musmanno, who was also unsuccessful in a bid for the Superior Court the following year.[15]

On December 15, 1942, Claude Trexler Reno was appointed by Governor James to fill the vacancy caused by the death of Judge Cunningham. Interestingly, Reno was the candidate originally selected by Republican state officials to run for governor in 1940, but he declined and James was substituted at the last minute.[16] Reno was born on April 4, 1882, in Lyons, Berks County. Thereafter, his family relocated to Allentown, and he was educated at Allentown High School, Muhlenberg College, and Dickinson School of Law. He also received honorary degrees from both Muhlenberg and Moravian Colleges. He was admitted to the Lehigh County bar in 1905, and served as solicitor from 1908 to 1912. He also served as a member of the legislature from 1910 to 1912. In November 1921, he was appointed judge of the Lehigh County Court of Common Pleas. He was elected to a full term in 1923 and ultimately became president judge, although he resigned at the end of his term. In January 1939, he was appointed attorney general by Governor James, and served until his appointment to the Superior Court in 1942. He was elected to a full term in 1943 and served until 1953.

The next opportunity presented to the Democrats occurred in 1944, when President Judge Keller announced his resignation. F. Clair Ross won the Democratic nomination to run for Keller's seat. The same year, Judge Rhodes, the only Democrat on the court, was required to run for reelection. The Republican candidates for the two contested seats were J. Frank Graff, who served on the court in 1930, and former Judge

---

14. *Philadelphia Public Ledger*, 3 Mar. 1939, p. 1, col. 3.
15. As noted, Musmanno lost to Judge Stadtfeld in the 1942 general election.
16. *Philadelphia Public Ledger*, 11 Dec. 1940, p. 1, col. 5.

The Superior Court in 1941. L. to R. (seated): Jesse E. B. Cunningham, William H. Keller (President Judge), Thomas J. Baldridge. L. to R. (standing): William E. Hirt, Joseph Stadtfeld, Chester H. Rhodes, Charles E. Kenworthey.

and Governor Arthur James, who was appointed upon the death of Judge Stadtfeld in 1943. In the fall election, Ross and Rhodes defeated the Republicans in an extremely close vote.[17] On January 18, 1945, as Ross joined Rhodes, the court had two Democrats for the first time. Ross was born at Sandy Lake, Mercer County, on January 3, 1895. He was educated in the public schools, at Grove City College, and at Columbia University Law School. During his final year at Columbia, he studied under Harlan Fiske Stone, later Chief Justice of the United States Supreme Court. Ross was a veteran of World War I, having served in the Flying Division of the Signal Corps. He also served two years as chairman of the National Defense Committee of the American Legion of Pennsylvania. He was admitted to the Butler County bar in 1924, and became associated with W. D. Brandon and J. Campbell Brandon, subsequently Brandon Brandon and Ross. In January 1935, Governor Earle appointed him attorney general. In November 1936 he was elected treasurer of Pennsylvania as the candidate of the Democratic Party. Four years later, he was elected auditor general. In 1942 he ran unsuccessfully as the Democratic candidate for governor. Following his election to the Superior Court in 1944, Ross was reelected in 1954 and served until his death two years later.

The remaining judges to join the court between 1944 and 1950 were Republicans. On December 29, 1945, W. Heber Dithrich was appointed by Governor James to fill the vacancy resulting from Judge Kenworthey's resignation. Dithrich was born on October 25, 1886, in Pittsburgh. He was educated in the public schools, Mercersburg

---

17. The vote was as follows: Ross (D), 1,888,194; Rhodes (D), 1,833,565; James (R), 1,809,349; and Graff (R), 1,781,326.

Academy, Washington and Jefferson College, and the University of Pittsburgh School of Law. He also received an honorary LL.D. from Washington and Jefferson College in 1948. During World War I, he served as a first lieutenant of cavalry. He served in the 1917, 1919, and 1921 terms of the Pennsylvania House of Representatives, including a term as chairman of the Judicial General Committee. Dithrich left the legislature and, from 1921 until 1924, served as first assistant United States attorney for the Western District of Pennsylvania. In 1924 he became solicitor of Allegheny County. In the summer of 1930, he was considered for appointment to the Allegheny County Court of Common Pleas, but Judge Stadtfeld received the appointment instead. Dithrich was finally appointed on September 4, 1930, with the support of W. L. Mellon and the Republican County Committee. He was elected to a full term in the fall of 1931, and reelected in 1941. Three years later, he was appointed to the Superior Court, and elected to a full ten-year term in 1945.

On April 2, 1945, John C. Arnold was appointed by Governor Martin to replace Judge James, who had been appointed to Judge Stadtfeld's seat and was unsuccessful in his attempt to unseat Judge Rhodes. Arnold was born in Curwensvillle, Clearfield County, on March 10, 1887. He was educated in the public schools and received an LL.B. from the University of Pennsylvania in 1909. He was admitted to the bar a year later and thereafter became solicitor for the borough of DuBois, later organizing it as a city. Reelected in 1921, he resigned to return to private practice in 1925. He later became a partner in the firm of Arnold and Chaplin. In 1935 he was elected president of the Clearfield County Bar Association, and seven years later became president of the Pennsylvania Bar Association. He was a member of the American Judicature Society, the Sociolegal Club of Philadelphia, the Board of Governance of the Supreme Court, and the Board of Managers of the Law Alumni Society of the University of Pennsylvania. He also served as a trustee of Dickinson School of Law. He remained in private practice until his appointment to the Superior Court in 1945. He was elected to a full term in the fall of that year.

On July 15, 1947, John S. Fine was appointed to replace Judge Baldridge. Fine was born on April 10, 1893, in Alden, Luzerne County. He later moved to Nanticoke, and was educated in the public schools. He graduated from Dickinson Law School in 1914 and was admitted to the bar of Luzerne County a year later. He remained in private practice until May 1917, when he entered military service. From 1916 to 1923, he served in various capacities, including chairman, with the Luzerne County Republican Committee. In 1919 he also completed postgraduate work at Trinity College in Dublin, Ireland. On January 3, 1927, he was appointed judge of the Court of Common Pleas of Luzerne County. He was elected to a full ten-year term in 1927, and reelected in 1937. Following his appointment to the Superior Court, Fine was elected to a full term in 1947. He served until March 1, 1950, when he resigned to campaign for governor. In the fall of 1950, he was elected. As governor, Fine stated his political beliefs as follows: "I like to give good government where I can, build up my organization, keep the confidence of the people, keep down the gripes, and refresh the organization with new blood."[18] Although this statement suggests that Fine was a pragmatic politician, he was also relatively progressive. He established the Governor's Industrial Race Relations Commission, a diverse group of religious, business, labor, and civic leaders that worked with local communities to eliminate discrimination. He also opened the state police to blacks and ended segregation in the National Guard. Further, he built rehabilitation centers to retrain injured workmen, increased the budget for public education, emphasized public works, and enhanced the state's public health delivery system.

---

18. Klein and Hoogenboom, *A History of Pennsylvania*, 477.

Because this spending increased the state's budget dramatically, Fine also proposed a variety of new taxes, including an income tax, which the legislature refused to enact. Lastly, Fine was a cold war warrior. He sponsored Senator Joseph McCarthy in a speech before the Veterans of Foreign Wars, and in his farewell address, he predicted war with Russia and spoke at length about the danger of surprise atomic attack. Fine left the governor's office when his term expired in January 1955. He died on May 21, 1978.

On April 25, 1950, Blair F. Gunther was appointed to replace Judge Fine. Gunther was born in Hastings, Cambria County, on June 20, 1903. He graduated from Kanty Preparatory and received an LL.B. from Duquesne University in 1927. He was admitted to the bar of Allegheny County a year later and engaged in private practice. From 1935 until 1938, he served as deputy attorney general of Pennsylvania. In 1942 he was appointed to the Allegheny County Court (since merged with the Common Pleas Court by the Constitutional Amendments of 1968), and elected to a full term in 1943. During his career, Gunther served as trustee of Alliance College, founder and director of the Committee to Stop World Communism, and national chairman of the American Resettlement Committee for Displaced Persons. He was also a member of the Rotary, Elks, Moose, and the Civic Club of Allegheny County. Following his appointment to the Superior Court, he was elected to a full term in 1950. His term expired on January 2, 1961 when he was replaced by Gerald F. Flood, the Democrat who defeated him in the 1960 election.

Although the accomplishment seems modest, the placement of two Democrats on the court between 1930 and 1950 was, in fact, significant. Prior to 1934, no Democrat had been elected to the court since 1905, and none had ever been elected without the assistance of a minority-representation statute. In the years since, Democrats have maintained their representation on the court, and the trend begun by Judge Rhodes has gradually but inexorably gained strength. In 1950 two Democrats sat on the court; in 1960, the number was three; and by 1965, Democrats were a majority on the court for the first time.

## THE COURT AT WORK: UNEMPLOYMENT COMPENSATION

While Pennsylvania benefited disproportionately from the nation's industrialization in the Gilded Age, so too did it share disproportionately in the misery of the Depression. The most tragic social consequence was unemployment. In the spring of 1933, with the national unemployment rate hovering at 25 percent, it reached a staggering 37.1 percent in Pennsylvania. Between 1929 and 1932, the state's industrial production was cut in half, wages paid in the metals industries fell by two-thirds, and per capita personal income decreased 40 percent. As companies failed in record numbers and consumer demand plummeted, the unemployed and homeless quickly overwhelmed local relief organizations. In Pittsburgh, shantytowns appeared virtually overnight, and in Philadelphia, officials of a local unemployment relief committee reported numerous cases of people eating dandelions to survive. As early as 1931, the State Department of Health reported dramatic increases in cases of malnutrition, disease, and even starvation. Although they were especially pronounced in Pennsylvania, these conditions prevailed throughout the nation for years, as federal and state officials experimented with methods to relieve the unprecedented suffering. Finally, in 1936, on the heels of Congress' passage of the Social Security Act, the Pennsylvania legislature enacted its own Unemployment Compensation Law.[19] The new statute established a system of employer-funded compensation for workers who became unemployed through

---

19. Pa. Act of December 5, 1936, PL 2897.

---

### In the Superior Court of Pennsylvania
SITTING AT PHILADELPHIA

No. 70 Order Book                              October Term, 19

RE:
Transfer of Wyoming County
from the Philadelphia District
to the Scranton District

Appeal from the

_____ Court

of _____

for the County of _____

No.                        Term, 19

May 12, 1938, Petition filed.

And now, May 23, 1938, pursuant to the foregoing
petition, signed by eleven of the fourteen resident
lawyers, members of the Bar of the County of Wyoming,
the said County of Wyoming is transferred from the
Philadelphia District to the Scranton District, to take
effect June 1, 1938.

By the Court

William H. Keller, P.J.

TRUE COPY FROM RECORD

**In Testimony Whereof,** *I have hereunto set my hand and the seal of*
*said Court, at Philadelphia, this* 24th *day of* May 19 38.

*Prothonotary.*

The administrative order of May 25, 1938, transferring Wyoming County
from the Scranton District to the Philadelphia District.

no fault of their own, and it created an Unemployment Compensation Board of Review to administer claims. The act further provided that claims would be filed with the Department of Labor and Industry, and appeals from the department's decisions would be taken to a referee, then to the board of review, and finally to the Superior Court.[20] In a series of decisions rendered over the next decade, the court construed important provisions of the Depression's most important law.

In two cases consolidated as *Department of Labor & Industry v. Unemployment Compensation Board of Review*,[21] the court construed the phrase "voluntarily leaving work," which the act declared in Section 402(b), shall render an employee ineligible for compensation.[22] The claimant in the first case, Elbert Bush, terminated his employment as a milk delivery driver after a physician advised that it was aggravating his

---

20. Pa. Act of December 5, 1936, PL 2897, sec. 510.

21. 133 Pa. Super. 518 (1938) (per curiam).

22. The section provided that "an employee shall be ineligible for compensation for any week. . . . [i]n which his unemployment is due to voluntarily leaving work."

rheumatic arthritis. In the second case, claimant John Priest was notified of his impending layoff and terminated his employment four days before the date specified in order to secure work out of town. The claims of Bush and Priest were denied by the Department of Labor and Industry on the basis that both men had "voluntarily [left] work" within the meaning of the act. This determination was reversed in both cases by the same referee, and the board of review affirmed the awards of compensation. The department appealed both cases to the Superior Court.

In a per curiam opinion filed on December 20, 1938, the court began by noting that its review was limited by the act to questions of law, and that the construction of the phrase "voluntarily leaving work" presented such a question. The court then found that, although the word "voluntarily" was subject to several definitions, "the most appropriate meaning or definition is, 'of one's own motion' (*Century Dictionary*); 'of one's own accord' (*Oxford Dictionary*); 'acting of one's self' (*Webster's New International Dictionary*)."[23] Relying on these definitions to fashion a test for the statute's application, the court concluded that "where the employe, without action by the employer, resigns, leaves or quits his employment, his action amounts to 'voluntarily leaving work,' such as to render him ineligible for unemployment compensation under the act."[24] The court then applied this standard to the cases at issue. As to Bush, the court noted, "He quit of his own motion or accord. He was not discharged, dismissed or laid off by his employer. To explore the reasons or mental processes which led the claimant to give up his employment . . . would result in too variable and uncertain results."[25] "Few actions are taken in this world," the court continued, "without some extraneous constraining or compulsive force or influence and to apply such an uncertain basis to 'voluntarily leaving work,' would be doing violence to the usual and ordinary meaning of the term in the light of the purpose of the enactment [to protect employees against discharge]."[26] Finally, the court rejected the argument raised on behalf of the claimant Bush, that the act offered compensation to an employee who terminates his employment due to a physical condition. "We are satisfied that the act . . . is not a health insurance measure," the court concluded. "The suggestion now being made in congressional circles that the Social Security Act, with which our Unemployment Compensation Act is closely connected, shall be enlarged so as to provide compensation for unemployment resulting from sickness is a potent reason for concluding that it is not now included."[27] On this basis, the court reversed the award of compensation in favor of Bush.

Turning to the facts involving claimant Priest, the court began by quoting from a letter, dated December 17, 1937, written to Priest by his employer. The letter stated that "because of reduction in schedule . . . you will be laid off on Fri. 12-24-37."[28] Three days later, with his employer's consent, Priest left his job in Erie to secure employment in Philadelphia. Finding that Priest was entitled to compensation, the court concluded:

> In our view of the case the claimant's employment was broken or severed as a result of the act of the employer in notifying him that he would be laid off on December 24, seven days later. His leaving was due to this positive act of the employer, which was never withdrawn or modified. His leaving a few days in advance of the time fixed for his lay-off, with the employer's full assent, cannot be construed as 'voluntarily leav-

---

23. 133 Pa. Super. 521.
24. 133 Pa. Super. 522.
25. 133 Pa. Super. 523-24.
26. 133 Pa. Super. 524.
27. See note 22.
28. See note 22.

Women in a typing pool during the changing years of the Great Depression and approaching war.

ing work,' but only as anticipating by a few days, with the consent of the employer, the effective date of his dismissal. He did not leave the work of his own motion or accord, but in consequence of the action of the employer laying him off.[29]

The court then affirmed the award of compensation to Priest. Thereafter, the Department of Labor and Industry pursued the appeal, but allocatur was denied by the Pennsylvania Supreme Court. In the years after it was rendered, the court's holding in *Labor & Industry* became the standard for defining the critical phrase "voluntarily leaving work" in the unemployment compensation law. It has been cited repeatedly for the proposition that an employee who resigns, leaves, or quits his employment "of his own motion or accord" and "without action by the employer" will be denied compensation.[30] This definition has also been utilized to construe the same phrase in subsequent amendments to the unemployment compensation statute.[31]

In 1942 the legislature amended Section 402(b) of the statute to provide that compensation is not available where unemployment is due to "voluntarily leaving work *without good cause.*"[32] Once again, in construing this broad phrase, the Superior Court rendered an influential series of decisions. In the first of these decisions, the *Teicher Unemployment Compensation Case*,[33] the court considered whether a wife who left her

---

29. 133 Pa. Super. 525.

30. *Monaco v. Unemployment Compensation Board of Review*, 523 Pa. 41 (1989) (Larsen, dissenting); *Mehlbaum Unemployment Compensation Case*, 175 Pa. Super. 497 (1954); *Cassell Unemployment Compensation Case*, 167 Pa. Super. 440 (1950); *MacFarland v. Unemployment Compensation Board of Review*, 158 Pa. Super. 418 (1946); *Torsky v. Unemployment Compensation Board of Review*, 81 Pa. Cmwlth. 642 (1984).

31. *Cassell*, supra; *Torsky*, supra; and *Stillman Unemployment Compensation Case*, 161 Pa. Super. 569 (1948).

32. Pa. Act of April 23, 1942, PL 60, amending the unemployment compensation statute (emphasis added).

33. 154 Pa. Super. 250 (1944) (Kenworthey, J.).

employment during World War II to join her soldier-husband at a military post had satisfied the "good cause" requirement of the amended statute. The wife received compensation despite the employer's claim that only employment-related reasons, and not personal reasons, would constitute "good cause" under the statute. The employer appealed to the Superior Court.

On appeal, the court began by acknowledging that the claimant had voluntarily quit her employment. Thus, the question became whether she had good cause to do so. Answering this question in the affirmative, the court rejected the employer's claim that only reasons arising from the employment relationship, and not purely personal reasons, could satisfy the "good cause" requirement of the act. Although noting that language from statutes in other states supported the employer's claim, the court nonetheless found it clear "that, if our legislature had intended a similar restriction, it would have said so. Causes which are purely personal are, therefore, permitted."[34] Since personal reasons could provide "good cause" for quitting employment, the court next considered whether claimant had such cause. Finding that she did, the court held:

> [I]t is difficult to conceive of a cause more impelling, more humanly justifiable, than the impulse which induces a devoted wife to spend with a husband, who is a member of the Armed Forces in time of war, what may prove to be the last days they shall ever be together on earth.[35]

Although the court ultimately denied compensation to claimant on the basis that she was not "available to work" at her new residence, as required by the statute, its holding that personal reasons may constitute "good cause" for leaving employment settled an extremely controversial issue relating to application of the unemployment compensation statute. In the following years, *Teicher* was cited repeatedly for this proposition.[36]

In an even more important decision rendered two years later, the court further refined the definition of "good cause" in the unemployment compensation statute. Like *Teicher*, the *Sturdevant Unemployment Compensation Case*[37] involved a wife who left her employment to join her soldier-husband at a distant military post. The review board awarded compensation on the basis the wife had established "good cause," and the employer appealed. A unanimous court began by noting the unique nature of unemployment compensation law, and the challenges it presented to courts attempting to construe its provisions:

> The statute, almost ten years old, introduced into our law a new concept of social obligation, extended the police power of the State into a virgin field, and created a body of rights and duties unknown to the common law. . . .
>
> The [compensation boards], state and federal, have produced an immense and impressive body of decisional law, but so far comparatively

---

34. 154 Pa. Super. 253.

35. See note 33. Judges Keller and Baldridge dissented, without opinion, from the finding of the majority that personal reasons could constitute "good cause."

36. See e.g., *Treon v. Unemployment Compensation Board of Review*, 499 Pa. 455 (1982); *Savage Unemployment Compensation Case*, 401 Pa. 501 (1960); *Dawkins Unemployment Compensation Case*, 358 Pa. 224 (1948); *Wolfson Unemployment Compensation Case*, 167 Pa. Super. 588 (1950); *Mills Unemployment Compensation Case*, 164 Pa. Super. 421 (1949); and *Donaldson v. Unemployment Compensation Board of Review*, 91 Pa. Cmwlth. 366 (1985).

37. 158 Pa. Super. 548 (1946) (Reno, J.).

few of the many vital questions arising out of the legislation have been presented to judicial scrutiny. Until more cases involving a wide variety of factual situations have been brought to the courts, judicial answers will necessarily lack the usual rigor of legal formulas, and tend to be tentative and groping in their nature. Concrete cases will develop general principles, and precise definition will issue from the wisdom acquired by greater experience.[38]

Proceeding in this "dawn of judicial interpretation," the court recited the holding of *Teicher* that personal reasons may constitute "good cause" for leaving employment. The court also found support for this holding in the fact that the legislature amended the compensation statute subsequent to *Teicher* without altering its definition of "good cause." Thus, the court stated, "[w]e must conclude that the legislature intended that the construction of [*Teicher*] should stand as the correct expression of the legislative will."[39] Although personal reasons *might* constitute good cause, this did not mean that they *must* constitute good cause, and the court fashioned a new standard for determining when compensation was appropriate:

When therefore the pressure of real not imaginary, substantial not trifling, reasonable not whimsical, circumstances *compel* the decision to leave employment, the decision is voluntary in the sense that the worker has willed it, but involuntary because outward pressures have *compelled* it. Or to state it differently, if a worker leaves his employment when he is compelled to do so by necessitous circumstances or because of legal or family obligations, his leaving is voluntary with good cause, and under the act he is entitled to benefits. The pressure of necessity, of legal duty, or family obligations, or other overpowering circumstances and his capitulation to them transform what is ostensibly voluntary unemployment into involuntary unemployment.[40]

As the emphasis in this statement indicates, the court believed that compulsion was the critical factor in determining whether personal reasons constituted good cause for leaving employment. Applying this standard to the facts at issue, the court stated that "[w]hen we approach the problem of a married woman who leaves her work to join her husband, we realize immediately that we are in the presence of a compulsion which readily supplies a personal reason and a good cause."[41] Moreover, since existing law vested in the husband the right to select the marital domicile, a wife was obligated to leave her employment when her husband secured work and moved to a distant region.[42] On this basis, the court concluded, claimant's "surrender to the compulsion of her legal obligations [to her husband] provided the good cause which justified the voluntary relinquishment of the employment."[43] The court affirmed the award of compensation to the claimant, and applied its holding to three other cases decided the same day.[44]

---

38. 158 Pa. Super. 553-54.

39. 158 Pa. Super. 555.

40. 158 Pa. Super. 557 (emphasis in original).

41. See note 39.

42. 158 Pa. Super. 558. The court was quick to point out, however, that a wife would not be justified in leaving her employment to join her husband on an extended vacation.

43. 158 Pa. Super. 559. The court also concluded that the claimant was "available for work" in South Carolina, as required by the statute, and that the "good cause" requirement was not modified by a 1943 amendment to the statute.

44. See *Dames Unemployment Compensation Case*, 158 Pa. Super. 564 (1946); *Felegy Unemployment Compensation Case*, 158 Pa. Super. 567 (1946); and *Miller Unemployment Compensation Case*, 158 Pa. Super. 570 (1946).

Community support for striking steelworkers during the 1946 walkout was considerable
(*Carnegie Library of Pittsburgh*).

In the five decades since it was rendered, *Sturdevant* has probably been the most important case defining the "good cause" requirement of the unemployment compensation statute. Indeed, its holding that the requirement is satisfied where personal reasons compel an employee to leave employment has been cited more than one hundred times, by all three appellate courts in Pennsylvania,[45] by courts from out of state,[46] and by scholarly texts, including *American Law Reports*,[47] and several law reviews.[48]

## *LABOR LEGISLATION*

In addition to these decisions applying the state's first unemployment compensation law, the court also played a critical role in construing the labor statutes of the "little New Deal." From the colonial period through the late nineteenth century, Pennsylvania courts endorsed the doctrine that laborers who combined to obtain mutual

---

45. See e.g., *Allegheny Valley School v. Unemployment Compensation Board of Review*, 548 Pa. 355 (1997) (Cappy, dissenting); *Du-Co Ceramics v. Unemployment Compensation Board of Review*, 546 Pa. 504 (1996); *Poola v. Unemployment Compensation Board of Review*, 520 Pa. 562 (1989); *Sledziowski v. Unemployment Compensation Case*, 195 Pa. Super. 337 (1961); *Cook Unemployment Compensation Case*, 194 Pa. Super. 652 (1961); *Naugle Unemployment Compensation Case*, 194 Pa. Super. 420 (1961); *Judd v. Unemployment Compensation Board of Review*, 91 Pa. Cmwlth. 372 (1985); *Brown v. Unemployment Compensation Board of Review*. 91 Pa. Cmwlth. 196 (1985).

46. See e.g., *Reep v. Department of Employment and Training Commissioner*, 412 Mass. 845, 593 N.E.2d 1297 (1992).

47. See e.g., 21 ALR 4th 317; 13 ALR 2d 874; 165 ALR 1382.

48. See e.g., 87 Dick. L. Rev. 507; 62 Dick. L. Rev. 315; 53 Dick. L. Rev. 187; 29 Duq. L. Rev. 447; 63 N.Y.U.L. Rev. 532; 17 Vill. L. Rev. 635.

economic benefit were engaged in a criminal conspiracy. It was not until 1869 that the legislature recognized the right of labor to establish unions for "mutual aid, benefit, and protection." Yet, the doctrine of conspiracy endured even after it was formally abolished in 1872. Indeed, although acknowledging the new rules legalizing concerted activity, the courts nonetheless found that they abolished only criminal liability for conspiracy, not civil liability. Even worse, beginning in the last decade of the nineteenth century, employers began to wield a powerful new weapon in labor disputes. For the next forty years, sweeping labor injunctions, often issued ex parte, virtually smothered the rights of labor to strike, picket, or engage in almost any other meaningful form of collective activity.[49] The most notorious of these injunctions even prohibited the singing of hymns by strikers gathered in church.[50]

So pervasive and notorious was the reign of the labor injunction that the period 1890-1930 has been known ever since as the era of "government by injunction." Yet this era, like so many other facets of American legal doctrine, was swept away by the Great Depression. In 1931 Pennsylvania passed a law granting the right to trial by jury and other protections to those charged with contempt of a labor injunction.[51] This law limited the arbitrary power of courts to suppress labor activity and placed the enforcement of injunctions in the hands of the alleged violators' peers. Three years after it was passed, the law was deemed constitutional by the Superior Court.[52] In 1932, as previously indicated, Congress passed the Norris-LaGuardia Act, which severely limited the authority of federal courts to issue labor injunctions. Following the invalidation of the National Industrial Recovery Act by the Supreme Court, Congress also passed the Wagner Act, which, along with Norris-LaGuardia, transformed the state of labor relations by granting unions broad new rights to picket, strike, and engage in collective bargaining. In 1937, spurred by the federal effort, Pennsylvania passed the State Labor Relations Act[53] and the Labor Anti-Injunction Act,[54] which, like their federal counterparts, expanded the rights of unions and restricted the authority of courts to issue labor injunctions.

While these statutes improved conditions for organized labor and sharply limited the issuance of labor injunctions, their broad terms required extensive judicial construction. In a line of cases decided between 1938 and 1940, for instance, the Superior Court considered the definition of the phrase "labor dispute." This definition was critical because, by their express terms, the new statutes applied only to such disputes.

---

49. Labor injunctions as a weapon in labor disputes rose to national prominence for the first time when one was issued with tremendous effect against Eugene V. Debs during the Pullman Strike of 1894. Such injunctions, which were a uniquely American contribution to legal history, were premised on the theory that an employer's labor supply is a property right that may not be interfered with.

50. The famous Rossiter Injunction, issued in 1927 by Judge Jonathan Langham of Indiana County against striking members of the United Mine Workers, prohibited virtually every collective activity, including the singing in a Presbyterian Church of what the judge deemed "hostile songs." A subsequent investigation by a subcommittee of the United States Senate determined that the prohibited songs included "Nearer My God to Thee," "Sound the Battle Cry," "Stand Up for Jesus," and "The Victory May Depend on You." The injunction, which was issued ex parte, remained in effect for six months before the strikers were afforded a hearing. Without a hint of overstatement, the *New York Times* referred to the Rossiter Injunction as "one of the most drastic injunctions in the history of labor disputes in this country." *New York Times*, 28 Dec. 1928, p. 1. See also, the *Daily Worker*, 27 Dec. 1927, p. 3, characterizing the Rossiter Injunction as "the most drastic injunction ever granted in [Pennsylvania]."

51. Pa. Act of June 23, 1931, PL 925. The rights provided by the law applied to indirect criminal contempt, or conduct that did not occur in the presence of the court. It did not affect the inherent authority of courts to punish contempt committed in their presence.

52. *Penn Anthracite Mining Co. v. Anthracite Miners of Pennsylvania,* 114 Pa. Super. 7 (1934).

53. See note 6.

54. See note 7.

The first significant case was *Dorrington v. Manning*,[55] in which both plaintiffs and defendants were employees of a bus company that executed a "closed shop" contract with the defendants' union providing that the company would employ only members of that union. Both plaintiffs and defendants were already employees at the time the contract was executed, and the plaintiffs thereafter attempted to join the defendants' union in order to retain their jobs. The defendants refused to allow the plaintiffs to join, and the union called a strike to protest the continued employment of the plaintiffs. The strike ultimately compelled the employer to discharge the plaintiffs. In response, the plaintiffs filed suit. After a hearing before a chancellor sitting in equity, they were awarded damages and an injunction prohibiting the defendants or other union members from interfering in their attempts to seek reinstatement to their jobs. On appeal to the Superior Court, the defendants argued that the case was subject to the Labor Anti-Injunction Act, which applied only to actions "involving or growing out of a labor dispute."[56] Since the act limited the issuance of injunctions to situations not relevant to their case, the defendants claimed the chancellor's award of an injunction was improper.

The court searched in vain for guiding precedent, and concluded that "[t]hus far, there are no decisions of our appellate courts interpreting the phrase 'labor dispute,' as used in our act."[57] The court then examined the broad definition provided by the statute:

> [Under Section 3(c) of the Act] the term "labor dispute" includes any controversy concerning terms or conditions of employment, or concerning the association or representation of persons in negotiating, fixing, maintaining, changing or seeking to arrange terms or conditions of employment or concerning employment relations or any other controversy arising out of the respective interests of employer and employe.[58]

Although acknowledging that the definition in Section 3(c) was "comprehensive," the court nonetheless emphasized that, by its express terms, the section only contemplated disputes that arose over "terms or conditions of employment" or the negotiation and arrangement of those terms.[59] "No one would say," the court noted, "that a dispute between two employees of the same employer over a right of way, division line of property, or some other private matter would be a labor dispute, because terms and conditions of employment would not be involved."[60] Similarly, the instant dispute:

> ...grew out of the plaintiffs' endeavoring to get into the union, under an agreement, while the union is trying to keep them out. There was no dispute as to what group should represent the employees for the purpose of collective bargaining; nor, in view of the defendants' unwarranted refusal to admit plaintiffs into membership, could defendants' action in forcing the employer to discharge the plaintiffs have had for its purpose the employment of none other than members of the defendant association. We can but conclude, therefore, that under the facts before us this was not a "labor dispute" within the provisions of our statute.[61]

---

55. 135 Pa. Super. 194 (1939) (Baldrige, J.).
56. 135 Pa. Super. 203, citing PL 1198.
57. 135 Pa. Super. 203.
58. 135 Pa. Super. 204, n. 1, citing PL 1198, sec. 3(c).
59. 135 Pa. Super. 205.
60. 135 Pa. Super. 205-06.
61. 135 Pa. Super. 206.

Since the defendants were not protected by the act, and since they had engaged in a tortious interference with the plaintiff's employment, the court found the injunction was properly issued. Following the Superior Court's ruling, the defendants appealed to the Pennsylvania Supreme Court, which denied allocatur.

In the years since it was rendered, *Dorrington* has been cited repeatedly for its seminal holding that, since the phrase "labor dispute" contemplates only conflicts arising out of the "terms or conditions of employment," the statute will not bar injunctions in conflicts between employees that are personal in nature.[62] Moreover, it has been cited by federal courts for the proposition that employers and employees are entitled to be free from meddling by third parties, even where the relationship is one of at-will employment.[63]

Two years after *Dorrington*, in *Brown v. Lehman*,[64] the court again considered the application of an injunction to concerted union activity aimed at securing the discharge of fellow employees by a "closed shop" employer. Like *Dorrington*, *Brown* established a new standard applicable to the relationship between employees in union-related disputes. The case involved a plaintiff who was employed as a truck driver by a grocer who executed a "closed shop" contract with the Teamsters Union. Although the plaintiff was originally a member of the union, he fell into arrears in the payment of dues. He was suspended pursuant to a union by-law and he later informed a union representative that he no longer desired to be a member. In order to pressure the grocer into discharging the plaintiff, several of his co-workers quit working and others picketed the grocer's premises. The plaintiff was discharged, and he was unsuccessful in securing employment with other local grocers, all of whom had "closed shop" agreements with the Teamsters. The plaintiff sought damages and an injunction prohibiting defendants from interfering with his attempts to secure employment with other "closed shop" grocers. The chancellor refused to issue an injunction, and the plaintiff appealed.[65]

The Superior Court began by noting that the "principal issue involved here, is whether a union employee, who . . . has been automatically suspended for failure to pay dues . . . is entitled to a decree restraining the members of the association from interfering with his employment by an employer who has entered into a closed shop contract."[66] Since the case involved the payment of union dues rather than "terms and conditions of employment," the court found initially that it was not a "labor dispute" within the meaning of the Labor Anti-Injunction Act. Although this finding was consistent with *Dorrington*, the court concluded that the cases were distinguishable on an important matter of fact. Specifically, the court noted that the plaintiff voluntarily chose not to pay union dues, whereas the plaintiff in *Dorrington* was precluded from joining the union. The court believed that this distinction was critical because an employee's refusal to join a union or pay dues is a threat to the very existence of the union. In support of this finding, the court turned to the rule set forth in Section 810 of the Restatement of Torts:

---

62. See *Mead v. Pennsylvania Railroad Co.*, 375 Pa. 325, 342 (1953); *Loerlein Unemployment Compensation Case*, 162 Pa. Super. 216, 220 (1948); *Ralston v. Cunningham*, 143 Pa. Super. 412 (1941); and 160 ALR 924.

63. See *Wells v. Thomas*, 569 F. Supp. 426, 434 (E.D. Pa. 1983); and *Geib v. Alan Wood Steel Co.*, 419 F. Supp. 1205 (E.D. Pa. 1976). The case also indicates that injunctions are properly awarded to stop third parties from procuring the breach of employment contracts. 26 ALR 2d 1237, 1277.

64. 141 Pa. Super. 467 (1940) (Stadtfeld, J.).

65. The chancellor did, however, award the plaintiff $25 in lost wages and issue an injunction against the defendants' interference with the plaintiff's attempts to secure employment from grocers not bound by a "closed shop" contract with the defendants' union. This ruling, which is a less significant aspect of *Brown*, was reversed by the Superior Court for lack of evidence. 141 Pa. Super. 478. Since it concluded that the plaintiff's discharge was proper, the court also reversed the award of damages.

66. 141 Pa. Super. 473.

Craftsmen creating model of Independence Hall during the Great Depression. Artists and craftsmen were employed under federal projects to create public works of art.

The justification for harm caused the individual employee who loses his job when he refuses to be—a term which includes both his becoming and his remaining—a member of the union rests in the necessity of united action by workers. They may correctly believe that the worker who belongs to a rival organization or to no organization and does not conform to their discipline, or contribute to the support of their united efforts, or join with them in their attempts to better themselves, is willing to compete with them outside of the union and constitutes a threat to the employment standards which they have won for themselves. They may, therefore, take action against him.[67]

According to the court, this rule was intended to focus judicial attention on the union's motives in seeking an employee's discharge, and not merely on the fact that the employee was discharged. So long as the union acted for "the legitimate advancement of its own interests," the court concluded, its conduct could not be enjoined. Thus, adopting Section 810 as Pennsylvania law, the court held, "In the absence of any maliciousness or wanton desire to injure an employee, the conduct of the union, seeking to enforce the provisions of its contract with the employer resulting in the discharge of an ineligible employee does not constitute a tortious interference with his employment."[68] On this basis, the court affirmed the chancellor's refusal to issue an injunction enjoining interferences with the plaintiff's attempt to secure employment with other "closed shop" grocers.

---

67. 141 Pa. Super. 476-77.
68. 141 Pa. Super. 477.

Most importantly, *Brown* stands for the proposition that an employee who is suspended for nonpayment of union dues is not entitled to an injunction restraining members of the union from interfering with his employment with a "closed shop" employer.[69] Similarly, it indicates that union members are bound by the organization's by-laws, unless those by-laws infringe upon constitutional rights or contravene public policy.[70] Like *Dorrington*, *Brown* has also been cited as indicating that differences between union members generally do not constitute "labor disputes" within the meaning of the Labor Anti-Injunction Act.[71]

Finally, *Brown* is significant because it indicates that unions have a particular interest in enforcing "closed shop" contracts, which were validated by the Pennsylvania Labor Relations Act in 1937.[72] Where such contracts do not exist, unions may be properly enjoined from compelling the discharge of an employee who voluntarily relinquishes his union membership. This was the holding of the Superior Court in the brief but important case of *Mische v. Kaminski*,[73] which was decided three years prior to *Brown*. In *Mische*, members of the defendant United Mine Workers Union (UMW) refused to work with the plaintiffs, former members of the UMW who resigned and joined a new union, the United Anthracite Miners of Pennsylvania. In addition to their refusal to work, the defendants also utilized threats, force, and violence to coerce the employer to discharge the plaintiffs. They were ultimately successful in compelling the employer to fire the plaintiffs. In response, the plaintiffs filed suit and received damages and an injunction prohibiting defendants from continuing to interfere with their attempts to gain reinstatement to their jobs. In a per curiam opinion which relied heavily on the decision of the trial court, the Superior Court upheld the damages and injunction. According to the court, since the plaintiffs "had the legal right to leave the [UMW]," they were entitled to damages and injunctive relief from the threats and violence of defendants aimed at preventing them from securing employment.[74] Thus, where the union was not attempting to enforce a "closed shop" contract, the employee had the right to resign, and the union's actions in compelling his discharge were not justified, particularly where those actions involved violence and coercion.[75] Despite its brevity, *Mische* has been cited repeatedly, including as recently as 1985 by the United States Supreme Court, as embodying the "traditional" rule that employees are free to resign from unions.[76]

## *Unfair Trade Practices*

While the court played a crucial role in construing Pennsylvania's "little New Deal" legislation, it also ensured that such legislation was not enacted in violation of

---

69. See *Seifing Unemployment Compensation Case*, 159 Pa. Super. 94, 103 (1946); 46 ALR 2d 1131.

70. See *Ralston v. Cunningham*, 143 Pa. Super. 420 (1941); *Underwood v. Maloney*, 152 F. Supp. 648, 666 (E.D. Pa. 1957).

71. See e.g., 160 ALR 545.

72. PL 1168.

73. 127 Pa. Super. 66 (1937).

74. 127 Pa. Super. 92.

75. Because of the violence involved, it is likely that the union conduct in *Mische* would also have been enjoined by the court in *Brown*, which held, as noted, that injunctions are not proper unless the union is motivated by "maliciousness or wanton desire to injure an employee." *Brown*, 141 Pa. Super. 477.

76. See *Pattern Makers' League of North America v. National Labor Relations Board*, 473 U.S. 95, 103 (1985). Although *Brown* did not address *Mische*, it appears that the latter case is distinguishable for the violence involved, and also because no "closed shop" contract was at issue.

the state constitution. In the prominent case of *Commonwealth v. Zasloff*,[77] for instance, the court deemed unconstitutional the Fair Sales Act of 1937.[78] This statute was modeled on the federal Robinson-Patman Act, which prohibited retailers from selling below cost with the intent to destroy competition, injure competitors, or create a monopoly.[79] The Pennsylvania law provided that "[a]ny retailer who shall sell, offer to sell, or sell at retail, any merchandise at less than cost to the retailer . . . shall be guilty of a misdemeanor."[80] It also provided exceptions for bona fide liquidation or clearance sales, sales of perishable or damaged goods, sheriffs' sales, sales for charity, and sales to meet the legal price of a competitor.[81] However, while the title of the act suggested that it sought to ensure "fair sales," its provisions did not express the legislature's purposes more clearly. In *Zasloff*, the defendant was charged with violating the act on three occasions by selling merchandise below cost. The trial court quashed the appeal on the basis that the act was unconstitutionally vague and the Commonwealth appealed.

A unanimous court began its analysis by noting that precedent of the United States Supreme Court established beyond question that the prohibition of unfair trade practices is a matter within the police power of the legislature, so long as the restrictions imposed were not unreasonable.[82] Thus, the question was whether the act bore a "true relation to the protection of fair trade practices . . . without imposing unreasonable and unnecessary restrictions."[83] The court had little doubt that such a relation was absent. "This inquiry convinces us," it held, "that the act as drawn is too broad in its application and prevents innocent transactions regardless of motive."[84] "Selling below cost is not an offense against the public," the court continued, "except where it is done with the intent to injure competitors or to destroy competition."[85] Thus, the "failure of the act to limit its application to sales made with that intent or to sales which actually result in injury regardless of intent, stamps the act invalid in that it exceeds the limits of legislative discretion and therefore is without justification under the police power of the State."[86] On this basis, the court deemed the Fair Sales Act unconstitutional. On appeal, the Pennsylvania Supreme Court affirmed.[87]

*Zasloff* has been cited repeatedly for the proposition that otherwise legitimate exercises of the legislature's police power will be invalidated where they do not specify with sufficient clarity the conduct proscribed.[88] In 1948, for instance, the case was relied upon by the Supreme Court to invalidate a law requiring those engaged in the business of renting motor vehicles to obtain licenses from the Public Utility Commission.[89]

---

77. 137 Pa. Super. 96, 8 A.2d 801 (1939) (Hirt, J.).
78. Pa. Act of July 1, 1937, PL 2672.
79. Pa. Act of June 19, 1936, chap. 592, 49 Stat. 1526.
80. PL 2672, sec. 3.
81. PL 2672, sec. 5.
82. 137 Pa. Super. 98, 8 A.2d 803, citing *Nebbia v. New York*, 291 U.S. 502 (1934).
83. 8 A.2d 803.
84. 8 A.2d 803-04.
85. 8 A.2d 804, citing *Wholesale Tobacco Dealers Bureau, Inc. v. National Candy & Tobacco Co.*, 82 P.2d 3 (Cal. 1938).
86. 8 A.2d 804, citing *Lief v. Packard-Bamberger & Co.*, 123 N.J.L. 95, 8 A.2d 98 (1939).
87. *Commonwealth v. Zasloff*, 338 Pa. 457 (1940).
88. See e.g., *Commonwealth v. Koczwara*, 397 Pa. 575 (1959) (Bell, dissenting); *Hertz Drivurself Stations v. Siggins*, 359 Pa. 25 (1948); *Commonwealth v. Gorodetsky*, 178 Pa. Super. 467 (1955); *Commonwealth v. Summons*, 157 Pa. Super. 95 (1945).
89. *Hertz Drivurself Stations v. Siggins*, 25.

The Indiantown Gap Barracks under construction in 1940 in preparation for anticipated enlargement of the armed forces *(Pennsylvania State Archives)*.

## DELEGATION OF ADMINISTRATIVE POWER

Broad and ambiguous provisions were not the only challenges presented to the Superior Court by the social and labor legislation of Pennsylvania's "little New Deal." Beginning in the Progressive Era and continuing through the 1930s, the promulgation of dozens of unprecedented laws extended legislative authority into vast new realms of the Commonwealth's affairs. As a result, the legislature's responsibilities grew dramatically, and it became increasingly unable to ensure that the new laws were being implemented and enforced. In response, the legislature created a dizzying array of oversight departments, boards, commissions, and agencies. These oversight bodies, many of which remain with us to this day, include the Department of Labor and Industry, the Health Department, the Board of Education, the Department of Agriculture, the Public Service Commission, the Workmen's Compensation Board, the Unemployment Compensation Board, and many others. All of these bodies are vested with broad investigatory, rule-making, and enforcement power. One of the Superior Court's central tasks has been reconciling this power with the provision of the state constitution prohibiting the delegation of legislative authority to administrative agencies.[90] Ironically, the court's most important decision in this regard arose from a statute enacted long before the New Deal.

In *Gima v. Hudson Coal Company*,[91] the Superior Court conclusively established the authority of the legislature to delegate administrative power. In that case, the plaintiff was injured in an explosion while working in a mine owned by the defendant coal company. A workmen's compensation claim was filed, but it was denied by a

---

90. Article II, Section 1, provides, "The legislative power of this Commonwealth shall be vested in a General Assembly which shall consist of a Senate and a House of Representatives."

91. 106 Pa. Super. 288 (1932) (Keller, J.).

World War II soldiers in transit via rail coach car, a frequent and common occurrence during the war years.

referee on the basis that the accident was caused by the plaintiff's violation of the Anthracite Mine Law of 1891. Specifically, the referee found that the plaintiff violated Rule 29 of the 1891 law by returning to the mine within twelve hours after he had reason to believe that one of the explosives used to loosen coal had misfired. As the plaintiff approached the face of the mine, the explosive detonated, and he was injured. The referee's denial of compensation was affirmed by the Workmen's Compensation Board, but the court of common pleas reversed on the basis that the plaintiff did not know he was returning to a misfire and that, even if negligent, he was nonetheless entitled to compensation because his conduct was not intentional. On appeal to the Superior Court, the plaintiff challenged the constitutionality of Rule 29 of the Anthracite Law. In particular, the plaintiff argued that because the rule was promulgated by the powder manufacturer and approved by the mine owner under authority granted by the legislature, it was an unconstitutional delegation of the legislature's power to make laws.[92]

The court rejected this claim. The court began by noting that the Anthracite Law was enacted to protect miners from the hazards of their occupation. "To destroy

---

92. Rule 29 provided:

When high explosives other than gun powder are used in any mine, the manner of storing, keeping, moving, charging, and firing or in any manner using such explosive, shall be in accordance with the special rules as furnished by the manufacturer of the same. The said rules shall be endorsed with his or their official signature and shall be approved by the owner, operator or superintendent of the mine in which such explosives are used. 106 Pa. Super. 296, n. 1.

the safeguard and protection of this law," the court stated, "in order to deal liberally in the allowance of compensation to a few men who were injured by failing to comply with its salutary provisions, would be a most short sighted policy."[93] Yet, the court relied on more than policy to reject the plaintiff's claim. First, the court examined a variety of state and federal laws delegating rule-making authority to administrative bodies. Quoting a decision of the Supreme Court construing the same constitutional provision at issue in the instant case, the court concluded that "[h]alf the statutes on our books are in the alternative depending on the discretion of some person or persons to whom is confided the duty of determining whether the proper occasion exists for executing them. But it cannot be said that the exercise of such a discretion is the making of the law."[94] Also relying on other precedents, the court stated the test to be applied as follows: "The legislature cannot delegate its power to make a law; but it can make a law to delegate a power to determine some fact or state of things upon which the law makes, or intends to make, its own action depend. To deny this would be to stop the wheels of government."[95] Applying this test to the plaintiff's claim, the court stated that Rule 29 was "no more a delegation of legislative power" than the many other rules regulating mining, the sale of food and drugs, and numerous other activities in which the state has an interest. The court held that no other conclusion was possible.

> The General Assembly cannot be expected to enact laws which shall in themselves keep abreast of every advance of science and invention in the explosive line, any more than it can of itself determine when a working place is free of gas and fit to work in; but it has established a means by which such advances can be utilized and made safe in mines, and in Rule 29 it has delegated its power to determine the safe method to store, charge, fire and use such explosives to the manufacturer and the mine owner jointly, knowing that they will not for their own interest err on the side of danger. . . . In doing so, the General Assembly has legislated—not the powder manufacturer or coal operator—no legislative power or authority has been delegated to them.[96]

On this basis, the court affirmed the order denying the plaintiff compensation. Thereafter, the Supreme Court affirmed the ruling of the Superior Court. In 1953 the Supreme Court stated that the "question of the delegation of power to an administrative officer was definitely settled by [*Gima*]."[97] The case has been cited repeatedly for the principle that the delegation of power to an administrative agency does not offend the constitution where the legislature provides sufficient standards to guide the agency in implementing a statute, and so long as the power delegated involves only the factual determination of whether the statute has been implicated.[98] This holding has been applied to reject constitutional challenges to the General State Authority,[99] the Department of Education,[100] the Secretary of Revenue,[101] the Liquor Control Act,[102] the Bor-

93. 106 Pa. Super. 297.
94. 106 Pa. Super. 300, quoting *Moers v. City of Reading*, 21 Pa. 188 (1853).
95. 106 Pa. Super. 298, quoting *Locke's Appeal*, 72 Pa. 491 (1873).
96. 106 Pa. Super. 300.
97. *Commonwealth v. Emerick*, 373 Pa. 388, 392 (1953).
98. See e.g., *Johnson v. Pa. Housing Finance Agency*, 453 Pa. 329 (1973); *Commonwealth v. Repplier Coal Co.*, 348 Pa. 372 (1944); *Chester County Institution District v. Commonwealth*, 341 Pa. 49 (1941); *National Transit Co. v. Boardman*, 328 Pa. 450 (1938); 99 ALR 613, 618; 83 ALR 1211, 1212, 1222.
99. *Kelley v. Earle*, 325 Pa. 337 (1937).
100. *In re Baldwin Township*, 103 Pa. Super. 106 (1931).
101. *Emerick*, supra; *Commonwealth v. Funk*, 323 Pa. 390 (1936).
102. *Weinstein Liquor Control Case*, 159 Pa. Super. 437 (1946).

In the Superior Court order of November 17, 1942, candidates recommended for admission to the bar of the Superior Court, who could not appear before the court due to service in the U. S. armed forces during the National Emergency, could be admitted in absentia *(Pennsylvania State Archives)*.

ough Code,[103] the School Reorganization Act,[104] the Housing Finance Law,[105] and numerous other statutes.[106] Also, in the realm of workmen's compensation, it indicates that injuries resulting from a willful violation of law are not compensable.[107]

## WAR CASES

Despite their unprecedented scope, the social and labor statutes of the New Deal were never adequate to cope with the Great Depression. More often than not, these statutes addressed the symptoms rather than the causes, and the result was that the nation's unemployment rate remained over 15 percent throughout the 1930s. In the end, it took the mobilization of a world war to break the Depression's stranglehold on the nation's economy. The manpower requirements of the military, coupled with the enormous need for industrial workers to produce war materials, quickly ended the prob-

103. *Nester Appeal*, supra.

104. *Chartiers Valley Joint Schools v. Allegheny County Board of School Directors*, 418 Pa. 520 (1965).

105. *Johnson v. Pa. Housing Finance Agency*, 453 Pa. 329 (1973). See also *Dornan v. Philadelphia Housing Authority*, 331 Pa. 209 (1938) (upholding the Housing Authority Act).

106. See e.g., *United States v. Dettra Flag Co.*, 86 F. Supp. 84 (1949) (18 U.S.C.A. 705); *H. A. Steen Industries v. Cavanaugh*, 430 Pa. 10 (1968) (Fairmount Park Commission); *Gulf Refining Co. v. Camp Curtin Trust Co.*, 323 Pa. 465 (1936) (Pa. Act of May 26, 1891, PL 129); *Rohrer v. Milk Control Board*, 322 Pa. 257 (1936) (Milk Control Board).

107. 73 ALR 4th 270.

In the Superior Court of Pennsylvania
SITTING AT PHILADELPHIA

No. 110                          Order Docket     xxxxxxxxxxxxxx

IN RE                                    Appeal from the

CONVENING HOUR                                        Court

HARRISBURG SESSION          of

                                         for the County of
                                         No.              Term, 19

O R D E R

        AND NOW, July 17, 1947, the Superior Court will
convene at 10 A. M. on the second Monday of March of each
year at Harrisburg instead of 1 P. M.

                              Chester H. Rhodes
                              President Judge

TRUE COPY FROM RECORD

In Testimony Whereof, I have hereunto set my hand and the seal of
said Court, at Philadelphia, this    22nd    day of    July    19 47

                                        Prothonotary.

This July 17, 1947, order changed the hour the court convened at Harrisburg
on the second Monday of March from 1:00 p.m. until 10:00 a.m.

lem of unemployment in Pennsylvania.[108] Although it improved the state's economic outlook, the Second World War, like its predecessor, presented the Superior Court with a number of challenging issues.

In *Penn Dairies v. Milk Control Commission of Pennsylvania*,[109] for instance, the court considered the extent to which state regulations could impact upon the federal government's procurement of supplies for its troops. *Penn Dairies* arose from the training of troops at Indiantown Gap in Lebanon County, the 1,600-acre National Guard reservation leased to the federal government in late September 1940. Throughout the fall of that year, the government spent $25,000,000 erecting buildings, power and water lines, roads, and other necessities in anticipation of the wartime personnel buildup. On February 1, 1941, with new recruits arriving daily, the quartermaster of the army solicited bids to supply the camp's milk requirements. The solicitation called for delivery of 135,000 one-quart bottles and 540,000 half-pint bottles between March 1 and June 30, 1941. At this point, a state law intervened. In order to ensure the purity of the state's milk supply, the legislature in 1937 passed the Milk Control Law, which established a commission with authority to set minimum prices for the sale of milk. Four

---

108. Between 1939 and 1943, for instance, nonagricultural employment grew from 2,700,600 to 3,512,200. Klein and Hoogenboom, *A History of Pennsylvania*, 469.

109. 148 Pa. Super. 261 (1942) (Kenworthey, J.).

days after the Indiantown Gap solicitation was issued, the commission notified prospective bidders that the minimum allowable price of milk was $.095 per quart and
$.025 per half-pint. Despite the commission's notice, the defendant, a Lancaster milk
dealer, bid on and was awarded the Indiantown Gap contract at $.079 per quart and
$.0215 per half-pint, both of which were below the state minimum. Thereafter, the
commission refused to renew the defendant's license to sell milk, and its decision was
sustained by the court of common pleas. The defendant, joined by the United States as
intervenor, appealed to the Superior Court on the basis that the Milk Control Law, as
applied to the defendant's bid on the Indiantown Gap contract, imposed an unconstitutional burden on the federal government.

The court began by noting that the difficult question of state authority to interfere with operations of the federal government "has long been the subject of controversy."[110] Finding no authority directly on point, the court turned to federal decisions
involving the authority of states to impose taxes that increase the expense of federal
activities. "From *McCullogh v. Maryland*, decided in 1824, down to *James v. Dravo
Contracting Co.*, decided in 1937," the court stated, "Chief Justice Marshall's dictum
that the power to tax is the power to destroy was the prevailing doctrine."[111] Under that
doctrine, virtually any law burdening the federal government was declared unconstitutional. Yet the court found that the old standard was replaced by the United States
Supreme Court in the late 1930s with one providing that a state tax is valid so long as
it "bears upon an independent contractor, does not discriminate, and is not so burdensome as seriously to interfere with governmental functions."[112] Applying this standard
for state tax statutes to exercises of the police power, the court noted that the minimum
price regulations established by the commission were directed at the defendant, an
independent contractor, and applied equally to the federal government and any other
consumer of milk. Moreover, since the regulations were neither barred by federal legislation nor discriminatory against the federal government, the fact that they increased
the price of milk sold to the government was merely incidental. Rejecting the claim of
the United States, the court also concluded that the regulations did not interfere with
the government's policy of competitive bidding because they merely "put all bidders on
an equal footing with regard to the minimum price."[113] On this basis, the court deemed
the Milk Control Law constitutional and dismissed the appeals of the defendant and
the United States.[114] On appeal, the Pennsylvania Supreme Court affirmed on the basis of the Superior Court opinion.

Thereafter, the defendant and the federal government pursued their case to the
United States Supreme Court. In 1943 the Supreme Court affirmed the state courts,
concluding as follows:

> We are unable to find in Congressional legislation, either as read in the
> light of its history or as construed by the executive officers charged
> with the exercise of the contracting power, any disclosure of a purpose
> to immunize government contractors from local price-fixing regulations

110. 148 Pa. Super. 269.

111. 148 Pa. Super. 269, citing *McCullogh v. Maryland*, 4 Wheat. 316, 17 U.S. 316 (1819), and *James v.
Dravo Contracting Co.*, 302 U.S. 134 (1937) (Kenworthey, J.).

112. 148 Pa. Super. 270, citing *Panhandle Oil Company v. Mississippi ex rel. Knox*, 277 U.S. 218, 223
(1928) (Holmes, dissenting); *Graves v. New York ex rel. O'Keefe*, 306 U.S. 466 (1939); *Alabama v. King &
Boozer*, 314 U.S. 1 (1941), and *James*, 302 U.S. 172 (Roberts, dissenting).

113. 148 Pa. Super. 272.

114. 148 Pa. Super. 272-73. Judge Rhodes dissented on the basis that the state minimum price regulations undermined the intent of the army's competitive bidding mandate to secure the lowest prices for goods
purchased.

which would otherwise be applicable. Nor, in the circumstances of this case, can we find that the Constitution, unaided by Congressional enactment, confers such an immunity. It follows that the Pennsylvania courts rightly held that the Constitution and laws of the United States did not preclude the application of the Pennsylvania Milk Control Law to appellant.[115]

In the half-century since *Penn Dairies* was decided, it has been cited more than a dozen times by the United States Supreme Court, by every circuit court of appeal, by courts in virtually every state, and repeatedly by Pennsylvania appellate courts. Most importantly, it stands for the proposition that the courts will not lightly infer congressional intent to set aside state regulations, and such regulations will not be invalidated by the supremacy clause merely because they have some impact upon federal activities.[116] Moreover, regulations directed at independent contractors dealing with the federal government will be sustained, despite the fact that they increase the price of goods purchased by the government.[117]

Two years after *Penn Dairies*, in *Commonwealth v. Reitz*,[118] the Superior Court considered the constitutionality of a state wartime defense law, the Air Raid Precautions Act. The act established a State Council of Defense with authority "to adopt, promulgate and enforce rules" intended to protect the civilian population, and also provided that the council's regulations shall have "the same force as if they formed a part of this Act."[119] One of the council's regulations provided that, upon the sounding of an air raid alarm, all persons "shall. . . immediately seek shelter and remain therein until the all clear signal is given." On July 22, 1942, an air raid alarm was sounded in the Washington County borough in which the defendant resided, and he was instructed by an air raid warden to extinguish the lights in his place of business and remain indoors. In violation of the instruction, the defendant remained outdoors and in the open and he was charged with a violation of the act. Following trial, the court of common pleas determined that the defendant had violated the act, but nonetheless deemed the act unconstitutional on the basis that it improperly delegated to the council the legislature's authority to establish and enforce rules of conduct. Since the defendant was discharged upon a pure question of law, the Commonwealth was permitted to appeal to the Superior Court.[120]

A unanimous court stated that the case "presents the important question whether the State, in time of war, or other serious emergency, may protect its citizens and their

---

115. *Penn Dairies v. Milk Control Commission of Pennsylvania*, 318 U.S. 261, 278 (1943). Like Judge Rhodes of the Superior Court, Justice Douglas, joined by Justices Black and Jackson, dissented on the basis that the army's competitive bidding regulations were intended to secure the lowest prices for goods purchased and, since the state milk regulations operate to increase milk prices, they must give way to the supremacy clause when government contracts are at issue. The same day the U.S. Supreme Court decided *Penn Dairies*, it invalidated California price controls on milk sold to the army at Moffett Field, outside of San Francisco. *Pacific Coast Dairy v. Dept. of Agriculture of California*, 318 U.S. 285 (1943). The court distinguished *Pacific Coast Dairies* from *Penn Dairies* on the basis that the federal government merely leased Indiantown Gap, whereas it retained sovereignty and exclusive jurisdiction over Moffett Field. 318 U.S. 295 ("Here we are bound to respect the relevant constitutional provision with respect to the exclusive power of Congress over federal lands.").

116. See e.g., *Bowen v. American Hospital Association*, 476 U.S. 610 (1986); *Hancock v. Train*, 426 U.S. 167 (1976); *Commonwealth v. Capitolo*, 324 Pa. Super. 61 (1984); and *Commonwealth v. Di Meglio*, 179 Pa. Super. 472 (1955).

117. See e.g., *Pennsylvania Liquor Control Board v. Publicker Commercial Alcohol Co.*, 347 Pa. 555 (1943); and *Appeal of Mesta Machine Co.*, 347 Pa. 191 (1943).

118. 156 Pa. Super. 122 (1944) (Hirt, J.).

119. Pa. Act of March 19, 1941, PL 6.

120. 156 Pa. Super. 124, citing *Commonwealth v. Simpson*, 310 Pa. 380 (1933) ("Upon the discharge of the defendant on this pure question of law the Commonwealth properly appealed to this court.").

property by legislation in the form presented."[121] After setting forth at some length the relevant provisions of the act and council regulations, the court described the situation prevailing early in the war, when the outcome was anything but certain:

> We have quoted enough of the acts in question to indicate the sense of imminent danger in the mind of the legislature and its serious effort to meet an unknown future through a flexible system of protection of persons and property. This state was not alone in enacting such legislation. The danger at the time was real. In the Pacific, following December 7, 1941, Japan's naval and air forces were superior; and in the Atlantic the battle was in the balance. We were unprepared. The danger was from the air and with a turn of events in favor of the Axis powers, Pennsylvania, with its capacity of production for materials and implements of war, well might have become a major target.[122]

The court then noted that a delegation of authority to a non-legislative body is not unconstitutional where the legislature prescribes "with reasonable clarity" the scope of power delegated. In such case, regulations promulgated by the body are administrative and not legislative. Since the state was threatened by "an enemy with a genius for new and effective instruments of aerial warfare," the court continued, it was not possible to foresee the precise measures required to combat the threat.[123] "Of necessity," it found, "the legislature was obliged to delegate some discretion as to the choice of means in protecting persons and property against an unknown future."[124] The court concluded that the act, which directed the council to regulate "the conduct of civilians and the movement and cessation of . . . traffic during attack or drill," was sufficiently clear to define the council's authority.[125] Since the regulations of the council were administrative and not legislative, the trial court erred in deeming the Air Raid Precautions Act an unconstitutional delegation of legislative authority. The record was then remitted to the trial court to enter a verdict of guilty against the defendant.

In the years since it was rendered, the court's decision in *Reitz* has stood for the proposition that the legislature may constitutionally delegate the responsibility to determine facts upon which the application or enforcement of the law is to depend, so long as the legislature sufficiently defines the scope of the delegation.[126] The case has also been cited repeatedly for the proposition that the Commonwealth may appeal where a defendant is discharged upon a pure question of law, or where the case involves the constitutionality of the act under which an indictment is drawn.[127]

A final type of case related to the war warrants consideration. Although the most obvious deaths resulting from war are combat casualties, soldiers are also killed while in training or on leave. These deaths raise difficult questions when estates or survivors attempt to collect on life insurance policies that commonly contain exclusions for deaths "resulting from" military service or occurring while the insured is "engaged in" military service. The Superior Court addressed two such questions of first impression in the wake of World War II.

---

121. 156 Pa. Super. 126.

122. 156 Pa. Super. 125.

123. 156 Pa. Super. 127.

124. 156 Pa. Super. 127, citing *Holgate Bros. Co. v. Bashore*, 331 Pa. 255 (1938)

125. 156 Pa. Super. 126.

126. *Commonwealth v. Collins*, 203 Pa. Super. 125 (1964); *Commonwealth v. Harrison*, 183 Pa. Super. 133 (1957); *Obradovich Liquor License Case*, 180 Pa. Super. 383 (1956) (Ervin, dissenting).

127. *Commonwealth v. Arnold*, 215 Pa. Super. 444 (1969); *Commonwealth v. Loyal Order of Moose*, 188 Pa. Super. 531 (1959); *Commonwealth v. Hartman*, 179 Pa. Super. 134 (1955); *Commonwealth v. Frank*, 159 Pa. Super. 271 (1946).

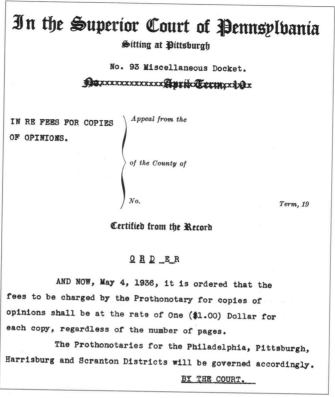

In the Superior Court of Pennsylvania
Sitting at Pittsburgh

No. 93 Miscellaneous Docket.

~~No.~~xxxxxxxxxxxxxx~~April Term, 19~~x

IN RE FEES FOR COPIES          Appeal from the
OF OPINIONS.

                               of the County of

                               No.                    Term, 19

Certified from the Record

O R D E R

AND NOW, May 4, 1936, it is ordered that the
fees to be charged by the Prothonotary for copies of
opinions shall be at the rate of One ($1.00) Dollar for
each copy, regardless of the number of pages.

The Prothonotaries for the Philadelphia, Pittsburgh,
Harrisburg and Scranton Districts will be governed accordingly.

BY THE COURT.

The order of May 4, 1936, applicable in each judicial district, established $1.00 to be the fee charged for copies of each opinion, regardless of the number of pages.

In *Selenack v. Prudential Insurance Co.*,[128] the defendant life insurance company issued two policies on the life of Joseph Selenack, a native of Pennsylvania. The policies contained double indemnity clauses that provided that an insured would receive twice the face value of the policy in the event that death was caused by accident. Selenack was a corporal in the army during the war and was stationed at Fort Knox, Kentucky. On May 31, 1943, he was riding in the turret of a tank, which was part of a convoy proceeding down a public road. To avoid an approaching school bus, the tank drove onto the berm of the road. The berm was too soft, however, and the tank overturned and killed Selenack. His estate commenced an action to recover under the double indemnity provisions of the policies issued by the defendant. At trial, the defendant conceded that, since Selenack had died as the result of an accident, the underlying condition of the indemnity clauses had been satisfied. The defendant raised in defense, however, another provision of the policy which provided, "No Accidental Death Benefit will be paid if the death of the Insured resulted . . . from having been engaged in military or naval service in time of war." The trial court found that this clause barred recovery by the plaintiff's estate. The estate appealed on the basis that the clause applied only to deaths resulting from combat.

The Superior Court noted that the "language of the exclusion clause in the present policies, has not been construed by our appellate courts."[129] Turning to the most common types of war-risk exclusion clauses, the court distinguished between so-

---

128. 160 Pa. Super. 242 (1947) (Hirt, J.).
129. 160 Pa. Super. 246.

```
                              In the
                    SUPERIOR COURT OF PENNSYLVANIA
                         Sitting at Harrisburg
                         ----------


In re:                   :
                         :
REVISED SCHEDULE         :    No.
                         :
OF FEES                  :


     April  12 , 1946, It is ordered that the fees to be charged
by the Prothonotary in each of the districts shall be in accord-
ance with the following schedule.   This order is to take effect
as of April 1, 1946.
                       SCHEDULE OF FEES

     Issuing Writ of Certiorari...........................$12.00
        "    "   "  Habeas Corpus.......................... 15.00
        "    "   "  Mandamus.............................. 15.00

     Petition, Stipulation, Agreement, Motion to
             quash, etc....................................  1.00

     Discontinuance........................................  5.00

     Non Pros..............................................  3.00

     Certificate of Transfer..............................  3.00
     Certificate of Order or Judgment.....................  2.00

     Short Certificate (certifying attorney has been
                     admitted to practice before
                     the Superior Court)................  1.00
     Certificate to practice in another State.............  1.00

     Admission of attorneys (Two Dollars of which shall
                     be paid to the Crier)........  5.00

     Copy of opinion of the Court, regardless of number
                             of pages................  1.50

     "Exemplification" with court seal to any opinion......  1.00

     Transcript of Record for petition for Certiorari to
     the United States Supreme Court, per page, first
                             10 pages.......   .50
                        Each succeeding page.......   .25

     Certifying case from Superior to Supreme Court
     where appeal is erroneously taken to Supreior Court...  6.00

               No charge for affixing seal to any paper
               connected with proceedings in Court.

          No charge for a copy of opinion to any
          lower court judge.
```

The order of April 12, 1946, established a schedule of fees to be charged by the prothonotary in each district for the named activities.

called "status" exclusions, which deny payment of benefits to an insured who is killed while a member of the military, and "resulting" exclusions, which, like the clause at issue, deny payment where death *results* from military service. While the court found unanimity among the nation's courts in upholding the validity of the former exclusions, it noted a conflict of opinion over the latter exclusions. Despite the conflict, however, the court found that the language of the exclusion clearly and unambiguously denied benefits where death occurred during wartime, regardless of whether it resulted from combat or training. To the court, the important distinction was not between combat and training, but between war and peacetime. Indeed, "one is much more liable to injury and death, by accidental means, from military training and other service in time of war than from like service at other times. The stepped-up tempo of the intensive effort in time of war increases the risk." Finding no express language limiting the exclusion to actual combat service, the court held that "[d]eath resulting from military service in time of war comprehends death in actual combat but is not so restricted as to exclude death under other circumstances, if actually resulting from military service, in time of war."[130] On this basis, the trial court's ruling was affirmed, and the Supreme Court subsequently denied allocatur. *Selenack* has been cited by numerous state and federal courts for the proposition that "resulting" clauses will bar the payment of double indemnity benefits where a death occurs while in training or other noncombat service.[131]

A year later, the court again construed a common war-risk exclusion. In *Wolford v. Equitable Life Insurance Co.*,[132] the decedent, an army captain, was insured under a policy issued by the defendant that contained a double indemnity clause for accidental death. On December 22, 1945, he was killed in an automobile accident in Pennsylvania while home on leave. The beneficiary of the life insurance policy filed suit for the double indemnity benefit. Although the defendant admitted that decedent was killed in an accident, it raised in defense clause 19 of the policy, which stated that the "provisions for the Disability and the Double Indemnity benefits . . . shall terminate: . . . (c) In the event that the insured shall engage in military or naval service in time of war. . . ." The beneficiary argued that the word "engage" in clause 19 meant more than simply being a member of the service; it meant active participation in the war in a manner that would have increased the risk to the insured. The trial court denied the beneficiary's claim and an appeal was taken.

The Superior Court began its analysis by noting that clause 19 was distinguishable from the "results" exclusion at issue in *Selenack* because it did not entail any causation between the service and the accident which killed decedent. Instead, clause (c) depended solely on the status of the decedent. "In the present contract," the court found, "the insurer, by plain words, provided for the termination of the double indemnity provisions upon the happening of an event. What event? The contract answers this without ambiguity: '[In] the event that the insured shall engage in military . . . service in time of war.'"[133] Since clause 19 did not require causation, the court "construe[d] the word 'engaged' to mean 'enter into' where used in the termination clause."[134] As a result, the double indemnity benefit terminated the moment decedent entered the armed forces, and the beneficiary's claim was properly denied by the trial court. The Supreme Court denied allocatur. Like *Selenack*, *Wolford* became an important precedent for courts

---

130. 160 Pa. Super. 247.

131. See e.g., *Mullen v. Pacific Mutual Life Insurance*, 179 F.2d 556 (3d Cir. 1950); *Hooker v. New York Life Insurance Co.*, 161 F.2d 852 (7th Cir. 1947); *Diamond Shamrock Chemicals Co. v. Aetna Casualty and Surety Co., et al.*, 609 A.2d 440 (N.J. Super. Ct. 1992); 39 ALR 2d 1018, 1029, 1034, 1045.

132. 162 Pa. Super. 259 (1948) (Arnold, J.).

133. 162 Pa. Super. 261.

134. 162 Pa. Super. 261 (noting that the word "engage" is derived from "gage," meaning "pledge").

The Superior Court in 1948. L. to R. (seated): William E. Hirt, Chester H. Rhodes (President Judge), Claude T. Reno. L. to R. (standing): John C. Arnold, W. Heber Dithrich, F. Clair Ross, John S. Fine.

construing provisions of life insurance policies issued to servicemen who are subsequently killed in noncombat activities.[135]

## CRIMINAL CASES

In addition to addressing difficult issues arising from the New Deal and World War II, the court also decided a number of important cases in the realm of criminal law. One such case was *Commonwealth v. Roller*,[136] the so-called "Talkie Confession" case, in which the court established an evidentiary standard for the admission of technological advances that has been cited around the country. In *Roller*, the defendant's confession to a series of robberies was recorded by the Philadelphia police on an early motion picture camera, known as a Movietone camera. The confession was played at trial and

135. See e.g., *Harding v. Pennsylvania Mutual Life Insurance Co.*, 171 Pa. Super. 236 (1952); *Janco v. John Hancock Mutual Life Insurance Co.*, 164 Pa. Super. 128 (1949); *Mullen,* supra. See also, 36 ALR 2d 1018, 1022, 1039, 1044, 1067.
136. 100 Pa. Super. 125 (1930) (Gawthrop, J.).

the defendant was convicted. On appeal, the defendant argued that the recording was improperly admitted at trial.

In affirming the defendant's conviction, the court held, "From time to time the courts have recognized new agencies for presenting evidential matters. The novelty of the talking motion picture is no reason for rejecting it if its accuracy and reliability, as aids in the determination of the truth, are established."[137] Quoting from the opinion of the trial court, it continued:

> [A]ll knowledge purveys to the law, and from the domains of every art and science it draws the weapons by which it discovers truth and confounds error. The still photograph, X-ray, dictagraph, the microscope and even the blood hound have all been used and received by judicial tribunals in proof of matters depending upon evidence. As photographs and phonographic reproductions of sound have been held to be admissible in evidence there would seem to be no reason for refusing to accept a talking moving picture, which is but a combination of the two, when it is shown to be accurate and reliable.[138]

The court then found that the recording of the defendant's confession was properly authenticated at trial. As a result, the court affirmed the trial court's decision admitting the recording into evidence. Based on this ruling, the Philadelphia police began the state's first routine use of cameras for recording confessions.[139] More importantly, *Roller* has been relied upon to validate the evidentiary use of a number of technological advances in law enforcement equipment, including standard motion picture cameras,[140] video cameras,[141] and two of the earliest versions of breathalyzers, intoximeters,[142] and drunkometers.[143] The case has also been cited by the Eighth Circuit Court of Appeals,[144] state courts in California,[145] Florida,[146] Louisiana,[147] Missouri,[148] New York,[149] North Carolina,[150] and Texas,[151] and a number of scholarly journals.[152]

Another important criminal decision was *Commonwealth ex rel. Lycett v. Ashe,*[153] in which the court considered the legislature's constitutional power to prescribe sentencing regulations. In order to understand *Lycett*, it is necessary to briefly consider the

---

137. 100 Pa. Super. 128.

138. See note 136.

139. The day of the court's ruling, Director Schofield of the Philadelphia Police "announced an intention to use the talking picture extensively if the higher court's judgment was one of approval." *Philadelphia Public Ledger*, 22 Nov. 1930, p. 1, col. 3 (discussing the "Talkie Confession" case).

140. *Reimer v. Delisio*, 296 Pa. Super. 205 (1982); *De Battiste v. Anthony Laudadio & Son*, 167 Pa. Super. 38 (1950).

141. *McNenamin v. Tartaglione*, 22 Phila. 133 (Pa. C. P. 1991).

142. *Commonwealth v. Hartman*, 179 Pa. Super. 134 (1955).

143. *Commonwealth v. Mummert*, 183 Pa. Super. 638 (1957).

144. *Hendricks v. Swenson*, 456 F.2d 503 (8th Cir. 1972).

145. *California v. Dabb*, 197 P.2d 1 (1948), and *California v. Hayes*, 71 P.2d 321 (1937).

146. *Hutchins v. Florida*, 286 So.2d 244 (Fla. Dist. Ct. App. 3d Dist. 1973).

147. *Louisiana v. Alleman*, 51 So.2d 83 (La. 1950).

148. *Missouri v. Hamell*, 561 S.W.2d 357 (Mo. Ct. App. 1977); *Missouri v. Lusk*, 452 S.W.2d 219 (Mo. 1970); *Missouri v. Perkins*, 198 S.W.2d 704 (Mo. 1946); and *Morris v. E.I. DuPont de Memours & Co.*, 139 S.W.2d 984 (Mo. 1940).

149. *New York v. Higgins*, 392 N.Y.S.2d 800 (1977).

150. *North Carolina v. Strickland*, 168 S.E.2d 697 (1969).

151. *Housewright v. Texas*, 225 S.W.2d 417 (1950).

152. 57 Dick. L. Rev. 1; 10 U. Pitt. L. Rev. 164; 41 ALR 4th 877; 100 ALR 2d 1257; 62 ALR 2d 686; 58 ALR 2d 1024; 9 ALR 2d 899.

153. 145 Pa. Super. 26 (1941) (Keller, J.).

law of sentencing in the 1930s. Prior to 1936, there existed no legislative authority for sentencing judges to aggregate consecutive sentences. In other words, to use a hypothetical, the judge was not empowered to convert two consecutive sentences of five to ten years into a single sentence of ten to twenty years. Instead, as a matter of custom, this aggregation was performed by prison authorities when they determined a prisoner's minimum and maximum terms for purposes of parole. Thus, in our hypothetical, when the prisoner was incarcerated, his sentences would be converted into a single sentence of ten to twenty years. Under this system of aggregation, the prisoner, at the end of five years (the minimum of the first sentence), could apply for "constructive" parole, which, if granted, meant that he began serving his second sentence at the same time he was on "parole" from the second half of his first sentence. Since he got "double" time for his second five years in prison, the aggregated maximum term of the prisoner's sentence was reduced from twenty to fifteen years. This difference became critical if the prisoner committed another crime while on parole from his second sentence. Again returning to our hypothetical, assume the prisoner was paroled after a total of ten years in prison, having satisfied either the minimum term of his aggregated sentence or the minimum terms of his two non-aggregated sentences. He immediately committed another crime, and thus became susceptible of being returned to prison to serve out his original sentences. If he did not receive a "constructive" parole, he would owe ten more years, or the final five years remaining on each sentence. However, if he received such parole, he would owe only five more years, the time remaining on his second sentence, because the same five years counted as the last half of his first sentence and the first half of his second sentence.

In 1936 the Supreme Court declared that neither courts nor prison authorities possessed authority to aggregate consecutive sentences. The court also noted that where a prisoner seeks and receives a "constructive" parole, the maximum term for which he is liable as a subsequent parole violator is reduced accordingly. Lynch, the prisoner at issue in *Commonwealth ex rel. Lynch v. Ashe*, [154] received two consecutive sentences of eighteen months to three years. After eighteen months, under prison rules and without filing a parole application, he was allowed to begin serving his second sentence. In effect, the prison granted him a "constructive" parole on the first sentence without a request. After serving three years, Lynch was paroled and reoffended. Thereafter, he was sentenced to the three years remaining on his original sentences. He argued that the first sentence had been fully discharged by the de facto "constructive" parole. The Supreme Court's ruling turned on the fact that the prisoner did not request "constructive" parole at the end of the minimum term of his first sentence, and that the prison had no authority to allow him to begin serving his second sentence in the absence of such a request. Accordingly, the court held that his subsequent commission of a crime while on parole from the second sentence meant that he must serve the remaining time on both sentences. The court stated, however, "If he had been granted a parole from further service of sentence No. 1 at the end of the first half of that sentence, he would have had for eighteen months the double status he now claims to have had, but he neither asked for nor obtained a parole."[155] A year later, in order to sanction aggregation and prohibit "constructive" paroles, the legislature enacted P.L. 2093, which required courts to aggregate consecutive sentences and mandated that parolees who committed new crimes must serve the maximum terms of the consecutive sentences originally imposed.[156] The act provided:

---

154. 320 Pa. 341 (1936).
155. 320 Pa. 346.
156. Pa. Act of June 25, 1937, PL 2093.

Whenever . . . two or more sentences to run consecutively are imposed by any court of this Commonwealth upon any person convicted of crime therein, there shall be deemed to be imposed upon such person a sentence the minimum of which shall be the total of the minimum limits of the several sentences so imposed, and the maximum of which shall be the total of the maximum limits of such sentence.[157]

By precluding the necessity of prisoners applying for "constructive" parole at the end of each of their various minimum terms, the act also relieved the probation and parole board of the burden of deciding those parole applications.[158]

Three years later, in *Lycett*, the constitutionality of P.L. 2093 was challenged before the Superior Court. The prisoner at issue received consecutive sentences of one and one-half to three years and one to three years. In supposed compliance with P.L. 2093, these sentences were aggregated into a single sentence of two and one-half to six years. Seven months after he was incarcerated, the prisoner escaped, but he was quickly apprehended. Although no parole violation was at issue, the prisoner's escape sentence, like the sentence for a parole violation, was based upon the length of the sentence originally imposed. Since the sentence was aggregated under P.L. 2093, the prisoner filed a writ of habeas corpus challenging the constitutionality of the statute. Specifically, he argued that by enacting a sentencing statute the legislature violated Article V, Section 1, of the state constitution, which vested the judicial power of the Commonwealth in the courts. The trial court rejected this claim, and the prisoner appealed.

A unanimous Superior Court also rejected the claim that P.L. 2093 was unconstitutional. This conclusion was based on the legislature's extensive power to regulate matters related to the criminal law. According to the court:

It is within the province of the legislature to pronounce what acts, in addition to those recognized at common law, are crimes, and to fix the punishment for all crimes, whether statutory or common law. The legislature has the right to classify crimes, and designate the procedure at trial or after sentence; it may fix the maximum penalty and likewise can, if it sees fit, name the minimum. The necessity or wisdom of its action is a question for its determination, and in so doing it does not violate Art. V, sec. 1 of the Constitution vesting the judicial power in the courts.[159]

---

157. See note 155.

158. See *Jamieson v. Pennsylvania Board of Probation and Parole*, 90 Pa. Cmwlth. 318 (1985).

159. 145 Pa. Super. 29 (citations omitted). The court modified the defendant's escape sentence from two and one-half to six years to one and one-half to three years. This modification reflected the length of his first consecutive sentence, which was the sentence he was serving at the time of escape. 145 Pa. Super. 33. In *Taylor v. Board of Probation and Parole*, 36 Pa. Cmwlth. 625 (1978), PL 2093 was deemed suspended by Pa.R.Cr.P. 1415(c) on the basis that it was inconsistent with Pa.R.Cr.P. 1406, which provided that sentences will be deemed concurrent unless the sentencing judge specifies otherwise. However, the legislature thereafter enacted section 1357 of the Crimes Code, 42 Pa.C.S., which required the trial court to determine the minimum sentence when consecutive sentences are imposed. The section made no reference to aggregation and, on this basis, the Commonwealth Court found in 1978 that PL 2093 had been revived. See *Blackwell v. Pennsylvania Department of Probation and Parole*, 36 Pa. Cmwlth. 31 (1978). For a later case discussing this point, see *Hamlin v. Pennsylvania Board of Probation and Parole*, 92 Pa. Cmwlth. 349 (1985).

In the years since it was decided, *Lycett* has been cited repeatedly as validating legislative authority over virtually every matter related to the criminal law.[160] It indicates, for instance, that "[t]he legislature is not encroaching upon the judiciary by determining what conduct is criminal, fixing the penalties, including maximum and minimum and indefinite sentences, and providing for probation and parole, and in establishing and regulating the institutions for incarceration and correction."[161] The case has also been cited to reject subsequent attacks on P.L. 2093,[162] its successor,[163] and other criminal statutes,[164] and to uphold the constitutionality of the Mandatory Minimum Sentencing Act,[165] and the penalty provisions of the state drunk driving statute.[166]

## PROPOSALS TO CHANGE THE COURT

In addition to the great societal events that influenced the political make-up and work of the court between 1931 and 1950, a number of proposals were also directed at its structure and operation. One such proposal emerged from the Governor's Advisory Committee on Constitutional Revision, which was appointed in 1935 by Democratic Governor George H. Earle to suggest alterations to the Constitution of 1874. A year later, the Committee issued a brief report in which it proposed a series of changes. The proposed judiciary article indicates the conservative nature of the Committee's recommendations:

### IV. The Judiciary

> Provision should be made for the more efficient handling of the work of the courts, but without changing in any fundamental respect our present judicial system as regards the supreme, superior, common pleas and orphan's courts, and without sacrificing the independence of the judiciary. All judges of the said courts shall be constitutional officers.[167]

Although the Committee recommended only modest change, its inclusion of the Superior Court within the judiciary article of the constitution would have removed the

---

160. See e.g., *United States ex rel. Monk v. Maroney*, 378 F.2d 55 (3d Cir. Pa. 1967); *Lowry v. Pennsylvania Board of Parole*, 415 Pa. 90 (1964); *Commonwealth v. Glover*, 397 Pa. 543 (1959); *Commonwealth ex rel. Banks v. Cain*, 345 Pa. 581 (1942); *Commonwealth ex rel. Baerchus v. Day*, 178 Pa. Super. 455 (1955); *Commonwealth ex rel. Tiscio v. Burke*, 173 Pa. Super. 350 (1953); *Commonwealth ex rel. Hill v. Burke*, 165 Pa. Super 583 (1949); *Commonwealth ex rel. Wolkiewicz v. Pennsylvania Parole Board*, 158 Pa. Super. 607 (1946); *Cunninghaam v. Pennsylvania Board of Probation and Parole*, 39 Pa. Cmwlth. 229 (1978); *Taylor v. Pennsylvania Board of Probation and Parole*, 36 Pa. Cmwwlth. 625 (1978); and 143 ALR 1486.

161. See Robert Woodside, *Pennsylvania Constitutional Law* (Sayre, Pa.: Murrelle Printing Co., 1985), 44.

162. *Commonwealth ex rel. Spader v. Myers*, 196 Pa. Super. 23 (1961); *Commonwealth ex rel. Tiscio v. Martin*, 180 Pa. Super. 462 (1956); *Commonwealth ex rel. Jamieson v. Pennsylvania Board of Probation and Parole*, 83 Pa. Cmwlth. 546 (1984).

163. *Gillespie v. Pennsylvania Department of Corrections*, 106 Pa. Cmwlth. 500 (1987) (construing Pa.R.Cr.P. 1406(b).

164. *Commonwealth ex rel. Salerno v. Banmiller*, 189 Pa. Super. 156 (1959) (construing the Pa. Act of August 24, 1951, PL 1401).

165. *Commonwealth v. Bates*, 10 Phila. 545 (Pa. C. P. 1984) (upholding 42 Pa.C.S. sec. 9712 et seq.).

166. *Commonwealth v. Gamber*, 352 Pa. Super. 36 (1986) (upholding 75 Pa.C.S. sec. 3731).

167. The Earle Committee's proposals are set forth in George D. Wolf, *Constitutional Revision in Pennsylvania; The Dual Tactic of Amendment and Limited Convention* (New York: National Municipal League, 1969), 13-15.

court's statutory status. However, like the similar proposal of the Sproul Commission in 1920, the Earle Committee's recommendation would not be incorporated into the constitution. In September 1935, the Committee's call for a constitutional convention was defeated by a public vote of 1,184,160 to 916,949.

Another proposal directed at the court arose from the unprecedented nature of New Deal legislation. On the federal level, as soon as the new statutes were passed, they were attacked on a variety of constitutional grounds, and the judiciary proved to be the principal obstacle to the success of President Roosevelt's program. Following the Supreme Court's invalidation of the National Industrial Recovery Act in 1935, Roosevelt's efforts to secure a friendly judiciary took on a new urgency. The most prominent of these efforts was the so-called "court-packing" plan, in which Roosevelt unsuccessfully attempted to increase the size of the Supreme Court and "pack" it with judges sympathetic to the New Deal. In Pennsylvania, the situation was similar, although somewhat less dramatic. Constitutional challenges to the state's "little New Deal" statutes flooded the courts. In 1938 Chief Justice Kephart told the *Philadelphia Public Ledger* that the judiciary was "loaded down with constitutionality cases."[168] Agreeing with the plaintiffs in many of these cases, the Supreme and Superior Courts in the late 1930s invalidated a series of "little New Deal" statutes,[169] including the 44-Hour Law,[170] the Full Crew Law,[171] the Liquor Floor Tax Act,[172] and, as noted, the Fair Sales Act.[173] In response to rulings such as these, legislators friendly to the New Deal proposed measures to limit the ability of courts to invalidate statutes on constitutional grounds. These proposals were advanced most forcefully during the administration of Governor Earle, who served from 1935 to 1939. In 1937, for instance, Democratic Representative Russell Marino of Washington County offered a bill requiring state appellate courts to agree unanimously before invalidating a statute as unconstitutional. However, many legislators objected to Marino's bill on the basis that it restricted too severely the power of judicial review. In response to these objections, the bill was modified to allow statutes to be invalidated upon a vote of five to two. Although the modified bill was reported out of the Judiciary General Committee, it again failed and was not revived.[174]

Another unsuccessful proposal arose from attempts to secure a new location for the Superior and Supreme Courts while convened at Philadelphia. Under state law existing since the nineteenth century, municipalities in which the courts sat were required to provide adequate facilities. In Philadelphia, both courts had convened in the Supreme Court's courtroom in City Hall since the Superior Court was created in 1895. Since they shared a courtroom, the courts could not sit in Philadelphia at the same time. By 1930, a number of judges and legislators believed that each court should be provided with its own courtroom. Since City Hall had become too congested, it was decided that a new building should be constructed, and a commission was appointed in 1930 to select a site.[175] The commission consisted of Chief Justice Robert Von Moschzisker, Attorney General Cyrus E. Woods, and Philadelphia attorney Francis Shunk Brown.[176] While it examined possible sites, the commission also had an archi-

---

168. *Philadelphia Public Ledger*, 10 Jan. 1938, p. 10, col. 1.

169. Constitutional challenges to the first three of these acts proceeded directly to the Supreme Court from the Dauphin County Court of Common Pleas, which handled cases involving the state and was the forerunner of the modern Commonwealth Court.

170. *Holgate Bros. Co. v. Bashore*, 331 Pa. 255 (1938).

171. *Pennsylvania Railroad Co. v. Driscoll*, 336 Pa. 310 (1939) (the Full Crew Law sought to ensure passenger safety on the state's railways by mandating certain minimum staffing requirements).

172. *Commonwealth ex rel. Department of Justice v. A. Overholt & Co.*, 331 Pa. 182 (1938).

173. *Commonwealth v. Zasloff*, 137 Pa. Super. 96, 8 A.2d 801 (1939).

174. Marino's proposals are discussed in the *Philadelphia Public Ledger*, 8 May 1937, p. 4, col. 2.

175. *Philadelphia Public Ledger*, 10 Oct. 1930, p. 1, col. 8.

176. *Philadelphia Public Ledger*, 5 Nov. 1930, p. 30, col. 3.

tect draw up plans for the new building. The commission began by searching for a site facing the parkway, but finding no lots available, it finally settled on a lot on 18th Street between Sumner and Vine, adjoining the Roman Catholic Cathedral.[177] However, a dispute arose over whether the city or state should bear the financial responsibility of acquiring the lot. In a report issued on March 7, 1931, the commission stated "that, in view of the present financial condition of the city, the Commonwealth itself should seriously consider acquiring the land and proceeding with the project."[178] In order to equalize the cost, the report further suggested that the expense of maintaining the new courthouse "could properly be placed on the County of Philadelphia, in place of the expenses to which it is now put in connection with the quarters presently furnished."[179] This suggestion proved inadequate, however, and the proposal for a new courthouse was apparently abandoned after the city and state could not agree on which entity would finance the purchase of a site.

A more successful proposal directed at the court arose from the economic privation of the Depression. In early 1933, with more than one-third of the state's work force unemployed, the Senate voted by a majority of forty-two to six to cut the pay of all judges in the state by 15 percent. Because the constitution prohibited the alteration of statutory salaries of officials during the term in which the alteration is enacted, the Senate also passed a resolution urging voluntary acceptance of the pay cut during 1933.[180] In compliance with this resolution, the Superior Court judges unanimously accepted the pay cut in April 1933.[181]

Perhaps the most significant proposals involving the state judiciary emerged from the Ruth Commission in 1938. This commission, chaired by Senator Frank W. Ruth, was established by the legislature in the spring of 1937 to "make a careful, thorough and impartial investigation of the general practice and procedure of the courts."[182] For more than a year, the commission conducted 135 hearings in 48 counties, heard 1,152 witnesses, and took 18,000 pages of testimony. The commission's final report, issued in August 1938, concentrated its proposals on the criminal courts, especially in Philadelphia. The commission found extensive problems in the administration of criminal justice, and assailed the courts, magistrates, district attorneys, the police, the mayor, and juries. Most of the improprieties identified by the commission occurred in Philadelphia. The commission documented instances, for example, in which defendants were kept in jail after acquittal, exorbitant bails were demanded, no records or notes of testimony were taken in important cases, and judges modified sentences in private after announcing a more lengthy sentence in open court and before the press. The commission's extensive proposals included the following: establishing the office of public defender to represent indigent defendants; requiring that criminal juries submit verdicts in writing; mandating that criminal proceedings be conducted in open court and on the record; abolishing the plea of nolo contendere; creating a police training academy; reducing the size of grand juries; allowing defendants the right to waive indictment; and permitting trial courts to appoint expert witnesses.[183]

However, the commission also offered proposals that effected appellate courts. For instance, it proposed creation of a Judicial Council composed of four lawyers and

---

177. *Philadelphia Public Ledger*, 9 Mar. 1931, p. 10, col. 1.

178. The report is quoted in the *Philadelphia Public Ledger*, 8 Mar. 1931, p. 1, col. 2.

179. See note 176. For a letter to the editor supporting state purchase of the site, see *Philadelphia Public Ledger*, 12 Mar. 1931, p. 12, col. 5.

180. *Philadelphia Public Ledger*, 25 Jan. 1933, p. 5, col. 2; 22 Feb. 1933, p. 6, col. 8.

181. *Philadelphia Public Ledger*, 14 Apr. 1933, p. 21, col. 6; 19 Apr. 1933, p. 11, col. 4.

182. The commission's charge is reprinted in the *Philadelphia Public Ledger*, 8 Aug. 1938, p. 12, col. 2.

183. *Philadelphia Public Ledger*, 8 Aug. 1938, p. 1, col. 1.

two laymen appointed by the governor with the approval of the Senate. As proposed, the council would also include the chief justice as ex-officio chairman, and a number of researchers, statisticians, and investigators. It would be vested with broad authority to continuously survey the courts, compile statistics, investigate criticism of the adminis-tration of justice, propose legislation, and adopt rules regulating the business of the courts.[184] For years after it was first offered, Senator Ruth continued to introduce this proposal, in the form of various bills, into the legislature, but it was not enacted. None-theless, it was the forerunner of the Judicial Council established in 1972 by the Su-preme Court.[185]

A more important proposal involved the method of selecting state judges. Un-der this proposal, when a judge's term expired, he would stand for reelection, without opposition, by a "yes" or "no" vote of the electorate. If the judge was successful, he would serve a ten-year term. If the judge was not reelected, the governor would appoint a successor with the approval of a qualification committee consisting of the appellate judges of the state and the attorney general. By requiring committee approval, this proposal sought to remove the overtly political aspects from gubernatorial appoint-ments. Finally, the proposal would allow for the removal of judges by a two-thirds vote of both branches of the legislature, whether or not there were sufficient grounds for impeachment. As the Ruth Commission recognized, implementation of this proposal required amendment of the constitutional provisions providing for the reelection of judges in the same manner as original elections.[186] This requirement operated to shelve the proposal, but it was the forerunner of the retention election system that was adopted by the Constitutional Convention of 1968.

These proposals having failed, the remainder of the court's operation changed very little between 1931 and 1950. Its jurisdictional limit remained at $2,500, and, until 1947, the court maintained its prior schedule, sitting in Scranton and Harrisburg in March, Pittsburgh in April and May, and Philadelphia in October, November, and December. In 1948, in order to reduce the time between sessions in the state's two largest cities, the court began sitting in Philadelphia in March and September, and Pittsburgh in April and November. The remainder of its schedule remained unchanged until 1965, when the court stopped sitting in Scranton.

As we have seen, the years 1910 to 1950 constitute a distinct phase in the his-tory of the Superior Court. More than any time before or since, the work of the court was influenced by great national events that altered the shape of existing law. Between 1910 and 1930, challenges to legislation arising from Progressivism and Prohibition required the court to consider a number of difficult issues, including the relationship of state law to treaties of the United States, constitutional amendments, a variety of fed-eral laws, and the commerce clause of the United States Constitution. The unprec-edented scope of World War I also presented the court with challenging issues related to the War Power, congressional authority over state industries during wartime, and the impact of world war on the civil justice system, particularly statutes of limitation. Even broader challenges were presented by the onset of the Depression and the result-ing extension of governmental authority into previously unregulated realms. Between

---

184. *Philadelphia Public Ledger*, 1 Feb. 1939, p. 10, col. 2.

185. This council, established in 1972 when the Supreme Court adopted the Rules of Judicial Adminis-tration, was composed of the chief justice as chairman, the appellate judges, and four members of the bar. Like the body proposed by Ruth, the council had broad authority to supervise the courts and promulgate rules for their operation. Ultimately, a number of judges came to feel that this authority was excessive, and the council receded into obscurity. No meetings were held after 1974, and the Supreme Court assumed the council's responsibilities. However, in October 1979, the council was revived, with restricted authority, by amendments to the Rules of Judicial Administration.

186. See note 183.

1931 and 1950, the court was repeatedly called upon to define the broad provisions of "little New Deal" statutes, and to ensure that those statutes were proper exercises of legislative authority. Its decisions relating to unemployment compensation and labor relations were particularly notable, and they established precedents that continue to be relied upon by courts both inside and outside of Pennsylvania. During World War II, the court rendered one of the nation's most important decisions construing the authority of states to impose financial burdens on the federal government. In other cases arising from the war, the court was required to define the authority of the state to protect its citizens in times of armed conflict, and to construe, in the first impression in Pennsylvania, war-risk provisions that were common features of insurance policies issued to hundreds of thousands of soldiers. All of these cases arose from great national events, and in resolving them the court rendered seminal opinions that contributed significantly to the development of Pennsylvania law. As the influence of such events diminished in the years after 1950, the court entered a new phase of its history. From the structural changes that accompanied this new phase, the Superior Court emerged in its modern form.

The Superior Court in 1956.
L. to R.: Harold L. Ervin, J. Colvin Wright, William E. Hirt, Chester H. Rhodes (President Judge), Blair F. Gunther, Robert E. Woodside, Phillip O. Carr.

# CHAPTER FIVE

# THE COURT IN TRANSITION: 1951-1968

## *THE COURT IN ITS FIFTH DECADE*

**A**s we have seen, in the four decades prior to 1950, the primary changes affecting the Superior Court were new types of cases resulting from broad social, economic, and political trends. The court's structure and operation changed only modestly and gradually. Its jurisdictional limit, which began at $1,000, was increased to $1,500 in 1899, and $2,500 in 1923.[1] Its subject matter jurisdiction was gradually expanded by the addition of appeals from the Public Service Commission in 1915 and the Workmen's Compensation Board in 1929. The court's caseload remained relatively constant, averaging between 500 and 600 cases per year in its first half-century. The only significant change in the court's schedule occurred in 1917, when it stopped sitting at Williamsport. More notable than these minor alterations, however, were the proposals directed at the court that did not succeed. The most prominent of these were the efforts within the bar association to abolish the court in 1909, and the recommendations of the Sproul Commission in 1919 and the Earle Committee in 1935 to include the court in the judiciary article of the state constitution. In the end, the court essentially remained in 1950 what it had been in 1895, a seven-member statutory tribunal that convened en banc and shared the state's appellate caseload in relatively equal parts with the Supreme Court.

Since 1950, virtually every aspect of the court has undergone dramatic change. The most important cause of this change has been the growth of the court's caseload. Although appellate courts in other states also experienced rapid caseload growth in the same period, few could match the experience of the Superior Court. In 1983, the American Bar Association published the results of a landmark study of appellate filings between 1952 and 1982 in fourteen states and the United States Court of Appeals. These results, which do not include Pennsylvania, are tabulated as follows:

| *State* | *% increase in appeals filed 1952-1982* | *% increase in population* |
|---|---|---|
| Arizona | 1,698 | 262 |
| California | 621 | 124 |
| Connecticut | 310 | 55 |
| Delaware | 1,011 | 87 |
| Hawaii | 449 | 93 |

---

1. In 1963 the jurisdictional limit was increased to $10,000. Pa. Act of August 14, 1963, PL 819.

| State | % increase in appeals filed 1952-1982 | % increase in population |
|-------|------|------|
| Maryland | 1,018 | 80 |
| Nebraska | 446 | 18 |
| New Hampshire | 665 | 73 |
| New Jersey | 680 | 52 |
| Oklahoma | 280 | 35 |
| Oregon | 1,803 | 73 |
| Utah | 346 | 112 |
| Virginia | 742 | 61 |
| Washington | 758 | 74 |
| U.S. Circuit | 808 | 50[2] |

The median state in this table, New Jersey, saw an increase in appellate filings of 680 percent. By comparison, the Superior Court's caseload grew from 543 in 1953[3] to 5,593 in 1982, an increase of 1,300 percent. Further, the only states with greater percentile increases, Arizona and Oregon, experienced population growth rates of 262 percent and 73 percent, respectively, between 1952 and 1982, whereas Pennsylvania's population grew by only 13 percent during roughly the same period.[4] Thus, when adjusted to account for disparities in population growth, the Superior Court's caseload increased more than the appellate caseload of any other state. Although the major caseload boom did not occur until the 1970s, the rapid upward trend began in the years with which this chapter is concerned, 1951 to 1968. In fact, while the court's caseload remained relatively constant in the fifty previous years, it more than tripled in this period.[5] The initial impact of this increase was on the court's schedule. In order to concentrate on the great center of litigation growth, it added new Philadelphia sessions in 1958 and 1960, and it stopped sitting at Scranton in 1965.[6]

In addition to the fact that the court's surging caseload signaled a larger boom in the following years, two other factors suggest that the court was in a period of transition between 1951 and 1968. The first was a concerted effort, beginning in 1953, to reform Pennsylvania's antiquated Constitution of 1874.[7] Although the initial stages of this drive were unsuccessful, proponents of reform, unlike their predecessors in the decades prior to 1950, continued to press the issue, and their efforts culminated with the calling of a constitutional convention in 1967. The convention reorganized the state judiciary and made a number of modifications that began to shape the Superior Court

---

2. This table is reprinted in *Judges' Journal* (summer 1986), 42.

3. Although the caseload figure for 1952 is not available, it would not have been much different from the 1953 figure of 543.

4. The 1950 census determined Pennsylvania's population to be 10,498,012; by 1980, the population was 11,866,728. See *The Pennsylvania Manual: 1951-52* (Harrisburg: Pa. Bureau of Publications), 997, and *The Pennsylvania Manual: 1980-81*, 732.

5. Again using the 1953 figure, the caseload increased from 543 to 1,697 by 1968.

6. From 1951 to 1958, the court convened at Scranton, Harrisburg, and Philadelphia in March, Pittsburgh in April, Philadelphia in September, and Pittsburgh in November. In 1958, the court maintained its prior schedule but added a Philadelphia session in June. Two years later, it also began meeting in Philadelphia in December. This schedule remained intact until 1965, when it stopped sitting at Scranton. The remainder of the schedule did not change.

7. Because the constitution became effective on January 1, 1874, it is commonly referred to as the Constitution of 1874. The legislature resolved some lasting confusion when it enacted 1 Pa.C.S. sec. 906, which provides, "The Constitution of Pennsylvania, as adopted by referendum of December 16, 1873, shall be known and may be cited as the 'Constitution of 1874.'" Since it completed its work on November 3, 1873, the convention which enacted the constitution is known as the Convention of 1873. See Robert Woodside, *Pennsylvania Constitutional Law* (Sayre, Pa.: Murrelle Printing Co., 1985), 576-77.

In the Superior Court of Pennsylvania

SITTING AT PHILADELPHIA

No. 130

ORDER DOCKET

IN RE:

FEE FOR ADMISSION TO

THE SUPERIOR COURT OF

PENNSYLVANIA

Appeal from the

_____ Court

of_____

for the County of _____

No. _____    Term, 19

O R D E R

AND NOW, this 17th day of January, 1952, it is ordered
that the fee to be charged for admission to the Superior
Court of Pennsylvania by the Prothonotary in each of the
four districts shall be Ten ($10.00) Dollars.    This order
is to take effect immediately.

CHESTER H..RHODES,
PRESIDENT JUDGE

TRUE COPY FROM RECORD

In Testimony Whereof, *I have hereunto set my hand and the seal of*
*said Court, at Philadelphia, this* ___21st___ *day of* ___January___ *19* 52

Prothonotary.

The order of January 17, 1952, setting the fee at $10 to be charged by the prothonotary for filing admission to Superior Court. It was signed by President Judge Chester H. Rhodes.

into its modern form. Decisions made by the convention also set the stage for subsequent changes in the court's structure.

Finally, the transition between the court's past and future is indicated by the rise of three important areas of substantive law that began to emerge in the 1950s and 1960s and have remained significant to the present. Numerous scholars have documented a general trend over the course of the twentieth century away from market-oriented areas of law such as contracts and property and toward nonmarket areas, especially criminal, family and tort law.[8] The few statistical studies that have been conducted also confirm this trend. For instance, a study conducted by the director of Court Studies, a Virginia-based judicial think tank, found that between 1950 and 1984, criminal cases increased by 555 percent[9] and family cases increased by 300 per-

8. See e.g., Robert A. Kagan, et al., "The Business of State Supreme Courts, 1870-1970," 30 Stan. L. Rev. 121 (1977); Burton M. Atkins and Henry R. Glick, "Environmental and Structural Variables as Determinants of Issues in State Courts of Last Resort", 20 A.J. Pol. Sci. 97 (1976); Lawrence Baum, Sheldon Goldman, and Austin Surat, "Research Note: The Evolution of Litigation in the Federal Courts of Appeals; 1895-1975," 16 Law & Soc'y Rev. 291 (1981-82).

9.The results of this study are tabulated and presented in Thomas B. Marvel, "Are Caseloads Really Increasing? Yes . . .", *Judges' Journal* (summer 1986), 43, Table 2. The states for which statistics were available, and the increases, are set forth as follows: Arizona - 830%; California - 285%; Colorado – 796%; Michigan – 523%; New Hampshire – 554%; Rhode Island – 493%; Texas - 403%. Dividing this number by the seven states yields an average increase of 555%.

cent.[10] The study also found a 349-percent increase in civil cases, although these cases were not differentiated beyond the exclusion of family law cases.[11] Additionally, scholars have noted the rise of tort law beginning in the middle of the century.[12]

Unfortunately, a lack of detailed caseload figures prevents the statistical demonstration of this trend in Pennsylvania. As a result, studies of other states are more suggestive than conclusive when applied to the Superior Court. Nonetheless, there is no reason to believe that Pennsylvania's experience was different from the states studied, all of which underwent dramatic increases in the number of criminal, family and tort cases in the years since 1950. Moreover, the factors that caused these increases in other states also operated in Pennsylvania.

Criminal law provides the most obvious example. Beginning in the early 1960s, a number of landmark decisions by the United States Supreme Court transformed existing law by granting criminal defendants broad new constitutional rights. All of these rights applied in the courts of all states, and the result was that the volume and importance of criminal appeals increased dramatically in relation to other areas of law.[13] Although the transformation of criminal law reached maturity in the 1960s, other changes that did not culminate until the 1970s began to emerge in the prior two decades.

The most notable of these changes occurred in tort law. While cases arose in a myriad of areas, the general thrust was in favor of dramatically expanded civil liability. Ancient principles restricting who could sue and be sued were shorn from the law and the reach of liability was extended into broad new areas of manufacturing and production. Old theories of negligence were expanded, new theories were developed, and in some areas negligence principles were abandoned entirely, as the previously narrow scope of strict liability, or liability without fault, was broadened to include a variety of new activities.

Finally, as new principles of gender equality emerged in the 1960s, family law began a process of change that, by the 1970s, significantly undermined traditional assumptions about marital and parental relationships. All of these changes profoundly influenced Pennsylvania law, and each is reflected in the important cases decided by the Superior Court. Thus, in addition to dramatic caseload increases and constitutional reform, the increasing significance of criminal, family and tort law suggests that the Superior Court was in a period of transition between 1951 and 1968.

While some trends began in the 1950s and 1960s, others reached maturity during that time. Most importantly, the decline in Republican political strength that began during the Great Depression culminated in the 1960s with the first Democratic majority in the Superior Court's history. Not surprisingly, this dramatic reversal of fortune

---

10. See note 9. The states for which statistics were available, and the increases, are set forth as follows: Arizona – 505%; California – 166%; Colorado – 640%; Kansas – 186%; New Hampshire – 354%; Rhode Island – 86%; Texas – 160%. Dividing this number by the seven states yields an average increase of 300%.

11. See note 9. The states for which statistics are available, and the increases, are set forth as follows: Arizona – 686%; California – 486%; Colorado – 380%; Kansas – 140%; New Hampshire – 106%; New Jersey – 425%; Rhode Island – 94%; Texas – 474%. Dividing this number by the eight states yields an average increase of 349%.

12. See e.g., Robert F. Blomquist, "'New Torts': A Critical History, Taxonomy, and Appraisal," 95 Dick. L. Rev. 23 (1990). Blomquist periodizes the rise of new causes of action sounding in tort. The period since 1940 has been one of "opening the floodgates." More narrowly, he designates the period from 1940 to 1969 as "Judicial Creativity Explored," 95 Dick. L. Rev. 23, 38-52; the period from 1970 to 1979 as "Judicial Creativity Embraced," 95 Dick. L. Rev. 23, 53-81; and the period after 1980 as "Judicial Creativity Consolidated," 95 Dick. L. Rev. 23, 82-123.

13. See Thomas B. Marvel, "Is There an Appeal from the Caseload Deluge," *Judges' Journal* (summer 1985), 34, 35-6 ("[State] criminal appeals shot up following the expansion of criminal procedural rights.").

The Superior Court in 1954. L. to R. (seated): William E. Hirt, Chester H. Rhodes (President Judge), F. Clair Ross. L. to R. (standing): Robert E. Woodside, Blair F. Gunther, J. Colvin Wright, Harold L. Ervin.

reflected the changing face of Pennsylvania politics. As late as 1952, Republicans out-numbered Democrats in the state by nearly one million. Thereafter, however, the Re-publican decline was rapid. By 1960, although their lead was extremely slim, Demo-crats were a majority for the first time since the Civil War.[14]

## THE NEW MEMBERS OF THE COURT

Before turning to important cases and structural changes, it is necessary to consider the court's political make-up between 1951 and 1968. The first new judge to join the court in this period was Republican J. Colvin Wright, who was appointed to replace Judge Dithrich on February 23, 1953. Wright was born in Bedford, Bedford County, on November 20, 1901. He graduated from Bedford High School in 1918, Haverford College in 1922, and the University of Pennsylvania Law School in 1925. He was a member of Phi Beta Kappa at Haverford and the Order of the Coif at Penn. In 1927, he was elected district attorney of Bedford County, and five years later he was appointed county solicitor. He was elected president judge of the Bedford County Court of Common Pleas in 1941, and reelected in 1951. A year later, he served as a delegate to the Republican National Convention from the Eighteenth Congressional District. Fol-lowing his appointment to the Superior Court, he was elected to a full term in the fall of

---

14. In 1952, Republicans numbered 3,130,078 and Democrats 2,136,511; in 1960, the numbers were Democrats 2,805,202, Republicans 2,802,237. This condition of relative equality between the two major par-ties has marked Pennsylvania politics ever since.

1953 and reelected in 1963. On January 1, 1968, Wright became president judge. He served until the expiration of his term in January 1974, at which time he was forced to retire, having reached the mandatory retirement age of seventy established by the Constitutional Convention of 1968.[15]

On October 1, 1953, Robert E. Woodside was appointed to replace Judge Arnold. Woodside was born on June 4, 1904, in Millersburg, Dauphin County. He graduated from Millersburg High School, Dickinson College, and in 1928 from Dickinson Law School. He worked his way through school serving as a senate page, mail carrier, and newspaper carrier. From 1928 to 1942, he engaged in private practice in Harrisburg and Millersburg. Beginning in 1932, Woodside also served five regular and six special sessions in the legislature. From 1939 to 1941, he was the Republican Leader. In 1942, he was elected judge of the Court of Common Pleas of Dauphin County. While in that capacity, he served as chairman of the Pennsylvania Council of Juvenile Court Judges. From March 7, 1951 until his appointment to the Superior Court, he served as attorney general of Pennsylvania. In 1954 he received the nominations of both parties for a full term. Although a long-time Republican, he was elected with more Democratic than Republican votes at the general election. This fact would take on particular significance six years later when the Democrats, counting Woodside as a Democrat, gained their first majority in the court's history. The candidates receiving the highest votes at the 1954 general election were Judges Ross and Rhodes, both of whom were reelected as Democrats. It was the first time in a Superior Court race that three candidates were elected as Democrats.[16] In 1964, while running as a Republican, Woodside was defeated for reelection. During his career as an attorney and judge, Woodside established himself as one of the foremost authorities on Pennsylvania government and constitutional law. In 1959, he served as chairman of the Commission on Constitutional Revision, known as the Woodside Commission, which recommended a number of changes to the structure of state government.[17] He also served as secretary of the Joint State Government Commission, and as a commissioner on Uniform State Laws. He had a long association with Dickinson Law School, where he served as trustee and adjunct professor of law for many years. In 1985, Woodside published *Pennsylvania Constitutional Law*, which remains an extremely influential text on the state constitution.[18]

In November 1953 Republican Harold L. Ervin was elected to the Superior Court to replace Judge Reno. Ervin was born in Catawissa, Delaware County, on April 5, 1895. He graduated from Catawissa High School in 1913 and Temple University in 1916. During World War I, he served as a lieutenant in the infantry. He graduated from the University of Pennsylvania Law School in 1920. Thereafter, he returned to Delaware County and engaged in private practice, serving as solicitor of numerous townships. In January 1929 he served as a presidential elector for Republican Herbert Hoover. He was appointed to the Court of Common Pleas of Delaware County on July 24, 1941, elected to a full term in the fall, and reelected in 1951. On January 5, 1948, he became president judge of that court. Following his election to the Superior Court in the fall of 1953, he was reelected in 1963 and became president judge on January 4, 1965.

---

15. Although he reached age seventy in 1971, Wright was permitted to complete his term since he had been elected under the Constitution of 1874. Constitution of 1968, art. V, Schedule to Judiciary Article, sec. 8. The establishment of the mandatory retirement age at the convention of 1968 is discussed infra.

16. The results of the extremely close election were as follows: Chester Rhodes, Democrat, 1,928,390; F. Clair Ross, Democrat, 1,916,191; Robert E. Woodside, Democrat, 1,851,033; Robert E. Woodside, Republican, 1,762,711; Ralph T. Bell, Republican, 1,755,292; George W. Griffith, Republican, 1,708,815; Charles Palmer, Prohibition, 22,003.

17. The work of the Woodside Commission is discussed infra.

18. *Pennsylvania Constitutional Law* has been extremely valuable in the research and writing of this book.

On February 1, 1956, Democrat Philip O. Carr was appointed to the Superior Court by Governor George Leader. Carr was born in Uniontown, Fayette County, on March 29, 1915. He graduated from the Westminster School in 1935 and Amherst College in 1939. He was admitted to the bar on September 2, 1942, after two years at the University of Pittsburgh Law School. That same month, he enlisted in the Army Air Corps and was commissioned a second lieutenant. Thereafter, he served as a bomber pilot in Italy and Africa, and received the Air Medal with clusters and the unit citation. He was discharged as a captain in January 1945. Returning home, he served as assistant United States attorney for the Western District of Pennsylvania for five years. Although he received the Democratic nomination for the Superior Court in the primary election of 1956, he was not elected at the general election of November 6, 1956.

Carr was defeated by Republican G. Harold Watkins, who was born in Girardville, Schuylkill County, on January 2, 1903. He graduated from Girardville High School in 1920 and Pennsylvania State University in 1924. He taught high school for two years after college and then went to Harvard Law School, graduating in 1929. Returning home, he was admitted to the bar of Schuylkill County in 1930 and served as counsel to the Selective Service Committee. He served as Schuylkill County solicitor from 1935 to 1947, as a Republican state senator from 1941 to 1944, and as chairman of the Schuylkill County Republican Party from 1941 to 1952. He also served as secretary of the Senate of Pennsylvania from 1944 to 1957. He was a trustee of Penn State from 1968 to 1972. Following his election to the Superior Court, he was reelected in 1966. In 1974, he became president judge. Since he reached age seventy in 1973, Watkins could not run for reelection at the end of his third term and his commission expired in January 1978.[19] Thereafter, he continued to serve as a senior judge until his retirement in 1988. Watkins, who served on the Superior Court for thirty-two years, died on August 5, 1991.

On November 3, 1959, Democrat Harry Milton Montgomery was elected to replace Judge Hirt. Montgomery was born in Pittsburgh on June 12, 1901. He graduated from Allegheny High School in 1919, the University of Pittsburgh in 1922, and the University of Pittsburgh Law School in 1924. On October 13, 1924, he established the firm of Ralph and Montgomery and engaged in private practice, except for serving one year as assistant county solicitor. While a practicing lawyer, he was also a member of the Pittsburgh Yellow Jackets, the city's professional hockey team. In 1943 Montgomery was elected to the County Court of Allegheny County, and in 1947 he was elected to the Court of Common Pleas of Allegheny County. He remained in that capacity until his election to the Superior Court in 1959. He was reelected in 1969. On June 12, 1971, he reached the mandatory retirement age of seventy, as established by the Constitutional Convention of 1968.[20] Thereafter, he served as a senior judge until his retirement in 1995. Judge Montgomery died on August 29, 1999.

The next change in the court's membership gave Democrats a technical majority for the first time. As of 1960, the court had Democrats Rhodes and Montgomery, and Judge Woodside, although a life-long Republican, had been elected as a Democrat. The

---

19. Although Watkins was originally scheduled to run for reelection in the fall of 1976, Article 13(a) of the judiciary article, promulgated at the convention of 1968, provides that judges must be elected at municipal elections which, pursuant to Article VII, Section 3, are to be held in odd-numbered years. As a result, Watkins' term was extended one year. However, in 1973, during his final term, he reached the mandatory retirement age of seventy. The timing of reelections for judges originally elected under the Constitution of 1874 was settled by a 1977 ruling of the Supreme Court. See *Barbieri v. Shapp*, 470 Pa. 463, 368 A.2d 721 (1977). This case was brought by Superior Court Judge William F. Cercone, whose biography and work on the court is discussed infra.

20. This change in the constitution is discussed infra.

Judge Theodore O. Spaulding. Spaulding was the first African American to sit on any appellate court in Pennsylvania.

fourth Democrat was Gerald F. Flood, who defeated the reelection bid of Republican Blair Gunther on November 6, 1960. Flood was born in Philadelphia on March 31, 1898. He graduated from Catholic High School in 1916 and enlisted in the United States Army in October 1918. He was assigned to the Officers' Training Camp in Fortress Monroe, Virginia. Thereafter, he graduated from the University of Pennsylvania in 1920 and Penn Law School in 1924 where he was president of his class. From March 15, 1935 to March 15, 1937, he served as special deputy attorney general. In 1937 he was elected judge of the Philadelphia County Court of Common Pleas, and reelected in 1947 and 1957. He also served as a judge advocate in the Pennsylvania National Guard from 1943 to 1945. In 1960 he was elected to the Superior Court and served until his death on December 26, 1965. During his career as a lawyer and judge, Flood served on the Council of the American Law Institute, the Civil Rules Committee of the Supreme Court of Pennsylvania, the Advisory Committee on Sentencing and Review, and the Appellate Judges Committee, Section of Judicial Administration.

The next two personnel changes gave Democrats an actual, as opposed to a technical, majority for the first time. On November 2, 1964, Democrats Robert Lee Jacobs and J. Sydney Hoffman defeated sitting judge Robert Woodside and Republican nominee Joseph C. Bruno. Jacobs and Hoffman joined Democrats Flood and Montgomery on the court in January 1965. Jacobs was born in Carlisle, Cumberland County, on December 17, 1910. He graduated from Carlisle High School, Dickinson College, and Dickinson Law School. During World War II, he served in the United States Navy. He served in the state senate from 1936 to 1940. In 1956 he was elected judge of the Court of Common Pleas of Cumberland County, and served in that capacity until 1964. Following his election to the Superior Court, he was reelected in 1975 and became president judge upon the retirement of Judge Watkins in 1978. He resigned on December 31, 1978.

The other Democrat elected in 1964, J. Sydney Hoffman, was born in Reading, Berks County, on July 14, 1908. He attended school there, graduated from Albright College, attended Dickinson Law School, and took graduate courses at the University of Pennsylvania and Temple University. During his early years, he took over his father's law practice in Reading and then moved to Philadelphia where he entered into practice with the daughter and son-in-law of Judge Adrian Bonnelley, a close friend of Judge Hoffman's father. This practice was located in the Kensington area of Philadelphia. Judge Hoffman was active in Democratic reform politics led by Joseph Clark and Richardson Dilworth in the early 1950s and was close to former Democratic city chairman William Green Sr. In 1956 Governor George Leader appointed Judge Hoffman to the Municipal Court (County Court) of Philadelphia. On May 17, 1956, he was elected to that court, where he developed a reputation for juvenile law expertise. In 1964 he was elected to the Superior Court. In 1971 he established the Philadelphia Accelerated Rehabilitation Disposition Program, known as ARD, which expedited the disposition of cases involving first-time offenders. Hoffman was specially appointed to this program by the Supreme Court and served two to three days per week adjudicating ARD cases in addition to his Superior Court duties. The Supreme Court later promulgated a rule adopting ARD throughout Pennsylvania. In 1980, together with then-President Judge William F. Cercone, Hoffman initiated the Supreme Court Settlement Conference Program to encourage the settlement of cases. The National Center for State Courts identified this program as one of the leading case settlement efforts in the nation. In July 1978, having reached the mandatory retirement age of seventy, Judge Hoffman was appointed by the Supreme Court as senior judge of the Superior Court. He served in that capacity full-time until his death on June 22, 1998.

The Democrats maintained their four-to-three majority when, on March 7, 1966, Theodore O. Spaulding was appointed to fill the vacancy caused by the death of Judge Flood. Spaulding was the first African American to sit on any appellate court in Pennsylvania. He was born in Concord, North Carolina, on February 18, 1902. He graduated from Howard University in 1924 and the University of Detroit Law School in 1928. During World War II, he served as a Selective Service attorney. In 1953, he was elected judge of the County Court of Philadelphia, and served in that capacity until 1966. Following his appointment to the Superior Court, he was elected to a full term in the fall of 1966. He retired in December 1973. During his career, Spaulding served as a member of numerous organizations, including the National Conference of State Trial Lawyers, the Lawyer's Club of Philadelphia, the YMCA, the NAACP, the National Conference of Christians and Jews, the Crime Commission of Philadelphia, and the United Fund of Philadelphia.

In January 1968 Republican John Beerne Hannum was appointed by Governor Raymond P. Shafer to replace President Judge Ervin. Hannum was born in Chester, Chester County, on March 19, 1915. He was educated at the Lawrenceville School, Princeton University, Franklin and Marshall College, and Dickinson Law School. During World War II, he served as a lieutenant in the United States Navy. Thereafter, he worked for the Philadelphia law firm of Pepper Hamilton & Scheetz, and later became a partner. In 1956 he served as chairman of Chester County Citizens for Eisenhower, and in 1960 he was a delegate to the Republican National Convention. He was also a delegate to the Pennsylvania Constitutional Convention of 1967-68, where he served as co-chairman of the Judiciary Committee's Subcommittee on the Tenure of Judges. Following his appointment to the Superior Court, Hannum ran for a full term in the fall of 1968, but he was not elected.

Hannum was defeated at the 1968 general election by Democrat William Franklin Cercone.[21] Cercone was born in Allegheny County on August 13, 1913. He graduated with a bachelor's degree from the University of Pittsburgh and received an LL.B. as well as an honorary J.D. from Duquesne University School of Law. During

---

21. *Harrisburg Patriot-News*, 6 Nov. 1968, 1.

The Superior Court in 1961. L. to. R. (seated): Harold L. Ervin, Chester H. Rhodes (President Judge), Gerald F. Flood. L. to R. (standing): Harry M. Montgomery, Robert E. Woodside, G. Harold Watkins, J. Colvin Wright.

World War II, he served as a lieutenant in the amphibious forces of the United States Navy. In 1942, he was an attorney for the Army Corps of Engineers in Pennsylvania and Ohio. From 1948 to 1953, he served as an assistant district attorney of Allegheny County. In this capacity, he prosecuted a number of prominent cases, including the 1950 sedition trial of Communist Steven Nelson, which garnered international media coverage. Cercone was president of the Stowe Township Board of Education from 1948 to 1954, solicitor of Stowe Township from 1949 to 1956, and solicitor of the Stowe School District from 1954 to 1956. He also served as special assistant United States attorney in 1952, and special deputy attorney general in 1954. In May 1956 he was appointed to the Court of Common Pleas of Allegheny County. He was elected to a full term in 1957 and reelected in 1967. In 1960 he received the merit award of the Academy of Trial Lawyers. He also served as president of the Pennsylvania Judicial Inquiry and Review Board. On January 1, 1979, he became president judge of the Superior Court, the first jurist from Allegheny County to hold that position. He was reelected at the 1979 general election. In the late 1970s, following unprecedented increases in the volume of appellate cases, Cercone became a prominent advocate in the ultimately successful effort to increase the size of the Superior Court. He served as a commissioned judge until August 1983, when he turned seventy and was forced to retire under the mandatory provision of the Constitution of 1968. Judge Cercone continues to serve as a senior judge.

These personnel changes indicate clearly that the court was in a period of transition between 1951 and 1968. Indeed, Republicans started this period with a five-to-two majority, yet Democrats attained a technical majority in 1960 and a true majority in 1964. With the election of Judge Cercone a mere four years later, the Democrats held the same five-to-two majority that Republicans had enjoyed eighteen years earlier. Yet even as this Democratic political trend reached fruition, a new legal trend had begun. The result of this new trend was that, for the first time, the most important cases decided by the court involved criminal law.

## THE COURT AT WORK

### CRIMINAL LAW

Of the numerous legal changes initiated in the 1950s and 1960s, none was greater than in the realm of criminal law. The most significant factor in this change was a series of landmark decisions by the United States Supreme Court. The first was *Mapp v. Ohio*[22] in 1961. Prior Pennsylvania law held that even where a search warrant was issued illegally (i.e., without probable cause), incriminating evidence seized as a result of the warrant was admissible in court.[23] This principle was completely obliterated by *Mapp*, which applied to state courts the long-standing federal rule that evidence obtained in violation of the constitution was inadmissible at trial.[24] The impact of this "exclusionary rule" on state criminal prosecutions is difficult to overstate. Most importantly, it gave a new impetus to hundreds of criminal defendants to file motions to suppress evidence seized as a result of allegedly unconstitutional searches. In 1962, Judge Ervin stated: "A hurricane, named *Mapp v. Ohio,* swept over our fair land last June. . . . [N]umerous appeals [have been] coming to our Court as part of the backlash. It now becomes our duty to endeavor to reassemble the machinery for law enforcement in our Commonwealth."[25] As Judge Ervin's comments suggest, a central task facing the Superior Court in the early 1960s was dealing with the "backlash" of *Mapp*.

Under both federal and state law, evidentiary searches are governed by constitutional provisions. The Fourth Amendment of the United States Constitution declares that the "right of the people to be secure in their persons, houses, papers, and effects, against unreasonable searches shall not be violated and no warrant shall issue but upon probable cause." A similar provision is found in Article I, Section 8, of the Pennsylvania Constitution, which provides, "The people shall be secure in their persons, houses, papers and possessions from unreasonable searches and seizures, and no warrant to search any place or to seize any person or things shall issue without describing them as nearly as may be, nor without probable cause." *Mapp* is significant in that it based the admissibility of evidence on the constitutionality of the search by which it was obtained. Since the state and federal constitutions prohibited "unreasonable" searches, the primary issue for state courts in the wake of *Mapp* was whether a given search was "reasonable." Yet *Mapp* gave no clear answer to whether courts should utilize state or federal standards in determining this issue.

In *Commonwealth v. Richards*,[26] the Superior Court addressed this difficult question for the first time in Pennsylvania. In *Richards*, the police received information from a reliable informant that the defendant had drugs in his apartment. They immediately proceeded, without a warrant, to the defendant's apartment building where, as they ascended the stairs, they were met by the defendant. A scuffle ensued, during which the defendant yelled to an individual in his apartment "they're here." As one of the officers subdued the defendant, the other officer heard someone running through the apartment. He kicked down the door in time to see a man dive through a rear window with a brown bag in his hand. The man was apprehended, and the bag was determined to contain 32.7 grams of marijuana. The defendant was charged with drug

---

22. 367 U.S. 643 (1961).

23. *Commonwealth v. Campbell*, 196 Pa. Super. 380, 175 A.2d 324 (1961) (Montgomery, J.).

24. 367 U.S. 655 (1961). The rule barring illegally obtained evidence from federal criminal trials was set forth in *Weeks v. United States*, 232 U.S. 383 (1914).

25. *Commonwealth v. One 1955 Buick Sedan*, 198 Pa. Super. 133, 182 A.2d 280, 281 (1962) (Ervin, J.).

26. 198 Pa. Super. 39, 182 A.2d 291 (1962) (Rhodes, J.).

The Superior Court in 1965. L. to R.: Robert L. Jacobs, Harry M. Montgomery, J. Colvin Wright, Harold L. Ervin (President Judge), G. Harold Watkins, Gerald F. Flood, J. Sydney Hoffman.

possession. Although it rendered a verdict of guilty following a bench trial, the trial court thereafter granted a motion in arrest of judgment. In a ruling that was typical of hundreds to reach the Superior Court in the early 1960s, the trial court relied upon *Mapp* to hold that the warrantless seizure of drugs from the defendant's apartment was illegal and that his arrest was therefore invalid. The Commonwealth appealed.

In a brief but extremely important decision, a five-judge majority of the Superior Court reversed the trial court's determination that *Mapp* rendered the search of the defendant's apartment unreasonable and therefore unconstitutional.[27] The majority's analysis turned on the finding that state courts are not bound to apply federal standards of "reasonableness." "The *Mapp* decision did not, as we interpret it, preclude [state] judicial determination of what constitutes a reasonable search and seizure."[28] The majority then reviewed Superior Court cases construing Article I, Section 8, of the state constitution and held, "In Pennsylvania '[w]hether search and seizure is or is not unreasonable must be determined from the facts in each particular case.'"[29] The court then applied this rule, which it found to be consistent with the federal rule, to the search of the defendant's apartment:

> In the instant case the arresting officer had probable cause to arrest defendant and reasonable grounds to believe that defendant had committed and was continuing to commit a felony. They had information from a reliable informer whose previous information led to at least ten arrests. In addition, defendant, without warning, shoved one of the officers against the wall prior to his being arrested. Since the arrest was lawful it is clear that a reasonable search of the premises under defendant's control is also lawful without a search warrant as being incident to the lawful ar-

27. Judges Watkins and Flood dissented on the basis of the trial court opinion.
28. 182 A.2d 293.
29. 182 A.2d 293, citing *Commonwealth v. Hunsinger*, 89 Pa. Super. 238, 241 (1926).

rest. Moreover, simultaneously with the arrest, they heard someone flee-ing from defendant's apartment. It subsequently appeared that he was attempting to escape with a quantity of marijuana. . . .

When we apply the test of "totality of facts" to the instant appeal, it is clear that the search and seizure by the narcotics squad were not un-reasonable. There was no invasion of defendant's constitutionally pro-tected right of privacy.[30]

On this basis the trial court's ruling was reversed. The defendant appealed to the Supreme Court but allocatur was denied. Thereafter, the United States Supreme Court denied certiorari.[31] *Richards* was the first important Pennsylvania case constru-ing the landmark holding of *Mapp*. It quickly became a leading case for the proposition that *Mapp* did not preclude state courts from assessing the reasonableness of searches and seizures under state law.[32] It was relied upon for this proposition in Maryland,[33] and cited in a variety of other early cases attempting to reconcile *Mapp* with state search and seizure law.[34]

*Richards* was also relied upon to reverse an order suppressing evidence in an-other Superior Court case decided the same day, which became the Pennsylvania Su-preme Court's first opportunity to consider the decision in *Mapp*. In *Commonwealth v. Bosurgi*,[35] a detective, who had investigated a jewelry store burglary earlier in the day, received information from an informant that the defendant was in a bar attempting to sell watches. The informant described the defendant's appearance with specificity and stated the location of the bar, which was close to the jewelry store. The detective pro-ceeded to the bar specified and found no one, but he located the defendant at another bar a block away. He approached the defendant, asked his name, and directed him to stand up. Observing the usual precaution to determine that a felony suspect was not armed, the officer "patted down" the defendant and felt a large bulge in a pocket. The officer retrieved ten watches, eight of which were determined to be proceeds of the burglary. The defendant stated that he did not know how the watches got in his pocket. He was arrested and particles removed from his clothing were subsequently matched to glass from a broken window at the location that had been burglarized. The defendant's motion to suppress the watches and glass fragments, however, was granted by the trial court on the basis that, under *Mapp*, the search of the defendant was unconstitutional. The Commonwealth appealed.

A five-judge majority of the Superior Court began its analysis by citing *Richards* for the proposition that *Mapp* "did not preclude the right of a [state] court to determine what is a reasonable search and seizure under the circumstances of the particular case."[36] The court then relied on well-established state law for the proposition that a police

---

30. 182 A.2d 295 (citations omitted).

31. 373 U.S. 376 (1963).

32. *See Commonwealth v. Bosurgi*, 411 Pa. 56, 190 A.2d 304 (1963) (the Supreme Court's first *Mapp* case).

33. *Stanley v. State*, 230 Md. 188, 186 A.2d 478 (1962).

34. *New York v. Estrialgo*, 233 N.Y.S.2d 558 (1962); *Commonwealth v. Geiger*, 209 Pa. Super. 369, 227 A.2d 920 (1967); *Commonwealth v. Gomino*, 200 Pa. Super. 160, 188 A.2d 784 (1963); *Commonwealth v. Kinderman*, 200 Pa. Super. 262, 188 A.2d 769 (1963); *Commonwealth v. Pittman*, 200 Pa. Super. 1, 186 A.2d 418 (1962); *Commonwealth v. Hodgester*, 199 Pa. Super. 469, 186 A.2d 65 (1962); *Commonwealth v. Johnson*, 198 Pa. Super. 51, 182 A.2d 541 (1962); *Commonwealth v. Czajkowski*, 198 Pa. Super. 511, 182 A.2d 298 (1962).

35. 198 Pa. Super. 47, 182 A.2d 295 (1962) (Rhodes, J.).

36. 182 A.2d 297.

officer may arrest without a warrant where he has probable cause and reasonable grounds to believe that the person arrested has committed a felony. Applying this rule, the court concluded:

> Here the police officer knew the burglary had just been committed in the immediate vicinity. He received information that defendant, described in detail by informant, was in the vicinity selling property of the type stolen. Defendant was apprehended and taken into custody in a taproom, approximately across the street from the jewelry store, carrying watches of the type taken by the burglar. Under all the circumstances, the officer had probable cause and reasonable grounds [to] believe that defendant had committed the crime and to arrest defendant.[37]

The court then held that "[t]he maintenance of a proper balance between the right of the individual to privacy and that of society in the apprehension of crime does not require suppression of the evidence . . . in this case."[38] On this basis the trial court's order suppressing the evidence recovered from the defendant was reversed. Thereafter, the defendant appealed to the Supreme Court, which granted allocatur. That court began its opinion by noting "[t]he first 'search and seizure' question to reach this Court since the decision in [Mapp} is presented upon this appeal."[39] After reviewing the holding of *Mapp*, the court stated the question at issue:

> In passing upon the "reasonableness" of a search and seizure, a preliminary, and most important, question is whether *Mapp* requires that state courts determine the "reasonableness of such search and seizure in accordance with federal or state standards. To that question *Mapp* gives no direct answer.[40]

Although this question was not answered directly by *Mapp*, the court had little difficulty resolving it. Citing *Richards* and two California cases, the court held that "a study of *Mapp* would indicate that, at least by implication, state courts are still free to apply their own, rather than the federal, criteria of 'reasonableness'."[41] The court then held, "We fully agree with the majority of the Superior Court" that the evidence recovered from the defendant's person was improperly suppressed by the trial court.[42] Following this ruling, the defendant pursued his appeal, but the United States Supreme Court denied certiorari.[43] Like *Richards*, *Bosurgi* became a leading case for the authority of courts to determine the reasonableness of searches under state law.[44]

Three years after *Mapp*, in *Escobedo v. Illinois*,[45] the United States Supreme Court rendered another landmark opinion that altered state criminal law. Prior to 1964,

---

37. See note 36.
38. See note 36.
39. 411 Pa. 56, 190 A.2d 304, 306 (1963).
40. 190 A.2d 309.
41. 190 A.2d 309, citing *Richards*, 182 A.2d 293, *People v. Cahan*, 44 Cal.2d 434, 282 P.2d 905 (1955), and *People v. Tyler*, 193 Cal. App.2d 728 (Cal. App. 1st Dist. 1961).
42. 190 A.2d 312.
43. 375 U.S. 910 (1963).
44. See *Commonwealth v. Wright*, 411 Pa. 81, 190 A.2d 709 (1963); *Commonwealth v. Devlin*, 221 Pa. Super. 175, 289 A.2d 237 (1972); *Commonwealth v. Zelnick*, 202 Pa. Super. 129, 195 A.2d 171 (1963); *Commonwealth v. Griffin*, 200 Pa. Super. 34, 186 A.2d 656 (1962); *Commonwealth v. Johnson*, 198 Pa. Super. 51, 182 A.2d 541 (1962); and *Gomino*, *Kinderman*, and *Czajkowski*, supra.
45. 378 U.S. 478 (1964).

Pennsylvania courts held that the primary test for the admissibility of a defendant's confession was whether it was "voluntary," and voluntariness was determined by the "totality of the circumstances."[46] In *Escobedo*, the United States Supreme Court ruled that a confession made by a suspect during a police investigation that "focused" on him was inadmissible if the suspect was not informed of his rights to remain silent and to be provided with counsel. Like *Mapp*, *Escobedo* dramatically increased the number of criminal appeals filed in state courts. In 1965, Pennsylvania Chief Justice John C. Bell made note of "the avalanche of petitions for habeas corpus and appeals which have been flooding Courts throughout our State and Country ever since [*Escobedo* and two similar cases]."[47] Chief Justice Bell also noted:

> These decisions have caused a stepped-up war of "Criminals vs. Society", with criminals being given by the Supreme Court of the United States greater and greater rights and law abiding people less and less protection. How often, after a criminal's conviction has been sustained by a Court, can he deluge Courts with petitions for a hearing and discharge (or for a new trial) because allegedly his confession was involuntary, or he was (psychiatrically speaking) insane, or for any technically-stretched reason he was denied newly-created "fundamentals" of a fair trial? Is there to be no finality to the law, and no protection for peaceful people in this constantly increasing and appalling crime wave?[48]

Not surprisingly, since the *Escobedo* rule was drawn so broadly, and because a violation of that rule resulted either in a new trial or complete discharge, criminal defendants attempted to extend it to a variety of new situations.

One such attempt was at issue in the 1966 case of *Commonwealth v. Anderson*,[49] in which the defendant was stopped by police for erratic driving. As they were talking to the defendant, who was known to the police as a drug violator, the officers noticed a cylindrical object wrapped in brown paper protruding from under the front seat. The defendant was asked to accompany the officers to the police station, and he complied. At the station, the defendant consented to a search of his car, and the officers recovered the cylindrical object, which was determined to contain narcotics. The defendant was then placed under arrest. Prior to trial, relying on *Mapp*, the defendant filed a motion to suppress the drugs on the basis that the search of his car was unconstitutional, having been conducted without a warrant. Suppression was denied and, following a bench trial, he was convicted.

On appeal, the defendant again relied on *Mapp* to argue that the search of his car was illegal. In addition to the basis for this claim advanced at trial, he argued that he should have been informed of his *Escobedo* rights prior to being asked to consent to a search of the car. The Superior Court rejected these claims. First, relying on its decision in a prior case, the Superior Court noted that constitutional prohibitions against unreasonable searches and seizures were not implicated when the officers noticed the cylindrical object protruding from beneath the front seat of the defendant's car. "The mere looking at an object which is plainly visible," the court held, "does not constitute a search, nor does its taking amount to a seizure."[50] Although the officers could not tell

---

46. See e.g., *Commonwealth ex rel. Gaito v. Maroney*, 422 Pa. 171, 220 A.2d 628 (1966).

47. *Commonwealth ex rel. Hilberry v. Maroney*, 417 Pa. 534, 545, 207 A.2d 794, 799 (1965) (Bell dissenting).

48. 207 A.2d 800.

49. 208 Pa. Super. 323, 222 A.2d 495 (1966) (Watkins, J.).

50. 222 A.2d 497, quoting *Commonwealth ex rel. Bowers v. Rundle*, 200 Pa. Super. 496, 189 A.2d 910 (1963).

what the package contained, its presence, combined with the officers' knowledge that the defendant was a drug user, gave the officers reasonable cause to investigate further. At that point, according to the court, the officers could have arrested the defendant on the motor vehicle violation, but they chose instead to ask that the defendant accompany them to the police station to complete the investigation. Since the defendant complied with the request and consented to a subsequent search of the vehicle, there was no constitutional violation. Relying upon decisions of the United States Supreme Court, the court concluded, "It is fundamental that the rights guaranteed by the Fourth Amendment prohibiting unreasonable searches and seizures may be waived by consent. This applies especially to an automobile so that one who voluntarily gives the keys of his car to an officer who finds contraband is not in a position to complain, having given his consent to the search."[51]

The court then turned to the defendant's claim that he was entitled to *Escobedo* rights before his consent to the search was obtained by the police. The court began by emphasizing the distinction between searches and confessions: "A search and seizure may be legally made against the wishes of the defendant in the course of a valid arrest or with a search warrant with reasonable cause shown. A confession or admission cannot be obtained against the wishes of the defendant even when he has been properly warned and has counsel."[52] Refusing to extend *Escobedo* to searches and seizures, the court held:

> The area covered by *Escobedo*, supra, is in the use of confessions or admissions obtained by police during the arrest or incarceration of a defendant accused of crime. We agree with the Commonwealth that 'The protection arises when the police are seeking inculpatory admissions which might subsequently be used in evidence. The request for appellant's consent to the examining of his automobile (which he readily could have refused) does not come remotely within the standards laid down in *Escobedo*.'[53]

The Superior Court affirmed the denial of the defendant's motion to suppress and the Supreme Court denied the defendant's petition for allocatur. Thereafter, appellant filed a habeas corpus petition in federal court, but the petition was denied on the basis that the search of his car and subsequent arrest were constitutionally valid.[54] In the years since it was rendered, *Anderson* has been a leading case in several areas of Pennsylvania search and seizure law, and it has been cited by the Supreme Courts of Iowa and Louisiana, and the Court of Appeals of California.[55] In particular, the case stands for the proposition that a voluntary consent to search will eliminate the warrant and probable cause requirements of the Fourth Amendment.[56] It has also been cited for the proposition that merely looking at that which is open to view is not a search.[57] More important, however, is *Anderson's* holding that the sweeping decision in *Escobedo* was

51. 222 A.2d 498, citing *Zap v. United States*, 328 U.S. 624 (1946), and *Grice v. United States*, 146 F.2d 849 (4th Cir. N.C. 1945).

52. 222 A.2d 499.

53. See note 52.

54. *United States ex rel. Anderson v. Rundle*, 274 F. Supp. 364 (E.D. Pa. 1967).

55. See *Iowa v. Gates*, 260 Iowa 772 (1967); *Louisiana v. Andrus*, 199 So.2d 867 (1967); and *California v. Beal*, 268 Cal. App. 2d 481 (Cal. App. 2d Dist. 1968).

56. *Commonwealth v. Danforth*, 395 Pa. Super. 1, 576 A.2d 1013 (1990); *Commonwealth v. Walsh*, 314 Pa. Super. 65, 460 A.2d 767 (1983); *Commonwealth v. Latshaw*, 242 Pa. Super. 233, 363 A.2d 1246 (1976); *Iowa v. Gates*, supra.

57. See e.g., *Commonwealth v. Chiesa*, 329 Pa. Super. 401, 478 A.2d 850 (1984); *Commonwealth v. Brayboy*, 209 Pa. Super. 10, 223 A.2d 878 (1966).

limited to confessions and admissions, and did not extend to requests for consent to search.[58]

In 1966 in another landmark opinion, *Miranda v. Arizona*,[59] the United States Supreme Court extended *Escobedo* by holding that, unless specific procedures are satisfied, a confession must be excluded regardless of whether the confession was "voluntary" under previous standards. As it did following the decisions in *Mapp* and *Escobedo*, the Superior Court played an important early role in applying the broad new *Miranda* decision to state law. The issue in *Commonwealth v. Bonser*,[60] for instance, was whether misdemeanor arrests were subject to the rule of *Miranda*, which had been applied almost exclusively in felony cases. In *Bonser*, the defendant was arrested and charged with drunk driving and, while being questioned on the way to the police station, he made a number of incriminating statements. At a subsequent hearing, the trial court determined that the defendant was too intoxicated to knowingly and intelligently waive his *Miranda* rights. Nonetheless, the court determined that *Miranda* did not apply to misdemeanor prosecutions. The defendant's incriminating statements were introduced and he was convicted. Thereafter, his motions for a new trial and in arrest of judgment were heard by the court en banc, which granted a new trial on the basis that the defendant was entitled to *Miranda* rights and that he was too intoxicated to waive those rights.

On appeal to the Superior Court, the Commonwealth relied on cases from Delaware, New Jersey, and Ohio to argue that *Miranda* warnings were inapplicable to drunk driving prosecutions. The defendant, represented by future Superior Court Judge Vincent A. Cirillo, argued that *Miranda* drew no distinction between felony and misdemeanor cases. A unanimous Superior Court rejected the contrary holdings of other jurisdictions and sided with the defendant. The court began by noting that, although *Miranda* and "the great bulk of cases following it" were felony cases, the United States Supreme Court gave "no indication that one accused of a misdemeanor, who faces the potential of a substantial prison sentence, must subject himself to police interrogation absent the fundamental safeguards afforded others." The court continued, "The 5th and 6th Amendments speak of criminal cases without distinction between felonies and misdemeanors."[61] The court also noted that drunk driving was an indictable offense that provided for both fines and up to three years in prison. "Consequently," the court concluded, "the appellee if convicted faces a substantial loss of liberty. Under these circumstances he is entitled to full protection under the Constitution as implemented by *Miranda*. Nor should there be any different holding because the offense is found in the Vehicle Code instead of the Penal Code."[62] On this basis, the court affirmed the award of a new trial to the defendant. The Commonwealth's petition for allocatur was denied by the Supreme Court.

In the years after it was rendered, *Bonser* was cited in other jurisdictions, and in one instance as the sole case, for the proposition that a suspect undergoing custodial interrogation for a misdemeanor traffic offense was entitled to *Miranda* warnings.[63] *Bonser* represented the minority view in this regard, and the Fourth Circuit Court of Appeals, and courts in Delaware, Florida, Missouri, North Carolina, New Hampshire,

---

58. See *Louisiana v. Andrus* and *California v. Beal*, supra.

59. 384 U.S. 436 (1966).

60. 215 Pa. Super. 452, 258 A.2d 675 (1969) (Jacobs, J.).

61. 258 A.2d 679.

62. 258 A.2d 680.

63. See *New Jersey v. Macuk*, 268 A.2d 1 (1970) (citing *Bonser* and two New York cases for the minority view); and *Missouri v. Neal*, 476 S.W.2d 547 (Mo. 1972) (citing cases from Delaware, North Carolina, New Hampshire, Louisiana, New York, Ohio, and New Jersey for the majority view that *Miranda* does not apply to motor vehicle offenses, and citing *Bonser* as the sole case for the minority view).

Louisiana, New York, Ohio, and New Jersey held otherwise.[64] In 1980, however, the Pennsylvania Supreme Court upheld suppression in a drunken driving case for failure to give *Miranda* warnings.[65] Four years later, in an Ohio case holding *Miranda* inapplicable to interrogation for a misdemeanor traffic offense, the United States Supreme Court "granted certiorari to resolve confusion in the federal and state courts regarding the applicability of our ruling in *Miranda* to interrogations involving minor offenses."[66] In reversing the Ohio court and a federal district court, the Supreme Court sided with the position taken by the Superior Court fifteen years earlier in *Bonser*. According to the Supreme Court, "[A] person subjected to custodial interrogation is entitled to the benefit of the procedural safeguards enunciated in *Miranda*, regardless of the nature or severity of the offense of which he is suspected or for which he was arrested."[67]

The same year it rendered *Bonser*, the Superior Court considered the precise language of the warnings required by *Miranda*. In *Commonwealth v. Baker*,[68] a police officer happened upon an overturned car and saw a man walking away from it. As he talked to the witness, the officer received a radio report that a vehicle matching the description of the overturned car had been stolen. The officer took the witness to police headquarters and took a statement implicating the defendant. Another officer then went to the defendant's apartment and requested that the defendant accompany him to the police station. The defendant complied. At the station, the officer read the defendant *Miranda* warnings from a card printed and distributed to the police by the York County District Attorney's Office. The card provided in relevant part: "The law requires that you be advised that you have the right to remain silent, that anything you say *can* be used against you in a Court of Law, that you have the right to the presence of an attorney."[69] After the card was read, the defendant asked the officer if he "could do something for him as far as making it easy on a sentence that he might get through this."[70] The defendant was charged with larceny of an automobile. At trial, he argued that the warning read to him was deficient in that it provided only that "anything you say *can* be used against you." This warning, the defendant argued, improperly deviated from the holding of a state Supreme Court case, *Commonwealth v. Medina*,[71] which quoted *Miranda* for the proposition that a defendant must be notified that an incriminating statement "can *and will*" be used against him. The trial court agreed with this argument, and granted the defendant's demurrer at the close of the Commonwealth's case. The Commonwealth appealed.

"The narrow issue presented" to the Superior Court was "whether an incriminatory statement made by one in custody is rendered inadmissible where, in warning of the right to remain silent, the questioner states that anything said 'can' be used adversely without adding the words 'and will' be so used."[72] The court began by discussing the language of *Miranda*, as quoted in *Medina*. The quoted portion was the following: "The warning of the right to remain silent must be accompanied by the explanation

---

64. See *Clay v. Riddle*, 541 F.2d 456 (4th Cir. Va. 1976); *State v. Bliss*, 238 A.2d 848 (Del. 1968); *County of Dade v. Callahan*, 259 So.2d 504 (Fla. Dist. Ct. App.3d Dist. 1971); *Neal*, supra; *State v. Beasley*, 10 N.C. App. 663 (1971); *State v. Desjardins*, 110 N.H. 511 (1970); *State v. Angelo*, 251 La. 250 (1967); *People v. Bliss*, 278 N.Y.S.2d 732 (1967); *Columbus v. Hayes*, 9 Ohio App.2d 38 (Ohio Ct. App., Franklin County 1967); *State v. Zucconi*, 93 N.J. Super. 380 (1967).

65. *Commonwealth v. Meyer*, 488 Pa. 297, 412 A.2d 517 (1980).

66. *Berkemer v. McCarty*, 468 U.S. 420, 426 (1984).

67. 468 U.S. 433.

68. 214 Pa. Super. 27, 251 A.2d 737 (1969) (Wright, J.).

69. 251 A.2d 738.

70. See note 69.

71. 424 Pa. 632, 227 A.2d 842 (1967).

72. See note 69.

that anything said *can and will* be used against the individual in court."[73] The court then reviewed the remainder of *Miranda* and concluded that the conjunctive phrase "can and will" was used only once, while the words "may" and "can" were used, standing alone, on three occasions.[74] The court also examined three state Supreme Court cases, all of which used the single word "can".[75] Based on this review, the court concluded:

> In brief, the entire purpose of the warning of a suspect as to the right to remain silent is to make sure that the person about to be questioned understands the consequences which "may" result if he chooses to speak. We are all of the opinion that the *Medina* decision is not to be construed as mandating a warning that the suspect's statement not only "may" but also "will" be used against him.[76]

On this basis the grant of a demurrer in favor of the defendant was reversed. The Supreme Court denied allocatur. The issue resolved in *Baker* has not arisen again in Pennsylvania, but a year after the decision was rendered it was relied upon by the New Mexico Supreme Court to reject the claim that *Miranda* requires notification that an incriminating statement "can and will" be used against a defendant at trial.[77]

In addition to construing landmark Supreme Court cases, the Superior Court also decided an important case involving the admissibility of scientific evidence that has defined Pennsylvania law ever since. Although the law regarding the admissibility of technological advances has long been ambiguous, the clearest governing standard is the broad language of *Frye v. United States*, a 1923 case in which the United States Court of Appeals for the District of Columbia stated the following:

> Just when a scientific principle or discovery crosses the line between the experimental and demonstrable stages is difficult to define. Some-where in this twilight zone the evidential force of the principle must be recognized, and while courts will go a long way in admitting expert testimony deduced from a well-recognized scientific principle or discov-ery, the thing from which the deduction is made must be sufficiently established to have gained general acceptance in the particular field in which it belongs.[78]

---

73. 251 A.2d 738, citing *Miranda*, 384 U.S. 436.

74. See note 69.

75. 251 A.2d 739, citing *Commonwealth v. Moody*, 429 Pa. 39, 239 A.2d 409 (1968); *Commonwealth v. Feldman*, 432 Pa. 428, 248 A.2d 1 (1968); *Commonwealth v. Leaming*, 432 Pa. 326, 247 A.2d 590 (1968).

76. 251 A.2d 739.

77. *State v. Briggs*, 81 N.M. 581, 469 P.2d 730 (N.M. Ct. App. 1970). Another decision of the United States Supreme Court that had a major impact on state law in the 1960s was *Fay v. Noia*, 372 U.S. 391 (1963), which held that states must provide an adequate procedure for reviewing and deciding claims of convicts that they had been deprived of federal rights after the period for direct appeal had expired. Prior to *Fay*, the procedure for deciding such claims in Pennsylvania was confused. Some courts reviewed writs of habeas corpus, others reviewed writs of coram nobis, and still others utilized a combination of the two. See Ethan Allen Doty and Stanley W. Bluestine, "The Purposes and Application of the Pennsylvania Post Convic-tion Hearing Act," 1974 Pa. B. A. Q. 480. In 1966, in order to comply with the mandate of *Fay*, the legislature passed the Post Conviction Hearing Act, which replaced the common law procedures and provided for the review of "sentences imposed without due process of law" after the direct appeal period had expired. Pa. Act of January 25, 1966, PL 780, sec. 2. The basic procedure established by this statute, although modified, continues to govern post- conviction proceedings in Pennsylvania. The modern successor of the statute is the Post Conviction Relief Act, 42 Pa.C.S. sec. 9541, et seq.

78. 54 U.S. App. D.C. 46, 293 F. 1013 (1923).

The Superior Court in 1968. L. to R. (seated): G. Harold Watkins, J. Colvin Wright (President Judge), Harry M. Montgomery. L. to R. (standing): Theodore O. Spaulding, Robert L. Jacobs, J. Sydney Hoffman, John B. Hannum.

Since scientific advances often acquire a mythic infallibility in the eyes of lay jurors, it is particularly important that such advances are approved by the scientific community before they are admitted in criminal trials. This is the purpose of the *Frye* "general acceptance" standard.[79] In 1955, the Superior Court considered for the first time under Pennsylvania law the admissibility of a scientific advance that has proven extremely important in law enforcement, the polygraph test.[80] In *Commonwealth ex rel. Riccio v. Dilworth*,[81] the defendant was convicted of robbery. Two years later, he initiated post-conviction proceedings arguing that he should have been permitted to take a polygraph test to establish his innocence. The trial court denied this claim.

On appeal, the defendant urged the Superior Court "to hold that the polygraph test has now reached the stage of scientific reliability that it should be so recognized in our law of evidence." In a brief but influential opinion, the court began by noting that since appellant had not actually taken a polygraph test, the court was not "squarely called upon to determine the reliability and admissibility of the test." Instead, the only question at issue was whether the trial court's refusal to administer the test was in error. Nonetheless, the court went on to consider whether the tests should be admitted. First, it found "no recognized authority which has ventured to state that the polygraph test is judicially acceptable."[82] Citing the *Frye* standard and reviewing other cases, the court concluded "[t]he reliability and scientific infallibility of the polygraph, lie detec-

---

79. See *United States v. Addison*, 162 U.S. App. D.C. 199, 498 F.2d 741, 744 (1974).

80. The polygraph, or lie detector test, was first developed in 1915 by William Moulton Marston, an attorney and Ph.D. at Harvard. See *Oregon v. Brown*, 687 P.2d 751, 770 (1984).

81. 179 Pa. Super. 64, 115 A.2d 865 (1955) (Ross, J.).

82. 115 A.2d 866.

tor, or other psychological deception test must be more definitely established before our courts will accept their results as credible."[83] On this basis, the defendant's petition for post-conviction relief was denied. *Riccio*'s holding that polygraph tests are inadmissible remains the law of Pennsylvania.[84] In 1976, the Supreme Court adopted this holding, ruling that polygraph tests were inadmissible for "any purpose."[85] *Riccio* has also been relied upon in other jurisdictions,[86] and in Pennsylvania to uphold the admissibility of breathalyzers,[87] to reject the admissibility of voice spectography,[88] and to refuse to sanction the discharge of employees for refusing to submit to polygraph tests.[89]

## CIVIL LIABILITY

Like criminal law, the law of civil liability, particularly in the realm of torts, changed dramatically between 1951 and 1968, as it occupied an increasing share of the court's work. No area was transformed as completely as the law of products liability. At common law, a party injured by a defective product had only two options of recovery against the manufacturer or seller of the product. The first, a negligence action, was unattractive because it required proof that the manufacturer or seller engaged in specific conduct that created the defect in the product. Evidence that the product was defective when it reached the end of the production line was insufficient. Due to the difficulty of proof in a negligence action, injured parties generally sued on the second available theory, warranty, which asserted that the manufacturer or seller breached an express or implied promise as to the condition of the product. Where a breach was established, this theory imposed what amounted to strict liability, or liability without fault, since it obviated the necessity of demonstrating negligence.[90]

Yet, the ability of injured parties to succeed on either negligence or warranty theories was extremely limited. The most significant limitation was privity, the legal requirement that injured parties could not sue, either in negligence or warranty, unless they were able to demonstrate a contractual relationship with the manufacturer or seller of a defective product. Privity could be established either "horizontally" or "vertically." Horizontal privity meant that lawsuits could be brought only by purchasers or those who had a particular "lateral" relationship to the purchaser, such as a family or household member. Vertical privity, on the other hand, meant that the injured party could sue only the individual with whom he had contracted for the product, such as a retailer, but could not sue others involved in the manufacturing and distribution of the product. As its name suggests, vertical privity allowed the injured party to sue only the

---

83. 115 A.2d 867.

84. See e.g., *Commonwealth v. Camm*, 443 Pa. 253, 277 A.2d 325 (1971); *Commonwealth v. Puchalski*, 310 Pa. Super. 199, 456 A.2d 569 (1983); *Carroll v. Unemployment Compensation Board of Review*, 113 Pa. Cmwlth. 596, 537 A.2d 969 (1988). See also, 23 ALR 2d 306; 34 Duq. L. Rev. 83, 815 (1996).

85. *Commonwealth v. Gee*, 467 Pa. 123, 354 A.2d 875 (1976).

86. *Marks v. United States*, 260 F.2d 377 (10th Cir. N.M. 1958); *Hawaii v. Chang*, 374 P.2d 5 (1962) (citing *Commonwealth v. Saunders*, 386 Pa. 149, 125 A.2d 442 (1956), which relied exclusively on *Riccio* to reject the admissibility of polygraph tests).

87. *Commonwealth v. McGinnis*, 336 Pa. Super. 601, 486 A.2d 428 (1984).

88. *Commonwealth v. Topa*, 471 Pa. 223, 369 A.2d 1277 (1977).

89. *Stape & DeVito v. Civil Service Commission*, 404 Pa. 354, 172 A.2d 161 (1961).

90. Joel R. Levine, "Buyer's Conduct as Affecting the Extent of Manufacturer's Liability in Warranty," 52 Minn. L. Rev. 627 (1968). This discussion of the law relating to breach of warranty, technically a contract action, is included in the tort section of this case review because breach of warranty is rooted in the law of torts. See William L. Prosser, *Handbook of the Law of Torts, 3d ed.* (St. Paul: West Publishing Co., 1964), 651-52 ("While breach of warranty is basically a contract rather than a tort action, it, nevertheless, has roots which spring essentially from a tort background.").

person directly "above" them in the chain of possession of the product. Needless to say, these privity requirements sharply limited both who could sue and who could be sued. As consumer goods flooded the market in the first decades of the twentieth century, courts were increasingly faced with individuals who sustained either bodily injury or property damage from defective products, but who were denied recovery because they could not establish privity with the manufacturer or seller. As a result, the "citadel" of privity came under heavy assault.[91] The first salvo was fired in 1916, when future United States Supreme Court Justice Benjamin Cardozo, at that time presiding on the Court of Appeals of New York, rendered his landmark opinion in *MacPherson v. Buick Motor Co.*,[92] which established a manufacturer's liability for negligently making a product regardless of whether a contractual relationship existed with the party it injured. The *McPherson* rule, which abolished the privity requirement in negligence actions, was adopted by other states, including Pennsylvania.[93] Yet, the privity requirement in the more common warranty actions proved more durable, and it entered the 1950s intact.[94]

In *Jarnot v. Ford Motor Co*,[95] the Superior Court decided a case that William Prosser, the nation's leading authority on tort law, identified as one of "seven spectacular decisions" of the late 1950s that hastened the decline of privity in warranty actions.[96] In *Jarnot*, the plaintiff had purchased a tractor-trailer from an authorized Ford dealer. On August 7, 1951, less than two months after delivery of the truck, the plaintiff's employee was using it to deliver 33,000 pounds of steel coils from Cincinnati to the Irvin Works of the United States Steel Corporation at Dravosburg. As the employee attempted to make a turn, the kingpin, a vital part of the steering mechanism, broke and the driver lost control. The trailer overturned and was destroyed, and the tractor was severely damaged as it slid to a halt on the side of the road. The plaintiff commenced an action against Ford and the dealer for breach of an implied warranty that the truck was of merchantable quality. At trial, he produced an expert metallurgist who testified that the kingpin broke at its "weakest point," a milled notch that allowed the pin to function. The company that supplied the pins to Ford admitted the possibility that a defect in the pin caused the accident. At the close of evidence, the jury found against Ford alone and rendered a verdict in favor of the plaintiff in the amount of the purchase price of the trailer and the repair cost of the tractor. The trial court, apparently believing that the plaintiff could not recover directly against Ford because of a lack of privity, molded the verdict to read "for the plaintiff and against the [dealer] with liability over against Ford."[97]

On appeal, Ford and the dealer argued that the contract signed by the plaintiff limited his recovery to replacement of the defective part. Ford also argued that the plaintiff, having dealt with the dealer and not Ford directly, lacked vertical privity of contract. The Superior Court rejected both claims. First, the court held that the con-

---

91. The reference is to Justice Cardozo's oft-quoted remark in *Ultramares Corp. v. Touche*, 255 N.Y. 170, 174 N.E. 441 (1931): "The assault upon the citadel of privity is proceeding in these days apace." See also William Prosser, "The Assault Upon the Citadel," 69 Yale L.J. 1099 (1960).

92. 217 N.Y. 382, 111 N.E. 1050 (1916), and Prosser, "The Fall of the Citadel," 50 Minn. L. Rev. 791 (1966).

93. *Foley v. Pittsburgh-Des Moines Co.*, 363 Pa. 1, 68 A.2d 517 (1949).

94. The only exception to this rule was in cases involving items of human consumption, such as food and beverages. In those cases, an injured plaintiff was allowed to recover against a remote manufacturer regardless of privity. See *Catani v. Swift & Co.*, 251 Pa. 52, 95 A. 931 (1915); *Nock v. Coca Cola Bottling Works*, 102 Pa. Super. 515, 156 A. 537 (1931).

95. 191 Pa. Super. 422, 156 A.2d 568 (1959) (Hirt, J.).

96. Prosser, "The Assault Upon the Citadel," 69 Yale L.J. 1112.

97. 156 A.2d 573.

tract provision relied upon by Ford did not preclude application of an implied warranty of merchantability imposed by state law.[98] This warranty provided that damages included "the loss directly and naturally resulting . . . from the breach of warranty."[99] The court also rejected Ford's claim that the plaintiff lacked privity:

> [A] manufacturer who by means of advertising extols his product, in an effort to persuade the public to buy, may thereby incur liability to a purchaser notwithstanding that privity between the purchaser and the manufacturer is wholly lacking.
>
> A person, who after purchase of a thing, has been damaged because of its unfitness for the intended purpose may bring an action in assumpsit against the manufacturer based on a breach of the implied warranty of fitness; and proof of a contractual relationship or privity between the manufacturer and the purchaser is not necessary to impose liability for the damage.[100]

Having found that a lack of privity did not bar the plaintiff's recovery directly against Ford, the court then modified the trial court's order to reflect the jury's verdict that Ford was directly liable to the plaintiff.[101]

By rejecting the well-established rule favoring privity in warranty actions, *Jarnot* helped to hasten what Prosser called "the most rapid and altogether spectacular overturn of an established rule in the entire history of the law of torts."[102] In the years after it was rendered, *Jarnot* was cited repeatedly by noted scholars as the leading case in Pennsylvania abolishing the vertical privity requirement in product liability actions based on breach of warranty.[103] In all, it was cited in twelve law reviews and by courts in nine states and five federal districts. It was expressly relied upon by the Supreme Courts of New Jersey and Florida, and an appeals court in Ohio, to abolish vertical privity in warranty actions.[104] It was also cited by the Supreme Courts of Delaware, Michigan, New Jersey, and North Carolina for the proposition that specific evidence of fault is not required in a warranty action.[105]

---

98. 156 A.2d 572. Section 15 of the Uniform Sales Act of May 19, 1915, PL 543, provided: "Where the goods are bought by description from a seller who deals in goods of that description (whether he be the grower or manufacturer or not), there is an implied warranty that the goods shall be of merchantable quality."

99. 156 A.2d 572, citing Section 69 of the Uniform Sales Act.

100. 156 A.2d 573 (citations omitted). Also, rejecting a claim apparently advanced by the dealer or Ford, the court found that the "plaintiff's contributory negligence does not arise here in an action of assumpsit on a contract as it does in trespass for personal injuries."

101. See note 97.

102. Prosser, "The Fall of the Citadel," 50 Minn. L. Rev. at 793-94.

103. See Robert S. Greenspan, H. Reginald Belden, and Libo B. Fineberg, "Sales," 27 U. Pitt. L. Rev. 345, 352 (1966) (identifying *Jarnot* as "a landmark case" in the field of breach of warranty); John E. Murray Jr., and Francis E. Holahan, "Commercial Transactions," 27 U. Pitt. L. Rev. 317, 334 (1966); Prosser, "The Assault Upon the Citadel," 69 Yale L.J. 1113 (although noting that cases relied upon by the *Jarnot* Court did not support the conclusion reached therein); Prosser, "The Fall of the Citadel," 50 Minn. L. Rev. 792, n. 4 (noting "the salutary result in the *Jarnot* case" despite the fact that the cases it relied on did not support its conclusion); Levine, "Buyer's Conduct as Affecting the Extent of Manufacturer's Liability in Warranty," 52 Minn. L. Rev. 632, n. 25; Dix W. Noel, "Strict Liability of Manufacturers," 50 A.B.A.J. 446, 449, n. 16 (1964).

104. *Santor v. A & M Karagheusian, Inc.,* 207 A.2d 305 (N.J. 1965); *Manheim v. Ford Motor Co.,* 201 So.2d 440 (Fla. 1967); *Lonzrick v. Republic Steel Corp.,* 205 N.E.2d 92 (Ohio Ct. App., Cuyahoga County 1965). See also *McQuaide v. Bridgeport Brass Co.,* 190 F. Supp. 252 (D. Conn. 1960), applying the *Jarnot* rule in a diversity of citizenship case where the manufacturer of insecticide was sued for breach of warranty by a remote buyer.

105. *Ciociola v. Delaware Coca-Cola Bottling Co.,* 172 A.2d 252 (Del. 1961); *Holloway v. General Motors*

Despite *Jarnot's* prominence, the Pennsylvania Supreme Court proved hesitant to join the vast majority of other jurisdictions in abandoning the privity requirement in warranty claims.[106] Indeed, in a 1966 ruling, the Supreme Court explicitly overruled *Jarnot*. In *Miller v. Preitz*,[107] a defective humidifier exploded and fatally scalded an infant. The humidifier was purchased by the aunt and next door neighbor of the infant, and the court held that, since the infant was not a purchaser, his administrator could not assert an implied warranty claim.[108] In overruling *Jarnot*, the court stated that the requirement of privity "still has great vitality in Pennsylvania."[109] In the dissenting portion of a concurring and dissenting opinion, Justice Jones noted *Jarnot* and stated, "I would favor the abolition of the requirement of privity in assumpsit actions in this field. The remote manufacturer of a product shown to be defective should be held liable to any person or persons who might be reasonably foreseen to use, consume or be affected by the defective product."[110] Justice Roberts, in a concurring and dissenting opinion joined by Justice Musmanno, agreed with Jones. "I believe that the time has arrived," he stated, "for this Court to settle the long perplexing problem of strict liability in cases involving defective products causing personal injuries by discarding privity as a predicate to the maintenance of such actions."[111] Two years later, the Pennsylvania Supreme Court reconsidered its ruling in *Miller* and expressly overruled it. In *Kassab v. Central Soya*,[112] the plaintiffs' cattle were injured by defective feed and they brought a warranty action against the feed manufacturer and distributor. The defendants received a verdict at trial and on appeal the manufacturer argued that the plaintiffs lacked privity to maintain their warranty action. In disposing of this claim, the court held:

> [W]ere we to continue to adhere to the requirement that privity of contract must exist between plaintiff and defendant in order to maintain an action in assumpsit for injuries caused by breach of implied warranty, there would be no doubt that [the manufacturer] could escape liability under the authority of *Miller*. However, we take this opportunity today to reconsider one of our holdings in that case, and accordingly this Court is now of the opinion that Pennsylvania should join the fast growing list of jurisdictions that have eliminated the privity requirement in assumpsit suits by purchasers against remote manufac-

---

*Corp.*, 271 N.W.2d 777 (Mich. 1978); *Pabon v. Hackensack Auto Sales, Inc.*, 164 A.2d 773 (N.J. 1960); *Tennessee-Carolina Transp. v. Strick Corp., Inc.*, 210 S.E.2d 181 (N.C. 1974). *Jarnot* also stands for the proposition that contributory negligence will not bar a warranty action.

106. See Prosser, "The Fall of the Citadel," 50 Minn. L. Rev. 799 (citing a State Supreme Court case and stating "it is only in Pennsylvania" that Section 2-318 of the Uniform Commercial Code has been interpreted to limit the expansion of liability outside the traditional bounds of privity).

107. 422 Pa. 383, 221 A.2d 320 (1966).

108. The court relied on its decision three years earlier in *Hochgertel v. Canada Dry Corp.*, 409 Pa. 610, 187 A.2d 575 (1963), which held that a manufacturer of bottled soda water sold to a fraternal lodge was not liable for breach of warranty to the lodge bartender who was injured when an unopened bottle exploded. The court held that the warranty extended from the manufacturer to the purchaser, but not to the bartender, an employee of the purchaser. Although it was not discussed, it appears that *Jarnot* was overruled by *Hochgertel*. The year that *Hochgertel* was rendered, an article co-authored by noted contract scholar John E. Murray Jr. called it "a giant step backward [in the] war against the archaic doctrine of privity." Murray and Holahan, 27 U. Pitt. L. Rev. 334-35.

109. 221 A.2d 324.

110. 221 A.2d 334 (Jones, concurring and dissenting).

111. 221 A.2d 340 (Roberts, concurring and dissenting).

112. 432 Pa. 217, 246 A.2d 848 (1968).

turers for breach of implied warranty. That aspect of *Miller* must therefore be overruled.[113]

Thus, nine years after the Superior Court rendered its decision in *Jarnot*, the Supreme Court formally abolished vertical privity in implied warranty actions. Six years later, in *Salvador v. I.H. English of Phila., Inc.*,[114] the Superior Court also abolished the requirement of horizontal privity, thereby allowing a nonpurchaser to maintain a claim for breach of implied warranty. With the holding in *Salvador*, the assault begun in *Jarnot* finally succeeded in destroying the "citadel" of privity.

Another important tort case decided by the court was *Schelin v. Goldberg*,[115] which is recognized as the case that initiated the modern law of dramshop, or liquor licensee, liability. In *Schelin*, the plaintiff had spent the evening of October 4, 1952 consuming double shots of whiskey at several bars. He was visibly intoxicated when he entered the defendant's bar, where he was served additional drinks. While in the bar, he annoyed several patrons and became involved in an argument with an individual named Richard Monk. When the plaintiff left the bar, he believed he was being followed by Monk, although he was not sure. As he walked toward the exit, he was struck on the side of the head. He was knocked to the floor and ultimately required hospitalization. The injuries he received required removal of his left eye. In July of 1954, the plaintiff filed suit against the defendants on the basis that they were negligent in providing him with alcohol after he was visibly intoxicated. At the close of evidence, the trial court instructed the jury that a visibly intoxicated person who is served alcohol is not contributorily negligent for accepting and consuming the alcohol. This instruction had the effect of charging the jurors that, as a matter of law, they could not consider the plaintiff's conduct in taking the alcohol furnished by the defendants and engaging in an altercation with Monk. The jury returned a verdict for $4,890.35. However, the court of common pleas, sitting en banc, awarded a new trial on the basis that the issue of the plaintiff's contributory negligence should have been submitted to the jury. The plaintiff appealed.

The issue presented to the Superior Court required it to construe two important liquor statutes. The first of these was P.L. 663, an 1854 law that made it a misdemeanor to furnish alcohol to an intoxicated person and provided for a civil cause of action for injuries resulting from the furnishing of alcohol in violation "of any existing law."[116] This law remained in effect until 1951, when it was replaced by the Liquor Code.[117] The new code incorporated the misdemeanor provision of the 1854 act, but it specifically repealed the civil liability provision.[118] Thus, the question presented to the Superior Court for the first time in *Schelin* was whether civil liability could be imposed upon a liquor licensee in the absence of statutory authorization. After setting forth the facts and relevant statutory provisions, the court began its analysis of this issue by

---

113. 246 A.2d 852. The court went on to state that its conclusion was compelled by the adoption of Section 402A of the Restatement of Torts two years earlier in *Webb v. Zern*, 422 Pa. 424, 220 A.2d 853 (1966). Section 402A provides, in subsection (b), that the seller of a defective product is liable when the product causes injury even though the injured party "has not bought the product from or entered into a contractual relationship with the seller." Section 402A effectively makes a manufacturer a guarantor of the safety of his product. *Salvador v. I.H. English of Phila., Inc.*, 224 Pa. Super. 377, 307 A.2d 398 (1973). The *Kassab* Court found that, since 402A abolishes privity where a product liability action is brought in tort, it would be anomalous to allow privity to bar such an action that is brought on a warranty theory in contract. According to the court, "To permit the result of a lawsuit to depend solely on the caption atop plaintiff's complaint is not now, and has never been, a sound resolution of identical controversies." 432 Pa. 229, 246 A.2d 853.

114. 224 Pa. Super. 377, 307 A.2d 398 (1973) (Cercone, J.), affirmed, 457 Pa. 24, 319 A.2d 903 (1974).

115. 188 Pa. Super. 341, 146 A.2d 648 (1958) (Woodside, J.).

116. Pa. Act of May 8, 1854, PL 663, No. 648, sec. 1, 3.

117. Pa. Act of April 12, 1951, PL 90, 179.

118. Pa. Act of April 12, 1951, sec. 901.

General Kin Chang Oh, chief of staff of the Republic of Korea Army, observes training with Major General Van H. Bond, commander of the XXI U.S. Army Corps (This U.S. Army Photograph was taken in 1963 by Pfc Cecil J. Smith Jr., Hqs. U.S. Army Garrison, Annville, Pennsylvania, now known as Indiantown Gap).

noting that "[w]hen an act embodying in expressed terms a principle of law is repealed by the legislature, then the principle as it existed at common law is still in force."[119] The court then found that the defendants' conduct in serving alcohol to an intoxicated person was negligent under established precedent, and the only remaining question was whether, under the common law, the plaintiff could have been contributorily negligent, thereby relieving the defendants of liability. To resolve this question, the court turned to the Restatement of Torts, Section 483, which provides, "If the defendant's negligence consists in the violation of a statute enacted to protect a class of persons from their inability to exercise self-protective care, a member of such class is not barred by his contributory negligence from recovery for bodily harm caused by the violation of such statute." Adopting this common law principle, the court found it obvious that the provision of the Liquor Code making it unlawful to sell alcohol to an intoxicated person was "enacted to protect [inebriates] from their inability to exercise self-protective care."[120] Accordingly, although the civil liability provision of the 1854 act was repealed, the common law, as set forth in Section 483 of the Restatement, nonetheless provided that the plaintiff was "not barred by his contributory negligence from recovery for bodily harm." On this basis, the court reversed the award of a new trial in favor of the defendants. An appeal was taken, but the Supreme Court denied allocatur. Thereafter, in 1960, *Schelin's* holding that liquor licensees were subject to civil liability at common law was followed by the Pennsylvania Supreme Court.[121] Recent cases continue to recognize the seminal

---

119. 146 A.2d 651, citing *American Rolling Mill Co. v. Hullinger*, 67 N.E. 986 (1903).
120. 146 A.2d 652
121. *Corcoran v. McNeal*, 400 Pa. 14, 161 A.2d A.2d 367 (1960).

role of *Schelin* in imposing common law civil liability on liquor licensees.[122] It has also been cited on numerous other occasions in Pennsylvania, by the Third Circuit Court of Appeals, and courts in Arkansas, Indiana, Louisiana, Michigan, Minnesota, Missouri, New Hampshire, New Jersey, New Mexico, New York, and Wisconsin.[123]

Another case that did not involve negligence but nonetheless represented the trend in favor of expanded civil liability was *Readinger v. Gottschall.*[124] In that case, the plaintiff was an employee of the defendants. On May 12, 1958, she was informed that her services were no longer required. Two days later, when she went to her former place of business to collect her final pay, a dispute arose over the amount of wages due. The plaintiff testified at trial that the defendants assaulted her and pushed her out the front door of the business. She suffered back injuries and, along with her husband, brought a trespass action. In defense, the defendants argued that the Workmen's Compensation Act was the sole means of compensation available to an employee injured in the course of employment. The jury returned a verdict in favor of the plaintiffs and the defendants appealed.

The question presented to the Superior Court, one of first impression in Pennsylvania, was whether the Workmen's Compensation Act contained an "intentional tort" exception.[125] The court began by surveying similar cases in other jurisdictions. Finding a difference of opinion, it concluded that the proper rule was suggested by decisions in New York and New Jersey holding that injuries caused by intentional conduct were not covered by the compensation statute. Citing these decisions, it held:

> If the injury is the result of an accident in the course of the employment, the Workmen's Compensation Act by its terms bars any recovery in trespass with certain exceptions. Nothing is said about an injury intentionally inflicted by the employer.

> The word "accident" is nowhere defined in the act but its language, covering only injury or death "by an accident" indicates no intention that deliberate injury to an employe by his employer is intended to be covered.[126]

Since "accident" had been defined to mean "an undesigned event," the court held that the act "creates no barrier to the plaintiffs' right to recover in trespass for the assault upon the wife-plaintiff by the defendants."[127] The jury verdict was affirmed on

---

122. See *Hiles v. Brandywine Club*, 443 Pa. Super. 462, 662 A.2d 16 (1995); appeal denied, 544 Pa. 631, 675 A.2d 1249 (1996); and *Mancuso v. Bradshaw*, 338 Pa. Super. 328, 487 A.2d 990 (1985).

123. See e.g., *Jardine v. Upper Darby Lodge*, 413 Pa. 626, 198 A.2d 550 (1964); *Smith v. Clark*, 411 Pa. 142, 190 A.2d 441 (1963); *Burkhart v. Brockway Glass Co.*, 352 Pa. Super. 204, 507 A.2d 844 (1986); *Mancuso v. Bradshaw*, 338 Pa. Super. 328, 487 A.2d 990 (1985); *Galvin v. Jennings*, 289 F.2d 15 (3d Cir. N.J. 1961); *Zygmuntowicz v. Hospitality Investments, Inc.*, 828 F. Supp. 346 (E.D. Pa. 1993); *Carr v. Turner*, 385 S.W.2d 656 (Ark. 1965); *Parrett v. Lebamoff*, 408 N.E.2d 1344 (Ind. Ct. App. 1980); *Pence v. Ketchum*, 326 So.2d 831 (La. 1976); *Hollerud v. Malamis*, 174 N.W.2d 626 (Mich. 1969); *Randall v. Excelsior*, 103 N.W.2d 131 (Minn. 1960); *Sampson v. W.F. Enterprises, Inc.*, 611 S.W.2d 333 (Mo. Ct. App. 1980); *Ramsey v. Anctil*, 211 A.2d 900 (N.H. 1965); *Soronen v. Olde Milford Inn, Inc.*, 218 A.2d 630 (N.J. 1966); *Romero v. Kendricks*, 390 P.2d 269 (N.M. 1964); *Berkeley v. Park*, 262 N.Y.S.2d 290 (N.Y. 1965); and *Olsen v. Copeland*, 280 N.W.2d 178 (Wis. 1979). See also 70 Cornell L. Rev. 1058; and 54 ALR 2d 1152.

124. 201 Pa. Super. 134, 191 A.2d 694 (1963) (Flood, J.).

125. The trial court also found that Mrs. Readinger was not an employee of the Gottschalls at the time of the assault, but the Superior Court did not reach this issue because of its resolution of the question relating to the Workmen's Compensation Act. The court noted that this latter question "has not heretofore reached our appellate courts." 191 A.2d 695.

126. 191 A.2d 696.

127. See note 126.

Superior Court Judge Robert E. Woodside,
chairman of the Commission on Constitutional
Revision (The Woodside Commission).

this basis.[128] In the past three decades, *Readinger* has been cited repeatedly by Pennsylvania courts, on more than a dozen occasions by the Third Circuit Court of Appeals, and by courts in California, Illinois, Michigan, Rhode Island, and Tennessee for its application of an "intentional tort" exception to workmen's compensation law.[129] Although its continuing validity was called into question by the 1972 amendments to the Workmen's Compensation Act that replaced "accident" with "injury," *Readinger* continues to be cited.[130]

## DOMESTIC RELATIONS

Although somewhat less dramatically than the criminal law, family law also changed in important ways between 1951 and 1968. In a series of important cases, the Superior Court initiated this change. At issue in the first of these cases, *Commonwealth ex rel. Ulmer v. Sommerville*,[131] was a 1959 order requiring the father to pay $40

---

128. 191 A.2d 697.

129. See e.g., *McGinn v. Valloti*, 363 Pa. Super. 88, 525 A.2d 732 (1987); *Brooks v. Marriot Corp.*, 361 Pa. Super. 350, 522 A.2d 618 (1987); *Jones v. P.M.A. Insurance Co.*, 343 Pa. Super. 411, 495 A.2d 203 (1985); *Wilson v. Asten-Hill Mfg. Co.*, 791 F.2d 30 (3d Cir. Pa. 1986); *Heilman v. United States*, 731 F.2d 1104 (1984); *Weldon v. Celotex Corp.*, 695 F.2d 67 (3d Cir. Pa. 1982); *Magliulo v. Superior Court of San Francisco*, 47 Cal. App.3d 760 (Cal. App.1st Dist. 1975); *Azevedo v. Abel*, 264 Cal. App. 2d 451 (Cal. App.3d Dist. 1968); *Collier v. Wagner Castings Co.*, 408 N.E.2d 198 (Ill. 1980); *Beauchamp v. Dow Chemical Co.*, 398 N.W.2d 882 (Mich. 1986); *Lopes v. G.T.E. Products Corp.*, 560 A.2d 949 (R.I. 1989); *Williams v. Smith*, 435 S.W.2d 808 (Tenn. 1968). See also 49 U. Pitt. L. Rev. 1127.

130. As the aforementioned citations indicate, *Readinger* has been relied upon repeatedly since the 1972 amendments.

131. 200 Pa. Super. 640, 190 A.2d 182 (1963) (Woodside, J.).

per week for support of his two daughters. The oldest daughter turned 18 on July 26, 1962, and she entered college two months later. Since the parties made no agreement respecting support for the daughter after high school, father petitioned for a $20 reduction in the support order. Mother then petitioned for an increase in support on the basis that father's income had increased since 1959. The trial court dismissed both petitions and father appealed, arguing that the court's action had the effect of requiring him to pay college support in violation of Pennsylvania law.

The court began its analysis of the defendant's claim by noting that the trial court's order must be vacated under existing law, which allowed college support only upon an express agreement. Moreover, the court stated, "[t]his Court has never affirmed an order for the support of a child in college except where an agreement to provide such support had been made."[132] Since no agreement existed, the case might have been terminated at this point. Nonetheless, the Superior Court broke new ground:

> [T]he majority of this Court thinks that an order may be entered against a father for the support of a child attending college. After finding there was no agreement by the father to send his daughter to college, we believe the Court cannot stop there but must examine the evidence further to determine whether under all the circumstances the father should be required without any agreement to continue to support his daughter while she is attending college.[133]

According to the court, it had long recognized that "parental duty involves, in addition to provision for mere physical needs, such instruction and education as may be necessary to fit the child reasonably to support itself and to be an element of strength, rather than one of weakness, in the social fabric of the state."[134] Finding that this duty could be extended to college support, the court then fashioned a two-prong test to determine if such support was justified. "In the first place," the court held, "before the father should be required by court order to support a child in college, the child should be able and willing to successfully pursue his course of studies." "In the second place, the father should have sufficient estate, earning capacity or income to enable him to pay the order without undue hardship." The court made a particular effort to distinguish this second requirement from the duty of "natural law" to provide food and shelter for children. The father might be made to suffer greater deprivation to fulfill the latter duty, the court held, but this did not mean that college support was warranted only where it imposed no burden. "No mathematical rule can be formulated," the court stated, "to determine how extensive the hardship upon a father must be before it will excuse him from supporting a child in college. It must be a matter of judgment in a field where the judgments of sincere and advised men differ materially."[135] The court then examined the father's financial condition and concluded that a college support order was not justified. On this basis, the trial court order refusing to reduce father's support obligation was vacated. Nonetheless, the court's willingness to award college support where it satisfied this two-prong test initiated an important trend in Pennsylvania family law. For the next thirty years, *Ulmer* was cited on dozens of occasions for the proposition that, under appropriate circumstances, parents owe a duty to pay college support.[136] In

---

132. 190 A.2d 183.

133. See note 132.

134. 190 A.2d 183, quoting *Commonwealth v. Gilmore*, 97 Pa. Super. 303, 308 (1929).

135. 190 A.2d 184.

136. See e.g., *McGettigan v. McGettigan*, 433 Pa. Super. 102, 639 A.2d 1231 (1994); *Cook v. Covey*, 415 Pa. Super. 353, 609 A.2d 560 (1992); *McCabe v. Krupinski*, 413 Pa. Super. 59, 604 A.2d 732 (1992); *O'Connell v. O'Connell*, 409 Pa. Super. 25, 597 A.2d 643 (1991).

1992, in the case of *Blue v. Blue*,[137] the Pennsylvania Supreme Court overruled *Ulmer* and its progeny. According to the *Blue* court, "In essence, the Superior Court has trans- ferred this 'principle of necessity' of a basic fundamental education to a requirement that each child be entitled to an 'enhanced' education. We do not agree with this trans- formation."[138] Seven months after *Blue*, the Pennsylvania legislature passed Act 62, which again established the duty to provide college support if certain requirements were met.[139] The preamble to the act stated that it was intended "to codify the decision of the Superior Court in the case of [*Ulmer*]." Yet the saga was not over. In 1995, the state Supreme Court deemed Act 62 unconstitutional. According to the court in *Curtis v. Kline*,[140] the act denied equal protection of the law under the Fourteenth Amendment to the U.S. Constitution because it entitled children of non-intact families to college support while making no similar provision to children of intact families. *Curtis* put to rest, at least for the time being, the issue of whether parents owe a duty of college support.

A year after its decision in *Ulmer*, the Superior Court again initiated a legal change, and this time it rejected a contrary Supreme Court precedent to do so. At issue in *Manley v. Manley*[141] was a husband's action for divorce on the ground of adultery. At trial, the evidence established beyond question that wife had indeed committed adul- tery. She testified that she had long been in love with her paramour, and evidence established that the telephone at wife's residence was listed jointly in the names of herself and her paramour and that her paramour had spent the night at wife's resi- dence on numerous occasions after the parties' separation. In defense to the claim of adultery, wife asserted her insanity. The master rejected this claim and granted the divorce.

The issue presented to the Superior Court by the wife's appeal was whether insanity could be raised in defense to an action for divorce based on adultery.[142] After reviewing the evidence, the court examined the sole precedent on point. In the 1847 case of *Matchin v. Matchin*,[143] the Supreme Court ruled that a wife's insanity was not a defense to an action against her for divorce on the ground of adultery. The court based this rule on the following rationale:

> [Adultery] is agreed by the civilians to be less grievous to the sufferer, though not less immoral, when it is committed by the husband, whose transgressions can not impose a supposititious offspring on the wife, than it is when committed by the wife, whose transgression may im- pose such an offspring on the husband, but the primary intent of [di- vorce based on adultery] is undoubtedly to keep the sources of genera- tion pure, and when they have been corrupted, the preventative rem- edy is to be applied without regard to the moral responsibility of the subject of it. . . . [I]nsanity might be a bar to divorce at the suit of a wife, when it would not, in similar circumstances, be a bar to divorce at the suit of the husband. . . . The great end of matrimony is not the comfort and convenience of the immediate parties, though these are necessarily

---

137. 532 Pa. 521, 616 A.2d 628 (1992).

138. 616 A.2d 632.

139. 23 Pa.C.S. sec. 4327.

140. 542 Pa. 249, 666 A.2d 265 (1995).

141. 193 Pa. Super. 252, 164 A.2d 113 (1960) (Woodside, J.).

142. At trial, the husband also alleged indignities as a ground for divorce, and the master ruled that the wife's insanity was a defense to this claim. This was not the important issue on appeal.

143. 6 Pa. 332 (1847).

embarked in it; but the procreation of a progeny having a legal title to maintenance by the father.[144]

The court found that the *Matchin* rule had been repeatedly cited as the law of Pennsylvania,[145] and that the legislature, in enacting the Divorce Code of 1929, omitted insanity as a defense.[146] The court also noted, however, that courts and commentators from around the country had "severely criticized" the rule.[147] Finding this criticism justified, the court stated:

> [T]he gist of the offense of adultery is not the possibility of illegitimate children but the unfaithfulness to the marriage vow, and, if the wife does not voluntarily indulge in sexual intercourse with a person other than her husband but it occurs rather by force, fraud, or by advantage of her insanity, she cannot be said to be guilty of any violation of her marital obligation."[148]

Yet the Superior Court recognized the basic principle that it was bound to follow precedents of the Supreme Court.[149] Nonetheless, the court decided to reject the *Matchin* rule. "We are of the opinion, that we should not blindly follow a rule which has failed to withstand the light of judicial and scholarly examination. If there was any reason for the rule in the light of the customs and thoughts of 1847, it is no longer evident in the light of 1960 thinking."[150] The court continued:

> [T]his Court has had jurisdiction over divorce appeals for 65 years, and as far as we have been able to determine, during this time the Supreme Court has made no reference in any divorce case to the rule on insanity stated in the *Matchin* case. The rule was pronounced many years ago, and there is authority for our ignoring an ancient higher court rule which is unreasonable and unjust by all known standards, and which has frequently been examined and universally rejected by legal authorities and by courts in other jurisdictions.[151]

Having rejected the *Matchin* rule, the court held that adultery could be asserted in defense to a divorce action based on insanity. The court then considered the test to be applied in determining insanity. Relying upon the test utilized by the criminal law, the court found that the wife's defense would lie "if it affirmatively appears from all of the evidence that at the time [she] committed adultery she did not know the nature and consequences of her acts, or have the ability to distinguish between right and wrong."[152] It then applied this test to the psychiatric evidence presented at trial, most of which related to a period prior to that in which the adultery occurred. The court determined the wife was not insane and on that basis affirmed the trial court order

---

144. 164 A.2d 118, quoting 6 Pa. 336-37 (1847).

145. 164 A.2d 118 (citations omitted).

146. 164 A.2d 118, citing the Pa. Act of May 2, 1929, PL 1237, sec. 52.

147. 164 A.2d 118-19.

148. 164 A.2d 120.

149. 164 A.2d 119. The court rejected the appellant's claim that Bannister's statement in *Matchin* was dicta.

150. 164 A.2d 119.

151. 164 A.2d 120, citing *Commonwealth v. Franklin*, 172 Pa. Super. 152, 92 A.2d 272 (1952).

152. See note 148.

Officers of the Constitutional Convention of 1967-68. L. to. R.: Robert P. Casey, first vice president, Raymond J. Broderick, president, Frank A. Orban Jr., second vice president, James A. Michener, secretary.

granting husband's petition for divorce.[153] The Supreme Court refused to hear the wife's appeal. Since 1960, *Manley* has been cited repeatedly by cases, law reviews, and articles considering the role of mental illness in divorce proceedings.[154] It is also perhaps the most important case in Pennsylvania standing for the proposition that a lower court need not follow an outdated decision where it appears that a higher court would not continue to follow the decision.[155]

---

153. 164 A.2d 121.

154. *Boggs v. Boggs*, 221 Pa. Super. 22, 289 A.2d 479 (1972); *Simons v. Simons*, 196 Pa. Super. 650, 176 A.2d 105 (1961); *Cox v. Cox*, 210 Pa. Super. 65, 231 A.2d 424 (1967) (Hoffman, dissenting); *Anonymous v. Anonymous*, 236 N.Y.S.2d 288 (1962) (recognizing *Manley* for applying the criminal mental illness standard to matrimonial law); annotation, "Insanity as Defense to Divorce or Separation Suit—Post-1950 Cases," 67 ALR 4th 277 (1996); 27 U. Pitt. L. Rev. 427, 23 U. Pitt. L. Rev. 465; 52 U. Va. L. Rev. 32; 23 Vill. L. Rev. 521; 45 S.C. L. Rev. 136.

155. See e.g., *Ayala v. Philadelphia Board of Public Education*, 223 Pa. Super. 171, 297 A.2d 495 (1972), reversed, 453 Pa. 584, 305 A.2d 877 (1973); and *Lovrinoff v. Pennsylvania Turnpike Commission*, 3 Pa. Cmwlth. 161, 281 A.2d 176 (1971);

## THE KOREAN "WAR"

Although the court's work in the realms of criminal law, torts, and domestic relations involved legal trends that remained important in the future, one important case decided in the 1950s also represented the court's work of the past. As we saw in the previous chapters, war presents challenging issues to state courts. In the wake of World War II, in particular, a number of such issues arose concerning insurance policies. In the leading cases of *Selenack v. Prudential Insurance Company of America* and *Wolford v. The Equitable Life Insurance Company of Iowa*, the Superior Court held that the phrases "in time of war" and "engaged in military service," respectively, precluded recovery of double indemnity by the estates of soldiers who died from causes other than actual combat.[156] In 1952, in a pair of cases that presented an issue of first impression nationally, the court again construed insurance policies issued to soldiers who subsequently died. The issue, whether the conflict in Korea constituted a "war," was presented in *Harding v. Pennsylvania Mutual Life Insurance Co.*[157] and *Beley v. Pennsylvania Mutual Life Insurance Co.*[158] In *Harding*, the defendant insurance company issued a policy to Clyde Harding on July 25, 1950, one month to the day after combat erupted in Korea. The face amount of the policy was $2,500, but it contained a provision for double indemnity if Harding died as a result of an accident. However, the policy further provided that the double indemnity provision "shall immediately terminate . . . if the Insured shall at any time, voluntarily or involuntarily, engage in military, air, or naval service in time of war."[159] On December 5, 1949, Harding enlisted in the National Guard, and on September 11, 1950, he was killed in a railroad accident while on his way to Camp Atterbury, Indiana, for military training. Thereafter, his widow brought an action to recover under the double indemnity provision of the policy. Citing *Wolford*, the trial court refused recovery on the basis that the provision terminated when Harding joined the National Guard in time of war. In *Beley*, the insurance company issued a policy to Andrew Beley on May 1, 1945. The policy contained the same provisions as that issued to Harding. Beley was killed in action in Korea on March 7, 1951, while a member of United Nations forces. Thereafter, his mother, the beneficiary, sought to recover under the double indemnity provision of the policy issued in 1945. Recovery was denied and she appealed.

On appeal, Harding's widow and Beley's mother argued that the conflict in Korea did not constitute a "war" within the meaning of the respective insurance policies. The Superior Court addressed this issue in *Harding* and applied its rationale to *Beley*. The court noted "Not only is the question one of first impression in this Commonwealth, but so far as we have been able to discover, both by our own and counsel's diligent and exhaustive research, the question has not heretofore been raised in the reported decision of any appellate court, either federal or state."[160] Since Congress was vested with the sole constitutional authority to formally declare war, and because it did not exercise this authority with regard to Korea, the court found initially that the hostilities there did not constitute a "declared war." Yet this did not resolve the case, and the court cited language from insurance policies at issue in federal cases that defined "war" to include "undeclared war." Thus, the court found "there is a marked distinction between the two

---

156. 160 Pa. Super. 242, 244, 50 A.2d 736, 737 (1947) (Hirt, J.); 162 Pa. Super. 259, 57 A.2d 581, 582 (1948) (Arnold, J.).
157. 171 Pa. Super. 236, 90 A.2d 589 (1952) (Dithrich, J.).
158. 171 Pa. Super. 253, 90 A.2d 597 (1952) (Dithrich, J.).
159. 90 A.2d 590.
160. 90 A.2d 592.

[types of war],"[161] and the question to be answered was whether the nation was "committed to an undeclared war of which we must take judicial notice." The court found nothing to assist its resolution of this issue. "The case for the appellee has been ably presented," the court noted, "but we have not been furnished with, nor have we been able to find, a direct precedent, either legal or factual, for the action of the President of the United States in dispatching troops to Korea." The court began by examining government documents and executive orders that referred to Korea as an "action" or "combat zone."[162] The court then reviewed a series of important wartime cases. It first looked to the famous *Prize Cases (The Brig Amy Warwick)*[163] arising from the Civil War in which the United States Supreme Court held five-to-four that President Lincoln's proclamation establishing a blockade of all Southern ports was a determination of a state of war that the courts must recognize. The court also looked to World War II, and found that the attack on Pearl Harbor "constituted a direct attack on the United States but, according to the weight of authority, war with Japan did not begin until the next day, following the declaration by Congress."[164]

Finding no clear answer, the court ultimately relied upon the fundamental rule of contract law that ambiguities are to be construed against the drafter. "The phraseology of the policy," the court stated, "was chosen by the insurer and tendered in fixed form to the prospective policyholder, and since its language is reasonably open to two constructions, we will adopt the construction which is more favorable to the insured."[165] On this basis, the court held that Korea was not a "war" within the meaning of the policy issued to Harding. Thus, the trial court decision refusing the award of double indemnity to Harding's widow was reversed.[166] This holding was applied the same day to reverse the denial of recovery to Beley's mother. Thereafter, the Supreme Court affirmed both decisions[167] and the United States Supreme Court denied certiorari.[168] In the years after they were decided, *Harding* and *Beley* were cited by other courts considering whether Korea was a "war," including the Ninth Circuit Court of Appeals, the Supreme Court of New Jersey, and the Court of Appeals of Texas.[169]

## CONSTITUTIONAL REFORM

The personnel changes and important cases in the years 1951 to 1968 represented both the court's past and its future. The Democratic majority attained in the 1960s was the culmination of a political trend that began in the Great Depression. The insurance cases arising from the conflict in Korea were reminiscent of the court's work

---

161. 90 A.2d 593, citing *New York Life Insurance Co. v. Durham*, 166 F.2d 874 (10th Cir. 1948); and *Stinson v. New York Life Insurance Co.*, 167 F.2d 233 (D.C. Cir. 1948).

162. 90 A.2d 594.

163. 90 A.2d 595, citing *The Brig Amy Warwick*, 67 U.S. 635 (1863).

164. 90 A.2d 597.

165. See note 164 (citations omitted).

166. See note 164. The policies in both cases also provided that the "company shall not be liable for the Additional Accidental Death Benefit specified above if said death shall result by reason of . . . (d) Military, air or naval service in time of war." At trial and on appeal in *Harding*, the insurance company conceded that Harding's death did not result from military service in time of war. In *Beley*, the company did assert this provision, but it was also disposed of on the basis that Korea was not a war. 90 A.2d 599.

167. *Harding v. Pennsylvania Mutual Life Insurance Co.*, 373 Pa. 270, 95 A.2d 221 (1953); *Beley v. Pennsylvania Mutual Life Insurance Co.*, 373 Pa. 231, 95 A.2d 202 (1953).

168. 346 U.S. 812 (1953); 346 U.S. 820 (1953).

169. *Weissman v. Metropolitan Life Insurance Co.*, 112 F. Supp. 420 (D. Cal. 1953); *In re Estate of Knight*, 11 N.J. 83 (1952); *Western Reserve Life Insurance Co. v. Meadows*, 256 S.W.2d 674 (Tex. Civ. App. 1953).

during World War II.[170] Yet in applying the landmark Supreme Court cases of the 1960s, the court dealt with criminal law issues that have remained contested to the present, and its resolution of negligence and domestic relations cases foreshadowed the larger role those areas of law would occupy in the future. In all of these ways, the court was in transition between 1951 and 1968. Yet the clearest indication of this transition was the structural changes that occurred during this period. In its first decades, as we have seen, the structure of the court changed very little. Indeed, to someone familiar with the court only as it exists today, its structure and operation in 1950 would have been barely recognizable. The first step in the process that shaped the modern court was a reform effort that culminated in the Constitutional Convention of 1967-68.

Throughout the colonial period, the judiciary of Pennsylvania consisted of an assortment of different courts, each operating pursuant to its own rules and often with overlapping jurisdiction. Some were the legacy of the Duke of York, who ruled the territory from 1664 to 1673, others were inherited from William Penn, and still others, like the Supreme Court, were established by Pennsylvania's provincial assembly. Although attempts were made from time to time to organize and define the jurisdiction of these myriad courts, the colony's English overseers resisted change. The judiciary was not organized until ratification of the Constitution of 1776, which incorporated the Supreme Court and established in each county courts of quarter sessions, courts of common pleas, and orphans' courts. This nascent framework was further developed by the Constitution of 1790, which grouped the counties into judicial districts and provided for president judges of the courts of common pleas in order to ease the administrative burden on the Supreme Court. The jurisdiction of the courts and methods for selecting judges were further modified by the constitutions of 1838 and 1874.[171]

Although the Constitution of 1874 remained in effect for ninety-four years, it became increasingly outdated. As the twentieth century evolved, Pennsylvania's social, economic, and political environment changed dramatically. Government spending increased rapidly as state agencies, and the number of services they provided multiplied, yet the debt limit in the constitution limited spending to mid-nineteenth century levels. Moreover, as Pennsylvanians left the farms in droves and moved to the state's burgeoning cities and suburbs, they placed tremendous pressure on counties and municipalities whose activities were subject to narrow constitutional limits. By the middle of the

---

170. The court also decided a case that was reminiscent of the "Capitol Fraud" cases of 1909. This case, *Commonwealth v. Evans*, 190 Pa. Super. 179, 154 A.2d 57 (1959) (Rhodes, J.), received extensive publicity, although it made no new law. *Evans* involved a conspiracy related to the $149,000,000 construction of the Northeast Extension of the Pennsylvania Turnpike. Members of the Turnpike Commission, including its chairman, entered into a contract purportedly for engineering services with a company controlled by the chairman's son and the nephew of his wife. The work performed under the contract was actually construction, but by designating the agreement as an engineering contract the conspirators avoided normal bidding and oversight measures. The contract, which was urged upon the state by the conspirators, called for drilling holes and "slushing," or pouring fill material into, abandoned mines allegedly in order to prevent subsidence. At trial, it was established that the mines at issue were "robbed out," or collapsed, when they were abandoned, and that any subsidence was long since completed. The work performed under the contract, 95 percent of which was unnecessary, was billed at exorbitant rates. Although the contract was suspended when the fraud was discovered a year later, the company's profit was estimated at between four and ten million dollars. Five members of the conspiracy were ultimately convicted, and the Superior Court affirmed four of these convictions. The fifth was reversed for insufficient evidence. The majority opinion spanned ninety reporter pages, with seventy-seven headnotes. *Commonwealth v. Evans*, 154 A.2d 57-103. The state Supreme Court affirmed on the basis of the Superior Court opinion, *Commonwealth v. Evans*, 399 Pa. 387, 160 A.2d 407 (1960), and the United States Supreme Court denied certiorari, 364 U.S. 899 (1960). One commission member pursued his appeal on habeas corpus petitions, but his conviction was affirmed by a federal district court, *Torrance v. Salzinger*, 195 F. Supp. 804 (M.D. Pa. 1961), and the Third Circuit Court of Appeals, *Torrance v. Salzinger*, 297 F.2d 902 (3d Cir. 1962).

171. *The Philadelphia Manual of Admininistrative Office of PA Courts*, 1982-83 ed., 8.

twentieth century, reform was desperately needed. A noted constitutional historian described the situation as follows:

> Though one may assume the role of apologist for the constitution makers who designed the cramped constitutional quarters in which the commonwealth still dwells, one may justly inquire whether a more commodious functional design would not better meet the needs of its family now grown to ten and a half million. The old home admittedly was designed according to the best architectural ideas of the age that produced it, an age which . . . was astonished by the foreshadowing of the electric street railways. Now we Pennsylvanians, proud of our heritage, still climb its rickety stairways and peer through its narrow windows at the problems of an age that has witnessed such tremendous developments that it is beyond all astonishment![172]

In order to accommodate these "tremendous developments," Pennsylvanians repeatedly attempted to modernize the Constitution of 1874. The method they selected was the constitutional amendment. In the first half of the twentieth century, the voters were called upon to review no less than sixty amendments, and they approved forty-seven, most of which dealt with specific issues related to suffrage, election, taxation, and finance. This method of revision by amendment proved slow and cumbersome, and it was increasingly viewed as a poor alternative to the more comprehensive method of revision by constitutional convention.[173]

Voters proved extremely reluctant, however, and they defeated proposals calling for conventions on no less than six occasions. In 1891, Democratic Governor Robert E. Pattison initiated a program of constitutional reform, but he was opposed by the state's Republican machine, and his call for a convention was defeated by almost 250,000 votes out of a total 600,000 cast. So complete was the repudiation that no serious efforts arose again for nearly thirty years. The second attempt was initiated during the Progressive era, when, as noted, the Sproul Commission recommended complete revision of the constitution, including redrafting the judiciary article to make the Superior Court a constitutional court. However, when Governor William C. Sproul finally succeeded in getting the question to the voters in 1920, it was defeated by 100,000 votes, based largely on the belief among Pennsylvanians that Sproul was attempting to stack the convention by appointing all twenty-five members of the Sproul Commission as delegates. A similar effort six years later by Governor Gifford Pinchot was defeated by a three-to-one margin. Not even the Depression could shake the electorate's hesitance to reform the constitution. In 1935 the Earle Committee recommended a number of measures aimed generally at easing restrictions on the legislature's borrowing and spending authority imposed by the Constitution of 1874. The measures were needed, the committee believed, to allow the legislature to deal with the hardships of the Depression. However, after an extremely partisan feud between Democrats and Republicans, the latter won out and the call for a convention was defeated by more than 200,000 votes. This defeat put the issue of a constitutional convention to rest for nearly two decades.[174] It was not until the early 1950s that the issue reemerged. Unlike their predecessors, however, reformers in the 1950s did not let initial defeat stand in their way, and they initiated a process that culminated in the calling of a convention in 1967.

---

172. Rosalind L. Branning, *Pennsylvania Constitutional Development* (Pittsburgh: University of Pittsburgh Press, 1960), 127.

173. Branning, *Pa. Constitutional Development*, 127-43.

174. See note 172.

The Committee on the Judiciary, Co-chairmen William W. Scranton and Gustave G. Amsterdam.

The effort began slowly. In 1953 a proposal to call a convention was defeated by 150,000 votes, based largely on the belief that the convention would be utilized as a screen to pass a state income tax. In 1957 the issue arose anew and, from that point forward, the movement in favor of a convention became inevitable. The Commission on Constitutional Revision was created by an act of the 1957 General Assembly.[175] The chairman of the commission was Superior Court Judge Robert E. Woodside.[176] The Woodside Commission, as it came to be known, labored for more than a year, examining every section of the Constitution of 1874. In its report to the governor, issued on March 9, 1959, the commission recommended 123 specific changes. These changes were grouped into three categories, "critically needed," "very desirable," and "would improve the language and form of the constitution." In addition to significant revision of the legislative and executive branches, the commission urged comprehensive reform of the judiciary.[177]

175. Pa. Act No. 400, 1957, PL 927.
176. The commission was composed of fifteen members, five appointed by the governor, five by the president pro tem of the Senate, and five by the Speaker of the House. In addition to Judge Woodside, notables included the secretary of internal affairs, the mayor of Philadelphia, the former chief justice of the Supreme Court, and a number of businessmen, professors, and community activists. Branning, *Pa. Constitutional Development*, 148, n. 4.
177. As to the legislature, the commission recommended abolishing specific sessions and constituting the legislature "a continuing body" for the duration of the two-year term for which representatives were elected. These changes, the commission believed, would permit the legislature to function more effectively in managing the state's fiscal affairs, and would prevent otherwise worthy bills from dying at the end of each legislative session. The commission also proposed enforcement of the constitutional mandate of reapportionment at the end of each decennial census. Reapportionment of congressional districts did not occur once in the thirty-two years prior to 1953, and no Senate reapportionment had occurred since 1921. As to the execu-

Foremost among the "critically needed" changes was a major alteration of the manner of selecting judges. Endorsing the Pennsylvania Plan drafted by the state bar association, the commission recommended the appointment of judicial candidates and the replacement of partisan elections with what we now call retention elections. This plan would apply to the appellate judiciary and courts of record in Philadelphia and Allegheny Counties.[178] It would also establish a "judicial commission" that would nominate three candidates, one of whom the governor would appoint. The appointee would then be subject to a "yes" or "no" vote at the next election. Judges sitting at the time of the commission's proposal would also be subject to a "yes" or "no" vote when their term expired. By removing partisanship from judicial selection, the commission believed that this method would require judges to "run against their records."[179] Going beyond the Pennsylvania Plan, the commission also proposed barring judges from contributing to political campaigns, holding office in a political organization, or running for other elective office.[180] Aware of the voters' repeated refusals to sanction conventions, the Woodside Commission urged that its proposals be enacted by a series of constitutional amendments. However, the commission met with significant opposition in the legislature, and, in the end, none of its proposals relating to the judicial article reached the electorate.[181]

Even as the Woodside Commission was meeting with failure, however, the battle for constitutional reform opened on two new fronts. In the winter of 1961, the state bar association authorized a new reform effort to be led by its outgoing president, former Pennsylvania Attorney General William A. Schnader, who had served as a member of the Earle Committee in 1935. The new reform committee of 300 lawyers headed by Schnader was designated Project Constitution. Over the next two years, the committee engaged in an article-by-article study of the constitution. Not surprisingly, this group of lawyers directed much of its attention to the judicial article. In 1963, it released a report endorsing the proposals of the Woodside Commission and adding its own program of court reform. Included in this program was the creation of a unified judicial system organizing all courts in the state under the supervision of the Supreme Court. Significantly, the committee also recommended including the Superior Court within the text of the constitution, increasing the court to nine judges, and allowing it to sit in panels of three. Like the Woodside Commission, Project Constitution believed that amendment was the method most likely to achieve the desired revisions.[182]

At the same time the bar association was formulating its proposals, the Citizens Committee, a group of reform activists, called a meeting of leaders of several influential organizations, including the AFL-CIO, Americans for Democratic Action, the American Civil Liberties Union, the League of Women Voters, the Jaycees, and the

---

tive branch, the commission recommended a number of changes, the most significant of which would have made the governor eligible for reelection, although he would be barred from seeking a third term. Branning, *Pa. Constitutional Development*, 149-50.

178. Other judicial districts would have the option of adopting the plan.

179. This program is detailed in the *Report of the Commission on Constitutional Revision* (1959) (hereinafter *Report*), 35-6 (proposed amendment to art. V, sec. 25).

180. *Report*, 36 (proposed amendment to art. V, sec. 25f). The commission also recommended a number of changes to the minor judiciary, including a reduction in the number of justices of the peace, and replacement of the fee system with salaries as the method of compensating justices of the peace. *Report*, 29-30 (proposed amendment to art. V, sec. 11).

181. Only a proposal making the governor eligible for reelection made it to the voters, and that proposal was defeated.

182. This information is set forth in the *Report of the Preparatory Committee of the Convention of 1967* (hereinafter *Preparatory Report*), 10. The work of the various commissions is also described at length in George D. Wolf, *Constitutional Revision in Pennsylvania* (New York: National Municipal League, 1969), 8-21. The following discussion relies heavily on these works.

Junior Bar Association. Unlike the Woodside Commission and Project Constitution, the leaders at this meeting resolved that nothing short of a full constitutional convention was necessary to remedy the deficiencies of the Constitution of 1874. The meeting called on future Governor Milton J. Shapp to lead the convention effort. Complying with this request, Shapp, in April of 1962, presided over the first meeting of the Committee for State Constitutional Revision (CSCR). This new organization appealed to the legislature in 1963 to call a convention, although it refrained from advocating any specific constitutional changes.[183]

Thus, at the same time that Project Constitution was calling for a program of amendments encompassing the Woodside proposals and its own court reforms, the CSCR was advocating an unlimited convention. Convention advocates argued that the legislature, which had adopted a practice of initiating only one uncomplicated amendment per year, would not agree to the numerous amendments proposed by the bar association. On the other hand, the bar and its supporters argued that the state's history of rejecting conventions would doom the efforts of the CSCR. With the inauguration of Governor William W. Scranton in 1963, the tide shifted in favor of the convention advocates. With Scranton's active support, the CSCR bill was adopted by the legislature. In July 1963, with a referendum on the question fast approaching, Scranton established the "Vote Yes" Committee and the CSCR was merged into the new organization. Despite these efforts, the voters again proved hesitant to authorize a convention. The vote was extremely close, however, and the question failed by only 40,000 votes, out of a total 2,250,000 cast.[184]

Encouraged by the narrowness of their defeat, reformers once again pushed ahead. Only days after the referendum, Scranton formed the Governor's Commission on Constitutional Revision, and appointed Project Constitution's author William Schnader as chairman. Not surprisingly, the momentum shifted back to the advocates of amendment and, in January 1964, the Scranton Commission endorsed the bulk of the bar association's proposals and recommended their immediate submission to the legislature and the voters.[185] Like the bar association and the Woodside Commission, the Scranton Commission recommended replacing partisan elections with retention elections. It also recommended establishing a unified judiciary and making the Superior Court a constitutional court, increasing its size, and authorizing it to sit in panels. Its proposed amendment regarding the Superior Court read as follows:

### Section 3 - The Superior Court

(a) The Superior Court shall consist of nine judges, except that the Supreme Court may from time to time assign additional judges from among the judges of the District Court or the Estates Court to temporary service on the Superior Court as the business of the Superior Court may require. The number of judges of the Superior Court may be changed by the General Assembly but only upon prior certification of the necessity thereof by the Supreme Court. The Court may act in panels of three or more judges, and shall sit at such places and times as the Supreme Court shall by Rule prescribe.[186]

---

183. *Preparatory Report*, 10.

184. See note 183.

185. *Preparatory Report*, 10-11.

186. *Preparatory Report*, 10-11, Annex Number 9, 415. Section (b) of the proposed amendment set forth the jurisdiction of the court and section (c) mandated that one of its judges serve as president judge.

In the summer of 1964, at the request of Governor Scranton, a new nonprofit corporation, Modern Constitution for Pennsylvania, Inc., was chartered to educate the public on the various reform proposals. The corporation's efforts made a significant difference, and two of the commission's recommendations passed the legislature and were ratified by the voters in 1966. Shortly after his election in the same year, Governor-elect Raymond P. Shafer, sensing the electorate's new receptiveness to reform, renewed the drive for a constitutional convention. Realizing that the specter of an income tax had been a major impediment to prior efforts, the governor expressly excluded the issue from consideration at the proposed convention. He took his proposal for a limited convention to the Senate at the beginning of its 1967 term. The Senate complied and, as its first order of business, passed SB 1, a convention amendment to be submitted to the voters at the May primary election. In March, SB 1 was submitted for Shafer's signature. Cognizant of its historic import, the governor signed the bill in front of a crowd of witnesses at Independence Hall on March 15, 1967.[187]

To generate support for the proposed convention among the electorate, Shafer created a new citizens' group, the Committee for 9 Yes Votes, the name of which signified the number of amendments, including the one calling for a convention, that would be voted on at the primary election in May 1967. The new committee was headed by former Governors Scranton and George M. Leader. Its activities, combined with the elimination of the income tax issue and the strong commitment of Governor Scranton, achieved what had been impossible for nearly a century. On May 16, 1967, the electorate approved the amendment calling for a convention by an overwhelming plurality of 374,000 votes.[188] Since the amendments passed at the same time resolved numerous other issues, the convention was left to concentrate on four particularly important areas: local government, finance, legislative apportionment, and judicial reform.[189] The convention's work in this latter realm had significant implications for the Superior Court.

The selection of delegates for the convention was conducted in an orderly fashion. They were chosen from the state's fifty senatorial districts, with each political party nominating two candidates, and the three receiving the highest votes at the 1967 general election were deemed elected. This method of selection ensured that third party candidates could not be elected as delegates, although they could be placed on the ballot by submitting nominating petitions with 500 signatures. In addition to the elected delegates, thirteen members of the legislature were selected as ex officio delegates. These delegates included the lieutenant governor (who was president of the Senate), the president pro tem of the Senate, the Speaker of the House, the leaders and whips of the majority and minority parties in both the House and Senate, and the minority caucus chairmen of the House and Senate. This brought the delegate total to 163, consisting of 88 Republicans and 75 Democrats. Under the leadership of Lieutenant Governor Raymond J. Broderick, the convention was organized to avoid partisanship and it was extremely successful in this regard. Each committee received co-chairmen, one from each party. Four leadership posts were also established and each party received two: Republican Broderick was elected president; Democrat Robert P. Casey, former senator and unsuccessful candidate for governor, was elected vice president; Republican Frank A. Orban Jr., of Somerset County, a former legislator, was elected second vice president; and Democrat James A. Michener of Bucks County, the famous author and unsuccessful candidate for Congress, was elected secretary. The convention was called

---

187. Wolf, *Constitutional Revision in Pa.*, 28.
188. *Preparatory Report*, 11.
189. Wolf, *Constitutional Revision in Pa.*, 23.

to order in the House of Representatives in Harrisburg on December 1, 1967.[190] Although it completed its work and adjourned less than three months later, on February 29, 1968, the convention accomplished a great deal of work. As it had in 1873, the judiciary article received considerable attention.[191]

On December 11, 1967, the delegates organized a committee for each of the four topics they were charged with addressing. William Scranton and Gustave G. Amsterdam of Philadelphia were appointed co-chairmen of the judiciary committee, which was further divided into four subcommittees: selection of judges, incompatible activities of judges, retirement and post-retirement service of judges, and judicial administration and organization. The co-chairman of this latter subcommittee was former Superior Court Judge Robert E. Woodside. Although the records of the subcommittee meetings are not available, the debates on the convention floor provide extensive insight into the judicial issues focused upon by the delegates. Two of these issues were particularly important. The first involved organization of the state's myriad courts into an efficient hierarchy. In opening remarks outlining the issues facing the delegates, Judge Burton K. Laub described the condition of the courts:

> Now, what do we have in Pennsylvania with respect to the judicial system and what have students of government to say about an ideal arrangement? Actually, we do not have a judicial system organized along conventional lines. We have a collection of courts, some of which are traditional and inherited from our foreign ancestors, and some of which have been created by statute. Each court is relatively autonomous and operates without external supervision. . . .

> Students of government call our system a congeries or collection of courts and many advocate the substitution of a system which, it is claimed, would eliminate its adverse phases. One of the strongest indictments against our system appeared in the consensus of a citizen's conference held in Philadelphia on January 9-10, 1964. According to that consensus, our judicial system has failed time and time again to serve the needs of efficient administration of justice. A bewildering patchwork of courts with overlapping jurisdiction, unsupervised operations and, often, ill-trained judicial personnel has created congested dockets and costly delays which deprive the people of prompt, fair and equal justice under law.[192]

From the outset, the leading proposal to address the problems outlined by Judge Laub was a Unified Judicial System. This plan, supported by the bar association since Project Constitution in 1961, had been utilized by thirty-eight states, with minor variations, to organize court systems into a vertical structure with a single head.[193] At the convention, it was endorsed by the delegates with little recorded discussion. As passed

---

190. Wolf, *Constitutional Revision in Pa.*, 28-33.

191. Wolf, *Constitutional Revision in Pa.*, 41. Sixty-nine lawyers were among the 163 delegates.

192. See *Debates of the Constitutional Convention of 1967-1968* (hereinafter *Debates*), vol. I, 46. Judge Laub formerly sat on the Erie County Court of Common Pleas and at the time of his remarks he was dean of Dickinson Law School. He directed a task force that prepared background material for the convention.

193. The Unified Judicial System was modeled on the British Judicature Act of 1873, and was selected as the preeminent court organization plan by the President's Commission on Law Enforcement and Administration of Justice. *Debates*, vol. I, 46. The unification movement began after Roscoe Pound's noted 1906 speech to the American Bar Association, "The Causes of Popular Dissatisfaction with the Administration of Justice," reprinted at 35 F.R.D. 273 (1954). For an excellent history of the concept, see L. Berkson and S.

on the convention floor, the plan "reposed the supreme judicial power of the Common-wealth" in the Supreme Court.[194] For the first time in Pennsylvania's history, all courts in the state were placed under the direct supervision and administrative control of the Supreme Court.[195] The new system changed the existing structure so completely that the delegates found it necessary to repeal the entire judiciary article of the Constitution of 1874. Section 1 of the replacement article set forth the scope of the Unified Judicial System, and Section 2 established the Supreme Court as the head of that system. Section 3 provided as follows:

> Superior Court. - The Superior Court shall consist of seven judges, one of whom shall be the President Judge, and its jurisdiction shall be as provided by law.

As a result of this section, the Superior Court was finally included within the text of a document that it had been construing for more than seven decades. This change was of tremendous symbolic value, particularly because it occurred without a single recorded objection. Yet the change also had practical ramifications. Most importantly, it placed the structure, size, and even the existence of the Superior Court beyond legislative control. The legislature retained control only over the court's jurisdiction; any other changes required a constitutional amendment. The new section also meant that, for the first time, the court's operation was subject to direct supervision by the Supreme Court.

Another issue affecting the Superior Court, and perhaps the convention's most contentious topic, involved the method of selecting judges. Judge Laub described the difficulty of this issue as follows:

> [M]ore important and transcending all others is the problem of how to attract good men to the bench and how to devise a satisfactory method of selecting them. Many good men will not seek the judgeship because it involves a partisan political election in the first instance and a partisan political election for another term in the second instance. . . . Just how to select good men for the office without partisan politics and yet, at the same time, preserve a modicum of control in the people is a hard nut to crack.[196]

Ironically, it appeared that this issue was settled until it reached the convention floor. As early as 1959, the Woodside Commission proposed gubernatorial appointment of judges based upon the recommendation of an advisory board. The bar association also supported this proposal and it was overwhelmingly endorsed at the convention by the judiciary subcommittee on the selection of judges.[197] The subcommittee's first draft, which tracked the bar proposal, was introduced by delegate and future Gov-

---

Carbon, *Court Unification: History, Politics and Implementation* (1978). See also, John C. Bell, State of the Judiciary Address to Pennsylvania Bar Association, *Pennsylvania Bar Association Quarterly* (March 1971), 268 (indicating that Pennsylvania was the thirty-ninth state to adopt the plan).

194. *Debates*, vol. II, 1414, citing proposed Constitution of 1968, art. V, sec. 2(a).

195. To accomplish its new administrative duties, the Pennsylvania Supreme Court was authorized to appoint a court administrator.

196. *Debates*, vol. I, 47. Judge Laub encouraged the delegates to compromise in dealing with the difficult issues confronting them. Quoting Benjamin Franklin's remarks to the federal Constitutional Convention 190 years earlier, Laub stated: "I have always observed that when a carpenter joins two boards together, he takes a little off of each one." *Debates*, vol. I, 48.

197. *Debates*, vol. II, 1007. Statement of Delegate Bruce Kauffman ("[I]n an area that was otherwise very controversial, there was one basic concept that drew virtual unanimity in thpe sub-committee on the se-

ernor Richard L. Thornburgh of Allegheny County on December 12, 1967. It provided as follows:

> Section 7. Method of Selection of Judges. - (a) Whenever a vacancy occurs by death, resignation, removal from office, expiration of a term of office, or creation of an additional judgeship . . . the Governor shall fill the vacancy by appointment from a panel of persons qualified for the office, nominated to him by a Judicial Nominating Commission.[198]

The section further provided that reelections would be conducted by a simple "yes" or "no" vote of the electorate.[199] Despite the strong support of the bar and the subcommittee, this proposal was repeatedly challenged, and it was countered with other proposals seeking to retain full elections.[200] As the vote approached, the issue split the delegates nearly in half. The principal objection to the bar plan was that it deprived the voters of the right to choose important state officials. Delegate Gerald E. Ruth, York County, who offered a proposal to retain full elections, stated the objection as follows:

> It is in the courts that these issues affecting the life, liberty and property of the people are resolved, and thus the people should have the right to say who shall administer justice on the people's behalf. An appointed master to the selection of judges does not remove the politics but only changes the battleground and the judiciary, being the highest form of patronage, should not be added as another pawn on the government chessboard. Courts do not belong to the government and lawyers alone, they belong to the people.[201]

But others saw it differently. According to Delegate Herman M. Buck of Fayette County:

> The argument that the will of the people is and ought to be supreme in every respect and no institution should be allowed to exist except on the direct expression of the people, one must admit, is fundamental to our way of life. As applied, however, to the judicial department, it is a specious argument. . . . The idea that the voters themselves elect their judges is pure romance. The real electors are a few political leaders who do the nominating. . . .
>
> It is true that no human institution, not even this Convention, works perfectly at all times, but of all methods of judicial selection, the appointive-elective merit plan is, in my opinion, the best. It eliminates, perhaps not entirely, but as far as possible, the wrong political considerations. It sets up a mechanism dominated by laymen for actively searching out the best talent by nonpolitical people whose objective is to beat the bushes in an attempt to find the most qualified men.[202]

lection of judges, that is, we decided it was far better for all of this Commonwealth to have our judges of statewide election appointed, rather than elected as at present.").

198. *Debates*, vol. I, 96.

199. *Debates*, vol. I, 96, citing Section 7(d) of proposed Article V.

200. One such counter-proposal was offered by Delegates Gerald Ruth and Edwin G. Warman (Fayette Co.) on December 21, 1967. *Debates*, vol. I, 179.

201. *Debates*, vol. I, 184.

202. *Debates*, vol. II, 1008.

On February 20, 1968, a vote was taken on an amendment to the subcommittee proposal seeking to remove its provisions for merit selection and reinstate full elections. The vote was seventy-two in favor of the amendment and seventy-two against.[203] Following a claim of procedural irregularity, another vote was taken and the convention again deadlocked, this time seventy-five to seventy-five.[204] For the remaining week of the convention, the delegates were unable to agree on a proposal. In the end, they decided to submit the issue to the voters by including it on the ballot when the new constitution was submitted for ratification. In a vote that was surprising only for its closeness, the electorate chose to keep the right to elect judges.[205] However, subsequent terms were to be determined according to the retention election system, which was set forth as follows in the judiciary article:

> If a justice or judge files a declaration, his name shall be submitted to the electors without party designation, on a separate judicial ballot or in a separate column on voting machines . . . to determine only the question of whether he shall be retained in office. If a majority is against retention, a vacancy shall exist upon the expiration of his term of office. . . . If a majority favors retention, the justice or judge shall serve for the regular term of office provided herein, unless sooner removed or retained.[206]

In order to avoid confusion in the transition to the new system, judges elected under the old constitution were permitted to complete their terms, and subsequent terms were to be determined under the new retention election system. This system continues to govern the reelection of judges in Pennsylvania.

Another factor that proved extremely important for the Superior Court was the convention's creation of a new intermediate appellate court. Prior to the convention, issues involving the state were generally handled by the Dauphin County Court of Common Pleas, which presided in the county that encompassed Harrisburg. In its capacity in dealing with state issues, this court was referred to as the Commonwealth Court. As the number of state agencies increased throughout the twentieth century, the Commonwealth Court became overburdened. Expecting this situation to worsen, the convention included in the judiciary article a new statewide court, also known as the Commonwealth Court, to handle appeals involving the state. The court was established by the following addition to the judiciary article:

> Section 4. The Commonwealth Court shall be a statewide court, and shall consist of the number of judges and have such jurisdiction as shall be provided by law. One of its judges shall be the president judge.[207]

The section was drawn broadly so the legislature could make changes in jurisdiction, the number of judges, and the remainder of the court's structure without the need for a constitutional amendment. The convention's only specific instructions were that the court "shall come into existence on January 1, 1970," and that the initial terms of its members must be staggered so they do not all stand for reelection at the same

---

203. *Debates*, vol. II, 1021.

204. *Debates*, vol. II, 1023-24.

205. The vote was 643,960 in favor of elections and 624,453 in favor of appointment.

206. Pa. Constitution (1968), art. V, sec. 15(b). For a discussion of the rationale behind retention elections, see Susan B. Carbon, "Judicial Retention Elections: Are They Serving Their Intended Purpose," 64 *Judicature* 210 (1980).

207. Pa. Constitution (1968), art. V, sec. 4.

time.[208] It was left to the legislature to provide the new court with a workable structure, judges, and jurisdiction. As we will see, the legislature's performance of these tasks in the 1970s had a significant impact on the remainder of the Pennsylvania's appellate judiciary.

Although much of its work affected the Superior Court, the convention also rejected a number of proposals that would have resulted in more drastic change. In fact, so many proposals were offered that it is surprising the court emerged from the convention intact. For instance, the first proposed judiciary article, modeled on the bar association's Project Constitution and introduced by Delegate Thornburgh on December 12, 1967, called for a nine-member Superior Court with authority to sit in panels of three at places designated by the Supreme Court.[209] A proposal introduced on December 21 sought to retain the court at seven judges, although it authorized the General Assembly to increase the number of judges upon prior authorization of the Supreme Court.[210] On January 4, 1968, Delegate Robert P. Fohl, Allegheny County, proposed renaming the court the Court of Appeals. In support of this proposal, Fohl stated:

> Our present Superior Court, Mr. President, is statutory rather than a constitutional court. While a number of other proposals have provided for the constitutional recognition of this important court, this proposal is significantly different. . . .[I]t proposes that the name of the court be the Court of Appeals. This name is more descriptive and specific regarding the court's functions. The public will be fully aware of the nature of the activities and responsibilities of this court.[211]

A proposal four days later by Delegate Americo V. Cortese, Philadelphia, retained Fohl's title for an intermediate court and sought to constitute the Superior Court a trial court of four divisions, the court of common pleas, court of quarter sessions, estates court, and juvenile and domestic relations court. Under this plan, there would be one Superior Court in each judicial district, under the supervision of a president judge.[212] The following day, Delegate Richard M. Sharp, Centre County, submitted a proposal increasing the Superior Court to nine judges, but not authorizing it to sit in panels.[213] On January 10, 1968, a proposal was introduced increasing the court to fifteen judges and mandating that it sit in three panels of five judges each, as directed by the president judge.[214] The same day, Delegates Dante Mattioni, Philadelphia, and Richard L. Huggins, Allegheny County, proposed changing the court's name to the Intermediate Appellate Court.[215] Finally, a proposal offered by Delegate William J. Devlin, Philadelphia, sought to divide the court into three divisions, an estates court, a family court, and a trial court.[216]

The judiciary committee rejected these proposals, and its final submission to the convention retained the court at its pre-convention level of seven judges and abandoned the clause authorizing the court to sit in panels. Although it is not entirely clear why the committee decided not to increase the size of the court, a subsequent attempt to amend its proposed judiciary article on the convention floor provides some indica-

---

208. Pa. Constitution (1968), Schedule to Judiciary Article, art. V, sec. 3.
209. *Debates*, vol. I, 95.
210. *Debates*, vol. I, 178-79.
211. *Debates*, vol. I, 231.
212. *Debates*, vol. I, 279.
213. *Debates*, vol. I, 289.
214. *Debates*, vol. I, 309.
215. *Debates*, vol. I, 323.
216. *Debates*, vol. I, 325.

tion. On February 15, Delegate Israel C. Bloom, Washington County, offered an amendment that provided for "not less than seven nor more than nine" judges on the Superior Court. In support of this amendment, Bloom stated:

> The only remark I want to make is that the Superior Court is the workhorse. It gets practically all the appeals' cases in the first instance, and there is such a thing as an allocatur where the Supreme Court can refuse and can hear a case again. It is the workhorse, and, in my mind, if any court needs this amendment, the Superior court does.[217]

Bloom's amendment came under attack on the ground that additional judges were not necessary because the Commonwealth Court would relieve the Superior Court to a significant degree. Reiterating a previous statement he had made in opposition to a similar amendment, Delegate Scranton, the next governor of Pennsylvania, stated, "I repeat to you here again that we have a situation where the establishment of the Commonwealth Court was for the purpose of creating flexibility for appellate jurisdiction in the future."[218] Delegate Woodside agreed:

> The Superior Court is today one of the very few courts in the Commonwealth of Pennsylvania that is completely up to date with its work, it is completely up to date. They are willing, ready, and able to accept additional jurisdiction now. There is no need for any additional amendments. On top of that, if we do create or if the legislature in accordance with the mandate of this convention, at some future time finds the need to create a Commonwealth Court, that Commonwealth Court will take even more work away from the Superior Court and we will have an excellent appellate court system. There is no need now or in the foreseeable future. We must remember that the appellate work of this Commonwealth has been carried on for over 75 years by those two courts, and the Superior Court today is right up to date.[219]

Following Woodside's statement, Bloom's proposal was defeated by a vote of 102 to 31.[220] Thereafter, the convention completed its work on schedule and adjourned on February 29, 1968. The convention then submitted its proposals to the electorate. Despite the concerted opposition of prominent state judges, including Chief Justice John C. Bell Jr. and Justice Michael A. Musmanno, the judiciary article, along with the other proposals, were overwhelmingly approved at the primary election of April 23, 1968.[221] The new constitution became effective on January 1, 1969.[222]

While the Convention of 1873 is remembered primarily for its changes to the legislative branch of government, the Convention of 1968 is remembered for its changes to the judiciary.[223] In addition to creating a unified judicial system, making the Supe-

---

217. *Debates*, vol. I, 860.
218. See note 217.
219. See note 217.
220. *Debates*, vol. I, 860-61.
221. The votes on the convention five proposals were as follows: judiciary - 910,855 yes, 729,845 no; legislative apportionment - 1,063,603 yes, 583,091 no; state finance - 1,022 yes, 614,110 no; taxation - 882,116 yes, 763,745 no; local government - 986,855 yes, 633,323 no. Wolf, *Constitutional Revision in Pa.*, 62.
222. All members of the Superior Court sitting at the time the new constitution became effective, having been elected under the old constitution, could complete their terms, and they were permitted to run for new terms in retention elections.
223. Woodside, *Pennsylvania Constitutional Law*, 407.

rior Court constitutional, and allowing the voters to decide the method of selecting judges, the latter convention also made seventy the mandatory retirement age for all judges.[224] Moreover, the convention provided for a constitutional right to appeal in all criminal and civil cases.[225] Prior to 1968 no such right existed, and appeals were generally subject to a reviewing court's consent.[226]

The two conventions also differed in other respects. Delegates in 1873 believed that an intermediate court would create conflicts in state law and lead to a multiplicity of appeals. They ultimately rejected such a court as completely unnecessary. By 1968, the Superior Court had demonstrated beyond question the fallacy of those beliefs. Beginning with the Sproul Commission in 1919, every organization that examined the issue concluded that the court, as a necessary part of the Pennsylvania judiciary, should be included in the text of the constitution. By the 1950s, the issue was not even discussed; the conclusion was simply assumed. A decade later, the judiciary article was the most debated topic at the convention, yet the judiciary committee's significant decision to include the Superior Court in the constitution was not questioned a single time. The only question was whether and to what extent the court should be expanded or altered in form. Primarily for this recognition of the value of an intermediate appellate court, the Convention of 1968 differed from its predecessor.

Yet the conventions were also quite similar. Both spent tremendous effort debating the form and function of the state's appellate judiciary. Both were also unable to provide for the long-term needs of the judiciary. The delegates in 1873 chose to expand the Supreme Court rather than create a new intermediate appellate court, and this faulty decision necessitated the creation of the Superior Court a mere twenty-two years later. In 1968, the delegates apparently learned from the mistake of their predecessors and rejected numerous proposals to expand existing courts in favor of authorizing the creation of a new appellate court. Yet this decision also proved inadequate and, just as in 1873, the debates of 1968 unwittingly foreshadowed dramatic changes in the years ahead. In this regard, it is useful to recall the basis on which Judge Woodside rejected Delegate Bloom's amendment to authorize nine judges on the Superior Court. "There is no need for additional amendments," he stated, either "now or in the foreseeable future." Judge Woodside could not have known what was to come, but the need for new amendments arose quickly.[227] Within two years, the caseload growth that began in the 1950s and 1960s accelerated dramatically, and a decade later the voters authorized a constitutional amendment that more than doubled the size of the Superior Court. This amendment completed the transformation begun by the Convention of 1968, and the court emerged in its modern form.

---

224. Pa. Constitution (1968), art. V, sec. 16.

225. Pa. Constitution (1968), art. V, sec. 9. Other changes in Article V included revision of the justice of the peace system and magistrate court system (sec. 7), creation of a Judicial Inquiry and Review Board to investigate allegations against judges (sec. 18), and abolition of the orphans' court, courts of oyer and terminer, and courts of quarter session (sec. 5 and sched. 4, 5).

226. Prior to 1968, a constitutional right to appeal existed only in cases of felonious homicide. The earlier constitution also provided for appeals from courts not of record (justices of the peace and aldermen), but such appeals could be taken only upon allowance by the court of common pleas. Pa. Constitution (1874), art. V, sec. 14. Other appeals were regulated by statute and, where provided, they were in the nature of a broad certiorari, which meant that a reviewing court could examine the entire record. Where a statute provided that the decision of a tribunal should be final, appeal was allowable only on narrow certiorari, which limited the reviewing court to an examination of the regularity of the trial process, abuses of authority, and constitutional questions. Woodside, *Pa. Constitutional Law*, 424.

227. In his important 1985 text on state constitutional law, Judge Woodside acknowledged that "[t]he breakdown of the judicial system came much faster than conceived at the convention." Woodside, *Pa. Constitutional Law*, 414.

The Superior Court in 1975.
L. to R. (seated): Robert L. Jacobs, G. Harold Watkins (President Judge), J. Sydney Hoffman. L. to R. (standing): William F. Cercone, Gwilym A. Price Jr., Robert Van der Voort, Edmund B. Spaeth Jr.

# CHAPTER SIX

# THE NATION'S BUSIEST APPELLATE JUDGES: 1969-1980

## *ENTERING THE SEVENTH DECADE*

If the caseload pressure and structural changes that shaped the modern court began to emerge in the two decades prior to 1968, they reached fruition in the twelve years that followed. Change began almost immediately as the legislature undertook to implement the new judiciary article drafted by the Constitutional Convention of 1968. The primary task facing the legislature was establishing the operating structure and jurisdiction of the newly-created Commonwealth Court, which the convention believed would provide for the needs of the state's judiciary well into the foreseeable future.

On January 6, 1970, in order to complete this task, the legislature passed the Commonwealth Court Act, which provided the new court with seven judges.[1] The act also authorized the court to sit at Philadelphia and Pittsburgh, with special sessions elsewhere,[2] and to sit in panels of three. In addition to the Commonwealth Court Act, the legislature passed the Appellate Court Jurisdiction Act, which redistributed the jurisdiction of the state's three appellate courts. In order to relieve the Supreme Court of direct appeals in assumpsit and trespass matters, the act abolished the Superior Court's jurisdictional limit of $10,000.[3] As a result, all assumpsit and trespass matters, regardless of amount, were appealable to the Superior Court. As between the Superior and Commonwealth Courts, the act essentially created a system of mutually exclusive jurisdiction. The Superior Court retained jurisdiction over what might be termed private sector appeals, i.e., those involving business, property, contract, family, tort, and criminal law. The Commonwealth Court received jurisdiction over all public sector appeals, including those involving state and local governments, agencies, ordinances, workmen's compensation and occupational diseases, and cases decided by the Public Service Commission and the Unemployment Compensation Board of Review.[4] As a result of the Appellate Court Jurisdiction Act, which was reenacted by the Judicial Code of 1976, the Superior Court retained no original jurisdiction except in cases of mandamus and prohibition to courts of inferior jurisdiction where such relief is ancillary to

---

1. Pa. Act of January 6, 1970, PL 434, 17 PS 211.1, 211.3. The number of judges on the Commonwealth Court was increased from seven to nine by the Act of 1980, Oct. 5, PL 693, No. 142, sec. 204.
    2. 17 PS 211.4.
    3. 17 PS 211.6.
    4. Pa. Act of 1973, 17 PS 211.402, 211.403 (Supp. 1973). This act substantially expanded the jurisdiction originally provided by the Commonwealth Court Act. The court also received jurisdiction over zoning appeals, which were previously handled by the Supreme Court.

President Judge Emeritus William F. Cercone at Nagasaki following the explosion of the atom bomb and surrender of Japan in 1945.

matters within the Superior Court's appellate jurisdiction. The legislation also gave the court jurisdiction of all appeals from final orders of the courts of common pleas, except where those appeals are specifically reserved to the Supreme or Commonwealth Courts.

Despite the establishment of a new court and the redistribution of appellate jurisdiction, the Superior Court's caseload rose dramatically throughout the 1970s. The rate of increase is indicated by the following table, which begins in 1968, when the new constitution was submitted to the electorate:

**NUMBER OF APPEALS**

| _Year_ | _Filed_ |
|--------|---------|
| 1968 | 1,697 |
| 1969 | 2,070 |
| 1970 | 2,585 |
| 1971 | 2,337 |
| 1972 | 2,433 |
| 1973 | 2,670 |
| 1974 | 2,203 |
| 1975 | 2,996 |
| 1976 | 3,631 |
| 1977 | 3,700 |
| 1978 | 4,495 |
| 1979 | 4,047 |
| 1980 | 4,523 |

As we saw in the last chapter, the Superior Court's caseload remained relatively constant between 1895 and the early 1950s. By 1968, the 1953 figure of 543 cases had increased by more than 300 percent. By 1980, the rate of increase exceeded 800 percent. Although matters clearly would have been worse without the Commonwealth Court, the measures undertaken by the convention proved woefully inadequate, and the Superior Court became increasingly overwhelmed as the 1970s wore on. At the end of the decade, the National Center for State Courts (NCSC) published a landmark study in which it found that members of the Superior Court were the busiest appellate judges in the nation.[5] The study ranked state appellate courts in two categories: number of appeals filed per judge and number of appeals decided per judge. The Superior Court easily "won" each category, with 642 and 345, respectively. No other court came even close to matching this remarkable output. The nearest competitors were ranked as follows:

## INTERMEDIATE APPELLATE COURTS

| *Court: Appeals Filed Per Judge* | | *Court: Appeals Decided Per Judge* | |
|---|---|---|---|
| Pennsylvania Superior Court | 642 | Pennsylvania Superior Court | 345 |
| Pennsylvania Cmwlth. Court | 355 | Florida Court of Appeals | 213 |
| Florida Court of Appeals | 349 | Oregon Court of Appeals | 197 |
| Oregon Court of Appeals | 311 | Georgia Court of Appeals | 188 |
| Michigan Court of Appeals | 293 | Alabama Court of Appeals (Cr.Div.) | 168 |

## ALL APPELLATE COURTS

| *Court: Appeals Filed Per Judge* | | *Court: Appeals Decided Per Judge* | |
|---|---|---|---|
| Pennsylvania Superior Court | 642 | Pennsylvania Superior Court | 345 |
| Texas Supreme Court (Cr.Div.) | 538 | Texas Supreme Court (Cr.Div.) | 302 |
| Pennsylvania Cmwlth. Court | 355 | Florida Court of Appeals | 213 |
| Florida Court of Appeals | 349 | Oregon Court of Appeals | 197 |
| Oregon Court of Appeals | 311 | Georgia Court of Appeals | 188[6] |

Two years before the NCSC study, the American Judicature Society (AJS) also examined Pennsylvania's judiciary and found that the "Superior Court has for some years been one of the most overworked appellate courts in America in terms of caseload and number of written opinions per judge per year."[7] According to the AJS report, which was commissioned by the Supreme Court, "35-40 full-scale majority opinions is all that can be expected from a diligent and competent judge, and . . . 45 in a year is an absolute

---

5. See Thomas B. Marvell and Mae Kuykendall, "Appellate Court Facts and Figures," *State Court Journal* (spring 1980), 11-13. The authors tabulated the 1978 caseloads of all twenty-eight supreme courts and thirty-two intermediate appellate courts for which statistics were available.

6. See note 5. These tables are composites of tables set forth by Marvell and Kuykendall. The following table, which aggregates 1977 statistics for the Superior and Commonwealth Courts, also indicates the caseload disparity between Pennsylvania's intermediate appellate courts and those in other large states:

Intermediate Appellate Court Caseloads

| State | Total Judges | Total Cases Filed (1977) | Average Per Judge |
|---|---|---|---|
| California | 48 | 11,460 | 239 |
| Illinois | 47 | 4,381 | 93 |
| New York | 29 | 7,362* | 254 |
| New Jersey | 22 | 5,208 | 237 |
| Michigan | 18 | 4,544 | 252 |
| Pennsylvania | 14 | 11,046 | 789 |

*This is a 1978 figure; 1977's was not available.

The table appears in "Pennsylvania's Legal Crisis," *Pennsylvania Lawyer*, March 15, 1979, 7.

7. *Pennsylvania's Appellate Courts: A Report of the American Judicature Society to the Supreme Court of Pennsylvania* (hereinafter *Report of the AJS*) 8 November 1978, 15.

maximum."[8] In 1978, the year the report was released, the Superior Court completed 1,736 "full-scale majority opinions," or 248 per judge.[9] This number was more than five times the "absolute maximum" recommended by AJS.

Beyond general agreement that population growth and increased business activity lead to more litigation, the particular reasons for the caseload boom of the 1970s have long been the subject of debate. Some scholars have cited a general increase in the willingness of the population to litigate. Others have argued that the boom was the natural result of growth in the number of laws regulating society. As one bar leader put it, "There are more lawsuits in America because there is more *law* in America."[10] Still others have argued that appeals increased nationally as states, throughout the 1960s and 1970s, established intermediate appellate courts, expanded the jurisdiction of existing courts, and added judges to appellate courts.[11]

Since these measures expanded the opportunity to appeal, it is argued, an increase in the volume of appeals logically followed.[12] It is likely that each of these factors contributed to the litigation boom to some degree, although the precise causes will probably never be known.[13] As to the Superior Court, it appears that the abolition of the $10,000 jurisdictional limit also contributed to the increase, since appeals jumped by one-third within three years.[14] Moreover, as the Supreme Court's caseload increased throughout the 1970s, it transferred a number of cases to the Superior Court. In the first nine months of 1979, for instance, the Supreme Court transferred 259 cases, many of which were important criminal matters requiring full opinions.[15]

Finally, there is little question that the litigation boom of the 1970s resulted from continued growth in criminal, family and tort cases that first emerged in the 1950s and 1960s. This trend is confirmed by studies of other states. For instance, a study of appellate litigation in thirty-eight states found that between 1973 and 1983 criminal appeals increased by 107 percent and undifferentiated civil appeals increased by 114 percent.[16] Another study of trial court filings in twenty-two states between 1964 and 1984 indicates that criminal cases increased by 196 percent,[17] family law cases in-

---

8. The AJS Report is discussed in "Pennsylvania's Legal Crisis," 9.

9. See *Report of the Pennsylvania Bar Association Subcommittee on Enabling Legislation for the Superior Court* (hereinafter *Report on Enabling Legislation*), reprinted in the *Pennsylvania Law Journal*, March 31, 1980, 1, 7.

10. Pennsylvania Bar Association President Paul L. Stevens, Address to the Conference of County Bar Leaders, quoted in 18 *Pa. Law Weekly* 339, March 13, 1995, 11 (emphasis in original).

11. Beginning in the middle 1960s, states established intermediate appellate courts at the rate of one per year, and by 1985, thirty-six states had such courts. See Marvell, "Is There an Appeal from the Caseload Deluge?," 36.

12. See Victor E. Flango and Mary E. Elsner, "Advance Report: The Latest State Court Caseload Data," *State Court Journal* (winter 1983), 16, 17 ("Th[e] increase in appeals may be related to the increased opportunity to appeal in states that have established an intermediate appellate court, expanded the jurisdiction of the appellate courts, or added justices to existing appellate courts.").

13. One leading scholar has noted that, with regard to the increase in civil appeals, "no causes can be singled out." See Marvell, "Is There an Appeal from the Caseload Deluge?," 36.

14. In 1973, the year the legislature passed the Appellate Court Jurisdiction Act, 2,670 appeals were filed; by 1976, appellate filings totaled 3,631.

15. *Report on Enabling Legislation*, 7.

16. Marvell, "Is There an Appeal from the Appellate Case Deluge?," 36.

17. Marvell, "Are Caseloads Really Increasing? Yes. . ." 44, table 3. The states for which statistics were available, and the percentage increases, are set forth as follows: Arizona - 342; Arkansas - 311; California - 109; Hawaii - 147; Maryland - 121; Michigan - 265; Missouri - 100; New Hampshire - 233; New Mexico - 289; North Carolina - 108; Ohio - 159; Tennessee - 146; Texas - 218; Virginia - 155; Washington - 234. Dividing the total sum by 15 states yields an average increase of 196 percent.

Judge Israel Packel.

creased by 155 percent,[18] and civil cases increased by 114 percent.[19] Scholars have also identified the 1970s as a period in which courts "embraced" a variety of new causes of action in tort law.[20] Although it is hardly comprehensive, the available evidence suggests that these increases were replicated in Pennsylvania. For instance, between 1972 and 1973 criminal cases in the state's trial courts increased by 6.7 percent and divorce cases increased by 8.4 percent.[21] In the following year, criminal cases rose an additional 6.7 percent, divorce cases rose 4.4 percent, and, on the whole, domestic relations cases increased 11 percent.[22] Importantly, it has also been determined that appellate filings increased much more rapidly than trial court filings during the 1970s.[23] Thus,

---

18. See note 17. The states for which statistics were available, and the percentage increases, are set forth as follows: Arizona - 207; Arkansas - 166; California - 68; Hawaii - 314; Illinois - 85; Kansas - 141; New Hampshire - 202; Ohio - 78; Texas - 123; Vermont - 164. Dividing the total sum by 10 states yields an average increase of 155 percent.

19. See note 17. The states for which statistics were available, and the percentage increases, are set forth as follows: Arizona - 116; Arkansas - 199; California - 161; Hawaii - 242; Illinois - 27; Kansas - 46; New Hampshire - 20; New Jersey - 114; Ohio - 74; Texas - 151; Vermont - 99. Dividing the total sum by 11 states yields an average increase of 114 percent.

20. Robert F. Blomquist, "'New Torts': A Critical History, Taxonomy, and Appraisal," 95 Dick. L. Rev. 23 (1990), 53-81 (identifying the 1970s as a period of "Judicial Creativity Embraced" in terms of new tort actions).

21. The statistics are quoted in Chief Justice Michael J. Eagen's 1974 State of the Judiciary Address to the Bar Association, reprinted in 1974 *Pennsylvania Bar Association Quarterly* 159.

22. The statistics are quoted in Chief Justice Eagen's 1975 State of the Judiciary Address to the Bar Association, reprinted in 1975 *Pennsylvania Bar Association Quarterly* 399-400.

23. See Marvell, "Is There an Appeal from the Caseload Deluge?," 35 ("In recent years [1973-1983] both civil and criminal appeals have increased rapidly - much faster than trial court caseloads."). See also, Flango and Elsner, "Advance Report," 17 ("Appellate filings, especially appeals to intermediate appellate courts, are increasing at a faster pace than trial court filings." The authors cite statistics indicating that appellate caseloads increased by 11 percent annually between 1977 and 1981, while trial court litigation increased annually over the same period by 6.8 percent in civil matters and 9.4 percent in criminal matters.).

the rate of increase of appellate filings in these areas of law may well have exceeded the rate of trial court filings. Whatever its causes, the litigation boom of the 1970s overwhelmed the Superior Court and led to structural changes that gave the court its modern form.

## THE MEMBERS OF THE COURT

While these changes proceeded rapidly, the court's political make-up stabilized. In fact, the five-to-two Democratic majority attained by Judge Cercone's victory in the fall of 1968 endured for nearly a decade. Following Cercone's victory there were no changes until June 12, 1971, when Judge Montgomery reached the mandatory retirement age of seventy. In December, Governor Milton Shapp nominated his attorney, Democrat Israel Packel, to replace Montgomery. Packel was born in Philadelphia on December 28, 1907. He was a graduate of the Wharton School and the University of Pennsylvania Law School. He served in the U.S. Navy during World War II. From 1942 to 1943, he also served as the state rationing attorney for Pennsylvania. After the war, he engaged in private practice and lectured at Penn and Temple Law Schools. He also authored the four volume treatise, *Law of Cooperatives*. In January 1971 he became Governor Shapp's attorney and served in that capacity until his appointment to the Superior Court. He joined the court on January 3, 1972, but left on December 31, 1972 to become Governor Shapp's attorney general. In 1977 he was appointed to the state Supreme Court.

On January 2, 1973, Governor Shapp appointed Democrat Edmund B. Spaeth Jr. to replace Packel. Spaeth was born in Washington, D.C., on June 10, 1920. He was educated at Harvard College, graduating magna cum laude and Phi Beta Kappa in 1942. He served in the U.S. Navy during World War II. In 1948 he graduated from Harvard Law School. Thereafter, he engaged in private practice until 1964 when he was appointed to the Philadelphia County Court of Common Pleas. The following year, he was elected to a full ten-year term. While on the trial court, Spaeth's most noted case was *Jackson v. Hendricks*, in which he enjoined the continued operation of Holmesburg Prison until it remedied a variety of inhumane conditions.[24] Following his appointment to the Superior Court, Spaeth ran for a full term, but was defeated in the 1973 primary election. Although his appointive term expired on January 6, 1974, he began a new appointive term the next day, filling the vacancy caused by the retirement of Judge Spaulding. In the 1975 general election Spaeth won a full term on the court. While on the court, Spaeth also served as chairman of the Philadelphia Commission for Effective Criminal Justice, an organization of civic, bar, and minority leaders advocating reform of the criminal justice system.[25] On August 11, 1983, Spaeth became the thirteenth president judge of the Superior Court. He was the first president judge from Philadelphia County and served until 1985 when he left the court and entered private practice.

Two seats on the court were at stake in the general election of 1973. The first was the seat vacated by the retirement of Judge Montgomery, which was temporarily filled by the consecutive appointments of Judges Packel and Spaeth, the latter having failed in a bid for a full term in the primary election in 1973. The second seat opened as a result of President Judge Wright's retirement. The men elected to these seats were Republican Gwilym A. Price Jr. and Democrat Robert Van der Voort, both of whom took office on January 7, 1974. Since these men replaced Republican Watkins and Democrat

---

24. Spaeth wrote the opinion in *Jackson* on behalf of a three-judge panel of the Philadelphia Court of Common Pleas. See President Judge Induction Ceremony, October 6, 1983, 308 Pa. Super. XLVII (1983).

25. Induction Ceremony, October 6, 1983, XLVI-XLVII.

Montgomery, the political structure of the court did not change. Price was born in Pittsburgh on July 1, 1922. When World War II erupted, he left his studies at Allegheny College and enlisted as a private in the Army. He served forty-six months in the Pacific and was discharged as a first lieutenant. Returning home, he completed his undergraduate studies. He graduated from Dickinson Law School in 1948 and was admitted to the bar in 1950. Thereafter, he worked at the law firm of Nicholas & Lewis, which later became Lewis Drew Gregg & Price. In 1955 he left the firm and established a partnership with Loyal Herman Gregg, Esq. From 1960 to 1963, he also served as a commissioner of Mt. Lebanon Township. On March 1, 1963, he was appointed to the Allegheny County Court of Common Pleas. Following his election to the Superior Court, he served until his death in January 1983. [26]

Robert Van der Voort, who joined Price on the court in January 1974, was born in Crafton, Allegheny County, on April 15, 1909. In 1929 he received a bachelor's degree from Guilford College, North Carolina, and a year later he received a master's degree from Haverford College. In 1934 he graduated from the University of Pittsburgh Law School. From 1939 until his entry in the U.S. Navy, he served as an assistant district attorney in Allegheny County. He served in the Pacific during World War II. Although he entered the Navy as a lieutenant junior grade, he ultimately attained the rank of commander. In 1948 he became first assistant district attorney of Allegheny County and served in that capacity until 1952. Thereafter, he returned to private practice and ultimately became senior partner in the firm of Van der Voort Royston Robb & Leonard. He also served as president of the Allegheny County Bar Association. On March 3, 1959, he was appointed to the Allegheny County Court of Common Pleas. He was elected to a full term in the fall of 1959, and reelected in 1969. He served in the Orphan's Court and Civil Divisions of the Court of Common Pleas, and was administrative judge of the Criminal Division. He was also a member of the Supreme Court's Criminal Procedure Rules Committee. In the fall of 1973, he was elected to the Superior Court and served until 1984, when he acquired senior judge status. Judge Van der Voort died November 24, 1993. [27]

There were no further changes until 1978, when two judges joined the court. The first change gave Democrats their first six-to-one majority. Democrat John P. Hester, who was elected the previous November, joined the court in January 1978, to succeed retiring President Judge Watkins, a Republican. Hester was born in McKeesport, Allegheny County. He graduated from Duquesne University in 1940 and the University of Pittsburgh School of Law in 1943. He served as a councilman in Glassport Borough from 1942 to 1950 and, while in private practice, he served as a deputy attorney general and as solicitor of numerous boroughs, including Glassport, Millvale, Dravosburg, and Heidelberg, and school districts, including Glassport, Millvale, Heidelberg, North Fayette Township, South Park, and West Allegheny. He also served on the Allegheny County Hospital Development Authority, the Board of Trustees of Mercy Hospital, and the Mercy Hospital Foundation. Hester currently serves as chairman of the Allegheny District Chapter of the National Multiple Sclerosis Society and president of the Stephen Foster Community Center and the Catholic Youth Association. In February 1960 he was appointed to the County Court of Allegheny County and shortly thereafter to the Allegheny County Court of Common Pleas. He was elected to a full term on the Common Pleas Court in 1961 and reelected in 1971. From 1976 to 1977, he served as administrative judge of the Civil Division. Following his election to the Superior Court, he served as a commissioned judge until he reached the mandatory retirement age of seventy. Thereafter, he continued to serve as a senior judge. Hester has been recognized as

26. Memorial Service, March 28, 1983, 305 Pa. Super. XXXV (1983).
27. Resolution of the Board of Judges of Superior Court, April 28, 1995, 400 Pa. Super. LXV (1995).

one of the one hundred outstanding graduates of Duquesne University in its first century, and in 1979 he received the St. Thomas More Award from the Catholic Diocese of Pittsburgh for outstanding contributions to the courts, community, and legal profession.

On September 19, 1978, Democrat Donald E. Wieand was appointed by Governor Shapp to replace Judge Hoffman, who reached age seventy in July 1978. Wieand was born in Allentown on September 18, 1926. He graduated from Villanova University in 1948. Two years later, he graduated first in his class from Dickinson Law School. He served in the U.S. Naval Reserve during World War II. In 1951, he was admitted to the Lehigh County bar and two years later he joined the firm of Butz Hudders Tallman & Rupp. He became a partner in only two years, and the firm became Butz Hudders Tallman & Wieand.[28] In 1963 Wieand was elected to the Court of Common Pleas of Lehigh County. He was reelected in 1973 and served until 1978. His appointment to the Superior Court the same year was subject to a 1975 constitutional amendment requiring Senate confirmation of gubernatorial appointments,[29] and he was confirmed in October 1978. He was, however, defeated for a full term in the 1979 general election. He was reappointed to the court in 1980 and elected to a full term on November 3, 1981. In 1990 Wieand received the Outstanding Alumni Award from Dickinson Law School and received an honorary doctor of laws degree two years later from Muhlenberg College.[30] He was reelected in 1991 and served until his death in 1996.[31]

The Democrats' six-to-one majority lasted approximately eighteen months, and Republicans thereafter gained two seats. The Republican opportunity arose when the terms of three Democrats, Judges Jacobs, Hoffman, and Van der Voort, ended. Jacobs resigned, leaving the court on December 31, 1978, only days before the inauguration of Republican Governor Richard L. Thornburgh. Judges Hoffman and Van der Voort continued on the court as senior judges. The new governor appointed Republican James R. Cavanaugh to fill the vacancy that returned the Democratic majority to five-to-two. Cavanaugh was born in Philadelphia on August 26, 1931. He graduated from St. Joseph's College in 1953 and the University of Pennsylvania Law School in 1956. At the general election of 1968, he was elected to the Philadelphia County Court of Common Pleas. Although Cavanaugh was appointed to the Superior Court in early 1979, he was not confirmed by the Senate until he won both the Republican and Democratic nominations at the May primary election. He took office on July 31, 1979, and was elected to a full term in the fall of 1979, reelected in 1989 and again in 1999. During his career, Cavanaugh served as chairman of the advisory committee of the Prisoner's Family Welfare Association, counsel for the State Athletic Commission and as permanent secretary of the James Wilson Law Club. He also served on the Governor's Justice Commission and the Pennsylvania Board of Judicial Inquiry and Review.

The Democrats' majority was cut to four-to-three at the 1979 general election when the seats vacated by Democrats Hoffman and Van der Voort were filled by one Democrat and one Republican. The Democrat, John G. Brosky, was born on August 4, 1920. He received his bachelor's and law degrees from the University of Pittsburgh where he was captain of the track team and honored as a Varsity Letterman of Distinction. During World War II, he spent thirty-nine months as an artillery officer in the South Pacific, where he received both the Philippine Liberation Medal and the Bronze

---

28. Induction Ceremony, January 8, 1982, 288 Pa. Super. XXXIII (1982).

29. Pa. Constitution, art. V, sec. 13(b) (amended 1975).

30. During his career, Wieand was extremely active in the Y.M.C.A., serving on the national board of directors, and as president of the Pennsylvania and Allentown chapters. He received the organization's Member of the Year Award in 1971.

31. Memorial Service, 453 Pa. Super. XLVII (1996).

Pennsylvania State Police during early training exercises utilizing "stop and frisk" technique, later approved by the U. S. Supreme Court.

Star. He was also awarded the Pennsylvania Distinguished Service Medal and the Air Force Legion of Merit Award. He eventually rose to the rank of major general in the U.S. Air Force Reserves and the Pennsylvania National Guard. On June 22, 1965, he was cited by a resolution of the Pennsylvania House of Representatives for developing outstanding programs in Americanism. From 1951 to 1956, Brosky served as assistant solicitor of Allegheny County. On May 24, 1956, he was appointed to the Allegheny County Court and was elected to a full term the following year. On September 12, 1960, he was appointed to the Court of Common Pleas of Allegheny County. He was elected to a full term in 1961 and reelected in 1971. On February 13, 1970, Brosky became administrative judge of the Court of Common Pleas, Family Division.[32] While a trial judge, he served on the Juvenile Court Judges Commission and the Joint State Government Commission. Following his election to the Superior Court, Brosky served from January 7, 1980 until 1989, when he chose not to run for retention. However, he continued to serve as a senior judge. During his legal career, Brosky received numerous awards, including the Man of the Year—Field of Law Award from the Pittsburgh Junior Chamber of Commerce, the St. Thomas More Award from the Catholic Diocese of Pittsburgh, and doctor of public service degree, La Roche College. He was also president of the Pennsylvania Conference of State Trial Judges, national president of the Air Force Association, and president of the Pennsylvania National Guard Association.

The second judge elected in the fall of 1979, Republican Richard B. Wickersham, was born in Pittsburgh on April 4, 1929. He received his bachelor's degree from Dickinson College and law degree from Dickinson School of Law . From 1953 to 1956, he served in

---

32. Portrait Presentation Ceremony, December 9, 1986, 361 Pa. Super. XLIII (1986).

the U.S. Army Judge Advocate Generals' Corps. From 1956 to 1959, he was assistant district attorney of Dauphin County. Thereafter, he engaged in private practice, serving as solicitor of the Lower Paxton Township Board of Supervisors and general counsel of the Pennsylvania State Association of Township Supervisors. During his career, he served as a member of the Insurance, Negligence, and Workmen's Compensation Committees of the state bar association, the National Panel of the American Arbitration Association, and the International Association of Insurance Counsel. He also served as the Pennsylvania chairman of the Defense Research Institute. In 1971, he was elected to the Court of Common Pleas of Dauphin County. Wickersham assumed office with the Superior Court the same day as Brosky, January 7, 1980, and served until March 1988, when he resigned to return to private practice.

As these personnel changes indicate, the Democratic majority that first emerged in the 1960s stabilized in the 1970s. Not surprisingly, this stabilization reflected a broader political trend. While Democrats maintained a majority of the state's electorate during most of the 1960s, their lead never exceeded 130,000 registered voters and Republicans occasionally recaptured the advantage.[33] By the early 1970s, however, the Democrats held a decided majority and the lead grew for the remainder of the decade. In 1972, for instance, Democrats outdistanced Republicans by 300,000 votes; by 1980, the lead was 700,000.[34] As a result of this political strength, the Democrats maintained their majority on the Superior Court for the entire period, 1969-1980.

## THE COURT AT WORK: CRIMINAL LAW

The transformation of criminal law, begun by the rulings of the United States Supreme Court in *Mapp, Escobedo,* and *Miranda,* continued with other landmark decisions in the late 1960s and early 1970s. Unlike their predecessors, however, these latter decisions expanded the authority of law enforcement personnel and limited the rights of criminal defendants. Prior to 1968, probable cause was the standard formally required for police officers to detain persons or seize property. However, as a practical matter, police had long utilized the technique of "stop and frisk," whereby suspects were detained for interrogation and often "patted down" for weapons, despite the absence of probable cause. In *Terry v. Ohio,*[35] the United States Supreme Court approved the long-standing practice of "stop and frisk." According to the Court, approval of this practice was necessary to balance the governmental interests in crime detection and officer safety with the individual's right to be free of arbitrary governmental intrusion. The applicable test was set forth as follows:

> [W]here a police officer observes unusual conduct which leads him reasonably to conclude in light of his experience that criminal activity may be afoot and that the persons with whom he is dealing may be armed and presently dangerous, where in the course of investigating this behavior he identifies himself as a policeman and makes reasonable inquiries, and where nothing in the initial stages of the encounter serves to dispel his reasonable fear for his own or others' safety, he is entitled for the protection of himself and others in the area to conduct a care-

---

33. In 1960, for example, Democratic registered voters outnumbered Republicans 2,805,202 to 2,802,237; in 1964, the lead grew to 2,884,396 to 2,759,565. In 1968, however, Republicans outnumbered Democrats 2,775,456 to 2,715,507. *Pennsylvania Manual: 1984-85* (Harrisburg: Pa. Dept. of General Services), 723-24.

34. In 1972, Democrats outnumbered Republicans 2,993,092 to 2,697,694. In 1980, the lead was 3,072,700 to 2,374,303. *Pennsylvania Manual: 1984-85*, 723-24.

35. 392 U.S. 1 (1968).

fully limited search of the outer clothing of such persons in an attempt
to discover weapons which might be used to assault him.[36]

As a result of *Terry*, "reasonable suspicion" replaced probable cause as the appropriate standard for determining police authority to conduct brief investigatory stops.[37] Four years after *Terry*, the Supreme Court further elaborated this standard. In *Adams v. Williams*,[38] the Court interpreted *Terry* as indicating that "[t]he Fourth Amendment does not require a policeman who lacks the precise level of information necessary for probable cause to arrest to simply shrug his shoulders and allow a crime to occur or a criminal to escape." The court continued, "On the contrary, *Terry* recognizes that it may be the essence of good police work to adopt an intermediate response. . . . A brief stop of a suspicious individual, in order to determine his identity or to maintain the status quo momentarily while obtaining more information may be most reasonable in light of the facts known to the officer at the time."[39] Not surprisingly, the erosion of probable cause by the broad new standard enunciated in *Terry* and *Adams* significantly changed prior law and imposed upon lower courts, most often state courts, the duty to determine the validity of investigatory stops in individual cases.

In a series of novel decisions in the 1970s and early 1980s, the Superior Court adopted an expansive interpretation of police authority under *Terry* and *Adams*. In *Commonwealth v. Benson*,[40] for instance, the court considered for the first time whether the standard set forth in *Terry* and elaborated in *Adams* authorized an officer to rely solely on radio information to stop the vehicle of an individual suspected of criminal activity. The officer received a radio report to be "on the lookout for a dark-skinned Negro male, approximately 6 feet tall, in a brown leather coat, driving a late-model dark green Ford station wagon with the first two numbers of the license plate 4 and 0."[41] The suspect was being sought for the illegal sale of guns and a check-writing machine. One hour after hearing the radio report, the officer stopped Benson, a black male in a brown leather coat driving a green Ford station wagon with a license plate number starting with 4 and 0. When Benson was unable to produce a driver's license or owner's card, the officer placed him in the squad car and returned to the green station wagon, where he noticed a check-writing machine in the back seat. A subsequent investigation determined that the car had been stolen the evening before, and Benson was charged with theft, unauthorized use, and receiving stolen goods, all related to the green station wagon. His motion to suppress was denied and he was convicted.

On appeal, Benson argued that the evidence of his possession of the car should have been suppressed as fruit of an unlawful arrest, since the radio report and his subsequent detention were not based on probable cause. The Superior Court rejected this claim. According to the court, "We should permit our police in the early stage of their investigative work (before a warrant has been issued for specific individuals), to adopt the 'intermediate response' mentioned in *Adams*—to rely on radio information for the purpose of detaining individuals suspected of criminal activity, at least long enough to determine identity." "[I]f the stop discloses new information," the court continued, "then the police should be permitted to proceed in a reasonable manner, detain-

---

36. 392 U.S. 30-31.

37. Although the phrase "reasonable suspicion" does not appear in the *Terry* opinion, it was utilized by Justice Harlan in his concurring opinion in a related case handed down the same day. See *Sibron v. New York*, 392 U.S. 40, 71 (1968) ("Under the decision in *Terry* a right to stop may indeed be premised on reasonable suspicion and does not require probable cause.").

38. 407 U.S. 143 (1972).

39. 407 U.S. 145.

40. 239 Pa. Super. 100, 361 A.2d 695 (1976) (Van der Voort, J.).

41. 361 A.2d 696.

ing for further investigation, or, where appropriate, making an arrest."[42] Applying this standard to Benson's arrest, the court concluded:

> In the case before us, Officer Baker stopped a car which matched the description of a car suspected of having been used for criminal activity. A check of the driver's identification disclosed that the driver did not have a driver's license, and did not have the owner's card with him. Officer Baker acted reasonably in attempting to determine whether or not the car had been stolen—certainly a possibility under the circumstances.[43]

On this basis, Benson's conviction was affirmed. An appeal was taken to the Supreme Court, which affirmed in a per curiam opinion.[44] *Benson* has been cited on numerous occasions, including as recently as 1998, for its holding that police may rely on a radio report to stop an individual suspected of criminal activity, even where the detaining officer did not witness any suspicious behavior.[45] The case has proven especially important in cases where the Commonwealth justifies or attempts to justify a vehicle stop on the basis that an officer learned via radio of a report by a private citizen that an individual is driving under the influence of alcohol near the officer's location.[46] Finally, the case has been cited for the proposition that a driver's inability to produce a license or an owner's card will convert reasonable suspicion for the stop into probable cause for an arrest.[47]

In an automobile case that eventually went to the United States Supreme Court, the court considered police authority to conduct investigative searches during traffic stops. In *Commonwealth v. Mimms*,[48] two officers observed an individual driving with an expired license plate. The officers made a traffic stop and asked the driver, Mimms, to step out of the car and produce his license and owner's card. One officer noticed a large bulge on Mimms' hip under his sport jacket. Fearing that the bulge was a weapon, the officer conducted a "pat down" and discovered a .38 caliber revolver. Mimms was arrested and subsequently convicted of weapons offenses.[49]

On appeal, the Superior Court considered Mimms' argument that the search of his person and the seizure of the revolver violated his constitutional rights. The court began its analysis by reviewing the decisions of the United States Supreme Court in *Terry* and *Adams*, and the Pennsylvania cases applying those decisions. "As a general proposition," the court found, "the arrest of the driver of an automobile for an ordinary traffic offense does not, without more, permit a warrantless search."[50] Yet the court had little doubt that the general rule did not apply where the officer, during a valid traffic stop, becomes aware of a potential danger. In this case, the court held the officers' observation of a bulge under Mimms' jacket gave them the right to conduct a protective

---

42. 361 A.2d 698.
43. See note 42 (Price, concurring).
44. 482 Pa. 1, 393 A.2d 348 (1978).
45. See e.g., *Commonwealth v. Lohr*, 715 A.2d 459 (Pa. Super. 1998); *Commonwealth v. Janiak*, 368 Pa. Super. 626, 534 A.2d 833 (1987); *Commonwealth v. Seip*, 285 Pa. Super. 551, 428 A.2d 183 (1981).
46. See *Lohr, Janiak*, supra.
47. See e.g., *Commonwealth v. Lawrence*, 311 Pa. Super. 326, 457 A.2d 909 (1983); *Commonwealth v. Prengle*, 293 Pa. Super. 64, 437 A.2d 992 (1981).
48. 232 Pa. Super. 486, 335 A.2d 516 (1975) (Watkins, J.).
49. 335 A.2d 517.
50. 335 A.2d 518, citing *Commonwealth v. Dussell*, 439 Pa. 392, 266 A.2d 659 (1970).
51. 335 A.2d 518, citing *Terry* and *Adams*.

search. "Such searches," the court reasoned, "are encouraged by the Supreme Court of the United States for the protection of law enforcement officers."[51] Mimms' judgment of sentence was then affirmed.[52]

On appeal, the Pennsylvania Supreme Court reviewed the principles underlying *Terry* and reversed the Superior Court on the basis that the officers' order to Mimm's to get out of his car was an unconstitutional seizure under the Fourth Amendment.[53] Thereafter, the Commonwealth pursued an appeal in federal court, and on December 5, 1977, the United States Supreme Court reversed the decision of Pennsylvania's high court.[54] Initially, as to the officers' conduct in ordering Mimms from his car, the court considered the interests involved and held that "[w]hat is at most a mere inconvenience [to Mimms] cannot prevail when balanced against legitimate concerns for the officers' safety."[55] Moreover, finding the search of Mimms constitutional, the court held:

> Under the standard enunciated in [*Terry*]—whether "the facts available to the officer at the moment of the seizure or the search 'warrant a man of reasonable caution in the belief' that the action taken was appropriate"—there is little question the officer was justified. The bulge in the jacket permitted the officer to conclude that Mimms was armed and thus posed a serious and present danger to the safety of the officer. In these circumstances, any man of "reasonable caution" would likely have conducted the "pat-down."[56]

The Superior Court's decision in *Mimms*, like *Benson*, was an expansive interpretation of police authority to conduct searches with less than probable cause. In addition to these decisions in automobile cases, the court also interpreted the Supreme Court decisions to authorize police entry into a residence with less than probable cause. In *Commonwealth v. Daniels*,[57] two police officers were informed by an anonymous caller that a screaming white female was being taken from a car into a building. The officers went to the building and one of them knocked on the door of the apartment identified by the caller. The officer announced his presence and asked if everything was "all right." Daniels opened the door, but did not respond to the officer's questions. Instead, he walked away from the open door and into a bedroom. The officer followed Daniels into the bedroom, where he saw, sitting on a bureau in plain view, a box containing numerous bundles of a tan powder subsequently determined to be heroin. The other officer also entered the apartment and found a white female sitting in the front room near a plant, later identified as marijuana, and rolling a marijuana cigarette. Daniels was arrested and charged with possession of a controlled substance, possession with intent to deliver, and manufacturing with intent to deliver. His motion to suppress the heroin was denied, the female testified against him at trial, and he was convicted.

---

52. 335 A.2d 519. Judge Hoffman dissented on the basis that the sole defense witness was improperly questioned as to his religion.

53. 471 Pa. 546, 370 A.2d 1157 (1977). The Supreme Court concluded that the order was issued as a matter of routine, rather than on the basis of a reasonable suspicion that Mimms posed a threat to the officers' safety.

54. *Pennsylvania v. Mimms*, 434 U.S. 106 (1977) (per curiam).

55. 434 U.S. 111.

56. 434 U.S. 112 (citations omitted). Following its decision that the search of Mimms was not invalid, the United States Supreme Court remanded to the Pennsylvania Supreme Court for further proceedings. On remand, the state Supreme Court held that Mimms was entitled to a new trial on the basis that his sole defense witness had been improperly questioned as to his religion. *Commonwealth v. Mimms*, 477 Pa. 553, 385 A.2d 334 (1978). This was the basis of Judge Hoffman's dissent when the case was decided by the Superior Court.

57. 280 Pa. Super. 278, 421 A.2d 721 (1980) (Brosky, J.).

On appeal, Daniels argued that the heroin should have been suppressed since the officers lacked probable cause to enter the apartment. A unanimous Superior Court rejected this claim. The court began by noting that Daniels, by opening the front door to his apartment, not answering questions directed at him, and walking away from the open door, had consented to the officers' entry into his apartment. Since the issue of consent was "not clearcut," however, the court also went on to consider whether the officers had authority to enter the apartment in the absence of consent.[58] "The *Terry* line of cases," the court stated, "has been expanded in Pennsylvania to include an 'intermediate response' applicable to circumstances where facts may not warrant an arrest."[59] Given Daniels' "suspicious conduct [in walking away from the door], viewed in light of the anonymous call," the court found that the officers adopted a proper intermediate response by following Daniels into his bedroom. The officers "are duty bound," the court concluded, "to assure the safety of the woman and to inquire into the circumstances which induced their arrival. . . . Of course, under the facts in this case, the police could not continue their inquiry without following Daniels."[60] Finally, utilizing a balancing test, the court found that the state's interest in encouraging effective police investigation outweighed Daniels' privacy interests under the facts presented.[61] Since the officers legally entered the apartment, and because the heroin was in plain view in the bedroom, the court held that the trial court properly denied suppression. Thus, unlike *Terry* and *Adams*, which involved stops on a public street and in a public parking lot, respectively, *Daniels* sanctioned police entry into the confines of a private dwelling. In the years since it was rendered, the court's opinion has been cited as indicating that the expectation of privacy in one's property is not absolute, and that not all entries onto private property without probable cause are unreasonable.[62] It has also been cited in other states to justify police entry without probable cause into a private home[63] and a motel room.[64] Finally, *Daniels* has been cited for the proposition that the public policy of Pennsylvania strongly encourages police to investigate reports of ongoing crimes, and that a citizen's right to privacy must be balanced against this public policy.[65]

Finally, in 1977 the Superior Court held that a criminal suspect might be removed from the scene of an alleged crime although the police did not possess probable cause for an arrest. In *Commonwealth v. Harper*,[66] an individual on a Philadelphia trolley had been approached by three young black males, two of whom attacked and repeatedly stabbed the individual. When the trolley stopped, the three men fled, and the screams of other passengers alerted a nearby police officer, who summoned backup and emergency vehicles. The officer learned that the three men had boarded a bus across the street. When backup arrived, the officer boarded the bus and found six young black males. All six, along with another man from the street, were taken to the hospital and, less than one hour after the attack, were paraded individually before the victim. The victim identified two of the men, including Harper, as his attackers. Both men were convicted for the knife assault.

---

58. 421 A.2d 723.
59. 421 A.2d 724.
60. 421 A.2d 724-25.
61. See note 60.
62. See e.g., *Commonwealth v. Oglialoro*, 377 Pa. Super. 317, 547 A.2d 387 (1988); *Commonwealth v. Carelli*, 377 Pa. Super. 17, 546 A.2d 1185 (1988); *Commonwealth v. Shannon*, 320 Pa. Super. 552, 467 A.2d 850 (1983).
63. *Conway v. Commonwealth*, 12 Va. App. 711, 407 S.E.2d 310 (1991).
64. *Servis v. Commonwealth*, 6 Va. App. 507, 371 S.E.2d 156 (1988); see also *Kentucky v. Johnson*, 777 S.W.2d 876 (1989) (Wintersheimer, dissenting).
65. *Commonwealth v. Dennis*, 289 Pa. Super. 305, 433 A.2d 79 (1981); see also *Commonwealth v. Campbell*, 418 Pa. Super. 391, 614 A.2d 692 (1992).
66. 248 Pa. Super. 344, 375 A.2d 129 (1977) (Price, J.).

On appeal, Harper argued that the hospital identification was the fruit of an illegal arrest because the officer lacked probable cause to remove him from the bus and transport him to the hospital. In a brief opinion, the Superior Court rejected this claim. Initially, the court found that no arrest had occurred when Harper was removed from the bus. Instead, it was a valid investigatory stop. The officer was justified, the court held, "in momentarily detaining all persons who reasonably fitted the description of the attackers until an identification could be made. Once the victim identified [Harper], probable cause for the arrest existed." Although the court did not refer to *Terry* or *Adams*, it found that the conduct of the police in transporting Harper and the others was reasonable in light of the "heinous nature of the crime and the small number of suspects" detained.[67] On this basis, the court affirmed Harper's conviction. The Supreme Court denied allocatur to hear an appeal. Like the decisions in *Benson, Mimms*, and *Daniels, Harper's* authorization of the removal of suspects from the scene of a stop represents an expansive interpretation of police authority under *Terry* and *Adams* to conduct investigations without probable cause.[68]

In addition to construing *Terry* and *Adams*, the Superior Court also rendered an important decision that extended its seminal holding twenty-five years earlier in *Riccio v. Dilworth*,[69] which established the inadmissibility of polygraph tests. In *Commonwealth v. Pfender*,[70] the court considered in the first impression case whether a polygraph test might be admitted in a criminal trial where the Commonwealth and the defendant consent to its admission. In that case, Pfender was charged with arson and related offenses and he agreed to undergo a polygraph test. Before the test was conducted, he and the Commonwealth stipulated that it would be admissible at trial. The test implicated Pfender in the arson and he sought suppression. The trial court suppressed the polygraph results but certified the issue for immediate appeal.[71]

The Superior Court began by stating "Pennsylvania cases still adhere to the principle set forth in [*Riccio*]."[72] Yet it also noted that the courts had not considered whether a stipulation affects the general rule of inadmissibility. Turning to cases in other states, the court found no unanimity of opinion. Courts in Arizona and New Jersey ruled polygraphs admissible by stipulation, while courts in West Virginia, Alaska, and Oklahoma held to the contrary. The court sided with the latter cases:

> We think these last cases illustrate the proper view for Pennsylvania Courts on this issue. . . . [O]ur cases have held that the reliability of polygraphic test results have not as yet been sufficiently demonstrated. No Pennsylvania case has undertaken a review of the science of polygraphy in order to evaluate its present reliability. Our research dis-

---

67. 375 A.2d 131.

68. For an article critical of *Daniels* and *Harper* in this regard, see Robert Berkley Harper, "Has the Pennsylvania Superior Court Misread *Terry* & *Adams*," 20 Duq. L. Rev. 585, 598-99, 601-02 (1982). In 1982, the Supreme Court reversed a Superior Court holding that the transportation of a suspect to the scene of a burglary was a valid investigatory procedure. The Supreme Court held that the transportation constituted an arrest and was thus illegal, having been conducted without probable cause. The Supreme Court further emphasized that the police easily could have transported the burglary victim to the scene of the defendant's detention. See *Commonwealth v. Lovette*, 498 Pa. 665, 450 A.2d 975 (1982), reversing 271 Pa. Super. 250, 413 A.2d 390 (1979). The impact of *Lovette* on the continuing validity of *Harper* is uncertain since the victim in the latter case had been seriously wounded and required seven weeks' hospitalization, and thus presumably could not have been transported to the scene where the defendant and the others were detained.

69. Discussed supra.

70. 280 Pa.Super. 417, 421 A.2d 791 (1980) (Cavanaugh, J.).

71. See note 70. The Pa. Act of July 9, 1976, PL 586, 42 Pa.C.S. sec. 702(b), permits an immediate appeal where it will materially advance the termination of the case.

72. 421 A.2d 794.

The Superior Court in 1978.
L. to R. (seated): J. Sydney Hoffman, Robert L. Jacobs (President Judge), William F. Cercone. L. to R. (standing): Gwilym A. Price Jr., Robert Van der Voort, Edmund B. Spaeth Jr., John P. Hester.

closes that there is no jurisdiction where the test is held to be generally admissible at trial. This has been the result even after an exhaustive analysis of the legal and scientific value of polygraphic evidence. We believe that the reception of such evidence even by stipulation before our courts undertake to evaluate and accept polygraphy generally is fraught with danger.[73]

On this basis, the court held "that evidence of results of the polygraphic tests is not admissible . . . even in the face of a knowing, voluntary and intelligent stipulation that they may be submitted in evidence."[74] Like *Riccio, Pfender* has defined Pennsylvania law regarding polygraphs since it was rendered.[75] It has also been cited by courts in other states considering the admissibility of polygraphs by stipulation.[76]

---

73. 421 A.2d 796.

74. See note 73.

75. See e.g., *Commonwealth v. Osborn*, 364 Pa. Super. 505, 528 A.2d 623 (1987); *Commonwealth v. Rodriguez*, 343 Pa. Super. 486, 495 A.2d 569 (1985); *Commonwealth v. Watts*, 319 Pa. Super. 179, 465 A.2d 1288 (1983).

76. See *North Carolina v. Grier*, 300 S.E.2d 351 (1983) (refusing to admit polygraphs by stipulation); *Wynn v. Alabama*, 423 S.O.2d 294 (1982) (admitting polygraphs by stipulation). See also *Oregon v. Brown*, 687 P.2d 751 (1984) (admitting polygraphs in certain circumstances).

## TORTS

The evolution of tort law that began in the 1950s and 1960s accelerated in the 1970s. Once again, the trend favored expanded liability, and the Superior Court recognized new causes of action and diminished or abolished traditional bars to liability. No tort case ever decided by the court involved issues as profound as those presented in *Speck v. Finegold.*[77] In that case, the plaintiffs, Frank and Dorothy Speck, were a married couple with two children, each of whom was afflicted with neurofibromatosis, a crippling and disfiguring disease of the fibrous tissues of the nerves.[78] In order to avoid conceiving a third child with the disease, Mr. Speck decided to undergo sterilization. He consulted with one of the co-defendants, Dr. Finegold, a urologist and surgeon, who stated that a vasectomy was an effective means of sterilization. Finegold performed the operation on April 28, 1974. Following the operation, Finegold informed Speck that he could engage in sexual relations with his wife without risking pregnancy. Despite Finegold's reassurances, Mrs. Speck became pregnant. Fearing that the baby would be born with neurofibromatosis, the Specks consulted with the other co-defendant, Dr. Schwartz, an obstetrician and gynecologist. On December 27, 1974, Schwartz performed an abortion on Mrs. Speck. After the operation, Schwartz informed the Specks that the operation had been a success and that the pregnancy had been terminated. Thereafter, Mrs. Speck returned to Dr. Schwartz and stated that she felt the pregnancy was continuing. Schwartz assured her that the fetus had been aborted. On April 29, 1975, Mrs. Speck gave birth to a premature child, Francine, who was afflicted with severe neurofibromatosis. The Specks filed a multiple-count complaint against Finegold and Schwartz seeking damages for themselves and their children, and on behalf of Francine, for the financial cost of past and future medical care, and for the pain, suffering, and emotional distress caused by Francine's birth and life.[79] The complaint asserted two causes of action that had not been recognized by Pennsylvania law. The first was "wrongful life," an action brought by parents on behalf of a child who is asserting that his or her very existence is wrongful. The second action, "wrongful birth," is brought by the parents in their own right to recover for damages sustained as the result of an unwanted pregnancy and birth.[80] The lower court denied these claims on the basis that they were not recognized by law and that the damages claimed were so speculative as to be immeasurable. The court also found that the claims were contrary to public policy since determining the value of life as against non-life was a task beyond human understanding.[81] The only actions allowed by the court were the traditional medical malpractice claims of the Specks relating to the negligent vasectomy and abortion.[82] Since the court's ruling had the effect of terminating a significant portion of the Speck's lawsuit, an appeal was taken.

The Superior Court, in a five-judge majority opinion, began its analysis of the Speck's claims by quoting from a New York case that recognized the difficulty of the issues presented: "Even as a pure question of law, unencumbered by unresolved issues of fact, the weighing of the validity of a cause of action seeking compensation for a wrongful causation of life itself casts an almost Orwellian shadow, premised as it is

---

77. 268 Pa. Super. 342, 408 A.2d 496 (1979) (Cercone, J.).

78. The children inherited the disease from their father.

79. 408 A.2d 500.

80. See 53 *Temple L.Q.* 176 n. 3.

81. 408 A.2d 501.

82. In its initial ruling, the court allowed Mr. Speck's claim relating to the vasectomy, but disallowed Mrs. Speck's claim relating to the abortion because her complaint had not been properly drafted. Thereafter, the court allowed Mrs. Speck to amend her complaint. 408 A.2d 501.

upon concepts of genetic predictability once foreign to the evolutionary process. It borders on the absurdly obvious to observe that resolution of this question transcends the mechanical application of legal principles."[83] The court emphasized that the important distinction between wrongful birth and wrongful life claims was that the former pitted the parents against the doctors for expenses and other damages relating to the care of the child, while the latter pitted the child against the doctors for injuries resulting from life itself.[84] Turning first to the Specks' claims against the doctors, the court surveyed cases around the nation, and found that those which denied recovery did so on the basis that "the sanctity of life precludes a cognizable action in law and/or that it is impossible to measure damages between a child being born, defectively or not, and not being born at all."[85] But the court found that these arguments, which the lower court found convincing, missed the point. "The question is not the worth and sanctity of life," the court reasoned, "but whether the doctors were negligent in their surgical attempts at vasectomy and abortion."[86] Although the court also noted that recent cases in other jurisdictions supported its conclusion, the court's analysis turned on this basic fact: the issue presented, stripped to its essentials, was one of simple negligence. If Finegold and Schwartz had breached a duty of care that resulted in injuries to the Specks, "it is axiomatic that [they are] liable for all damages which ordinarily and in the natural course of things have resulted from the commission of the tort."[87] Thus, the court concluded, in addition to their traditional malpractice claims for injuries to themselves, the Specks could also maintain their wrongful birth action for the expense of Francine's past and future care.[88]

Francine's claim for wrongful life, however, was not as successful. Initially, although the court acknowledged that the negligence of Finegold and Schwartz caused Francine's "defective birth,"[89] it found no precedent establishing the fundamental right of a human being to be born free of abnormalities. Moreover, the court stated:

> Whether it is better not to have been born at all rather than to have been born with serious mental defects is a mystery more properly left to the philosophers and theologians, a mystery which would lead us into the field of metaphysics, beyond the realm of our understanding or ability to solve. The law cannot assert a knowledge which can resolve this inscrutable and enigmatic issue.[90]

Similarly, on the issue of damages, the court noted that successful maintenance of a cause of action alleging that one should not have been born would require "a calcu-

---

83. 408 A.2d 499, quoting *Becker v. Schwartz*, 413 N.Y.S.2d 895, 898, 386 N.E.2d 807, 810 (1978). The court hastened to add that its task was not to consider whether the Specks should ultimately prevail, but only to determine if their claims were cognizable under Pennsylvania law. 408 A.2d 502.

84. Although he noted that the parents' claims might be divided into an action for "wrongful conception" against Finegold and an action for "wrongful birth" against Schwartz, the court analyzed these claims together for the remainder of the opinion. 408 A.2d 502.

85. 408 A.2d 503.

86. The court also found that the legalization of abortion by the United States Supreme Court in *Roe v. Wade*, 410 U.S. 113 (1973), undermined any claim that the procedure underwent by Mrs. Speck was against public policy. 408 A.2d 503-04.

87. 408 A.2d 508.

88. The cases cited in support of this conclusion were *Sherlock v. Stillwater Clinic*, 260 N.W.2d 169 (Minn. 1977); *Karlsons v. Guerinot*, 394 N.Y.S.2d 933 (N.Y. App. Div. 4th Dep't 1977); *Ziemba v. Sternberg*, 357 N.Y.S.2d 265, 45 A.D.2d 230 (1974); *Martineau v. Nelson*, 247 N.W.2d 409 (Minn. 1976); *Rivera v. State*, 404 N.Y.S.2d 950 (1978); *Becker v. Scwartz* and *Park v. Chessin*, 386 N.E.2d 807 (N.Y. 1978) (consolidated cases).

89. 408 A.2d 508.

90. See note 89.

lation of damages dependent on a comparison between Hobson's choice of life in an impaired state and nonexistence. This the law is incapable of doing."[91] The court also denied the claim for emotional distress arising from Francine's birth on the basis that the Specks could not be distinguished from other parents who suffered such distress in the course of raising handicapped or injured children. "The fact that plaintiffs did not want Francine," the court held, "does not alter the sameness in the quality and nature of pain and suffering in the everyday work of parenthood." On this basis, the five-judge majority remanded the case for trial on the Specks' medical malpractice and wrongful birth claims against Doctors Finegold and Schwartz.[92]

In a concurring and dissenting opinion, Judge Price agreed with the majority that the Specks could not recover damages for emotional distress, and that Francine should not be able to maintain an action for wrongful life. He dissented, however, from that portion of the majority opinion allowing the Specks' a cause of action for wrongful birth. "[P]ublic policy and social necessity," he stated, "mandate a holding that the birth of *any* child is not a wrong that results in 'damage' to the parents."[93]

Judge Spaeth also concurred and dissented. First, he noted his agreement with the majority that Francine should not be permitted to maintain an action for wrongful life and that the Specks should be able to recover damages for wrongful birth.[94] Unlike the majority, however, he would have allowed the Specks to recover for emotional distress resulting from Francine's birth. This recovery, he reasoned, was consistent with ordinary negligence principles requiring a party who commits a tort to compensate for all foreseeable injuries resulting from the tort.[95]

To summarize, the *Speck* court was unanimous in rejecting a wrongful life cause of action under Pennsylvania law. With the exception of Judge Price, however, the court agreed to recognize an action for wrongful birth on behalf of the parents. As to damages, all but Judge Spaeth agreed that the parents should not be permitted to pursue damages for emotional distress.

Following the Superior Court's decision, an appeal was taken. On December 31, 1981, a sharply-divided Supreme Court affirmed in part and reversed in part.[96] First, by a vote of five-to-one, the court affirmed the Superior Court's recognition of a wrongful birth cause of action under Pennsylvania law. The court divided three-to-three on the issue of wrongful life, and this split had the effect of affirming the Superior Court's refusal to recognize a cause of action. However, by a vote of five-to-one, the court reversed the determination that the Specks could not recover for emotional distress. In the following years, the Supreme and Superior Courts applied the principles established in *Speck*.[97] The Superior Court's opinion was also cited by several federal courts,[98]

---

91. See note 89.

92. 408 A.2d 509.

93. 408 A.2d 510.

94. Spaeth would have allowed the jury to deduct from the parents' recovery an amount representing the benefit that Francine brought to her parents. 408 A.2d 513.

95. 408 A.2d 513-14.

96. 497 Pa. 77, 439 A.2d 110 (1981). Only six justices participated in the consideration of the appeal. Chief Justice O'Brien and Justices Flaherty, Larsen, Kaufman, and Roberts upheld the Superior Court's recognition of a "wrongful birth" cause of action and reversed the Superior Court's determination that the Specks could not recover for emotional distress. Justice Nix would not have allowed a "wrongful birth" cause of action under any circumstances. Finally, Justices Flaherty, Larsen, and Kaufman supported a cause of action for "wrongful life," and Chief Justice O'Brien and Justices Roberts and Nix opposed it.

97. See *Mason v. Western Pennsylvania Hospital*, 499 Pa. 484, 453 A.2d 974 (1982) (authorizing recovery of costs associated with pregnancy and delivery after allegedly improper sterilization procedure); *Ellis v. Sherman*, 330 Pa. Super. 42, 478 A.2d 1339 (1984), affirmed, 512 Pa. 14, 515 A.2d 1327 (1986) (Pennsylvania law does not recognize action for wrongful life); and *Rubin v. Hamot Medical Center*, 329 Pa. Super. 439, 478 A.2d 869 (1984) (Pennsylvania law does not recognize action for wrongful life).

98. *Hartke v. McKelway*, 707 F.2d 1544 (D.C. Cir. 1983); *Robak v. United States*, 658 F.2d 471 (7th Cir. 1981); *Phillips v. United States*, 508 F.Supp. 544 (D.S.C. 1981).

courts in eight states,[99] law reviews,[100] and other sources.[101] In 1988, however, the legislature enacted a statute abolishing the cause of action for wrongful birth recognized in *Speck*.[102] The statute also prohibited a cause of action for wrongful life.[103]

In addition to *Speck*, the court rendered two other important decisions that expanded liability in the realm of medical malpractice. The first of these decisions, *Hamil v. Bashline*,[104] was endorsed by the Pennsylvania Supreme Court and initiated a national trend toward reducing the standard of proof in certain suits alleging negligence against physicians and hospitals. As a general rule, plaintiffs in medical malpractice actions, like other negligence plaintiffs, are required to prove that a physician's lack of due care was a substantial factor in causing the injury at issue. This burden of proof was extremely difficult to meet in cases where the plaintiff was treated for a preexisting condition, because the condition might have resulted in injury even if the physician was not negligent. In other words, because the plaintiff could not prove that the condition would not have resulted in injury in the absence of the physician's negligence, he or she was often unable to prevail at trial.[105] In *Hamil*, the Superior Court reconsidered the traditional burden of proof in cases where there is a possibility that harm would have occurred even without negligence. The facts of *Hamil* began on May 31, 1968, when Kenneth Hamil arrived at the defendant-hospital suffering from severe chest pains. The emergency room doctor could not be located, but another physician, Dr. J.F. Johnston, was present and ordered an electrocardiogram (EKG) test. Due to a faulty electrical outlet, the EKG machine failed to function. Dr. Johnston directed that another machine be used and he then left the hospital. The staff could not locate another machine and, receiving no aid, Hamil was taken by his wife to the office of a private physician, Dr. Raymond Saloom. Hamil died of a heart attack while Dr. Saloom was attempting to perform an EKG. Mrs. Hamil filed suit arguing that the hospital failed to employ recognized methods to treat her husband. At trial, Hamil called noted pathologist Dr. Cyril Wecht as an expert witness. Wecht testified that if the hospital had employed available methods of treatment, which he described, Mr. Hamil would have had a 75 percent chance of survival. Wecht testified that the hospital's negligence terminated this significant chance of survival. The defendant's expert, Dr. John Treadway, testified that death was imminent when Hamil arrived at the hospital, and that he would have died regardless of any treatment rendered by the hospital. Following the submission of evidence, the trial court ruled that Wecht's testimony failed to meet the common law standard of expert testimony requiring reasonable medical certainty that the hospital's negligence was the proximate cause of Mr. Hamil's death. On this basis, the trial court directed a verdict in favor of the hospital.

---

99. *Boone v. Mullendore*, 416 So.2d 718 (Ala. 1982); *Turpin v. Sortini*, 643 P.2d 954 (Cal. 1982); *Moores v. Lucas*, 405 So.2d 1022 (Fla. 1981); *Goldberg v. Ruskin*, 499 N.E.2d 406 (Ill. 1986); *Eisbrenner v. Stanley*, 308 N.W.2d 209 (Mich. 1981); *Kingsbury v. Smith*, 442 A.2d 1003 (N.H. 1982); *Procanik v. Cillo*, 478 A.2d 755 (N.J. 1984); *Nelson v. Krusen*, 678 S.W.2d 918 (Tex. 1984).

100. 1995 U. Ill. L. Rev. 761; 66 Temp. L. Rev. 1087 (1993); 26 Duq. L. Rev. 925; 18 Duq. L. Rev. 857.

101. 74 ALR 4th 798; 99 ALR 3d 303; 83 ALR 3d 15; 27 ALR 3d 906.

102. 42 Pa.C.S. sec. 8305(a) provided in relevant part, "There shall be no cause of action or award of damages on behalf of any person based on a claim that, but for an act or omission of the defendant, a person once conceived would not or should not have been born."

103. 42 Pa.C.S. sec. 8305(b).

104. 224 Pa. Super. 407, 307 A.2d 57 (1973) (Cercone, J.).

105. See e.g., Post, Peters, and Stahl, *The Law of Medical Practice in Pennsylvania and New Jersey*, sec. 4:35, 416 (1984) ("It is often difficult for a patient-plaintiff to demonstrate that a physician's negligence was a substantial factor in causing injury, because a patient-plaintiff cannot prove the events which would have occurred, had the physician not acted negligently. If the physician proves that the injury would have been sustained without his or her negligence, then the physician is not liable for the injury. Since the burden is on the patient-plaintiff, however, this standard often treated the patient-plaintiff unfairly.").

On appeal, Mrs. Hamil urged the Superior Court to reject the common law standard and adopt in its stead the test set forth in the Restatement of Torts, 2d, Section 323, which provides:

> One who undertakes, gratuitously or for consideration, to render services to another which he should recognize as necessary for the protection of the other's person or things, is subject to liability to the other for physical harm resulting from his failure to exercise reasonable care to perform his undertaking, if (a) his failure to exercise such care increases the risk of such harm. . . .[106]

The importance of this section was that, in cases such as *Hamil*, it would allow the jury to consider testimony that a defendant's conduct "increase[d] the risk" of harm, even though such testimony fell short of the traditional standard of proof requiring evidence that the conduct *caused* the harm. The court found that Section 323 suggested the proper approach. Initially, the court acknowledged that Dr. Wecht's testimony was insufficient to satisfy the common law standard for proof of causation. Nonetheless, the court held, Mrs. Hamil should have been permitted to "rely on section 323 which is hereby expressly accepted as the law of Pennsylvania and interpreted as allowing causal connection between the death and the defendant's conduct to be proved by evidence that the risk of death was increased by the defendant's failure to exercise reasonable care." In light of this conclusion, the court found that the trial court improperly prevented the jury from considering Dr. Wecht's testimony that the hospital's conduct diminished Mr. Hamil's 75 percent chance of survival. Yet the court also hastened to add that Section 323 does not impose liability upon every defendant who increases the risk of harm to a plaintiff. Instead, it dictates only that evidence of the increased risk must be submitted for the jury's consideration on the issue of whether the defendant's conduct caused the plaintiff's harm. Accordingly, a new trial was awarded to Mrs. Hamil, and the trial court was instructed to allow the jury to consider whether the hospital failed to exercise reasonable care and "whether or not such failure, which according to Dr. Wecht's testimony increased the risk of death, did in fact cause decedent's death."[107]

This ruling, which is referred to hereinafter as *Hamil I*, was not the last time the case appeared before the Superior Court. Following a retrial, the jury rendered a verdict in favor of the hospital, and Mrs. Hamil again appealed. In *Hamil II*,[108] the Superior Court was sharply divided. An opinion by Judge Price, joined by President Judge Watkins and Judge Van Der Voort, argued that *Hamil I* should be overruled on the basis that it allowed the jury to find causation merely upon evidence of increased risk of harm, a standard that was believed to be insufficient. Since the trial court's directed verdict after the first trial was therefore proper, the court affirmed the result in the second trial without reaching Mrs. Hamil's appellate issues. In separate opinions, Judges Hoffman, Cercone, and Spaeth argued that *Hamil I* should not be overruled.[109] However, Judge Hoffman believed that the jury charge in the second trial was proper and he concurred in the result reached by Judge Price's opinion. Judge Jacobs also concurred in the result of Judge Price's opinion. Thus, a majority of five judges rejected Mrs. Hamil's appeal.[110] She appealed and the Supreme Court granted alloca-

---

106. Restatement of Torts, 2d, sec. 323, Negligent Performance of Undertaking to Render Services.

107. 307 A.2d 62.

108. 243 Pa. Super. 227, 364 A.2d 1366 (1976) (Price, J.).

109. Although he stated that *Hamil I* should not be overruled, Judge Jacobs concurred in the result of the court's opinion because he believed the trial court had properly charged the jury at the second trial. 364 A.2d 1371. Judges Cercone and Spaeth dissented. 364 A.2d 1380, 1386.

110. 364 A.2d 1371.

tur (*Hamil III*).[111] Following a lengthy review, the Supreme Court endorsed the analysis of *Hamil I*:

> We agree with the view of the Superior Court majority expressed in [*Hamil I*] that the effect of Section 323(a) is to relax the degree of certitude normally required of plaintiff's evidence in order to make a case for the jury as to whether a defendant may be held liable for the plaintiff's injuries: Once a plaintiff has introduced evidence that a defendant's negligent act or omission increased the risk of harm to a person in plaintiff's position, and that the harm was in fact sustained, it becomes a question for the jury as to whether or not that increased risk was a substantial factor in producing the harm.[112]

On this basis, the Supreme Court vacated the Superior Court's decision in *Hamil II*.[113] The test set forth in *Hamil I* and endorsed by the Supreme Court in *Hamil III* remains the law of Pennsylvania, and the state's courts have consistently held that when proof of causation cannot meet the common law standard in a case where there is a possibility of harm, even without negligence, evidence of increased risk will nonetheless be permitted to reach the jury under Section 323 of the Restatement of Torts, 2d.[114] The Supreme or Superior Court versions of *Hamil* have been cited on more than one hundred occasions in Pennsylvania, and by courts in twenty-nine states and numerous federal circuits and districts.[115]

Seven years after *Hamil I*, in *Capan v. Divine Providence Hospital*,[116] the court reconsidered a long-standing rule limiting the liability of hospitals for the malpractice of their physicians. Historically, hospitals could not be held liable for the negligence of physicians, since the physicians were considered independent contractors and not employees of the hospital.[117] This rule was rejected in *Capan*, in which the plaintiff's decedent, Frank Capan, was admitted to Divine Providence Hospital on November 17, 1972, with a severe nosebleed. While in the hospital, Mr. Capan developed delirium tremens[118] and became violent. Six days after he was admitted, Dr. Pollice was the "on call" physician when he was notified that the patient had become combative with hospital staff. Pollice administered a series of drugs to Capan in order to calm him. After Pollice left, Capan suffered cardiac arrest and died. Thereafter, Capan's wife sued the hospital and

---

111. *Hamil v. Bashline*, 481 Pa. 256, 392 A.2d 1280 (1978).

112. 392 A.2d 1286.

113. A third trial was ordered, and this trial also resulted in a verdict for the hospital. Mrs. Hamil again appealed. Although the decision did not involve the standard of causation, the Superior Court once again reversed the trial court, finding that the jury was improperly precluded from considering the joint liability of the defendants. See *Hamil v. Bashline*, 309 Pa. Super. 518, 455 A.2d 1204 (1982). On this basis, the case was remanded for a fourth trial, and it did not reappear in the appellate courts.

114. See e.g., *Martin v. Evans,* 551 Pa. 496, 711 A.2d 458 (1998); *Welsh v. Bulger*, 548 Pa. 504, 698 A.2d 581 (1997); *Mitzelfelt v. Kamrin*, 526 Pa. 54, 584 A.2d 888 (1990); *Jones v. Montefiore Hospital*, 494 Pa. 410, 431 A.2d 920 (1981); *Gradel v. Inouye*, 491 Pa. 534, 421 A.2d 674 (1980).

115. See e.g., *Thompson v. Sun City Community Hospital*, 688 P.2d 605 (Ariz. 1984); *Williams v. Wraxall*, 33 Cal.App. 4th 120 (Cal. 1995); *Holton v. Memorial Hospital*, 679 N.E.2d 1202 (Ill. 1997); *Scafidi v. Seiler*, 543 A.2d 95 (N.J. 1988); *Coffran v. Hitchcock Clinic*, 683 F.2d 5 (1st Cir. 1982); *Redland Soccer Club v. Department of the Army*, 55 F.3d 827 (3d Cir. Pa. 1995); *Waffen v. U.S. Dept. of Health and Human Services*, 799 F.2d 911 (4th Cir. 1986); *Keir v. U.S.,* 853 F.2d 398 (6th Cir. Tenn. 1988); *Miller v. U.S.*, 530 F. Supp. 611 (E.D. Pa. 1982); *Blessing v. U.S.*, 447 F. Supp. 1160 (E.D. Pa. 1978). See also, 100 Dick. L. Rev. 29; 30 Duq. L. Rev. 639; 65 B. U. L. Rev. 275; 13 ALR 5th 289; 54 ALR 4th 10.

116. 287 Pa. Super. 364, 430 A.2d 647 (1980) (Hoffman, J.).

117. Hospitals were also commonly afforded the protections of charitable immunity, but this immunity was abolished by the Supreme Court in *Flagiello v. Pennsylvania Hospital*, 417 Pa. 486, 208 A.2d 193 (1965).

The Superior Court in 1980 (the last seven-member court).
L. to R. (standing): James R. Cavanaugh, John P. Hester, Gwilym A. Price Jr., Edmund B. Spaeth Jr., John G. Brosky, Richard B. Wickersham. Seated is William F. Cercone (President Judge).

numerous doctors, who joined Dr. Pollice as an additional defendant. The case went to trial and, following the close of Mrs. Capan's case, the trial court granted nonsuits in favor of all doctors except Dr. Pollice. The case was then submitted to the jury with special interrogatories, one of which asked whether Pollice was an employee of the hospital. The jury answered the question in the negative and, on this basis, the trial court entered a verdict in favor of the hospital. Capan's wife appealed on the basis that the trial court should have instructed the jury that it could have found the hospital vicariously liable for the negligence of Dr. Pollice, regardless of whether he was an employee.[119]

The court began its analysis of this issue by noting the general rule that an employer is not liable for the torts committed by an independent contractor in his employ.[120] The court noted, however, that an exception to this general rule exists under Section 429 of the Restatement of Torts, 2d, which provides:

> One who employs an independent contractor to perform services for another which are accepted in the reasonable belief that the services are being rendered by the employer or by his servants, is subject to liability for physical harm caused by the negligence of the contractor in

118. Delirium tremens is normally associated with alcohol withdrawal. Symptoms can include sweating, tremors, dyspepsia, restlessness, increased heart rate, fever, anxiety, chest pains, mental confusion and hallucinations that are often tactile

119. When the appeal first reached the Superior Court, it found that this issue had not been preserved for review. *Capan v. Divine Providence Hospital*, 270 Pa. Super. 127, 410 A.2d 1282 (1979). The Supreme Court vacated the Superior Court's order, however, and remanded for consideration of the hospital's vicarious liability.

120. 430 A.2d 648, citing *McDonough v. United States Steel Corp.*, 228 Pa. Super. 268, 324 A.2d 542 (1974).

supplying such services, to the same extent as though the employer were supplying them himself or by his servants.[121]

The court noted that the theory underlying Section 429 has been designated as "ostensible agency," since it imposes liability based upon the injured party's reasonable belief that a contractor is acting as an agent at the time of the accident. This theory had been applied in other states to impose liability for medical malpractice on hospitals. According to the court, the extension of liability was premised on two factors. The first was the increasing tendency of the public to look to hospitals, rather than to individual physicians, for medical care. The court quoted from a New York case to emphasize this point:

> The conception that the hospital does not undertake to treat the patient, does not undertake to act through its doctors and nurses, but undertakes instead simply to procure them to act upon their own responsibility, no longer reflects the fact. Present-day hospitals, as their manner of operation plainly demonstrates, do far more than furnish facilities for treatment. They regularly employ on a salary basis a large staff of physicians, nurses and interns, as well as administrative and manual workers, and they charge patients for medical care and treatment, collecting for such services, if necessary, by legal action.[122]

The court reasoned that it would be anomalous in the modern world of medicine to require a patient to inquire as to which of his treating physicians was an employee and which was an independent contractor. "Similarly," the court continued, "it would be unfair to allow the 'secret limitations' on liability contained in a doctor's contract with the hospital to bind the unknowing patient." The court also found that patients are often led to believe that the physician is an employee of the hospital. This was particularly true in the case of emergency room physicians, since the hospital opens its doors to the public and provides care without informing patients that the physician is not an employee. In such a case, the court found, the hospital "holds out" the physician as its employee.[123] In the case at issue, for instance, Capan entered the hospital through the emergency room and was treated not by his personal physician, but by Pollice, a house physician. For these reasons, the court held, the jury should have been able to determine whether Capan was relying on the hospital, and not Pollice, for treatment, and whether the hospital had "held out" Pollice as its employee. In this regard, the court emphasized that there was no evidence in the record that Capan knew or should have known that Pollice was an independent contractor rather than an employee. In light of this ostensible agency, the court awarded Mrs. Capan a new trial. The court established the rule, followed since, that hospitals may be held vicariously liable under the theory of ostensible agency for medical malpractice committed by physicians in their employ.[124] *Capan* has been cited by a number of federal courts[125] and by courts in eight states.[126]

---

121. 430 A.2d 648, citing Restatement of Torts, 2d, sec. 429, Negligence in Doing Work Which is Accepted in Reliance on the Employer's Doing the Work Himself.

122. 430 A.2d 649, quoting *Bing v. Thunig*, 163 N.Y.S.2d 3, 11, 143 N.E.2d 3, 8 n. 3 (1957).

123. See note 122.124. See e.g., *Thompson v. Nason Hospital*, 527 Pa. 330, 591 A.2d 703 (1991); *McClellan v. Health Maintenance Organization of Pennsylvania*, 413 Pa. Super. 128, 604 A.2d 1053 (1992).

125. See e.g., *Menzie v. Windham Community Memorial Hospital*, 774 F. Supp. 91 (D. Conn. 1991); *Stipp v. Kim*, 874 F.Supp. 663 (E.D. Pa. 1995).

126. *Richmond County Hospital Authority v. Brown*, 361 S.E.2d 164 (1987); *Gilbert v. Sycamore Munici-*

In addition to recognizing new causes and expanding liability in the realm of medical malpractice, the court also rendered an important decision in the realm of products liability, which was at the vanguard of the tort law boom of the 1970s.[127] As we saw in the last chapter, the Superior Court's decision in *Jarnot v. Ford Motor Co.* signaled the demise of vertical privity, which generally prohibited a purchaser injured by a defective product from recovering in a warranty action against the product's manufacturer. Yet even after the Supreme Court formally abolished vertical privity in *Kassab et ux. v. Central Soya*,[128] horizontal privity, the other principle obstacle to recovery, remained intact. Horizontal privity, as noted, prohibited a nonpurchaser from recovering for breach of warranty against either the seller or manufacturer of a defective product. Recovery was denied on the basis that the nonpurchaser had no contractual relationship with anyone involved in the manufacture or sale of the product.

Fourteen years after its decision in *Jarnot*, the Superior Court abolished horizontal privity. In *Salvador v. I.H. English of Philadelphia, Inc.*,[129] an employee was injured by the explosion of a steam boiler purchased by his employer. The employee instituted an action against the manufacturer of the boiler asserting breach of an implied warranty of fitness.[130] In granting the manufacturer's preliminary objections to this claim, the trial court relied on *Hochgertel v. Canada Dry Corp.*,[131] in which the Supreme Court ruled that an employee could not recover for injuries sustained when a bottle purchased by his employer exploded. The basis of the *Hochgertel* decision was that the employee, not having purchased the bottle, lacked horizontal privity with the manufacturer.

On appeal, Salvador argued that *Hochgertel* had been implicitly overruled by the Supreme Court's decision in *Kassab*. A five-judge majority of the court agreed. The court began by examining the two Supreme Court decisions. *Hochgertel*, it noted, was based on the rationale that "to grant such an extension of the warranty [to an employee] would in effect render the manufacturer a guarantor of his product and impose liability in all such accident cases even if the utmost degree of care were exercised." However, the court stated, ever since the adoption of strict liability under Section 402A, Pennsylvania law has indeed regarded a manufacturer as a guarantor of his product. Thus, the rationale of *Hochgertel* "no longer finds support in the law."[132] The court then turned to *Kassab*, in which the Supreme Court held that, because the adoption of Section 402A authorized a tort action against the manufacturer, it would be anomalous to

---

*pal Hospital*, 622 N.E.2d 788 (1993); *Paintsville Hospital v. Rose*, 683 S.W.2d 255 (1985); *Hardy v. Brantley*, 471 So.2d 358 (Miss. 1985); *Martell v. St. Charles Hospital*, 523 N.Y.S.2d 342 (N.Y. Sup. Ct. 1987); *Clark v. Southview Hospital Family & Health Center*, 628 N.E.2d 46 (1994); *Torrence v. Kusminsky*, 408 S.E.2d 684 (1991); *Pamperin v. Trinity Memorial Hospital*, 423 N.W.2d 848 (Wis. 1988). See also 108 Harv. L. Rev. 381; 58 ALR 5th 613; 51 ALR 4th 235.

127. See e.g., Donald J. Farge and Edward B. McDaid, "Annual Survey of the Law—Torts," 45 Pa. B.A.Q. 247, 276 ("From the sheer volume of cases reported in the various advance sheets this year, it would seem that, at the present time, the products liability controversy is the most active in the torts field.").

128. 432 Pa. 217, 246 A.2d 848 (1968).

129. 224 Pa. Super. 377, 307 A.2d 398 (1973) (Cercone, J.), affirmed, 457 Pa. 24, 319 A.2d 903 (1974). As with *Jarnot*, *Salvador* is, strictly speaking, a warranty and not a tort action. Nonetheless, it is included in the tort section of this case review because breach of warranty is rooted in tort law. See William L. Prosser, *Handbook of the Law of Torts, 3d ed.* (St. Paul: West Publishing Co., 1964), 651-52 ("While breach of warranty is basically a contract rather than a tort action, it, nevertheless, has roots which spring essentially from a tort background.").

130. The employee did not file suit in time to assert a tort claim, which was subject to a two-year statute of limitations. 42 Pa.C.S. sec. 5524. The warranty action, on the other hand was subject to a six-year statute of limitations. 42 Pa.C.S. sec. 5527.

131. 409 Pa. 610, 187 A.2d 575 (1963).

132. 307 A.2d 400, quoting *Hochgertel*.

preclude a suit for identical injuries merely because it was styled as a warranty action.[133] Since *Kassab* also held that the Uniform Commercial Code was "co-extensive with Restatement Section 402a in the case of product liability," and thus eliminated vertical privity, the court reasoned that the code must also have eliminated horizontal privity. "Plaintiff's right of recovery," the court held, "should not be made to depend on a narrow distinction between horizontal privity and vertical privity, which is a distinction without a difference as far as concerns lack of contractual relationship. If either horizontal or vertical privity is lacking between plaintiff and defendant, the result is the same: a lack of contractual relationship."[134] Moreover, the court continued:

> Since such lack of contractual relationship was held in *Kassab* not to be a bar to recovery in assumpsit for breach of implied warranty, we determine that in this case as well, plaintiff-employee is not barred from his assumpsit action based on implied warranty. Since plaintiff's rights and defendant's liabilities in an assumpsit action can now be determined, as stated in the *Kassab* decision, in a scope co-extensive with that of Section 402A, the basis of the *Hochgertel* decision no longer exists. Today, the elimination of the requirement of horizontal privity would not, as it would have at the time of the *Hochgertel* decision, impose upon a seller any greater liability to the purchaser's employee than would otherwise exist in tort.[135]

On this basis, the court reinstated the employee's complaint and remanded the case to the trial court.[136] The decision was affirmed on appeal by the Supreme Court. In overruling *Hochgertel*, the court held, "*Kassab* dealt with only vertical privity. The Superior Court nevertheless concluded that *Kassab*'s rationale likewise required the abolition of the requirement of horizontal privity in breach of warranty cases. We believe the Superior Court is correct."[137] Thus, fourteen years after the Superior Court's assault on privity began in *Jarnot*, it was completed in *Salvador*.[138]

### DOMESTIC RELATIONS

Like its work in criminal and tort law, the court's work in family law was marked by a willingness to reconsider long-standing rules and principles. In 1973, for instance, the court overturned a rule backed by more than a century of precedent. The rule at issue denied to wives the right to recover for loss of consortium resulting from injuries to their husbands.[139] Husbands, on the other hand, had always been able to recover for

---

133. 307 A.2d 401, citing *Kassab* ("[W]ith Pennsylvania's adoption of Restatement 402a, the same demands of legal symmetry which once supported privity now destroy it.").

134. 307 A.2d 401.

135. See note 133. Although the employee's action would have been barred by the two-year statute of limitations if it had been commenced in tort, the court noted that it was timely under the four-year statute of limitations applicable to warranty actions.

136. See note 133. Judge Spaulding concurred in the result, and Judges Watkins and Jacobs dissented.

137. 457 Pa. 24, 31, 319 A.2d 903, 907 (1974).

138. The case has been cited repeatedly: *Williams v. West Penn Power Co.*, 502 Pa. 557, 467 A.2d 811 (1983); *Fredly v. Crandall Filling Machinery, Inc.*, 234 Pa. Super. 530, 342 A.2d 757 (1975); *Hahn v. Atlantic Richfield Co.*, 625 F.2d 1095 (3d Cir. Pa. 1980); *Hafer v. Firestone*, 523 F.Supp. 1216 (E.D. Pa. 1981); *Morrow v. New Moon Homes*, 548 P.2d 279 (Alaska 1976). The case is discussed in John E. Murray Jr., "Products Liability—Another Word," 35 U. Pitt. L. Rev. 255, 257-61 (1973); 49 ALR 5th 1, 17 ALR 3d 1010; and 37 ALR 2d 703.

139. "Consortium" was defined by the common law as the aid, affection, comfort, and society a wife was expected to render to her husband. It implied both conjugal and domestic factors.

loss of consortium. The continuing validity of the common law rule was called into question by Pennsylvania's 1971 ratification of the Equal Rights Amendment to the Pennsylvania Constitution. The amendment provided, "[e]quality of rights under the law shall not be denied or abridged in the Commonwealth of Pennsylvania because of the sex of the individual."[140]

In *Hopkins v. Blanco*,[141] a husband had been injured allegedly as the result of medical malpractice, but the trial court held that his wife's claim for consortium was not recognized by Pennsylvania law. The question on appeal was whether the Equal Rights Amendment mandated abolition of the common law rule denying consortium damages to wives. The Superior Court began its analysis of this question by explaining the basis for the common law rule:

> The Commonwealth's refusal to extend the right to consortium to women is founded upon the common law rationale that a woman-spouse was her husband's property. "She owed him duties much the same as did a servant his master. If he by injury to her suffered a loss of some feudal service owing to him by her, he and he alone—for she was too inferior a subject to have any such right, much less the privilege to assert it—was allowed to sue to recover, just as he would sue for injuries done to his cattle. He for all technical purposes, owned her at common law. . . ."[142]

Yet, the court found that the Equal Rights Amendment clearly altered this rule by abolishing sexual discrimination. Thus, there were only two choices. "[T]his Court must either abolish the husband's right to consortium or extend the right to the wife." In order to determine "which route to take," the court examined cases from other jurisdictions. Following this review, the court concluded, "[o]ur neighboring states have logically expressed the belief that consortium is a valuable right in today's world. Their reasoning is persuasive and compels us to extend this valuable right of consortium to women. The alternative method of equalizing the rights of men and women—abolishing the common law right to consortium—would merely compound the wrongful denial of the right."[143] In further support of its conclusion, the court relied on the fact that "courts have increasingly recognized that tort law must protect the individual's interest in protecting one's essentially emotional interests."[144] The court then remanded the wife's consortium claim for trial.[145] On appeal, the Supreme Court affirmed, holding, "[w]e agree that if the husband may recover for loss of consortium, to deny the wife an equal right would be invalid under the Pennsylvania Constitution."[146] The *Blanco* rule remains the law in Pennsylvania[147] and has been cited by commentators[148] and courts in other jurisdictions.[149] This case had its counterpart in a long string of cases which

---

140. Pa. Constitution, art. I, sec. 28, Prohibition against denial or abridgement of equality of rights because of sex, adopted May 18, 1971.

141. 224 Pa. Super. 116, 302 A.2d 855 (1973) (Hoffman, J.).

142. 302 A.2d 856, citing *Neuberg v. Bobowicz*, 401 Pa. 146, 150, 162 A.2d 662 (1960).

143. 302 A.2d 857-58.

144. 302 A.2d 858.

145. 302 A.2d 859. The court also consolidated wife's claim, which had been filed separately, with that of her husband for trial.

146. 457 Pa. 90, 320 A.2d 139, 140 (1974).

147. See e.g., *Buttermore v. Aliquippa Hospital*, 522 Pa. 325, 561 A.2d 733 (1989); *Manzitti v. Amsler*, 379 Pa. Super. 454, 550 A.2d 537 (1988); *McHugh v. Litvin*, 379 Pa. Super. 95, 549 A.2d 922 (1988).

148. 90 ALR 3d 158; 36 ALR 3d 900.

149. See e.g., *Quinones v. United States*, 492 F.2d 1269 (3d Cir. Pa. 1974); *Rodriguez v. Bethlehem Steel Corp.*, 525 P.2d 669 (1974).

rectified sexual bias in custody, support, divorce, age at marriage, and domestic relations in general.

Five years after *Blanco*, the court also terminated a long-standing practice that some have referred to as "legalized kidnapping." This practice arose, in relation to Pennsylvania, when the parents of a child divorced and one of the parents, who lived out-of-state, received a custody award in his or her state of residence. At some point, the child would go on a scheduled visitation trip to the home of the noncustodial parent in Pennsylvania. The noncustodial parent would then decide not to return the child at the end of the visitation period. Instead, he or she would file a petition for custody in Pennsylvania.[150] Prior to 1977, this tactic was generally sanctioned by Pennsylvania courts, which assumed jurisdiction and adjudicated the custody petition regardless of the prior decree entered in the custodial parent's state and despite the child's de minimis contacts with Pennsylvania.[151] This interstate "child snatching"[152] also occurred in the intrastate context, where children were taken across county lines and a new trial court would assume jurisdiction regardless of an existing custody order in another county.[153] In both situations, Pennsylvania law encouraged parents to transport children across state and county lines in order to avoid adverse custody orders.[154] In order to prevent this practice, the Pennsylvania Legislature enacted the Uniform Child Custody Jurisdiction Act (UCCJA) in 1977.[155] The purpose of the UCCJA was to limit custody jurisdiction to courts of "the state where the child has his home or where there are other strong contacts with the child and his family."[156] The following year, the legislature enacted the Commonwealth Child Custody Jurisdiction Act, which limited custody jurisdiction to courts of the child's home county and thus applied to intrastate custody disputes, the same provisions the UCCJA applied to interstate disputes.[157]

Even before these acts became effective, however, the Superior Court abandoned the prior jurisdictional approach to custody disputes. *In re Custody of Sagan*[158] involved a custody petition filed on July 1, 1977, ten months before the effective date of the UCCJA. In *Sagan*, a custody award was entered in New York in favor of the mother on December 24, 1975. On September 1, 1976, the parties' son traveled from New York to visit with his father, a resident of Lawrence County, Pennsylvania. The following day, the father filed a petition for custody in the Lawrence County Court of Common Pleas and thereafter kept the child with him, although the visitation was scheduled to end on September 7, 1976. In November and December, hearings were held on the father's custody petition, and on February 10, 1977, the court awarded custody to the father.

---

150. For excellent discussions of this practice, see Frederick N. Frank, "The End of Legal Kidnapping in Pennsylvania: The Development of a Decided Public Policy," 25 Vill. L. Rev. 784, 790 (1979-80); and Comment, "Legalized Kidnapping of Children by their Parents," 80 Dick. L. Rev. 305 (1976).

151. A good example is *In re Custody of Irizarry*, 195 Pa. Super. 104, 169 A.2d 307 (1961), cert. denied, 368 U.S. 928 (1961) (The Superior Court held that the child's presence for visitation constituted residence sufficient to confer jurisdiction on Pennsylvania courts.) Although custody orders were technically subject to the Full Faith and Credit Clause, many courts, including the United States Supreme Court, found ways to avoid application of the clause. See *Ford v. Ford*, 371 U.S. 187 (1962) (holding that the custody decree lacked finality); and *May v. Anderson*, 345 U.S. 528 (1953) (holding the custody decree invalid).

152. Frederick N. Frank, "The End of Legal Kidnapping in Pennsylvania," 790.

153. See *Commonwealth ex rel. Freed v. Freed*, 172 Pa. Super. 276, 93 A.2d 863 (1953).

154. Frank, "The End of Legal Kidnapping in Pennsylvania," 790.

155. 11 PS 2301 et seq.

156. UCCJA, *Commissioners' Prefatory Note*, reprinted in 9 Uniform Laws Ann. 111, 114 (1979). The act defined the "home" state as the one in which the child resided for six or more consecutive months or, if the child is less than six months old, since birth. 11 PS 2303.

157. 11 PS 2401 et seq.

158. 261 Pa. Super. 384, 396 A.2d 450 (1978) (Jacobs, J.).

On appeal, the mother argued that the Lawrence County court lacked jurisdiction over the child and, therefore, was powerless to alter the custody award entered in New York. In a brief opinion, the Superior Court agreed. The father, it noted, "would have us equate residence with mere physical presence within the jurisdictional borders, without reference to the understanding which the parents have with respect to the duration of that presence."[159] Although the court acknowledged that prior case law supported father's claim, it nonetheless concluded:

> The experience of recent years, however, has demonstrated that the most appropriate way to reconcile this dilemma of the state's *parens patriae* concern for the welfare of those children living within its boundaries, on the one hand, and "legalized abduction" on the other is to restrict jurisdiction. . . .

Consequently, we hold that unless there is evidence that a minor child has been abandoned or physically abused, where another state's court has awarded custody to the parent domiciled in that other state, and that parent has allowed the child to *visit temporarily* with the other parent in Pennsylvania, the child is not a resident of Pennsylvania, nor does Pennsylvania have a sufficient interest in that child's well being to merit the assumption of jurisdiction by its courts to relitigate the matter of custody.[160]

On this basis, the court vacated the order awarding custody to the father.[161] In a footnote, the court also noted that the result would have been the same under the provisions of the UCCJA.[162] As this footnote suggests, *Sagan* accomplished under the common law what the legislature intended to accomplish by statute, the end of "legalized kidnapping" in Pennsylvania.

In addition to rejecting dubious family law practices in *Blanco* and *Sagan*, the court clarified an important aspect of family law that had been clouded by conflicting standards. *In re Custody of Hernandez*[163] involved the appropriate standard to be applied in cases where a third party seeks custody of a child in a suit against the child's parent or parents. In *Hernandez*, a fifteen-year-old mother, while living in Florida, found herself unable to support her young child. At the suggestion of a church organization, she sent the child to live with Robert and Twila Peterson, a couple from Clearfield County, Pennsylvania, with whom the mother also had lived as a child. Eighteen months later, she and the child's father, who had recently married, sought return of their child. The Petersons refused to return the child and the parents filed a custody petition in Clearfield County, Pennsylvania. After a series of hearings, the court awarded custody to the Petersons. In so doing, the court stated, "while natural parents may have a prima facie right to custody, nevertheless, if the best interests and welfare of the child require it, custody may be placed in a non-relative."[164]

The issue on appeal was whether the court applied the correct standard. In a lengthy review, the Superior Court found that Pennsylvania courts "have used various, and it would seem inconsistent, expressions in describing the burden of proof that the third party bears" in a custody dispute with a parent.[165] According to the court:

---

159. 396 A.2d 453.
160. See note 158 (citations omitted; emphasis in original).
161. See note 158.
162. See note 158, n. 5.
163. 249 Pa. Super. 274, 376 A.2d 648 (1977) (Spaeth, J.).
164. 376 A.2d 656.
165. 376 A.2d 653.

Sometimes it has been said that the parents have a "primary right" to custody of the child, although the right is not absolute and must yield to the child's best interest. Other times it has been said that absent "compelling reasons" to the contrary, it will be "presumed" that the child's best interest will be served by being raised by its parents. Still other times it has been said that the parents have a "prima facie right to custody," which "may be forfeited if convincing reasons appear that the best interests of the child will be served by awarding custody to someone else."[166]

The court rejected the first two of these standards and found the phrase "primary right" objectionable because it "connotes a property interest as though a child were a chattel." Moreover, the remainder of the standard did not specify the evidentiary burden imposed on the third party.[167] The second standard was unacceptable because, by invoking a presumption, it mistakenly focused on the respective rights of the parties, rather than on the best interests of the child.[168] The court favored the third standard. Initially, since it afforded the parent a prima facie right to custody, this standard "properly allocates the burden of proof to the third party who is opposing the parent." Further, the requirement of "convincing reasons" focuses the trial court's attention on the best interests of the child, rather than on some characteristic of either party that the court might regard unfavorably.[169]

Applying this standard, the court found that the trial court had "depreciate[d] the parents' status" by stating only that they "may" have a prima facie right to custody. "They *do* have a prima facie right," the court emphasized.[170] Moreover, the trial court failed to recite the evidence that overcame the parents' right to custody. The court then reviewed the record and found no "convincing reasons" justifying the award to the Petersons. On this basis, the court awarded custody to the parents.[171] Three years later, the Supreme Court expressly adopted the *Hernandez* analysis,[172] and the Superior Court's opinion has become the standard for courts considering custody contests between parents and third parties. Indeed, it has been cited nearly two hundred times by Pennsylvania and federal courts,[173] law reviews,[174] and other sources.[175]

Following passage of the Juvenile Act of 1972, the court also altered long-standing practices regarding the housing of juvenile offenders in adult institutions.[176] For nearly a century before the Juvenile Act was passed, the State Correctional Institution at Camp Hill was required by statute to house and provide rehabilitation services to "all male criminals, between the ages of fifteen and twenty-five."[177] Given the age ranges specified, Camp Hill housed both juvenile and young adult offenders, and these groups were not separated. In passing the Juvenile Act of 1972, the legislature mandated, in

---

166. See note 164 (citations omitted).
167. See note 164.
168. 376 A.2d 653-54.
169. 376 A.2d 654.
170. 376 A.2d 656 (emphasis in original).
171. 376 A.2d 663. Judge Price dissented without opinion.
172. *Ellerbe v. Hooks*, 490 Pa. 363, 416 A.2d 512 (1980).
173. See e.g., *Rowles v. Rowles*, 542 Pa. 443, 668 A.2d 126 (1995); *Commonwealth ex. rel. Zaffarano v. Genaro*, 500 Pa. 256, 455 A.2d 1180 (1983); *Albright v. Commonwealth ex. rel. Fetters*, 491 Pa. 320, 421 A.2d 157 (1980); *Wiseman v. Wall*, 718 A.2d 844 (Pa. Super. 1998); *J.A.L. v. E.P.H.*, 453 Pa. Super. 78, 682 A.2d 1314 (1996).
174. 70 Va. L. Rev. 879; 54 U. Pitt. L. Rev. 211; 25 Vill. L. Rev. 752.
175. 15 ALR 5th 692; 22 ALR 4th 971.
176. Pa. Act of December 6, 1972, PL 1464, now codified at 42 Pa.C.S. sec. 6301 et seq.
177. Pa. Act of June 8, 1881, PL 63.

Section 25, that a delinquent child could be committed only to a "special facility for children operated by the Department of Justice."[178] Section 27 of the act further provided that where no separate juvenile facilities were available, children must be kept segregated from adult inmates at all times.[179] When the act was passed, Camp Hill was Pennsylvania's only "special facility for children operated by the Department of Justice," yet it did not segregate juvenile and adult offenders.

In *In re Parker v. Patton*,[180] the Superior Court considered the conflict between the Juvenile Act and the long-standing practice at Camp Hill. Following a hearing, the juvenile court ruled that Camp Hill no longer qualified as a facility for delinquent children. Reviewing this decision, the court began by noting that Pennsylvania had no institution satisfying the mandate of the Juvenile Act, and the legislature had not undertaken establishment of such an institution.[181] Thus, the court was left with the language of the Juvenile Act, and, finding its mandate clear, directed authorities at Camp Hill to undertake one of two measures: either establish separate facilities for juveniles and adults or provide for the separate use of existing facilities. "These arrangements may be difficult to achieve," the court concluded, "but they can and must be done, if the objectives of the Juvenile Act are to be presently realized in Pennsylvania."[182] Two years later, in *In the Interest of Haas*,[183] the court relied on the analysis in *Patton* to invalidate the commitment of a female juvenile offender to the State Correctional Institute at Muncy, which housed only serious adult criminals and had no rehabilitative programs or facilities with which to accommodate a juvenile. Thereafter, in 1977 the legislature amended the Juvenile Act so that it would no longer authorize commitment of a juvenile to a "special facility for children operated by the Department of Justice." The amended act authorized commitment only to institutions operated by the courts or other public authorities and approved by the Department of Public Welfare.[184] Since Camp Hill was operated by the Department of Justice, the amendment expressly prohibited commitments to that institution, and the Superior Court so held in *In the Interest of Scott W.*[185]

The Superior Court's work in the realm of juvenile delinquency was also influenced by two decisions of the United States Supreme Court. First, *In re Gault*[186] held that children involved in juvenile court proceedings must receive a number of constitutional due process protections, including notice, an opportunity to be heard, the right against self-incrimination, the right to an attorney, the right to contact witnesses, and a standard of proof equivalent to that required in adult criminal proceedings. Four years later, in *McKeiver v. Pennsylvania*,[187] the Court held that jury trials were not required in juvenile court proceedings. In a series of decisions during the 1970s, the Superior Court further developed and enunciated the scope of protections available in state juvenile court proceedings. In *In the Interest of Anderson*,[188] for instance, the court held that the Juvenile Act codified the common law rule that corpus delecti must be established before a juvenile's confession can be admitted into evidence. Two years later,

---

178. Pa. Act of December 6, 1972, sec. 25.

179. Pa. Act of December 6, 1972, sec. 27.

180. 225 Pa. Super. 217, 310 A.2d 414 (1973) (Cercone, J.).

181. 310 A.2d 415. The court noted, "The debate that rages over Camp Hill is reminiscent of Mark Twain's observation that, 'Everybody talks about the weather, but no one does anything about it.'"

182. 310 A.2d 416.

183. 234 Pa. Super. 422, 339 A.2d 98 (1975) (Hoffman, J.).

184. The Juvenile Act was amended by Pa. Act of August 3, 1977, PL 155.

185. 250 Pa. Super. 226, 378 A.2d 909 (1977) (Cercone, J.).

186. 387 U.S. 1 (1967).

187. 403 U.S. 528 (1971).

188. 227 Pa. Super. 439, 313 A.2d 260 (1973) (Watkins, J.).

President Judge William F. Cercone presided from 1979 to 1983, during the transition to an expanded Superior Court.

in *Commonwealth v. McNaughton*,[189] the court held that a juvenile could not be adjudicated delinquent based upon inadmissible hearsay evidence. Finally, in *In Interest of Dreslinski*,[190] the court held that reasonable doubt is the appropriate standard of proof to be applied in delinquency proceedings.

## RELIEVING THE CASELOAD CRISIS

These and many other cases are indicative of the changes in criminal, tort and family law that contributed to the unprecedented caseload increases of the 1970s. By the middle of the decade, with the Superior Court overwhelmed, the deficiencies of the Constitution of 1968 became apparent. Most importantly, by freezing the court at seven judges, the constitution prevented the most obvious solution to the case load crisis, legislation increasing the number of judges. As it stood, a constitutional amendment was required to authorize the legislature to expand the court, yet for such an amendment to be submitted to the voters, the constitution further provided that it must first pass two consecutive sessions of the legislature.[191] With few other options, this laborious process was initiated on June 23, 1977, when a joint resolution proposing a constitutional amendment was introduced into the legislature. The proposed amendment began in the House, where it was designated HB 1395 and sponsored by Representatives K. Leroy Irvis, James J. Manderino, Norman S. Berson, Anthony J. Scirica, William H. Yohn, and Harry A. Englehart.[192] Its purpose was to amend Article V, Section 3,

189. 252 Pa. Super. 302, 381 A.2d 929 (1977) (Hoffman, J.).
190. 254 Pa. Super. 539, 386 A.2d 81 (1978) (Cercone, J.).
191. Pa. Constitution of 1968, art. XI.
192. *History of House Bills*, 1978, A-186.

of the constitution to provide that the Superior Court "shall consist of the number of judges, which shall be not less than seven judges, and have such jurisdiction as shall be provided by this Constitution or by the General Assembly."[193] On April 18, 1978, the House passed this proposed amendment by a vote of 120 to 70.[194] The following day, the amendment was introduced into the Senate by Senators Edward M. Early and Michael P. Schaefer. Designated SB 3, the proposed amendment was passed by a vote of forty-two to zero on June 12, 1978.[195] Having passed one session of the legislature, the amendment required passage by a second session before it could be submitted to the voters.

In the meantime, relief of the caseload crisis became a significant issue outside of the legislature. The Pennsylvania Bar Association, in particular, brought to the crisis the same energy that it had earlier focused on the drive to reform the judiciary article of the constitution.[196] In early 1977, the bar planned an extensive study of the operations of the appellate judiciary. However, the proposed study was delayed by the death of the bar's executive director, Frederick H. Bolton, who was one of two men designated to lead the study.[197] As the new executive director was preparing to launch the study, the *Philadelphia Inquirer* began publishing a series of editorials that were highly critical of the state's appellate operations, particularly those of the Supreme Court.[198]

In February 1978, in the midst of the intense publicity generated by the *Inquirer's* coverage, the bar organized the Special Committee on the Appellate Courts to conduct the proposed study. The committee was composed of ten prominent lawyers. According to Louis J. Goffman, president of the state bar, these lawyers "would be listened to above any tumult."[199] In May 1978, the committee submitted an interim report to Chief Justice Michael J. Eagen in which it recommended a number of measures. The most important of these was expansion of the Superior Court. In order to increase manpower while the amendment process continued, the committee recommended assigning senior judges, i.e., those who had reached the mandatory retirement age of seventy, to sit on the Superior Court on an interim basis. The committee also urged that the court sit in panels of three, rather than the current practice of the entire court sitting in judgment of each case.[200] On May 9, 1978, consistent with this latter recommendation, the Supreme Court utilized its constitutional role as head of the unified judicial system and ordered the Superior Court to begin sitting in three-judge panels.[201] This measure was necessary, the Supreme Court concluded, to address the "exceedingly heavy volume of appeals coming to the Superior Court, presently at the rate of 3,000 per year, and the emergency created thereby."[202] On September 1, 1978, as a result of the Supreme Court's order, the Superior Court stopped sitting en banc, i.e., as an entire body,

---

193. The proposed amendment is set forth in full in *Laws of Pennsylvania*, 1978, 1427.

194. *History of House Bills*, 1978, A-186. On February 15, when the amendment was first considered for final passage, it was defeated by a vote of 101 to 86. The same day, however, the vote was reconsidered and the amendment was postponed. Thereafter, it was postponed until the vote of April 18. Although the basis of the significant resistance is not entirely clear, subsequent events indicate that a number of legislators were concerned with the cost of court expansion. This concern is discussed infra.

195. *History of House Bills*, 1978, A-186. The amendment was filed in the Office of the Secretary of the Commonwealth on June 20, 1978.

196. The bar's early efforts to address the caseload crisis are chronicled in "Pennsylvania's Legal Crisis," *Pennsylvania Lawyer*, March 15, 1979, 6-9, 24.

197. Frederick H. Bolton died in August 1977.

198. "Pennsylvania's Legal Crisis," 8.

199. "Pennsylvania's Legal Crisis," 7.

200. "Pennsylvania's Legal Crisis," 8, discussing the interim report.

201. The court began sitting in panels in September. The panels frequently included a specially assigned common pleas judge.

202. The Supreme Court's order is quoted in James E. Rowley, comp., *100 Years of Justice: The Superior Court of Pennnsylvania's First Century: 1895-1995* (Superior Court of Pennsylvania, 1995), 7-8.

for the first time in its eighty-three-year history. Thereafter, the court was authorized to convene en banc only in particularly difficult or contentious cases.[203] However, since each of the seven judges still had to decide the same number of cases whether sitting in panels or en banc, the panel system was intended only to allow the Superior Court to *hear* more cases. Yet the court's major problem was the inability to *decide* the cases. To resolve this problem, further reform was needed, and the bar's special committee continued its examination of the appellate judiciary.

On September 1, 1978, the committee released its final report. In addition to reiterating its earlier recommendation that the Superior Court be "increased substantially in size," the committee also proposed a number of other changes. It recommended, for instance, that the appellate courts sit in a single location at which all judicial and administrative functions would be performed. Significantly, the committee also recommended relieving the Supreme Court of its duty to hear appeals except those to which it consents. The committee believed that this proposal, which was analogous to the certiorari system of the United States Supreme Court, would allow the state high court to concentrate on appeals that presented significant legal issues. This recommendation had tremendous ramifications for the Superior Court, because it sought to impose upon the court the vast majority of Pennsylvania's appellate workload. The committee further recommended establishing timetables for the efficient adjudication of appeals, and reactivating the Judicial Council, which would assist the courts in their administrative duties. Finally, the committee endorsed creation of a merit selection system for judges.[204] This proposal, which would have established an advisory body to evaluate judicial candidates and submit a limited list of names to the governor, was another step in the continuing process to limit the governor's appointment authority. Prior to 1975, gubernatorial appointments were subject to Senate confirmation only if the Senate was in session at the time of the appointment. When it was not in session, the appointee automatically assumed the bench. In 1975, voters approved a new appointment system, which required Senate confirmation by a two-thirds vote of all judicial appointments.[205]

Immediately after submitting its final report, the committee began a statewide campaign to see that its recommendations were implemented. First on its list was lobbying the legislature to approve the proposed constitutional amendment authorizing the expansion of the Superior Court.[206] The committee's goal was to have the proposed amendment placed on the ballot at the general election on November 6, 1979. Leaders of the state bar, including bar association president Goffman, also began to publicly advocate the proposed amendment. They toured the state urging their local counterparts to speak out in favor of the amendment, and they promised support from the state organization for local pro-amendment efforts. In the meantime, Chief Justice Eagen lobbied legislators. Numerous members of the legislative, executive, and judicial branches of government also joined the effort. In an address to the Thirteenth Annual Seminar of the Conference of County Bar Officers, Judge Cercone advocated the proposed amendment and stated that the size of the Superior Court might have to be tripled to meet the caseload growth. Judge Wieand echoed Cercone's concern and stated that when he joined the court, he found its "workload truly staggering."[207] Support for the amendment also came from groups with a wide array of political, economic, and social interests, and from a number of media sources.[208]

---

203. The composition of the en banc Superior Court is set forth in Pa. R.A.P. 3103, Court En Banc.

204. "Pennsylvania's Legal Crisis," 8-9.

205. Jonathan P. Nase, "Pennsylvania's Appellate Judges, 1969-1994," 33 Duq. L. Rev. 377 (1995).

206. See note 198.

207. "Cercone Calls on PBA to Back Larger Court," *Pennsylvania Lawyer*, March 15, 1979, 9.

208. See *Report on Enabling Legislation* reprinted in the *Pennsylvania Law Weekly*, March 31, 1980, 6-7.

These efforts received a boost on November 8, 1978, when the American Judicature Society (AJS) released its high-profile report on the condition of Pennsylvania's appellate judiciary.[209] The following statement of its project director suggested the scope of the examination conducted by AJS:

> The purpose of this study was to review and make recommendations with regard to the constitutional, statutory and rule provisions relating to the appellate courts and the appellate process; the administration of the appellate courts and the judicial system of the commonwealth; the internal operating procedures of the appellate courts and their case management practices.[210]

In its lengthy report, AJS reviewed the operation and workload of each court and issued a number of recommendations. As to the Superior Court, it found "a great amount of work" and a number of procedural inadequacies.[211] AJS found that, although statistics were available for the court's current workload, there were inadequate figures available to determine its backlog, which must have been "tremendous" given the sheer volume of appeals. In the end, the only evidence of the extent of the backlog was a statement by President Judge Jacobs on July 31, 1978, that the court had not rendered opinions in forty-one cases dating from 1976 and that its docket contained one thousand cases that had been argued but not resolved by opinion.[212] Based on this sketchy evidence, AJS concluded that "the Court's real backlog is not in unargued and unsubmitted cases, but in cases that have been argued or submitted on briefs and in which opinions have not yet been handed down."[213] The report also surveyed published opinions and found that the time between submission and decision averaged between ten and one-half and fourteen and one-half months.[214] In order to reduce the delay and backlog, AJS recommended the establishment of a central location for the court, which would foster cooperation and communication between the judges. It also endorsed the Supreme Court's order of May 9, 1978, directing the Superior Court to sit in three-judge panels. Finally, the report found that the use of senior judges was a worthwhile, although partial, solution.[215]

AJS then turned to "a major difficulty with the Pennsylvania system," namely, that the Superior Court handled the bulk of the appellate caseload while constitutionally limited to seven members. "It is humanly impossible," the report noted, "for seven persons, no matter how able, to perform this task as is evidenced by the fact that other states of similar size have far more intermediate appellate judges than Pennsylvania. Ohio, for example, has 38; Illinois 34; New Jersey 22; Missouri 24; Florida 28; and Michigan 18."[216] Finding that "[o]nly one ultimate solution is possible," the report then recommended a constitutional amendment authorizing the legislature to increase the size of the Superior Court. Based on 1978 figures, AJS concluded that the court needed

---

209. As noted, this report was commissioned by the Supreme Court.

210. Cover letter to the *Report of the AJS*, submitted by Mayo H. Steigler, November 8, 1978.

211. *Report of the AJS*, 15.

212. *Report of the AJS*, 15. President Judge Jacobs indicated that opinions were prepared but not yet filed in thirty-one of the forty-one cases dating from 1976.

213. *Report of the AJS*, 16.

214. *Report of the AJS*, 17-18. AJS concluded that this delay was caused by a variety of factors, the most important of which was the volume of cases filed. Other causes included the "excessive" number of dissenting and concurring opinions filed by judges of the court and the fact that their offices were "scattered over the state."

215. *Report of the AJS*, 18-19.

216. *Report of the AJS*, 19.

sixteen or seventeen judges, so that five panels could sit regularly with two or three judges in reserve.[217]

AJS also made a number of additional recommendations that would have affected the Superior Court. These recommendations included promulgation of a rule providing for publication only of opinions of precedential value, much improved record-keeping, focusing on caseload statistics, creation of a central legal staff to coordinate the work of the court, and transfer of two or three of the judges' four law clerks to the new central staff. The report also recommended that the president judge of each appellate court be selected by other members of the court, rather than by tenure. Moreover, like the bar association, AJS recommended making the Supreme Court a certiorari court, establishing a merit selection system for all appellate judges,[218] and reactivating the Judicial Council.[219] Finally, the report urged consolidation of the Superior and Commonwealth Courts on the basis that "they could operate far more efficiently as a single court, there could be more unity in the State's entire body of law [and] more collegiality in the judicial system as a whole."[220]

## THE AMENDMENT OF *1979*

The efforts of the state bar and many others, combined with the publicity generated by the *Inquirer* articles and the AJS report, had significant ramifications for the proposed amendment when it was resubmitted to the legislature on January 16, 1979. Beginning in the Senate, the amendment sped through first and second consideration, and it was submitted for third and final consideration on March 12, 1979. Prior to the final vote, Senator Michael O'Pake urged his colleagues to vote in the affirmative. He noted that the Superior Court's caseload had increased nearly ten-fold between 1953 and 1978, and he emphasized that as of July 1978, the court had 1,140 undecided cases remaining on its docket. "As long as the total number of judges is kept at seven," he argued, "[the court] will never be able to keep up with the backlog."[221] The senators apparently agreed with O'Pake, and they passed the amendment by a vote of forty-seven to zero. The amendment was then submitted to the House. On March 26, 1979, a mere two weeks after Senate passage, it was submitted for a final vote and passed by a margin of 107 to 89. Thus, although it took one year to pass the legislature for the first time, the amendment passed the second time in just over two months. The high-profile campaign to expedite passage through the legislature then focused on the electorate, and the results were similar. On November 6, 1979, the amendment was passed by a vote of 793,474 to 703,736.[222]

With the amendment authorizing expansion ratified, the question then became how many judges the legislature should add to the Superior Court. Recommendations

217. *Report of the AJS*, 20. The report also cautioned that "doctrinal unity" among the panels could be assured only by rotating the membership of the panels.

218. *Report of the AJS*, iii (Summary of Major Recommendations). Despite the AJS recommendation, and similar proposals made by the bar and other organizations, the legislature and the voters showed little interest in a merit selection system.

219. *Report of the AJS*, 55.

220. *Report of the AJS*, 32. The AJS report also made a number of detailed recommendations regarding case flow management in the appellate judiciary. *Report of the AJS*, 35-54.

221. *Senate Legislative Journal*, Pennsylvania General Assembly, March 12, 1979, 284. Senator Henry G. Hager also supported the amendment, but only "to keep it moving through the legislative and electoral process." Hager's preference was a bill he introduced a month earlier to create a separate criminal court of appeals. He also noted that former Judge Robert Woodside supported his bill.

222. *History of Senate Bills*, 1979, A-1.

varied a great deal. In his speech to the Conference of County Bar Officers, Judge Cercone suggested the possibility that the court needed twenty-one judges to handle its yearly caseload.[223] AJS recommended an increase to sixteen or seventeen judges.[224] On March 21, 1980, Sidney L. Krawitz, president of the Pennsylvania Bar Association, informed the House Appropriations Committee that "the statistics on the caseload in Pennsylvania suggest very strongly that we need a total of thirty-eight, and not seven, judges on the Superior Court."[225] Krawitz also submitted to the Appropriations Committee a report of the bar association's Subcommittee on Enabling Legislation for the Superior Court. The purpose of the report was "to provide to the legislature and the people of Pennsylvania the recommendation of the PBA as to the appropriate size to which the Superior Court should be increased."[226] The subcommittee relied on the AJS standard of forty-five opinions per judge per year to arrive at its recommendation. Utilizing the 1978 figure of 1,736 majority opinions filed by the Superior Court, divided by the workload recommended by AJS, the subcommittee determined that the court needed thirty-eight judges to handle its duties. However, in light of "cost considerations," the subcommittee limited its recommendation to a minimum of twenty-five new judges. "Anything less tha[n] this number," the report concluded, "will require the use of judges temporarily assigned from the ranks of senior and retired judges. This stop-gap system should not be continued except as an emergency device."[227]

## *HB 2000*

It is unclear how long the legislature considered these various recommendations, but the legislation authorized by the amendment proceeded rapidly. On November 26, 1979, twenty days after the amendment was approved, a bill to add eight judges to the court was introduced in the House. The bill, designated HB 2000, was sponsored by Representatives Berson, Manderino, and Scirica, who also sponsored HB 1395, and by Representatives Warren H. Spencer, Matthew J. Ryan, and William D. Hutchinson.[228] Just three days after it was introduced, the bill was submitted for final passage in the House. Prior to the vote, Representative Jeffrey Piccola offered a last-minute amendment that would have increased the court to nine, rather than fifteen judges. According to Piccola, this amendment would have permitted the court to sit in three panels of three while saving a significant portion of the $2.4 million dollars the increase proposed by HB 2000 would cost.[229] Representative Warren H. Spencer then rose in opposition to the amendment. "Our intermediate courts," he noted, "consist of 9 in the Commonwealth Court and 7 in the Superior, a total of 16. This compares with California that has 56 intermediate judges in the appellate courts; Texas, 47; Ohio, 38; Illinois, 34; and little New Jersey, 27."[230] He also indicated that the Superior Court had a backlog of 2,500 cases. "The eight additional judges were done after careful study." He concluded, "It has the approval of all parties involved, including the appellate courts, and I respectfully

223. See "Pennsylvania's Legal Crisis," 9.

224. *Report of the AJS*, 20.

225. Krawitz's statement is reprinted in the *Pennsylvania Law Journal*, March 31, 1980, 1, 6.

226. *Report on Enabling Legislation*, 6.

227. *Report on Enabling Legislation*, 7.

228. *History of House Bills*, 1979, A-249.

229. *House Legislative Journal*, Pennsylvania General Assembly, November 29, 1979, 2455. Piccola noted that HB 2000 "will only be a stopgap measure unless we reform the jurisdictional system of our appellate court system and make the Supreme Court a court of certiorari." He did not explain how the Superior Court would cope with the dramatic caseload increase that would have been caused if the Supreme Court became a certiorari court.

230. *House Leg. Journal*, November 29, 1979, 2455-56.

*Legislation*  1980 — Act 63    *Vol II No 25*

PAGE 4    PENNSYLVANIA LAW JOURNAL, JUNE 23, 1980

# Thornburgh Signs Ct. Expansion Bill, Says Help is Finally on the Way

### By FRANK CHRISTOPHER
*Staff Writer*

HARRISBURG — Commenting that his function — affixing his signature — was the easiest part of the entire operation, Gov. Thornburgh signed legislation creating eight new judges for Superior Court. It became Act 63.

Chief Justice Michael J. Eagen of the Supreme Court and President Judge William F. Cercone of Superior Court took part in the bill-signing ceremonies at the Governor's reception room.

Gov. Thornburgh said the measure, which stemmed from a constitutional referendum, brings "relief to Superior Court in particular and the entire judicial system in general."

### Backlog Still Growing

The Governor pointed out that in spite of accelerated efforts of the present Superior Court complement, there exists a backlog of 4500 cases — and more coming.

He added that this creates a delay in the dispensation of justice and a major concern to those in and out of the judicial system.

### Merit Selection Slated

The selection process — for the eight new judgeships — "is very important to me," the Governor observed. He added that he would be guided by the recommendations of his Merit Selection Commission in making those appointments.

Speaking directly to Judge Cercone, the Governor commented that "help is on the way." Echoing the sentiments expressed by Chief Justice Eagen before a Joint House-Senate hearing earlier this year, he said, "It's a good day for the judicial system."

In addition to the legislators who sponsored and guided H.B. 2000 through the General Assembly, Pennsylvania Bar Association President Sidney L. Krawitz and State Court Administrator Alexander F. Barbieri took part in the ceremony.

### Supreme Court Jurisdiction

Expansion of the Superior Court bench removes a substantial impediment to pending legislation that would make the Supreme Court one of discretionary jurisdiction. This has been a fond hope of Chief Justice Eagen for many years. He has indicated his intention to work toward that objective — even beyond his scheduled retirement next September, if necessary.

Prior to attending the Act 63 ceremonies, he appeared before the Senate Judiciary Committee, which was considering legislation outlining the jurisdiction of the high court.

### Senate Follows House

The committee speeded up the legislative process by focusing its attention on a bill of similar intent which already had cleared the House. H.B. 2184 contained all of the provisions that were in S.B. 1207 to delineate the jurisdiction of the Supreme Court.

In the course of its deliberations, however, the Senate Judiciary Committee deleted language requiring the court to hear matters prescribed by general rule and then reported H.B. 2184 to the Senate floor for action.

## CCH Offers New Sales Guide To Federal Tax Requirements

CHICAGO — To assist salespersons in keeping posted on current federal taxation law as it applies to them both professionally and personally, Commerce Clearing House has published the *1980 Tax Guide for Sales Representatives.*

CCH noted that from its inception in 1913, the Federal Income Tax Code has increased in size and complexity to the extent it now affects many of the common activities that make up our daily lives. Many people now keep a record of where they eat, how much gas they buy and whom they entertain because the Internal Revenue Service may require a detailed account of such events if an audit is made of an individual's taxes.

### Business, Personal Records

Salespeople are particularly burdened with record-keeping requirements that involve making a distinction between travel and entertainment expenses that are business-related and those that are personal. They must pay quarterly estimated taxes, which take the place of an employee's withholding taxes, but the quarterly payments may be on money yet to be earned.

The 168-page *1980 Tax Guide for Sales Representatives* provides the sales person with a clear, concise explanation of what expenses qualify as business expenses and how to keep acceptable records of them. Topics range from conventions to traffic tickets and from business is hired. Also, the book covers the routine deductions and credits with which all taxpayers are concerned, CCH said.

### Help Come April

With this book as a reference tool, salespersons will be able to take advantage of the deductions and credits to which they are entitled and thus alleviate the burden of digging for tax records in April.

### Examples Given

The book includes a number of examples scattered throughout the text, in addition to comprehensive examples at the end. Some of the examples include completed IRS forms, but they should be examined with the realization they reflect the tax law as it applies to the 1979 tax year. In the event salespersons are filing for a year other than 1979, they should examine an official IRS form for that year and make the necessary adjustments.

The appendix includes nine checklists covering categories such as taxable income, nontaxable income, and deductions. These should be checked for items not specifically covered in the text. The appendix also includes a list of abbreviations and acronyms used in the guide.

## Human Rel. Comm. Checking Legality of Anti-Bias Bill

### By ROBIN ENRIGHT

## National News

WASHINGTON, D.C.—The U.S. that incriminating statements ma while a defendant is incarcerate prosecution. Chief Justice Burge: Brennan, Stewart, Powell and Ste ion. Dissenting in the case wer Rehnquist. Billy Gale Henry wa: tially on the basis of incriminatin FBI informant Edward Nichols, Henry's conviction, the court note uation in which a defendant is n statements without counsel prese ment right to counsel.

—Man-made life forms may be pa Supreme Court decision by Chief eral Electric microbiologist Anar perbug" bacterium that ravenous case rested on the patentability nature or which is created by hu tion being a chemical product. were Justices Brennan, White, M. lative intent in the patent laws as ria here.

—The number of prisoners held stitutions reached a record high year, the Bureau of Justice Statis ports. The total rose by 2.3 perc Dec. 31. Prisoners under federal 12 percent from 1978. The number There were 12,927 minimum prisone both state and federal prisons. Fo ade, the rate of increase for wom

PROVIDENCE, R.I. (UPI)—The ruled that four-letter words share Amendment, and people can't be police. Joanne E. McKenna, con shouting vulgarities at policemen for throwing rocks at pedestrian: the court concluded that, "While language the defendant used, ou does not permit us to sanction it speech includes the right to use "fighting words" that are "inherent tion [or] incite imminent disorde Bevilacqua."

MADISON, WIS. (UPI)—The stat Wisconsin's obscenity law, saying not comply with requirements se unanimous decision overturned t charges filed against the Princes kee police seized 20 motion pictu filed obscenity charges."Our gene tie or no guidance as to what peo tice Roland Day, who wrote the has remained silent for 25 years scene.

HARRISBURG, PA.—A woman for spinal surgery, instead of a gla have, is suing Philadelphia's Gra Charging gross negligence, Annie vania's Arbitration Panels for He pensatory damages and nonspecif in addition to the hospital, are ne Jr., and anesthesiologists John Bi spinal surgery was intended for a son, who has not disclosed wheth

CHICAGO—ABA officials have d Jordan Jr. President of the Nat

---

An article in the *Pennsylvania Law Journal*, June 23, 1980, regarding the signing of HB 2000 by Governor Dick Thornburgh, effectuating the expansion of the Superior Court.

---

urge that this amendment be rejected and the bill be adopted as submitted." Representative Hardy Williams then rose in agreement with Spencer, arguing that "the critical need for [fifteen] judges immediately was thoroughly laid out in our committee hearings on this matter very, very effectively, and I believe that we are in [an] emergency situation."[231] Finally, Representative Joseph R. Zeller, supporting the Piccola amendment, argued that the proposed court expansion was yet another example of the "lawyer's welfare state that has been creating these [caseload] problems."[232] Following Zeller's statement, the Piccola amendment was rejected by a vote of 89 to 84.[233] Immediately

---

231. *House Leg. Journal*, November 29, 1979, 2456.

232. *House Leg. Journal*, November 29, 1979, 2456-57. Zeller also claimed that the legislators who were lawyers would not support the Piccola amendment "because one of these days they are going to before one of these judges, and they do not want to have it on their record that they went against the [amendment]." *House Leg. Journal*, November 29, 1979, 2457.

233. *House Leg. Journal*, November 29, 1979, 2457.

thereafter, HB 2000 was submitted for final passage, and it succeeded by a vote of 105 to 71.[234] The bill was then sent to the Senate, where it passed by a vote of 49 to 0 on May 28, 1980.[235] Governor Richard Thornburgh signed the bill into law on June 11, 1980.[236]

  With the expansion authorized by the new law, the Superior Court reached its current complement of fifteen judges, and the panel system mandated by the Supreme Court in 1978, as well as reliance on senior judges, have continued to the present. These measures were the final significant steps in the reform process that began in the 1950s, continued through the Constitutional Convention of 1968, and acquired new urgency during the litigation boom of the 1970s. When this reform process culminated with the passage of HB 2000, the court's original structure—a seven-member, statutory tribunal with limited jurisdiction that sat en banc—had been completely transformed, and its modern structure emerged. Perhaps this transition from past to present is most effectively symbolized by an event that occurred on December 3, 1980. On that date, for the first time in its history, the court stopped sitting at City Hall during its visits to Philadelphia and relocated to the old Federal Building at Ninth and Market Streets. Although it occasionally returned in the years that followed, the court's continuous use of its first home, like its original structure, had become a thing of the past.

---

234. *House Leg. Journal*, November 29, 1979, 2457-58.
235. *History of House Bills*, 1979, A-249.
236. Pa. Act of June 11, 1980, PL 213, No. 63.

Members of the Superior Court, 1984.

L. to R. (seated): John P. Hester, Abraham H. Lipez*, Harry M. Montgomery, Edmund B. Spaeth Jr. (President Judge), G. Harold Watkins, J. Sydney Hoffman, William F. Cercone, Samuel J. Roberts*.

L. to R. (standing): James E. Rowley, John G. Brosky, Patrick R. Tamilia, Zoran Popovich, Justin M. Johnson, Stephen J. McEwen Jr., Phyllis W. Beck, Vincent A. Cirillo, James R. Cavanaugh, Donald E. Wieand, Richard B. Wickersham, Joseph A. Del Sole. Missing from photograph: Peter Paul Olszewski, Frank J. Montemuro Jr.

* Served by designation of the Pennsylvania Supreme Court.

# Chapter Seven

# The Modern Court: 1981-1995

## The Ninth Decade – 100 Years and Counting

**W**ith passage of the act expanding the Superior Court, it became necessary to select appointees for the eight additional judgeships. The new law provided that the appointments were to be made by the governor, with the advice and consent of two-thirds of the Senate.[1] It also provided that the terms of the eight new judges would be staggered. Four of the judges would serve terms ending in January 1982, two would serve terms ending in January 1984, and two would serve terms ending in January 1986.[2] The law further mandated that no more than half of the new appointees could be members of the same political party.[3] At the end of their initial terms, the appointees were required to run in contested, not retention, elections.[4]

## The Enlarged Court and Its Members

Following passage of the new law, the Appellate Court Nominating Committee, a merit selection panel utilized by Governor Thornburgh, formulated and submitted a list of possible appointees. Thornburgh selected eight candidates, four from each party.[5] For the terms scheduled to expire in January 1982, he appointed Democrats Richard DiSalle and Donald Wieand and Republicans Stephen J. McEwen Jr. and Perry Shertz. DiSalle and Shertz assumed office on December 16, 1980.[6]

Judge DiSalle was born on January 16, 1927 in Canonsburg, Washington County. From 1945 to 1946 he served in the U.S. Army. He graduated from the University of Pittsburgh with a bachelor's degree in 1948, and a law degree in 1951. In 1970 he was elected to the Washington County Court of Common Pleas. Seven years later, he was elected to the Commonwealth Court, and served until his appointment to the Superior Court. He was defeated in the general election in November 1981, and he left the court when his appointive term expired in January 1982. During his career, DiSalle served

---

1. Pa. Act of June 11, 1980, No. 1980-63. 1980 PL 213, sec. (b), Initial appointments.
2. 1980 PL 213, sec. (b) (1) - (3).
3. 1980 PL 213, sec. (b) (3).
4. 1980 PL 213, sec. (d).
5. Although Thornburgh named his nominees in September 1980, none of the nominees assumed the bench before December 1980. Others took office in 1981. For this reason, the nominees are discussed in this, rather than the previous, chapter.
6. Wieand's biographical sketch is set forth at page 234.

on the Pennsylvania Judicial Council, the Governor's Justice Commission, and the Juvenile Court Judges Commission.[7]

Judge McEwen commenced service on the Superior Court on May 15, 1981, after his appointment by Governor Thornburgh. McEwen was elected to a full ten-year term in November 1981, was retained for a further ten-year term in the general election of November 1991, and was elected president judge by the members of the Superior Court for a five-year term commencing January 1996. While a judge on the Superior Court, he was twice appointed by the Pennsylvania Supreme Court to the Board of Judicial Inquiry and Review, and, in 1996, was appointed by Governor Tom Ridge to the Court of Judicial Discipline and elected president judge by the members of that court.

McEwen pursued his study of the law at St. Joseph's College and the University of Pennsylvania Law School and in 1986, upon completion of graduate study, was awarded the degree of master of laws by the University of Virginia Law School. A native of Upper Darby, McEwen was an active trial lawyer during twenty-three years of private practice, and was district attorney of Delaware County from 1967 through 1976. He served as general counsel for the Pennsylvania District Attorneys Association and, for ten years commencing in 1975, was a professor of Trial Advocacy at Villanova University Law School. In 1997 he published *Not Even Dicta*, a collection of judicial/personal lessons in the law. McEwen has lectured at various law schools, universities, and Pennsylvania Bar Institute seminars, and authored articles published by the St. John's *Journal of Legal Commentary*, the Notre Dame *Journal of Law, Ethics and Policy*, the *Dickinson Law Review*, the Philadelphia *Legal Intelligencer*, and the Journal of the American Judges Association, *Court Review*.

Perry J. Shertz was born in Wilkes-Barre on May 26, 1928. From 1946 to 1948 he served in the U.S. Navy and continued in the Naval Reserve until 1949. Thereafter, he joined the Marine Corps, serving on active duty from 1952 to 1954 and in the reserves from 1958 to 1976, when he retired as a colonel.[8] He graduated from Dickinson College in 1952 and Temple Law School in 1957. As an attorney, Shertz was a lecturer for the American Trial Lawyers Association, the Pennsylvania Bar Institute, and the Dickinson Forum. He was also a fellow of the American Academy of Trial Lawyers and, from 1969 to 1971, he served on the board of governors of the Pennsylvania Trial Lawyers Association. He also chaired the state bar's insurance, negligence, and compensation section. Following his appointment to the Superior Court, Shertz ran for a full term, but he was defeated in the 1981 general election.[9]

For the terms set to expire in January 1984, Governor Thornburgh appointed Democrat Phyllis W. Beck and Republican Frank J. Montemuro Jr. Beck was the first woman to serve on the Superior Court. She graduated magna cum laude and Phi Beta Kappa from Brown University and was first in her class at Temple Law School. From 1967 to 1974 she engaged in private practice. She then became an associate professor at Temple Law School and served until 1976, when she became vice-dean of Penn Law School. She remained at Penn until her appointment to the Superior Court. Beck's nomination, like that of Judge McEwen's, was blocked by the Senate Rules and Executive Nominations Committee, but she was ultimately confirmed and assumed office on

---

7. DiSalle was also a member of the Fraternal Order of Eagles, Sons of Italy, and the Italian Sons and Daughters of America.

8. Induction ceremony, December 16, 1980, 272 Pa. Super. XXXVI, LVI (1980).

9. During his career, Shertz was an active member of numerous organizations, including the B'nai B'rith, the Northeastern Pennsylvania Heart Association, Kiwanis International, the Jewish Home of Eastern Pennsylvania, the Westbrook Park Civic Association, the Jewish Community Center, the Jewish Welfare Board, Veterans of Foreign Wars, the American Legion, AMVETS, and the Marine Corps League.

June 23, 1981.[10] She was elected to a full term on November 8, 1983, and retained in 1993. In July 1987 Beck was appointed by Governor Robert Casey to chair the twenty-three-member Commission on Judicial Reform. This commission submitted an extensive report to the governor in January 1988, in which it recommended significant structural reform of the state judicial system. Beck served as a commissioned judge until she reached the mandatory retirement age of seventy, and she continues to serve as a senior judge.[11]

In 1983 Phyllis W. Beck was the first woman to be elected to the Superior Court.

Frank Montemuro Jr., born in Philadelphia on October 27, 1925, joined the Superior Court on December 16, 1980. During World War II, he served in the Pacific for two and one-half years. Returning home, he graduated from Temple University and, in June of 1952, he received his bachelor of laws degree from the Duke University School of Law. Thereafter, he engaged in private practice in Philadelphia. On January 4, 1965, he was appointed to the Philadelphia County Court of Common Pleas. He was elected to a full term in the fall of 1965 and reelected in 1975. He served three terms as administrative judge of the Family Division. On September 18, 1992, Governor Casey appointed him to the Supreme Court, where he remained until October 27, 1995, when he reached the mandatory retirement age of seventy. Thereafter, Montemuro was designated a senior justice of the Supreme Court and continued in that position until the vacancy he occupied was filled by the election of Justice Nigro in November 1996. Since January 1997, Justice Montemuro has served on the Superior Court as a senior judge.[12]

The two judges appointed to the terms expiring in January 1986 were Democrat Justin M. Johnson and Republican Zoran Popovich, who both assumed office on December 16, 1980. Johnson was born in Wilkinsburg, Allegheny County, on August 19, 1933. He received bachelor's and law degrees from the University of Chicago. He also studied in a nondegree program at the University of Virginia. From 1954 to 1959 he served on active duty in the U.S. Air Force, and he remained in the reserves until 1973. Following his active duty service, Johnson engaged in private practice, and ultimately became a partner in the firm of Berkman Ruslander Pohl Lieber & Engel.[13] He also

---

10. Frank Christopher, "Two Thornburgh Nominees Blocked by Rules Committee," *Pennsylvania Law Journal,* November 24, 1980, 1.

11. During her career, among other positions, Beck served as associate trustee of the University of Pennsylvania, overseer of Penn Nursing School, and president of the Foundation for Cognitive Therapy and Research at Penn. She also received the Judicial Administration Award from the Pennsylvania Bar Association, and the Herbert Harley Award for Judicial Reform from the American Judicature Society.

12. By special assignment of the Pennsylvania Supreme Court, Justice Montemuro was appointed Master in the *Allegheny County* case, infra, to prepare a report on the transition to state funding of the Unified Judicial System. The transfer of funding from the counties to the state was deemed to be required by the 1968 constitutional amendments mandating a unified judiciary. *Allegheny County v. Commonwealth of PA*, 517 Pa. 65, 534 A.2d 760 (1987). In 1993, in response to an action of mandamus against the Commonwealth of Pennsylvania to restore funding levels to the counties at the pre-1992-93 level, the Supreme Court stayed judgment in order to afford the General Assembly an opportunity to enact appropriate funding legislation consistent with its Order. *County of Allegheny v. Commonwealth of PA*, 534 Pa. 8, 626 A.2d 492 (1993). Justice Montemuro completed his task, which is the basis for ongoing efforts to achieve the necessary results without a constitutional crisis.

Justice Montemuro was a member of numerous professional organizations and served as national president of the Order of Sons of Italy in America. In 1968 he was decorated with the rank of "Knight of the Order of Merit of the Republic of Italy" by the president of Italy. In 1982 Pope John Paul II conferred upon Justice Montemuro the Papal Honor of Knight Commander of the Order of St. Gregory the Great.

13. Induction ceremony, December 16, 1980, 272 Pa. Super. XXXVI, LI (1980).

served on the Pennsylvania Crime Commission from 1977 to 1980, and on the Pennsylvania Board of Law Examiners from 1969 to 1989. Following his appointment to the Superior Court, he ran for a full term in the general election of November 5, 1985. He received the nominations of both political parties and was elected. In 1993 he was also appointed a judge of the Court of Judicial Discipline.[14] In the general election of 1995 he was retained for an additional ten years.

Zoran Popovich was born in Akron, Ohio, on February 4, 1933. From 1951 to 1953 he served in the U.S. Air Force. In 1954, he graduated from the University of Pittsburgh and three years later he graduated from the university's law school. Thereafter, he engaged in private practice in McKeesport, Allegheny County. In 1973 he finished first on both the Republican and Democratic ballots for common pleas judge, ahead of sixty-three other candidates.[15] He served as a trial judge until his appointment to the Superior Court. He was elected to a full term on November 5, 1985, and was retained in 1995.

Since these eight new judges had to run in partisan elections following their appointments, the next few years saw a number of open seats on the Superior Court. The first changes occurred in the 1981 general election, at which Judges Wieand, McEwen, DiSalle, and Shertz ran for full ten-year terms. Wieand and McEwen won, but DiSalle and Shertz were defeated by Vincent A. Cirillo and James E. Rowley.

Cirillo was born in Ardmore, Montgomery County, on December 19, 1927. He graduated from Villanova University in 1951 and received an LL.B. in 1955 and a J.D. in 1969, both from Temple Law School. He also served in the Korean Conflict. From 1955 to 1958, he was a law clerk to President Judge Harold G. Knight of the Montgomery County Court of Common Pleas. For five years thereafter, he was assistant district attorney of Montgomery County, and he served as assistant solicitor of that county from 1966 to 1971. On December 31, 1971, he was appointed judge of the court of common pleas and served in that capacity until his election to the Superior Court. He also served as vice-chairman of the Judicial Education Committee of the Pennsylvania Conference of State Trial Judges and as a member of the executive board of Temple Law School.

On January 8, 1986, Cirillo succeeded Judge Spaeth as president judge. He was the first president judge to be elected by his colleagues on the court. Previously, the commissioned judge with the longest tenure automatically became president judge. However, this practice was changed by a 1979 amendment to the state constitution, which provided that the judge with the longest service would become president judge only if he or she was a member of the court on or before the first Monday of January 1977.[16] When no sitting judge had been a member of the court on that date, the president judge was to be elected by the commissioned judges. Since the retirement of President Judge Spaeth left the court without a member who had served since the first Monday of January 1977, the constitutional amendment was employed and Cirillo was elected.[17] He served as president judge until 1990, the same year he was retained for

---

14. During his career, Johnson was a Fellow of the American Bar Foundation and a member of the Permanent Judicial Council of the General Assembly, the Disciplinary Board of the Pennsylvania Supreme Court, the National Conference of Bar Examiners, and the Homer S. Brown Law Association. He also received numerous awards, including the President's Award of the Pennsylvania Trial Lawyer's Association, the St. Thomas More Award of the Catholic Diocese of Pittsburgh, the Dr. Martin Luther King Citizen's Award, the Humanitarian and Community Service Award, and the Bond Medal from the University of Chicago.

15. Induction ceremony, December 16, 1980, 272 Pa. Super. XXXVI, LIV (1980).

16. This amendment is considered more fully, infra.

17. On May 8, 1990, the Supreme Court issued an order providing that the president judge of a court with eight or more members could not serve consecutive terms.

another ten-year term. He reached the mandatory retirement age of seventy in 1997 and continues to serve as a senior judge.[18]

James E. Rowley was born in Tarentum, Allegheny County, on April 8, 1926. He served in the U.S. Army from 1944 to 1946. He graduated from Washington and Jefferson College in 1949 and the University of Pittsburgh Law School in 1952. From 1963 to 1966 he served as special assistant attorney general. On June 11, 1966, he was appointed to the Court of Common Pleas of Beaver County. He was elected to a full term a year later and reelected in 1977. He was elected to the Superior Court in 1981 and was reelected in 1991. In January of 1991 Rowley succeeded Judge Cirillo as president judge. Upon the Superior Court's centennial anniversary in 1995, President Judge Rowley published a pamphlet entitled *100 Years of Justice*, which set forth the personnel and significant events that have shaped the court's history. While on the court, Rowley also served on the Judicial Inquiry and Review Board and the Advisory Committee of the Center for Judicial Conduct Organizations. From 1987 to 1991 he was chairman of the Superior Court's Internal Operating Committee. Rowley served on the court until his retirement in 1995. He then elected to assume senior status in the Common Pleas Court of Beaver County where he continues to serve.[19]

Five seats were on the ballot at the general election of 1983. Judges Beck and Montemuro won full terms. The third opening resulted from the death of Judge Price in January 1983. Governor Thornburgh initially nominated Ward F. Clark of Doylestown to replace Judge Price, but he later withdrew the nomination.[20] The two final vacancies were caused when Judges Hester and Cercone achieved senior status in July and August, respectively. Along with Judge Price's seat, these seats remained vacant until the end of 1983, leaving the court with only twelve active judges. Patrick R. Tamilia, Joseph A. Del Sole, and Peter Paul Olszewski filled the seats at the 1983 general election and assumed office on January 2, 1984.

Patrick R. Tamilia was born in Pittsburgh. He graduated from Duquesne University in 1952 and Duquesne School of Law in 1959. He also engaged in post-graduate studies in psychology and sociology at Duquesne. From 1946 to 1948 he served in the U.S. Marine Corps, and in 1952 he served as an officer with the U.S. Army Artillery. Prior to assuming the bench, Tamilia worked in juvenile detention and juvenile probation, and he served as director of the Domestic Relations Division of the Allegheny County Court. He also served as chairman of the Pennsylvania Bar Association Family Law Section. He was elected to the Allegheny County Court of Common Pleas in 1969 and was retained in 1979. In the intervening fourteen years, he served in the juvenile, family, and criminal divisions. He was elected to the Superior Court in 1983 without endorsement of either political party and Tamilia was retained in 1993. He reached the mandatory retirement age of seventy in 1998, but continues to serve as a senior judge. From 1970 until 2000 he served as an adjunct professor of Family Law at Duquesne University School of Law. While a trial judge, Tamilia was chairman of the Family Law Section of the Allegheny County Bar Association and the Juvenile Judges Section of the Pennsylvania Conference of State Trial Judges.[21]

---

18. During his career, Cirillo received Man of the Year Awards from the Catholic War Veterans and the Optimist Club of Norristown. He also received the Distinguished Service Award from the Phi Alpha Delta Law Fraternity, and the Medal of Honor from the Italian American Press Association.

19. During his career, Rowley received the Judicial Award of the Pennsylvania Bar Association, the George Ross Award from the Lancaster Bar Association, the Liberty Bell Award from the Beaver County Bar Association, and an honorary doctor of laws degree from Washington and Jefferson College.

20. See Senate Legislative Journal, Pennsylvania General Assembly, June 27, 1983, 757.

21. Tamilia has authored numerous articles on juvenile delinquency, family law, and mental health. He was instrumental in creating numerous programs for delinquent and dependent children, unwed mothers, and mentally handicapped children. Tamilia played a significant role in creating the Domestic Relations

The court in 1980, following the induction ceremony of six newly appointed judges to the enlarged court, Supreme Court Justice Henry X. O'Brien officiating.
Front row, L. to R.: Richard DiSalle, Donald E. Wieand, Zoran Popovich, Perry J. Shertz, Justin M. Johnson, Frank J. Montemuro Jr.
Second row, L. to R.: Harry M. Montgomery, Richard B. Wickersham, James. R. Cavanaugh, J. Sydney Hoffman.
Third row, L. to R.: John G. Brosky, John P. Hester, Gwilym A. Price Jr., Justice O'Brien, William F. Cercone (President Judge), Edmund B. Spaeth Jr.

Joseph A. Del Sole was born in Pittsburgh on November 16, 1940. He received a bachelor of science degree from Carnegie Institute of Technology, an LL.B. degree from Duquesne University, and a master of laws degree from the University of Virginia. In 1978, he was appointed to the Court of Common Pleas of Allegheny County and elected to a full term a year later. Following his election to the Superior Court, he was retained in 1993 and continues to serve. Del Sole was the first chairman of the Judicial Conduct Board of Pennsylvania, and chairman of the Court of Common Pleas Computerization Project. He is an adjunct professor at Duquesne University School of Law, and a member of numerous organizations, including the Supreme Court's Statewide Steering Committee on Automation.[22]

Manual published by the Administrative Offices of the Supreme Court and in establishing the Shuman Center's Neuropsychiatric Assessment Unit for Violent Children and the "Lessons Learned" program for Allegheny County Children and Youth Services. He also served as chairman of the Allegheny County 2001 Public Safety and Criminal Justice Committee, as a member of the Judicial College of the Pennsylvania Supreme Court, and was national president of the Italian Sons and Daughters of America. Tamilia was a charter member of the Duquesne University Century Club and, among other awards, he received the Distinguished Alumnus Award from Duquesne University and the Phi Delta Kappa Lay Leader Award in Education. In conjunction with the Duquesne University School of Law and the Pittsburgh Council for International Visitors, he also has engaged as an escort/instructor for international visitors from the law schools and courts of Africa, China, Central America, Europe, Russia, and the Ukraine.

22. Del Sole has served as a member of the Pennsylvania Defense Institute, the Academy of Trial Lawyers of Allegheny County, Italian Sons and Daughters of America, and the Serbian National Federation. In 1995, Del Sole received the Century Club Distinguished Alumnus Award from Duquesne University. He has also authored numerous law review articles.

Peter Paul Olszewski was born in Plains, Luzerne County, on May 12, 1925. He graduated from Wyoming Seminary in 1942, and served with the U.S. Army in the China-Burma-India theater from 1943 to 1946. Returning home, he graduated from Lafayette College in 1948 and St. John's University Law School in 1952. In 1955 he was a law clerk to Judge Thomas M. Lewis of the Luzerne County Common Pleas Court. For the next seven years, he was city solicitor of Wilkes-Barre. In 1968 he became judge of the Court of Common Pleas of Luzerne County. He served until his election to the Superior Court in 1983. He was retained in 1993. Although he reached mandatory retirement age two years later, Olszewski continues to serve as a senior judge. Olszewski has served as a member of numerous judicial organizations, including vice president of the Pennsylvania State Conference of Trial Judges, the Appellate Judges Conference, and the Long Range Planning Commission of the American Bar Association.[23]

Following the 1983 general election, there were no further changes on the court for two years. At the 1985 general election, three seats were on the ballot. Judges Johnson and Popovich, whose appointive terms were set to expire, were elected to full terms. The other opening resulted from Judge Spaeth's decision not to run for retention. John T.J. Kelly Jr. was elected to this seat.

Kelly was born on December 29, 1930. He served in the U.S. Army from 1952 to 1956. He graduated from LaSalle University in 1956 and Creighton Law School in 1961. From 1963 to 1966 he served as assistant attorney general and chief counsel of the Pennsylvania Department of Public Welfare. He served as an assistant to Lieutenant Governor Raymond J. Broderick from 1967 to 1971, and in 1968 he was chief of staff of the Pennsylvania delegation to the Republican National Convention. He was also executive director of Governor Thornburgh's Inaugural Committee from 1978 to 1979 and the national field director of John B. Connally's presidential campaign from 1979 to 1980. From 1980 to 1985 he was deputy secretary for industry of the Pennsylvania Department of Labor and Industry. In 1985 Kelly won the nominations of both parties for a seat on the Superior Court, and he was elected. On December 9, 1988, Kelly commenced a four-year term on the Judicial Inquiry and Review Board. He was retained on the Superior Court in 1995 and continues to serve as a commissioned judge.

Following Kelly's election, the next change occurred in 1988, when Judge Wickersham resigned. Governor Robert P. Casey first nominated Levan Gordon to this vacancy, but the nomination was defeated in the Senate.[24] Casey then nominated James R. Melinson and this nomination was confirmed. Melinson, who assumed office on February 10, 1988, was born in Philadelphia on September 6, 1939. In 1961 he graduated from LaSalle University and, the following year, he served as an artillery unit commander in the U.S. Army. In 1968 he graduated from Temple Law School, where he was president of his class. Five years later he also received a master's degree in education from Temple. Following law school, he was a general practitioner for nineteen years, a chief negotiator for the School District of Philadelphia, a special advisor to the U.S. Department of Defense, and chief counsel of the International Association of Machinists and Aerospace Workers, Local Lodge 159, AFL-CIO. While on the Superior Court, Melinson was a member of numerous judicial organizations, including the Appellate

---

23. Olszewski is a fellow of the American Bar Foundation, the American Legion, and Veterans of Foreign Wars. He has also received numerous awards, including the Fraternal Order of Eagles "Liberty under Law" Award, the Man of the Year Award from the Polish American Citizens League of Pennsylvania, the Distinguished Law and Justice Award from the Deputy Sheriffs Association of Pennsylvania, and the Distinguished Law and Justice Award from the County and State Detectives Association of Pennsylvania. He was the Catholic chairman of the Interfaith Council, a board member of Pennsylvania State University, Wilkes-Barre Campus, a trustee of College Misericordia, and a lifetime director of the St. John's University Law School Alumni Association.

24. Leg. Journal, Pa. Senate, October 20, 1987, 1222-23.

Judge James R. Melinson

Judges Conference of the American Bar Association, Pennsylvania Conference of State Trial Judges, and the American Judges Association. After his appointment, Melinson unsuccessfully sought a full term in the 1989 general election.

In addition to the seat occupied by Melinson, the seat of Judge Brosky, who decided not to run for retention, was on the ballot for the 1989 general election. Melinson was defeated and Kate Ford Elliott and Joseph A. Hudock were elected. Ford Elliott received a bachelor's degree from the University of Pittsburgh in 1971, a master's degree in education from Duquesne University in 1973, and a law degree from Duquesne's School of Law in 1978. From 1971 to 1977 she was a reading specialist with the Pittsburgh Board of Education. Following law school, she served for two years as a law clerk to Judge Montgomery of the Superior Court. From 1980 to 1982 she also served as administrative assistant to President Judge Cercone. For the next six years, she was chief staff attorney of the Superior Court's Central Legal Staff. Prior to her election to the Superior Court, she was associated with the firm Kirkpatrick & Lockhart in Pittsburgh. From 1987 to 1988 she chaired the Appellate Practice Committee of the Allegheny County Bar Association. She presently serves as vice-chair of the Pennsylvania Futures Commission and as a member of the National Association of Women Judges. Judge Ford Elliott was reelected in the general election of November 1999.

Joseph A. Hudock was born in Greensburg, Westmoreland County, on November 21, 1937. He graduated from St. Vincent College in 1959 and Duquesne University School of Law in 1962. From 1963 to 1966 he served as a judge advocate in the U.S. Navy. In 1978 he was elected to the Court of Common Pleas of Westmoreland County and served in that capacity until his election to the Superior Court in 1989. He was retained in the 1999 general election. Hudock has served as a member of the Supreme Court Appellate Rules Committee, a member of the Editorial Board of the American Bar Association publication, *The Practical Litigator*, and president of the Westmoreland County American Inn of Court.[25]

25. In 1959, Hudock received the American Jurisprudence Award for Excellence in Bills and Notes, and two years later he received the American Jurisprudence Award for Excellence in Wills. He was recognized as a distinguished alumnus of St. Vincent College in 1986. He also was a member of numerous organizations, including the Pennsylvania Conference of State Trial Judges, the American Judicature Society, the United Way of Westmoreland County, Salvation Army Advisory Board, the Regional Planning Council of the Governor's Justice Commission, the Latrobe Area Task Force of the Diocese of Greensburg, and the Alumni Council of St. Vincent College.

No further changes occurred on the court until 1992, when Judge Montemuro was appointed to the Supreme Court. Governor Casey nominated Robert D. Mariani to fill Montemuro's seat, but the nomination was recalled.[26] Acting Governor Mark Singel[27] then nominated John Pushinsky of Pittsburgh, but that nomination was also recalled.[28] Montemuro's seat remained vacant until the 1993 general election, when it was filled by Thomas G. Saylor. Saylor was born in Meyersdale, Somerset County, on December 14, 1946. He graduated from the University of Virginia in 1969 and Columbia Law School in 1972. From 1973 to 1976 he served as first assistant district attorney of Somerset County. In 1982 he served as director of the Pennsylvania Bureau of Consumer Protection and two years later he became first deputy attorney general of Pennsylvania. He was also a litigation partner with the firm of Eckert Seamans Cherin & Mellott. Following his election to the Superior Court in 1993, Saylor served until the end of 1997, when he was elected to the Supreme Court.

Since the court had four Democrats and three Republicans prior to its expansion, the appointment of four members from each party maintained the Democrats' one-judge majority as of 1981. The subsequent changes also maintained the relative balance between the parties. Once again, this balance reflected Pennsylvania's electorate, which saw a minor Republican rebound after the heavy Democratic majorities of the late 1960s and 1970s. For instance, although Democrats outnumbered Republicans by nearly 800,000 in 1976, the lead was cut in half within twenty years.[29]

## THE COURT AT WORK – TORT LAW

The most significant development in tort law during the 1980s and early 1990s was the increase of so-called toxic tort cases, in which the plaintiffs alleged injury from exposure to harmful substances. The most notable of these substances was asbestos. One study found that more than 21 million Americans had been exposed to asbestos and approximately 200,000 would die from asbestos-related cancers by the end of the century.[30] Not surprisingly, the vast exposure and injury figures translated into a tremendous volume of new litigation. In fact, asbestos cases accounted for one-third to one-half of all product liability actions filed during the 1980s.[31] The volume of these cases swamped federal and state trial courts and necessitated a variety of new administrative procedures. In 1991 a federal judicial panel studying the issue found that asbestos litigation "has reached a magnitude . . . that threatens the administration of

26. Leg. Journal, Pa. Senate, April 20, 1993, 504.

27. Singel, the lieutenant governor, was acting governor while Robert Casey recovered from heart transplant surgery.

28. Leg. Journal, Pa. Senate, December 6, 1993, 1397-98. Pushinsky was the unsuccessful Democratic candidate for the seat in the 1993 general election.

29. In 1976, there were 3,152,450 registered Democrats and 2,387,197 registered Republicans in Pennsylvania. In 1996, Democrats numbered 3,336,933 and Republicans 2,910,615.

30. Kimberly V. Rest, "'Fear of Cancer': Pennsylvania's Temporary Respite from Inadequate Compensation for Victims of Asbestos Exposure," 13 *Temp. Envtl. L. & Tech. J.* 319, 330 (1994), citing Robert V. Percival et al., *Environmental Regulation: Law, Science, and Policy,* 629 (1992).

31. See Michael J. Saks, "Do We Really Know Anything About the Tort Litigation System—and Why Not?," 140 U. Pa. L. Rev. 1147, 1192 (1992) ("One-third of all product liability cases in the system in the mid-1980s were attributable to a single product: asbestos."), citing Ad Hoc Committee on Asbestos Litigation, Report to the Judicial Conference of the U.S., 7-10 (1991); J. Mark Ramseyer, "Products Liability Through Private Ordering: Notes on a Japanese Experiment," 144 U. Pa. L. Rev. 1823, 1837 (1996) ("Perhaps half of the recent cases have been asbestos cases."), citing W. Kip Viscusi, "The Dimensions of the Products Liability Crisis," 20 J. Legal Stud. 147, 154-157 (1991) (stating that 55 percent of all product liability actions filed in 1987 were asbestos-related).

justice and that requires a new, streamlined approach."[32] This panel ultimately ordered the transfer of 26,639 pending asbestos cases from 87 district courts to a single forum designated for such cases.[33] The volume of asbestos cases was especially great in Pennsylvania. As early as 1982, for instance, the Philadelphia court system was third highest in the nation in the number of asbestos cases filed. Up to a dozen cases were filed for every case adjudicated. In response to the flood of new cases, Philadelphia courts established a separate docket with a specially-appointed asbestos judge.[34]

As the new asbestos cases strained the capacity of trial courts, they also presented the Superior Court with a number of challenging issues. In fact, throughout the 1980s and early 1990s, the court probably convened en banc more often in asbestos cases than any other type of case.[35] In these cases, the court was repeatedly called upon to modify or abolish several traditional rules of tort law.

For instance, the court reconsidered the long-standing rule in personal injury actions that all claims against a defendant arising from a single event must be asserted in a single lawsuit. This rule was intended to protect defendants from repeated exposure to liability while ensuring judicial efficiency by avoiding the time and expense of multiple claims. Although it worked well in traditional tort cases, where the full extent of harm is generally known at or near the time of injury, the rule proved extremely unjust in latent disease cases, where it was referred to as the "single disease" rule. In a typical asbestos case, for instance, pleural thickening[36] is the first manifestation of asbestos exposure. Although this condition is often accompanied by no physiological impairments, it was nonetheless held to commence the two-year statute of limitations for "injuries to the person."[37] Thus, the plaintiff had two years to file suit and, under the "single disease" rule, this suit must seek compensation for the pleural thickening and all future diseases related to asbestos-exposure, even though the plaintiff was unaware of what further conditions might arise. Due to the fact that pleural thickening was asymptomatic, and because future damages were extremely speculative, the plaintiff generally received little or no compensation. Years or even decades later, the plaintiff might acquire a serious condition, particularly lung cancer, but, under the "single disease" rule, the statute of limitations had expired two years after the diagnosis of pleural thickening and the plaintiff was barred from filing a second action for asbestos-related cancer. Because of this harsh result, the Superior Court abolished the "single disease" rule.

In the en banc case of *Marinari v. Asbestos Corp., Ltd.*,[38] Anthony Marinari claimed that he was exposed to asbestos while employed by two manufacturing estab-

---

32. See *In Re Asbestos Products Liability Litigation* (No. VI), 771 F. Supp. 415, 418 (Judicial Panel on Multidistrict Litigation, 1991).

33. See note 32. The cases were transferred to the United States District Court for the Eastern District of Pennsylvania.

34. Comment, "The King's Bench Power in Pennsylvania: A Unique Power That Provides Efficient Results," 101 Dick. L. Rev. 671, 690 (1997).

35. See e.g., *Marinari v. Asbestos Corp., Ltd.*, 417 Pa. Super. 440, 612 A.2d 1021 (1992) (Wieand, J.); *Ottavio v. Fibreboard Corp.*, 421 Pa. Super. 284, 617 A.2d 1296 (1992) (per curiam); and *Altiere v. Fibreboard Corp.*, 421 Pa. Super. 297, 617 A.2d 1302 (1992) (per curiam); *Doe v. Johns-Manville Corp.*, 324 Pa. Super. 469, 471 A.2d 1252 (1984) (Cavanaugh, J.); *Cathcart v. Keene Industrial Insulation*, 324 Pa. Super. 123, 471 A.2d 493 (1984) (Hester, J.); *Giffear v. Johns-Manville Corp.*, 429 Pa. Super. 327, 632 A.2d 880 (1993) (Cirillo, J.).

36. Pleural thickening is "the formation of calcified tissue on the membranes surrounding the lungs . . . [which] may occur independent of or in conjunction with asbestosis." See *Giffear*, 632 A.2d 881.

37. The current statute of limitations is codified at 42 Pa.C.S. sec. 5524(2). Pleural thickening was held to commence the statute of limitations in a number of cases, the most prominent of which were the en banc decisions in *Doe* and *Cathcart*, supra.

38. 417 Pa. Super. 440, 612 A.2d 1021 (1992) (Wieand, J.).

The 26,000-ton tanker under construction at the Sun Shipyards, Chester, Pa., illustrates the basis for the enormous amount of litigation involving asbestos-related diseases arising from shipbuilding and related industries in Pennsylvania (photo credit: Standard Oil Co., N.J.).

lishments between 1928 and 1972. In 1983 a routine chest x-ray prior to hip-replacement surgery revealed that he had pleural thickening. Despite this condition, Marinari suffered no symptoms or other impairments, and he chose not to file suit at that time. In July of 1987, however, Marinari was diagnosed with lung cancer and he died in November of the same year. Marinari's wife thereafter filed suit. Prior to trial, the asbestos manufacturers filed motions for summary judgment claiming that the statute of limitations began to run when the asymptomatic pleural thickening was diagnosed in 1983, and Mrs. Marinari's lawsuit, which was not filed until 1987, was therefore time-barred. Believing itself bound by the "single disease" rule, the trial court granted summary judgment in favor of the asbestos manufacturers.[39] Mrs. Marinari appealed.

The Superior Court, sitting en banc, reversed the decision of the trial court. The court began by acknowledging that, under the "single disease" rule, Mrs. Marinari's lawsuit was barred by the statute of limitations. Yet, the court found that this rule had been viewed with disfavor by a number of courts.[40] First, the court noted a 1991 panel decision of the Superior Court that deemed it proper for a trial court to instruct the jury that, if it determined that the plaintiff's pleural thickening was non-compensable, the plaintiff could bring another action if he later developed cancer.[41] The court then found that a majority of other jurisdictions considering the issue had abolished the "single disease" rule in asbestos actions.[42] The court discussed these cases as follows:

> Those jurisdictions which permit more than one action for separate asbestos related injuries have done so in recognition that asbestos exposure does not result in only one disease. The damage to the human body

---

39. 612 A.2d 1022.
40. 612 A.2d 1023. The court found, "This rule, which has generally proven fair and workable in the context of actions for personal injury, has given rise to an unworkable process and a potential for unfair results in the context of asbestos litigation."
41. 612 A.2d 1023, citing *Manzi v. H.K. Porter Co.*, 402 Pa. Super. 595, 587 A.2d 778 (1991).
42. See note 41.

which may result from asbestos exposure does not occur as a seamless progression of a single pathology. Instead, exposure to asbestos may result in a variety of benign and malignant conditions, each of which may occur at widely divergent times.[43]

Further, the court reasoned, the "single disease" rule encouraged speculative and inequitable damage awards in cases involving latent diseases. For instance, because the statute of limitations has commenced, a plaintiff diagnosed with pleural thickening but not cancer is forced to file suit and claim damages only for the fear that he might later develop cancer. "Allowing recovery for risk of cancer damages," the court noted, "not only encourages anticipatory lawsuits but runs counter to the goal that cases be decided on the best quality evidence available and that jury verdicts speak the truth."[44] "In latent disease cases," the court concluded, "these principles of fair adjudication are not well served by the 'rules developed against the relatively unsophisticated backdrops of barroom brawls, intersection collisions and slips and falls. . . .' The rigid rules designed to limit plaintiffs to a single lawsuit must yield."[45] On this basis, the court adopted the "separate disease" rule, which provides that "an asbestos plaintiff may assert, in a second lawsuit, a claim for a distinct, separate disease if and when it develops at a later time." Since this rule permitted a subsequent action for cancer, the court also held that risk of cancer was no longer a viable cause of action. Applying the "separate disease" rule to the facts at issue, the court then concluded Mrs. Marinari's claim for compensation for her husband's cancer, being a distinct cause of action, was not barred by the statute of limitations.[46] *Marinari's* holding that separate diseases result in separate causes of action has been expressly followed by the Supreme Court,[47] and it has been cited on dozens of other occasions by courts in Pennsylvania and elsewhere.[48]

*Marinari* was also relied upon by the court en banc one year later in another important asbestos case. In *Giffear v. Johns-Manville Corp.*, William Giffear had been exposed to asbestos in several occupations between 1964 and 1982. In 1982 an annual medical checkup revealed that he had extensive pleural thickening. Thereafter, Giffear and his wife filed suit against a number of asbestos manufacturers for physical injury and for increased risk and fear of cancer. All but three of the manufacturers reached a settlement and trial commenced against the remaining three. Although Giffear's medical expert testified as to his diagnosis of pleural thickening, he was unable to identify any physiological impairment resulting from the condition. Further medical testimony also indicated that, as a result of his asbestos exposure, Giffear's risk of contracting cancer was two to five times greater. The jury returned a verdict in the Giffears' favor in the amount of $300,000. The trial court granted judgment notwithstanding the verdict in favor of the manufacturers, however, on the basis that Mr. Giffear had suffered no

---

43. 612 A.2d 1024.

44. 612 A.2d 1026, quoting *Eagle-Picher Industries, Inc. v. Cox*, 481 So.2d 517 (Fla. 1985). Wieand also noted that a plaintiff who recovers damages on the basis that he may develop cancer in the future, but does not develop cancer, receives a windfall. "Second, and perhaps worse," he continued, "an asbestosis plaintiff who is unsuccessful in his efforts to recover risk of cancer damages, but later contracts cancer, has the disease but no damages." Finally, the very fact that the possibility of contracting cancer is indeterminate tends to make awards unnecessarily speculative.

45. 612 A.2d 1027.

46. 612 A.2d 1028.

47. *Simmons v. Pacor, Inc.*, 543 Pa. 664, 674 A.2d 232 (1996); see also *McNeil v. Owens-Corning Fiberglas Corp.*, 545 Pa. 209, 680 A.2d 1145 (1996).

48. See e.g., *Randt v. Abex Corp.*, 448 Pa. Super. 224, 671 A.2d 228 (1996); *Giordano v. A.C. & S. Inc.*, 446 Pa. Super. 232, 666 A.2d 710 (1995); *In re TMI*, 89 F.3d 1106 (3d Cir. 1996); *In re Paoli Railroad Yard PCB Litigation*, 35 F.3d 717 (3d Cir. 1994); *In re Celotex Corp.*, 175 B.R. 98 (11th Cir. 1994); *Richmond v. A.P. Green Industries, Inc.*, 66 Cal.App. 4th 878 (Cal. 1998).

damages since his pleural thickening was accompanied by no "symptoms, illness or impairment of any sort."[49] The Giffears appealed, arguing that pleural thickening, even if unaccompanied by physiological impairments, was a compensable injury.

Although a number of factually similar asbestos cases had been presented to the Superior Court during the 1980s and early 1990s, the question of whether asymptomatic pleural thickening was compensable was an issue of first impression. It was addressed by the court en banc in *Giffear*.[50] The court's analysis turned on the change in law occasioned by *Marinari*. Under the "single disease" rule, the court noted that plaintiffs were required to commence suit based upon pleural thickening because discovery of this condition commenced the statute of limitations, and a failure to file suit within two years would forever bar a subsequent action for a more serious asbestos-related condition. In other words, prior to the decision in *Marinari*, plaintiffs had a single chance to recover for all present and possible future asbestos-related harms, and that chance endured for only two years after pleural thickening was diagnosed. Subsequent to *Marinari*'s adoption of the "separate disease" rule, however, plaintiffs could file an action for cancer if and when it arose, regardless of when pleural thickening was diagnosed. "This being the case," the court reasoned, "plaintiffs no longer have a valid reason to bring a lawsuit for asymptomatic pleural thickening."[51] In addition to the fact that *Marinari* had obviated the legal necessity of an action for asymptomatic pleural thickening, the court also found that practical considerations precluded such an action. Following a review of similar cases in other jurisdictions and Pennsylvania trial courts, the court concluded:

> While we sympathize with Mr. Giffear's disturbing discovery, his diagnosis does not warrant compensation. Where we cannot find that one has suffered a symptomatic injury, how is it possible to assess damages? . . . It remains that, but for the fact that x-rays were taken revealing a pleural condition, Mr. Giffear would not have realized that such a condition even existed. It would hardly be fair to compensate him for something that has yet to manifest itself into a functional impairment. If and when such impairment does occur, Mr. Giffear may then bring an action for damages. Until that time, however, he is without a legally cognizable claim; there is, at this point, no legal injury.[52]

The court also found that the jury verdict in favor of the Giffears could not be justified on the basis of increased risk or fear of cancer. Again relying on *Marinari*, it noted that a new action could be commenced if and when Mr. Giffear contracted cancer. "To allow recovery under these circumstances based on [Giffear's] fear alone," the court concluded, "would fly in the face of our recent adoption of the separate disease rule."[53] Having found that the Giffears' claims for asymptomatic pleural thickening and fear of cancer were not recognized by Pennsylvania law, the Superior Court affirmed the trial court's grant of judgment notwithstanding the verdict in favor of the asbestos manufacturers. *Giffear* was affirmed on appeal by the Supreme Court,[54] and it has been cited on

---

49. 632 A.2d 881.

50. See note 49.

51. See note 49.

52. 632 A.2d 887-88. The court overruled two previous decisions to the extent that they recognized pleural thickening as a viable cause of action. Overruling in part, *Morrison v. Fibreboard Corp.*, 428 Pa. Super. 114, 630 A.2d 436 (1993), and *Higginbotham v. Fibreboard Corp.*, 428 Pa. Super. 26, 630 A.2d 14 (1993).

53. 632 A.2d 889.

54. *Giffear* was affirmed in *Simmons*, supra.

Superior Court of 1987.
L. to R. (seated): James E. Rowley, James R. Cavanaugh, Vincent A. Cirillo (President Judge), John G. Brosky, Donald E. Wieand. L. to R. (standing): Zoran Popovich, Patrick R. Tamilia, Peter Paul Olszewski, Stephen J. McEwen Jr., Joseph A. Del Sole, John T. J. Kelly Jr., Justin M. Johnson. Missing from photograph: Phyllis W. Beck, Frank J. Montemuro Jr.

dozens of occasions for its holdings that asymptomatic asbestos-related conditions and fear of contracting a disease are not compensable injuries.[55] Also, following the Superior Court's holding, the Philadelphia Court of Common Pleas established an inactive docket for cases which failed to meet the *Giffear* requirements. As a result of the new docket, cases in which a plaintiff has been diagnosed with an asbestos-related condition, but the condition is asymptomatic, are deferred with the right to pursue reinstatement if the condition becomes symptomatic.[56]

In another important case, the court extended *Giffear's* holding that fear of cancer was not a cognizable cause of action to another deadly disease. In *Lubowitz v. Albert Einstein Medical Center*,[57] physicians performed an in vitro fertilization procedure on Robyn Lubowitz. An egg was removed from Lubowitz and combined with her husband's sperm in a placental serum provided by an anonymous donor. The embryo was implanted in Mrs. Lubowitz in August 1985. On November 18, 1985, Mrs. Lubowitz was informed that a test of the donated placental serum determined that it contained the AIDS antibody, HTLV-III. A test of Mrs. Lubowitz' blood conducted five days later returned a negative result. Over the next two months, additional testing of the donated serum and Mrs. Lubowitz' blood found no evidence of the AIDS antibody. Based on this testing, the physicians believed that the initial test of the placental serum was a false positive. Nonetheless, Lubowitz and her husband filed suit for fear of AIDS and related physical ailments. The trial court entered summary judgment in favor of the defendants on the basis that Pennsylvania law did not recognize a claim for fear of AIDS.

---

55. For cases citing the former holding, see e.g., *Alexander v. Carlisle Corp.*, 449 Pa. Super. 416, 674 A.2d 268 (1996); *Randt v. Abex Corp.*, 448 Pa. Super. 224, 671 A.2d 228 (1996); and *White v. Owens-Corning Fiberglas Corp.*, 447 Pa. Super. 5, 668 A.2d 136 (1995). For cases citing *Giffear* for its holding that fear of disease is not compensable, see e.g., *Cleveland v. Johns-Manville Corp.*, 547 Pa. 402, 690 A.2d 1146 (1997); *Didio v. Philadelphia Asbestos Corp.*, 434 Pa. Super. 191, 642 A.2d 1088 (1994).

56. The Philadelphia court's docket is described in *Taylor v. Owens-Corning Fiberglas Corp.*, 446 Pa. Super. 174, 666 A.2d 681 (1995).

57. 424 Pa. Super. 468, 623 A.2d 3 (1993) (Beck, J.).

On appeal, the Superior Court affirmed the ruling of the trial court. It began by acknowledging that the issue presented was one of first impression. Nonetheless, the court concluded that the issue was guided by the analysis of *Marinari* and two subsequent cases that rejected "risk of contracting disease" claims.[58] Relying on these cases, it reasoned that, based on the "separate disease" rule, Lubowitz could file a second action if and when she contracted AIDS. Prior to that time, however, no action could be maintained. "Because there is no legally cognizable injury," it concluded, "there can be no recovery for the alleged negligence." On this basis, the court held that summary judgment was properly entered in favor of the defendants.[59] *Lubowitz* has been cited repeatedly in Pennsylvania, and by courts in seven states considering fear of AIDS claims.[60]

## DOMESTIC RELATIONS

Like its work in the realm of torts, the court's family cases involved a variety of claims that were unknown to the common law. Perhaps the most notable of these was a claim for enforcement of an alleged oral agreement between unmarried cohabitants to share property. Nationally, the most famous case involving this issue was *Marvin v. Marvin*,[61] in which the California Supreme Court held that an oral property agreement between unmarried cohabitants would be enforced if established by adequate evidence. The viability of an action for enforcement of such an agreement under Pennsylvania law was first considered by the Superior Court in *Knauer v. Knauer*.[62] In that case, Florence Todd began to cohabitate with Lewis Knauer, her paramour, allegedly based upon his promise to "share everything" with Todd and to take care of her for the rest of her life. Thereafter, Todd quit her employment as a waitress and began working for Knauer's construction company. She also performed all domestic tasks at the parties' residence. The parties ultimately built another house and, although it was titled solely in Knauer's name, the parties executed a written agreement whereby "the survivor's interest shall be the net equity in the property as of the date of death."[63] Todd also lent Knauer $9,200 to buy two undeveloped lots for construction projects. In making the loan, Todd stated that it was part of the parties' sharing agreement and that she did not expect repayment. Eight years after the parties began to cohabitate, Knauer left Todd and married another woman. Todd filed suit based on the express oral agreement to share assets and for proceeds from the sale of the home the parties built. Following trial, Todd received a verdict of $30,000.

On appeal, Knauer argued that the alleged agreement to "share everything" was void because it was based on a meretricious relationship and thus against public policy. Specifically, Knauer argued that the only consideration for his promise was Todd's promise of sexual services. Rejecting "this careless description of the parties' relationship," the Superior Court began by noting that, although an agreement based solely on the procurement of sexual services was void as contrary to public policy, mere cohabita-

---

58. 623 A.2d 5, citing *Marinari*, *Ottavio* and *Altiere*, supra. Since *Lubowitz* was decided prior to *Giffear*, the court did not have the benefit of the latter opinion to further support its holding.

59. 623 A.2d 5. The court also rejected the Lubowitz' claim for alleged physical symptoms because it was premised on an invalid cause of action.

60. See e.g., *Williamson v. Waldman*, 696 A.2d 14 (N.J. 1997); *Kerins v. Hartley*, 27 Cal.App. 4th 1062 (Cal. 1994); *Brzoska v. Olson*, 668 A.2d 1355 (Del. 1995); *Doe v. Surgicare of Joliet*, 643 N.E.2d 1200 (Ill. 1994); *K.A.C. v. Benson*, 527 N.W.2d 553 (Minn. 1995); *Madrid v. Lincoln County Medical Center*, 909 P.2d 14 (N.M. 1995); *Tischler v. Dimenna*, 609 N.Y.S.2d 1002 (N.Y. 1994). See also, 55 U. Pitt. L. Rev. 291, 59 ALR 4th 535.

61. 18 Cal.3d 660, 134 Cal.Rptr. 815, 557 P.2d 106 (1976).

62. 323 Pa. Super. 206, 470 A.2d 553 (1983) (Cercone, J.).

63. 470 A.2d 556.

tion does not render parties incapable of forming a binding contract. The court then examined "palimony" cases from around the nation, including *Marvin*. "It is the general view [of these cases]," it held, "that an agreement to accumulate or transfer property and the legally viable consideration, such as household or personal services, upon which the agreement is based can be enforced to the extent that the contract is independent of any agreement to pay for sexual services."[64] The court also rejected the claim, raised in other jurisdictions, that enforcing such agreements would convert the relationship between cohabiting parties into a common law marriage. "Parties to a common law marriage," it stated, "are legally married in Pennsylvania and can, by virtue of their status as spouses, make claims to property even absent an agreement. Cohabitors, on the other hand, acquire no automatic claims to property from cohabitation."[65] Finally, in concluding that Knauer's promise to "share everything" was enforceable, the court emphasized that legal recognition of agreements between unmarried cohabitants did not undermine the institution of marriage:

> We do not mean by this opinion to in any way reflect a diminution of the sanctity of marriage, which brings to society an orderliness and stability which no other social institution can bring. All we say is that two adults not married to each other, who agree to establish a financial and economic relationship based on adequate consideration which is not predominantly based on sexual consideration create an agreement cognizable and binding in law.[66]

*Knauer* has been cited repeatedly by courts in Pennsylvania, other states, and various federal districts.[67] Moreover, it was also relied on in an important case decided a year later in which the Superior Court considered an issue of first impression in the nation, whether common law marriage was available to gay couples. In *DeSanto v. Barnsley*,[68] John DeSanto sought a divorce from a common law marriage that he had allegedly entered into with William Barnsley in 1970. The parties lived together until 1980. DeSanto also sought equitable distribution, alimony, alimony pendente lite, and costs. The trial court rejected DeSanto's claims on the basis that Pennsylvania law did not recognize gay marriages and that, in addition, DeSanto had failed to produce sufficient evidence establishing a common law marriage between the parties.

The Superior Court affirmed the trial court's holding that Pennsylvania common law did not recognize gay marriages. Although no other court had addressed the validity of gay common law marriages, the Superior Court found that cases in other states considering gay statutory marriages were analogous because "'marriage' presumably has the same meaning" in both instances.[69] These cases had consistently refused to acknowledge gay marriages under statutory law. Turning to Pennsylvania law, the court also noted that state-licensing law referred to the "male and female applicant,"[70] and that case law defined marriage as a civil contract between "husband and wife."[71] Finally, it noted that leading dictionaries defined marriage as a union between

---

64. 470 A.2d 563.
65. 470 A.2d 564.
66. 470 A.2d 566.
67. See e.g., 328 Pa. Super. 206, 470 A.2d 553 (1984); *In re Murphy*, 226 B.R. 601 (U.S.B.C., Tenn. 1998); *Cook v. Cook*, 691 P.2d 664 (Ariz. 1984); *Bright v. Kuehl*, 650 N.E.2d 311 (Ind. 1995); *Shaw v. Smith*, 964 P.2d 428 (Wyo. 1998). See also, 3 ALR 4th 13, and 69 *Temple L.Q.* 655.
68. 328 Pa. Super. 181, 476 A.2d 952 (1984) (Spaeth, P.J.).
69. 476 A.2d 954.
70. 476 A.2d 954, citing 48 P.S. 1-3.
71. 476 A.2d 954, citing *In re Estate of Manfredi*, 399 Pa. 285, 159 A.2d 697 (1960).

Superior Court of 1991.
L. to R. (seated): Peter Paul Olszewski, Vincent A. Cirillo, James R. Cavanaugh, James E. Rowley (President Judge), Donald E. Wieand, Stephen J. McEwen Jr., Joseph A. Del Sole.
L. to R. (standing): John G. Brosky, J. Sydney Hoffman, Kate Ford Elliott, Justin M. Johnson, John T. J. Kelly Jr., Phyllis W. Beck, Frank J. Montemuro Jr., Patrick R. Tamilia, Zoran Popovich, Joseph A. Hudock, Harry M. Montgomery, William F. Cercone.

members of the opposite sex.[72] Based on this review, the court concluded "that up until now common law marriage has been regarded as a relationship that can be established only between two persons of opposite sex."[73] It then considered whether it should sanction an extension to persons of the same sex and found that neither history nor public policy warranted such an extension. Historically, the court noted, common law marriage was necessitated by the "social conditions of pioneer society [which] made access to clergy or public officials difficult." Although required by necessity, however, common law marriages were tolerated only reluctantly and they were narrowly interpreted. Extending the institution to same-sex couples, the court held, "would be, not simply inconsistent with such reluctant toleration, but an about-face." In this regard, it cited *Knauer's* careful distinction between utilizing contract principles to enforce a property agreement and extending common law marriage to unmarried cohabitants. "Certainly the law should take into account changes in social relationships," the court stated, "but [as in *Knauer*] that may be done without expanding common law marriage." Finally, the Superior Court concluded that recognition of gay marriage was for the legislature, not the judiciary. "If, under the guise of expanding the common law," it reasoned, "we were to create a form of marriage forbidden by statute, we should abuse our judicial power: our decision would have no support in precedent, and its practical effect would be to amend the Marriage Law—something only the legislature can do."[74] For these reasons, the court declined DeSanto's invitation to recognize gay common law marriages.[75] Like *Knauer*, *DeSanto* remains Pennsylvania law and it has been cited by courts in a number of other jurisdictions.[76]

72. 476 A.2d 954, citing *Black's Law Dictionary,* 876 (5th ed. 1979) (defining marriage as a "legal union of one man and one woman as husband and wife"); and *Webster's Third International Dictionary* 1384 (1976) (defining marriage as a "state of being united to a person of the opposite sex as husband or wife").

73. 476 A.2d 954.

74. 476 A.2d 956.

75. The court also refused to consider DeSanto's claim that denial of common law marriage to gays violated the Equal Rights Amendment of the Pennsylvania Constitution because this claim was not raised before the trial court. See note 73.

76. See e.g., *Constant A. v. Paul C.A.,* 344 Pa. Super. 49, 496 A.2d 1 (1985); *Africa v. Vaughan*, 998 F. Supp.

In addition to considering whether to adopt new rules of family law, the court also considered whether to abolish old rules. *In the Interest of Miller*,[77] for instance, involved the common law principle that men over the age of fourteen and women over twelve could enter a valid common law marriage. In *Miller*, a thirty-six-year-old school teacher, Edward Christoph, and his fourteen-year-old student, Melissa Miller, entered into a common law marriage in a ceremony witnessed by Christoph's sister and brother-in-law. On July 22, 1981, one day after the marriage, Miller's mother filed a petition alleging that Miller was a dependent. The trial court ordered Miller detained at a foster home and thereafter adjudicated her dependent and forbade any contact with Christoph. The court also ruled that Christoph married Miller to prevent her from testifying against him in a prosecution for corrupting the morals of a minor. Since Christoph's motives were fraudulent, the court held, he lacked the assent necessary to create a valid marriage and his marriage to Miller was therefore void.[78]

The Superior Court began its analysis by rejecting the trial court's conclusion that Christoph agreed to marry Miller solely to avoid prosecution. According to the court, the evidence indicated that Christoph's motives were mixed; he wanted to avoid prosecution, but he also loved Miller.[79] At any rate, the court continued, controlling precedent dictated that the motive for a marriage is irrelevant so long as the parties possessed a present intention to marry at the time of the ceremony.[80] Thus, "[t]he fact—as the lower court found it to be—that Mr. Christoph's motive was to avoid prosecution could not render invalid their otherwise valid common law marriage."[81] Similarly, the court rejected the trial court's conclusion that since Christoph's motives were fraudulent the marriage was void. Discussing at length the distinction between void and voidable marriages, the court found that the trial court "blurred the distinction" between the two. Specifically, it emphasized that under Section 204(a)(3) of the Divorce Code, as relied on by the trial court, a marriage was void only if one of the parties "lacked capacity to consent or did not assent" to the marriage. Since both parties intended to assent, regardless of their motives for doing so, the marriage between Christoph and Miller was not void. Instead, since it was arguably induced by fraud, the marriage was at most voidable under Section 205(a)(5) of the Divorce Code. However, under well-established principles of common and statutory law, a voidable marriage, unlike a void marriage, can be annulled only by one of the parties thereto and it continues "unless and until" challenged by one of them.[82] Since neither party challenged the marriage, the court reasoned, it remained valid. Finally, the Superior Court considered the argument of counsel for Miller's mother that the court should abolish common law marriage, or at least modify it to conform to statutory marriage laws, which provided that eighteen was the minimum age for marriage. The court found that neither the judiciary nor the legislature had altered the status of common law marriage, despite numerous opportunities to do so.[83] "If common law marriage is to be abolished, or the requirements for

---

552 (E.D. Pa. 1998); *Shahar v. Bowers*, 70 F.3d 1218 (11th Cir. 1995); *Dean v. District of Columbia*, 653 A.2d 307 (D.C. 1995); *Baehr v. Lewin*, 852 P.2d 44 (Hawaii 1993); *Rutgers Council of AAUP Chapters v. Rutgers State Univ.*, 689 A.2d 828 (N.J. 1997). See also, 144 U. Pa. L. Rev. 1, 79 Va. L. Rev. 1419, 1994 Wis. L. Rev. 1033.

    77. 301 Pa. Super. 511, 448 A.2d 25 (1982) (Spaeth, J.).

    78. 448 A.2d 25-26.

    79. 448 A.2d 29.

    80. 448 A.2d 29, citing *In re Estate of Gower*, 445 Pa. 554, 284 A.2d 742 (1971).

    81. 448 A.2d 29-30.

    82. 448 A.2d 32, citing Perlberger, *Pennsylvania Divorce Code* 3.2.3. (1980).

    83. 448 A.2d 32, citing *Buradus v. General Cement Products Co.*, 159 Pa. Super. 501, 48 A.2d 883 (1946), The Marriage Law, Act of August 22, 1953, PL 1344, 48 P.S. 1-23, The Divorce Code of 1980, Act of April 2, 1980, PL 63, Act No. 26, 23 P.S. 101 et seq.

entering into it changed," the court held, "it must be done by the Legislature, not the courts." Finally, the court acknowledged the anguish the marriage had caused Miller's mother and the court expressed hope that the marriage would endure. Yet these factors could not influence the court's decision. "Our responsibility is to interpret and apply the law," the court concluded. "If a marriage is lawful, that is the end of our inquiry. For as judges, we are agents of the State, and whether a lawful marriage is happy or unhappy is none of the State's affair."[84] On this basis, the order of the trial court invalidating the marriage and adjudicating Miller delinquent was reversed.

Although the court believed that its holding was mandated by the common law, it was extremely controversial. In a lengthy dissent, Judge Johnson argued that the 3:00 a.m. exchange of vows between Christoph and Miller "constituted a mockery of this respected institution [of marriage]"[85] and that "the purpose of the surreptitious ceremony was something other than to establish the solemn and permanent relationship of husband and wife."[86] The legislature reacted to the notoriety engendered by this case and subsequently enacted a statute permitting the parent or guardian of a child under the age of eighteen who enters a common law marriage to bring a declaratory judgment action to annul the marriage.[87]

The legislature also codified a family law rule established by the Superior Court in the 1989 case of *In re Quick*.[88] In that case, three children were adjudicated dependent after they had been sexually abused by their step-father and another man. The children's mother was also convicted of endangering their welfare. Thereafter, Allegheny County Children and Youth Services filed a petition for the involuntary termination of both parents' rights. Father's rights were terminated without contest on June 3, 1987. At this point, the court of common pleas invoked a standing administrative order to determine which judge should hear the mother's termination proceeding. The July 13, 1987, order issued by the president judge of the court of common pleas provided that in contested parental termination proceedings involving a dependent child, the juvenile court judge who decided the dependency disposition could be assigned to preside over the proceeding for the termination of parental rights. Pursuant to this order, the trial judge who had adjudicated the children dependent while sitting in the juvenile section of the family division was assigned to orphan's court division to hear the termination proceeding against mother. The mother then presented a motion seeking recusal of the trial judge which was denied. A decree nisi was entered terminating the mother's parental rights. On August 2, 1988, following argument before the orphan's court en banc, the decree was made final.[89]

On appeal, the mother claimed that her constitutional right to a fair hearing was violated by the administrative order providing that the same judge would hear the dependency and termination proceedings. Specifically, the mother argued that since the prior dependency proceeding was subject to a lesser evidentiary standard, the trial judge considered hearsay and inflammatory statements that were inadmissible in the subsequent termination proceeding, and that this evidence prejudiced him in determining whether to terminate the mother's parental rights. In a lengthy opinion, this court rejected the mother's argument and validated the administrative order of the court of common pleas. First, it drew a distinction between the lenient standard for admission of evidence in dependency proceedings and the more stringent standard—

---

84. 448 A.2d 32.
85. 448 A.2d 37.
86. 448 A.2d 38.
87. See 23 Pa.C.S. sec. 3303(b).
88. 384 Pa. Super. 412, 559 A.2d 42 (1989) (Tamilia, J.).
89. 559 A.2d 42-43.

clear and convincing evidence—required for an adjudication of dependency. "The fact that a lesser standard is applied for admission of evidence," it reasoned, "does not obviate the rigorous requirement of finding clear necessity."[90] Experienced trial judges, the court stated, could be relied on to apply the separate standards without bias or prejudice. Moreover, the administrative order providing for the same judge at dependency and termination proceedings was supported by strong policy considerations. According to the court:

> [A]doption and termination procedures are logically and traditionally construed to be family matters. The consistent thread, over many years flowing through the management of family cases, has been that so far as possible the judge who initially heard the family matter should remain with it to its conclusion. Indeed, one of the most disruptive and disconcerting factors in multi-judge jurisdictions is the fragmentation of different aspects of a family case resulting from the hearing by several judges of different stages of a particular proceeding. Family matters are complex but intricately intertwined so that the best treatment so far as the parties are concerned, particularly in regard to children, as well as the most consistent and efficient approach from the judicial point of view, is for the same judge to remain involved with the family along the continuum of the particular case.[91]

The court found further support for its conclusion in the commitment of federal and state family law guidelines to the concept of permanency planning, which sought to prevent children from spending their lives in the limbo of foster care by emphasizing adoption where the family cannot be rehabilitated within a reasonable time.[92] Under this concept, the juvenile court judge who initially deals with the child is primarily responsible for monitoring and expediting the child's movement through the child welfare system, up to and including the termination of parental rights. It would undermine the goals of Permanency Planning, the court stated, to replace the juvenile court judge once the process is initiated, since the new judge "will not have the benefit of recall of hearings, reports and directions not fully detailed in the cold or abbreviated reports [of prior proceedings]."[93] The court also found that the mother had cited no prejudicial or inflammatory evidence, either in support of her recusal motion or on appeal, which was presented at the dependency action and would not have been admissible at the termination proceeding. Nor did a review of the record indicate such evidence. Finally, after a review of relevant constitutional and statutory provisions, the court concluded that the assignment of a juvenile judge to hear a termination proceeding in orphan's court violated no legislative mandate. On this basis, the order terminating the mother's parental rights was affirmed.[94,95] In 1996, seven years after this court's holding in *Quick*, the

---

90. 559 A.2d 46.
91. See note 90.
92. Permanancy Planning is defined at 559 A.2d 47.
93. 559 A.2d 47.
94. 559 A.2d 49.
95. The result of the ruling in *In Re Quick*, coupled with changes in policy by Children and Youth Services, fostered by the federal legislation requiring permanency planning, has dramatically increased the adoption of children formerly placed in long-term or permanent foster homes. In a report in the *Pittsburgh Post-Gazette*, July 22, 1999, there were 84 adoptions following termination of parental rights in 1989, the year of the *Quick* decision. According to Allegheny County Children and Youth Services, there were 1,682 such adoptions in 1998-99, and approximately 2,500 in 1999-2000.

legislature enacted an amendment to the Juvenile Act as to dependency, which provided that the same judge would hear both dependency and termination proceedings.[96]

Like *Knauer, DeSanto, Miller,* and *Quick*, the case of *In the Interest of Jones*[97] also involved an important issue of first impression. The question in that case was whether a fundamental constitutional right available to criminal defendants—the right to personally confront adverse witnesses—should be afforded to parents in dispositional hearings regarding the custody of their children. In *Jones*, two children were adjudicated dependent, removed from the home of their mother, and placed in the custody of their maternal aunt, Ernestine Taylor. Thereafter, the mother underwent counseling and petitioned for a hearing to regain custody. Children and Youth Services (CYS) indicated that it would recommend to the juvenile court that mother be awarded custody. However, at a hearing on the mother's petition, CYS elicited testimony from Ernestine Taylor that she had received reports from an unnamed source that the mother was continuing a lesbian relationship with a male impersonator, Aznif Smith, who had committed acts of violence against the mother while the children still lived with her. Based on this testimony, CYS recommended further investigation. At a subsequent hearing, the unnamed source was permitted to testify in camera after he refused to testify if his identity was revealed to the mother. Identified only as Mr. C, the source testified that he was a frequent visitor to the mother's house, that the mother had maintained a relationship with Aznif Smith, and that the relationship was at times violent. Although the mother's attorney was permitted to cross-examine Mr. C, the mother was not informed of his identity or permitted to be present during the testimony. Based on Mr. C's testimony, both CYS and the juvenile court reversed their initial position and concluded that the mother should not be awarded custody. The court entered an order awarding custody to CYS.[98]

On appeal, the mother argued that, regardless of whether her attorney was permitted to cross-examine Mr. C, she had the constitutional right to know his identity and to personally confront him. The Superior Court agreed. Noting the novel nature of the mother's claim, the court began by acknowledging that, although the right to confrontation is well established in criminal proceedings, such a right is not "universally applicable to all hearings."[99] To determine whether the right should apply to dispositional proceedings in juvenile court, the court examined the propriety of the in camera procedure utilized to elicit Mr. C's testimony.

Citing a two-factor test established by the United States Supreme Court, the court considered the risk of error and the consequences that flowed from the procedure utilized by the juvenile court. As to the first factor, risk of error, it found that the failure to inform the mother of Mr. C's identity deprived her of the opportunity to confront him with any evidence of bias or vindictiveness. Since dispositional hearings turn on factual determinations, the deprivation of the mother's critical opportunity to attack Mr. C's credibility might well have resulted in the loss of custody of her children. This risk of error, the court held, "cannot be overstated."[100]

The Superior Court then turned to the consequences of the juvenile court's in camera procedure. First, it found that allowing damaging testimony against a parent,

---

96. Pa. Act of July 11, 1996, PL 607, 23 Pa.C.S. sec. 6351, Disposition of Dependent Child, (i) Assignment to orphans' court.

97. 286 Pa. Super. 574, 429 A.2d 671 (1981) (Cavanaugh, J.).

98. 429 A.2d 671-674.

99. 429 A.2d 675. The court further stated, "The facts of this case raise a difficult question as to the nature of the parent's right to due process in a dispositional hearing. The answer to this question is most troublesome in that it involves the delicate determination of when the integrity of the family may be sacrificed in an effort to protect its individual members." 429 A.2d 674.

100. 429 A.2d 675, citing *Wolff v. McDonnell*, 418 U.S. 539 (1974).

without also allowing the parent an opportunity to challenge the truthfulness of the testimony, might result in a situation where a parent is unjustifiably deprived of his or her children. Worse yet, this situation would also deprive the children of their parent. Since the court's most important consideration is the best interests of the children, it held that this consequence was impermissible. Having found that the risk of error and the consequences flowing from the trial court's refusal to allow the mother to confront Mr. C were too great, it further concluded that the mother's due process rights had been violated. Yet this did not end the case.

The Superior Court next considered whether the unconstitutional procedure employed by the trial court had been sanctioned by the Juvenile Act. In this regard, the court emphasized Section 6341(d) of the act, which provides, "Sources of information given in confidence need not be disclosed."[101] Because this "troublesome" provision was so broadly drawn, the court found it arguably authorized Mr. C's in camera testimony. Given the conclusion that Mr. C's testimony deprived the mother of her due process right, the court had little choice but to conclude that Section 6341(d) was unconstitutional. "The statement that sources of information need not be disclosed," the court held, "is, in fact, clearly, palpably, and plainly violative of the Constitution in its unqualified allowance of testimony into evidence regardless of the opportunity provided to test the veracity and reliability of the declarant." Since the procedure authorized by the Juvenile Act and employed by the trial court was unconstitutional, the Superior Court reversed the award of custody to CYS and remanded for a new dispositional hearing.[102] In a lengthy dissent, Judge Hester argued that the risk of error and consequences flowing from the in camera procedure were minimal because the mother's attorney cross-examined Mr. C, and Mr. C's testimony was supported by other evidence. Hester also emphasized that Mr. C would not have testified if the mother knew his identity. As a result, Hester argued, requiring confrontation would have deprived the court of Mr. C's critical testimony and the children would have been returned to a potentially dangerous environment. Finally, Hester emphasized that the right of confrontation provided to criminal defendants is not available in all types of hearings, and the Juvenile Act properly authorized a lesser standard in dispositional proceedings.[103] The majority holding in *Jones* has endured, and dispositional hearings in juvenile court continue to be subject to the constitutional right to confront adverse witnesses.[104]

## THE FAMILY LAW REVOLUTION

The most significant legislative development in family law in the past two decades was passage of the Divorce Code of 1980.[105] The Divorce Code, which has generated a tremendous volume of appellate litigation, dramatically altered the manner in which the courts processed dissolution of marriages, spousal support, and distribution of marital property. As detailed earlier in Chapter II, the slow, steady progression of dealing with marital problems evolved from ecclesiastical courts to remedies at common law and ultimately to statutory procedure.

The preamble to the Divorce Code of 1990, formerly the preamble to the Divorce Code of 1980, establishes:

---

101. 429 A.2d 677.

102. 429 A.2d 678.

103. 429 A.2d 680-82.

104. See e.g., *Commonwealth v. Taylor*, 346 Pa. Super. 599, 500 A.2d 110 (1985); *In Interest of Leslie H.*, 329 Pa. Super. 453, 478 A.2d 876 (1984); *Commonwealth ex rel. Grimes v. Yack*, 289 Pa. Super. 495, 433 A.2d 1363 (1981).

105. PL 63, No. 26, April 2, 1980. Since the Superior Court construed the Code in the years after 1980, it is considered in this chapter.

§ 3102. Legislative findings and intent

(a) Policy.—The family is the basic unit in society and the protection and preservation of the family is of paramount public concern. Therefore, it is the policy of the Commonwealth to:

(1) Make the law for legal dissolution of marriage effective for dealing with the realities of matrimonial experience.

(2) Encourage and effect reconciliation and settlement of differences between spouses, especially where children are involved.

(3) Give primary consideration to the welfare of the family rather than the vindication of private rights or the punishment of matrimonial wrongs.

(4) Mitigate the harm to the spouses and their children caused by the legal dissolution of the marriage.

(5) Seek causes rather than symptoms of family disintegration and cooperate with and utilize the resources available to deal with family problems.

(6) Effectuate economic justice between parties who are divorced or separated and grant or withhold alimony according to the actual need and ability to pay of the parties and insure a fair and just determination and settlement of their property rights.

(b) Construction of part.—The objectives set forth in subsection (a) shall be considered in construing provisions of this part and shall be regarded as expressing the legislative intent.

The provision in Section 3102(b) has been the underlying premise, which has guided the courts both at the trial level and on appeal in the resolution of marital difficulties. The courts, standing free of the limitation of actions in divorce and its ancillary matters, have done extremely well in developing and interpreting the legislative mandates of Sections 3102(a)(1)(3) and (6).

In creating a new means for obtaining marital dissolution, where proof of fault based on grounds for divorce was not required, the legislature responded to national and local public pressure in permitting divorce to be obtained without the necessity of proving fault.

Under Section 3301, "Grounds for divorce," subsection (a), the Divorce Code retained the traditional fault grounds for divorce. Subsection (c), "Mutual consent," however, provides that the court "may grant a divorce where it is alleged that the marriage is irretrievably broken and 90 days have elapsed from the date of commencement of an action under this part and an affidavit has been filed by each of the parties evidencing that each of the parties consent to the divorce." This is the no-fault ground which has cleared the way for divorce without the difficulty and additional trauma of bitter and acrimonious laundering of a family's dirty linen in court. A more stringent ground, which also does away with proof of fault and the ensuing acrimony, is provided by Section 3301(d), "Irretrievable breakdown."

> (1)  The court may grant a divorce where a complaint has been filed alleging that the marriage is irretrievably broken and an affidavit has been filed alleging that the parties have lived separate and apart for a period of at least two years and that the marriage is irretrievably broken.

This section is known as the "living apart grounds." Section 3301(e), "No hearing required in certain cases," provides, "If grounds for divorce alleged in the complaint or counterclaim are established under subsection (c) or (d), the court shall grant a divorce without requiring a hearing on any other grounds."

Thus, this legislation virtually eliminated all divorce hearings and the number of divorce complaints requesting fault ground divorces are infinitesimal. Since the inception of no-fault grounds in 1980, divorces have been processed routinely, almost as an administrative matter. This has not, however, reduced the number of matters heard in divorce cases as the activity has shifted from the dissolution proceeding to the determination of custody and economic issues, including support, alimony, and counsel fees.

Highlighting the flood of appellate cases relating to the newly enacted Divorce Code were those which dealt with the treatment of marital property. Pursuant to the Divorce Code, Section 3104, "Bases of jurisdiction":

> The courts shall have original jurisdiction in cases of divorce ... and shall determine, in conjunction with any decree granting a divorce or annulment . . . if raised in the pleadings. . . .

> (1)  The determination and disposition of property rights and interests between spouses. . . .

Chapter 35, "Property Rights," Section 3501, "Definitions," provides:

> (a) General rule.—As used in this chapter, "marital property" means all property acquired by either party during the marriage, including the increase in value, prior to the date of final separation, of any nonmarital property acquired pursuant to paragraphs (1) [Property acquired prior to marriage or property acquired in exchange for property acquired prior to the marriage] and (3) [Property acquired by gift, except between spouses, bequest, devise or descent].

There are several exceptions which are self-explanatory. Section 3501(b), "Presumption," provides, "All real or personal property acquired by either party during the marriage is presumed to be marital property regardless of whether title is held individually or by the parties in some form of co-ownership such as joint tenancy, tenancy in common or tenancy by the entirety."

Typical of the cases reaching the Superior Court were those relating to types of property which could be construed as marital property subject to equitable distribution. One of the first cases in this regard was *Hodge v. Hodge*,[106] which called upon this

---

106. 337 Pa. Super. 151, 486 A.2d 951 (1984) (Del Sole, J.).

Judge Vincent Cirillo holds up for display to guests, at a Superior Court recognition dinner in 1992, the sterling silver plaque presented to him by the court for his outstanding contributions during his term as president judge, 1986-1990.

court to determine whether a professional degree (M.D.) obtained during the marriage was subject to equitable distribution based upon the increased earning capacity acquired due to the schooling. *Hodge* involved a couple who, during the marriage, in what can only be described as a joint effort, worked together to enable the husband to acquire a medical degree. During the marriage, three children were born. Upon completion of his training, the husband entered into private practice, leaving his wife and family and taking up residence with a nurse he met during his internship. The period of training began in January 1971 and concluded in January 1977, during which time the wife contributed to support of the family, contributed to husband's educational costs, and helped maintain the family in other ways. The issue was framed as whether the medical degree, earned with the assistance of the wife, qualified as marital property subject to equitable distribution. A second issue was whether increased earning capacity could also be considered an asset divisible as marital property. The court stated:

> A clear majority of courts that have considered the question of whether the advanced degree itself, or the increased earning capacity it represents, are divisible marital assets, have concluded they are not. . . .

> The question then becomes: Is potential increased earning capacity marital property if developed during the marriage? . . .

> Our analysis of the Divorce Code also supports the conclusion that the legislature did not intend increased earning capacity to be a divisible asset. Section 401(d)(4) provides that one of the factors to be considered in distributing marital property is 'the contribution by one party to the education, training, or increased earning power of the other party' . . . It is logical to conclude from that statement that increased earning power *itself* is not marital property.[107]

Judge Richard Wickersham, in a vigorous dissent, would have held that the Divorce Code, in mandating economic justice, manifested the legislature's intent that

---

107. 486 A.2d 953.

the medical degree and the increased earnings were subject to equitable distribution. Despite Wickersham's argument, the majority's holding was affirmed by the Supreme Court.[108]

In addition to professional degrees, the court also considered whether a number of other assets acquired during the marriage were subject to equitable distribution. For instance, in *King v. King*,[109] the court considered whether pensions could be divided as marital property. Holding in the affirmative, the court stated:

> Although he does not raise the question as a separate issue, appellant does suggest in the body of his argument that perhaps his pension fund is not subject to equitable distribution. . . .
>
> We believe it is clear that the pension is marital property subject to equitable distribution and agree with the decisions of other jurisdictions that have so found.[110]

One year later, in *Braderman v. Braderman*,[111] the court reaffirmed that pensions are marital property. According to the court:

> Plaintiff-wife and defendant-husband were married when defendant-husband was employed by the Commonwealth, as well as at the time he terminated his employment and his interest [in the pension] matured. These benefits constitute deferred compensation for services defendant-husband performed during the marriage and therefore he acquired his interest in these benefits while married to plaintiff-wife.[112]

The court went on to say, "We believe it is clear that the pension is marital property subject to equitable distribution and agree with the decisions of other jurisdictions that have so found."[113]

In the 1988 case of *Ciliberti v. Ciliberti*,[114] the court considered whether disability benefits were subject to equitable distribution. Distinguishing such benefits from pensions, the court began by noting:

> Although the pertinent section of the Divorce Code does not otherwise refer to retirement pension benefits, it is now firmly established that retirement pension benefits, vested and non-vested, military and civilian, are deemed marital property subject to equitable distribution. Whether disability payments are to be deemed marital property, however, has not previously been decided by an appellate court in this Commonwealth.
>
> The courts of other jurisdictions have reached varying results. Several courts have held that disability benefits are not marital property but, rather, compensation for loss of earning capacity. Such compensation, these courts have held, is the separate property of the employee spouse.[115]

---

108. *Hodge v. Hodge*, 513 Pa. 264, 520 A.2d 15 (1986).
109. 332 Pa. Super. 526, 481 A.2d 913 (1984) (Brosky, J.).
110. 481 A.2d 916 n. 2.
111. 339 Pa. Super. 185, 488 A.2d 613 (1985) (Montemuro, J.).
112. 488 A.2d 618.
113. 488 A.2d 619.
114. 374 Pa. Super. 228, 542 A.2d 580 (1988) (Wieand, J.).
115. 542 A.2d 581 (citations omitted).

Judge Cirillo (left) was presented with his portrait at the 1992 commemorative dinner in recognition of his stellar performance as president judge, 1986-1990. The portrait now hangs in the Founder's Court Room in Philadelphia. Accompanying Judge Cirillo is Judge Donald Wieand.

Although other courts deemed disability pensions to be marital property, the Superior Court held to the contrary:

> We decline to hold that true disability payments are marital property subject to equitable distribution. Such benefits are intended to compensate the employee spouse for lost earning capacity. They are paid in lieu of the earnings which would have been paid to the employee if he or she had been able to work. They replace the future salary or wages which the employee, because of physical or mental disability, will not be able to earn. They are comparable to Workmen's Compensation disability payments. Post-divorce payments intended to compensate for an inability to work are not marital property.[116]

This holding relating to pensions and disability payments continues to be the law of Pennsylvania.

The above issues presented the initial policy matters to be reviewed and interpreted. While there were numerous other issues concerning equitable distribution, none set forth the basic interpretation of a law, new in concept and in many ways a departure from the past, that these issues presented.

---

116. 542 A.2d 582.

A third issue related to the Divorce Code of 1980 was considered by this court in *Fratangelo v. Fratangelo*.[117] In employing the equitable distribution provisions of the new Code, trial courts frequently ordered a mechanical fifty-fifty division of marital property, regardless of other equitable considerations. This practice was rejected by the Superior Court in *Fratangelo*, in which the court began by noting:

> This is the first instance where this Court has taken the opportunity to review what has quickly become the widespread practice of using a fifty-fifty distribution of marital property as the starting point in marital distribution. By utilizing a semantic inversion, "starting point" without consideration of its defacto nature and effect, the legislative provisions have been subverted.[118]

In reviewing the facts of record, the court stated:

> The sum and substance of these facts leads to the conclusion that but for the in-kind contribution estimated at $9,000 by the husband, the purchase of the lot, payment of the mortgage, property maintenance and protection from foreclosure, were primarily through the efforts and sacrifice of the wife with the assistance of her family.[119]

If, without more, the trial court considered the above factors in relation to 23 P.S. Section 401(d)(7), "[t]he contribution or dissipation of each party in the acquisition . . . of marital property," it would be hard pressed, in equity, to find that the husband was entitled to any but a token share of the marital home which is the only significant property. The court also stated:

> Turning to section 401(d), the clear statement of the law is that the court will equitably distribute or assign marital property (which is determined pursuant to section 401(e)) *"[A]fter considering all relevant factors including. . . ."* (emphasis added), and then lists ten factors. The starting point is unequivocally the consideration of all relevant factors. This requires compilation, computation, weighing and balancing considerations, and then applying the sound discretion of the court to achieve economic justice. This is more difficult than beginning (and likely ending with minor variation) at a fifty-fifty starting point. It is, however, no more difficult than in other areas of domestic relations where the legislature and our courts have rejected presumptions such as shared custody, the tender years doctrine or arbitrary support levels for wife or children.[120]

Prior to introduction of the concept of equitable distribution to Pennsylvania law, all property held by parties to a marriage was held individually or by the entireties. At divorce, solely-owned property was retained by the party and where property was acquired during marriage, it was generally acquired as entireties property. Upon divorce, absent agreement, the parties would "thereafter hold the property as tenants

---

117. 360 Pa. Super. 487, 520 A.2d 1195 (1987) (Tamilia, J.).
118. 520 A.2d 1199.
119. 520 A.2d 1204.
120. 520 A.2d 1203. The court then went on to analyze the continuation and evolution of the law relating to division of marital property.

in common of equal one-half shares in value, and either of them may bring an action against the other to have the property sold and the proceeds divided between them."[121] This section was incorporated into the Divorce Code of 1980, and while applicable in divorce actions where neither party makes a claim for equitable distribution, it is not applicable when equitable distribution is claimed.

The effect of the Divorce Code of 1980 was to define marital property in a more expansive manner than prior law had defined it for purposes of distribution. Moreover, it provides for a means of distribution, which is equitable but not necessarily equal.

The *Fratangelo* court, supra, directly addressed this issue in firm fashion. "When a fifty-fifty starting point is utilized, this Court will scrutinize that process very carefully to determine whether the lower court proceeded in a presumptive fashion or properly and fully considered all 401(d) [now 23 Pa.C.S. Section 3502] factors before making distribution."[122] The clarification of the proper weight to be given the factors enumerated by the legislature in equitable distribution of marital property is critical to the mandate to effectuate economic justice between parties who are divorced or separated and will result in litigants, who otherwise would have been denied justice, receiving the justice to which they are entitled.

In the realm of child custody, the Superior Court was again involved at the threshold of expanding concepts in the field of family law that, at best, had been difficult and onerous and, at worst, wrenching and debilitating. For the families involved, particularly the children, the effect of separation, divorce, or out-of-wedlock relationships involving children has never left practitioners in the field of family law with a sense of accomplishment.

Following extensive review, the legislature passed the Child Custody Act of 1985.[123] The policy of the new law was set forth as follows:

§ 5301. Declaration of policy

The General Assembly declares that it is the public policy of this Commonwealth, when in the best interest of the child, to assure a reasonable and continuing contact of the child with both parents after a separation or dissolution of the marriage and the sharing of the rights and responsibilities of child rearing by both parents and continuing contact of the child or children with grandparents when a parent is deceased, divorced or separated.[124]

In the years after 1985, the Superior Court was called upon to apply the new custody law to a myriad of factual scenarios. Preliminarily, the court needed to reaffirm the doctrinal change initiated by our Supreme Court in *Commonwealth ex rel. Spriggs v. Carson*,[125] which eliminated the presumption of tender years. This presumption was found to be a violation of the Equal Rights Amendment of Article I, Section 28, of the Pennsylvania Constitution. The elimination of the presumption forced the courts to carefully review case-specific factual situations in order to determine what is in the best interests of the child. In *Commonwealth ex rel. Jordan v. Jordan*,[126] the Superior

---

121. 68 P.S. sec. 501, 503 (repealed), now 23 Pa.C.S. sec. 3507, Division of entireties property between divorced persons.

122. 520 A.2d 1201.

123. PL 264, No. 66, October 30, 1985, 23 Pa.C.S. sec. 5301-66.

124. 23 Pa.C.S. sec. 5301. The sections following the declaration of policy expand and more fully define the section 5301 principles.

125. 470 Pa. 290, 368 A.2d 635 (1977).

126. 302 Pa. Super. 421, 448 A.2d 1113 (1982) (Beck, J.). Also see *Hugo v. Hugo*, 288 Pa. Super. 1, 430

Court wrote, "[a] child of tender years should not be lightly removed from a parent with whom the child has lived since birth." The court also indicated that "[i]f in the past, the primary caretaker has tended to the child's physical needs and has exhibited love, affection, concern, tolerance, discipline and a willingness to sacrifice, the trial judge may predict that these qualities will continue."[127] Thus, the primary caretaker doctrine was pronounced. Subsequently, this court has utilized the doctrine as both a fact-finding process and a determinant to supplant the reliance on the tender years presumption.

A second major source of litigation under the Custody Act has to do with shared custody. Section 5304 of the act provides as follows:

§ 5304. Award of shared custody

The court may award an order for shared custody when it is in the best interest of the child:

(1)  upon application of one or both parents;
(2)  when the parties have agreed to an award of shared custody; or
(3)  in the discretion of the court.

The legislation of this position was highly debated with strong emphasis by some proponents for creating a presumption that shared custody is in the best interest of the child. This view did not prevail. Illustrative of the debate is the editorial carried in the *Pittsburgh Post-Gazette,* dated Saturday, August 2, 1980:

Joint custody as an option

The concept of granting divorced parents "joint custody" of their children is an increasingly popular idea, and a good one in terms of providing flexibility to parents and judges.

Much of the impetus for joint custody has come from fathers who have felt unfairly shut out of their children's lives by the prevailing "sole custody" arrangements. Testimony at recent hearings here on two legislative proposals on "joint custody" revealed that in 90 percent of Pennsylvania cases custody has been granted to the mother. Some fathers assert that former presumptions in favor of the mother on grounds she would be at home all the time to care for the children no longer are as applicable with so many mothers working. . . .

Obviously, such an arrangement would be ideal if the divorcing parents were on sufficiently good terms to be able to work things out. Otherwise, there is a danger of a continuing battle. And encouraging that sort of friction flouts the idea that, in the end, custody should be granted on the basis of what's best for the child, not for the parent.

That is where SB 1411 particularly and SB 1282 to an extent appear to go farther than necessary. They would put joint custody first on the judge's priority list, rather than making it just one of the options. This

---

A.2d 1183 (1981) (Cavanaugh, J.) (With the demise of the tender years presumption, the continuation of the child in his environment is a factor which should be considered and may be controlling.).

127. 448 A.2d 1115.

could give a judge an easy way out in a sticky situation—just throw it back in the laps of both parents rather than deciding that the child's best interests require selecting one parent.

A spokesperson for the Governor's Commission for Women made the point well with the comment that "joint custody is desirable only when both parents want it. No legislation can make it work unless both parents are committed to that concept."

Legislation that clearly spelled out joint custody as one option would be valuable. It also could help overcome any presumption that the mother always is the proper person to whom to award custody. But the purpose of such a statute should be to increase flexibility, rather than substitute a new presumption for the present one.

The editorial clearly summarized the debate and foretold the actual outcome of the legislation. Relatively soon after the effective date of the legislation, the Superior Court enunciated the criteria to be met in an order of shared custody.

*In re Wesley J.K.*[128] adopted standards that have been utilized in other jurisdictions and in treatises. Specifically, the court emphasized that the law recognized no presumption of shared custody and held that trial courts should consider an award of joint custody when:

1) both parents are "fit",
2) both parents desire continuing involvement with their child,
3) both parents are seen by the child as sources of security and love, and
4) both parents are able to communicate and cooperate in promoting the child's interests.[129]

Another aspect of the Custody Act of 1985 has been the provision for review of family relocation.

§ 5308. Removal of party or child from jurisdiction

If either party intends to or does remove himself or the child from this Commonwealth after a custody order has been made, the court, on its own motion or upon motion of either party, may review the existing custody order.

In *Fatemi v. Fatemi,*[130] the court employed this provision and concluded that removal of a child from the United States to the father's native country, Iran, was not in the child's best interest in light of the turmoil and warfare occurring in that country.

Further, in 1990, the court considered the standard to be applied by a trial court in determining under what circumstances a parent who has primary custody may relocate outside the jurisdiction of the court. In *Gruber v. Gruber,*[131] the court held that

---

128. 299 Pa. Super. 504, 445 A.2d 1243 (1982) (Beck, J.).

129. 445 A.2d 1249. In subsequent cases, the court insisted on trial court compliance with these factors. See e.g., *Schwarcz v. Schwarcz,* 548 A.2d 556 (Pa. Super. 1988), appeal denied 522 Pa. 578, 559 A.2d 39 (1989), certiorari denied 498 U.S. 815 (1990), and *Wiseman v. Wall,* 718 A.2d 844 (Pa. Super. 1998).

130. 371 Pa. Super. 101, 537 A.2d 840 (1988) (Cirillo, J.).

131. 400 Pa. Super. 174, 583 A.2d 434 (1990) (Beck, J.).

in order to decide whether a custodial parent and children should be permitted to relocate some distance away from a non-custodial parent, a court must consider the integrity of the motives of the custodial parent and whether the move substantially would improve the quality of life of the custodial parent and children and is not the result of a momentary whim of the custodial parent. Motives for moving on the part of the custodial parent must withstand close scrutiny.

Two other family law acts that affected the work of the court in the 1980s and early 1990s were the Protection from Abuse Act[132] and the Child Protective Services Law.[133] The Protection from Abuse Act defines spousal and domestic abuse and mandates a registry in which courts must list certified copies of court orders entered pursuant to the act. It also provides, among other things, a means for seeking relief by adults, and children, through a parent, adult household member, or guardian, by filing petitions and acquiring service of the petitions to obtain expeditious court hearings, and a means to gain relief in the form of restraining orders, temporary custody and support orders, and temporary relinquishment of weapons. It empowers law enforcement officials to arrest without warrant, upon probable cause, any person in violation of the registered order.

Cases arising under the Protection from Abuse Act have created an enormous volume of litigation in the district and trial courts, and this volume indicates the widespread nature of domestic violence in our society.[134] While the number of appeals under the act has been relatively limited, the Superior Court has consistently construed the act broadly in an effort to enhance its implementation throughout the Commonwealth.[135]

Finally, the Child Protective Services Law was passed by the legislature to encourage and require the reporting of child physical, sexual, and emotional abuse. It empowers the appropriate state and county agencies to investigate and, when required, to provide protection for children from further abuse and furnish rehabilitative services for children and parents so as to preserve and stabilize family life. Importantly, the act also creates a child abuse registry, hot lines, and a means of expunging records when appropriate, and it empowers appropriate agencies to take children into custody, and to petition the court under the Juvenile Act[136] to render appropriate treatment and rehabilitation. As with the Protection from Abuse Act, the volume of Child Protective Services cases in the trial courts is great but the number of appeals is not significant.[137] Most appeals arising under the act are heard in Commonwealth Court, since they generally involve the activities of governmental agencies and departments such as the Department of Public Welfare and Children and Youth Services. The Superior Court does, however, consider matters relating to the act when, in the context of a criminal case, there is an issue as to whether a crime has been committed which requires interpretation of the definition of abuse and the sufficiency or weight of the evidence. This court has also been required to distinguish between the Juvenile Act and its jurisdiction to hear and decide abuse charges and The Protection From Abuse Act as an admin-

---

132. PL 1090, October 7, 1976, 23 Pa.C.S. sec. 6101-18.

133. PL 438, No. 124, November 26, 1975, 23 Pa.C.S. sec. 6301-84.

134. The 1998 Annual Report of the Common Pleas Court of Allegheny County states 3,947 applicants were processed with total dispositions by means of conciliation in direct criminal contempt hearings totaling 8,988 cases.

135. See *Cipolla v. Cipolla*, 264 Pa. Super. 53, 398 A.2d 1053, 1054 n. 1 (1979) ("The Protection From Abuse Act is a vanguard measure dealing with problems of wife and child abuse."). *Eichenlaub v. Eichenlaub*, 340 Pa. Super. 552, 490 A.2d 918, 922 (1985) ("The primary goal of the Act was therefore not retrospective punishment, but rather, 'advance' prevention of physical and sexual abuse.").

136. 42 Pa.C.S. sec. 6301-65.

137. Initial appeals related primarily to review of the scope and purpose of the act. See e.g., *Commonwealth v. Arnold*, 356 Pa. Super. 343, 514 A.2d 890 (1986).

istrative procedure to identify and prevent abuse short of the power to mandate custodial changes and compel treatment.[138] The juvenile court alone, upon a petition charging neglect or abuse, may assume legal custody of and/or jurisdiction over the child for treatment and placement purposes.

As this brief review indicates, the Superior Court between 1981 and 1995 significantly shaped Pennsylvania family law relating to divorce, equitable distribution, custody and, to a lesser extent, domestic abuse. The enormity of the litigation handled in the trial courts of Pennsylvania, reflected in large numbers of appeals to this court, is suggested by the activity of only one county. In 1998 Allegheny County disposed of 17,900 support cases, 1,251 custody cases and 3,065 divorce cases. Even more striking is the collection of $123,623,470 in support payments by the Allegheny County Domestic Relations Division. Magnify these figures by those compiled in the remaining sixty-seven counties (sixty judicial districts), and it is obvious that the work of this court in reviewing the proceedings of the trial courts of Pennsylvania is a crucial aspect bearing on the welfare of the people of this Commonwealth.[139]

## CRIMINAL LAW

In the 1980s and early 1990s, the most significant challenge presented to the Superior Court in the realm of criminal law involved implementation of the legislature's new sentencing guidelines. The primary purpose of the guidelines was to foster uniformity in criminal sentencing. As the court noted in 1986, "The sentencing guidelines were formulated in order to weave rationality out of an all-too chaotic sentencing system wherein sentences sometimes varied widely from one county to the next, and even from one courtroom to the next in the same county."[140] In 1978, in order to address persistent sentencing disparities, the legislature established the Commission on Sentencing and vested it with authority to develop standards for trial courts to consider in imposing sentences upon individuals convicted of similar crimes. The first set of guidelines promulgated by the commission became effective on July 22, 1982.[141] These guidelines, which remain in effect in amended form, assign numerical values, or "scores," to the seriousness of the offender's instant crime ("offense gravity score") and the extent and seriousness of the offender's prior criminal record ("prior record score").[142] Based on the combination of these scores, three sentencing ranges are provided; a mitigated range where the combined score is low; a standard range applicable to most cases; and an aggravated range where the combined score is high.[143] Sentences are generally expected to be in the standard range, and where a trial court sentences in the mitigated or aggravated ranges, it must provide a "contemporaneous written statement" of the

---

138. See *In re Morgan L.*, 716 A.2d 658 (Pa. Super. 1998) (Child Protective Services Law does not provide for legal determination of abuse, rather it is a vehicle for reporting abuse and invoking the involvement of county protective services for a child's care).

139. The Public Welfare Department, Office of Child Support Collections, reported the collection of $1,095,655,688 in 1998.

140. See *Commonwealth v. Chesson*, 353 Pa. Super. 255, 509 A.2d 875, 876-77 (1986) (Cavanaugh, J.).

141. The commission initially submitted guidelines in 1981, but these guidelines were rejected by the legislature as too brief and narrow. The guidelines were rewritten and submitted to the legislature one year later. They were deemed effective on July 22, 1982. However, in 1987, the Pennsylvania Supreme Court ruled the guidelines invalid for lack of gubernatorial approval. *Commonwealth v. Sessoms*, 516 Pa. 365, 532 A.2d 775 (1987). The legislature quickly enacted new guidelines, which became effective on April 25, 1988.

142. 204 Pa.Code sec. 303.2(a).

143. 204 Pa.Code sec. 303.8, 303.12, 303.16. The guidelines also authorize an enhanced sentence where an offense involves youths in drug trafficking, where drugs are distributed within 1,000 feet of a school, or where a deadly weapon is used. 204 Pa.Code sec. 303.9.

Superior Court of 1994.
L. to R. (seated): John T. J. Kelly Jr., Phyllis W. Beck, Stephen J. McEwen Jr., James R. Cavanaugh, James E. Rowley (President Judge), Donald E. Wieand, Vincent A. Cirillo, Patrick R. Tamilia, Zoran Popovich.
L. to R. (standing): John P. Hester, J. Sydney Hoffman, Thomas G. Saylor, Joseph A. Hudock, Justin M. Johnson, Harry M. Montgomery, Kate Ford Elliott, William F. Cercone, John G. Brosky.
Missing from photograph: Peter Paul Olszewski, Joseph A. Del Sole.

reasons for doing so. Finally, the guidelines are mandatory in the sense that they must be considered by sentencing courts.[144]

Although the guidelines were relatively specific as applied to trial courts, they provided little guidance to appellate courts reviewing criminal sentences.[145] For instance, sentences could be reversed where the guidelines were erroneously applied, where a sentence within the guidelines was "clearly unreasonable," or where a sentence outside the guidelines was unreasonable.[146] The Commission on Sentencing hoped that appellate decisions would supplement these broad provisions and develop a body of law to assist trial courts in implementing the guidelines.[147]

Between 1981 and 1995, the Superior Court developed the "common law of sentencing" desired by the commission. However, its work in this regard was subject to two opposing theories of appellate review. The first held that appellate courts should grant trial courts broad deference in sentencing matters generally, and in application of the guidelines specifically, since the latter courts are in a better position to weigh the defendant's character, the nature of the crime, and other factors that become apparent at trial. The second theory held that trial courts should be required to set forth at length their reasons for sentencing above or below the guidelines and that appellate courts should engage in a searching examination of those reasons, as well as other factors relating to the appropriateness of sentencing. In light of these opposing theories, the Superior Court's work in sentencing matters between 1981 and 1995 can be

---

144. 42 Pa.C.S. sec. 9721(b).

145. As to the appealability of sentences generally, both the Commonwealth and the defendant had the right to appeal where an issue was raised regarding the legality of sentence. 1978 PL 319, 1386(a). Discretionary aspects of sentencing were reviewable only where a substantial question existed that the sentence was inappropriate. 1978 PL 319, 1386(b).

146. 42 Pa.C.S. sec. 9781(c).

147. See Jodeen M. Hobbs, "Structuring Sentencing Discretion in Pennsylvania: Are Guidelines Still a Viable Option in Light of *Commonwealth v. Devers*," 69 Temple L. Rev. 941, 946 n. 44 (1996), citing Interview with John H. Kramer, Executive Director of the Pennsylvania Commission on Sentencing, in State College, Pa. (Sept. 1, 1995).

divided into two equal periods. Between 1981 and 1988, the court basically endorsed the second theory. As a result, it took an extremely activist approach to enforcing both the letter and the spirit of the sentencing guidelines, and it granted trial courts little discretion to deviate from either.[148] In 1988, however, the Supreme Court rendered its decision in *Commonwealth v. Devers*,[149] which sharply limited the Superior Court's authority to vacate a criminal sentence where the trial court indicates that it was informed by a presentence report. Thereafter, the Superior Court struggled to reestablish standards for appellate review of criminal sentences.

Prior to *Devers*, the court rendered dozens of decisions that defined and interpreted the broad provisions of the sentencing guidelines. These decisions indicate that the court took an activist approach to sentencing review, and it did not hesitate to overturn sentences on both procedural and substantive grounds. For instance, sentences were vacated repeatedly on the basis that a trial court did not indicate awareness of the correct guideline ranges on the record at the time of sentencing.[150] The court also vacated sentences that departed from the guidelines where the trial court did not provide a contemporaneous written statement of its rationale.[151] In 1984 the court defined the "contemporaneous written statement" required for a departure to be justified. In *Commonwealth v. Royer*, the court held that this requirement is satisfied only where the trial court's reasons for departure are delivered at the sentencing proceeding, in the defendant's presence, and recorded and ultimately transcribed so that they may be examined by the defendant and reviewed on appeal. The court further held that trial courts must advise defendants of the permissible sentencing ranges that might be imposed.[152] In *Commonwealth v. Mullen*,[153] an en banc case decided a year earlier, the court also held that, even where there is no departure from the guidelines, the reasons for a sentence must be recorded at the sentencing hearing and in the defendant's presence.

Although these cases indicate that the court strictly applied procedural mandates, its activist approach to appellate review of sentencing is most clearly indicated by a willingness to engage in substantive analysis of the reasons provided by trial courts to justify sentences. For instance, in *Commonwealth v. Mattis*[154] and *Commonwealth v. Septak*,[155] the court vacated sentences as too lenient where the trial court focused more on the rehabilitative needs of the defendant than on the nature of the offense and its impact on the victim and society. Similarly, in *Commonwealth v. Fluellen*,[156] the court vacated a lenient sentence that was based on the ineffectiveness of prison drug rehabilitation programs, and in *Commonwealth v. Bullicki*,[157] the court vacated a lenient sentence premised on the fact that the defendant committed a crime while on parole and thus faced additional incarceration as a parole violator.

---

148. Hobbs, "Structuring Sentencing Discretion," 946 (noting that, between 1982 and 1988, the court considered 321 appeals involving the discretionary aspects of sentencing). Many of the cases considered herein are grouped and analyzed in Hobbs' excellent article.

149. 519 Pa. 88, 546 A.2d 12 (1988).

150. See e.g., *Commonwealth v. Royer*, 328 Pa. Super. 60, 476 A.2d 453 (1984); *Commonwealth v. Johnakin*, 348 Pa. Super. 432, 502 A.2d 620 (1985); *Commonwealth v. Catapano*, 347 Pa. Super. 375, 500 A.2d 882 (1985).

151. See e.g., *Catapano*, supra; *Commonwealth v. Smith*, 340 Pa. Super. 72, 489 A.2d 845 (1985).

152. 328 Pa. Super. 60, 476 A.2d 453 (1984) (Cavanaugh, J.).

153. 321 Pa. Super. 19, 467 A.2d 871 (1983) (en banc) (Cercone, J.).

154. 352 Pa. Super. 144, 507 A.2d 423 (1986) (Montemuro, J.).

155. 359 Pa. Super. 375, 518 A.2d 1284 (1986) (Montgomery, J.).

156. 345 Pa. Super. 167, 497 A.2d 1357 (1985) (Hester, J.).

157. 355 Pa. Super. 416, 513 A.2d 990 (1986) (Hester, J.).

In 1995, in commemoration of the Superior Court's 100th anniversary, President Judge James E. Rowley and members of the court accepted a resolution from the Allegheny County Board of Commissioners commending the achievements and contributions of the court (see page 311). This presentation was made at a weekly meeting of the county commissioners with media and the public in attendance.
L. to R. (standing): Judges Patrick R. Tamilia, Zoran Popovich, James E. Rowley (President Judge), Kate Ford Elliott, John G. Brosky, William F. Cercone (President Judge Emeritus), John P. Hester.
L. to R. (seated): Commissioner Pete Flaherty, Chairman of the Board Tom Foerster, and Commissioner Larry Dunn.

The court also repeatedly held that deviations from the guidelines may not be based on reasons that are already accounted for under the guidelines. In *Commonwealth v. Stevens*,[158] for example, the trial court relied solely on the defendant's extensive criminal record to justify sentencing outside of the guidelines. Noting that the "prior record score" of the guidelines accounted for the defendant's previous crimes, the court held that a "sentencing court should not impose a sentence entirely outside of the guideline ranges solely based on a criterion already incorporated in other provisions of the guidelines."[159] This rationale was also applied in *Commonwealth v. Drumgoole*[160] to vacate a sentence below the guidelines where the sentence was based on the defendant's lack of a prior criminal record. Similarly, since the "offense gravity score" of the guidelines contemplated the seriousness of the offense, in *Commonwealth v. Plasterer*[161] the court held that trial courts may not base sentencing solely on that factor.

Finally, the court identified factors that would justify departure from the guidelines. For instance, in *Commonwealth v. Vanderhorst*,[162] the court held that a sentence of probation for manslaughter was justified where the defendant had been attacked by the victim, he had a supportive family and a stable work history, had no convictions in

158. 349 Pa. Super. 310, 503 A.2d 14 (1986) (Hoffman, J.).
159. 503 A.2d 16.
160. 341 Pa. Super. 468, 491 A.2d 1352 (1985) (Rowley, J.).
161. 365 Pa. Super. 190, 529 A.2d 37 (1987) (Hoffman, J.).
162. 347 Pa. Super. 648, 501 A.2d 262 (1985) (Cercone, J.).

the prior eleven years, and had shown remorse. In *Commonwealth v. Darden*,[163] the court upheld a sentence exceeding the guidelines where the trial court indicated that the defendant had an extensive juvenile record that was not included in his prior record score, that he was a drug addict who had not attempted to improve himself, and that the victim was an elderly woman. Similarly, in *Commonwealth v. Ward*,[164] the court found that a sentence in excess of the guidelines was justified where the burglary defendant was on probation at the time of the offense, and that he had subjected the victim to indignities while burglarizing her home.[165]

In all of these cases, the court granted trial courts little deference in implementing the sentencing guidelines. In procedural matters, the court enforced the mandate that the guidelines were properly considered and calculated, and it defined the type of statement necessary to justify departure from the guidelines. In substantive matters, the court actively examined the reasons relied upon by trial courts to justify criminal sentences, and it distinguished between appropriate and inappropriate reasons. The theory of appellate review that emerged from these cases was that the guidelines supplied the presumptive sentence to be applied in a given case, and that a trial court's departure from the guidelines would be closely scrutinized.[166]

The Superior Court's activist approach to sentencing review was largely rejected by the Supreme Court in *Devers*. In that case, the defendant pled guilty to third degree murder and robbery. At sentencing, the trial court had before it a presentence report and a variety of other information relevant to the defendant's background and character and the nature of the crime. In imposing sentences of ten to twenty years for murder and five to ten years for robbery, however, the trial court did not place on the record a lengthy explanation of its rationale. In a per curiam memorandum for a divided panel of the Superior Court, the majority remanded for resentencing on the basis that the trial court "failed to make a meaningful explanation of which factors it considered to be significant and what weight it allotted to these factors."[167] In dissent, Judge Tamilia argued "that running down the check list of sentencing provisions is not required when it appears from the record that the court was fully aware of the relevant factors and considerations. . . . [A] simple lack of articulation on the record of each of the factors contained in the sentencing code in no way prevents an adequate review by this court of the trial judge's reasoning."[168]

On appeal, the Supreme Court agreed with the dissent. The court began by noting that its own cases considering the sufficiency of a trial court's sentencing rationale "offered little guidance as to the sufficiency of detail and particularity required to pass review. That task has fallen largely to the Superior Court."[169] Next, the court considered a number of Superior Court cases that vacated sentences based on an insufficient explanation of the trial court's rationale.[170] Finding these cases in error, the court stated, "We emphatically reject . . . interpretations of our law in this area which call for separate, written opinions embodying exegetical thought."[171] The court then concluded:

---

163. 366 Pa. Super. 597, 531 A.2d 1144 (1987) (Kelly, J.).

164. 369 Pa. Super. 94, 534 A.2d 1095 (1987) (Watkins, J.), vacated 524 Pa. 48, 568 A.2d 1242 (1990).

165. The defendant directed the victim to undress and lie under her bed until he had finished burglarizing her home. 534 A.2d 1095. The sentence was vacated on other grounds. 534 A.2d 1099.

166. Hobbs, "Structuring Sentencing Discretion," 949.

167. *Commonwealth v. Devers*, 352 Pa. Super. 611, 505 A.2d 1030 (1985).

168. 505 A.2d 1030.

169. 519 Pa. 88, 546 A.2d 12 (1988).

170. 546 A.2d 15.

171. 546 A.2d 18.

In order to dispel any lingering doubt as to our intention of engaging in an effort of legal purification, we state clearly that sentencers are under no compulsion to employ checklists or any extended or systematic definitions of their punishment procedure. Having been fully informed by the pre-sentence report, the sentencing court's discretion should not be disturbed. This is particularly true, we repeat, in those circumstances where it can be demonstrated that the judge had any degree of awareness of the sentencing considerations, and there we will presume also that the weighing process took place in a meaningful fashion. It would be foolish, indeed, to take the position that if a court is in possession of the facts, it will fail to apply them to the case at hand.[172]

In 1989 the court stated, "With the broad discretion accorded trial judges [by *Devers*], [and with] the Sentencing Code and the Sentencing Guidelines to guide them, trial judges who diligently conduct their sentencing procedures are very unlikely to be reversed by this Court. Only the most exceptional cases are subject to reversal."[173] As this statement suggests, appellate review in the years after *Devers* changed significantly. By creating a presumption that a sentence is justified where the trial court is informed by a presentence report, *Devers* sharply limited the Superior Court's authority to examine the reasons behind a given sentence.[174] Thereafter, the court continued to strictly enforce the procedural requirements of the guidelines,[175] and it occasionally found that the *Devers* presumption was rebutted where the trial court failed to consider or apply relevant evidence in a presentence report.[176] In general, however, the court felt constrained to affirm sentences where the trial court reviewed a presentence report and placed on the record some minimal statement of reasons for the sentence imposed. In these latter cases, the court frequently noted the "essentially unfettered" discretion of sentencing courts.[177]

## BLOOD TESTING

The rapidly evolving science of blood testing played a significant role in a number of important cases decided by the Superior Court between 1981 and 1995. This was particularly true in the realms of family and criminal law. In *Turek v. Hardy*,[178] for instance, the court considered the admissibility of advanced DNA testing in paternity

---

172. See note 168.

173. *Commonwealth v. Simpson*, 384 Pa. Super. 18, 557 A.2d 751, 757 (1989) (Tamilia, J.).

174. See Hobbs, "Structuring Sentencing Discretion," 951 ("In *Devers*, the Supreme Court undermined the ability of the Superior Court to analyze the reasons for a particular sentence and determine whether the reasons were appropriate on a state-wide basis. . . . Substantive review of a sentencing decision is nearly abolished under *Devers*.").

175. See e.g., *Commonwealth v. Rich*, 392 Pa. Super. 380, 572 A.2d 1283 (1990) (vacating a sentence where the defendant was not advised of the permissible guidelines ranges and where the trial court failed to state any reasons for departing from the guidelines); and *Commonwealth v. Dutter*, 420 Pa. Super. 565, 617 A.2d 330 (1992) (vacating a sentence where the trial court failed to state any reasons for departing from the guidelines).

176. See e.g., *Commonwealth v. Moore*, 420 Pa. Super. 484, 617 A.2d 8 (1992); and *Commonwealth v. Masip*, 389 Pa. Super. 365, 567 A.2d 331 (1989).

177. See e.g., *Commonwealth v. Jones*, 418 Pa. Super. 93, 613 A.2d 587, 591 (1992) (en banc) (noting "the essentially unfettered discretion of the trial judge at sentencing"); and *Commonwealth v. Hallock*, 412 Pa. Super. 340, 603 A.2d 612, 616 (1992) (related to *Jones*, supra; noting the "unfettered discretion in sentencing").

178. 312 Pa. Super. 158, 458 A.2d 562 (1983) (Brosky, J.).

actions. As early as 1961, when the legislature enacted the Uniform Act on Blood Tests to Determine Paternity, blood test results were admissible to establish nonpaternity. Until *Turek* was decided in 1983, however, it remained unclear whether such testing also could be used affirmatively to establish paternity. In *Turek*, Albert Hardy sought blood testing to determine whether he could be excluded as the father of a child born to Mary K. Turek. The court ordered testing and the parties stipulated that the results would be admissible at trial. The test that was ultimately performed, a Human Leukocyte Antigen (HLA) test, indicated a probability that Hardy was the baby's father. Despite the stipulation, however, the trial court refused to admit the results of the HLA test. Following trial, the jury found that Hardy was not the father of Turek's baby.

On appeal, Turek argued that the HLA test should have been admitted not only to establish that Hardy could not be excluded as the baby's father, but also as affirmative evidence that he was in fact the father. The Superior Court agreed with Turek. The court began by citing the statute providing for the admission of blood test results to establish nonpaternity and also noted that, in enacting the statute, the legislature refused to authorize tests to establish paternity. Nonetheless, based on its review of available literature and cases in other states, the court found that the HLA test, which involved the tissue typing of white blood cells, was far more reliable than the tests available when the statute was passed in 1961.[179] The court also relied on a California case which held that the legislature's previous refusal to authorize blood test results to establish paternity would not prevent the subsequent use of more advanced tests for that purpose. "We conclude as the California court did," the court held, "that rejection of the affirmative use of blood test results by the legislature was not a rejection of the HLA test, which was at that time not yet accepted scientific method." The court also found that admission of HLA tests as evidence of paternity furthered several public policy considerations, including "protecting children from the stigma of illegitimacy, preservation of the family, and insuring that individuals rather than the government bear responsibility for child support."[180] Finally, the court emphasized that its holding was only that HLA tests were admissible as *some evidence* of paternity, not to conclusively establish paternity. In addition to the necessity of establishing a traditional evidentiary foundation, the court held those seeking to admit the tests must demonstrate:

1) the effect of racial and ethnic variables;
2) any factors which might invalidate the test or affect its accuracy;
3) the procedures of the actual test;
4) the qualifications of witnesses called to explain the test.[181]

Having set forth these guidelines for the admissibility of HLA tests, the case was remanded for a new trial. In a concurring opinion, Judge Johnson agreed that HLA tests were sufficiently reliable and that such tests should be admitted as evidence of paternity. However, he expressed concern that the guidelines set forth by the majority would be utilized to the exclusion of other relevant factors. Johnson preferred instead "to leave to our trial courts the admittedly difficult task of formulating any special rules which may be required [to admit HLA tests], secure in the belief that our appellate system remains available to guard against manifest abuse which results in prejudice to either contending party."[182] Since *Turek*, HLA tests supported by an adequate

---

179. Earlier tests examined only red blood cells.
180. 458 A.2d 565.
181. 458 A.2d 565, relying on factors set forth in *Phillips v. Jackson*, 615 P.2d 1228 (Utah 1980).
182. 458 A.2d 566.

foundation have been admitted as evidence of paternity, and the court's holding in this regard has been cited by courts in Pennsylvania, federal districts, and other states.[183] As genetic tests have become more reliable, their evidentiary value has continued to increase. In 1991, for instance, the legislature decreed that a genetic test indicating a 99 percent or greater probability of paternity creates a presumption of paternity that can be rebutted only by clear and convincing evidence that the test was not reliable in that particular case.[184]

The Superior Court also addressed the admissibility of blood test results in the realm of criminal law. In *Commonwealth v. Hipp*,[185] the defendant was involved in an automobile accident and transported to a hospital, where blood was drawn and tested for alcohol content pursuant to hospital procedure. A police officer investigating the accident visited Hipp in the emergency room and noticed that he smelled of alcohol, had bloodshot eyes, and spoke with slurred speech. Believing that Hipp was intoxicated, the officer asked hospital personnel to conduct a blood test. This request was authorized by Section 1547(a) of the Motor Vehicle Code, which provides that an officer may ask hospital personnel to conduct a blood alcohol test where probable cause exists to believe that an individual has driven under the influence of alcohol. Under Section 3755 of the Vehicle Code, hospital personnel must comply with the officer's request. Following his request, the officer was informed that Hipp's blood had already been tested pursuant to hospital procedure and that it revealed that Hipp was intoxicated. After placing Hipp under arrest, the officer asked him to submit to a blood test. Exercising a right provided by the Vehicle Code, Hipp refused the blood test, and the officer left the hospital. The Commonwealth subpoenaed the results of the blood test conducted by the hospital and, at trial, a laboratory technician testified as to the results of the test. The Commonwealth also elicited testimony as to Hipp's refusal to submit to a second blood test. Hipp was convicted of driving under the influence of alcohol.

On appeal, the question was whether the results of a blood alcohol test conducted for medical purposes, offered to a police officer by hospital personnel, are admissible at trial where a defendant exercises his statutory right to refuse to submit to a second blood alcohol test. This broad issue had a number of constitutional implications. Most importantly, Hipp argued that his constitutional right to privacy was violated when hospital personnel offered the results of the blood alcohol to the police and when the results were subpoenaed and introduced at trial by the Commonwealth. The Superior Court, sitting en banc, rejected this claim. Although acknowledging that Hipp had a reasonable expectation of privacy in his medical records, the court emphasized that the state and federal constitutions restrain not all searches, but only "intrusions which are not justified in the circumstances, or which are made in an improper manner."[186] Applying this rule, the court found that, since the officer had probable cause to believe that Hipp had driven while drunk, he was authorized by Section 1547(a) to request a blood test, and hospital personnel were required by Section 3755 of the Vehicle Code to comply with the officer's request. Since the test was justified, hospital personnel acted properly when they volunteered its results, even though the test had been conducted prior to the officer's request. As a result, the court found that Hipp's constitutional rights

---

183. See e.g., *Rodgers v. Woodin*, 448 Pa. Super. 598, 672 A.2d 814 (1996); *Wawrykow v. Simonich*, 438 Pa. Super. 340, 652 A.2d 843 (1994); *Zearfoss v. Frattaroli*, 435 Pa. Super. 565, 646 A.2d 1238 (1994); *Government of the Virgin Islands v. Byers*, 941 F. Supp. 513 (D. Virgin Islands 1996); *State ex rel. Munoz v. Bravo*, 678 P.2d 974 (Ariz. 1984); *E.M.F. v. N.N.*, 717 P.2d 961 (Colo. 1985); *Imms v. Clarke*, 654 S.W.2d 281 (Mo. 1983); *Kofford v. Flora*, 744 P.2d 1343 (Utah 1987); *L.M. v. O.F.*, 452 S.E.2d 436 (W.Va. 1994).

184. See 23 Pa.C.S. sec. 4343(c)(2).

185. 380 Pa. Super. 345, 551 A.2d 1086 (1988) (en banc) (McEwen, J.).

186. 551 A.2d 1090, citing *Schmerber v. California*, 384 U.S. 757, 758 (1966).

against unreasonable searches had not been violated. The court also rejected Hipp's claim that, since he exercised the statutory right to refuse the officer's request for a blood test, the officer lacked authority to request a blood sample from hospital personnel. Specifically, the court emphasized that the test conducted by the hospital was not performed at the officer's request. Since the test was conducted by a hospital employee, a private individual, it did not violate any constitutional rights, which bar only unreasonable searches by state agents. Moreover, the court found that even if the hospital employee was regarded as a state agent, the test would nonetheless have been valid since the officer had probable cause for the request. Also, the fact that Hipp exercised his statutory right to refuse the officer's request for a blood test was irrelevant to the admissibility of a test already conducted pursuant to hospital policy. Finally, the court held that the trial court did not err in admitting Hipp's refusal to submit to a subsequent test, after it admitted the initial test results, since the admissibility of the refusal was expressly authorized by Section 1547(e) of the Vehicle Code.[187] Having rejected Hipp's claims, his judgment of sentence was affirmed.[188] Dozens of cases in Pennsylvania and other states have cited the court's holding that the right to privacy in medical records is subject to reasonable searches and seizures, and that an officer who possesses probable cause may obtain the results of medical tests without a warrant.[189] *Hipp* has also been followed by the Supreme Court.[190] Finally, the case has been cited repeatedly for the proposition that the right to refuse a blood test where an officer possesses probable cause that an individual has been driving drunk is statutory, not constitutional.[191]

In another case decided the same year, the court considered the admissibility of a certain type of blood test, called electrophoresis, which linked an individual to his blood by identifying genetic markers. In *Commonwealth v. Middleton*,[192] the defendant was charged with murder and robbery. At trial, the prosecution produced a serologist who testified concerning the incriminating results of an electrophoresis test upon dried blood stains found at the scene of the crime. The serologist testified that, based upon his own experience as well as his review of scientific studies, electrophoresis is generally accepted as reliable by experts in the field of forensic serology. The serologist also opined that the test was accurate when applied to dried blood stains. Middleton was convicted of first degree murder and sentenced to life imprisonment.

On appeal, Middleton argued the trial court committed reversible error when it admitted the results of the electrophoresis test because the prosecution had presented only one witness to establish the scientific validity and acceptability of the test when conducted on dried blood stains. The court rejected Middleton's challenge to the electrophoresis test. It began by reciting the established standard for the admission of new scientific evidence at trial:

---

187. 551 A.2d 1093. Section 1547(e) provides:

(e) Refusal admissible in evidence—In any summary proceeding or criminal proceeding in which the defendant is charged with a violation of section 3731 or any violation of this title arising out of the same action, the fact that the defendant refused to submit to chemical testing as required by subsection (a) may be introduced in evidence along with other circumstances of the refusal.

188. 551 A.2d 1094.

189. See e.g., *Commonwealth v. Barton*, 456 Pa. Super. 290, 690 A.2d 293 (1997); *Commonwealth v. Moore*, 430 Pa. Super. 575, 635 A.2d 625 (1993); *Commonwealth v. Franz*, 430 Pa. Super. 394, 634 A.2d 662 (1993); *State v. Rains*, 574 N.W.2d 904 (Iowa 1998); *People v. Perlos*, 462 N.W.2d 310 (Mich. 1990); *State v. Johnston*, 779 P.2d 556 (N.M. 1989); *State v. Vandergrift*, 535 N.W.2d 428 (S.D. 1995); *Ashford v. Skiles*, 837 F. Supp. 108 (E.D. Pa. 1993). See also, 25 ALR 2d 1407; 65 *Temple L.Q.* 865.

190. See *Commonwealth v. Riedel*, 539 Pa. 172, 651 A.2d 135 (1994).

191. See e.g., *Riedel*, supra; *Commonwealth v. Mordan*, 419 Pa. Super. 214, 615 A.2d 102 (1992); *Kostyk v. Dept. of Transportation*, 131 Pa. Cmwlth. 455, 570 A.2d 644 (1990).

192. 379 Pa. Super. 502, 550 A.2d 561 (1988) (McEwen, J.).

Just when a scientific principle or discovery crosses the line between the experimental and demonstrable stages is difficult to define. Somewhere in this twilight zone the evidential force of the principle must be recognized, and while courts will go a long way in admitting expert testimony deduced from a well-recognized scientific principle or discovery, the thing from which the deduction is made must be sufficiently established to have gained general acceptance in the particular field in which it belongs.[193]

Applying this standard, the court rejected Middleton's claim that a single expert could not provide an adequate evidentiary foundation for a new scientific procedure. The court reasoned that so long as the expert's testimony went beyond his own personal view or the view of a small segment of the scientific community and demonstrated general acceptance of the new procedure among the scientific community as a whole, a new procedure could be admitted without the necessity of calling multiple experts. Reviewing the record of trial, the court emphasized that the "extended interrogation" of the prosecution's expert demonstrated that electrophoresis was generally accepted by the national community of forensic serologists. The court also cited a number of cases in other states that admitted electrophoresis, and it considered relevant scientific literature that deemed the test reliable and generally accepted, even when conducted on dried bloodstains.[194] Finally, the court noted that Middleton had not introduced "any evidence whatsoever" undermining the serologist's testimony. For these reasons, the court held that the trial court properly admitted the electrophoresis test results.[195] In 1992, the Superior Court's holding was followed by the Supreme Court, which deemed electrophoresis tests admissible in *Commonwealth v. Zook*.[196]

## THE CASELOAD

The litigation growth of the 1970s continued unabated throughout the 1980s and early 1990s. In 1979, the last full year prior to the court's expansion, 4,523 appeals were filed; by 1995, the number was 7,606, an increase of 68 percent. With the structural modifications of the late 1970s largely complete, the court took other measures to deal with the ongoing litigation growth. For instance, in order to ease legal research, the court began employing LEXIS, an online legal database. In 1981, the court also began to use word processors, and a year later it established a computerized docketing system to track appeals. Further, in the late 1980s, the court implemented an integrated system of computerization that linked the judges' chambers and administrative offices.

President Judge Cirillo, in particular, made a concerted effort to improve and standardize the court's administrative functioning. When Cirillo joined the court in 1982, there was a significant lack of uniformity. Some judges had one secretary, others had two. Some judges had two law clerks, others had three. More prosperous counties even provided their resident Superior Court judges with a fourth law clerk. Numerous judges were required to share a single copy machine and many secretaries still worked

---

193. 550 A.2d 565, quoting *Commonwealth v. Topa*, 471 Pa. 223, 230, 369 A.2d 1277, 1281 (1977), quoting *Frye v. United States*, 293 F. 1013, 1014 (D.C. 1923).

194. One of the articles considered by the court concluded, "There is widespread agreement in the relevant scientific community that reliable, accurate determination of genetic marker . . . types in dried blood and body fluid stains is possible using these techniques and procedures." 550 A.2d 567 n. 2.

195. 550 A.2d 567.

196. 532 Pa. 79, 615 A.2d 1 (1992).

with manual typewriters. During his tenure as president judge (1986 to 1990), Cirillo ensured that each judge, whether senior or commissioned, had four law clerks, two secretaries, and a copy machine. Each law clerk and secretary was also provided with a computer and upgraded software, and the court even purchased laptop computers for employees who were injured or otherwise unable to complete their tasks at their usual workplace. In order to fund these innovations, Cirillo persistently lobbied the legislature and he succeeded in increasing the court's budget from $6 million to $13 million.

The combination of these administrative improvements and the structural modifications of the late 1970s—expansion to fifteen judges, implementation of a panel system, and the addition of senior judges—significantly enhanced the Superior Court's ability to deal with the ongoing flood of appeals. In particular, the combination of court expansion and implementation of the panel system increased the number of days that judges were able to sit in judgment of cases. In 1977, for instance, the final full year before the Supreme Court ordered implementation of a panel system, the seven-member Superior Court sat for forty-two days. In 1981, the first full year the expanded court utilized panels, judges sat a total of 120 days. These changes allowed the court to resolve many more cases. In 1977, for instance, the court resolved 1,550 cases by filed decision; in 1995, it resolved 7,558 cases. This increase of 388 percent outstripped the 250 percent growth in new appeal filings over the same period. The court's progress in dealing with its expanding caseload is also reflected in the reduction in the average number of days between filing and disposition. In the late 1970s, it routinely took the court more than 350 days to dispose of a case. By the 1990s, the average disposition time was reduced to approximately 300 days.[197]

As these statistics indicate, the measures of the late 1970s enhanced the court's ability to deal with its caseload. While these measures gave the court its modern structure, a final significant change also increased the court's role within Pennsylvania's appellate judiciary. In 1981, the Supreme Court became an allocatur court, which meant that, in the vast majority of cases, the court was no longer required to hear appeals unless it agreed to do so by granting allocatur. Implementation of an allocatur system had significant ramifications for the Supreme Court's caseload. In 1980, for instance, the year before the new system was implemented, the court resolved 667 cases by filed opinion. A year later, the court decided only 246 cases. The impact of the allocatur system on the appellate judiciary is indicated by the following chart, which utilizes the years 1980 (the first full year prior to implementation of the allocatur system) and 1995:

---

197. In 1991, for instance, average disposition time was 290 days; the next year it was 307 days and, in 1995, the number was 302. As intended, the court's expansion also significantly reduced the number of appeals filed per judge. Between 1976 and 1979 (the last full year before expansion), appeals averaged 567 per judge. Between 1981 (the first full year after expansion) and 1984, the number was reduced to 360.

*Total Appeals Resolved by Opinion*[198]

|      | Supreme Court | Superior Court | Commonwealth Court |
|------|---------------|----------------|--------------------|
| 1980 | 667[199]      | 1,750[200]     | 1,029[201]         |
| 1995 | 197[202]      | 4,936[203]     | 1,896[204]         |

As the comparison of appeals above indicates, the Superior Court resolved 4,936 of 7,029, or 70 percent, of Pennsylvania's appellate cases in 1995, the year of its centennial anniversary. Although the allocatur system was a significant factor in creating the Superior Court's dominant role within the appellate judiciary, it was only the final stage in a century of growth. At the end of the century, the Superior Court had been transformed from a mere adjunct, created to relieve the Supreme Court of low-end litigation, into the tribunal of last resort for a large majority of Pennsylvania's appellate cases.

---

198. It is somewhat difficult to compare the three appellate courts because each categorizes its work product differently. The designation "Total Appeals Resolved by Opinion" attempts to isolate only those appeals that were disposed of on the merits by filed opinion. It does not include appeals withdrawn, dismissed, transferred or remanded.

199. The designation for this category in the Supreme Court's statistics is "Number of Cases in which Opinions were Filed."

200. See note 199.

201. The designation for this category in the Commonwealth Court's statistics is "Appeals Disposed of by Order or Panel." The figure does not include cases remanded or transferred (248), withdrawn or dismissed (1,052), consolidated with other appeals (138), or resolved by stipulation (234).

202. The statistics for cases resolved by the Supreme Court in 1995 are categorized as "Per Curiam [Order], "Full Opinion," or "Other." The figure above includes cases resolved by full opinion; it does not include cases resolved by per curiam Order (110) or by other means (17).

203. The statistics for cases resolved by the Superior Court in 1995 are categorized as "Filed Decision," or "By Order or Discontinuance." The figure above includes cases resolved by filed decision; it does not include cases resolved by order or discontinuance (2,622).

204. The statistics for cases resolved by the Commonwealth Court in 1995 are categorized as "Majority Opinions," "Consolidated," "By Stipulation," "Withdrawn/Dismissed/Remanded," "Transferred," and "Other." The figure above includes cases resolved by majority opinion; it does not include cases resolved by consolidation (277), stipulation (443), withdrawal/dismissal/remand (1,808), transfer (87) or otherwise (170).

# County of Allegheny

## Board of County Commissioners
### Pittsburgh, Pennsylvania

## Resolution

WHEREAS, the greatest heritage of American citizenship is a system of government under laws devised by elected representatives of the people and administered by independent courts in which every American enjoys equal standing; and our legal and judicial systems are foundation stones upon which rest our democratic form of government, our economic well-being, and our entire social order; and

WHEREAS, the judicial system of Pennsylvania was founded during its colonial period by early settlers and advanced by William Penn through his Provincial Council, eventually evolving into the Supreme Court, which, even with the increased number of justices, the caseload became unbearably heavy by 1895 when the Legislature established an additional appellate court, the Superior Court of Pennsylvania, with no original jurisdiction but appellate jurisdiction in all civil actions, claims and disputes with no more than $1,000 in controversy; and

WHEREAS, while there have been some changes to the role, structure and jurisdiction of the Court during its first century, some elements have remained relatively constant with the number of new appeals increasing annually into the thousands, and its learned judges and capable staffs engaging high-tech automation and computers to process the court's work to maintain its respected reputation of resolving cases speedily; and

WHEREAS, with its 15 qualified and elected judges and five senior judges from throughout the state, the Superior Court is one of the busiest intermediate appellate courts in the United States, more than 7,500 appeals being filed in 1994, its decisions touching almost every aspect of life and commerce in the Commonwealth, including family matters such as child custody, visitation, adoption, divorce, and support; criminal matters, wills and estates, property disputes, and cases involving personal injury or breach of contract;

NOW, THEREFORE, BE IT RESOLVED that this Board of County Commissioners hereby does commend President Judge James E. Rowley and the Superior Court of Pennsylvania, judges past and present, from which has emerged two governors, upon its Centennial Anniversary year of 1995; in recognition of the analytical and learned members who have displayed extraordinary acumen for justice, and who continue to serve our grateful citizens by inspiring them to reaffirm the democratic form of government and the supremacy of law in our lives.

RESOLVED and ENACTED this          12th day of October, 1995

                                   COUNTY OF ALLEGHENY

                                   BY _____
                                   Chairman

                                   _____

                                   _____
                                   Board of County Commissioners

APPROVED:

_____
Chief Clerk

Resolution of the Allegheny Board of County Commissioners, October 12, 1995.

# Supreme Court of Pennsylvania

## Resolution Honoring the
## Superior Court of Pennsylvania on
## Its Centennial

*Whereas, the Superior Court of Pennsylvania is one of the oldest state intermediate appellate courts in the nation, formed under the Superior Court Act of June 24, 1895 to help alleviate the burgeoning caseload of the Supreme Court of Pennsylvania;*

*Whereas, the Superior Court of Pennsylvania, as one of few intermediate appellate courts whose jurisdiction is statewide, has been a court readily accessible to the citizens of the Commonwealth. The Superior Court Act of 1895 ensured this accessibility by stipulating that the Court must meet at least once a year in Philadelphia, Pittsburgh, Harrisburg, Scranton and Williamsport and emphasized its role as the "poor man's Supreme Court," through which a case could be resolved speedily;*

*Whereas, the Superior Court of Pennsylvania, which was created by the Legislature, became a constitutionally mandated court incorporated under the state Constitution of 1968, and retained the same jurisdiction assigned to it by the 1895 Act and its subsequent amendments;*

*Whereas, the Appellate Court Jurisdiction Act of 1970 and the Judicial Code of 1976 established that the Superior Court has no original jurisdiction except in cases of mandamus and prohibition to courts of inferior jurisdiction where such relief is ancillary to matters within its appellate jurisdiction. Superior Court judges also were given full authority to issue writs of habeas corpus;*

*Whereas, through the 1970 and 1976 legislation, the Superior Court obtained exclusive appellate jurisdiction of all appeals from final orders of Common Pleas Courts in all matters and amounts in controversy, the only exceptions being those appeals within the exclusive jurisdiction of the Supreme Court or Commonwealth Court.*

*Whereas, to deal with the heavy volume of appeals, the people of Pennsylvania in 1979 approved a constitutional amendment authorizing the Legislature to increase the number of judges on the Superior Court from seven to fifteen;*

*Whereas, the Superior Court of Pennsylvania today is one of the busiest intermediate appellate courts in the nation, with its decisions touching upon almost every aspect of life and commerce in the Commonwealth;*

*Whereas, the Superior Court of Pennsylvania has been blessed with the leadership of wise, patient and honorable President Judges beginning with the first President Judge Charles E. Rice and continuing through the years to current President Judge James E. Rowley;*

*Whereas, the Superior Court of Pennsylvania has been served nobly by outstanding jurists selected from throughout the Commonwealth. The 72 distinguished men and women who have served as judges on the Superior Court have displayed a remarkable commitment to justice and the law that has earned them the respect and appreciation of every citizen of this great Commonwealth;*

*Therefore, Be It Resolved this 19th day of October in the year nineteen hundred ninety five that the Supreme Court of Pennsylvania pays tribute to the Superior Court of Pennsylvania and salutes its one hundred years of jurisprudence in the Commonwealth.*

Resolution of the Pennsylvania House of Representatives, June 12, 1996, recognizing the Superior Court as "one of the most efficient in the nation."

COMMONWEALTH OF PENNSYLVANIA
OFFICE OF THE GOVERNOR
HARRISBURG

THE GOVERNOR

**GREETINGS:**

It gives me great pleasure to congratulate The Superior Court of Pennsylvania as you celebrate 100 years of justice.

This country, founded on the precepts of freedom, liberty and the pursuit of happiness, recognizes the critical role of justice in our society. Law, as a shared sense of being, encourages us to comprehend the boundaries of fairness, equality and independence. As a nation, we look to our judges and our courts as icons of probity, integrity and honor. The Superior Court of Pennsylvania has, for one century, maintained the exacting tenets of legal acumen, interpretive vision and human justness. We gather to applaud these virtues and ask that these ideals continue to reflect our Commonwealth's pursuit of justice, democracy and wisdom.

On behalf of all Pennsylvanians, I commend The Superior Court of Pennsylvania for 100 years of distinguished and honorable service.

*Tom Ridge*
**TOM RIDGE**
Governor

Letter from Governor Tom Ridge congratulating the Superior Court on "100 years of justice."

### House of Representatives

COMMONWEALTH OF PENNSYLVANIA
OFFICE OF THE SPEAKER

*In the House, June 12, 1996*

*Whereas, The Superior Court of Pennsylvania, created by the General Assembly in 1895 and having intermediate appellate jurisdiction in this Commonwealth, has been recognized as one of the most efficient courts in the nation; and*

*Whereas, The President Judge of the Superior Court of Pennsylvania, the Honorable Stephen J. McEwen, Jr., has received notice from the National Center for State Courts that, compared with other courts from across the country, the Superior Court of Pennsylvania is one of the most expeditious courts in the nation, despite the large number of case filings per judge. The Superior Court of Pennsylvania has achieved this timeliness with one of the nation's heaviest workloads, with 7,606 appeals filed in 1995 and 7,558 appeals disposed of in that same year; and*

*Whereas, The Superior Court of Pennsylvania has been designated an exemplary institution, a prestigious designation shared only by the Georgia Court of Appeals; therefore be it*

*Resolved, That the House of Representatives express its sincere and heartfelt congratulations to the Superior Court of Pennsylvania for receiving this distinction in recognition of the splendid jurisprudential skills of all of the members of the court, both commissioned and senior judges; and be it further*

*Resolved, That a copy of this resolution be transmitted to the Honorable Stephen J. McEwen, Jr., President Judge of the Superior Court of Pennsylvania.*

*I certify that the foregoing is a true and correct copy of House Resolution No. 402, introduced by Representatives Dennis M. O'Brien, Matthew J. Ryan, Edward J. Lucyk, Robert E. Belfanti, Jr., Albert Masland, Robert J. Flick, Robert W. Godshall, Don Walko, Linda Bebko-Jones, Susan Laughlin, Thomas R. Caltagirone, Matthew E. Baker, Fred A. Trello, Elinor Z. Taylor, Timothy L. Pesci, James E. Shaner, Sheila M. Miller, Kathy M. Manderino, Paul S. Clymer, William Russell Robinson, John Taylor, Lisa M. Boscola, Gene DiGirolamo, Julie Harhart, Arthur D. Hershey, and adopted by the House of Representatives of the Commonwealth of Pennsylvania.*

*Matthew J. Ryan*

Matthew J. Ryan, Speaker

Resolution of the Pennsylvania House of Representatives, June 12, 1996, recognizing the Superior Court as "one of the most efficient in the nation."

# RECAPITULATION

The story of the Superior Court is essentially one of progress ordained out of necessity. The necessity of an intermediate appellate court first became apparent to many of the state's political and legal leaders at the Constitutional Convention of 1873 when Pennsylvania's rapid industrialization caused a litigation expansion that strained and then overwhelmed the Supreme Court. A number of proposals were considered, some of which ultimately helped to shape the Superior Court.

Initially, the convention majority saw significant disadvantages in an intermediate appellate court; the most prominent of which were delayed justice, increased cost, and conflicting precedent. These perceived flaws doomed the intermediate court proposals and the convention opted instead to increase the number of members of the Supreme Court. When this measure proved inadequate, the necessity for further reform became apparent. Ironically, by amending the judiciary article to the constitution to authorize new courts, the very convention that declined to create an intermediate appellate court in 1873 enabled the legislature to do so two decades later.

With proposals to increase the size of the Supreme Court demonstrably in error, a majority of legislators in 1895 rejected numerous arguments advanced against creation of an intermediate appellate court. Although they recognized the need for a new court, the legislators disagreed sharply on the court's structure and operation. All of the options that were considered by the delegates in 1873 remained available, but a variety of factors led to selection of the Superior Court model. Fear of conflicting decisions and the state's disastrous experiment with a *nisi prius* court undermined proposals to create circuit courts of appeal, and a fear of partiality made legislators wary of staffing a new appellate court through assignment of common pleas judges. These factors led to the creation of a court composed of elected appellate judges that convened en banc. Moreover, Pennsylvania's heavy Republican majority dictated the court's political structure for the first third of its history.

In addition to surmounting numerous criticisms and competing models, the early court also accomplished its primary mission—relief of the Supreme Court's caseload. Indeed, the high court's caseload was cut in half by the turn of the twentieth century. The Superior Court also reviewed a number of difficult issues, the most important of which involved the relationship between the legislature and the economy, the respective powers of the branches of state government, the duties of contractors dealing with state officials, the effect of gubernatorial pardons, and state authority over political subdivisions.

Perhaps the early court's most important task was enunciating the proper relationship between the state and the economy. Mediating between industrial reformers and advocates of laissez faire, the court fashioned standards by which to assess statutes governing employment and other economic regulations. In developing these standards, the court was confronted with constitutional provisions and doctrines, including police power, prohibitions against special legislation, and liberty of contract, that were hardly well-defined in the early years of the new industrial order. Despite its decisions in these and other cases, the early court's existence was somewhat tenuous and a significant effort within the state bar to abolish the court was defeated by a single vote in 1909.

Although it indicated that the necessity of the Superior Court was not yet a settled issue, the state bar effort was the final convulsion of concerted opposition to the court. Its failure put to rest many of the criticisms that had been advanced against intermediate appellate courts since the Constitutional Convention of 1873. The failure of the bar effort also marked the first important shift in the court's history. Prior to 1910, as stated earlier, the court's history was shaped almost entirely by factors that made Pennsylvania unusual, if not unique, in the nation.

In the decades after 1910, however, the tremendous influence of these Pennsylvania-centered factors began to diminish, and the work of the court increasingly was shaped by events that occurred beyond the state's borders. For instance, some of the court's most important decisions rendered between 1911 and 1930 involved the constitutionality and construction of progressive social legislation. Additionally, in resolving cases arising from World War I, the court rendered a number of important and far-reaching decisions. Even the criminal cases appearing before the court involved issues that transcended state borders.

The most important of these cases, which arose from prosecutions under Pennsylvania Prohibition enforcement law, required the Superior Court to construe the relationship of state law to the Eighteenth Amendment and the federal Volstead Act. Similarly, a number of cases involving the scope of personal freedoms under the state constitution arose from the sedition convictions of Socialists and Communists in the wake of the Bolshevik Revolution. Due to the importance of these issues, an unprecedented number of Superior Court decisions were reviewed by the United States Supreme Court between 1911 and 1930. During this period, the Superior Court's jurisdictional limit and subject matter jurisdiction was increased and, by 1930, the limited jurisdiction it originally received had grown to include all civil cases in which the amount in controversy did not exceed $2,500, all criminal cases except felonious homicides, all cases from the Public Service Commission, and all workmen's compensation cases. Despite its increased responsibilities, the court continued to relieve the workload of the Supreme Court, which was routinely clearing its docket by the early 1920s. Significantly, in 1919, the Sproul Commission became the first of several judicial reform bodies to recommend that the Superior Court be included in the state constitution.

As in the two decades prior to 1930, issues of national importance dominated the two decades that followed. Most importantly, the court was regularly called upon to construe and apply Pennsylvania's "little New Deal" statutes, which involved unprecedented extensions of legislative authority into the state's economic, social, and labor affairs. Since many of these statutes also established administrative bodies, the court's most significant decisions involved distinguishing between legitimate delegations of rule—making authority and unconstitutional delegations of legislative authority. Like the social and economic statutes of the New Deal, the scope of World War II was unprecedented, and for years after the fighting ended, it influenced the cases brought before the Superior Court.

In the four decades prior to 1950, the most important changes affecting the Superior Court were new types of cases resulting from broad social, economic, and political trends. Yet, the court's structure and operation changed very little, especially in relation to the decades that followed. Between 1895 and 1950 the court's subject matter jurisdiction expanded slowly, with the addition of appeals from the Public Service Commission in 1915 and the Workmen's Compensation Board in 1929. Moreover, its caseload remained relatively constant, averaging between 500 and 600 cases per year in the first half-century, and its jurisdictional limit, which began at $1,000, was increased to $1,500 in 1899, and $2,500 in 1923. The only significant change in the court's schedule occurred in 1917, when it stopped sitting at Williamsport. More notable than these minor alterations, however, were the proposals directed at the court that did not succeed. The most prominent of these were the effort within the bar association to abolish the court in 1909, and the recommendations of the Sproul Commission in 1919 and the Earle Committee in 1935 to include the court in the judiciary article of the constitution. In the end, the Superior Court essentially remained in 1950 what it had been in 1895, a seven-member statutory tribunal that convened en banc and shared the state's appellate caseload with the Supreme Court in relatively equal parts.

In the decades after 1950, the court underwent dramatic change in virtually every respect. Although this change was spurred by growth in Pennsylvania's appellate caseload, its most important catalyst was the Constitutional Convention of 1967-68. The convention reorganized the state judiciary and made a number of modifications that began to shape the Superior Court in its modern form. Decisions made at the convention also set the stage for subsequent changes in the court's structure. The court's transition in the years between 1951 and adjournment of the convention is further indicated by the rise of criminal, tort and family law. Change in the criminal law was generated by the landmark holdings of the United States Supreme Court during the 1960s, and many of the Superior Court's important cases involved the application of these holdings to state law. The general thrust of change in tort law was toward expanded liability and the Superior Court played an important role in facilitating this expansion. Moreover, as new principles of gender equality emerged in the 1960s, family law began a process of change that, by the 1970s, significantly undermined traditional assumptions about marital and parental relationships. All of these changes profoundly influenced Pennsylvania law, and each is reflected in the important cases decided by the Superior Court. Finally, the decline in Republican political strength that began during the Great Depression culminated in the 1960s with the first Democratic majority in the Superior Court's history. These legal and political changes, as well as the dramatic caseload increases and constitutional reform effort culminating in the Constitutional Convention of 1967-68, established beyond question that the court entered a new phase in its history in the years after 1950.

The changes initiated in the two decades prior to the convention culminated in the twelve years that followed. Initially, creation of the Commonwealth Court and the redistribution of jurisdiction essentially gave the state's appellate judiciary its modern form. Further changes occurred in the late 1970s as the litigation growth, commenced in the prior two decades, reached unprecedented heights. The ensuing litigation explosion of the 1970s overwhelmed the Superior Court and led to structural changes that completed the court's transformation. Spurred by high profile reports from national judicial research organizations, these changes included a legislative amendment expanding the court to fifteen judges, a Supreme Court order mandating a panel system, and a statute authorizing the utilization of senior judges. These measures were the final significant steps in a reform process that began in the 1950s, continued through the Constitutional Convention of 1968, and acquired new urgency during the litigation boom of the 1970s. When this reform process culminated in the passage of the act establishing fifteen judgeships, the court's original structure, a seven-member statutory tribunal with limited jurisdiction that sat en banc, had been completely transformed, and its modern structure emerged. When the Supreme Court implemented an allocatur system, the Superior Court became the tribunal of last resort for the great majority of Pennsylvania's appellate litigants.

Fortuitously, the evolution, which reshaped and redefined the court after 1980, prepared it for another onslaught of appellate litigation following enactment of the Divorce Code of 1980, the expansion of criminal law in the areas of drunk driving, mandatory sentences for drug and gun related crimes, and the increased litigation in asbestos and other creeping disease cases in the tort field. While the court was reformed to meet the demands of existing litigation, serendipitously, it also had been structured to adjust to a further wave of unanticipated litigation. As a result, by the end of its first century, the Superior Court had indeed become the keystone of Pennsylvania's appellate judiciary.

The Superior Court in 1999.
L. to R. (seated): J. Michael Eakin, Joseph A. Hudock, Zoran Popovich, James R. Cavanaugh, Stephen J. McEwen Jr. (President Judge), Joseph A. Del Sole, Justin Morris Johnson, Kate Ford Elliott, Michael T. Joyce. L. to R. (standing): Patrick R. Tamilia, Peter Paul Olszewski, John P. Hester, Maureen E. Lally-Green, Joan Orie Melvin, Correale F. Stevens, John L. Musmanno, Berle M. Schiller, William F. Cercone, John G. Brosky, Vincent A. Cirillo, Phyllis W. Beck.

# EPILOGUE

## TRANSITION TO THE SECOND CENTURY

One hundred years of justice achieved by the Superior Court of Pennsylvania, from its inception on June 24, 1895, to its centennial celebration in 1995, has been described in the preceding pages. Beginning in 1996, the Superior Court entered into its second century and in many ways the challenges and expectations of the second century are as great and unpredictable as those faced by the court at its creation.

The birthing process of the Superior Court, which ended in 1895, began as early as 1873 and was achieved only when necessity and political will came together in the legislative process after attempts through constitutional amendment proved unworkable. In the subsequent century, as the court invented itself, it became essential to the dispensation of justice in the Commonwealth of Pennsylvania, becoming the true intermediary between the trial courts and the Supreme Court. The Superior Court became indispensable and established a standard of judicial performance and productivity matched by few, if any, intermediate appellate courts in the country.[1] For the vast majority of litigants, the Superior Court is the court of last resort.

The Superior Court attained constitutional status during the Constitutional Convention of 1968, which also enlarged and realigned the court's jurisdiction under the unified judicial system, which is overseen by the Supreme Court. In 1980 the General Assembly enlarged the number of members of the court from seven to fifteen, a process fully documented in the preceding chapters. With the enlargement of the court and concomitant staff increase, commensurate with the expanding caseload, new administrative structures were necessary and were created and refined by succeeding administrations to meet the various and changing demands faced by the court. With the advent of computers, the Superior Court became Pennsylvania's most advanced court in the use of computer technology. These computer advancements, as documented in prior chapters, were accomplished during the administrations of Judges William Cercone, Edmund Spaeth, Vincent Cirillo, James Rowley and now, Stephen McEwen Jr.

The administration of President Judge McEwen began in 1996 and has carried the Superior Court into the twenty-first century. This administration has progressed with vigor and energy to secure the gains of the past century and is poised to proceed boldly and innovatively in the coming millennium. Among the immediate effects of the McEwen administration is a solid and productive relationship with the legislature, particularly leaders such as Speaker of the House Matthew Ryan.

Early in his administration, Judge McEwen, recognizing that the co-equal

---

1. Reports of Center of State Courts, Chapter VI.

branches of government, as well as the trial courts, are intricately involved with this court in addressing the daunting challenges which have confronted it, initiated a program known as "Commonwealth Partners." This program, through regional meetings throughout the state, gathers Superior Court judges, trial judges, and members of the General Assembly to consider the manner in which the Superior Court may better assist these partners to achieve a creative balance between (a) the de jure doctrine of separation of powers, and (b) the de facto interdependence of the three branches of government. These meetings successfully have brought together other participants in the justice systems, including legislators, trial judges, and appellate jurists, so as to gain the benefit of the personal experience and particular perspectives of those other participants on justice system issues. This has served to establish a spirit of mutuality reflective of the relationship between the branches which emphasizes the reality of their interdependence. In true fashion, the Superior Court has become a keystone of justice in Pennsylvania.

The public profile of the court has been raised through several recent innovations. In 1998 the court became one of only a few intermediate appellate courts in the nation to have its own Web site, serving the public by providing access to opinions, as well as the court's history, procedures, schedules, and other topics of interest. In 1999, for the first time, sessions of the court were broadcast on television; the Pennsylvania Cable Network televised the court's en banc sessions held in each of the three districts.

One of the most noteworthy achievements occurring during President Judge McEwen's tenure was the establishment of a courtroom in Philadelphia to serve the Superior Court's Eastern District. At its inception, the Superior Court held its Eastern District sessions in Philadelphia City Hall, in the courtroom created for the Supreme Court of Pennsylvania before the turn of the twentieth century. Subsequently, when the Robert N.C. Nix Sr. Federal Courthouse at Ninth and Market Streets in Philadelphia became available, the Superior Court, and the recently-created Commonwealth Court, took advantage of the opportunity and established administrative offices, docketing and filing facilities, a library, courtroom, conference room, and visiting judges chambers there. Judges Spaeth, Cavanaugh, Montemuro, Kelly, and Hoffman also established their chambers in that location.

By the end of the 1980s, however, the federal courts needed to reacquire this space, and, after an intensive search by President Judges Cirillo and Rowley, new quarters were established in the Penn Mutual Building at Walnut and Sixth Streets in Philadelphia, adjacent to and overlooking Independence Hall. This became the location of the court's Eastern District courtroom and administrative offices from 1990 to the present time, except that in 1996-1997 cases again were heard at the Supreme Court Courtroom in City Hall, returning the court to its historical beginning. The search for a permanent courtroom continued, and the efforts of President Judge McEwen led to the acquisition of the former corporate offices and board room of the Penn Mutual Insurance Company on the seventeenth floor of the Penn Mutual Building.

In the fall of 1997 renovations began to turn this space into a courtroom, conference room, and visiting judges' chambers and to provide space and amenities for counsel. The completion reunited the court with its administrative offices and provides an outstanding facility in Philadelphia commensurate with the dignity of the court and on par with the facilities in Harrisburg and Pittsburgh. The dedication of the courtroom took place on May 13, 1998, with many legislators, judicial officers, public officials, local and state bar association representatives, and friends of the court in attendance.

The Founders Court Room is so named because the facility overlooks Independence Hall, the edifice where the Declaration of Independence was debated and adopted in 1776, where the Articles of Confederation were drafted in 1776 and ratified in 1781, and where George Washington in 1787 chaired the Convention which drafted the Constitution. The courtroom also provides a view of Washington Square, the site of the Tomb of the Unknown Soldier of the Revolutionary War, and the burial ground for hundreds of other unknown Continental Army patriots who died in the struggle for freedom. In keeping with its historical surroundings, the courtroom features a counsel's podium, which originally was installed as the clerk's desk in a Woonsocket, Rhode Island, courtroom in 1895, the year the Pennsylvania Superior Court was established. The courtroom should serve the court and the public well into the twenty-first century.

Another hallmark of President Judge McEwen's administration is the Heritage Conferences. These conferences, an annual retreat/seminar of the court, held at a historical site, provide an opportunity to review the operations of the court and obtain meaningful legal instruction from respected lecturers in a location of distinct jurisprudential and historical ambiance. The first of these was in May 1996 in the Brandywine Valley, where future Chief Justice John Marshall had fought in 1777 at the Battle of the Brandywine. In May 1997, the court visited Monticello, home of Thomas Jefferson, and the town of Charlottesville, where Jefferson, James Madison, and James Monroe all practiced law, and where Jefferson founded the University of Virginia. The court found itself in historical Annapolis in 1998 with classes at the United States Naval Academy. In 1999, approaching the close of the twentieth century, the court convened in St. Louis, which played such a crucial role, not only in United States history, where Lewis and Clark wintered before their Expedition of Discovery, but in legal history, as the site of the law suit brought by Dred Scott to win his freedom from slavery.

Finally, in recognition of the great bond between the bench and the bar, President Judge McEwen began the practice of annually honoring those members of the bar who celebrate their golden anniversary of the practice of law by publicly recognizing them at ceremonies preceding en banc sessions in Philadelphia, Harrisburg, and Pittsburgh. This program has been well received and promises to be a continuing ritual of the court in the new century.

## THE COURT'S COMPOSITION IN THE FINAL YEAR OF THE TWENTIETH CENTURY

By the mid-1990s, the court's caseload had risen to such a level that the judges, even working at their nationally recognized level of efficiency, were barely able to remain afloat amid this rising tide of appeals. About the time Judge McEwen assumed the position of president judge, the court benefited by a number of judges reaching retirement age and providing an opportunity to meet the challenge of exploding litigation and appeals.

Fortunately, the court does not have to do without the wisdom and efforts of its retired judges. With the approval of the Supreme Court, upon request of the president judge, a judge may, upon reaching age seventy, remain on the court as a senior judge. Except that they do not sit on the court en banc, senior judges retain a full workload and they produce as many opinions and memoranda as the commissioned judges. At the close of 1999, the court under President Judge McEwen's administration enjoyed the benefit of eight senior judges.

The influx of new judges began in 1996 when J. Michael Eakin filled the position created by the assumption of senior judge status by Judge Peter Paul Olszewski. Eakin was elected to a ten-year term on the Superior Court in November 1995. Born in Mechanicsburg, Pennsylvania, on November 18, 1948, he graduated from Franklin & Marshall College in 1970 and earned a J.D. from the Dickinson School of Law in 1975.

Looking up at the eighth floor of the City-County Building in Pittsburgh, the location of the Supreme and Superior Courts from 1918 to the present. The courtroom is the site of the 1999 Superior Court portrait on page 320.

From 1975 to 1983 Eakin served as an assistant district attorney in Cumberland County, and in 1983 was elected district attorney, an office that he held through 1995. He also maintained a private law practice from 1980 to 1989. Eakin served on the executive committee of the Pennsylvania District Attorneys Association for seven years, and in 1992-93, served as president of that organization. He served on the board of directors and as president of the Pennsylvania District Attorneys Institute, and on the Criminal Law Symposium Planning Committee of the Pennsylvania Bar Institute. Eakin is currently chairman of Pennsylvania Supreme Court Criminal Rules Committee.

Michael T. Joyce, Correale F. Stevens, John L. Musmanno, and Joan Orie Melvin were elected to the court in 1997 when vacancies were created by the retirement of President Judge Emeritus James E. Rowley, Judge Schiller's decision not to run to fill his appointed position, and the assumption of senior judge status by Judge Phyllis W. Beck and President Judge Emeritus Vincent A. Cirillo.

Judge Michael T. Joyce was born on February 24, 1949, in Pittsburgh. He received his B.A. from the Pennsylvania State University in 1973 and was awarded a J.D. from the Franklin Pierce Law Center in 1977. Joyce served in U.S. Army Intelligence from 1967-70 and served as a staff sergeant with the 25th Infantry Division in Vietnam from 1969-70. During his tour of duty, he was awarded the Bronze Star Medal and two Army Commendation Medals. He was a presidential law clerk in the White House in 1975, and maintained a private law practice from 1977-85. After winning both the Republican and Democratic judicial primaries, he was appointed to serve on the Erie County Court of Common Pleas in July 1985, elected to a ten-year term in November 1985, and retained for an additional term in November 1995. Joyce was the first designated family law judge in Erie County and subsequently served in both the criminal and civil divisions of the court before being elected to the Superior Court in 1997. He is a member of the Pennsylvania Trial Lawyers Association, Pennsylvania Trial

Judges Association, American Judicature Society, and the Domestic Relations Association of Pennsylvania.

Judge Correale F. Stevens was born in Hazleton, Pennsylvania. He graduated from the Pennsylvania State University with a B.A. in Political Science and received his J.D. from the Dickinson School of Law. While in law school, Stevens served as an associate editor of the *Dickinson Law Review*. He was engaged in the private practice of law, served as Hazleton City Solicitor from 1976-79 and as Hazleton City Authority Solicitor from 1979-84. He was named Outstanding Young Pennsylvanian by the state Jaycee organization and served on the executive board of the Wilkes-Barre Law and Library Association. In 1980 Stevens was elected to the Pennsylvania House of Representatives and was re-elected in 1982, 1984, and 1986. In 1987 he was elected district attorney of Luzerne County and in 1991, after winning both nominations for the Court of Common Pleas of Luzerne County, he was appointed to fill a vacancy and later won election to a full term. Stevens was elected to the Superior Court of Pennsylvania in 1997.

Judge John L. Musmanno was born March 31, 1942, in McKees Rocks. He received a B.A. from Washington & Jefferson College in 1963, (Magna Cum Laude, Phi Beta Kappa), and a J.D. from Vanderbilt University School of Law in 1966, where he was an assistant editor of the *Vanderbilt Law Review*. Judge Musmanno is a member of the American, Pennsylvania, and Allegheny County Bar Associations and a member of the Sons of Italy, Italian Sons and Daughters of America, and the Italian Heritage Society. He received the President's Award from the Pennsylvania Trial Lawyers Association in 1991, and the Academy of Trial Lawyers of Allegheny County award in 1993. He was an elected district justice from 1970 through 1981 (specially assigned city court magistrate 1970-73) and was elected judge of the Allegheny Court of Common Pleas in November 1981. He was the administrative judge of the civil division of that court from 1990 through 1997. In November 1997 he was elected to the Superior Court.

Judge Joan Orie Melvin was born in Pittsburgh. She attended the University of Notre Dame, where she received a B.A. in Economics in 1978, and the Duquesne University School of Law, where she was awarded a J.D. in 1981. From 1981 until 1985 Orie Melvin served as corporate counsel and was engaged in a private law practice, concentrating in civil litigation before she was appointed magistrate of the City of Pittsburgh Municipal Courts. She was named chief magistrate in 1987 and while holding this position, Orie Melvin established Pennsylvania's first Domestic Violence Court. In 1990 she was appointed to a vacancy on the Allegheny County Court of Common Pleas and was elected to a full term in 1991. She served in the civil, criminal, and family divisions before being elected to the Superior Court in 1997. Orie Melvin is a member of the Allegheny County Bar Association and the Allegheny County Women's Bar Association. She is past president of the Allegheny County Prison Board and was the recipient of the YMCA of Greater Pittsburgh, A Tribute to Women Leadership Award in Government/Public & Civic Service.

Judge Berle M. Schiller was appointed to the Superior Court in May 1996, following the death of Judge Donald Wieand. He did not seek election to the Superior Court in 1997, but following the election of Judge Thomas Saylor to the Supreme Court of Pennsylvania, Governor Tom Ridge again appointed him to the Superior Court in January 1998. Schiller was born June 17, 1944, in Brooklyn, New York. He received a B.A. from Bowdoin College in 1965 and a J.D. from New York University Law School in 1968. In 1971 he served as deputy director of personnel for the Commonwealth of Pennsylvania and in 1971-72, while a member of the Pennsylvania Department of Justice, he established and directed the Narcotics Strike Force. He was commissioned a captain in the Pennsylvania National Guard, Judge Advocate General Corps. Schiller was a litigator and senior partner with Astor Weiss & Newman from 1972 to 1994. The Supreme Court of Pennsylvania appointed Schiller to the Disciplinary Board of the Supreme Court, where he served from 1989 to 1995. Schiller was named chief counsel for the Federal Transit Administration of the U.S. Department of Transportation, a post he held from 1994 to 1996. In May 1999 he won the Democratic nomination for the Superior Court, but was not elected in the November 1999 general election.

Debra M. Todd

Judge Maureen E. Lally-Green was appointed in 1999 to fill the vacancy created by retirement and senior judge status of Judge Patrick R. Tamilia. Lally-Green was born in Sharpsville, Pennsylvania. She graduated from Duquesne University with a degree in Secondary Mathematics Education in 1971 and graduated from Duquesne's School of Law in 1974. Judge Lally-Green's early career spanned work as an associate with a private law firm in Pittsburgh, as counsel to the Commodity Futures Trading Commission in Washington, D.C., and as both major litigation and corporate counsel to Westinghouse Electric Corporation (now CBS). In 1983, she joined the faculty of Duquesne University School of Law and upon being appointed to the Superior Court, took a leave of absence from that position. For ten years, Lally-Green served as a consultant to Chief Justice John P. Flaherty, Supreme Court of Pennsylvania, and earlier with former Justice Nicholas P. Papadakos. She won election to a full term on the Superior Court in November 1999. Among other activities, Lally-Green served on the Criminal Procedural Rules Committee of the Supreme Court, the Hearing Committee of the Disciplinary Board of the Supreme Court, the Pennsylvania Bar Association's Commission on Women in the Profession, and as a Duquesne University representative on a Diocese Committee to study *Ex Corde Ecclesiae.* Having served the Allegheny County Bar Association on numerous boards and committees, she is currently a member of its board of governors. She now serves as an adjunct professor of law at Duquesne University School of Law.

To round out the full complement of the court as it entered the twenty-first century, the court's newest judge, Debra McClosky Todd, was elected in the general election of November 1999. Todd was born on October 15, 1957, in Ellwood City, Pennsylvania. In 1979, she graduated with honors from Chatham College and in 1982 she received a J.D. from the University of Pittsburgh School of Law where she served on the Law Review. Between 1982 and 1999 Todd maintained a civil litigation practice in Pittsburgh. Among her achievements are election to the Academy of Trial Lawyers of Allegheny County and service as a board member of the Leadership Pittsburgh Program. From 1989 through 1999 Todd served as a court-appointed special master for the Allegheny County Court of Common Pleas. She is a member of the Allegheny, Pennsylvania, and American Bar Associations.

In order of seniority, the court at the beginning of the twenty-first century was composed of Stephen J. McEwen Jr., President Judge (R), James R. Cavanaugh (R), Joseph A. Del Sole (D), John T. J. Kelly Jr. (R), Zoran Popovich (R), Justin M. Johnson (D), Joseph A. Hudock (D), Kate Ford Elliott (D), J. Michael Eakin (R), Michael T. Joyce (R), Correale F. Stevens (R), John L. Musmanno (D), Joan Orie Melvin (R), Maureen E. Lally-Green (R), Debra McClosky Todd (D), Senior Judges William F. Cercone, President Judge Emeritus (D), John P. Hester (D), John G. Brosky (D), Peter Paul Olszewski (D), Frank J. Montemuro Jr. (R), Phyllis W. Beck (D), Vincent A. Cirillo, President Judge Emeritus (R), and Patrick R. Tamilia (D).

At the end of the nineteenth century, the political affiliation of the court was one Democrat and six Republicans. At the end of the twentieth century, there were eleven Republicans and twelve Democrats. Despite a Democratic majority in registration, Republicans, since the early 1990s, have fared better than Democrats in gubernatorial, legislative, and statewide judicial elections. A Democratic dominance of statewide judicial elections began in the 1970s and continued to the early 1990s, providing for Democratic majorities on the appellate courts. A return to Republican dominance, however, began in 1985 with the election of Judges Kelly and Popovich, the last two Superior Court judges who were permitted by law to cross-file and run on both the Republican and Democratic primary ballots. At that time, it was not uncommon for Democratic judicial candidates, particularly from Philadelphia or Allegheny County, to win both nominations because of the regional identity and the overwhelming Democratic registration in those counties, the two most populous in the state. In 1986 the General Assembly eliminated cross-filing in statewide judicial elections, and all judges now run solely on the ticket of their party affiliation. In an anomaly that occurred only once before in the court's history, Judge Popovich, a Republican, was denied the Republican nomination but won the Democratic nomination in the primary election. In the November 1985 general election, he was elected to the Superior Court as a Democrat.

Despite maintaining party affiliation while running for office, political party plays no factor in the decisions of the judges of the Superior Court, and analysis of the voting patterns of the individual judges would fail to provide information from which a judge's political party could be discerned. The Superior Court has, through its history, been a court, not of political parties, but of legal principles.

## *Court Computerization*

The essential work of the court has changed little since 1895. Appeals are briefed and argued, opinions are written, circulated, and filed. Enormous advances in technology, however, have revolutionized the way all of this is accomplished. Until 1979, only minor changes had occurred in the way cases were docketed, legal research was conducted, and memoranda, opinions, and orders were produced and circulated.

The first application of computer technology to the work of the court occurred in 1979 with the installation of Lexis terminals in some court offices to assist in legal research. At about this time, the Administrative Office of Pennsylvania Courts (AOPC) became interested in the use of computers for docketing of cases. The Superior Court, as the court that handled the greatest volume of the three appellate courts, was chosen as the first court to have such a system. When it was installed, this system ran on the same computer used by the AOPC for financial and payroll applications.

In 1981 each judge's chambers was provided with a word processor to expedite the writing of opinions. This was a significant improvement in the mechanical process of writing, revising, and polishing the final work of the judges for circulation and filing. Also in 1981, the process of electronically docketing cases began with terminals being installed at each of the three district offices of the Superior Court, Philadelphia, Harrisburg, and Pittsburgh. Starting in 1982, all new cases were docketed electronically and, in essence, the foundation had been established for an integrated computerized system that could link all chambers of the court with each other and to each prothonotary's office.

The first step toward this system was taken in 1987 with the installation of networked personal computers in each judge's chambers and administrative office. With these computers came greatly improved word processing, electronic mail, and the ability to access Lexis and Westlaw without the need for separate, single-purpose terminals. Individual offices could now also maintain their own customized programs for information storage and retrieval. In 1989 an improved version of the original docketing program was deployed. With this, the vision of having legal research, word processing, and docketing integrated into a single system was realized and the Superior Court became one of the leaders in the country in the utilization and application of computer technology to the work of the judiciary at the appellate level.

With the updated equipment, the various offices could transmit mail, memoranda, and opinions electronically. Cases could be filed directly with the court's official publisher, West Publishing, through our recorder's office. Selected offices could search the docketing system for cases filed in the Superior Court concerning any of the areas of the law subject to the court's jurisdiction. The central legal staff had a readily accessible research tool to determine whether circulated opinions were in conflict with previous rulings of the court and thereby minimize conflicts between new memoranda and opinions and those previously published. In 1997 the court improved its system by upgrading to a Microsoft Windows-based operating system, providing even more flexibility and potential for diversification into a broader system which will eventually comprise every judicial level and function under the Unified Judiciary of Pennsylvania.

A computer network with high-speed, dedicated lines now links all judicial chambers and administrative offices of the court. The efficiency of the court has been demonstrably increased and the court provides an advanced docketing and case management system so that any judge, law clerk, or administrative staff member of the court may access information on any given appeal, including the status of the circulating proposed opinions, the nature and status of motions, inter-chambers correspondence, and votes of panel members.

While the heart and soul of the operation of the Superior Court still is and always will be the intellectual application and knowledge brought by the judges and their support staffs to the legal issues presented by appeals, the process would be curtailed considerably, in light of the constantly increasing volume, were it not for the efficient application of computer technology to the work of the court. As the use of the typewriter advanced the operation and efficiency of the court as it entered the twentieth century, the application of computer technology will permit the court to keep pace with the mounting volume of appellate litigation without diminishing in any way the quality of the work of the court.

In a retrospective comparison, it is important to note that in 1899, the end of the nineteenth century, the seven judges of Superior Court were assigned 609 appeals of which to dispose, for an average of 87 cases per judge[2]. At the close of the twentieth century, the Superior Court filed 6,046 decisions, an average of 263 decisions for each of the 23 judges on the court.[3] This is in keeping with the pace maintained by the court[4] throughout 1997 to 1999.

## THE COURT IN THE TWENTY-FIRST CENTURY

What challenges and expectations lie before us in the years 2000 and beyond? This is the question to be asked, if not answered, as we move to the dawn of the twenty-first century and the second century of the existence of the Superior Court.

We must acknowledge that the greatest number of fundamental decisions, opin-

2. See Chapter II.
3. Statistical Report, Superior Court Recorder's Office, Dec. 31, 1999.
4. See note 2 above.

ions, and legal treatises began with pen being applied to paper. Only in this century did the typewriter, as a mechanical aid, supplant what was a very personal, physically, and mentally involved process. The word processor became an adjunct to, but not a substitute for, that process. Reading, personal exchange and hands-on review, evaluation, and revision still play a major role in the intellectual activity that is fundamental to judicial review and opinion writing.

The relationship between the elbow clerk and the judge is critical to the effective work of each. In the Superior Court, virtually all memoranda, opinions, and orders are done in chambers by staff selected and trained by each particular judge. This court has not succumbed to the practice of many, if not most appellate courts, whereby the work product of the court is created in a central office by a battery of clerks, who forward the memorandum or opinion to an individual judge for approval and filing. It is the practice in some courts to have the memoranda prepared on the basis of the briefs and circulated to the assigned judge before the case is heard at oral argument. The practice of reducing involvement by the judges with the appellate judicial process, while promoting efficiency, does not promote justice, since it trivializes the very heart of the system: cases being decided on their merits, after review by a judge chosen by the people.

These advances in technology must always be the servant, while knowledgeable, experienced, and dedicated judges and staff remains the heart and soul of a system of justice which requires human input and interaction as contemplated by our Constitution and as shaped by our predecessors on this court.

To predict what this court will face as major legal challenges in the not-too-distant future is beyond our powers of prescience and foreseeability. It is not difficult, however, to determine what faces this state and country at this time and, as we have seen in the chapters of this book, what engages society as issues, problems, and conditions, which immediately impact upon the court.

## FAMILY AND SOCIAL CONCERNS IN THE LAW

The most fundamental issues today, despite unparalleled economic achievement and wealth, concern the state of the nation's family stability, moral commitment, human values, and political integrity. The legislature and the courts will be tested in extreme measure to retain the balance required to continue the existence of a civilization unequaled in human history. The performance of science and medicine increasingly outpaces our capacity to maintain an ethical and/or legal system to guard against unanticipated destructive results. Scientifically, human reproduction has progressed far from natural conception and the fundamental process of procreation. The centuries of law which govern our handling of reproduction and parenting have been tested by discoveries which surpass even the predictions in James Orwell's "1984" and Aldous Huxley's "Brave New World." New drugs and medical procedures give promise to an attainable longevity of 100 to 120 years which will have a dramatic impact on allocation of resources available for pension and health care.

While progressing in science and computer technology, we are losing ground in family stability, child rearing practices, ecology, moral and ethical accountability, and in achievement of freedom with responsibility. A recent study from the National Marriage Project at Rutgers University, "The State of Our Unions: The Social Health of Marriage in America," depicts marriage in great difficulty, rates having dropped to a forty year low, with young women particularly pessimistic about achieving long and happy unions. It remains to be seen whether governmental policies can have an impact on this regression in the face of television influences, and now Internet preemption of character development from families, schools, and religious institutions.

In early August 1999 the American Academy of Pediatrics publicized recommendations that children under two years of age not be permitted to view television but rather be actively engaged in interaction with adults and playmates to foster necessary mental development. It also recommended that viewing by older children be limited and that television, computer games, and other electronic devices not be utilized to baby-sit children. The political will, supported by definitive studies and evaluations by our institutions of higher learning and research, must guide the way with the courts supporting the social developments of the fundamental protection of value systems.

The concepts of government, justice, and institutions devoted to the common good will be as important in the coming years as they have been in the past. A most critical concern, going to the heart of family life and function, is the right to privacy. In every aspect of our lives, from day to day existence to criminal culpability, the protection from an invasion of privacy, and the security that protection brings, will be a critical legal issue for the courts in this century. It is but a short step to DNA typing at birth for all citizens, entered into a national computer bank, to elimination of any semblance of privacy or anonymity which we have enjoyed up until now. For better or worse, even the deep recesses of the brain will be explored routinely and memories of previously concealed information dredged from its depths. "Farwell brain fingerprinting" is fast becoming a reality. This procedure permits the measuring of brainwaves emitted in response to keywords proposed to the subject, which unequivocally establishes the subject's knowledge of the matter tendered. As prepared and submitted by highly skilled operators, the key words can elicit information, which could only be known by the criminal, terrorist, spy, or other candidate for questioning. The technique is far superior to the polygraph and should meet the *Frye v. United States*[5] and *Daubert v. Merrell Dow*[6] tests of scientific reliability. The problem for the legislators and the courts is how the privacy rights of the individual can be protected from both government and multinational business intrusion with the availability of these scientific advances. This is perhaps what is really meant by the "New World Order."

The seeming ease by which malignant minded terrorists and enemies of democracy can interdict critical programs of economic, governmental, and defense computer operated and controlled functions presages unthinkable destruction of the computer managed operation of systems upon which our civilization has come to depend. The reaction by government necessarily must be to provide a superior blanket of interception of the electronic plague, which in turn may introduce a degree of intrusion into personal activities dependent upon the electronic medium. The guarantees of privacy under the Constitution will be tested as never before.

We have been able to adjust the fundamentals of constitutional protection to electronic interceptions of telephone and cellular phone transmissions. It remains to be seen if a super surveillance that is total, unremitting, and exhaustive can be implemented by the government while retaining any degree of privacy, particularly for the family.

---

5. 54 App.D.C. 46, 293 F. 1013 (D.C. Cir. 1923).
6. 509 U.S. 579, 113 S.Ct. 2786, 125 L.Ed.2d 469 (1993).

L. to R.: Judge Del Sole, former Pennsylvania Governor Robert Casey, Judge Tamilia, and Judge Popovich seated at a luncheon held in conjunction with a court function.

## CIVIL AND ECONOMIC DEVELOPMENT

Economic and industrial development in the coming years has unparalleled potential for impacting on the judicial system of this country and the world. In the past ten years the Internet alone has accelerated economic productivity and growth through the exchange of information and creation of worldwide markets beyond our wildest imagination. New concepts of contract liability, intellectual property, criminal misuse of the World Wide Web, and the practice of medicine and the dispensing of drugs over the Internet have taxed legislatures, the courts, and governmental agencies to the limit. New products, medicines, engineering, biomedical agents, genetic creation or alteration, and electronic devices will demand expanded knowledge and legal concepts to provide the degree of judicial balance required. We must accept as dogma that for every right there is a correlative duty, and for every benefit a corresponding cost. Most important is the evolving relationship between federal preemption and state sovereignty in dealing with these rapidly emerging scientific and medical discoveries. It is also conceivable that the mastery of near space, as inconceivable to us at this junction as traveling to the moon was in 1895, will provide legal issues and tests similar to those concerning aviation and intercontinental transportation. Already, estimates are being made that private, as opposed to governmental, space enterprises are poised to generate trillions of dollars in economic productivity. It may well be that the era of the expert jury may need to supplant the time-honored lay jury in some cases or the creation of specialized courts, much as we have seen for bankruptcy, patents, family, and criminal cases, may be necessary.

In an editorial, Mortimer B. Zuckerman, editor-in-chief of *U.S. News and World Report*, commented on the explosive economy, quoting Alan Greenspan, chairman of the Federal Reserve System Board of Governors, as attributing the economy's "phenomenal" performance to technological innovation wrought by computers and other information-processing equipment. Zuckerman continued his analysis stating:

> The United States enjoys a unique capacity to move financial and human resources to the cutting edges of technology. This is the fifth industrial revolution of American history. The first was in the 18th century, with waterpower, textiles, and iron. In the mid-19th century came steam, rail, and steel. The turn of the 20th century brought electricity, chemicals, and internal combustion. Fifty years later, it was electronics, aviation, and mass production. The current revolution is based on semiconductors, fiber optics, genetics, and software.[7]

Throughout these revolutions, the Superior Court, as reviewed in earlier chapters, has played an active and constructive role in the evolution of the law maintaining pace with the economic and industrial changes. We are confident that progress will continue.

## LITIGATION IN THE NEXT CENTURY

It is unquestionable that the volume and rate of litigation in the future will continue the unending acceleration experienced from the inception of the Superior Court in 1895. What is not clearly predictable is the area which will create the greatest volume and challenge to the court in the second century.

Speculation logically leads to the conclusion that, for the foreseeable future, present trends will continue. Recognizing that laws are driven by political considerations and legislators' response to public and societal pressures, it is evident the Superior Court will respond in like fashion. As in the immediate past, major demands on the court have arisen from criminal, tort and family law.

## CRIMINAL LAW

The crisis in criminal law is less than we experienced thirty to forty years ago resulting in the refinement and articulation of rights derived from the Constitution and the Bill of Rights and which produced the exclusionary rule of *Mapp v. Ohio*,[8] *Miranda v. Arizona*,[9] and *Escobedo v. Illinois*[10] as discussed in Chapter V. This rule has become embedded in the law, with recent tightening and restricting of its effect, as pragmatic and logical considerations require. The new crisis is related more to the international drug trade and the uncontrolled use of firearms, which has resulted in widespread violence spreading to younger children, into our schools, and across the social and cultural landscape. The advent of mandatory sentences, promulgated by legislators, and the expansion of criminal laws to meet real or perceived threats to life and public safety, have increased the number and extent of periods of incarceration across the breadth of criminal prosecution. Accordingly, a present and expanding crisis in criminal law is the number of persons incarcerated and the amount of time each person spends in prison. It is conceivable that the courts may be faced with a constitutional crisis if the legislature fails to deal with the problem.

---

7. Mortimer B. Zuckerman, "The Time of Our Lives," *U.S. News and World Report*, 17 May 1999, 72.
8. 367 U.S. 643 (1961).
9. 384 U.S. 436 (1966).
10. 378 U.S. 478 (1964).

The Founder's Courtroom was dedicated May 13, 1998.
Top left is the litigants' view; Top right the judges' view. Bottom, L. to R.: William C. Archbold, Media, Pennsylvania, attorney; Matthew J. Ryan, Speaker of the Pennsylvania House; President Judge McEwen.

Already, in states such as California, more money is being spent on prisons than education. A trend has begun whereby states and federal correction systems are building prisons dedicated entirely to geriatric prisoners with the myriad of health and mental problems which are the corollary to the aging process. This may require a rethinking of mandatory sentencing and sentences which bring about incarceration long beyond the time when a prisoner can or will be a threat to society. As prisons become increasingly overcrowded, less funding is available for drug rehabilitation, retraining, and treatment. This results in a greater probability that inmates, once paroled, are more likely to fail and return to prison.

From another direction is the increased federalization of crime by the United States Congress. In a recently issued report of the Task Force on Federalization of the Criminal Law, an eminent bipartisan committee's examination of a serious criminal justice concern concluded "[t]he Federalization trend is inconsistent with long established allocation of power and promises a troubling series of adverse consequences."[11] The report recommends retention of basic jurisdiction in criminal law enforcement in the state justice system while suggesting Congress carefully and cautiously promulgate any new federal criminal legislation by imposing on itself limits on federalization of local crime. The Superior Court will be called upon to play its part in determining issues which unquestionably will arise as a result of overlapping jurisdiction and it may well be one of the leaders, as in the past, in bringing order out of conflict.

A seamless web of deviance has evolved starting with family breakdown, an increase in mental disabilities, and a lack of conscience or remorse which, coupled with real or imagined slights, results in the senseless, unexplainable brutality and violence permeating society. The response from government and the courts will determine the quality of life in the next century. Prisons are reflecting deviance at every level with 12 to 13 percent of prisoners suffering from mental illness. The lack of trust in governmental institutions and politics is leading increasingly to splinter groups and self-styled militia who see the government as their enemy and who have a willingness to attack and destroy it. The threats to our country from within are real and, to some degree, ominous. Nor are we isolated from militants offshore in many countries, particularly third world dictatorships, who see the United States as the enemy, and who are increasingly willing and able to attack the United States and its citizens wherever they can, including here at home.

For this country to survive, its institutions must be strong and stable and its defenses impenetrable. Particularly, the courts must be clear of vision, purpose, and values, and have the courage to confront and deal with the problems presented by a society and culture with accelerating tendencies to spin out of control. The Superior Court must remain true to its heritage. As in the past one hundred years, when the problems it faced and resolved appeared equally as daunting as those it now faces, the court will report to those to whom it is entrusted in the twenty-second century, a job well done. One only needs to refer to the chapters of this book regarding prohibition, the depression, the wars, sedition, and communist threats to be aware that the same concerns in different forms remain with us today.

---

11. James Starzella and William W. Taylor III, "Federalizing Crime," *ABA Criminal Justice*, 14 (spring 1999), No. 1.

# TORT LAW

The major innovations of the past century have created the foundation upon which the future of tort litigation will evolve. An accelerating trend due to the enormous growth of tort litigation arising from industrial developments, transportation, medical practices, the interaction between the public and service industries, and the environmental impact of new technologies, has created an enormous volume of cases at the trial level. Increasingly, the legislature and affected businesses are looking to non-judicial resolution of disputes such as compulsory binding arbitration, caps on damages, and limitations on liability. The pressure on the intermediate appellate courts will be to provide a balance between expediting cases and appeals and assuring that due process and substantial justice are maintained.

# FAMILY LAW

The revolution, begun in 1903 in juvenile and child welfare law and culminating in 1980 with no-fault divorce and equitable distribution, which created new standards of economic justice relating to valuing and distributing marital property, will continue unabated into the twenty-first century. Issues which will command increased attention of the legislature and the courts are treatment of delinquent and dependent children, custody, joint or shared custody, relocation of households as related to primary custody, adoption, termination of parental rights, and gay marriages and adoptions. Domestic violence has demanded increased legislation and court involvement and will be a significant factor in family court activity. The juvenile law in both the areas of delinquency and dependency has experienced congressional and state legislative attention which will impact on the trial courts and this court as the legislation works its way through the system. A two-part package of bills introduced in the legislature in January 2000 calls for the revamping of the family courts and proposes an amendment to the Pennsylvania Constitution and implementation of legislation that would allow the General Assembly to change the way the state court system deals with divorce, custody, child and spousal support, and the division of marital property. We have worked through incredible changes in these areas since the 1980 divorce code, support laws, and custody laws, and are now standing on the threshold of still greater changes.

The Joint State Government Commission, by joint resolution, adopted in 1996 by the Senate and the House, has established a task force which will undertake a total review of the adoption law on an ongoing basis and make recommendations to the General Assembly. The last major adoption legislation was implemented in 1980 and has been construed by this court during the past twenty years to give the adoption law its present form. The impact of this work on adoption legislation will be felt by this court for years to come.

# CONCLUSION

The charge to the court in its second century is every bit as great as in its first century. Its ability to deal with issues and volume will be taxed to the greatest extent and a full measure of dedication, character, and expertise will be necessary. The court believes in keeping with its tradition it will respond with resolute vision and that the challenges of the future will be met and mastered.

The president judges who have served on the Pennsylvania Superior Court since 1895. Clockwise, starting at top center: Charles E. Rice (1895-1915), George B. Orlady (1915-1925), William D. Porter (1925-1930), Frank M. Trexler (1930-1935), William H. Keller (1935-1945), Thomas J. Baldridge (1945-1947), Chester H. Rhodes (1947-1965), Harold L. Ervin (1965-1967).

Superior Court president judges (continued). Clockwise, starting at top center: J. Colvin Wright (1968-1974), G. Harold Watkins (1974-1978), Robert Lee Jacobs (1978-1979), William F. Cercone (1979-1983), Edmund B. Spaeth Jr. (1983-1985), Vincent A. Cirillo (1986-1990), James. E. Rowley (1991-1995), and Stephen J. McEwen Jr. (1995-2000).

## SUPERIOR COURT JUDGES OF PENNSYLVANIA
### 1895 - 2000

| | | | |
|---|---|---|---|
| Charles E. Rice | 1895 | Jesse E. B. Cunningham | 1926 |
| James Addams Beaver | 1895 | Thomas J. Baldridge | 1929 |
| George B. Orlady | 1895 | J. Frank Graff | 1930 |
| John J. Wickham | 1895 | John G. Whitmore | 1930 |
| Edward Newell Willard | 1895 | James B. Drew | 1931 |
| Howard J. Reeder | 1895 | Joseph Stadtfeld | 1931 |
| Henry J. McCarthy | 1895 | William M. Parker | 1932 |
| Peter P. Smith | 1896 | Arthur H. James | 1933 |
| William W. Porter | 1897 | Chester H. Rhodes | 1935 |
| William D. Porter | 1898 | William E. Hirt | 1939 |
| Dimner Beeber | 1899 | Charles E. Kenworthey | 1941 |
| John I. Mitchell | 1900 | Claude T. Reno | 1942 |
| Thomas A. Morrison | 1902 | F. Clair Ross | 1945 |
| John J. Henderson | 1903 | W. Heber Dithrich | 1945 |
| John B. Head | 1906 | John C. Arnold | 1945 |
| Frank M. Trexler | 1914 | John S. Fine | 1947 |
| John W. Kephart | 1914 | Blair F. Gunther | 1950 |
| J. Henry Williams | 1916 | J. Colvin Wright | 1953 |
| William Heustis Keller | 1919 | Robert E. Woodside | 1953 |
| William B. Linn | 1919 | Harold L. Ervin | 1954 |
| Robert S. Gawthrop | 1922 | Philip O. Carr | 1956 |

# SUPERIOR COURT JUDGES OF PENNSYLVANIA
## 1895 ✦ 2000

| | | | |
|---|---|---|---|
| G. Harold Watkins | 1957 | Perry J. Shertz | 1980 |
| Harry M. Montgomery | 1960 | Phyllis W. Beck | 1981 |
| Gerald F. Flood | 1961 | Stephen J. McEwen, Jr. | 1981 |
| Robert Lee Jacobs | 1965 | Vincent A. Cirillo | 1982 |
| J. Sydney Hoffman | 1965 | James E. Rowley | 1982 |
| Theodore O. Spaulding | 1966 | Peter Paul Olszewski | 1984 |
| John B. Hannum | 1968 | Joseph A. Del Sole | 1984 |
| William Franklin Cercone | 1969 | Patrick R. Tamilia | 1984 |
| Israel Packel | 1972 | John T. J. Kelly, Jr. | 1986 |
| Edmund B. Spaeth, Jr. | 1973 | James R. Melinson | 1988 |
| Gwilym A. Price, Jr. | 1974 | Joseph A. Hudock | 1990 |
| Robert Van der Voort | 1974 | Kate Ford Elliott | 1990 |
| John P. Hester | 1978 | Thomas G. Saylor | 1994 |
| Donald E. Wieand | 1978 | J. Michael Eakin | 1996 |
| James R. Cavanaugh | 1979 | Berle M. Schiller | 1996 |
| John G. Brosky | 1980 | Michael T. Joyce | 1998 |
| Richard B. Wickersham | 1980 | Correale F. Stevens | 1998 |
| Richard DiSalle | 1980 | John L. Musmanno | 1998 |
| Justin M. Johnson | 1980 | Joan Orie Melvin | 1998 |
| Frank J. Montemuro, Jr. | 1980 | Maureen E. Lally-Green | 1999 |
| Zoran Popovich | 1980 | Debra M. Todd | 2000 |

# *Proclamation*

***Whereas*** the American Bar Association on the basis of extensive national research has determined that the public's knowledge of and confidence in our judicial systems will be enhanced through increased participation by judges in programs designed to explain the role of the courts and the importance of an independent judiciary; and

***Whereas*** the American Bar Association supports judicial initiatives that allow the public to learn about courts and to interact with judges consistent with judicial ethical obligations; and

***Whereas*** the American Bar Association urges judges to participate actively in public education programs about the role of law and justice systems; and

***Whereas*** the Pennsylvania Superior Court has undertaken a number of initiatives to further public understanding of the role of the courts in our society; and

***Whereas*** the Pennsylvania Superior Court has televised its proceedings with helpful commentary about the cases under consideration; and

***Whereas*** the Pennsylvania Superior Court has demonstrated leadership in the field of public education and awareness of the importance of the role of law and the justice systems; and

***Whereas*** the Pennsylvania Superior Court has initiated steps to foster increased understanding among the branches of government;

***Now, Therefore,*** on behalf the American Bar Association, pursuant to the authority vested in me as President, I congratulate the Pennsylvania Superior Court for its leadership, commitment and creativity in establishing replicable programs to enhance public knowledge about and confidence in the rule of law and our justice systems.

***Executed*** on behalf of the American Bar Association on this 8th day of August, 1999, in Atlanta, Georgia.

Philip S. Anderson
President, American Bar Association

# Sidebar

The American Bar Association paid tribute to the Superior Court's educational and judicial participation in public and international programs designed to strengthen the role and public perception of the court in today's world. On August 8, 1999, Judge Kate Ford Elliott and Judge James Cavanaugh accepted the proclamation for the court from ABA President Phillip Anderson at the ABA meeting in Atlanta, Georgia (photo 1).

An important initiative of the modern Superior Court is to combine working business and educational conferences at locations that stimulate recognition of and pride in the history of our nation. Since 1996, the administration of President Judge Stephen J. McEwen Jr. has instituted court conferences in the Brandywine Valley, at the University of Virginia, at the Naval Academy in Annapolis, and in St. Louis.

At the Brandywine Conference in 1996, in addition to the business session at Widener University, experts in the field of Death and Dying Jurisprudence engaged the court in lectures and discussion. The second day of lecture involved the new rules of evidence being considered by the Pennsylvania Supreme Court. The historical and cultural aspects of the conference were supplied by touring both the Brandywine River Museum and

(1) L-R: Judge Ford Elliott, Mr. Anderson, and Judge Cavanaugh.

(2) President Judge McEwen presented Superior Court commemorative seals to lecturers. L-R: Judge James Harry Michael Jr. who introduced us to the local history of the judicial system which saw James Madison, John Adams, and Thomas Jefferson appear in the court at Charlottesville, Virginia; Judge McEwen; George Meredith Cohen, Associate Professor of Law, who spoke on law and economics; and Professor Earl C. Dudley Jr. who spoke on constitutional law.

(3) The business conference at Annapolis.

(4) The famous courthouse in St. Louis, now a federal monument, which was the site of the Dred Scott Decision by Chief Justice Taney in 1857.

(5) Members of the Pennsylvania Superior Court behind the bench in the courtroom in which the Dred Scott case was heard.

(6) L-R: Professor Barlett, Professor Ellman and Professor Blumberg.

the Winterthur, the former estate of one of the Dupont heirs.

In June 1997, the court conference convened at the University of Virginia. In addition to the business sessions, lectures and discussions concerning the law and economics and constitutional law accounted for interesting and informative educational benefits (photo 2).

The Naval Academy at Annapolis, Maryland, was site of the annual court conference in May 1998 (photo 3). In addition to the business sessions, the conference included several educational sessions. The first pertained to the new Restatement on Products Liability and was presented by reporters of the American Law Institute. The second dealt with the presentation of expert evidence with a focus on the Daubert Rule. It was presented by Philadelphia Attorney Dave Binder, author of *Binder on Evidence* and Practicing Law Institute lecturer, Laura Ellsworth, author of a paper titled *Scientific Evidence in Pennsylvania*. The third educational session pertained to judicial independence and was presented by Edward Maeira.

Additionally, members of the court had the privilege of having dinner at the officer's dining hall and hearing a stimulating and inspiring talk by Rear Admiral (retired) Eugene G. Fluckey, a true World War II hero and commander of the submarine Barb, which sank the greatest tonnage of any submarine during World War II. Admiral Fluckey was awarded four Navy crosses and the Congressional Medal of Honor for his valor under fire.

In May 1999, the court's Business and Educational Conference took place in St. Louis (photos 4, 5), with educational seminars conducted at the University of St. Louis. Speakers at the first seminar were Katherine T. Bartlett, Professor of Law at Duke University, Ira Mark Ellman, Professor at Arizona State University College of Law, and Grace Ganz Blumberg, Law Professor at UCLA (photo 6). All are experts, writers, and researchers in family law and related fields.

Speakers at the second seminar dealing with bioethics were Reverend Kevin O'Rourke, O. P., a priest of the Dominican Order and member of the faculty of St. Louis University Medical School, where he founded the center for healthcare and ethics, and Jesse A. Goldner, A.B., M.A., J.D., a professor of law, psychiatry, and pediatrics of St. Louis University Medical School (photo 7).

The Legal Education and Judiciary Exchange Program, sponsored by Duquesne University and supported by the Pennsylvania Superior Court, is illustrated in the presentment of Lic. Dunia Chacón, Superior Court of Costa Rica, accompanied by Professor Robert S. Barker of Duquesne, who directs the program with Central and South American countries (photo 8). Judge Tamilia is a liaison to the court for this program.

(7) L-R: Judge McEwen, Rev. O'Rourke, and Mr. Goldner.

(8) L-R: Professor Barker, Judge Tamilia, Judge Chacón, Judge McEwen, Judge Hudock, and Judge Hester.

(9) L–R (standing): Judge Tamilia and the Ukrainian delegation, (seated): Panel members Judge Popovich, Judge Del Sole, and Judge Hester.

(10) L-R: Judge Brosky, International Assistance Group Attorney Barbara Clements, Judge Schiller, Judge Ford Elliott, International Assistance Group Director Larisa Mason, Judge Mazkov, Lauren Posati, and Judge Tamilia.

(11) L. to R.: Justice Zappala, Judge Mazkov, and Judge Tamalia.

(12) L-R: Professor Jiang, Xingguo, China University of Political Science and Law (CUPL), Beijing, China, Judge Tamilia, Professor Frank Y. Liu, Duquesne University, and Professor Wang, Ping, CUPL, Professor Du, Zinli, CUPL.

Following a lecture on the American system of justice, due process, and constitutional issues, and our method of selecting judges by election, a group of Ukrainian judges and lawyers (photo 9), referred to Judge Tamilia by the Pittsburgh Council for International Visitors, was introduced to a panel of the Superior Court and to members of the Court of Common Pleas of Allegheny County and the Third Circuit Court of Appeals.

Appellate Judge Mikhail Mazkov of St. Petersburg, Russia, who was assigned to process the first foreign adoptions under Russia's judicial proceedings, rather than the previous administrative proceedings, was invited to visit Pittsburgh and the Superior Court. Judge Mazkov presided over the first adoption under the new process, a child adopted by Richard and Lauren Posati through the International Assistance Group. Lauren is Judge Tamilia's administrative clerk. Judge Mazkov was introduced to the panel of Superior Court, sitting at the time of his visit, which provided a great opportunity for country-to-country exchange (photo 10). In further promoting an exchange between Pennsylvania and Russian appellate judiciaries, Judge Mikhail Mazkov of St. Petersburg, Russia, was presented to Justice Stepehn A. Zappala (photo 11). Chinese officials (photo 12) are representative of the many visitors from the Peoples Republic of China who are involved with Duquesne

University in a legal exchange program. The Superior Court is an important part of the program, presenting an opportunity to educate judges and professors from China in the elements of the judicial and legal process in America.

In 1999 Mr. Justice A. I. Hayanga of the High Court of Kenya in eastern Africa and his wife, Mrs. Christine Hayanga, an attorney who practices family law, were introduced to a panel of the Superior Court (photo 13). Justice and Mrs. Hayanga were in the United States for the graduation of their daughter, Lulu Hayanga, from Duquesne University School of Law. Lulu was a member of Judge Tamilia's family law class and an intern in his office during the summer of 1998. The Hayangas expressed their appreciation for the kindness and treatment by the Superior Court in both Pittsburgh and Philadelphia, where Justice Hayanga attended a Superior Count en banc session in the Founder's Courtroom.

The Commonwealth Partners program, created by President Judge McEwen in 1998, brings together Superior Court judges, trial judges and members of the Legislature in regional meetings. Photographs taken at the Judicial/Legislative Partnership meeting held at the Mountain View Inn in Greensburg, Pennsylvania, in 1999, illustrate the partnership program (photos 14, 15).

(13) L-R: Judge Tamilia, Justice Hayanga, Mrs. Hayanga, Judge Johnson, Judge Lally-Green, and Judge Hester.

(14) L-R: Judge Hudock and Judge Charles Marker, Judge Gilbert Mahalich, and Judge John Blahovec of the Westmoreland County Common Pleas Court.

(15) At the Commonwealth Partners work session are L-R: Representative Timothy J. Solobay, Representative Terry E. Van Horne, Senator Allen G. Kukovich and Judge McEwen.

# GLOSSARY OF LEGAL TERMS

**Action at law**
An action that seeks recovery of damages for negligence, breach of contract, or recovery of real or personal property, as opposed to equitable relief.

**Action in equity**
An action that seeks equitable relief, such as an injunction or specific performance, as opposed to damages.

**Adjudication**
The legal process of resolving a dispute. The formal giving or pronouncing a judgment or decree in a court proceeding; also the judgment or decision given. The entry of a decree by a court in respect to the parties in a case.

**Aggregate sentence**
A sentence that arises from a conviction on multiple counts in an indictment. Entire number, sum, mass, or quantity of something; total amount; complete; whole; i.e. the total sentence imposed.

**Alimony**
A court-ordered allowance that one spouse pays to the other spouse for maintenance and support while they are separated, while they are involved in a matrimonial lawsuit, or after they are divorced.

**Alimony pendente lite**
Temporary alimony. An allowance made pending a suit for divorce or, separate maintenance including a reasonable allowance for preparation of the suit as well as for support.

**Allocatur**
It is allowed. It is used in Pennsylvania to denote permission to appeal.

**Amount in controversy**
The damages claimed or relief demanded by the injured party in a lawsuit.

**Appeal as of right**
An appeal to a higher court from which permission need not be first obtained.

**Appellate**
Pertaining to or having cognizance of appeals and other proceedings for the judicial review of adjudications. The term has a general meaning, and it has a specific meaning indicating the distinction between original jurisdiction and appellate jurisdiction.

**Assessor**
An officer chosen or appointed to appraise, value, or assess property. A person learned in some particular science or industry, who sits with the judge on the trial of a cause requiring such special knowledge and gives his advice.

**At-will employment**
Employment that is usually undertaken without a contract and that may be terminated at any time, by either the employer or the employee, without cause.

**Causation**
The fact of being the cause of something produced or of happening. The act by which an effect is produced. An important doctrine in fields of negligence and criminal law.

**Certiorari**
To be informed of. A writ of common law origin issued by a superior to an inferior court requiring the latter to produce a certified record of a particular case tried therein. The writ is issued in order that the court issuing the writ may inspect the proceedings and determine whether there have been any irregularities. It is most commonly used to refer to the Supreme Court of the United States, which uses the writ of certiorari as a discretionary device to choose the cases it wishes to hear.

## Chancellor (in equity)
A judge serving on a court of chancery or presiding in an equity action.

## Circuit court
Courts whose jurisdiction extends over several counties or districts, and of which terms are held in the various counties or districts to which their jurisdiction extends.

## Closed shop
Exists where workers must be members of a union as a condition of their employment. This practice was made unlawful by the Taft-Hartley Act.

## Common law marriage
A marriage not solemnized in the ordinary way (i.e. non-ceremonial) but created by an agreement to marry, followed by cohabitation. A consummated agreement to marry, between persons legally capable of making a marriage contract, per verba de praesenti (words of present intent), followed by cohabitation. Such marriage requires a positive mutual agreement, permanent and exclusive of all others, to enter into a marital relationship, cohabitation sufficient to warrant a fulfillment of necessary relationship of man and wife, and an assumption of marital duties and obligations.

## Consecutive sentences.
When one sentence of confinement is to follow another in point of time, the second sentence is deemed to be consecutive to the first. May also be applied to suspended sentences.

## Constructive (parole)
That which is established by the mind of the law in its act of construing facts, conduct, circumstances, or instruments inferred, implied or made out by legal interpretation (parole implied).

## Corpus delicti
"Body of the crime." The fact of a transgression. Loosely, the material substance on which a crime has been committed; the physical evidence of a crime, such as the corpse of a murdered person, requires the criminal agency of a person.

## Court en banc
Court in bank (en banc). A meeting of all the judges of a court, usually for the purposes of hearing arguments on demurrers, motions for new trial, etc., as distinguished from sessions of the same court presided over by a single judge or panel of judges

## Court of Oyer and Terminer and General or Jail Delivery
In American law, formerly, a court of criminal jurisdiction in the state of Pennsylvania. It was held at the same time with the court of quarter sessions, as a general rule, and by the same judges. Pa.Const. art. 5, § 1.

## Court of Quarter Sessions
Formerly, a court of criminal jurisdiction in the state of Pennsylvania, having power to try misdemeanors, and exercising certain functions of an administrative nature.

## Demurrer
A pleading stating that although the facts alleged in a complaint may be true, they are insufficient for the plaintiff to state a claim for relief and for the defendant to frame an answer. In most jurisdictions, such a pleading is now termed a motion to dismiss, but demurrer is still used in a few states, including Pennsylvania.

## Dictum
A statement of opinion or belief considered authoritative because of the dignity of the court making it. Plural: dicta.

## Discontinuance
The termination of a lawsuit by the plaintiff; a voluntary dismissal or nonsuit.

## Divorce "a vinculo matromonii"
A divorce from the bond of marriage. A total, absolute divorce of husband and wife, dissolving the marriage tie, and releasing

the parties wholly from their matrimonial obligations.

### Double indemnity clause
Payment of twice the basic benefit in event of loss resulting from specified causes or under specified circumstances. Provision in life insurance contract requiring payment of twice the face amount of the policy by the insurer in the event of death by accidental means.

### Emotional distress
A highly unpleasant mental reaction (such as anguish, grief, fright, or humiliation) that results from another person's conduct; emotional pain and suffering. Emotional distress, when severe enough, can form a basis for the recovery of tort damages.

### Entirety (Entireties Property)
The whole, in contradistinction to a moiety or part only. When land is conveyed to husband and wife, they do not take by moieties, but both are seised of the entirety. Parceners, on the other hand, have not an entirety of interest, but each is properly entitled to the whole of a distinct moiety.

### Equitable distribution
No-fault divorce statutes in certain states grant courts the power to distribute equitably, upon divorce, all property legally and beneficially acquired during marriage by husband and wife, or either of them, whether legal title lies in their joint or individual names. Equitable does not necessarily mean equal.

### Exclusionary rule.
This rule commands that where evidence has been obtained in violation of the search and seizure protections guaranteed by the U.S. Constitution, the illegally obtained evidence cannot be used at the trial of the defendant. Under this rule evidence which is obtained by an unreasonable search and seizure is excluded from admissibility under the Fourth Amendment, and this rule has been held to be applicable to the States.

### Execution
Carrying out some act or course of conduct to its completion. Completion of an act; putting into force. The completion, fulfillment, or perfecting of anything, or carrying it into operation and effect.
- Execution of contract includes performance of all acts necessary to render it complete as an instrument and imports idea that nothing remains to be done to make a complete and effective contract.
- Execution upon a money judgment is the legal process of enforcing the judgment, usually by seizing and selling property of the debtor. Form of process whereby an official (usually a sheriff) is directed by way of an appropriate judicial writ to seize and sell so much of the debtor's nonexempt property as is necessary to satisfy a judgment. Process of carrying into effect the directions in a decree or judgment.
- In criminal law, refers to carrying out a death sentence (capital punishment).
- Body execution. An order of court which commands the officer to take the body of the defendant or debtor; generally to bring him before court to pay debt.

### Felonious homicide
Killing of human being without justification or excuse.

### Felony
A crime of a graver or more serious nature than those designated as misdemeanors; e.g., aggravated assault (felony) as contrasted with simple assault (misdemeanor). Under many state statutes, any offense punishable by death or imprisonment for a term exceeding one year.

### Frye standard
The federal common-law rule of evidence on the admissibility of scientific evidence. It requires that the tests or procedures must have gained general acceptance in their particular field.

## Good cause

Generally means a substantial reason amounting in law to a legal excuse for failing to perform an act required by law. Legally sufficient ground or reason. Phrase "good cause" depends upon circumstances of individual case, and finding of its existence lies largely in discretion of officer or court to which decision is committed.

• Unemployment compensation. "Good cause" for leaving employment, so as not to render one ineligible for unemployment compensation benefits, must be objectively related to the employment and be such cause as would compel a reasonably prudent person to quit under similar circumstances.

## Habeas corpus

"You have the body." A writ employed to bring a person before a court, most frequently to ensure that the party's imprisonment or detention is not illegal. In addition to being used to test the legality of an arrest or commitment, the writ may be used to obtain review of (1) the regularity of extradition process, (2) the right to or amount of bail, or (3) the jurisdiction of a court that has imposed a criminal sentence.

## In camera

In chambers; in private. A judicial proceeding is said to be heard in camera either when the hearing is conducted before the judge in his private chambers or when all spectators are excluded from the courtroom.

## In re

In the matter of; in regard to; the typical method of entitling a judicial proceeding in which the parties are not formally adversarial. For example, adoption, juvenile, or estate proceedings.

## Injunction

A court order commanding or preventing an action. To get an injunction, the complainant must show that there is no plain, adequate, and complete remedy at law and that an irreparable injury will result unless the relief is granted.

## Intentional tort

A tort in which the actor is expressly or impliedly judged to have possessed intent or purpose to injure.

## Intermediate court

Those courts which have general jurisdiction, either trial or appellate or both, but which are below the court of last resort in the jurisdiction.

## Intermediate response (stop and frisk)

Applicable to circumstances where facts may not warrant arrest – where police are duty bound to assure the safety of the person and to inquire into circumstance which induced their arrival.

## Involuntary termination of parental rights

Termination hearings are held to determine whether parental rights will be taken away from parents of a child who has become the court's ward, usually because of parental neglect or abuse.

## Judgment non obstante veredicto

Notwithstanding the verdict. A judgment entered by order of court for the plaintiff (or defendant) although there has been a verdict for the defendant (or plaintiff). Judgment non obstante veredicto in its broadest sense is a judgment rendered in favor of one party notwithstanding the finding of a verdict in favor of the other party. A motion for a directed verdict is a prerequisite to a subsequent grant of judgment notwithstanding the verdict.

## Latent disease

Hidden, dormant, concealed, not apparent; that which does not present itself initially but develops without symptoms for sometimes prolonged periods of time.

## Loss of consortium

A loss of the benefits that one spouse is

entitled to receive from the other, including companionship, cooperation, aid, affection, and sexual relations. Loss of consortium can be recoverable as damages in a personal-injury or wrongful-death action.

## Magistrate's courts

A court with jurisdiction over minor criminal offenses. Such a court also has the power to bind over for trial persons accused of more serious offenses. A court with limited jurisdiction over minor criminal and civil matters.

## Mandamus

"We command." A writ which issues from a court of superior jurisdiction, and is directed to a private or municipal corporation, or any of its officers, or to an executive, administrative, or judicial officer, or to an inferior court, commanding the performance of a particular act therein specified, and belonging to his or their public, official, or ministerial duty, or directing the restoration of the complainant to rights or privileges of which he has been illegally deprived.

## Mandatory minimum sentence

Mandatory sentence. A sentence set by law with no discretion for the judge to individualize punishment. Statutes generally provide the sentence may not be suspended and that no probation may be imposed.

Minimum sentence. The least amount of time that a defendant must serve in prison before becoming eligible for parole.

## Marital property

Property of spouses subject to equitable distribution upon termination of marriage. Property purchased or otherwise accumulated by spouses while married to each other and which, in most jurisdictions, on dissolution of the marriage is divided in proportions, as the court deems fit.

## Medical malpractice

In medical malpractice litigation, negligence is the predominant theory of liability. In order to recover for negligent malpractice, the plaintiff must establish the following elements: (1) the existence of the physician's duty to the plaintiff, usually based upon the existence of the physician-patient relationship; (2) the applicable standard of care and its violation; (3) a compensable injury; and, (4) a causal connection between the violation of the standard of care and the harm complained of.

## Meretricious relationship

Of the nature of unlawful sexual connection. The term is descriptive of the relationship sustained by persons who contract a marriage that is void by reason of legal incapacity.

## Miranda warnings

Prior to any custodial interrogation (questioning initiated by law enforcement officers after a person is taken into custody or otherwise deprived of his freedom in any significant way) the person must be warned: 1. that he has a right to remain silent; 2. that any statement he does make may be used as evidence against him; 3. that he has a right to the presence of an attorney; 4. that if he cannot afford an attorney, one will be appointed for him prior to any questioning if he so desires. Unless and until these warnings or a waiver of these rights are demonstrated at the trial, no evidence obtained in the interrogation may be used against the accused.

## Misdemeanor

An offense graded lower than a felony and generally punishable by fine, penalty, forfeiture or imprisonment other than in a penitentiary. Under federal law and most state laws, any offense other than a felony is classified as a misdemeanor.

## Natural law

This expression, "natural law," or jus naturale, was largely used in the philosophical speculations of the Roman jurists of the Antonine age, and was intended to denote a system of rules and principles for the guidance of human conduct which, independently of enacted law or of the systems peculiar to any one people, might be discovered by the rational intelligence of man, and would be found to grow out of and conform to his nature, meaning by that word his whole mental, moral, and physical constitution.

## Negligence

The failure to exercise the standard of care that a reasonably prudent person would have exercised in a similar situation; any conduct that falls below the legal standard established to protect others against unreasonable risk of harm, except for conduct that is intentionally, wantonly, or willfully disregardful of others' rights.

## Nisi prius court

The nisi prius courts are such as are held for the trial of issues of fact before a jury and one presiding judge. In America the phrase formerly was used to denote the forum in which the cause was tried to a jury, as distinguished from the appellate court. Though frequently used as a general designation of any court exercising general, original jurisdiction in civil cases (being used interchangeably with "trial-court"), it belonged as a legal title only to a court which formerly existed in the city and county of Philadelphia, and which was presided over by one of the judges of the Supreme Court of Pennsylvania. This court was abolished by the constitution of 1874.

## Non pros

He does not prosecute. Abbreviation of non prosequitur. The judgment rendered against a plaintiff who has not pursued the case.

## Original jurisdiction

A court's power to hear and decide a matter before any other court can review the matter.

## Orphans' court

In Pennsylvania, a court, elsewhere known as a "Probate" or "Surrogates" court, with general jurisdiction over matters of probate and administration of estates, orphans, wards, and guardians.

## Ostensible agency

An implied or presumptive agency, which exists where one, either intentionally or from want of ordinary care, induces another to believe that a third person is his agent, though he never in fact employed him. It is, strictly speaking, no agency at all, but is in reality based entirely upon estoppel. Estoppel is a bar that prevents one from asserting a claim or right which contradicts what one has said or done before.

## Palimony

Term has meaning similar to "alimony" except that award, settlement or agreement arises out of nonmarital relationship of parties (i.e. nonmarital partners). It has been held that courts should enforce express contracts between nonmarital partners except to the extent the contract is explicitly founded on the consideration of meretricious sexual services, despite contention that such contracts violate public policy; that in the absence of express contract, the court should inquire into the conduct of the parties to determine whether that conduct demonstrates implied contract, agreement of partnership or joint venture, or some other tacit understanding between the parties, and may also employ the doctrine of quantum meruit (reasonable value) or equitable remedies such as constructive or resulting trust, when warranted by the facts of the case.

## Parens patriae

"Parent of the country." The state regarded as a sovereign; the state in its capacity as provider of protection to those unable to care for themselves. A doctrine by which a government has standing to prosecute a lawsuit on behalf of a citizen, especially on behalf of someone who is under a legal disability to prosecute the suit. The state ordinarily has no standing to sue on behalf of its citizens, unless a separate, sovereign interest will be served by the suit.

### Per curium opinion
An opinion handed down by an appellate court which does not identify the individual judge who wrote the opinion.

### Plain view doctrine
The rule permitting a police officer's warrantless seizure and use as evidence of an item observed in plain view from a lawful position or during a legal search when the officer has probable cause to believe that the item is evidence of a crime.

### Police power
The inherent and plenary power of a sovereign to make all laws necessary and proper to preserve public security, order, health, morality, and justice. It is a fundamental power essential to government, and it cannot be surrendered by the legislature or irrevocably transferred away from government.

### Polygraph
A device used to evaluate veracity by measuring and recording involuntary physiological changes in the human body during interrogation. Polygraph results are inadmissible as evidence in most states. Also termed lie detector.

### Prima facie
At first sight; on the first appearance; on the face of it; so far as can be judged from the first disclosure; presumably; a fact presumed to be true unless disproved by some evidence to the contrary.

### Primary caretaker doctrine
If in the past the primary caretaker has tended to the child's physical, emotional, educational, and moral needs, exhibiting love, affection, tolerance, discipline, and a willingness to sacrifice, a court may predict these qualities will continue in adjudicating custody of a child, giving them substantial weight.

### Privity
Horizontal privity. Such privity is not, in reality, a state of privity but rather one of nonprivity. The term refers to those who are not in the distributive chain of a product but who, nonetheless, use the product and retain a relationship with the purchaser, such as a member of the purchaser's family.

Vertical privity. Refers to the relationship between those who are in the distributive chain of a product.

### Probable cause
A reasonable ground to suspect that a person has committed or is committing a crime, or that a place contains specific items connected with a crime. Under the Fourth amendment, probable cause – which amounts to more than a bare suspicion but less than evidence that would justify a conviction—must be shown before an arrest warrant or search warrant may be issued. "Probable cause" to arrest exists where facts and circumstances within officers' knowledge and of which they had reasonably trustworthy information are sufficient in themselves to warrant a person of reasonable caution in the belief that an offense has been or is being committed.

### Quash
To overthrow; to abate; to vacate; to annul; to make void; e.g. to quash an indictment.

### Quo warranto
A common law writ designed to test whether a person exercising power is legally entitled to do so. An extraordinary proceeding, prerogative in nature, addressed to preventing a continued exercise of authority unlawfully asserted. It is intended to prevent exercise of powers that

are not conferred by law, and is not ordinarily available to regulate the manner of exercising such powers.

### Reasonable doubt
The standard used to determine the guilt or innocence of a person criminally charged. To be convicted of a crime, one must be proved guilty "beyond a reasonable doubt." Reasonable doubt which will justify acquittal is doubt based on reason and arising from evidence or lack of evidence, and it is doubt which a reasonable man or woman might entertain, and it is not fanciful doubt, is not imagined doubt, and is not doubt that juror might conjure up to avoid performing an unpleasant task or duty. Reasonable doubt is such a doubt as would cause prudent men to hesitate before acting in matters of importance to themselves. Doubt based on reason that arises from evidence or lack of evidence.

### Reasonable suspicion
A particularized and objective basis, supported by specific and articulable facts, for suspecting a person of criminal activity. A police officer must have a reasonable suspicion to stop a person in a public place.

### Restitution
An equitable remedy under which a person is restored to his or her original position prior to loss or injury, or placed in the position he or she would have been, had the breach not occurred. Act of restoring; restoration; restoration of anything to its rightful owner; the act of making good or giving equivalent for any loss, damage or injury; and indemnification. In criminal law, the courts of many states have restitution programs under which the criminal offender is required to repay, as a condition of his sentence, the victim or society in money or services.

### Search and seizure
A "search" to which the exclusionary rule may apply is one in which there is a quest for, a looking for, or a seeking out of that which offends against the law by law enforcement personnel or their agents.

Unlawful or unreasonable search. Within constitutional immunity (Fourth Amendment) from unreasonable searches and seizures, an examination or inspection without authority of law of premises or person with view to discovery of stolen, contraband, or illicit property, or for some evidence of guilt to be used in prosecution of criminal action.

Amendment of the U.S. Constitution guaranteeing people the right to be secure in their homes and property against unreasonable searches and seizures and providing that no warrants shall issue except upon probable cause and then only as to specific places to be searched and persons and things to be seized.

### Statute of limitations
Running of the statute of limitations. A metaphorical expression, meaning that the time specified in the statute of limitations is considered as having passed and hence the action is barred.

### Stop and frisk
A police officer's brief detention, questioning, and search of a person for a concealed weapon when the officer reasonably suspects that the person has committed or is about to commit a crime. The stop and frisk, which can be conducted without a warrant or probable cause, was held to be constitutional by the United States Supreme Court.

### Summary judgment
Procedural device available for prompt and expeditious disposition of controversy without trial when there is no dispute as to either material fact or inferences to be drawn from undisputed facts, or if only question of law is involved.

### Suppression of evidence

A trial judge's ruling that evidence that a party has offered should be excluded because it was illegally acquired. Concept of "suppression", as that term is used in rule that suppression by the prosecution of material evidence favorable to an accused on request violates due process, implies that the government has information in its possession of which the defendant lacks knowledge and which could exculpate the defendant.

### Tender years doctrine.

Under this doctrine courts generally award custody of children of tender years to mother unless she is found to be unfit. In many states this doctrine has been abolished by statute or by case law, and replaced by either the Primary Caretaker Doctrine or joint custody.

### Tort law

A private or civil wrong or injury, including an action for bad faith breach of contract, for which the court will provide a remedy in the form of an action for damages. A violation of a duty imposed by general law or otherwise upon all persons occupying the relation to each other which is involved in a given transaction. There must always be a violation of some duty owing to plaintiff, and generally such duty must arise by operation of law and not by mere agreement of the parties. A legal wrong committed upon the person or property independent of contract. It may be either (1) a direct invasion of some legal right of the individual; (2) the infraction of some public duty by which special damage accrues to the individual; (3) the violation of some private obligation by which like damage accrues to the individual.

• Intentional tort. Tort or wrong perpetrated by one who intends to do that which the law has declared wrong as contrasted with negligence in which the tortfeasor fails to exercise that degree of care in doing what is otherwise permissible.

• Personal tort. One involving or consisting of an injury to the person or to the reputation or feelings, as distinguished from an injury or damage to real or personal property, called a "property tort."

### Tortious interference

Wrongful; of the nature of a tort. The word "tortious" is used throughout the Restatement, Second, Torts, to denote the fact that conduct, whether of act or omission, is of such a character as to subject the actor to liability, under the principles of the law of torts. To establish "tortious act" plaintiff must prove not only existence of actionable wrong, but also that damages resulted therefrom.

### Totality of circumstances

Test used to determine the constitutionality of various search and seizure procedures and investigative stops. This standard focuses on all the circumstances of a particular case, rather than any one factor.

### Toxic tort

A civil wrong arising from exposure to a toxic substance, such as asbestos, radiation, or hazardous waste. A toxic tort can be remedied by a civil lawsuit, usually a class action, or by administrative action.

### Void marriage

A marriage not good for any legal purpose, the invalidity of which may be maintained in any proceeding between any parties. A void marriage is invalid from its inception, and parties thereto may simply separate without benefit of a court order of divorce or annulment.

### Voidable marriage

One which is valid (not void) when entered into and which remains valid until either party secures a lawful court order dissolving the marital relationship. Major difference between "void marriage" and "voidable marriage" is that the latter is treated as binding until its nullity is ascertained and declared by competent court, whereas former does not require such judgment because parties could not enter into valid marital relationship.

## Warranty
A promise that a proposition of fact is true. An assurance by one party to agreement of existence of fact upon which other party may rely. It is intended precisely to relieve promisee of any duty to ascertain facts for himself, and amounts to a promise to indemnify promisee for any loss if the fact warranted proves untrue. A promise that certain facts are truly as they are represented to be and that they will remain so, subject to any specified limitations. In certain circumstances a warranty will be presumed, known as an "implied" warranty.

## Writ of certiorari
An order by an appellate court which is used by that court when it has discretion on whether or not to hear an appeal from a lower court. If the writ is denied, the court refuses to hear the appeal and, in effect, the judgment below stands unchanged. If the writ is granted, then it has the effect of ordering the lower court to certify the record and send it up to the higher court which has used its discretion to hear the appeal. In the U.S. Supreme Court, a review on writ of certiorari is not a matter of right, but of judicial discretion, and will be granted only when there are special and important reasons therefore.

## Writ of error
A writ issued from a court of appellate jurisdiction, directed to the judge or judges of a court of record, requiring them to remit to the appellate court the record of an action before them, in which a final judgment has been entered, in order that examination may be made of certain errors alleged to have been committed, and that the judgment may be reversed, corrected, or affirmed, as the case may require.

## Wrongful birth
A medical malpractice claim brought by the parents of an impaired child, alleging that negligent treatment or advice deprived them of the opportunity to avoid conception or terminate the pregnancy.

## Wrongful life
A medical malpractice claim brought on behalf of a child born with birth defects, alleging that the child would not have been born but for negligent advice to, or treatment of, the parents.

*This Glossary of Legal Terms was derived from Black's Law Dictionary, (6th ed. 1990) (7th ed. 1999).*

# About the Authors

*Patrick R. Tamilia*

*John J. Hare*

Patrick R. Tamilia is the son of an Italian immigrant father, who at fifteen years of age began life in the foundries of Pittsburgh. Tamilia's earliest recollections are of the 1929 depression with its concomitant hardships. The "Gilded Age", the "New Deal" and Pennsylvania's "Little New Deal" detailed herein have personal meaning to Tamilia.

With Pearl Harbor came the end of the depression and revolutionary changes which involved individuals, families and the nation. As a teenager Tamilia was recruited in the war effort as a "gandy dancer," rebuilding railroads in and around Pittsburgh during summers and weekends.

Following Marine Corps service and college under the G.I. Bill, Tamilia's career began with the judiciary as a Juvenile Court detention home worker, followed by the positions of probation officer, while attending both graduate and law school at night, director of family court, and in 1970, judge. As a trial and appellate judge for thirty years and thirty years as an adjunct professor of law, *Keystone of Justice* is a reflection of the totality of Tamilia's experiences.

John J. Hare is an attorney with the Philadelphia law firm of Marshall Dennehey Warner Coleman & Goggin, where he practices in the area of defense litigation. Following his graduation from Duquesne University Law School in 1993, and his subsequent admission to the Pennsylvania bar, Hare was employed as a law clerk to the Honorable Patrick R. Tamilia of the Pennsylvania Superior Court, the co-author of this book. Following his clerkship with Judge Tamilia, Hare returned to school and received an M.A. degree in legal history from the University of California, Berkeley. In 1999, he completed the coursework for a Ph.D. in legal history at Princeton University. Hare lives with his wife, Jennifer, in Doylestown, Bucks County.

John J. Hare Photo: Maggie Wallace-Cullen

# INDEX